M000191389

Microsoft® C/C++
Run-Time Library Reference

Covers version 7

SECOND EDITION

Microsoft PRESS

PUBLISHED BY
Microsoft Press
A Division of Microsoft Corporation
One Microsoft Way, Redmond, Washington 98052-6399

Copyright © 1990, 1992 by Microsoft Corporation

All rights reserved. No part of the contents of this book may be reproduced or trans-
mitted in any form or by any means without the written permission of the publisher.

Library of Congress Cataloging-in-Publication Data
Microsoft C/C++-run-time library reference/author, Microsoft
    Corporation. -- 2nd ed.
        p.   cm.
    Includes index.
    ISBN 1-55615-382-1 (softcover)
    1. C (Computer program language)   2. Microsoft C (Computer
program)   I. Microsoft Corporation.
QA76.73.C15M52   1992
005'.13'3--dc20   91-39268
                                          CIP

Printed and bound in the United States of America.

1 2 3 4 5 6 7 8 9   RDRD   7 6 5 4 3 2

Distributed to the book trade in Canada by Macmillan of Canada, a division of
Canada Publishing Corporation.

Distributed to the book trade outside the United States and Canada by Penguin Books Ltd.

Penguin Books Ltd., Harmondsworth, Middlesex, England
Penguin Books Australia Ltd., Ringwood, Victoria, Australia
Penguin Books N.Z. Ltd., 182-190 Wairau Road, Auckland 10, New Zealand

British Cataloging-in-Publication Data available.

AT&T® and UNIX® are registered trademarks of American Telephone and Telegraph
Company. Hercules® is a registered trademark of Hercules Computer Technology. Olivetti® is
a registered trademark of Ing. C. Olivetti. IBM® is a registered trademark of International
Business Machines Corporation. Microsoft®, MS-DOS®, QuickC®, and XENIX® are registered
trademarks and Windows™ is a trademark of Microsoft Corporation.

Writers:	Editors:	Sample Programs:	Reviewers:
Chris Burt	Amanda Clark	Bruce McKinney	Greg Fowler
Ted Chiang	Moira Macdonald		James MacCalman
Phil Nelson	Marjorie Manwaring		Georgio Papagiannakopoulos
Chuck Sphar	Bill Nolan		Jeff Robbins
Terry Ward	Rod Wilkinson		Karl Simonsen

Document No. 410840021-520-R00-1088
Part No. 04412

Contents Overview

Contents

Part 2   Run-Time Functions

Tables

Tables

Tables

Introduction

The Microsoft® run-time library is a set of more than 550 ready-to-use functions and macros designed for use in C and C++ programs. The run-time library makes programming easier by providing

- Fast and efficient routines to perform common programming tasks (such as string manipulation), sparing you the time and effort needed to write such routines
- Reliable methods of performing operating-system functions (such as opening and closing files)

The run-time library is important because it provides basic functions not provided by the C and C++ languages themselves. These functions include input and output, memory allocation, process control, graphics, and many others.

This book describes the run-time library routines included with Microsoft C/C++ version 7.0. These comprise all of the routines included with earlier versions of Microsoft C, as well as many new routines.

About the Microsoft® Run-Time Library

The Microsoft run-time library contains routines and features that support American National Standards Institute (ANSI) C and UNIX C compatibility, DOS and Microsoft Windows™ programming, and sophisticated graphics programming.

To ease the task of transporting programs between operating systems and compilers, the description of each run-time library routine includes a compatibility section. A routine with full compatibility has the following entries:

Standards: ANSI, UNIX

16-Bit: DOS, QWIN, WIN, WIN DLL

32-Bit: DOS32X

(In this book, references to UNIX systems also encompass XENIX® and other UNIX-like systems.)

ANSI C Compatibility

The run-time library routines are designed for compatibility with the ANSI C standard, which the Microsoft C and C++ compilers support. Functions that are ANSI C compatible are marked as ANSI in the compatibility section.

Type Checking

The major innovation of ANSI C is to permit argument-type lists in function proto-types (declarations). Given the information in the function prototype, the compiler can check later references to the function to make sure that the references use the correct number and type of arguments and the correct return value.

To take advantage of the compiler's type-checking ability, the include files that accompany the run-time library have been expanded. In addition to the definitions and declarations required by library routines, the include files now contain function declarations with argument-type lists. Several new include files have also been added. The names of these files are chosen to maximize compatibility with the ANSI C standard and with UNIX and XENIX names.

Underscores and OLDNAMES.LIB

With Microsoft C/C++, all Microsoft-specific run-time functions, constants, variables, type definitions, structures, and macros (such as, respectively, **_open**, **_VRES16COLOR**, **_cpumode**, **_HEAPINFO**, **_heapinfo**, and **__isascii**) are ANSI compatible. The Microsoft-specific run-time functions, constants, variables, type definitions, and structures begin with a single underscore; Microsoft-specific run-time macros begin with two underscores.

For compatibility with previous versions of Microsoft C, Microsoft C/C++ provides a library named OLDNAMES.LIB, which contains alias records mapping the names to the new names. For instance, **open** is mapped to **_open**.

You have to link with OLDNAMES.LIB to link Microsoft C/C++ programs with object files created by previous versions of Microsoft C. However, by default the compiler emits a library search record—the only time you must link explicitly with OLDNAMES.LIB is under one of the following situations:

- Compiling with a combination of the default /Ze option (use Microsoft extensions) and the /Zl option (omit default library name from object file)

- Compiling with the default /Ze option (use Microsoft extensions) and a combination of the /link option (linker-control) and the /NOD option (no default-library search)

For more information on the CL command-line options, see Chapter 13 of *Environment and Tools* (in the Microsoft C/C++ version 7.0 documentation set).

Note The compiler views a structure with both an old name and a new name as two different types; you cannot copy from an old type to a new type. Also, old prototypes that take **struct** pointers use the old **struct** names in the prototype. So, you must be consistent—match the old names for routines with the old names for the parameters and be similarly consistent with the new routine names and parameters.

UNIX C Compatibility

Most of the functions in the Microsoft run-time library are compatible with like-named UNIX routines. For additional compatibility, the math library functions have been extended to provide exception handling in the same manner as the UNIX System V math functions. Functions that are UNIX and XENIX compatible are marked as UNIX in the compatibility section.

DOS and Microsoft Windows™ Programming

Microsoft run-time library routines are designed to maintain maximum compatibility between DOS, Windows, and UNIX or XENIX systems. The run-time library offers a number of operating-system interface routines that allow you to take advantage of specific DOS and Windows features. Functions that are DOS and Windows compatible are marked, respectively, as DOS and WIN in the compatibility section. Note that for Windows the compatibility section also contains information on dynamic-link library (DLL) compatibility.

Many run-time library functions are designed to work with the Microsoft DOS Extender. The DOS Extender is a shell between a program and DOS that allows the program to run in the 32-bit flat memory model. Currently, the Microsoft C and C++ compilers are hosted under the DOS Extender; when Microsoft C/C++ provides 32-bit targeting, you can use the functions listed as DOS32X compatible to develop and run 32-bit flat model programs under DOS.

QuickWin

The Microsoft run-time library now contains several QuickWin functions that make it possible to compile non-Windows DOS programs as simple text-only Windows applications. DOS programs compiled with the /Mq compiler option have a limited Windows user interface, including a standard menu bar, standard online help (for the QuickWin features), and a client (or application) window with a child (document) window for the C input/output streams **stdin**, **stdout**, and **stderr**. You can also add other child windows of your own. QuickWin applications support the Windows Clipboard, and you can use standard C functions to write to and read from a QuickWin application's windows, which behave as streams. Functions that are QuickWin compatible are marked as QWIN in the compatibility section.

Expanded Graphics Library

The Microsoft run-time library contains more than one hundred graphics routines. The core of this library consists of several dozen low-level graphics routines that allow your programs to select video modes, set points, draw lines, change colors, and draw shapes such as rectangles and ellipses. You can display real-valued data, such as floating-point values, within windows of different sizes by using various coordinate systems.

The graphics library includes presentation graphics and fonts. The presentation-graphics library provides powerful tools for adding presentation-quality graphics to your programs. These routines can display data as a variety of graphs, including pie charts, bar and column charts, line graphs, and scatter diagrams.

The fonts library allows your programs to display various styles and sizes of text in graphics images or charts. You can use font-manipulation routines with any graphics routines that display text, including presentation graphics.

About This Book

This book provides a guide to the run-time library provided with Microsoft C/C++.

This book has two parts. Part 1, "Overview," introduces the Microsoft run-time library. It describes general rules for using the library and summarizes the main categories of library routines. Part 1 contains the following chapters:

- Chapter 1, "Using the Run-Time Library," gives general rules for understanding and using library routines and mentions special considerations that apply to certain routines. It is recommended that you read this chapter before using the run-time library; you may also want to turn to Chapter 1 when you have questions about library procedures.

- Chapter 2, "Run-Time Routines by Category," lists the library routines by category and discusses considerations that apply to each category. This chapter makes it easy to locate routines by task. Once you find the routine you want, turn to the reference page in Part 2 for a detailed description.

- Chapter 3, "Global Variables and Standard Types," describes variables and types that are used by library routines. Global variables and standard types are also described in the reference descriptions of the routines that use them.

Part 2, "Run-Time Functions," describes the library routines in alphabetical order. Once you are familiar with the run-time library rules and procedures, you will probably use this part most often.

Other Books of Interest

The following books cover a variety of topics that you may find useful. They are listed only for your convenience. With the exception of its own publications, Microsoft does not endorse these books or recommend them over others on the same subject.

- Barkakati, Nabajyoti. *The Waite Group's Microsoft C Bible*. Indianapolis, IN: Howard W. Sams, 1988.

  A topical guide to the Microsoft C run-time library. A similar volume is available for the Microsoft QuickC® product.

- Campbell, Joe. *C Programmer's Guide to Serial Communications*. Indianapolis, IN: Howard W. Sams & Company, 1987.

  A comprehensive guide to the specialized area of serial communication programming in C.

- Christian, Kaare. *C++ Programming*. Redmond, WA: Microsoft Press, 1992.

  An introduction to object-oriented programming concepts, C++ fundamentals, and Microsoft C/C++ version 7.0, particularly the Foundation class libraries.

- Harbison, Samuel P., and Guy L. Steele, Jr. *C: A Reference Manual*, 2d ed. Englewood Cliffs, NJ: Prentice Hall, 1987.

  A comprehensive guide to the C language and the standard library.

- Kernighan, Brian W., and Dennis M. Ritchie. *The C Programming Language*, 2d ed. Englewood Cliffs, NJ: Prentice Hall, 1988.

  The first edition of this book is the classic definition of the C language. The second edition includes new information on the ANSI C standard.

- Lafore, Robert. *Microsoft C Programming for the IBM*. Indianapolis, IN: Howard W. Sams & Company, 1987.

  The first half of this book teaches C. The second half concentrates on specifics of the PC environment, such as BIOS calls, memory, and video displays.

- Mark Williams Company. *ANSI C: A Lexical Guide*. Englewood Cliffs, NJ: Prentice Hall, 1988.

  A dictionary-style guide to the ANSI C standard.

- Plauger, P. J., and Jim Brodie. *ANSI and ISO Standard C: A Guide for Programmers*. Redmond, WA: Microsoft Press, 1992.

  A reference to the ANSI and ISO C implementation by the secretary and chairman of the ANSI- and ISO-authorized C Programming Language Standards Committee.

- Plum, Thomas. *Reliable Data Structures in C*. Cardiff, NJ: Plum Hall, 1985.

  An intermediate-level look at data structures using the C language.

- Plum, Thomas, and Jim Brodie. *Efficient C*. Cardiff, NJ: Plum Hall, 1985.

  A guide to techniques for increasing the efficiency of C programs.

- Press, William H., Brian P. Flannery, Saul A. Teukolsky, and William T. Vetterling. *Numerical Recipes in C: The Art of Scientific Computing*. New York: Cambridge University Press, 1988.

  A comprehensive look at numerical techniques using the C language.

- Schustack, Steve. *Variations in C: Building Professional Applications with Microsoft C*. Second Edition. Redmond, WA: Microsoft Press, 1989.

  An intermediate-level guide to developing business applications in C.

- Ward, Robert. *Debugging C*. Indianapolis, IN: Que Corporation, 1986.

  An advanced guide to the theory and practice of debugging C programs.

- Wilton, Richard. *Programmer's Guide to PC and PS/2 Video Systems: Maximum Video Performance from the EGA, VGA, HGC, & MCGA*. Redmond, WA: Microsoft Press, 1987.

  An advanced guide to all the PC and PS/2 video modes.

Document Conventions

This book uses the following typographic conventions:

Example	Description
STDIO.H	Uppercase letters indicate filenames, segment names, registers, and terms used at the operating-system command level.
char, **_setcolor**, **__far**	Bold type indicates C and C++ keywords, operators, language-specific characters, and library routines. Within discussions of syntax, bold type indicates that the text must be entered exactly as shown.
	Many functions and constants begin with either a single or double underscore. These are part of the name and are mandatory. For example, to have the **__cplusplus** manifest constant be recognized by the compiler, you must enter the leading double underscore.
expression	Words in italics indicate placeholders for information you must supply, such as a filename.

Example	Description
[[*option*]]	Items inside double square brackets are optional.
#pragma pack {1 | 2}	Braces and a vertical bar indicate a choice among two or more items. You must choose one of these items unless double square brackets ([[ ]]) surround the braces.
`#include <io.h>`	This font is used for examples, user input, program output, and error messages in text.
CL [[*option...*]] *file...*	Three dots (an ellipsis) following an item indicate that more items having the same form may appear.

`while()`
`{`
`    .`
`    .`
`    .`
`}`
	A column or row of three dots tells you that part of an example program has been intentionally omitted.

CTRL+ENTER	Small capital letters are used to indicate the names of keys on the keyboard. When you see a plus sign (+) between two key names, you should hold down the first key while pressing the second.
	The carriage-return key, sometimes marked as a bent arrow on the keyboard, is called ENTER.
"argument"	Quotation marks enclose a new term the first time it is defined in text.
`"C string"`	Some C constructs, such as strings, require quotation marks. Quotation marks required by the language have the form " " and ' ' rather than " " and ' '.
Color Graphics Adapter (CGA)	The first time an acronym is used, it is usually spelled out.

Note Microsoft documentation uses the term "DOS" to refer to both the MS-DOS® and IBM Personal Computer DOS operating systems. The name of a specific operating system is used to note features unique to that system.

Overview

Overview

The first part of this book provides an overview of the run-time library provided with Microsoft C/C++.

Chapter 1 is a general guide to the use of the run-time library routines.

Chapter 2 lists the routines by category.

Chapter 3 tells how to access global variables and types defined in the run-time library.

Using the Run-Time Library

This chapter provides basic information about how to use the Microsoft run-time library routines. It also describes some special rules, such as path-name and filename conventions, that apply to particular routines. You should read this chapter before you begin to use the run-time library routines, and you may also want to refer back to it if you have questions about library procedures.

1.1 Calling Library Routines

To use a library routine, simply call it in your program, just as if it is defined there. For instance, suppose you write the following program and name it SAMPLE.C:

```
#include <stdio.h>
void main( void )
{
    printf( "Microsoft C/C++\n" );
}
```

The program prints `Microsoft C/C++` by calling the **printf** routine, which is part of the run-time library. Calling a library routine normally involves two groups of files:

- Header ("include") files that contain declarations, constants, and type definitions required by library routines

- Library files that contain the library routines in compiled form

Header files and library files are both included with Microsoft C/C++. Header files are used when compiling, and library files are used when linking.

You include the necessary header files in your program source code with **#include** directives. The description of each library routine in Part 2, "Run-Time Functions," tells you what header file the routine requires. Since **printf** requires the STDIO.H header file, the SAMPLE.C program contains the following line:

```
#include <stdio.h>
```

This line causes the compiler to insert the contents of STDIO.H into the source file SAMPLE.C.

After you compile the source file, you link the resulting object (.OBJ) file with the appropriate library (.LIB) file to create an executable (.EXE) file. Your object file contains the name of every routine that your program calls, including library routines. If a routine is not defined in your program, the linker searches for its code in a library file and includes that code in the executable file.

Normally, the code for standard library routines is contained in the "default library" that you create when installing Microsoft C/C++. Since the linker automatically searches the default library, you do not need to specify that library's name when linking your program. The following command links the example program with the default library:

```
link sample,,,;
```

If you call a library routine that is not contained in the default library, you must give the linker the name of the library file that contains the routine. For instance, if your program uses a Microsoft graphics routine, you would link the program using a line that includes GRAPHICS.LIB:

```
link sample,,, graphics.lib;
```

For more information about installing libraries and linking, see *Getting Started* and Part 3 of *Environment and Tools* (both are in the Microsoft C/C++ version 7.0 documentation set) or consult the installation documentation for your compiler.

1.2 Using Header Files

As stated in the previous section, you should include header files when using library routines. This section describes particular reasons why header files are required.

Including Necessary Definitions

Many run-time library routines use constants, type definitions, or macros defined in a header file. To use the routine, you must include the header file containing the needed definition(s). The following list gives examples:

Definition	Example
Macro	If a library routine is implemented as a macro, the macro definition appears in a header file. For instance, the **toupper** macro is defined in the header file CTYPE.H.

Definition	Example
Manifest constant	Many library routines refer to constants that are defined in header files. For instance, the **_open** routine uses constants such as **_O_CREAT**, which is defined in the header file FCNTL.H.
Type definition	Some library routines return a structure or take a structure as an argument. For example, stream input/output routines use a structure of type **FILE**, which is defined in STDIO.H.

Including Function Declarations

The run-time library header files also contain function declarations for every function in the run-time library. These declarations are in the style recommended by the ANSI C standard. Given these declarations, the compiler can perform "type checking" on every reference to a library function, making sure that you have used the correct return type and arguments. Function declarations are sometimes called "prototypes," since the declaration serves as a prototype or template for every subsequent reference to the function.

A function declaration lists the name of the function, its return type, and the number and type of its arguments. For instance, this is the declaration of the **pow** library function from the header file MATH.H:

double pow(double x, double y);

The example declares that **pow** returns a value of type **double** and takes two arguments of type **double**. Given this declaration, the compiler can check every reference to **pow** in your program to ensure that the reference passes two **double** arguments to **pow** and takes a return value of type **double**.

The compiler can perform type checking only for function references that appear after the function declaration. Because of this, function declarations normally appear near the beginning of the source file, prior to any use of the functions they declare.

Function declarations are especially important for functions that return a value of some type other than **int**, which is the default. For example, the **pow** function returns a **double** value. If you do not declare such a function, the compiler treats its return value as **int**, which can cause unexpected results.

It is also a good practice to provide declarations for functions that you write. If you do not want to type the declarations by hand, you can generate them automatically by using the /Zg compiler option. This option causes the compiler to generate ANSI-standard function declarations for every function defined in the current source file. Redirect this output to a file, then insert the file near the beginning of your source file.

Your program can contain more than one declaration of the same function, as long as the declarations do not conflict. This is important if you have old programs whose function declarations do not contain argument-type lists. For instance, if your program contains the declaration

```
char *calloc( );
```

you can later include the following declaration:

```
char *calloc(unsigned, unsigned);
```

Because the two declarations are compatible, even though they are not identical, no conflict occurs. The second declaration simply gives more information about function arguments than the first. A conflict would arise, however, if the declarations gave a different number of arguments or gave arguments of different types.

Some library functions can take a variable number of arguments. For instance, the **printf** function can take one argument or several. The compiler can perform only limited type checking on such functions, a factor that affects the following library functions:

- In calls to **_cprintf**, **_cscanf**, **printf**, and **scanf**, only the first argument (the format string) is type checked.

- In calls to **fprintf**, **fscanf**, **_snprintf**, **sprintf**, and **sscanf**, only the first two arguments (the file or buffer and the format string) are type checked.

- In calls to **_open**, only the first two arguments (the path name and the **_open** flag) are type checked.

- In calls to **_sopen**, only the first three arguments (the path name, the **_open** flag, and the sharing mode) are type checked.

- In calls to **_execl**, **_execle**, **_execlp**, and **_execlpe**, only the first two arguments (the path name and the first argument pointer) are type checked.

- In calls to **_spawnl**, **_spawnle**, **_spawnlp**, and **_spawnlpe**, only the first three arguments (the mode flag, the path name, and the first argument pointer) are type checked.

1.3 Paths and Filenames

Many library routines take strings representing paths and filenames as arguments. If you plan to transport your programs to the UNIX (or XENIX) operating system, you should remember that UNIX uses path-name and filename conventions that are different from those used by DOS. If you do not plan to transport your programs to UNIX, you can skip this section.

Case Sensitivity

The DOS operating system is not case sensitive (it does not distinguish between uppercase and lowercase letters). Thus, SAMPLE.C and Sample.C refer to the same file. However, the UNIX operating system is case sensitive. In UNIX, SAMPLE.C and Sample.C refer to different files. To transport programs to UNIX, choose path names and filenames that work correctly in UNIX, since either case works in DOS. For instance, the following directives are identical in DOS, but only the second works in UNIX:

```
#include <STDIO.H>
#include <stdio.h>
```

Subdirectory Conventions

Under UNIX, certain header files are normally placed in a subdirectory named SYS. Microsoft C follows this convention to ease the process of transporting programs to UNIX. If you do not plan to transport your programs, you can place the SYS header files elsewhere.

Path-Name Delimiters

UNIX uses the slash (/) in path names, while DOS uses the backslash (\). To transport programs to UNIX, it is advantageous to use path-name delimiters that are compatible with UNIX whenever possible.

1.4 Choosing Between Functions and Macros

This book uses the words "routine" and "function" interchangeably. However, the term "routine" actually encompasses both functions and macros. Because functions and macros have different properties, you should pay attention to which form you are using. The descriptions in the reference section indicate whether routines are implemented as functions or as macros.

Most routines in the Microsoft run-time library are functions. They consist of compiled C code or assembled Microsoft Macro Assembler (MASM) code. However, a few library routines are implemented as macros that behave like functions. You can pass arguments to library macros and invoke them in the same way you invoke functions.

The main benefit of using macros is faster execution time. Every library macro is defined with a **#define** directive in a header file. A macro is expanded (replaced by its definition) during preprocessing, creating inline code. Thus, macros do not have the overhead associated with function calls. On the other hand, each use of a macro inserts the same code in your program, whereas a function definition occurs only once regardless of how many times it is called. Functions and macros thus offer a trade-off between speed and size.

Apart from speed and size issues, macros and functions have some other important differences:

- Some macros treat arguments with side effects incorrectly when the macro evaluates its arguments more than once (see the example that follows this list). Not every macro has this effect. To determine if a macro handles side effects as desired, examine its definition in the appropriate header file.

- A function name evaluates to an address, but a macro name does not. Thus, you cannot use a macro name in contexts requiring a function pointer. For instance, you can declare a pointer to a function, but you cannot declare a pointer to a macro.

- You can declare functions, but you cannot declare macros. Thus, the compiler cannot perform type checking of macro arguments as it does of function arguments. However, the compiler can detect when you pass the wrong number of arguments to a macro.

The following example demonstrates how some macros can produce unwanted side effects. It uses the **toupper** routine.

```
#include <ctype.h>

int a = 'm';
a = toupper(a++);
```

The example increments `a` when passing it as an argument to the **toupper** routine, which is implemented as a macro. It is defined in CTYPE.H:

```
#define toupper(c) ( (islower(c)) ? _toupper(c) : (c) )
```

The definition uses the conditional operator (**? :**). The conditional expression evaluates the argument `c` twice: once to check if it is lowercase and again to create the result. This macro evaluates the argument `a++` twice, increasing `a` by 2 instead of 1. As a result, the value operated on by **islower** differs from the value operated on by **_toupper**.

Like some other library routines, **toupper** is provided in both macro and function versions. The header file CTYPE.H not only declares the **toupper** function but also defines the **toupper** macro.

Choosing between the macro version and function version of such routines is easy. If you wish to use the macro version, you can simply include the header file that contains the macro definition. Because the macro definition of the routine always appears after the function declaration, the macro definition normally takes precedence. Thus, if your program includes CTYPE.H and then calls **toupper**, the compiler uses the **toupper** macro:

```
#include <ctype.h>

int a = 'm';
a = toupper(a);
```

You can force the compiler to use the function version of a routine by enclosing the routine's name in parentheses:

```
#include <ctype.h>

int a = 'm';
a = (toupper) (a);
```

Because the name **toupper** is not immediately followed by a left parenthesis, the compiler cannot interpret it as a macro name. It must use the **toupper** function.

A second way to do this is to "undefine" the macro definition with the **#undef** directive:

```
#include <ctype.h>
#undef toupper
```

Since the macro definition no longer exists, subsequent references to **toupper** use the function version.

A third way, not generally recommended, to make sure the compiler uses the function version is to declare the function explicitly:

```
#include <ctype.h>
int toupper(int _c);
```

Since this function declaration appears after the macro definition in CTYPE.H, it causes the compiler to use the **toupper** function.

1.5 Stack Checking on Entry

For certain library routines, the compiler performs stack checking on entry. (The "stack" is a memory area used for temporary storage.) Upon entry to such a routine, the stack is checked to determine if it has enough room for the local variables used by that routine. If it does, space is allocated by adjusting the stack pointer. Otherwise, a "stack overflow" run-time error occurs. If stack checking is disabled, the compiler assumes there is enough stack space; if there is not, you might overwrite memory locations in the data segment and receive no warning—unpredictable program behavior may result.

Typically, stack checking is enabled only for functions with large local-variable requirements (more than about 150 bytes), since there is enough free space between the stack and data segments to handle functions with smaller requirements. If the function is called many times, stack checking slows execution slightly.

Stack checking is enabled for the following library functions:

_execvp	scanf	system
_execvpe	_spawnvp	vprintf
fprintf	_spawnvpe	_write
fscanf	sprintf	
printf	sscanf	

You can enable or disable stack checking with the /Gs and /Ge compiler options (see Chapter 13 of *Environment and Tools*) or the **check_stack** pragma (see Chapter 7 of the *C Language Reference*). Both books are in the Microsoft C/C++ version 7.0 documentation set.

1.6 Handling Errors

Many library routines return a value that indicates an error condition. To avoid unexpected results, your code should always check such error values and handle all of the possible error conditions. The description of each library routine in the reference section lists the routine's return value(s).

Some library functions do not have a set error return. These include functions that return nothing and functions whose range of return values makes it impossible to return a unique error value.

To aid in error handling, some functions set the value of a global variable named **errno**. If the reference description of a routine states that it sets the **errno** variable, you can use **errno** in two ways:

- Compare **errno** to the values defined in the header file ERRNO.H.

- Handle **errno** with the **perror** or **strerror** library routine. The **perror** routine prints a system error message to the standard error (**stderr**). The **strerror** routine stores the same information in a string for later use.

When you use **errno, perror**, and **strerror**, remember that the value of **errno** reflects the error value for the last call that set **errno**. To avoid confusion, you should always test the return value to verify that an error actually occurred. Once you determine that an error has occurred, use **strerror** or **perror** immediately. Otherwise, the value of **errno** may be changed by intervening calls.

Library math routines set **errno** by calling the **_matherr** or **_matherrl** library routine; both are described in the reference section. If you wish to handle math errors differently from these routines, you can write your own routine and name it **_matherr** or **_matherrl**. Your routine must follow the rules listed in the **_matherr** reference description.

The **ferror** library routine allows you to check for errors in stream input/output operations. This routine checks if an error indicator has been set for a given stream. Closing or rewinding the stream automatically clears the error indicator. You can also reset the error indicator by calling the **clearerr** library routine.

The **feof** library routine tests for end-of-file on a given stream. An end-of-file condition in low-level input and output can be detected with the **_eof** routine or when a **_read** operation returns 0 as the number of bytes read.

The **_grstatus** library routine allows you to check for errors after calling certain graphics library operations. See the reference page on the **_grstatus** function for details.

1.7 Operating-System Considerations

The library routines listed in this section behave differently under different operating-system versions. For more information on an individual routine, see the description of that routine in the reference section.

Routine	Restrictions
_locking **_sopen** **_fsopen**	These routines are effective only in DOS versions 3.0 and later.
_dosexterr	The **_dosexterr** routine provides error handling for system call 0x59 (get extended error) in DOS versions 3.0 and later.
_dup **_dup2**	The **_dup** and **_dup2** routines can cause unexpected results in DOS versions earlier than 3.0. If you use **_dup** or **_dup2** to create a duplicate file handle for **stdin**, **stdout**, **stderr**, **stdaux**, or **stdprn**, calling the **_close** function with one handle causes errors in later I/O operations that use the other handle. This anomaly does not occur in DOS versions 3.0 and later.
_exec **_spawn**	When using the **_exec** and **_spawn** families of functions under DOS versions earlier than 3.0, the value of the *arg0* argument (or *argv*[0] to the child process) is not available to the user; a null string (**""**) is stored in that position instead. In DOS versions 3.0 and later, the *arg0* argument contains the complete command path.

Microsoft C/C++ defines global variables that indicate the version of the current operating system. You can use these to determine the operating-system version in which a program is executing. See Chapter 3, "Global Variables and Standard Types," for more information.

1.8 Floating-Point Support

Microsoft math library routines require floating-point support to perform calculations with real numbers (numbers that can contain fractions). This support can be provided by the floating-point libraries that accompany your compiler software or by an 8087, 80287, or 80387 coprocessor. The names of the functions that require floating-point support are listed below:

acos	cos	_fmodl	_powl
_acosl	_cosl	_fmsbintoieee	sin
asin	cosh	_fpreset	_sinl
_asinl	_coshl	frexp	sinh
atan	_dieeetomsbin	_frexpl	_sinhl
_atanl	difftime	_gcvt	sqrt
atan2	_dmsbintoieee	_hypot	_sqrtl
_atan2l	_ecvt	_hypotl	_status87
atof	exp	ldexp	strtod
_atold	_expl	_ldexpl	_strtold
Bessel	fabs	log	tan
_cabs	_fabsl	_logl	_tanl
_cabsl	_fcvt	log10	tanh
ceil	_fieeetomsbin	_log10l	_tanhl
_ceill	floor	modf	
_clear87	_floorl	_modfl	
_control87	fmod	pow	

Note that the Bessel routine does not correspond to a single function, but to 12 functions named **_j0, _j1, _jn, _y0, _y1, _yn, _j0l, _j1l, _jnl, _y0l, _y1l**, and **_ynl**. Also note that the **_clear87** and **_control87** functions are not available with the /FPa compiler option.

Also requiring floating-point support is the **printf** family of functions (_ **cprintf**, **fprintf**, **printf**, _ **snprintf**, **sprintf**, **vfprintf**, **vprintf**, _ **vsnprintf**, and **vsprintf**). These functions require support for floating-point input and output if used to print floating-point values.

The compiler tries to detect whether floating-point values are used in a program so that supporting functions are loaded only if required. This behavior saves a considerable amount of space for programs that do not require floating-point support.

When you use a floating-point type specifier in the format string for a **printf** or **scanf** call, make sure you specify floating-point values or pointers to floating-point values in the argument list. These must correspond to any floating-point type specifiers in the format string. The presence of floating-point arguments allows the compiler to detect that floating-point support code is required. If a floating-point type specifier is used to print an integer argument, for example, floating-point values will not be detected because the compiler does not actually read the format string used in the **printf** and **scanf** functions. For instance, the following program produces an error at run time:

```
void main( void )  /* This example causes an error */
{
    long f = 10L;
    printf("%f", f);
}
```

In the preceding example, the functions for floating-point support are not loaded because

- No floating-point arguments are given in the call to **printf**.

- No floating-point values are used elsewhere in the program.

As a result, the following error occurs:

```
Floating point not loaded
```

Here is a corrected version of the above call to **printf** in which the long integer value is cast to **double**:

```
void main( void )  /* This example works correctly */
{
    long f = 10L;
    printf("%f", (double) f);
}
```

1.9 Using Huge Arrays with Library Functions

In programs that use small, compact, medium, and large memory models, the compiler allows you to use arrays exceeding the 64K (kilobyte) limit of physical memory in these models by explicitly declaring the arrays as **__huge**. However, generally, you cannot pass huge pointers as arguments to run-time library functions. In the compact-model library used by compact-model programs and in the large-model library used by both large-model and huge-model programs, only the functions listed below use pointer arithmetic that works with huge items:

bsearch	_fmemmove	memcmp
fread	_fmemset	memcpy
fwrite	_halloc	_memicmp
_fmemccpy	_hfree	memmove
_fmemchr	_lfind	memset
_fmemcmp	_lsearch	qsort
_fmemcpy	_memccpy	
_fmemicmp	memchr	

With this set of functions, you can read from, write to, search, sort, copy, initialize, compare, or dynamically allocate and free huge arrays; the huge array can be passed without difficulty to any of these functions in a compact-, large-, or huge-model program. The model-independent routines in the above list (those beginning with **_f**) are available in all memory models.

The **memset**, **memcpy**, and **memcmp** library routines are available in two versions: as C functions and as intrinsic (inline) code. The function versions of these routines support huge pointers in compact and large memory models, but the intrinsic versions do not support huge pointers. (The function version of such routines generates a call to a library function, whereas the intrinsic version inserts inline code into your program. For information on how to select the intrinsic versions of library routines, see the /Oi option in Chapter 13 of *Environment and Tools* (in the Microsoft C/C++ version 7.0 documentation set) or consult your compiler documentation.)

Run-Time Routines by Category

Microsoft run-time library routines handle various kinds of tasks. If you know the type of task you need done, but don't know exactly which routine to use, the categorized lists of routines in this chapter can help. The descriptions here are intended only to give you a brief overview of the capabilities of the run-time library. For a complete description of the behavior, syntax, and use of each routine, see Part 2, "Run-Time Functions."

The main categories of library routines are

- Buffer manipulation
- Character classification and conversion
- Data conversion
- Directory control
- File handling
- Graphics
- Input and output
- Internationalization
- Math
- Memory allocation
- Process and environment control
- QuickWin
- Searching and sorting
- String manipulation
- System calls
- Time
- Variable-length argument lists
- Virtual memory allocation

2.1 Buffer Manipulation

The buffer-manipulation routines are useful for working with areas of memory on a byte-by-byte basis. A "buffer" is an array of bytes, similar to a character string. However, unlike strings, buffers are not usually terminated with a null character ('\0') and can contain non-ASCII data. Therefore, the buffer-manipulation routines always take a *length* or *count* argument. Function declarations for the buffer-manipulation routines are given in the include files MEMORY.H and STRING.H, except for the **_swab** function, which appears in STDLIB.H.

Routines beginning with **_f** are model independent; the **_f** stands for **far**. These routines are useful in writing mixed-model programs because they can be called from any program, regardless of the memory model being used.

Routine	Use
_memccpy, _fmemccpy	Copy characters from one buffer to another until a given character or a given number of characters has been copied
memchr, _fmemchr	Return a pointer to the first occurrence, within a specified number of characters, of a given character in the buffer
memcmp, _fmemcmp	Compare a specified number of characters from two buffers
memcpy, _fmemcpy	Copy a specified number of characters from one buffer to another
_memicmp, _fmemicmp	Compare a specified number of characters from two buffers without regard to the case of the letters (uppercase and lowercase treated as equivalent)
memmove, _fmemmove	Copy a specified number of characters from one buffer to another
memset, _fmemset	Use a given character to initialize a specified number of bytes in the buffer
_swab	Swaps bytes of data and stores them at the specified location

When the source and target areas overlap, only the **memmove** and **_fmemmove** functions are guaranteed to copy the full source properly. (The **memcpy** and **_fmemcpy** routines do not always copy the full source in such cases.)

2.2 Character Classification and Conversion

The character classification and conversion routines allow you to test individual characters in a variety of ways and to convert between uppercase and lowercase characters.

Routine	Use
isalnum	Tests for alphanumeric character
isalpha	Tests for alphabetic character
__isascii	Tests for ASCII character
iscntrl	Tests for control character
__iscsym	Tests for letter, underscore, or digit
__iscsymf	Tests for letter or underscore
isdigit	Tests for decimal digit
isgraph	Tests for printable character except space
islower	Tests for lowercase character
isprint	Tests for printable character
ispunct	Tests for punctuation character
isspace	Tests for white-space character
isupper	Tests for uppercase character
isxdigit	Tests for hexadecimal digit
__toascii	Converts character to ASCII code
tolower	Tests character and converts to lowercase if uppercase
_tolower	Converts character to lowercase (unconditional)
toupper	Tests character and converts to uppercase if lowercase
_toupper	Converts character to uppercase (unconditional)

The classification routines identify characters by finding them in a table of classification codes. Using these routines to classify characters is generally faster than writing a test expression such as the following:

```
if ((c >= 0) || (c <= 0x7f))
```

All of these routines are implemented in two versions: as functions and as macros. The function prototypes and macro definitions appear in CTYPE.H. "Choosing Between Functions and Macros" on page 9 explains how to choose the appropriate version. The **toupper** and **tolower** functions are also declared in the STDLIB.H header file.

2.3 Data Conversion

The data-conversion routines convert numbers to strings of ASCII characters and vice versa. These routines are implemented as functions, all of which are declared in the include file STDLIB.H. The **atof** function, which converts a string to a floating-point value, is also declared in MATH.H.

Routine	Use
abs	Finds absolute value of integer
atof	Converts string to **float**
atoi	Converts string to **int**
atol	Converts string to **long**
_atold	Converts string to **long double**
_ecvt	Converts **double** to string
_fcvt	Converts floating-point number to string
_gcvt	Converts floating-point number to string and stores it in a buffer
_itoa	Converts **int** to string
labs	Finds absolute value of **long** integer
_ltoa	Converts **long** to string
strtod	Converts string to **double**
strtol	Converts string to a **long** integer
_strtold	Converts string to **long double**
strtoul	Converts string to an **unsigned long** integer
_ultoa	Converts **unsigned long** to string

2.4 Directory Control

The directory-control routines let a program access, modify, and obtain information about the directory structure. These routines are functions and are declared in DIRECT.H.

Routine	Use
_chdir	Changes current working directory
_chdrive	Changes current drive
_getcwd	Gets current working directory for the specified drive
_getdrive	Gets current working directory
_mkdir	Makes a new directory
_rmdir	Removes a directory
_searchenv	Searches for a given file on specified paths

2.5 File Handling

The file-handling routines let you create, manipulate, and delete files. They also set and check file-access permissions.

File-handling routines work on a file designated by a path name or by a "file handle," an integer assigned by the operating system that identifies an open file. These routines modify or give information about the designated file. Most of them are declared in the include file IO.H, with the exceptions being the **_fstat** and **_stat** functions (declared in SYS\STAT.H), the **_fullpath** routine (declared in DIRECT.H), and the **remove** and **rename** functions (also declared in STDIO.H).

Routine	Use
_access	Checks file-permission setting
_chmod	Changes file-permission setting
_chsize	Changes file size
_filelength	Gets file length
_fstat	Gets file-status information on handle
_fullpath	Makes an absolute path name from a relative path name
_isatty	Checks for character device
_locking	Locks areas of file (available with DOS versions 3.0 and later)
_makepath	Merges path-name components into a single, full path name
_mktemp	Creates unique filename
remove	Deletes file
rename	Renames file
_setmode	Sets file-translation mode
_splitpath	Splits a path name into component pieces
_stat	Gets file-status information on named file
_umask	Sets default-permission mask
_unlink	Deletes file

The **_access**, **_chmod**, **_fullpath**, **_makepath**, **remove**, **rename**, **_splitpath**, **_stat**, and **_unlink** routines operate on files specified by a path name or filename.

The **_chsize**, **_filelength**, **_fstat**, **_isatty**, **_locking**, and **_setmode** routines work with files designated by a file handle.

The **_mktemp** and **_umask** routines have functions that are slightly different from the other routines. The **_mktemp** routine creates a unique filename; you can use **_mktemp** to create unique filenames that do not conflict with the names of existing files. The **_umask** routine sets the default permission mask for any new files created in a program. The mask can override the permission setting given in the **_open** or **_creat** call for the new file.

2.6 Graphics

The Microsoft run-time library includes a set of graphics routines that offer a wide variety of graphics functions, low-level graphics primitives, font functions, and presentation graphics (displays such as graphs and pie charts).

Graphics functions are supplied in two libraries that must be explicitly linked with your program. The GRAPHICS.LIB library provides support for low-level graphics and character-font routines. The library PGCHART.LIB supports presentation-graphics routines.

Low-Level Graphics and Character-Font Functions

The low-level graphics and font functions are declared in the include file GRAPH.H.

The library can be divided into the eight categories listed below, which correspond to the different tasks involved in creating and manipulating graphic objects.

Category	Task
Configuring mode and environment	Selects the proper display mode for the hardware and establishes memory areas for writing and displaying images
Setting coordinates	Specifies the logical origin and the active display area within the screen
Setting low-level graphics palettes	Specifies a palette mapping for low-level graphics routines
Setting attributes	Specifies background and foreground colors, fill masks, and line styles for low-level graphics routines
Creating graphics output	Draws and fills figures
Creating text output	Writes text on the screen
Transferring images	Stores images in memory and retrieves them
Displaying fonts	Displays text in character fonts compatible with Microsoft Windows

The following sections explain each of these categories.

Configuring Mode and Environment

Routines that configure the mode and environment establish the graphics or text mode of operation, determine the current graphics environment, and control the display of the cursor.

Routine	Use
_clearscreen	Erases the screen and fills it with the current background color
_getactivepage	Gets the current active page number
_getbkcolor	Returns the current background color
_getvideoconfig	Obtains status of current graphics environment
_getvisualpage	Gets the current visual page number
_grstatus	Returns the status of the most recent graphics function call
_setactivepage	Sets memory area for the active page for writing images
_setbkcolor	Sets the current background color
_settextrows	Sets the number of text rows
_setvideomode	Selects an operating mode for the display screen
_setvideomoderows	Sets the video mode and the number of rows for text operations
_setvisualpage	Sets memory area for the current visual page

Setting Coordinates

The "set coordinates" routines set the current text or graphics position and convert pixel coordinates between the various graphics coordinate systems.

The Microsoft graphics functions recognize three sets of coordinates:

- Fixed physical coordinates
- View coordinates defined by the application
- Window coordinates that can include floating-point values

The functions in this category establish window and view coordinate systems and translate between physical, view, and window coordinate systems.

Routine	Use
_getcurrentposition	Determines current position in view coordinates
_getcurrentposition_w	Determines current position in window coordinates
_getphyscoord	Converts view coordinates to physical coordinates
_getviewcoord	Converts physical coordinates to view coordinates
_getviewcoord_w	Converts window coordinates to view coordinates
_getviewcoord_wxy	Converts window coordinates in **_wxycoord** structure to view coordinates
_getwindowcoord	Converts view coordinates to window coordinates
_setcliprgn	Limits graphic output to a region of the screen
_setvieworg	Positions the view-coordinate origin

Routine	Use
_setviewport	Limits graphics output to a region of the screen and positions the view-coordinate origin to the upper-left corner of that region
_setwindow	Defines a floating-point window coordinate system

The default view coordinate system is identical to the physical screen coordinate system. The physical origin (0, 0) is always in the upper-left corner of the display. The x axis extends in the positive direction left to right, while the y axis extends in the positive direction top to bottom.

The physical horizontal and vertical dimensions depend on the hardware display configuration and the selected mode. These values are accessible at run time by examining the **numxpixels** and **numypixels** fields of the **_videoconfig** structure returned by **_getvideoconfig**. (The **_getvideoconfig** routine is listed in the previous section.)

The **_setvieworg** function allows you to move the viewport origin to a new position relative to the physical screen.

Routines that refer to coordinates on the physical screen or viewport require integer values. However, in real-world graphing applications, you might wish to use floating-point values, such as stock prices or average rainfall. The window coordinate system allows you to display graphics using floating-point values instead of integers.

The **_getcurrentposition** and **_getcurrentposition_w** routines allow you to determine the location of the current graphics-output point.

The **_setcliprgn** function defines a restricted active display area on the screen. The **_setviewport** function does the same thing and also resets the viewport origin to the upper-left corner of the restricted active display area.

The physical coordinates of any view-coordinate point can be determined with the **_getphyscoord** function, and the view coordinates of any physical point can be determined with the **_getviewcoord** function.

The view coordinates of any window coordinate can be determined with the **_getviewcoord_w** and **_getviewcoord_wxy** functions. The window coordinates of any view coordinate can be determined with the **_getwindowcoord** function.

The **_setwindow** function defines the current viewport as a real-coordinate window bound by the specified floating-point values.

Setting Low-Level Graphics Palettes

Use the low-level palette routines to select or remap color palettes.

Routine	Use
_remapallpalette	Changes all color indexes in the current palette
_remappalette	Changes a single color index in the current palette
_selectpalette	Selects a predefined palette

Some video modes support a "color palette," which is a table of the color values that can be displayed together on the screen at any given time. A "color value" is a **long** integer representing a color that can be displayed on your system.

In CGA color graphics modes, you can use the **_selectpalette** routine to choose one of several predefined palettes.

On EGA, MCGA, VGA, and SVGA video systems, you can "remap" (change) the palette using the **_remappalette** or **_remapallpalette** routines. For instance, the EGA **_ERESCOLOR** mode offers a total of 64 color values, of which 16 can be displayed at a time. In this mode, the palette contains 16 "color indices," or slots to which you can assign color values.

The **_remappalette** routine changes a single color index to a specified color value. The **_remapallpalette** routine changes all of the available palette entries simultaneously.

Setting Attributes

The low-level output functions that draw lines, arcs, ellipses, and other basic figures do not specify color or line-style information. Instead, the low-level graphics functions rely on a set of attributes that are set independently by the following functions:

Routine	Use
_getarcinfo	Determines the endpoints in viewport coordinates of the most recently drawn arc or pie
_getcolor	Gets the current color
_getfillmask	Gets the current fill mask
_getlinestyle	Gets the current line-style mask
_getwritemode	Gets the current logical write mode
_setcolor	Sets the current color
_setfillmask	Sets the current fill mask
_setlinestyle	Sets the current line-style mask
_setwritemode	Sets logical write mode for line drawing

The _getcolor and _setcolor functions get or set the current color index for graphics and font output. The _getbkcolor and _setbkcolor functions get or set the current background color. (The _getbkcolor and _setbkcolor functions are listed in "Configuring Mode and Environment" on page 22.)

The _getfillmask and _setfillmask functions get or set the current fill mask. The mask is an 8-by-8-bit template array, with each bit representing a pixel. If a bit is 0, the pixel in memory is left untouched, as the mask is transparent to that pixel. If a bit is 1, the pixel is assigned the current color value. The template is repeated as necessary over the entire fill area.

The _getlinestyle and _setlinestyle functions get or set the current line style. The line style is determined by a 16-bit template buffer with each bit corresponding to a pixel. If a bit is 1, the pixel is set to the current color. If a bit is 0, the pixel is not changed. The template is repeated for the length of the line.

The _getwritemode and _setwritemode functions get or set the logical write mode for straight-line drawing. The default mode, _GPSET, causes lines to be drawn in the current graphics color. Other modes combine the current graphics color and the original screen image using various logical operations.

Creating Graphics Output

The graphics output functions use a set of specified coordinates and draw various figures. They use the current or default attributes for line-style mask, fill mask, write mode, background color, and foreground color.

The name of each function announces its task or the figure it draws, as the following list indicates:

Routine	Use
_arc, _arc_w, _arc_wxy	Draw an arc
_ellipse, _ellipse_w, _ellipse_wxy	Draw an ellipse or circle
_floodfill, _floodfill_w	Flood-fill an area of the screen with the current color
_getcurrentposition, _getcurrentposition_w	Obtain the current graphic-output position used by _lineto and _outgtext
_getpixel, _getpixel_w	Obtain a pixel's color
_lineto, _lineto_w	Draw a line from the current graphic-output position to a specified point
_moveto, _moveto_w	Move the current graphic-output position to a specified point
_pie, _pie_w, _pie_wxy	Draw a pie-slice-shaped figure
_polygon, _polygon_w, _polygon_wxy	Draw or scan-fill a polygon

Routine	Use
_rectangle, **_rectangle_w,** **_rectangle_wxy**	Draw or scan-fill a rectangle
_setpixel, _setpixel_w	Set a pixel's color

Most of these routines are available in several forms, which are indicated by their names. Output functions without a suffix use the view coordinate system. Functions that end with **_w** take **double** values as arguments and use the window coordinate system. Functions that end with **_wxy** use **_wxycoord** structures to define the coordinates and use the window coordinate system.

Circular figures, such as arcs and ellipses, are centered within a "bounding rectangle" specified by two points that define the diagonally opposed corners of the rectangle. The center of the rectangle becomes the center of the figure, and the rectangle's borders determine the size of the figure.

Creating Text Output

The next group of routines provides text output in both graphics and text modes. Unlike the standard console I/O library routines, these functions recognize text-window boundaries and use the current text color.

Routine	Use
_displaycursor	Sets the cursor on or off upon exit from a graphics routine
_gettextcolor	Obtains the current text color
_gettextcursor	Returns the current cursor attribute (text modes only)
_gettextposition	Obtains the current text-output position
_gettextwindow	Gets the current text window boundaries
_outmem	Prints text of a specified length from a memory buffer
_outtext	Outputs a text string to the screen at the current text position
_scrolltextwindow	Scrolls the current text window up or down
_settextcolor	Sets the current text color
_settextcursor	Sets the current cursor attribute (text modes only)
_settextposition	Relocates the current text position
_settextwindow	Defines the current text-display window
_wrapon	Enables or disables line wrap

The **_outtext** and **_outmem** routines provide no formatting. If you want to output integer or floating-point values, you must convert the values into a string variable (using the **sprintf** function) before calling these routines.

The **_outtext** routine recognizes the **\n** (newline character) and **\r** (carriage return) sequences. The **_outmem** routine treats these sequences as printable graphics characters.

Transferring Images

The functions in this category transfer screen images between memory and the display, using a buffer allocated by the application, or determine the size in bytes of the buffer needed to store a given image.

The functions that end with **_w** or **_wxy** use window coordinates; the other functions in this set use view coordinates.

Routine	Use
_getimage, **_getimage_w,** **_getimage_wxy**	Store a screen image in memory
_imagesize, **_imagesize_w,** **_imagesize_wxy**	Return the size (in bytes) of the buffer needed to store the image
_putimage, **_putimage_w**	Retrieve an image from memory and display it

In some cases, the buffer needed to store an image with the **_getimage** functions must be larger than 64K (65,534) bytes. Use the **_halloc** routine to allocate a buffer larger than 64K.

Displaying Fonts

The functions listed in this section control the display of font-based characters on the screen.

Routine	Use
_getfontinfo	Obtains the current font characteristics
_getgtextextent	Determines the width in pixels of specified text in the current font
_getgtextvector	Gets orientation of font text output
_outgtext	Outputs text in the current font to the screen at the specified pixel position
_registerfonts	Initializes font library
_setfont	Finds a single font that matches a specified set of characteristics and makes this font the current font for use by the **_outgtext** function

Routine	Use
_setgtextvector	Sets the current orientation for font text output
_ungisterfonts	Frees memory allocated by **_registerfonts**

Presentation-Graphics Functions

The presentation-graphics functions are declared in the PGCHART.H include file. The library can be divided into the three categories listed below, corresponding to the different tasks involved in creating and manipulating graphic objects:

Category	Task
Displaying presentation graphics	Initializes video structures for presentation graphics and establishes the default chart type. Displays presentation-graphics chart: bar, column, pie, scatter, or line chart.
Analyzing presentation-graphics data	Analyzes data (does not display chart).
Manipulating presentation-graphics structures	Modifies basic chart structures (e.g., palettes, cross-hatching styles).

Displaying Presentation Graphics

The functions listed in this section initialize the presentation-graphics library and display the specified graph type.

Because the **_pg_initchart** routine initializes the presentation-graphics library, it must be called before any other function in the presentation-graphics library. The **_pg_defaultchart** function initializes the variables in the chart environment.

The other routines in this category display the specified graph. The single-series versions plot one set of data, and the multiseries versions (those ending with an **ms** suffix) plot several sets of data in the same chart style.

Presentation-graphics programs can display text in different font sizes by taking advantage of font-based characters (see the previous section, "Displaying Fonts"). Call the **_registerfonts** and **_setfont** routines to select a font before calling the **_pg_initchart** routine. Subsequent charts use the selected font. You can later call the **_unregisterfonts** routine to restore the default character font and free the memory previously allocated for fonts.

Note If your program uses the alternate math package—if it is compiled with /FPa—it cannot use the PGCHART.LIB module.

Routine	Use
_pg_chart	Displays a single-series bar, column, or line chart
_pg_chartms	Displays a multiseries bar, column, or line chart
_pg_chartpie	Displays a pie chart
_pg_chartscatter	Displays a scatter diagram for a single series of data
_pg_chartscatterms	Displays a scatter diagram for more than one series of data
_pg_defaultchart	Initializes all necessary variables in the chart environment for a specified chart type
_pg_initchart	Initializes the presentation-graphics library

Analyzing Presentation-Graphics Charts

These routines calculate default values for the specified graph type but do not display the chart. The single-series versions analyze one set of data, and the multiseries versions analyze several sets of data in the same chart style.

Routine	Use
_pg_analyzechart	Analyzes a single series of data for a bar, column, or line chart
_pg_analyzechartms	Analyzes a multiseries of data for a bar, column, or line chart
_pg_analyzepie	Analyzes data for a pie chart
_pg_analyzescatter	Analyzes a single series of data for a scatter diagram
_pg_analyzescatterms	Analyzes a multiseries of data for a scatter diagram

Manipulating Presentation-Graphics Structures

These functions control low-level aspects of the presentation-graphics package.

Routine	Use
_pg_getchardef	Retrieves the current 8-by-8-pixel bit map for a specified character
_pg_getpalette	Retrieves current colors, line styles, fill patterns, and plot characters for all presentation-graphics palettes
_pg_getstyleset	Retrieves the contents of the current styleset
_pg_hlabelchart	Writes text horizontally on the screen
_pg_resetpalette	Sets current colors, line styles, fill patterns, and plot characters to the default values for the current screen mode
_pg_resetstyleset	Resets the contents of the current styleset to the default value for the current screen mode
_pg_setchardef	Sets the 8-by-8-pixel bit map for a specified character

Routine	Use
_pg_setpalette	Sets current colors
_pg_setstyleset	Sets the contents of the current styleset
_pg_vlabelchart	Writes text vertically on the screen

2.7 Input and Output

The input and output (I/O) routines allow you to read and write data to and from files and devices. In C, there are no predefined file structures; all data items are treated as sequences of bytes. The following three types of I/O functions are available:

- Stream
- Low-level
- Console and port

The stream I/O functions treat data as a stream of individual characters. By choosing among the many stream functions available, you can process data in different sizes and formats, from single characters to large data structures. Stream I/O also provides buffering, which can significantly improve performance.

The low-level I/O routines do not perform buffering and formatting. Instead, they invoke the operating system's input and output capabilities directly. These routines let you access files and peripheral devices at a more basic level than the stream functions.

The console and port I/O routines allow you to read or write directly to a console (keyboard and screen) or an I/O port (such as a printer port). The port I/O routines simply read and write data in bytes. With console I/O routines, some additional options are available, such as detecting whether a character has been typed at the console. You can also choose between echoing characters to the screen as they are read or reading characters without echoing.

The run-time library also provides a number of direct DOS I/O system-call routines. These are described in "System Calls" on page 55.

You can perform file I/O operations in two modes: text and binary. The following section describes these modes and their use. You can also ensure that the **fflush** and **_flushall** routines write data to storage media rather than to just the operating system's buffers. See "Stream Routines" on page 33.

Warning! Because stream routines are buffered and low-level routines are not, the two types of routines are generally incompatible. You should use either stream or low-level routines consistently for processing a given file.

Text and Binary Modes

Many C and C++ programs use data files for input and output. With DOS, data files are normally processed in text mode. In this mode, each carriage-return–line-feed (CR-LF) combination is translated into a single line-feed character during input. During output, each line-feed character is translated into a CR-LF combination.

Sometimes you may want to process a file without making those translations. In these cases you use binary mode, which suppresses CR-LF translations.

You can control the file translation mode in the following ways:

- To process a few selected files in binary mode, while retaining the default text mode for most files, you can specify binary mode when you open the selected files. The **fopen** routine opens a file in binary mode when you specify the letter **b** in the access-mode string for the file. The **_open** routine opens a file in binary mode when you specify the **_O_BINARY** flag in the *oflag* argument. For more information about **fopen** and **_open**, see the reference description of each routine.

- To process most or all files in binary mode, you can change the default mode to binary. The global variable **_fmode** controls the default translation mode, which is normally text. If you set **_fmode** to **_O_BINARY**, the default mode is binary except for **stdaux** and **stdprn**, which are opened in binary mode by default.

You can change the value of **_fmode** in two ways:

- Link with the file BINMODE.OBJ (supplied with Microsoft C/C++). This changes the initial setting of **_fmode** to the **_O_BINARY** flag, causing all files except **stdin**, **stdout**, and **stderr** to be opened in binary mode.

- Change the value of **_fmode** directly by setting it to the **_O_BINARY** flag in your program. This has the same effect as linking with BINMODE.OBJ.

You can still override the default mode (now binary) for a particular file by opening it in text mode. Specify the letter **t** when using **fopen**, or specify the **_O_TEXT** flag when using **_open**.

By default, the **stdin**, **stdout**, and **stderr** files are opened in text mode, and the **stdaux** and **stdprn** files are opened in binary mode. The **_setmode** routine allows you to change these defaults or change the mode of a file after it has been opened. See the reference description of **_setmode** for details.

Stream Routines

Stream I/O functions handle data as a continuous stream of characters. To use the stream functions, you must include the file STDIO.H in your program. This file defines constants, types, and structures used in the stream functions, and contains function declarations and macro definitions for the stream routines.

When a file is opened for I/O using the stream functions, the opened file is associated with a structure of type **FILE** (defined in STDIO.H) containing basic information about the file. A pointer to the **FILE** structure is returned when the stream is opened. Subsequent operations use this pointer (also called the "stream pointer," or just "stream") to refer to the file.

The stream functions provide for buffered, formatted, or unformatted input and output. When a stream is buffered, data that is read from or written to the stream is collected in an intermediate storage location called a "buffer." In write operations, the output buffer's contents are written to the appropriate final location when the buffer is full, the stream is closed, or the program terminates normally. The buffer is said to be "flushed" when this occurs. In read operations, a block of data is placed in the input buffer. When the input buffer is empty, the next block of data is transferred into the buffer.

Buffering produces efficient I/O because the system can transfer a large block of data in a single operation rather than performing an I/O operation each time a data item is read from or written to a stream. However, if a program terminates abnormally, output buffers may not be flushed, resulting in loss of data.

You can use the **fflush** and **_flushall** routines to ensure that the buffer associated with the specified file or all of the open buffers are flushed to the operating system. If a file was opened with **fopen** or **_fdopen** and the **c** flag, or if the program is linked with COMMODE.OBJ, the contents of a flushed buffer are written to disk.

Some of the constants defined in STDIO.H may be useful in your program. The manifest constant **EOF** is defined to be the value returned at end-of-file. **NULL** is the null pointer. **FILE** is the structure that maintains information about a stream. **BUFSIZ** defines the default size of stream buffers, in bytes.

Routine	Use
clearerr	Clears the error indicator for a stream
fclose	Closes a stream
_fcloseall	Closes all open streams
_fdopen	Associates a stream with an open file handle
feof	Tests for end-of-file on a stream
ferror	Tests for error on a stream
fflush	Flushes a stream

Routine	Use
fgetc	Reads a character from a stream (function version)
_fgetchar	Reads a character from **stdin** (function version)
fgetpos	Gets the position indicator of a stream
fgets	Reads a string from a stream
_fileno	Gets the file handle associated with a stream
_flushall	Flushes all streams
fopen	Opens a stream
fprintf	Writes formatted data to a stream
fputc	Writes a character to a stream (function version)
_fputchar	Writes a character to **stdout** (function version)
fputs	Writes a string to a stream
fread	Reads unformatted data from a stream
freopen	Reassigns a **FILE** pointer to a new file
fscanf	Reads formatted data from a stream
fseek	Moves file position to a given location
fsetpos	Sets the position indicator of a stream
_fsopen	Opens a stream with file sharing
ftell	Gets current file position
fwrite	Writes unformatted data items to a stream
getc	Reads a character from a stream
getchar	Reads a character from **stdin**
gets	Reads a line from **stdin**
_getw	Reads a binary **int** item from a stream
printf	Writes formatted data to **stdout**
putc	Writes a character to a stream
putchar	Writes a character to **stdout**
puts	Writes a line to a stream
_putw	Writes a binary **int** item to a stream
rewind	Moves file position to beginning of a stream
_rmtmp	Removes temporary files created by **tmpfile**
scanf	Reads formatted data from **stdin**
setbuf	Controls stream buffering
setvbuf	Controls stream buffering and buffer size
_snprintf	Writes formatted data of a specified length to a string
sprintf	Writes formatted data to a string
sscanf	Reads formatted data from a string

Routine	Use
_tempnam	Generates a temporary filename in given directory
tmpfile	Creates a temporary file
tmpnam	Generates a temporary filename
ungetc	Places a character in the buffer
vfprintf	Writes formatted data to a stream
vprintf	Writes formatted data to **stdout**
_vsnprintf	Writes formatted data of a specified length to a string
vsprintf	Writes formatted data to a string

Opening a Stream

A stream must be opened using the **_fdopen**, **fopen**, **freopen**, or **_fsopen** function before input and output can be performed on that stream. When opening a stream, the named stream can be opened for reading, writing, or both, and it can be opened in either text or binary mode.

The **_fdopen**, **fopen**, **freopen**, and **_fsopen** functions return a **FILE** pointer. You normally assign the pointer value to a variable and use the variable to refer to the opened stream. For instance, if your program contains the lines

```
FILE *infile
infile = fopen ("test.dat", "r");
```

you can use the **FILE** pointer variable `infile` to refer to the stream.

Using Predefined Stream Pointers

When a program begins execution, the startup code automatically opens several streams: standard input, standard output, and standard error. By default, the standard input, standard output, and standard error streams are directed to the console (keyboard and screen). This means that when a program expects input from the "standard input," it receives that input from the console. Similarly, a program that writes to the "standard output" prints its data to the console. Error messages generated by the library routines are sent to the "standard error," meaning that error messages appear on the user's console.

With DOS, two additional streams are opened: standard auxiliary and standard print. The assignment of standard auxiliary and standard print depends on the machine configuration. These streams usually refer to the first serial port and a printer port, but those ports may not be available on some systems. Be sure to check your machine configuration before using these streams.

You can refer to the standard streams with the following predefined stream pointers:

Pointer	Stream
stdin	Standard input
stdout	Standard output
stderr	Standard error
stdaux	Standard auxiliary (DOS only)
stdprn	Standard print (DOS only)

You can use these pointers in any function that requires a stream pointer as an argument. Some functions, such as **getchar** and **putchar**, are designed to use **stdin** or **stdout** automatically. The pointers **stdin**, **stdout**, **stderr**, **stdaux**, and **stdprn** are constants, not variables; do not try to assign them a new stream pointer value.

DOS allows you to redirect a program's standard input and standard output at the operating-system command level. See your operating-system user's manual for a complete discussion of redirection.

Within your program, you can use **freopen** to redirect **stdin**, **stdout**, **stderr**, **stdaux**, or **stdprn** so that it refers to a disk file or to a device. See the reference description of **freopen** for more details.

Controlling Stream Buffering

As mentioned earlier, stream routines can use in-memory buffers to speed I/O operations. Files opened using the stream routines are buffered by default, except for **stdaux** and **stdprn**, which are normally unbuffered. The **stdout** and **stderr** streams are flushed whenever they are full or (if you are writing to a character device) after each library call.

By using the **setbuf** or **setvbuf** function, you can cause a stream to be unbuffered, or you can associate a buffer with an unbuffered stream. Buffers allocated by the system are not accessible to you, but buffers allocated with **setbuf** or **setvbuf** refer to arrays in your program and can be manipulated. Buffers can be any size up to **INT_MAX** bytes. This size is set by the manifest constant **BUFSIZ** in STDIO.H if you use **seftbuf**; if you use **setvbuf**, you can set the size of the buffer yourself. (See the descriptions of **setbuf** and **setvbuf** in the reference section for more details.)

Note These routines affect only buffers created by the run-time library routines. They have no effect on buffers created by the operating system.

Committing Buffer Contents to Disk

Normally, both the **fflush** and the **_flushall** functions pass the contents of a program buffer to the operating system, which can cache data before writing it to disk. In the case of a system failure, data cached by the operating system will be lost. The commit-to-disk feature ensures that the flushed contents of a buffer are written to storage media.

There are two ways to commit buffer contents to disk:

- Link with the file COMMODE.OBJ (provided with Microsoft C/C++) to set a global commit flag. The default setting of the global flag is "no-commit."

- Set the **c** "commit" flag with **fopen** or **_fdopen** to open the file in commit mode. The **n** flag specifies the "no-commit" mode.

COMMODE.OBJ allows existing code to use the commit feature. Any file specifically opened with either the **c** or the **n** flag will behave according to the flag, regardless of the state of the global commit/no-commit flag. Thus, some files can be opened with committing contents to disk and some without.

Closing Streams

The **fclose** and **_fcloseall** functions close a stream or streams. The **fclose** routine closes a single specified stream; **_fcloseall** closes all open streams except **stdin**, **stdout**, **stderr**, **stdaux**, and **stdprn**. If your program does not explicitly close a stream, the stream is automatically closed when the program terminates. However, it is a good practice to close a stream when your program is finished with it, as the number of streams that can be open at a given time is limited.

Reading and Writing Data

The stream functions allow you to transfer data in a variety of ways. You can read and write binary data (a sequence of bytes), or specify reading and writing by characters, lines, or more complicated formats.

Reading and writing operations on streams always begin at the current position of the stream, known as the "file pointer" for the stream. The file pointer is changed to reflect the new position after a read or write operation takes place. For example, if you read a single character from a stream, the file pointer is increased by one byte so that the next operation begins with the first unread character. If a stream is opened for appending, the file pointer is automatically positioned at the end of the file before each write operation.

When switching directly between output and input, there must be an intervening call to the **fflush** function or to a file-positioning function (**fseek**, **fsetpos**, or **rewind**). Input can be directly followed by output without an intervening call to a file-positioning function if the input operation encounters end-of-file.

The **fseek** and **fsetpos** functions allow you to position the file pointer anywhere in a file. The next operation occurs at the position you specified. The **rewind** routine positions the file pointer at the beginning of the file. Use the **ftell** or **fgetpos** routine to determine the current position of the file pointer.

The **feof** macro detects an end-of-file condition on a stream. Once the end-of-file indicator is set, it remains set until the file is closed, or until **clearerr**, **fseek**, **fsetpos**, or **rewind** is called.

Streams associated with a character-oriented device (such as a console) do not have file pointers. Data coming from or going to a console cannot be accessed randomly. Routines that set or get the file-pointer position (such as **fseek**, **fgetpos**, **fsetpos**, **ftell**, or **rewind**) have undefined results if used on a stream associated with a character-oriented device.

Detecting Errors

When an error occurs in a stream operation, an error indicator for the stream is set. You can use the **ferror** macro to test the error indicator and determine whether an error has occurred. Once an error has occurred, the error indicator for the stream remains set until the stream is closed, or until you explicitly clear the error indicator by calling **clearerr** or **rewind**.

Low-Level Routines

Low-level input and output calls do not buffer or format data. Declarations for the low-level functions are given in the include files IO.H, FCNTL.H, SYS\TYPES.H, and SYS\STAT.H. Unlike the stream functions, low-level functions do not require the include file STDIO.H. However, some common constants are defined in STDIO.H; for example, the end-of-file indicator (**EOF**) may be useful. If your program requires these constants, you must include STDIO.H.

Routine	Use
_close	Closes a file
_commit	Flushes a file to disk
_creat	Creates a file
_dup	Creates a second handle for a file
_dup2	Reassigns a handle to a file
_eof	Tests for end-of-file

Routine	Use
_lseek	Repositions file pointer to a given location
_open	Opens a file
_read	Reads data from a file
_sopen	Opens a file for file sharing
_tell	Gets current file-pointer position
_umask	Sets default file-permission mask
_write	Writes data to a file

Opening a File

You must open a file before performing I/O functions on it. The **_open** function opens a file; it can also create the file when opening it. With DOS versions 3.0 and later, you can use **_sopen** to open a file with file-sharing attributes. The **_creat** function can create and open a file.

The file can be opened for reading, writing, or both, and opened in either text or binary mode (see "Text and Binary Modes" on page 32). The include file FCNTL.H must be included when opening a file, as it contains definitions for flags used in **_open**. In some cases, the files SYS\TYPES.H and SYS\STAT.H must also be included; for more information, see the reference description for the **_open** function.

These functions return a file handle, which is normally assigned to an integer variable. You use the variable to refer to the opened file.

Reading and Writing Data

Use the **_read** and **_write** routines to read and write to files. These operations begin at the current position in the file. The current position is updated each time a read or write operation occurs.

The **_lseek** function allows you to place the file pointer anywhere in the file. The next operation occurs at the position you specified. The **_tell** function indicates the current position of file pointer. The **_eof** routine tests for the end of the file.

Low-level I/O routines set the **errno** variable when an error occurs. Chapter 3, "Global Variables and Standard Types," describes **errno**.

Character-oriented devices, such as the console, do not have file pointers. The **_lseek** and **_tell** routines have undefined results if used on a handle associated with a device.

Closing Files

The **_close** function closes an open file. Open files are automatically closed when a program terminates. However, it is a good practice to close a file when your program is finished with it, as there is a limit to the number of files that can be open at one time.

Using Predefined Handles

When a program begins execution, five files are automatically opened: standard input, standard output, standard error, standard auxiliary, and standard print.

Low-level routines can access these files using the following predefined handles:

Stream	Handle
stdin	0
stdout	1
stderr	2
stdaux (DOS only)	3
stdprn (DOS only)	4

You can use these file handles without previously opening the files. The files are opened and the handles are assigned when the program starts.

The **_dup** and **_dup2** functions allow you to assign multiple handles for the same file. These functions are typically used to associate the predefined file handles with different files.

With DOS and Windows, you can redirect the standard input and standard output at the operating-system command level. See your operating-system user's manual for a complete discussion of redirection.

Increasing the Maximum Number of File Handles and Streams

You can change the maximum number of file handles and streams that your program can handle. The process is simple and involves changing some constants in the startup source files, which are provided with Microsoft C/C++, and then compiling and linking the new startup code with your program. The following sections describe the process.

Increasing File Handles

DOS, Windows, and QuickWin use the value of the constant _NFILE_ to establish the maximum number of available file handles. To increase the number of file handles, edit the startup source file CRT0DAT.ASM and change the line

```
_NFILE_ = 20
```

so that _NFILE_ is set to the desired maximum. For example, to increase the maximum number of available file handles to 40, change the line as shown here:

```
_NFILE_ = 40
```

CRT0DAT.ASM contains a section of conditional code that is automatically enabled when you change the value of _NFILE_.

QuickWin uses the constant _WFILE_ to establish the maximum number of available text child windows. You can edit CRT0DAT.ASM to change _WFILE_. Change the line

```
_WFILE_ = 20
```

so that _WFILE_ is set to the desired maximum. For example, to increase the maximum number of available text child windows to 40, change the line as shown here:

```
_WFILE_ = 40
```

Note Increasing the number of file handles allows you to use low-level I/O functions, such as **_open** and **_read**, with more files. However, it does not affect the number of stream-level I/O files (that is, the number of **FILE *** streams).

Increasing Streams

To increase the maximum number of streams, edit one or more of the following source files and constants:

System	Source File	Constant
DOS	_FILE.C	_NFILE_
Windows and QuickWin	FILE.ASM	_NFILE_
QuickWin	WFILE.ASM	_WFILE_

For DOS, Windows, and QuickWin, change the line

```
_NFILE_ equ 20
```

to set `_NFILE_` to the desired maximum. For example, to allow a maximum of 40 streams, change the line as shown here:

```
_NFILE_ equ 40
```

In addition, you can change the value of the constant _WFILE_, found in WFILE.ASM, to increase the maximum number of available QuickWin text child windows.

Increasing the number of streams allows you to use stream-level I/O functions, such as **fopen** and **fread**, with more files.

Note The number of low-level file handles must be greater than or equal to the number of stream-level files. For example, if you increase the value of _NFILE_ in the module _FILE.C, you must also increase the value of _NFILE_ in the module CRT0DAT.ASM. Similarly, if you increase the value of _WFILE_ in the module WFILE.ASM, you must also increase the value of _WFILE_ in the module CRT0DAT.ASM.

Increasing the System Limit

To use more than 20 files at a time, you must increase the file limit imposed on your process by the operating system.

To increase the system-wide limit, increase the number of files available on your system as a whole by editing your system configuration file (CONFIG.SYS). For example, to allow 50 open files at a time on your system, put this statement in the configuration file:

```
FILES=50
```

Using the Modified Startup Files

After you modify one or more of the startup source files, you need to recompile the file(s) using the batch file CSTARTUP.BAT. Be sure to read the file README.TXT, which is located in the same directory as CSTARTUP.BAT, before running the batch file.

To use a new object file, either explicitly link your program with it or replace it in the appropriate model of the run-time library. For example, after you assemble CRT0DAT.ASM, the object file will be CRT0DAT.OBJ.

Console and Port I/O

The console and port I/O routines are implemented as functions and are declared in the include file CONIO.H. These functions perform reading and writing operations on your console or on the specified port. The **_cgets**, **_cscanf**, **_getch**, **_getche**, and **_kbhit** routines take input from the console, while **_cprintf**, **_cputs**, **_putch**, and **_ungetch** write to the console. The input or output of these functions can be redirected.

Routine	Use
_cgets	Reads a string from the console
_cprintf	Writes formatted data to the console
_cputs	Writes a string to the console
_cscanf	Reads formatted data from the console
_getch	Reads a character from the console
_getche	Reads a character from the console and echoes it
_inp	Reads one byte from the specified I/O port
_inpw	Reads a two-byte word from the specified I/O port
_kbhit	Checks for a keystroke at the console
_outp	Writes one byte to the specified I/O port
_outpw	Writes a two-byte word to the specified I/O port
_putch	Writes a character to the console
_ungetch	"Ungets" the last character read from the console so that it becomes the next character read

Note Programs that need only run under DOS can also use a number of direct DOS I/O system calls (**_dos_open**, **_dos_read**, **_dos_close**, etc.). These are described in detail in "System Calls" on page 55.

The console or port does not have to be opened or closed before I/O is performed, so there are no open or close routines in this category. The port I/O routines **_inp** and **_outp** read or write one byte at a time from the specified port. The **_inpw** and **_outpw** routines read and write two-byte words, respectively.

The console I/O routines allow reading and writing of strings (**_cgets** and **_cputs**), formatted data (**_cscanf** and **_cprintf**), and characters. Several options are available when reading and writing characters.

The **_putch** routine writes a single character to the console. The **_getch** and **_getche** routines read a single character from the console: **_getche** echoes the character back to the console, while **_getch** does not. The **_ungetch** routine "ungets" the last character read; the next read operation on the console begins with the "ungotten" character.

The _**kbhit** routine determines whether a key has been struck at the console. This routine allows you to test for keyboard input before you attempt to read from the console.

Note The console I/O routines are not compatible with stream or low-level library routines and should not be used with them.

2.8 Internationalization

Internationalization routines are useful for creating different versions of a program for international markets. These routines are declared in the header file LOCALE.H, except for **strftime**, which is declared in TIME.H.

Routine	Use
localeconv	Sets a structure with appropriate values for formatting numeric quantities
setlocale	Selects the appropriate locale for the program
strcoll	Compares strings using locale-specific information
strftime	Formats a date and time string
strxfrm	Transforms a string based on locale-specific information

Currently only the "C" locale is supported by Microsoft C/C++.

2.9 Math

The math routines allow you to perform common mathematical calculations. All math routines work with floating-point values and therefore require floating-point support (see "Floating-Point Support" on page 14).

The math library provides two versions of some routines. The first version of the routine supports **double** arguments and return values. The second version supports an 80-bit data type, allowing the routine to take **long double** arguments and return a **long double** value. The second version usually has the same name with the suffix **l**. For instance, the **acos** routine supports **double** arguments and return values, while _**acosl** supports **long double** arguments and return values.

Routines which support **long double** values are not available when you compile with the /FPa (alternate math) compiler option. The same is true of the _**clear87**, _**control87**, and _**status87** routines.

Most math declarations are in the include file MATH.H. However, the **_clear87**, **_control87**, **_fpreset**, and **_status87** routines are defined in FLOAT.H; the **abs** and **labs** functions are defined in MATH.H and STDLIB.H; and the **div** and **ldiv** routines are declared in STDLIB.H.

Routine	Use
acos, _acosl	Calculate the arccosine
asin, _asinl	Calculate the arcsine
atan, _atanl	Calculate the arctangent
atan2, _atan2l	Calculate the arctangent
Bessel	Calculates Bessel functions
_cabs, _cabsl	Find the absolute value of a complex number
ceil, _ceill	Find the integer ceiling
_clear87	Gets and clears the floating-point status word
_control87	Gets the old floating-point control word and sets a new control-word value
cos, _cosl	Calculate the cosine
cosh, _coshl	Calculate the hyperbolic cosine
_dieeetomsbin	Converts IEEE double-precision number to Microsoft (MS) binary format
div	Divides one integer by another, returning the quotient and remainder
_dmsbintoieee	Converts Microsoft binary double-precision number to IEEE format
exp, _expl	Calculate the exponential function
fabs, _fabsl	Find the absolute value
_fieeetomsbin	Converts IEEE single-precision number to Microsoft binary format
floor, _floorl	Find the largest integer less than or equal to the argument
fmod, _fmodl	Find the floating-point remainder
_fmsbintoieee	Converts Microsoft binary single-precision number to IEEE format
_fpreset	Reinitializes the floating-point-math package
frexp, _frexpl	Calculate an exponential value
_hypot, _hypotl	Calculate the hypotenuse of a right triangle
ldexp, _ldexpl	Calculate the product of the argument and 2^{exp}
ldiv	Divides one **long** integer by another, returning the quotient and remainder
log, _logl	Calculate the natural logarithm
log10, _log10l	Calculate the base-10 logarithm
_lrotl, _lrotr	Shift an **unsigned long int** item left (**_lrotl**) or right (**_lrotr**)

Routine	Use
_matherr, **_matherrl**	Handle math errors
__max, __min	Return the larger or smaller of two values
modf, _modfl	Split the argument into integer and fractional parts
pow, _powl	Calculate a value raised to a power
rand	Gets a pseudorandom number
_rotl, _rotr	Shift an **unsigned int** item left (**_rotl**) or right (**_rotr**)
sin, _sinl	Calculate the sine
sinh, _sinhl	Calculate the hyperbolic sine
sqrt, _sqrtl	Find the square root
srand	Initializes a pseudorandom series
_status87	Gets the floating-point status word
tan, _tanl	Calculate the tangent
tanh, _tanhl	Calculate the hyperbolic tangent

The Bessel routine does not correspond to a single function, but to 12 functions named **_j0, _j1, _jn, _y0, _y1, _yn, _j0l, _j1l, _jnl, _y0l, _y1l,** and **_ynl.**

The **_matherr** and **_matherrl** routines are invoked by the math functions when errors occur. The **_matherr** routine handles functions that return a **double** value, and **_matherrl** handles routines that return a **long double**.

These routines are defined in the library, but you can redefine them for different error handling. The user-defined function, if given, must follow the rules given in the reference description of **_matherr** and **_matherrl**.

You are not required to supply a definition for the **_matherr** routines. If no definition is present, the default error returns for each routine are used. The reference description of each routine describes that routine's error returns.

2.10 Memory Allocation

The memory-allocation routines allow you to allocate, free, and reallocate blocks of memory. Memory-allocation routines are declared in the include file MALLOC.H. The C++ **_set_new_handler** functions allow you to redefine the action of the C++ **new** operator and are declared in include file NEW.H.

Routine	Use
_alloca	Allocates a block of memory from the program's stack
_bfreeseg	Frees a based heap
_bheapseg	Allocates a based heap
calloc, _bcalloc, _fcalloc, _ncalloc	Allocate storage for an array
_expand, _bexpand, _fexpand, _nexpand	Expand or shrink a block of memory without moving its location
free, _bfree, _ffree, _free	Free an allocated block
_freect	Returns approximate number of items of given size that could be allocated in the near heap
_halloc	Allocates storage for huge array
_heapadd, _bheapadd	Add memory to a heap
_heapchk, _bheapchk, _fheapchk, _nheapchk	Check a heap for consistency
_heapmin, _bheapmin, _fheapmin, _nheapmin	Release unused memory in a heap
_heapset, _bheapset, _fheapset, _nheapset	Fill free heap entries with a specified value
_heapwalk, _bheapwalk, _fheapwalk, _nheapwalk	Return information about each entry in a heap
_hfree	Frees a block allocated by **_halloc**
malloc, _bmalloc, _fmalloc, _nmalloc	Allocate a block of memory
_memavl	Returns approximate number of bytes available for allocation in the near heap
_memmax	Returns size of largest contiguous free block in the near heap
_msize, _bmsize, _fmsize, _nmsize	Return size of an allocated block
realloc, _brealloc, _frealloc, _nrealloc	Reallocate a block to a new size
_set_new_handler, _set_bnew_handler, _set_fnew_handler, _set_hnew_handler, _set_nnew_handler	Enable an error-handling mechanism
_stackavail	Returns size of stack space available for allocation with **_alloca**

Some memory-management routines, such as **malloc**, are available in different versions that begin with **_b**, **_f**, or **_n**. These variations are described in the following section.

The **malloc** and **free** routines allocate and free memory space, respectively, while a program runs. The **malloc** routine allocates memory from the "heap," which is a pool of memory not otherwise used by your program. In tiny-, small-, and medium-model programs, the heap consists of unused memory in your program's default data segment. In compact-, large-, and huge-model programs, it is unused memory outside the default data segment.

The **malloc** and **free** routines satisfy the memory-allocation requirements of most programs. More specialized memory-management routines are discussed below.

The **realloc** and **_expand** routines can expand or shrink an allocated memory block. They behave differently in cases in which there is not enough room to expand the block in its current location. In this case, **realloc** moves the block as needed, but **_expand** does not.

The **calloc** routine allocates memory for an array and initializes every byte in the allocated block to 0.

The **_halloc** routine is similar to **calloc**, except that it can allocate memory for a huge array (one that exceeds 64K in size). This routine is useful when you need a very large data object, or if you need to return allocated memory to the operating system for subsequent calls to the **_spawn** family of functions.

Near and Far Heaps

As mentioned in the previous section, heap memory can reside inside or outside your program's default data segment, depending on what memory model your program uses. When it lies inside the default data segment, the heap is called the "near heap," since it can be accessed with near pointers. The "far heap" is memory that spans one or more segments outside the default data segment. The far heap can be accessed only with far pointers.

In various memory models, **malloc** automatically allocates memory from the near heap or far heap, as appropriate. The run-time library also includes near and far versions of **malloc**, **free**, and other memory-management routines, which allow you to specify the near and far heaps explicitly. These have the same names as standard memory routines, but are preceded by **_n** (for **near**) or **_f** (for **far**).

For instance, the **_nmalloc** routine always allocates memory from the near heap and returns a near pointer, no matter which memory model your program uses. Use **_nfree** to release memory allocated with **_nmalloc**.

Similarly, **_fmalloc** always allocates memory from the far heap and returns a far pointer, regardless of memory model. Use the **_ffree** routine to release memory allocated with **_fmalloc**.

Based Heaps

You can also allocate memory from a "based heap," which is a single segment that lies outside the default data segment. Based-heap routines generally use the same names as standard memory routines, but begin with **_b**. For instance, **_bmalloc** allocates a memory block from the based heap and **_bfree** frees the block.

Based heaps offer the following advantages:

- Localized data. Based heaps allow you to group related data in a single segment. This can simplify the management of related data.

- Faster pointer arithmetic. Although the based heap lies in the far data segment, pointers to its data items are the same size as near pointers. Thus, pointer arithmetic on items in a based heap is faster than pointer arithmetic on items in the far heap.

The **_bheapseg** routine allocates a based heap segment, from which you can then allocate blocks of memory. You can call **_bheapseg** more than once to allocate as many based-heap segments as needed (within the confines of available memory).

The **_bfreeseg** routine frees a based-heap segment. This routine frees every block in the based-heap segment, whether or not you previously freed the blocks individually.

Note Near-, far-, and based-heap calls are not ANSI compatible and will make your program less portable.

2.11 Process and Environment Control

The process-control routines allow you to start, stop, and manage processes from within a program. Environment-control routines allow you to get and change information about the operating-system environment.

A "process" is a program being executed by the operating system. It consists of the program's code and data, plus information about the process, such as the number of open files. Whenever you execute a program at the operating-system level, you start a process. All process-control functions except **signal** are declared in the include file PROCESS.H. The **signal** function is declared in SIGNAL.H. The **abort**, **exit**, and **system** functions are also declared in the STDLIB.H include file. The environment-control routines (**getenv** and **_putenv**) are declared in STDLIB.H.

Routine	Use
abort	Aborts a process without flushing buffers or calling functions registered by **atexit** and **_onexit**
assert	Tests for logic error
atexit	Schedules routines for execution at program termination
_cexit	Performs the **exit** termination procedures (such as flushing buffers) and returns control to the calling program
_c_exit	Performs the **_exit** termination procedures and returns control to the calling program
_execl	Executes child process with argument list
_execle	Executes child process with argument list and given environment
_execlp	Executes child process using PATH variable and argument list
_execlpe	Executes child process using PATH variable, given environment, and argument list
_execv	Executes child process with argument array
_execve	Executes child process with argument array and given environment
_execvp	Executes child process using PATH variable and argument array
_execvpe	Executes child process using PATH variable, given environment, and argument array
exit	Calls functions registered by **atexit** and **_onexit**, then flushes all buffers and closes all open files before terminating the process
_exit	Terminates process without processing **atexit** or **_onexit** functions or flushing buffers
_fatexit	Schedules routines for execution at program termination (memory-model independent)
_fonexit	Schedules routines for execution at program termination (memory-model independent)
getenv	Gets the value of an environment variable
_getpid	Gets process ID number
longjmp	Restores a saved stack environment

Routine	Use
_onexit	Schedules routines for execution at program termination
perror	Prints error message
_putenv	Adds or changes the value of an environment variable
raise	Sends a signal to the calling process
setjmp	Saves a stack environment
signal	Handles an interrupt signal
_spawnl	Executes child process with argument list
_spawnle	Executes child process with argument list and given environment
_spawnlp	Executes child process using PATH variable and argument list
_spawnlpe	Executes child process using PATH variable, given environment, and argument list
_spawnv	Executes child process with argument array
_spawnve	Executes child process with argument array and given environment
_spawnvp	Executes child process using PATH variable and argument array
_spawnvpe	Executes child process using PATH variable, given environment, and argument array
system	Executes an operating-system command

The **atexit** and **_onexit** routines create a list of functions to be executed when the calling program terminates. The only difference between the two is that **atexit** is part of the ANSI standard. The **_onexit** function is offered for compatibility with previous versions of Microsoft C.

The **_exit** routine terminates a process immediately, whereas **exit** terminates the process only after flushing buffers and calling any functions previously registered by **atexit** and **_onexit**. The **_cexit** and **_c_exit** routines are identical to **exit** and **_exit**, respectively, except that they return control to the calling program without terminating the process.

The **setjmp** and **longjmp** routines save and restore a stack environment. These allow you to execute a nonlocal **goto**.

The **_exec** and **_spawn** routines start a new process called the "child" process. The difference between the **_exec** and **_spawn** routines is that the **_spawn** routines are capable of returning control from the child process to its caller (the "parent" process). Both the parent process and the child process are present in memory (unless **_P_OVERLAY** is specified). In the **_exec** routines, the child process overlays the parent process, so returning control to the parent process is impossible (unless an error occurs when attempting to start execution of the child process).

There are eight forms each of the **_exec** and **_spawn** routines (see Table 2.1). The differences among the forms involve the method of locating the file to be executed as the child process, the method for passing arguments to the child process, and the method of setting the environment.

Passing an argument list means that the arguments to the child process are listed separately in the **_exec** or **_spawn** call. Passing an argument array means that the arguments are stored in an array, and a pointer to the array is passed to the child process. The argument-list method is typically used when the number of arguments is constant or is known at compile time. The argument-array method is useful when the number of arguments must be determined at run time.

Table 2.1   Forms of the _spawn and _exec Routines

Routines	Locating the File	Argument-Passing Convention	Environment Settings
_execl, _spawnl	Do not use PATH	Argument list	Inherited from parent
_execle, _spawnle	Do not use PATH	Argument list	Pointer to environment table for child process passed as last argument
_execlp, _spawnlp	Use PATH	Argument list	Inherited from parent
_execlpe, _spawnlpe	Use PATH	Argument list	Pointer to environment table for child process passed as last argument
_execv, _spawnv	Do not use PATH	Argument array	Inherited from parent
_execve, _spawnve	Do not use PATH	Argument array	Pointer to environment table for child process passed as last argument
_execvp, _spawnvp	Use PATH	Argument array	Inherited from parent
_execvpe, _spawnvpe	Use PATH	Argument array	Pointer to environment table for child process passed as last argument

The **assert** macro is typically used to test for logic errors. It prints a message when a given "assertion" fails to hold true. Defining the identifier **NDEBUG** to any value causes occurrences of **assert** to be removed from the source file, thus allowing you to turn off assertion checking without modifying the source file.

2.12 QuickWin

The QuickWin functions make it possible to compile non-Windows DOS programs as simple text-only Windows applications. DOS programs compiled with the /Mq compiler option have a limited Windows user interface, including a standard menu bar, standard online help (for the QuickWin features), and a client (or application) window with a child (document) window for the input/output streams **stdin**, **stdout**, and **stderr**. You can also add other child windows of your own. QuickWin applications support the Windows Clipboard, and you can use standard C and C++ functions to write to and read from a QuickWin application's windows, which behave as streams.

Unless you use the functions covered in this section, you do not need to alter your program's source code. However, by using these functions in your source, you can take advantage of enhanced capabilities in your QuickWin programs.

Note that there are some restrictions on the kinds of DOS programs that can be compiled with QuickWin. Programs that use graphics or that spawn processes cannot take advantage of QuickWin. For full details about QuickWin, see Chapter 8 of *Programming Techniques* (in the Microsoft C/C++ version 7.0 documentation set).

QuickWin programs cannot be run in real mode.

QuickWin uses Windows libraries and the QWIN.LIB library. QuickWin constants, structures, and functions are declared in the Windows version of IO.H and STDIO.H. The /Mq compiler option defines the **_WINDOWS** constant, declared in the Windows version of STDIO.H.

Routine	Use
_fwopen	Opens a new window stream
_wabout	Sets the string that appears in the About dialog box
_wclose	Closes a window's file handle
_wgetexit	Gets a QuickWin program's current exit behavior setting
_wgetfocus	Returns a file handle to the window with the input focus
_wgetscreenbuf	Gets a window's current screen-buffer size
_wgetsize	Gets a window's current size and position on the screen
_wmenuclick	Chooses a menu command
_wopen	Opens a window, returning a file handle to it
_wsetexit	Sets the way a QuickWin program behaves when **exit** is called
_wsetfocus	Makes a window the active window (sets its focus)
_wsetscreenbuf	Sets a window's screen-buffer size
_wsetsize	Sets a window's size and position on the screen
_wyield	Yields processor time to Windows for queue servicing

2.13 Searching and Sorting

Search and sort routines provide binary-search, linear-search, and quick-sort capabilities. They are all declared in SEARCH.H.

Routine	Use
bsearch	Performs binary search
_lfind	Performs linear search for given value
_lsearch	Performs linear search for given value, which is added to array if not found
qsort	Performs quick sort

2.14 String Manipulation

The string functions are declared in the include file STRING.H. They allow you to compare strings, copy them, search for strings and characters, and perform various other operations.

Routines beginning with **_f** are model-independent versions of the corresponding routines and are useful in mixed-model programs. These routines can be called from any point in the program, regardless of which model is being used.

Routine	Use
strcat, _fstrcat	Append one string to another
strchr, _fstrchr	Find first occurrence of a given character in a string
strcmp, _fstrcmp	Compare two strings
strcpy, _fstrcpy	Copy one string to another
strcspn, _fstrcspn	Find first occurrence of a character from a given character set in a string
_strdup, _fstrdup, _nstrdup	Duplicate a string
strerror	Maps an error number to a message string
_strerror	Maps a user-defined error message to a string
_stricmp, _fstricmp	Compare two strings without regard to case
strlen, _fstrlen	Find length of string
_strlwr, _fstrlwr	Convert string to lowercase
strncat, _fstrncat	Append characters of a string
strncmp, _fstrncmp	Compare characters of two strings
strncpy, _fstrncpy	Copy characters of one string to another
_strnicmp, _fstrnicmp	Compare characters of two strings without regard to case

Routine	Use
_strnset, _fstrnset	Set characters of a string to a given character
strpbrk, _fstrpbrk	Find first occurrence of a character from one string in another
strrchr, _fstrrchr	Find last occurrence of a given character in string
_strrev, _fstrrev	Reverse a string
_strset, _fstrset	Set all characters of a string to a given character
strspn, _fstrspn	Find first substring from a given character set in a string
strstr, _fstrstr	Find first occurrence of a given string in another string
strtok, _fstrtok	Find next token in a string
_strupr, _fstrupr	Convert a string to uppercase

All string functions work on null-terminated character strings. When working with character arrays that do not end with a null character, you can use the buffer-manipulation routines, described in "Buffer Manipulation" on page 18.

2.15 System Calls

The following routines give access to IBM-PC BIOS interrupts and DOS system calls. These routines are for DOS application programs only.

BIOS Interface

The functions in this category provide direct access to the BIOS interrupt services. They are all declared in BIOS.H.

Routine	Use
_bios_disk	Issues service requests for both hard and floppy disks, using INT 0x13
_bios_equiplist	Performs an equipment check, using INT 0x11
_bios_keybrd	Provides access to keyboard services, using INT 0x16
_bios_memsize	Obtains information about available memory, using INT 0x12
_bios_printer	Performs printer output services, using INT 0x17
_bios_serialcom	Performs serial communications tasks, using INT 0x14
_bios_timeofday	Provides access to system clock, using INT 0x1A

Note BIOS routines are hardware dependent. Some of them may not work as expected on machines whose hardware differs from the IBM PC.

DOS Interface

These routines are implemented as functions and declared in DOS.H.

Routine	Use
_bdos	Invokes DOS system call; uses only DX and AL registers
_chain_intr	Chains one interrupt handler to another
_disable	Disables interrupts
_dos_allocmem	Allocates a block of memory, using DOS system call 0x48
_dos_close	Closes a file, using DOS system call 0x3E
_dos_commit	Flushes a file to disk, using DOS system call 0x68
_dos_creat	Creates a new file and erases any existing file having the same name, using DOS system call 0x3C
_dos_creatnew	Creates a new file and returns an error if a file having the same name exists, using DOS system call 0x5B
_dos_findfirst	Finds first occurrence of a given file, using DOS system call 0x4E
_dos_findnext	Finds subsequent occurrences of a given file, using DOS system call 0x4F
_dos_freemem	Frees a block of memory, using DOS system call 0x49
_dos_getdate	Gets the system date, using DOS system call 0x2A
_dos_getdiskfree	Gets information on a disk volume, using DOS system call 0x36
_dos_getdrive	Gets the current default drive, using DOS system call 0x19
_dos_getfileattr	Gets current attributes of a file or directory, using DOS system call 0x43
_dos_getftime	Gets the date and time a file was last written, using DOS system call 0x57
_dos_gettime	Gets the current system time, using DOS system call 0x2C
_dos_getvect	Gets the current value of a specified interrupt vector, using DOS system call 0x35
_dos_keep	Installs terminate-and-stay-resident (TSR) programs using DOS system call 0x31
_dos_open	Opens an existing file, using DOS system call 0x3D
_dos_read	Reads a file, using DOS system call 0x3F
_dos_setblock	Changes the size of a previously allocated block, using DOS system call 0x4A
_dos_setdate	Sets the current system date, using DOS system call 0x2B
_dos_setdrive	Sets the default disk drive, using DOS system call 0x0E
_dos_setfileattr	Sets the current attributes of a file, using DOS system call 0x43
_dos_setftime	Sets the date and time that the specified file was last written, using DOS system call 0x57
_dos_settime	Sets the system time, using DOS system call 0x2D

Routine	Use
_dos_setvect	Sets a new value for the specified interrupt vector, using DOS system call 0x25
_dos_write	Sends output to a file, using DOS system call 0x40
_dosexterr	Obtains in-depth error information from DOS system call 0x59
_enable	Enables interrupts
_FP_OFF	Returns offset portion of a far pointer
_FP_SEG	Returns segment portion of a far pointer
_harderr	Establishes a hardware error handler
_hardresume	Returns to DOS after a hardware error
_hardretn	Returns to the application after a hardware error
_int86	Invokes DOS interrupts
_int86x	Invokes DOS interrupts with segment register values
_intdos	Invokes DOS system call using registers other than DX and AL
_intdosx	Invokes DOS system call using registers other than DX and AL with segment register values
_segread	Returns current values of segment registers

The **_dosexterr** function obtains and stores the error information returned by DOS system call 0x59 (extended error handling). This function is provided for use with DOS versions 3.0 and later.

The **_bdos** routine is useful for invoking DOS calls that use either or both of the DX (DH/DL) and AL registers for arguments. However, **_bdos** should not be used to invoke system calls that return an error code in AX if the carry flag is set; since your program cannot detect whether the carry flag is set, it cannot determine whether the value in AX is a legitimate value or an error value. In this case, the **_intdos** routine should be used instead, since it allows the program to detect whether the carry flag is set. The **_intdos** routine can also be used to invoke DOS calls that use registers other than DX and AL.

The **_intdosx** routine is similar to the **_intdos** routine, but is used when ES is required by the system call, when DS must contain a value other than the default data segment (for instance, when a far pointer is used), or when making the system call in a large-model program. When calling **_intdosx**, give an argument that specifies the segment values to be used in the call.

The **_int86** routine can be used to invoke any interrupt. The **_int86x** routine is similar; however, like the **_intdosx** routine, it is designed to work with large-model programs and far items, as described in the preceding paragraph.

The **_FP_OFF** and **_FP_SEG** routines allow easy access to the segment and offset portions of a far pointer value. **_FP_OFF** and **_FP_SEG** are implemented as macros and defined in DOS.H.

The **_segread** routine returns the current values of the segment registers. This routine is typically used with the **_intdosx** and **_int86x** routines to obtain the correct segment values.

The **_chain_intr** routine is useful for chaining interrupt handlers together. The **_enable** routine enables interrupts, while the **_disable** routine disables interrupts.

The routines prefixed with **_dos_** are all direct system interfaces that use the system calls noted above. More detailed information on these system calls can be found in the *MS-DOS Encyclopedia* (Duncan, ed.; Redmond, WA: Microsoft Press, 1988) or the *Programmer's PC Sourcebook* 2nd ed. (Hogan; Redmond, WA: Microsoft Press, 1991).

Note The DOS interface I/O routines are generally incompatible with console, low-level, and stream I/O routines. Do not mix different types of I/O routines in the same source file.

2.16 Time

The time functions allow you to obtain the current time, then convert and store it according to your particular needs. The current time is always taken from the system time.

Routine	Use
asctime	Converts time from type **struct tm** to a character string
clock	Returns the elapsed CPU time for a process
ctime	Converts time from type **time_t** to a character string
difftime	Computes the difference between two times
_ftime	Puts current system time in variable of type **struct _timeb**
gmtime	Converts time from type **time_t** to **struct tm**
localtime	Converts time from type **time_t** to **struct tm** with local correction
mktime	Converts time to a calendar value
_strdate	Returns the current system date as a string
strftime	Formats a date and time string
_strtime	Returns the current system time as a string
time	Gets current system time as type **time_t**
_tzset	Sets external time variables from the environment time variable
_utime	Sets file-modification time

The **time** and **_ftime** functions return the current time as the number of seconds elapsed since midnight, on December 31, 1899, Universal Coordinated Time. This value can be converted, adjusted, and stored in a variety of ways by using the

asctime, **ctime**, **gmtime**, **localtime**, and **mktime** functions. The **_utime** function sets the modification time for a specified file, using either the current time or a time value stored in a structure.

Note In versions of Microsoft C/C++ prior to 7.0, the **time** and **_ftime** functions return the current time as the number of seconds elapsed since midnight, on January 1, 1970.

The **clock** function returns the elapsed CPU time for the calling process.

The **_ftime** function requires two files: SYS\TYPES.H and SYS\TIMEB.H. It is declared in SYS\TIMEB.H. The **_utime** function also requires two include files: SYS\TYPES.H and SYS\UTIME.H. It is declared in SYS\UTIME.H. The remainder of the time functions are declared in the include file TIME.H.

When you want to use **_ftime** or **localtime** to make adjustments for local time, you must define an environment variable named TZ. For more information on TZ and the global variables **_daylight**, **_timezone**, and **_tzname**, refer to "_daylight, _timezone, and _tzname" on page 62. TZ is also described on the **_tzset** reference page in Part 2 of this book.

The **_strdate** and **_strtime** routines return strings containing the current date and time, respectively, in the DOS and Windows date and time format rather than in the UNIX-style formats.

The **strftime** function is useful for creating international versions of a program. See "Internationalization" on page 44.

2.17 Variable-Length Argument Lists

The **va_arg**, **va_end**, and **va_start** routines are macros that provide a portable way to access the arguments to a function when the function takes a variable number of arguments. Two versions of the macros are available: the macros defined in the VARARG.H include file, which are compatible with the UNIX System V definition, and the macros defined in STDARG.H, which conform to the ANSI C standard.

Routine	Use
va_arg	Retrieves argument from list
va_end	Resets pointer
va_start	Sets pointer to beginning of argument list

For more information on the differences between the two versions and for an explanation of how to use the macros, see their descriptions in Part 2 of this book.

2.18 Virtual Memory Allocation

The virtual memory functions allow you to allocate, free, reallocate, lock, and unlock blocks of memory. The virtual memory functions are declared in the include file VMEMORY.H.

Routine	Use
_vfree	Frees an allocated block of virtual memory
_vheapinit	Initializes the virtual memory manager
_vheapterm	Terminates the virtual memory manager
_vload	Loads an allocated block of virtual memory
_vlock	Locks an allocated block of virtual memory
_vlockcnt	Returns the number of locks held on a block of virtual memory
_vmalloc	Allocates a block of virtual memory
_vmsize	Returns the size of an allocated block of virtual memory
_vrealloc	Reallocates a block of virtual memory to a new size
_vunlock	Unlocks a locked block of virtual memory

The **_vheapinit** function specifies how much DOS memory the virtual memory manager can use and whether it should use expanded memory, extended memory, or disk storage. You must call this function before calling any of the other virtual memory functions.

The **_vmalloc** function returns a handle of type **_vmhnd_t**, which is used to refer to a block of virtual memory.

The **_vfree**, **_vrealloc**, **_vload**, **_vlock**, **_vunlock**, **_vlockcnt**, and **_vmsize** functions work on blocks of virtual memory specified by handles of type **_vmdhnd_t**.

The **_vheapterm** function frees all the resources used by the virtual memory manager. You must call this function after you have finished using virtual memory.

Global Variables and Standard Types

The Microsoft run-time library contains definitions for a number of variables and standard types used by library routines. You can access these variables and types by including in your program the files in which they are declared, or by giving appropriate declarations in your program, as shown in the following sections.

3.1 _amblksiz

The **_amblksiz** variable controls memory heap granularity.

It is declared in the MALLOC.H include file as follows:

extern unsigned int _amblksiz;

The value of **_amblksize** is used to control how memory is obtained from the operating system for the heap. The initial requested size for a segment of memory for the heap manager is based on the amount of current allocation request plus overhead for the heap manager's bookkeeping chores—that is, just enough to satisfy the allocation request at hand (for example, a **malloc** or **calloc**). However, when the heap manager grows a segment, it does so in multiples of **_amblksize**. The value of **_amblksize** represents a trade-off between the number of times the operating system must be called to grow a segment to its maximum size (no more than 640K for DOS) and the amount of memory potentially wasted (available but not used) at the end of the heap.

The default value of **_amblksize** is 8K. The value can be changed by direct assignment in your program. For example:

```
_amblksize = 2048;
```

The actual value used internally by the heap manager will be the given value, rounded up to the nearest whole power of 2 (so an **_amblksize** value of 4K–1 is the same as a value of 4K).

Note that adjusting the value of **_amblksize** affects allocation in the near, far, and based heaps. The value of **_amblksize** has no effect on huge memory blocks (those allocated with **_halloc** and similar functions).

3.2 _daylight, _timezone, _tzname

The **_daylight**, **_timezone**, and **_tzname** variables are global time-zone variables used in time functions.

They are declared in the TIME.H include file as follows:

extern int _daylight;

extern long _timezone;

extern char *_tzname[2];

Some time and date routines use the **_daylight**, **_timezone**, and **_tzname** variables to make local-time adjustments. Whenever a program calls the **_ftime**, **localtime**, or **_tzset** function, the value of **_daylight**, **_timezone**, and **_tzname** is determined from the value of the TZ environment variable. If you do not explicitly set the value of TZ, the default value of "PST8PDT" is used. The following list shows each variable and its value:

Variable	Value
_daylight	Nonzero if a daylight-saving-time zone (DST) is specified in TZ; otherwise, 0. Default value is 1.
_timezone	Difference in seconds between Universal Coordinated Time and the local time. Default value is 28,800.
_tzname[0]	Three-letter time-zone name derived from the TZ environment variable. Default value is "PST" (Pacific standard time).
_tzname[1]	Three-letter daylight-saving-time-zone name derived from the TZ environment variable. Default value is "PDT" (Pacific daylight time). If the DST zone is omitted from TZ, **_tzname[1]** is an empty string.

3.3 _doserrno, errno, sys_errlist, sys_nerr

The **_doserrno**, **errno**, **sys_errlist**, and **sys_nerr** variables contain error codes and are used by the **perror** and **strerror** routines to print error information.

These variables are declared in the STDLIB.H include file. Manifest constants for the **errno** variables are declared in the ERRNO.H include file. The declarations are as follows:

extern int _doserrno;

extern int errno;

extern char *sys_errlist[ ];

extern int sys_nerr;

The **errno** variable is set to an integer value to reflect the type of error that has occurred in a system-level call. Each **errno** value is associated with an error message, which can be printed with the **perror** routine or stored in a string with the **strerror** routine.

Note that only some routines set the **errno** variable. If a routine sets **errno**, the description of the routine in the reference section says so explicitly.

The value of **errno** reflects the error value for the last call that set **errno**. However, this value is not necessarily reset by later successful calls. To avoid confusion, test for errors immediately after a call.

The include file ERRNO.H contains the definitions of the **errno** values. However, not all of the definitions given in ERRNO.H are used in DOS. Some of the values in ERRNO.H are present to maintain compatibility with the UNIX (and XENIX) operating system.

The **errno** values in DOS are a subset of the values for **errno** in XENIX systems. Thus, the **errno** value is not necessarily the same as the actual error code returned by a DOS system call. To access the actual DOS error code, use the **_doserrno** variable, which contains this value.

In general, you should use **_doserrno** only for error detection in operations involving input and output, since the **errno** values for input and output errors have DOS error-code equivalents. In other cases, the value of **_doserrno** is undefined.

The **sys_errlist** variable is an array; the **perror** and **strerror** routines use it to process error information. The **sys_nerr** variable tells how many elements the **sys_errlist** array contains.

Table 3.1 gives the **errno** values for DOS, the system error message for each value, and the value of each constant. Note that only the **ERANGE** and **EDOM** constants are specified in the ANSI standard.

Table 3.1   errno Values and Their Meanings

Constant	Meaning	Value
E2BIG	Argument list too long	7
EACCES	Permission denied	13
EBADF	Bad file number	9
EDEADLOCK	Resource deadlock would occur	36
EDOM	Math argument	33
EEXIST	File exists	17
EINVAL	Invalid argument	22
EMFILE	Too many open files	24
ENOENT	No such file or directory	2
ENOEXEC	Exec format error	8
ENOMEM	Not enough memory	12
ENOSPC	No space left on device	28
ERANGE	Result too large	34
EXDEV	Cross-device link	18

3.4   _fmode

The **_fmode** variable controls the default file-translation mode.

It is declared in the STDLIB.H include file as follows:

extern int _fmode;

By default, the value of **_fmode** is **_O_TEXT**, causing files to be translated in text mode (unless specifically opened or set to binary mode). When **_fmode** is set to **_O_BINARY**, the default mode is binary. You can set **_fmode** to the flag **_O_BINARY** by linking with BINMODE.OBJ or by assigning **_fmode** the **_O_BINARY** value.

3.5 Locale Macros

The two ANSI macros, **MB_LEN_MAX** and **MB_CUR_MAX**, are useful when writing portable programs for international markets. The following list describes them and gives the include file where each is defined.

Macro	Description
MB_CUR_MAX	The **MB_CUR_MAX** macro, defined in STDLIB.H, expands to the maximum number of bytes in a multibyte character of the current locale.
MB_LEN_MAX	The **MB_LEN_MAX** macro, defined in LIMITS.H, gives the maximum number of bytes in a multibyte character.

3.6 _osmajor, _osminor, _osmode, _osversion, _cpumode

The **_osmajor**, **_osminor**, **_osmode**, **_osversion**, and **_cpumode** variables specify the version number of the operating system or the current mode of operation.

They are declared in the STDLIB.H include file as follows:

extern unsigned char _osmajor;

extern unsigned char _osminor;

extern unsigned char _osmode;

extern unsigned char _osversion;

extern unsigned char _cpumode;

The **_osmajor**, **_osminor**, and **_osversion** variables specify the version number of DOS or Windows in use. The **_osmajor** variable holds the "major" version number, and the **_osminor** variable stores the "minor" version number. Thus, under DOS version 5.0, **_osmajor** is 5 and **_osminor** is 0. The **_osversion** variable holds both values: its low byte contains the major version number and its high byte contains the minor version number.

These variables are useful for creating programs that run in different versions of DOS and Windows. For example, you can test the **_osmajor** variable before making a call to **_sopen**; if the major version number is earlier (less) than 3, **_open** should be used instead of **_sopen**.

The **_osmode** variable indicates the currently running operating system—
_DOS_MODE, which is defined as 0, and **_WIN_MODE**, which is defined as 2.

The **_cpumode** variable indicates the mode of the currently running operating
system—**_REAL_MODE**, which is defined as 0, and **_PROT_MODE**, which is
defined as 2.

3.7 environ

The **environ** variable is a pointer to the strings in the process environment.

It is declared in the STDLIB.H include file as follows:

extern char *environ[ ];

The **environ** variable provides access to memory areas containing process-specific
information.

The **environ** variable is an array of pointers to the strings that constitute the
process environment. The environment consists of one or more entries of the form

NAME=*string*

where NAME is the name of an environment variable and *string* is the value of
that variable. The string can be empty. The initial environment settings are taken
from the operating-system environment at the time of program execution.

The **getenv** and **_putenv** routines use the **environ** variable to access and modify
the environment table. When **_putenv** is called to add or delete environment settings, the environment table changes size; its location in memory may also change,
depending on the program's memory requirements. The **environ** variable is adjusted in these cases and always points to the correct table location.

3.8 _psp

The **_psp** variable contains the segment address of the program segment prefix
(PSP) for the process. It is declared in the STDLIB.H include file as follows:

extern unsigned int _psp;

The PSP contains execution information about the process, such as a copy of the
command line that invoked the process and the return address on process termination or interrupt. The **_psp** variable can be used to form a long pointer to the PSP,
where **_psp** is the segment value and 0 is the offset value.

Note that the **_psp** variable is supported only in DOS.

3.9 _pgmptr

The **_pgmptr** variable is automatically initialized at startup to point to the full path of the executing program. It is defined as a global variable in the run-time library and declared in CRT0DAT.ASM, which is part of the startup code. This code is linked to any module that contains a **main** function. Declaring **_pgmptr** in your own code is all that is required to make the full path available to your program:

extern char __ far *_pgmptr;

The following program demonstrates the use of **_pgmptr**:

```
#include <stdio.h>

extern char __far *_pgmptr;

void main( void )
{
    printf("The full path of the executing program is : %Fs\n",
            _pgmptr);
}
```

In DOS versions 3.0 and later, *argv*[0] also contains a pointer to the full path of the executing program.

3.10 Standard Types

A number of library routines use values whose types are defined in include files. The following list describes these types and gives the include file where they are defined.

Standard Type	Description
clock_t	The **clock_t** type, defined in TIME.H, stores time values. It is used by the **clock** function.
_complex	The **_complex** structure, defined in MATH.H, stores the real and imaginary parts of complex numbers. It is used by the **_cabs** function.
_diskfree_t	The **_diskfree_t** structure, defined in DOS.H, stores disk information used by the **_dos_getdiskfree** routine.
_diskinfo_t	The **_diskinfo_t** structure, defined in BIOS.H, records information about disk drives returned by the **_bios_disk** routine.

Standard Type	Description
div_t, ldiv_t	The **div_t** and **ldiv_t** structures, defined in STDLIB.H, store the values returned by the **div** and **ldiv** functions, respectively.
_dosdate_t	The **_dosdate_t** structure, defined in DOS.H, records the current system date used in the **_dos_getdate** and **_dos_setdate** routines.
_dostime_t	The **_dostime_t** structure, defined in DOS.H, records the current system time used in the **_dos_gettime** and **_dos_settime** routines.
_DOSERROR	The **_DOSERROR** structure, defined in DOS.H, stores values returned by DOS system call 59H (available with DOS versions 3.0 and later).
_exception	The **_exception** structure, defined in MATH.H, stores error information for math routines. It is used by the **_matherr** routine.
FILE	The **FILE** structure, defined in STDIO.H, is the structure used in all stream input and output operations. The fields of the **FILE** structure store information about the current state of the stream.
_find_t	The **_find_t** structure, defined in DOS.H, stores file-attribute information returned by the **_dos_findfirst** and **_dos_findnext** routines.
fpos_t	The **fgetpos** and **fsetpos** functions use the **fpos_t** object type, defined in STDIO.H, to record all the information necessary to uniquely specify every position within the file.
jmp_buf	The **jmp_buf** type, defined in SETJMP.H, is an array type rather than a structure type. A buffer of this type is used by the **setjmp** and **longjmp** routines to save and restore the program environment.
lconv	The **lconv** type, defined in LOCALE.H, is a structure containing formatting rules for numeric values in different countries.
_onexit_t	The **_onexit** routine is declared as an **_onexit_t** pointer type, which is defined in STDLIB.H.
ptrdiff_t	The **ptrdiff_t** type is used for the signed integral result of the subtraction of two pointers.
_REGS	The **_REGS** union, defined in DOS.H, stores byte and word register values to be passed to and returned from calls to the DOS interface functions.
sig_atomic_t	The **sig_atomic_t** type, defined in SIGNAL.H, is the integral type of an object that can be modified as an atomic entity, even in the presence of asynchronous interrupts. It is used in conjunction with the **signal** routine.
size_t	The **size_t** type, defined in STDDEF.H and several other include files, is the unsigned integral result of the **sizeof** operator.

Standard Type	Description
_SREGS	The **_SREGS** structure, defined in DOS.H, stores the values of the ES, CS, SS, and DS registers. This structure is used by the DOS interface functions that require segment register values (**_int86x**, **_intdosx**, and **_segread**).
_stat	The **_stat** structure, defined in SYS\STAT.H, contains file-status information returned by the **_stat** and **_fstat** routines.
time_t	The **time_t** type, defined in TIME.H, represents time values in the **mktime** and **time** routines.
_timeb	The **_timeb** structure, defined in SYS\TIMEB.H, is used by the **_ftime** routine to store the current system time.
tm	The **tm** structure, defined in TIME.H, is used by the **asctime**, **gmtime**, and **localtime** functions to store and retrieve time information.
_utimbuf	The **_utimbuf** structure, defined in SYS\UTIME.H, stores file access and modification times used by the **_utime** function to change file-modification dates.
va_list	The **va_list** array type, defined in STDARG.H, is used to hold information needed by the **va_arg** macro and the **va_end** routine. The called function declares a variable of type **va_list**, which can be passed as an argument to another function.
_vmhnd_t	The **_vmhnd_t** type, defined in VMEMORY.H, represents the handles to blocks of virtual memory. Handles of this type are returned by **_vmalloc** and used by the virtual memory routines.
wchar_t	The **wchar_t** type, defined in STDDEF.H and STDLIB.H, is the internal type of a wide character. It is required by the ANSI standard for the C language and is useful when writing portable programs for international markets.
_wopeninfo	The **_wopeninfo** type is a structure containing information needed to open a new QuickWin window. It is defined in IO.H.
_wsizeinfo	The **_wsizeinfo** type is a structure containing information needed to initialize the size of a new QuickWin window, to examine the size of an existing QuickWin window, or to resize an existing QuickWin window. It is defined in IO.H.

Run-Time Functions

Part

2

Run-Time Functions

The second part of this book is the reference section. It describes, in alphabetical order, each function of the run-time library provided with Microsoft C/C++.

Each reference entry gives syntax, return values, and other useful information about the library functions. Information on compatibility is supplied to assist you in writing portable programs.

About the Run-Time Reference

The following pages describe, in alphabetical order, the more than 550 functions and macros in the Microsoft run-time library. In some cases, related routines are clustered in the same description. For example, the based, near, and far versions of **_heapwalk** are in the same discussion, as are the regular and long double versions of the math functions, such as **acos** and **atan**. Differences are noted where appropriate. Refer to Chapter 2, "Run-Time Routines by Category," or to the index to locate any function that does not appear in the expected position within the alphabetical reference.

The discussion of each function (or group of functions) is divided into the following sections:

- **Description**. Summarizes the routine's effect, names the include file(s) containing its declaration, illustrates the syntax, and briefly describes the arguments.
- **Remarks**. Gives a more detailed description of the routine and how it is used.
- **Return Value**. Describes the value returned by the routine.
- **Compatibility.** Tells whether the routine is compatible with ANSI C, UNIX, DOS, QuickWin, Windows, and the DOS Extender (DOS32X).
- **See Also**. Names related routines.
- **Example**. Gives a complete program showing the use of the routine.
- **Output**. Shows the output from the example program.

abort

Description   Aborts the current process and returns an error code.

#include <process.h> **#include <stdlib.h>**	Required only for function declarations; use either PROCESS.H or STDLIB.H

void abort(void);

Remarks   The **abort** function prints the message

```
abnormal program termination
```

to **stderr**, then calls **raise(SIGABRT)**. The action taken in response to the **SIGABRT** signal depends on what action has been defined for that signal in a prior call to the **signal** function. The default **SIGABRT** action is for the calling process to terminate with exit code 3, returning control to the parent process or operating system.

In Windows, the **abort** function does not call **raise(SIGABRT)**. Instead, it terminates the process with an "Abnormal Program Termination" pop-up message. In Windows multithread libraries, the **abort** function does not call **raise(SIGABRT)**. Instead, it terminates the process with exit code 3.

The **abort** function does not flush stream buffers or do **atexit /_onexit** processing.

Return Value   The **abort** function does not return control to the caller. Rather, it terminates the process and, by default, returns an exit code of 3 to the parent process.

Compatibility   Standards: ANSI, UNIX
                    16-Bit: DOS, QWIN, WIN, WIN DLL
                    32-Bit: DOS32X

See Also   **_exec** functions, **exit**, **_exit**, **raise**, **signal**, **_spawn** functions

Example   /* ABORT.C: This tries to open a file and aborts if the attempt fails. */

```
#include <stdio.h>
#include <stdlib.h>

void main( void )
{
   FILE *stream;

   if( (stream = fopen( "NOSUCHF.ILE", "r" )) == NULL )
   {
      perror( "Couldn't open file" );
      abort();
   }
   else
      fclose( stream );
}
```

Output   Couldn't open file: No such file or directory

abnormal program termination

abs

Description   Calculates the absolute value.

      #include <stdlib.h>   Required only for function declarations; use either
      #include <math.h>   STDLIB.H or MATH.H

      int abs(int *n* **);**

      n   Integer value

Remarks   The **abs** function returns the absolute value of its integer argument *n*.

Return Value   The **abs** function returns the absolute value of its argument. There is no error
return.

Compatibility   Standards: ANSI, UNIX

         16-Bit: DOS, QWIN, WIN, WIN DLL

         32-Bit: DOS32X

See Also   **_cabs, fabs, labs**

Example
```
/* ABS.C: This program computes and displays the absolute values of
 * several numbers.
 */

#include <stdio.h>
#include <math.h>
#include <stdlib.h>

void main( void )
{
    int    ix = -4, iy;
    long   lx = -41567L, ly;
    double dx = -3.141593, dy;

    iy = abs( ix );
    printf( "The absolute value of %d is %d\n", ix, iy);

    ly = labs( lx );
    printf( "The absolute value of %ld is %ld\n", lx, ly);
```

```
        dy = fabs( dx );
        printf( "The absolute value of %f is %f\n", dx, dy );
}
```

Output   The absolute value of -4 is 4
The absolute value of -41567 is 41567
The absolute value of -3.141593 is 3.141593

_access

Description

Determines file-access permission.

#include <io.h>	Required only for function declarations
#include <errno.h>	Required for definition of **errno** constants

int _access(char *___pathname___, int ___mode___);

___pathname___	File or directory path name
___mode___	Permission setting

Remarks

With files, the **_access** function determines whether the specified file exists and can be accessed in ___mode___. The possible mode values and their meanings in the **_access** call are as follows:

Value	Meaning
00	Check for existence only
02	Check for write permission
04	Check for read permission
06	Check for read and write permission

With directories, **_access** determines only whether the specified directory exists; in DOS, all directories have read and write access.

Return Value

The **_access** function returns the value 0 if the file has the given mode. A return value of −1 indicates that the named file does not exist or is not accessible in the given mode, and **errno** is set to one of the following values:

Value	Meaning
EACCES	Access denied: the file's permission setting does not allow the specified access.
ENOENT	File or path name not found.

Compatibility	Standards:	UNIX
	16-Bit:	DOS, QWIN, WIN, WIN DLL
	32-Bit:	DOS32X

Use **_access** for compatibility with ANSI naming conventions of non-ANSI functions. Use **access** and link with OLDNAMES.LIB for UNIX compatibility.

See Also   **_chmod, _fstat, _open, _stat**

Example
```
/* ACCESS.C: This example uses _access to check the file named "data"
 * to see if it exists and if writing is allowed.
 */

#include <io.h>
#include <stdio.h>
#include <stdlib.h>

void main( void )
{
    /* Check for existence */
    if( (_access( "access.c", 0 )) != -1 )
    {
        printf( "File exists\n" );

        /* Check for write permission */
        if( (_access( "access.c", 2 )) != -1 )
            printf( "File has write permission\n" );
    }
}
```

Output
```
File exists
File has write permission
```

acos Functions

Description   Calculate the arccosine.

#include <math.h>

#include <errno.h>   Required for definition of **errno** constant

double acos(double *x* **);**

long double _acosl(long double *x* **);**

x Value whose arccosine is to be calculated

Remarks   The **acos** functions return the arccosine of x in the range 0 to π radians. The value
of x must be between -1 and 1. The **_acosl** function is the 80-bit counterpart,
which uses an 80-bit, 10-byte coprocessor form of arguments and return values.
See the reference page on the long double functions for more details on this
data type.

Return Value   The **acos** functions return the arccosine result. If x is less than -1 or greater than 1,
the function sets **errno** to **EDOM**, prints a **_DOMAIN** error message to **stderr**,
and returns 0. Error handling can be modified with the **_matherr** (or **_matherrl**)
routine.

Compatibility   **acos**

Standards:	ANSI, UNIX
16-Bit:	DOS, QWIN, WIN, WIN DLL
32-Bit:	DOS32X

_acosl

Standards:	None
16-Bit:	DOS, QWIN, WIN, WIN DLL
32-Bit:	None

See Also   **asin** functions, **atan** functions, **cos** functions, **_matherr**, **sin** functions, **tan**
functions

Example

```
/* ASINCOS.C: This program prompts for a value in the range -1 to 1.
 * Input values outside this range will produce _DOMAIN error messages.
 * If a valid value is entered, the program prints the arcsine and the
 * arccosine of that value.
 */

#include <math.h>
#include <stdio.h>
#include <stdlib.h>
#include <errno.h>

void main( void )
{
    double x, y;

    printf( "Enter a real number between -1 and 1: " );
    scanf( "%lf", &x );
    y = asin( x );
    printf( "Arcsine of %f = %f\n", x, y );
    y = acos( x );
    printf( "Arccosine of %f = %f\n", x, y );
}
```

Output

```
Enter a real number between -1 and 1: .32696
Arcsine of 0.326960 = 0.333085
Arccosine of 0.326960 = 1.237711
```

_alloca

Description

Allocates memory on the stack.

#include <malloc.h>   Required only for function declarations

void *_alloca(size_t *size* **);**

size   Bytes to be allocated from stack

Remarks

The **_alloca** routine allocates *size* bytes from the program's stack. The allocated space is automatically freed when the calling function is exited.

Observe the following restrictions when using **_alloca**:

- When you compile with optimization on (either by default or by using one of the /O options), the stack pointer may not be restored properly in functions that have no local variables and that also reference the **_alloca** function. (This restriction does not apply to DOS32X.) The following program demonstrates the problem:

```
/* Compile with CL /AM /Ox /Fc */
#include <malloc.h>

void main( void )
{
    func( 10 );
}
void func( register int i )
{
    _alloca( i );
}
```

  To ensure that the stack pointer is properly restored, make sure that any function referencing **_alloca** declares at least one local variable.

- The pointer value returned by **_alloca** should never be passed as an argument to **free**.

- The **_alloca** function should never be used in an expression that is an argument to a function.

Return Value   The **_alloca** routine returns a **void** pointer to the allocated space, which is guaranteed to be suitably aligned for storage of any type of object. To get a pointer to a type other than **char**, use a type cast on the return value. The return value is **NULL** if the space cannot be allocated.

Compatibility   Standards: UNIX
                16-Bit: DOS
                32-Bit: DOS32X

Use **_alloca** for compatibility with ANSI naming conventions of non-ANSI functions. Use **alloca** and link with OLDNAMES.LIB for UNIX compatibility.

See Also   **calloc** functions, **malloc** functions, **realloc** functions

Example
```
/* ALLOCA.C: This program checks the stack space available before
 * and after using the _alloca function to allocate space on the stack.
 */

#include <malloc.h>
#include <stdio.h>

void main( void )
{
    char *buffer;

    printf( "Bytes available on stack: %u\n", _stackavail() );

    /* Allocate memory for string. */
    buffer = _alloca( 120 * sizeof( char ) );
    printf( "The _alloca function just allocated" );
    printf( " memory from the program stack.\n" );

    printf( "Enter a string: " );
    gets( buffer );
    printf( "\"%s\" was stored in the program stack.\n", buffer );
    printf( "Bytes available on stack: %u\n", _stackavail() );
}
```

Output
```
Bytes available on stack: 1744
The _alloca function just allocated memory from the program stack.
Enter a string: Store this on the stack.
"Store this on the stack." was stored in the program stack.
Bytes available on stack: 1614
```

_arc Functions

Description   Draw elliptical arcs.

#include <graph.h>

short __far _arc(short *x1*, short *y1*, short *x2*, short *y2*, short *x3*, short *y3*,
    short *x4*, short *y4*);

short __far _arc_w(double *x1*, double *y1*, double *x2*, double *y2*, double *x3*,
    double *y3*, double *x4*, double *y4*);

short __far _arc_wxy(struct _wxycoord __far *pwxy1*,
    struct _wxycoord __far *pwxy2*, struct _wxycoord __far *pwxy3*,
    struct _wxycoord __far *pwxy4*);

x1, y1	Upper-left corner of bounding rectangle
x2, y2	Lower-right corner of bounding rectangle
x3, y3	Second point of start vector (center of bounding rectangle is first point)
x4, y4	Second point of end vector (center of bounding rectangle is first point)
pwxy1	Upper-left corner of bounding rectangle
pwxy2	Lower-right corner of bounding rectangle
pwxy3	Second point of start vector (center of bounding rectangle is first point)
pwxy4	Second point of end vector (center of bounding rectangle is first point)

Remarks   The **_arc** functions draw elliptical arcs. The center of the arc is the center of the
bounding rectangle, which is defined by points $(x1, y1)$ and $(x2, y2)$ for **_arc** and
_arc_w and by points *pwxy1* and *pwxy2* for **_arc_wxy**. The arc starts where it in-
tersects an imaginary line extending from the center of the arc through $(x3, y3)$ for
_arc and **_arc_w** and through *pwxy3* for **_arc_wxy**. It is drawn counterclock-
wise about the center of the arc, ending where it intersects an imaginary line extending from the center of the arc through $(x4, y4)$ for **_arc** and **_arc_w** and
through *pwxy4* for **_arc_wxy**.

The **_arc** routine uses the view coordinate system. The **_arc_w** and **_arc_wxy** functions use the real-valued window coordinate system.

In each case, the arc is drawn using the current color. Since an arc does not define a closed area, it is not filled.

Return Value   These functions return a nonzero value if the arc is successfully drawn; otherwise, they return 0.

Compatibility

Standards: None
16-Bit: DOS
32-Bit: None

See Also   **_ellipse** functions, **_lineto** functions, **_pie** functions, **_rectangle** functions, **_setcolor**

Example

```
/* ARC.C: This program draws a simple arc. */

#include <graph.h>
#include <stdlib.h>
#include <conio.h>

void main( void )
{
    short x, y;
    struct _xycoord xystart, xyend, xyfill;

    /* Find a valid graphics mode */
    if( !_setvideomode( _MAXRESMODE ) )
        exit( 1 );

    /* Draw arcs            */
    x = 100; y = 100;
    _arc( x - 60, y - 60, x, y, x - 30, y - 60, x - 60, y - 30 );
    _arc( x + 60, y + 60, x, y, x,      y + 30, x + 30, y );

    /* Get endpoints of second arc and enclose the figure, then fill it. */
    _getarcinfo( &xystart, &xyend, &xyfill );
    _moveto( xystart.xcoord, xystart.ycoord );
    _lineto( xyend.xcoord,   xyend.ycoord );
    _floodfill( xyfill.xcoord, xyfill.ycoord, _getcolor() );

    _getch();
    _setvideomode( _DEFAULTMODE );
}
```

asctime

Description

Converts a **tm** time structure to a character string.

#include <time.h>

char *asctime(const struct tm *timeptr);

timeptr   Time/date structure

Remarks

The **asctime** function converts a time stored as a structure to a character string. The timeptr value is usually obtained from a call to **gmtime** or **localtime**, both of which return a pointer to a **tm** structure, defined in TIME.H. (See **gmtime** for a complete description of the **tm** structure fields.)

The **tm** structure contains the following elements:

Element	Description
int tm_sec	Seconds after the minute (0–59)
int tm_min	Minutes after the hour (0–59)
int tm_hour	Hours since midnight (0–23)
int tm_mday	Day of the month (0–31)
int tm_mon	Months since January (0–11)
int tm_year	Years since 1900
int tm_wday	Days since Sunday (0–6)
int tm_yday	Days since January 1 (0–365)
int tm_isdst	Daylight-saving-time flag

The string result produced by **asctime** contains exactly 26 characters and has the form of the following example:

```
Wed Jan 02 02:03:55 1980\n\0
```

A 24-hour clock is used. All fields have a constant width. The newline character (**\n**) and the null character (**'\0'**) occupy the last two positions of the string. The **asctime** function uses a single statically allocated buffer to hold the return string. Each call to this routine destroys the result of the previous call.

Return Value

The **asctime** function returns a pointer to the character string result. There is no error return.

Compatibility	Standards: ANSI, UNIX
	16-Bit: DOS, QWIN, WIN, WIN DLL
	32-Bit: DOS32X

See Also   **ctime, _ftime, gmtime, localtime, time, _tzset**

Example

```
/* ASCTIME.C: This program places the system time in the long integer aclock,
 * translates it into the structure newtime and then converts it to
 * string form for output, using the asctime function.
 */

#include <time.h>
#include <stdio.h>

struct tm *newtime;
time_t aclock;

void main( void )
{
    time( &aclock );                        /* Get time in seconds */

    newtime = localtime( &aclock );     /* Convert time to struct tm form */

    /* Print local time as a string */
    printf( "The current date and time are: %s\n", asctime( newtime ) );
}
```

Output

```
The current date and time are: Tue Jun 15 06:57:59 1999
```

asin Functions

Description

Calculate the arcsine.

#include <math.h>

#include <errno.h>

double asin(double *x*);

long double _asinl(long double *x*);

x   Value whose arcsine is to be calculated

Remarks

The **asin** functions calculate the arcsine of *x* in the range $-\pi/2$ to $\pi/2$ radians. The value of *x* must be between -1 and 1. The **_asinl** function is the 80-bit counterpart, which uses an 80-bit, 10-byte coprocessor form of arguments and return values. See the reference page on the long double functions for more details on this data type.

Return Value

The **asin** functions return the arcsine result. If *x* is less than -1 or greater than 1, **asin** sets **errno** to **EDOM**, prints a **_DOMAIN** error message to **stderr**, and returns 0.

Error handling can be modified by using the **_matherr** (or **_matherrl**) routine.

Compatibility

asin

Standards:	ANSI, UNIX
16-Bit:	DOS, QWIN, WIN, WIN DLL
32-Bit:	DOS32X

_asinl

Standards:	None
16-Bit:	DOS, QWIN, WIN, WIN DLL
32-Bit:	None

See Also

acos functions, **atan** functions, **cos** functions, **_matherr**, **sin** functions, **tan** functions

Example

```
/* ASINCOS.C: This program prompts for a value in the range -1 to 1.
 * Input values outside this range will produce _DOMAIN error messages.
 * If a valid value is entered, the program prints the arcsine and the
 * arccosine of that value.
 */

#include <math.h>
#include <stdio.h>
#include <stdlib.h>
#include <errno.h>

void main( void )
{
    double x, y;

    printf( "Enter a real number between -1 and 1: " );
    scanf( "%lf", &x );
    y = asin( x );
    printf( "Arcsine of %f = %f\n", x, y );
    y = acos( x );
    printf( "Arccosine of %f = %f\n", x, y );
}
```

Output

```
Enter a real number between -1 and 1: .32696
Arcsine of 0.326960 = 0.333085
Arccosine of 0.326960 = 1.237711
```

assert

Description

Prints an error message and aborts the program.

#include <assert.h>

#include <stdio.h>

void assert(int *expression* **);**

expression   C expression specifying assertion being tested

Remarks

The **assert** routine prints a diagnostic message and calls the **abort** routine if *expression* is false (0). The diagnostic message has the form

```
Assertion failed: expression, file filename, line linenumber
```

where *filename* is the name of the source file and *linenumber* is the line number of the assertion that failed in the source file. No action is taken if *expression* is true (nonzero).

In Windows, the diagnostic message appears in an "Assertion Failed" pop-up window.

The **assert** routine is typically used in program development to identify program logic errors. The given expression should be chosen so that it holds true only if the program is operating as intended. After a program has been debugged, the special "no debug" identifier **NDEBUG** can be used to remove **assert** calls from the program. If **NDEBUG** is defined (by any value) with a /D command-line option or with a **#define** directive, the C preprocessor removes all **assert** calls from the program source.

The **assert** routine is implemented as a macro.

Return Value

None.

Compatibility

Standards: ANSI, UNIX
16-Bit: DOS, QWIN, WIN, WIN DLL
32-Bit: DOS32X

See Also

abort, raise, signal

Example

```
/* ASSERT.C: In this program, the analyze_string function uses the
 * assert function to test several conditions related to string and
 * length. If any of the conditions fails, the program prints a
 * message indicating what caused the failure.
 */

#include <stdio.h>
#include <assert.h>
#include <string.h>

void analyze_string( char *string );   /* Prototype */

void main( void )
{
   char   test1[] = "abc", *test2 = NULL, test3[] = "";

   printf ( "Analyzing string '%s'\n", test1 );
   analyze_string( test1 );
   printf ( "Analyzing string '%s'\n", test2 );
   analyze_string( test2 );
   printf ( "Analyzing string '%s'\n", test3 );
   analyze_string( test3 );
}

/* Tests a string to see if it is NULL, empty, or longer than 0 characters */
void analyze_string( char * string )
{
   assert( string != NULL );       /* Cannot be NULL */
   assert( *string != '\0' );      /* Cannot be empty */
   assert( strlen( string ) > 2 ); /* Length must be greater than 2 */
}
```

Output

```
Analyzing string 'abc'
Analyzing string '(null)'
Assertion failed: string != NULL, file assert.c, line 28

abnormal program termination
```

atan Functions

Description

Calculate the arctangent of x (**atan** and **_atanl**) and the arctangent of y/x (**atan2** and **_atan2l**).

```
#include <math.h>
```

double atan(double *x*);

double atan2(double *y*, double *x*);

long double _atanl(long double *x*);

long double _atan2l(long double *y*, long double *x*);

x, y Any number

Remarks

The **atan** family of functions calculates the arctangent of x, and the **atan2** family of functions calculates the arctangent of y/x. The **atan** group returns a value in the range $-\pi/2$ to $\pi/2$ radians, and the **atan2** group returns a value in the range $-\pi$ to π radians. The **atan2** functions use the signs of both arguments to determine the quadrant of the return value. The **atan2** functions are well defined for every point other than the origin, even if x equals 0 and y does not equal 0.

Return Value

The **atan** family of functions returns the arctangent result. If both arguments of **atan2** or **_atan2l** are 0, the function sets **errno** to **EDOM**, prints a **_DOMAIN** error message to **stderr**, and returns 0.

Error handling can be modified by using the **_matherr** (or **_matherrl**) routine.

Compatibility

atan, atan2

Standards:	ANSI, UNIX
16-Bit:	DOS, QWIN, WIN, WIN DLL
32-Bit:	DOS32X

_atanl, _atan2l

Standards: None

16-Bit: DOS, QWIN, WIN, WIN DLL

32-Bit: None

See Also   **acos** functions, **asin** functions, **cos** functions, **_matherr**, **sin** functions, **tan** functions

Example
```
/* ATAN.C: This program calculates the arctangent of 1 and -1. */

#include <math.h>
#include <stdio.h>
#include <errno.h>

void main( void )
{
    double x1, x2, y;

    printf( "Enter a real number: " );
    scanf( "%lf", &x1 );
    y = atan( x1 );
    printf( "Arctangent of %f: %f\n", x1, y );
    printf( "Enter a second real number: " );
    scanf( "%lf", &x2 );
    y = atan2( x1, x2 );
    printf( "Arctangent of %f / %f: %f\n", x1, x2, y );
}
```

Output
```
Enter a real number: -862.42
Arctangent of -862.420000: -1.569637
Enter a second real number: 78.5149
Arctangent of -862.420000 / 78.514900: -1.480006
```

atexit, _fatexit

Description   Process the specified function at exit.

#include <stdlib.h>   Required only for function declarations

int atexit(void (_ _cdecl * *func* **)(void));**

int _ _far _fatexit(void (_ _cdecl _ _far * *func* **)(void));**

func   Function to be called

Remarks   The **atexit** function is passed the address of a function (*func*) to be called when the program terminates normally. Successive calls to **atexit** create a register of functions that are executed in LIFO (last-in-first-out) order. No more than 32 functions can be registered with **atexit** or **_onexit**. The functions passed to **atexit** cannot take parameters.

For DOS32X, **atexit** and **_onexit** use the heap to hold the "register of functions." Thus, the number of functions that can be registered is limited only by heap memory.

The **_fatexit** function is a far version of **atexit**; it can be used with any memory model.

Return Value   Both **atexit** and **_fatexit** return 0 if successful, or a nonzero value if an error occurs (e.g., if there are already 32 exit functions defined).

Compatibility   **atexit**

Standards: ANSI
16-Bit: DOS, QWIN, WIN, WIN DLL
32-Bit: DOS32X

Use the ANSI-standard **atexit** function (rather than the similar **_onexit** function) whenever ANSI portability is desired.

_fatexit

Standards: None

16-Bit: DOS, QWIN, WIN, WIN DLL

32-Bit: None

See Also   **abort, exit, _exit, _onexit**

Example
```
/* ATEXIT.C: This program pushes four functions onto the stack of functions
 * to be executed when atexit is called. When the program exits, these
 * programs are executed on a "last in, first out" basis.
 */

#include <stdlib.h>
#include <stdio.h>
void fn1( void ), fn2( void ), fn3( void ), fn4( void );

void main( void )
{
    atexit( fn1 );
    atexit( fn2 );
    atexit( fn3 );
    atexit( fn4 );
    printf( "This is executed first.\n" );
}

void fn1()
{
    printf( "next.\n" );
}

void fn2()
{
    printf( "executed " );
}

void fn3()
{
    printf( "is " );
}

void fn4()
{
    printf( "This " );
}
```

Output
```
This is executed first.
This is executed next.
```

atof, atoi, atol, _atold

Description

Convert strings to double (**atof**), long double (**_atold**), integer (**atoi**), or long (**atol**).

#include <math.h>	atof, _atold
#include <stdlib.h>	atof, _atold, atoi, atol

double atof(const char *string);

long double _atold(const char *string);

int atoi(const char *string);

long atol(const char *string);

string   String to be converted

Remarks

These functions convert a character string to a double-precision floating-point value (**atof**), an integer value (**atoi**), a long integer value (**atol**), or a long double value (**_atold**). The input string is a sequence of characters that can be interpreted as a numerical value of the specified type.

The string size that can be handled by the **atof** or **_atold** function is limited to 100 characters.

The function stops reading the input string at the first character that it cannot recognize as part of a number. This character may be the null character ('\0') terminating the string.

The **atof** and **_atold** functions expect *string* to have the following form:

[[*whitespace*]] [[*sign*]] [[*digits*]] [[*.digits*]] [[{**d** | **D** | **e** | **E**}[[*sign*]]*digits*]]

A *whitespace* consists of space and/or tab characters, which are ignored; *sign* is either plus (+) or minus (–); and *digits* are one or more decimal digits. If no digits appear before the decimal point, at least one must appear after the decimal point. The decimal digits may be followed by an exponent, which consists of an introductory letter (**d**, **D**, **e**, or **E**) and an optionally signed decimal integer.

The **atoi** and **atol** functions do not recognize decimal points or exponents. The *string* argument for these functions has the form

[[*whitespace*]] [[*sign*]]*digits*

where *whitespace*, *sign*, and *digits* are exactly as described above for **atof**.

Return Value   Each function returns the **double**, **long double**, **int**, or **long** value produced by interpreting the input characters as a number. The return value is 0 (for **atoi**), 0L (for **atol**), and 0.0 (for **atof** and **_atold**) if the input cannot be converted to a value of that type. The return value is undefined in case of overflow.

Compatibility   **atof, atoi, atol**

Standards: ANSI, UNIX
16-Bit: DOS, QWIN, WIN, WIN DLL
32-Bit: DOS32X

_atold

Standards: None
16-Bit: DOS, QWIN, WIN, WIN DLL
32-Bit: DOS32X

See Also   **_ecvt, _fcvt, _gcvt, strtod**

Example
```
/* ATOF.C: This program shows how numbers stored as strings can be
 * converted to numeric values using the atof, atoi, and atol functions.
 */

#include <stdlib.h>
#include <stdio.h>

void main( void )
{
    char *s; double x; int i; long l;

    s = "  -2309.12E-15";    /* Test of atof */
    x = atof( s );
    printf( "atof test:  ASCII string: %s\tfloat:     %e\n", s, x );

    s = "7.8912654773d210";  /* Test of atof */
    x = atof( s );
    printf( "atof test:  ASCII string: %s\tfloat:     %e\n", s, x );
```

```
        s = "  -9885 pigs";        /* Test of atoi */
        i = atoi( s );
        printf( "atoi test:  ASCII string: %s\t\tinteger: %d\n", s, i );

        s = "98854 dollars";       /* Test of atol */
        l = atol( s );
        printf( "atol test:  ASCII string: %s\t\tlong:    %ld\n", s, l );
}
```

Output

```
atof test:  ASCII string:  -2309.12E-15      float:    -2.309120e-012
atof test:  ASCII string: 7.8912654773d210   float:     7.891265e+210
atoi test:  ASCII string:  -9885 pigs        integer: -9885
atol test:  ASCII string: 98854 dollars      long:    98854
```

_bdos

Description

Invokes the DOS system call.

#include <dos.h>

int _bdos(int *dosfunc***, unsigned int** *dosdx***, unsigned int** *dosal* **);**

dosfunc	Function number
dosdx	DX register value
dosal	AL register value

Remarks

The **_bdos** function invokes the DOS system call specified by *dosfunc* after placing the values specified by *dosdx* and *dosal* in the DX and AL registers, respectively. The **_bdos** function executes an INT 21H instruction to invoke the system call. When the system call is complete, **_bdos** returns the contents of the AX register.

The **_bdos** function is intended to be used to invoke DOS system calls that either take no arguments or take arguments only in the DX (DH, DL) and/or AL registers.

Do not use the **_bdos** function to call interrupts that modify the DS register. Instead, use the **_intdosx** or **_int86x** function. The **_intdosx** and **_int86x** functions load the DS and ES registers from the *segregs* argument and also store the DS and ES registers into *segregs* after the function call.

This call should not be used to invoke system calls that indicate errors by setting the carry flag. Since C programs do not have access to this flag, your program cannot determine whether the return value is an error code. The **_intdos** function should be used in these cases.

Return Value

The **_bdos** function returns the value of the AX register after the system call has completed.

Compatibility

Standards: None
16-Bit: DOS, QWIN, WIN, WIN DLL
32-Bit: None

See Also

_intdos, _intdosx

Example   ```
/* BDOS.C: This example calls DOS function 0x9 (display string)
 * to display a $-terminated string.
 */

#include <dos.h>

/* Function 0x09 assumes that DS will contain segment of the string.
 * This will be true for all memory models if the string is declared near.
 */
char __near str[] = "Hello world!\r\n$";

void main(void)
{
    /* Offset of string must be in DX, segment in DS. AL is not needed,
     * so 0 is used.
     */
    _bdos(0x09, (int)str, 0);
}
```

**Output**    ```
Hello world!
```

Bessel Functions

Description

Compute the Bessel function.

#include <math.h>

double _j0(double x **);**

double _j1(double x **);**

double _jn(int n**, double** x **);**

double _y0(double x **);**

double _y1(double x **);**

double _yn(int n**, double** x **);**

long double _j0l(long double x **);**

long double _jnl(int n**, long double** x **);**

long double _j1l(long double x **);**

long double _y0l(long double x **);**

long double _y1l(long double x **);**

long double _ynl(int n**, long double** x **);**

x	Floating-point value
n	Integer order

Remarks

The **_j0**, **_j1**, and **_jn** routines return Bessel functions of the first kind—orders 0, 1, and n, respectively.

The **_y0**, **_y1**, and **_yn** routines return Bessel functions of the second kind— orders 0, 1, and n, respectively. The argument x must be positive.

The long double versions of these functions are the 80-bit counterparts and use the 80-bit, 10-byte coprocessor form of arguments and return values. See the reference page on the long double functions for more details on this data type.

The Bessel functions are explained more fully in most mathematics reference books, such as the *Handbook of Mathematical Functions* (Abramowitz and Stegun; Washington: U.S. Government Printing Office, 1964). These functions are commonly used in the mathematics of electromagnetic wave theory.

Return Value

These functions return the result of a Bessel function of *x*.

For **_y0**, **_y1**, or **_yn**, if *x* is negative, the routine sets **errno** to **EDOM**, prints a **_DOMAIN** error message to **stderr**, and returns –**HUGE_VAL**.

Error handling can be modified by using the **_matherr** (or **_matherrl**) routine.

Compatibility

_j0, _j1, _jn, _y0, _y1, _yn

Standards:	UNIX
16-Bit:	DOS, QWIN, WIN, WIN DLL
32-Bit:	DOS32X

Use **_j0, _j1, _jn, _y0, _y1**, and **_yn** for compatibility with ANSI naming conventions of non-ANSI functions. Use **j0, j1, jn, y0, y1**, and **yn** and link with OLDNAMES.LIB for UNIX compatibility.

_j0l, _j1l, _jnl, _y0l, _y1l, _ynl

Standards:	None
16-Bit:	DOS, QWIN, WIN, WIN DLL
32-Bit:	None

See Also

_matherr

Example

```
/* BESSEL.C: This program illustrates Bessel functions, including:
 *    _j0        _j1        _jn        _y0        _y1        _yn
 */

#include <math.h>
#include <stdio.h>
```

```
void main( void )
{
    double x = 2.387;
    int n = 3, c;

    printf( "Bessel functions for x = %f:\n", x );
    printf( "  Kind\t\tOrder\t\Function\tResult\n\n" );
    printf( "  First\t\t0\t_j0( x )\t\t%f\n", _j0( x ) );
    printf( "  First\t\t1\t_j1( x )\t\t%f\n", _j1( x ) );
    for( c = 2; c < 5; c++ )
        printf( "  First\t\t%d\t_jn( n, x )\t%f\n", c, _jn( c, x ) );

    printf( "  Second\t0\t_y0( x )\t\t%f\n", _y0( x ) );
    printf( "  Second\t1\t_y1( x )\t\t%f\n", _y1( x ) );
    for( c = 2; c < 5; c++ )
        printf( "  Second\t%d\t_yn( n, x )\t%f\n", c, _yn( c, x ) );
}
```

Output

```
Bessel functions for x = 2.387000:
    Kind        Order   Function        Result

    First       0       _j0( x )        0.009288
    First       1       _j1( x )        0.522941
    First       2       _jn( n, x )     0.428870
    First       3       _jn( n, x )     0.195734
    First       4       _jn( n, x )     0.063131
    Second      0       _y0( x )        0.511681
    Second      1       _y1( x )        0.094374
    Second      2       _yn( n, x )     -0.432608
    Second      3       _yn( n, x )     -0.819314
    Second      4       _yn( n, x )     -1.626833
```

_bfreeseg

Description

Frees a specified based heap.

#include <malloc.h>   Required only for function declarations

int _bfreeseg(__segment *seg* **);**

seg   Segment selected

Remarks

The **_bfreeseg** function frees a based heap. The *seg* argument is a based heap returned by an earlier call to **_bheapseg**. It specifies the based heap to be freed.

The specified segment is freed completely regardless of whether the blocks it contains are free or allocated. After a **_bfreeseg** call, the *seg* value is invalid and should not be used.

Return Value

The **_bfreeseg** function returns 0 if successful and –1 in the case of an error.

Compatibility

Standards: None
16-Bit: DOS, QWIN, WIN, WIN DLL
32-Bit: None

See Also

_bheapseg, **calloc** functions, **free** functions, **malloc** functions, **realloc** functions

Example

See the example for **_bheapseg**.

_bheapseg

Description

Allocates a based heap.

#include <malloc.h>   Required only for function declarations

__segment _bheapseg(size_t *size* **);**

size   Segment size to allocate

Remarks

The **_bheapseg** function allocates a based-heap segment of at least *size* bytes. (The block may be larger than *size* bytes because of space required for alignment and for maintenance information.)

The value returned by **_bheapseg** is the identifier of the based-heap segment. This value should be saved and used in subsequent calls to other based-heap functions. If the original block of memory is depleted (e.g., by calls to **_bmalloc** and **_brealloc**), the run-time code will try to enlarge the heap as necessary.

The **_bheapseg** function can be called repeatedly. For each call, the run-time library will allocate a new based-heap segment.

Return Value

The **_bheapseg** function returns the newly allocated segment selector; save this value for use in subsequent based-heap functions. A return value of **_NULLSEG** indicates failure.

Always check the return from the **_bheapseg** function (especially when it is used in real mode), even if the amount of memory requested is small.

Compatibility

Standards:	None
16-Bit:	DOS, QWIN, WIN, WIN DLL
32-Bit:	None

See Also

calloc functions, **free** functions, **malloc** functions, **realloc** functions

Example

```
/* BHEAPSEG.C: This program C illustrates dynamic allocation of based
 * memory using functions _bheapseg, _bfreeseg, _bmalloc, and _bfree.
 */

#include <stdio.h>
#include <malloc.h>
#include <stdlib.h>
#include <string.h>

void main( void )
{
    __segment seg;
    char __based( seg ) *outstr, __based( seg ) *instr;
    char __based( seg ) *pout,   __based( seg ) *pin;
    char tmpstr[80];
    int  len;

    printf( "Enter a string: " );
    gets( tmpstr );

    /* Request a based heap. Use based so that memory won't be taken from
     * near heap.
     */
    if( (seg = _bheapseg( 1000 )) == _NULLSEG )
        exit( 1 );

    /* Allocate based memory for two strings. */
    len = strlen( tmpstr );
    if( ((instr  = _bmalloc( seg, len + 1 )) == _NULLOFF) ||
        ((outstr = _bmalloc( seg, len + 1 )) == _NULLOFF) )
        exit( 1 );

    /* Copy a lowercased string to dynamic memory. The based memory is
     * far when addressed as a whole.
     */
    _fstrlwr( _fstrcpy( (char __far *)instr, (char __far *)tmpstr ) );

    /* Copy input string to output string in reversed order. When reading
     * and writing individual characters from a based heap, the compiler will
     * try to process them as near, thus speeding up the processing.
     */
    for( pin = instr + len - 1, pout = outstr;
                pout < outstr + len; pin--, pout++ )
        *pout = *pin;
    *pout = '\0';
```

```
                /* Display strings. Again, strings as a whole are far. */
                printf( "Input:  %Fs\n", (char __far *)instr );
                printf( "Output: %Fs\n", (char __far *)outstr );

                /* Free blocks and release based heap. */
                _bfree( seg, instr );
                _bfree( seg, outstr );
                _bfreeseg( seg );
        }
```

Output
```
Enter a string: Was I god
Input:  was i god
Output: dog i saw
```

_bios_disk

Description

Calls BIOS disk services, using INT 0x13.

#include <bios.h>

unsigned _bios_disk(unsigned *service*, **struct _diskinfo_t** **diskinfo* **);**

service	Disk function desired
diskinfo	Disk parameters

Remarks

The **_bios_disk** routine uses INT 0x13 to provide several disk-access functions. The *service* parameter selects the function desired, while the *diskinfo* structure provides the necessary parameters. Note that the low-level disk operations allowed by the **_bios_disk** routine are very dangerous to use because they perform direct manipulation of the disk.

The *diskinfo* structure provides the following parameters:

Element	Description
unsigned drive	Drive number
unsigned head	Head number
unsigned track	Track number
unsigned sector	Starting sector number
unsigned nsectors	Number of sectors to read, write, or compare
void far *buffer	Memory location to write to, read from, or compare

The *service* argument can be set to one of the following manifest constants:

Constant	Function
_DISK_FORMAT	Formats the track specified by *diskinfo*. The *head* and *track* fields indicate the track to format. Only one track can be formatted in a single call. The *buffer* field points to a set of sector markers. The format of the markers depends on the type of disk drive; see a technical reference to the PC BIOS to determine the marker format. The high-order byte (AH) of the return value contains the status of the call; 0 equals success. If there is an error, the high-order byte will contain a set of status flags, as defined below under Return Value.

Constant	Function
_DISK_READ	Reads one or more disk sectors into memory. This service uses all fields of the structure pointed to by *diskinfo*, as defined earlier in this section. If no error occurs, the function returns 0 in the high-order byte and the number of sectors read in the low-order byte. If there is an error, the high-order byte (AH) will contain a set of status flags, as defined below under Return Value.
_DISK_RESET	Forces the disk controller to do a hard reset, preparing for floppy-disk I/O. This is useful after an error occurs in another operation, such as a read. If this service is specified, the *diskinfo* argument is ignored. Status is returned in the 8 high-order bits (AH) of the return value. If there is an error, the high-order byte will contain a set of status flags, as defined below under Return Value.
_DISK_STATUS	Obtains the status of the last disk operation. If this service is specified, the *diskinfo* argument is ignored. Status is returned in the 8 low-order bits (AL) of the return value. If there is an error, the low-order byte (AL) will contain a set of status flags, as defined below under Return Value.
_DISK_VERIFY	Checks the disk to be sure the specified sectors exist and can be read. It also runs a CRC (cyclic redundancy check) test. This service uses all fields (except *buffer*) of the structure pointed to by *diskinfo*, as defined earlier in this section. If no error occurs, the function returns 0 in the high-order byte (AH) and the number of sectors compared in the low-order byte (AL). The error status flags are listed below under Return Value.
_DISK_WRITE	Writes data from memory to one or more disk sectors. This service uses all fields of the structure pointed to by *diskinfo*, as defined earlier in this section. If no error occurs, the function returns 0 in the high-order byte (AH) and the number of sectors written in the low-order byte (AL). If there is an error, the high-order byte will contain a set of status flags, as defined below under Return Value.

Return Value

The **_bios_disk** function returns the value in the AX register after the BIOS interrupt.

Bits	Meaning
0x00	No error
0x01	Invalid request or a bad command
0x02	Address mark not found
0x03	Disk write protected
0x04	Sector not found
0x05	Reset failed
0x06	Floppy disk removed
0x07	Drive parameter activity failed

Bits	Meaning
0x08	Direct Memory Access (DMA) overrun
0x09	DMA crossed 64K boundary
0x0A	Bad sector flag detected
0x0B	Bad track flag detected
0x0C	Media type not found
0x0D	Invalid number of sectors on format
0x0E	Control data access mark detected
0x0F	DMA arbitration level out of range
0x10	Data read (CRC or ECC) error
0x11	Corrected data read (ECC) error
0x20	Controller failure
0x40	Seek error
0x80	Disk timed out or failed to respond
0xAA	Drive not ready
0xBB	Undefined error
0xCC	Write fault on drive
0xE0	Status error
0xFF	Sense operation failed

Compatibility

Standards: None

16-Bit: DOS, QWIN, WIN, WIN DLL

32-Bit: None

Example

```
/* BDISK.C: This program first attempts to verify a disk by using an
 * invalid disk head number. After printing the return value error code,
 * the program verifies the disk by using a valid disk head code.
 */

#include <conio.h>
#include <stdio.h>
#include <bios.h>
```

```
void main( void )
{
    unsigned status = 0;
    struct _diskinfo_t disk_info;

    disk_info.drive    = 0;
    disk_info.head     = 10;      /* Invalid head number */
    disk_info.track    = 1;
    disk_info.sector   = 2;
    disk_info.nsectors = 8;

    printf( "Insert disk in drive A: and press any key\n" );
    _getch();
    status = _bios_disk( _DISK_VERIFY, &disk_info );
    printf( "Return value: 0x%.4x\n", status );
    if( status & 0xff00 )         /* Error if high byte is 0 */
       printf( "Seek error\n" );
    else
       printf( "No seek error\n" );

    printf( "Press any key\n" );
    _getch();
    disk_info.head = 0;           /* Valid head number */
    status = _bios_disk( _DISK_VERIFY, &disk_info );
    printf( "Return value: 0x%.4x\n", status );
    if( status & 0xff00 )         /* Error if high byte is 0 */
       printf( "Seek error\n" );
    else
       printf( "No seek error\n" );
}
```

Output

```
Insert disk in drive A: and press any key
Return value: 0x0400
Seek error
Press any key
Return value: 0x0008
No seek error
```

_bios_equiplist

Description

Calls BIOS equipment-list service, using INT 0x11.

#include <bios.h>

unsigned _bios_equiplist(void);

Remarks

The **_bios_equiplist** routine uses INT 0x11 to determine what hardware and peripherals are currently installed on the machine.

Return Value

The function returns the AX value, which is a set of bits indicating what equipment is installed, as defined below:

Bits	Meaning
0	True (1) if disk drive(s) installed
1	True (1) if math coprocessor installed
2–3	System RAM in 16K blocks (16–64K)
4–5	Initial video mode:
	00 = Reserved
	01 = 40 x 25 color
	10 = 80 x 25 color
	11 = 80 x 25 monochrome
6–7	Number of floppy-disk drives installed (00 = 1, 01 = 2, etc.)
8	False (0) if and only if a Direct Memory Access (DMA) chip is installed
9–11	Number of RS232 serial ports installed
12	True (1) if and only if a game adapter is installed
13	True (1) if and only if an internal modem is installed
14–15	Number of printers installed

Compatibility

Standards:	None
16-Bit:	DOS, QWIN, WIN, WIN DLL
32-Bit:	None

Example

```
/* BEQUIPLI.C: This program checks for the presence of diskettes. */

#include <bios.h>
#include <stdio.h>

void main( void )
{
   unsigned equipment;

   equipment = _bios_equiplist();
   printf( "Equipment bits: 0x%.4x\n", equipment );
   if( equipment & 0x1000 )        /* Check for game adapter bit */
      printf( "Game adapter installed\n" );
   else
      printf( "No game adapter installed\n" );
}
```

Output

```
Equipment bits: 0x4061
No game adapter installed
```

_bios_keybrd

Description   Calls BIOS keyboard services, using INT 0x16.

#include <bios.h>

unsigned _bios_keybrd(unsigned *service* **);**

service   Keyboard function desired

Remarks   The **_bios_keybrd** routine uses INT 0x16 to access the keyboard services. The *service* argument can be any of the following manifest constants:

Constant	Meaning
_KEYBRD_READ, **_NKEYBRD_READ**	Reads the next character from the keyboard. If no character has been typed, the call will wait for one. If the low-order byte of the return value is nonzero, the call contains the ASCII value of the character typed. The high-order byte contains the keyboard scan code for the character. The **_NKEYBRD_READ** constant is used with enhanced keyboards to obtain the scan codes for function keys F11 and F12 and the cursor control keys.
_KEYBRD_READY, **_NKEYBRD_READY**	Checks whether a keystroke is waiting to be read and, if so, reads it. The return value is 0 if no keystroke is waiting, or it is the character waiting to be read, in the same format as the **_KEYBRD_READ** or **_NKEYBRD_READ** return. This service does not remove the waiting character from the input buffer, as does the **_KEYBRD_READ** or **_NKEYBRD_READ** service. The **_NKEYBRD_READY** constant is used with enhanced keyboards to obtain the scan codes for function keys F11 and F12 and the cursor control keys.

Constant	Meaning
_KEYBRD_SHIFTSTATUS, **_NKEYBRD_SHIFTSTATUS**	Returns the current SHIFT-key status. **_KEYBRD_SHIFTSTATUS** returns only low byte. The **_NKEYBRD_SHIFTSTATUS** constant is used to get a full 16-bit status value. Any combination of the following bits may be set:

Bit	Meaning if True
00H	Rightmost SHIFT key pressed
01H	Leftmost SHIFT key pressed
02H	Either CTRL key pressed
3H	Either ALT key pressed
04H	SCROLL LOCK on
05H	NUM LOCK on
06H	CAPS LOCK on
07H	In insert mode (INS)
08H	Left CTRL key pressed
09H	Left ALT key pressed
0AH	Right CTRL key pressed
0BH	Right ALT key pressed
0CH	SCROLL LOCK key pressed
0DH	NUM LOCK key pressed
0EH	CAPS LOCK key pressed
0FH	SYS REQ key pressed

Return Value

With the **...READ** and **...SHIFTSTATUS** arguments, the **_bios_keybrd** function returns the contents of the AX register after the BIOS call.

With the **...READY** argument, **_bios_keybrd** returns 0 if there is no key. If there is a key, **_bios_keybrd** returns the key waiting to be read (i.e., the same value as **_KEYBRD_READ**).

With the **...READ** and the **...READY** arguments, the **_bios_keybrd** function returns −1 if CTRL+BREAK has been pressed and is the next keystroke to be read.

Compatibility

Standards: None

16-Bit: DOS, QWIN, WIN, WIN DLL

32-Bit: None

Example

```
/* BKEYBRD.C: This program prints a message on the screen until the
 * right SHIFT key is pressed.
 */

#include <bios.h>
#include <stdio.h>

void main( void )
{
    while( !(_bios_keybrd( _KEYBRD_SHIFTSTATUS ) & 0001) )
        printf( "Use the right SHIFT key to stop this message\n" );
    printf( "Right SHIFT key pressed\n" );
}
```

Output

```
Use the right SHIFT key to stop this message
Use the right SHIFT key to stop this message
Use the right SHIFT key to stop this message
Use the right SHIFT key to stop this message
Right SHIFT key pressed
```

_bios_memsize

Description

Calls the BIOS memory-size service, using INT 0x12.

#include <bios.h>

unsigned _bios_memsize(void);

Remarks

The **_bios_memsize** routine uses INT 0x12 to determine the total amount of main memory installed.

Return Value

The routine returns the total amount of installed memory in 1K blocks. The maximum return value is 640, representing 640K of main memory.

Compatibility

Standards: None
16-Bit: DOS, QWIN, WIN, WIN DLL
32-Bit: None

Example

```
/* BMEMSIZE.C: This program displays the amount of memory installed. */

#include <bios.h>
#include <stdio.h>

void main( void )
{
    unsigned memory;

    memory = _bios_memsize();
    printf ( "The amount of memory installed is: %dK\n", memory );
}
```

Output

```
The amount of memory installed is: 640K
```

_bios_printer

Description   Calls BIOS printer services, using INT 0x17.

#include <bios.h>

unsigned _bios_printer(unsigned *service*, **unsigned** *printer*, **unsigned** *data* **);**

service	Printer function desired
printer	Target printer port
data	Output data

Remarks   The **_bios_printer** routine uses INT 0x17 to perform printer output services for parallel printers. The *printer* argument specifies the affected printer, where 0 is LPT1, 1 is LPT2, and so forth.

Some printers do not support the full set of signals. As a result, the "Out of Paper" condition, for example, may not be returned to your program.

The *service* argument can be any of the following manifest constants:

Constant	Meaning
_PRINTER_INIT	Initializes the selected printer. The *data* argument is ignored.
_PRINTER_STATUS	Returns the printer status. The *data* argument is ignored.
_PRINTER_WRITE	Sends the low-order byte of *data* to the printer specified by *printer*.

Return Value   The **_bios_printer** function returns the value in the AX register after the BIOS interrupt. The high-order byte (AH) of the return value indicates the printer status after the operation, as defined below:

Bit	Meaning if True	Bit	Meaning if True
0	Printer timed out	4	Printer selected
1	Not used	5	Out of paper
2	Not used	6	Acknowledge
3	I/O error	7	Printer not busy

Compatibility   Standards: None

16-Bit: DOS, QWIN, WIN, WIN DLL

32-Bit: None

Example

```
/* BPRINTER.C: This program checks the status of the printer attached to
 * LPT1 when it is off line, then initializes the printer.
 */

#include <bios.h>
#include <conio.h>
#include <stdio.h>

#define LPT1 0

void main( void )
{
    unsigned status;

    printf ( "Place printer off line and press any key\n" );
    _getch();

    status = _bios_printer( _PRINTER_STATUS, LPT1, 0 );
    printf( "Status with printer off line: 0x%.4x\n\n", status );
    printf( "Put the printer on line and then\n" );
    printf( "Press any key to initialize printer\n" );
    _getch();

    status = _bios_printer( _PRINTER_INIT, LPT1, 0 );
    printf( "Status after printer initialized: 0x%.4x\n", status );
}
```

Output

```
Place printer off line and press any key
Status with printer off line: 0x0018

Put the printer on line and then
Press any key to initialize printer
Status after printer initialized: 0x0090
```

_bios_serialcom

Description

Calls BIOS communications services, using INT 0x14.

#include <bios.h>

unsigned _bios_serialcom(unsigned *service*, unsigned *serial_port*,
    unsigned *data*);

service	Communications service
serial_port	Serial port to use
data	Port configuration bits

Remarks

The **_bios_serialcom** routine uses INT 0x14 to provide serial communications services. The *serial_port* argument is set to 0 for COM1, to 1 for COM2, and so on.

The **_bios_serialcom** routine may not be able to establish reliable communications at baud rates in excess of 1,200 baud (**_COM_1200**) due to the overhead associated with servicing computer interrupts. Faster data communication rates are possible with more direct programming of serial-port controllers. See *C Programmer's Guide to Serial Communications* for more details on serial-communications programming in C.

The *service* argument can be set to one of the following manifest constants:

Constant	Service
_COM_INIT	Sets the port to the parameters specified in the *data* argument
_COM_SEND	Transmits the *data* characters over the selected serial port
_COM_RECEIVE	Accepts an input character from the selected serial port
_COM_STATUS	Returns the current status of the selected serial port

The *data* argument is ignored if *service* is set to **_COM_RECEIVE** or
_COM_STATUS. The *data* argument for **_COM_INIT** is created by combining
(with the OR operator) one or more of the following constants:

Constant	Meaning
_COM_CHR7	7 data bits
_COM_CHR8	8 data bits
_COM_STOP1	1 stop bit
_COM_STOP2	2 stop bits
_COM_NOPARITY	No parity
_COM_EVENPARITY	Even parity
_COM_ODDPARITY	Odd parity
_COM_110	110 baud
_COM_150	150 baud
_COM_300	300 baud
_COM_600	600 baud
_COM_1200	1,200 baud
_COM_2400	2,400 baud
_COM_4800	4,800 baud
_COM_9600	9,600 baud

The default value of *data* is 1 stop bit, no parity, and 110 baud.

Return Value   The function returns a 16-bit integer whose high-order byte contains status bits.
The meaning of the low-order byte varies, depending on the *service* value. The
high-order bits have the following meanings:

Bit	Meaning if Set
15	Timed out
14	Transmission-shift register empty
13	Transmission-hold register empty
12	Break detected
11	Framing error
10	Parity error
9	Overrun error
8	Data ready

When *service* is **_COM_SEND**, bit 15 will be set if *data* could not be sent.

When *service* is **_COM_RECEIVE**, the byte read will be returned in the low-order bits if the call is successful. If an error occurs, any of the bits 9, 10, 11, or 15 will be set.

When *service* is **_COM_INIT** or **_COM_STATUS**, the low-order bits are defined as follows:

Bit	Meaning if Set
7	Receive-line signal detected
6	Ring indicator
5	Data set ready
4	Clear to send
3	Change in receive-line signal detected
2	Trailing-edge ring indicator
1	Change in data-set-ready status
0	Change in clear-to-send status

Note that this function works only with IBM personal computers and true compatibles.

Compatibility

Standards: None

16-Bit: DOS, QWIN, WIN, WIN DLL

32-Bit: None

Example

```
/* BSERIALC.C: This program checks the status of serial port COM1. */

#include <bios.h>
#include <stdio.h>

void main( void )
{
    unsigned com1_status;

    com1_status = _bios_serialcom( _COM_STATUS, 0, 0 );
    printf ( "COM1 status: 0x%.4x\n", com1_status );
}
```

Output

```
COM1 status: 0x6000
```

_bios_timeofday

Description

Calls BIOS time and date services, using INT 0x1A.

#include <bios.h>

unsigned _bios_timeofday(unsigned *service*, long *timeval*);

service	Time function desired
timeval	Clock count

Remarks

The **_bios_timeofday** routine uses INT 0x1A to get or set the clock count. The *service* argument can be either of the following manifest constants:

Constant	Meaning
_TIME_GETCLOCK	Copies the current value of the clock count to the location pointed to by *timeval*. If midnight has not passed since the last time the system clock was read or set, the function returns 0; otherwise, the function returns 1.
_TIME_SETCLOCK	Sets the current value of the system clock to the value in the location pointed to by *timeval*. There is no return value.

Return Value

The **_bios_timeofday** function returns the value in the AX register after the BIOS interrupt.

Compatibility

Standards:	None
16-Bit:	DOS, QWIN, WIN, WIN DLL
32-Bit:	None

Example

```
/* BTIMEOFD.C: This program gets the current system clock count before and after
 * a "do-nothing" loop and displays the difference.
 */

#include <bios.h>
#include <stdio.h>

void main( void )
{
    long i, begin_tick, end_tick;

    _bios_timeofday( _TIME_GETCLOCK, &begin_tick );
    printf( "Beginning tick count: %lu\n", begin_tick );
    for( i = 1; i <= 900000; i++ )
        ;
    _bios_timeofday( _TIME_GETCLOCK, &end_tick );
    printf( "Ending tick count:    %lu\n", end_tick );
    printf( "Elapsed ticks:        %lu\n", end_tick - begin_tick );
}
```

Output

```
Beginning tick count: 1114255
Ending tick count:    1114287
Elapsed ticks:        32
```

bsearch

Description

Performs a binary search of a sorted array.

#include <stdlib.h>   Required for ANSI compatibility

#include <search.h>   Required only for function declarations

void *bsearch(const void **key***, const void ****base***, size_t** *num***, size_t** *width***,**
    int (__cdecl *compare **)(const void ****elem1***, const void ****elem2* **));**

key	Object to search for
base	Pointer to base of search data
num	Number of elements
width	Width of elements
compare	Function that compares two elements: *elem1* and *elem2*
elem1	Pointer to the key for the search
elem2	Pointer to the array element to be compared with the key

Remarks

The **bsearch** function performs a binary search of a sorted array of *num* elements, each of *width* bytes in size. The *base* value is a pointer to the base of the array to be searched, and *key* is the value being sought.

The *compare* argument is a pointer to a user-supplied routine that compares two array elements and returns a value specifying their relationship. The **bsearch** function calls the *compare* routine one or more times during the search, passing pointers to two array elements on each call. The routine compares the elements, then returns one of the following values:

Value	Meaning
< 0	*elem1* less than *elem2*
= 0	*elem1* identical to *elem2*
> 0	*elem1* greater than *elem2*

If the array you are searching is not in ascending sort order, **bsearch** does not work properly. If the array contains duplicate records with identical keys, there is no way to predict which of the duplicate records will be located by **bsearch**.

Return Value   The **bsearch** function returns a pointer to an occurrence of *key* in the array pointed
to by *base*. If *key* is not found, the function returns **NULL**.

Compatibility   Standards: ANSI, UNIX

16-Bit: DOS, QWIN, WIN, WIN DLL

32-Bit: DOS32X

See Also   **_lfind, _lsearch, qsort**

Example
```
/* BSEARCH.C: This program reads the command-line arguments, sorting them
 * with qsort, and then uses bsearch to find the word "cat."
 */

#include <search.h>
#include <string.h>
#include <stdio.h>

int compare( char **arg1, char **arg2 );  /* Declare a function for compare */

void main( int argc, char **argv )
{
    char **result;
    char *key = "cat";
    int i;

    /* Sort using Quicksort algorithm: */
    qsort( (char *)argv, argc, sizeof( char * ), compare );

    for( i = 0; i < argc; ++i )         /* Output sorted list */
        printf( "%s ", argv[i] );

    /*  Find the word "cat" using a binary search algorithm: */
    result = (char **)bsearch( (char *) &key, (char *)argv, argc,
                               sizeof( char * ), compare );
    if( result )
        printf( "\n%s found at %Fp\n", *result, result );
    else
        printf( "\nCat not found!\n" );
}

int compare( char **arg1, char **arg2 )
{
    /* Compare all of both strings: */
    return _strcmpi( *arg1, *arg2 );
}
```

Output
```
[C:\LIBREF] bsearch dog pig horse cat human rat cow goat
bsearch cat cow dog goat horse human pig rat
cat found at 0292:0FD0
```

_cabs, _cabsl

Description

Calculate the absolute value of a complex number.

#include <math.h>

double _cabs(struct _complex *z* **);**

long double _cabsl(struct _complexl *z* **);**

    z   Complex number

Remarks

The **_cabs** and **_cabsl** functions calculate the absolute value of a complex number, which must be a structure of type **_complex** (or **_complexl**). The structure *z* is composed of a real component *x* and an imaginary component *y*. A call to one of the **_cabs** routines is equivalent to the following:

sqrt($z.x*z.x + z.y*z.y$ **)**

The **_cabsl** function is the 80-bit counterpart and it uses the 80-bit, 10-byte co-processor form of arguments and return values. See the reference page on the long double functions for more details on this data type.

Return Value

On overflow, these functions call **_matherr** or **_matherrl**, return **HUGE_VAL**, and set **errno** to **ERANGE**.

Compatibility

    _cabs

Standards: UNIX
16-Bit: DOS, QWIN, WIN, WIN DLL
32-Bit: DOS32X

Use **_cabs** for compatibility with ANSI naming conventions of non-ANSI functions. Use **cabs** and link with OLDNAMES.LIB for UNIX compatibility.

_cabsl

Standards: None

16-Bit: DOS, QWIN, WIN, WIN DLL

32-Bit: None

See Also   **abs, fabs, labs**

Example
```
/* CABS.C: Using _cabs, this program calculates the absolute value of
 * a complex number.
 */

#include <math.h>
#include <stdio.h>

void main( void )
{
    struct _complex number = { 3.0, 4.0 };
    double d;

    d = _cabs( number );
    printf( "The absolute value of %f + %fi is %f\n",
            number.x, number.y, d );
}
```

Output   The absolute value of 3.000000 + 4.000000i is 5.000000

calloc Functions

Description

Allocate an array in memory with elements initialized to 0.

#include <stdlib.h>	For ANSI compatibility (**calloc** only)
#include <malloc.h>	Required only for function declarations

void *calloc(size_t *num*, **size_t** *size* **);**

void __ based(void) *_bcalloc(__segment *seg*, **size_t** *num*, **size_t** *size* **);**

void __ far *_fcalloc(size_t *num*, **size_t** *size* **);**

void __ near *_ncalloc(size_t *num*, **size_t** *size* **);**

num	Number of elements
size	Length in bytes of each element
seg	Segment selector

Remarks

The **calloc** family of functions allocates storage space for an array of *num* elements, each of length *size* bytes. Each element is initialized to 0.

In large data models (compact-, large-, and huge-model programs), **calloc** maps to **_fcalloc**. In small data models (tiny-, small-, and medium-model programs), **calloc** maps to **_ncalloc**.

The various **calloc** functions allocate storage space in the data segments shown in the list below:

Function	Data Segment
calloc	Depends on data model of program
_bcalloc	Based heap, specified by *seg* segment selector
_fcalloc	Far heap (outside default data segment)
_ncalloc	Near heap (inside default data segment)

Return Value

The **calloc** functions return a pointer to the allocated space. The storage space pointed to by the return value is guaranteed to be suitably aligned for storage of any type of object. To get a pointer to a type other than **void**, use a type cast on the return value.

The **_fcalloc** and **_ncalloc** functions return **NULL** if there is insufficient memory available. The **_bcalloc** function returns **_NULLOFF** in this case.

Compatibility

calloc

Standards: ANSI, UNIX
16-Bit: DOS, QWIN, WIN, WIN DLL
32-Bit: DOS32X

_bcalloc, _fcalloc, _ncalloc

Standards: None
16-Bit: DOS, QWIN, WIN, WIN DLL
32-Bit: None

See Also   **free** functions, **_halloc**, **_hfree**, **malloc** functions, **realloc** functions

Example

```
/* CALLOC.C: This program uses calloc to allocate space for 40 long integers.
 * It initializes each element to zero.
 */

#include <stdio.h>
#include <malloc.h>

void main( void )
{
   long *buffer;

   buffer = (long *)calloc( 40, sizeof( long ) );
   if( buffer != NULL )
      printf( "Allocated 40 long integers\n" );
   else
      printf( "Can't allocate memory\n" );
   free( buffer );
}
```

Output

```
Allocated 40 long integers
```

ceil, _ceill

Description

Calculate the ceiling of a value.

#include <math.h>

double ceil(double *x* **);**

long double _ceill(long double *x* **);**

x   Floating-point value

Remarks

The **ceil** and **_ceill** functions return a **double** (or **long double**) value representing the smallest integer that is greater than or equal to *x*.

The **_ceill** function is the 80-bit counterpart and it uses the 80-bit, 10-byte co-processor form of arguments and return values. See the reference page on the long double functions for more details on this data type.

Return Value

These functions return the **double** or **long double** result. There is no error return.

Compatibility

ceil

Standards:	ANSI, UNIX
16-Bit:	DOS, QWIN, WIN, WIN DLL
32-Bit:	DOS32X

_ceill

Standards:	None
16-Bit:	DOS, QWIN, WIN, WIN DLL
32-Bit:	None

See Also

floor, fmod

Example   /* FLOOR.C: This example displays the largest integers less than or equal
                 * to the floating-point values 2.8 and -2.8. It then shows the smallest
                 * integers greater than or equal to 2.8 and -2.8.
                 */

```c
#include <math.h>
#include <stdio.h>

void main( void )
{
    double y;

    y = floor( 2.8 );
    printf( "The floor of 2.8 is %f\n", y );
    y = floor( -2.8 );
    printf( "The floor of -2.8 is %f\n", y );

    y = ceil( 2.8 );
    printf( "The ceil of 2.8 is %f\n", y );
    y = ceil( -2.8 );
    printf( "The ceil of -2.8 is %f\n", y );
}
```

Output   The floor of 2.8 is 2.000000
               The floor of -2.8 is -3.000000
               The ceil of 2.8 is 3.000000
               The ceil of -2.8 is -2.000000

_cexit, _c_exit

Description

Perform cleanup operations and return without terminating the process.

#include <process.h>

void _cexit(void);

void _c_exit(void);

Remarks

The **_cexit** function calls, in LIFO ("last in, first out") order, the functions registered by **atexit** and **_onexit**. Then the **_cexit** function flushes all I/O buffers and closes all open streams before returning.

The **_c_exit** function is the same as the **_exit** function but returns to the calling process without processing **atexit** or **_onexit** or flushing stream buffers.

The behavior of the **exit**, **_exit**, **_cexit**, and **_c_exit** functions is described in the following list:

Function	Action
exit	Performs complete C library termination procedures, terminates the process, and exits with the supplied status code
_exit	Performs "quick" C library termination procedures, terminates the process, and exits with the supplied status code
_cexit	Performs complete C library termination procedures and returns to caller, but does not terminate the process
_c_exit	Performs "quick" C library termination procedures and returns to caller, but does not terminate the process

Return Value

None.

Compatibility

Standards: None
16-Bit: DOS, QWIN, WIN, WIN DLL
32-Bit: DOS32X

See Also

abort, **atexit**, **_exec** functions, **exit**, **_onexit**, **_spawn** functions, **system**

_cgets

Description

Gets a character string from the console.

#include <conio.h>   Required only for function declarations

char *_cgets(char **buffer***);**

buffer   Storage location for data

Remarks

The **_cgets** function reads a string of characters directly from the console and stores the string and its length in the location pointed to by *buffer*. The *buffer* argument must be a pointer to a character array. The first element of the array, *buffer*[0], must contain the maximum length (in characters) of the string to be read. The array must contain enough elements to hold the string, a terminating null character ('\0'), and two additional bytes.

The **_cgets** function continues to read characters until a carriage-return–line-feed (CR-LF) combination is read, or the specified number of characters is read. The string is stored starting at *str*[2]. If a CR-LF combination is read, it is replaced with a null character ('\0') before being stored. The **_cgets** function then stores the actual length of the string in the second array element, *buffer*[1].

Because all DOS editing keys are active when you call **_cgets**, pressing F3 repeats the last entry.

Return Value

The **_cgets** function returns a pointer to the start of the string, at *buffer*[2]. There is no error return.

Compatibility

Standards: None
16-Bit: DOS, QWIN, WIN, WIN DLL
32-Bit: DOS32X

See Also

_getch, _getche

Example

```
/* CGETS.C: This program creates a buffer and initializes the first byte
 * to the size of the buffer - 2. Next, the program accepts an input string
 * using _cgets and displays the size and text of that string.
 */

#include <conio.h>
#include <stdio.h>

void main( void )
{
    char buffer[82] = { 80 };  /* Maximum characters in first byte */
    char *result;

    printf( "Input line of text, followed by carriage return:\n");
    result = _cgets( buffer );  /* Input a line of text */
    printf( "\nLine length = %d\nText = %s\n", buffer[1], result );
}
```

Output

```
Input line of text, followed by carriage return:
This is some text
Line length = 17
Text = This is some text
```

_chain_intr

Description   Chains an interrupt from one handler to another.

#include <dos.h>

void _chain_intr(void(__cdecl __interrupt __far * *target* **)( ));**

target   Target interrupt routine

Remarks   The **_chain_intr** routine passes control from one interrupt handler to another. The
stack and the registers of the first routine are passed to the second, allowing the
second routine to return as if it had been called directly.

The **_chain_intr** routine is generally used when a user-defined interrupt handler
begins processing, then chains to the original interrupt handler to finish processing.

Chaining is one of two techniques, listed below, that can be used to transfer control from a new interrupt routine to an old one:

- Call **_chain_intr** with the interrupt routine as an argument. Do this if your
  routine is finished and you want the second interrupt routine to terminate the interrupt call.

```
void __interrupt new_int( unsigned _es, unsigned _ds,
  unsigned _di, unsigned _si,... )
{
    ++_di;                     /* Initial processing here */
    _chain_intr( old_int ); /* New DI passed to old_int */
    --_di;                     /* This is never executed   */
}
```

- Call the interrupt routine (after casting it to an interrupt function if necessary).
  Do this if you need to do further processing after the second interrupt routine
  finishes.

```
void __interrupt new_int( unsigned _es, unsigned _ds,
  unsigned _di, unsigned _si,... )
{
    ++_di;                     /* Initial processing here */
    (*old_int)();              /* New DI passed to old_int */
    __asm mov _di, di          /* Put real DI from old_int */
                               /*   into _di for return    */
}
```

Note that the real registers set by the old interrupt function are not automatically set to the pseudoregisters of the new routine.

Use the **_chain_intr** function when you do not want to replace the default interrupt handler, but you do need to see its input. An example is a TSR (terminate-and-stay-resident) program that checks all keyboard input for a particular "hot key" sequence.

The **_chain_intr** function should be used only with C functions that have been declared with **__interrupt**. The **__interrupt** declaration ensures that the procedure's entry/exit sequence is appropriate for an interrupt handler.

Return Value   The **_chain_intr** function does not return to the caller.

Compatibility   Standards: None

16-Bit: DOS

32-Bit: None

See Also   **_dos_getvect**, **_dos_keep**, **_dos_setvect**

_chdir

Description

Changes the current working directory.

#include <direct.h>   Required only for function declarations

#include <errno.h>   Required for **errno** constants

int _chdir(char *_dirname_);

dirname   Path name of new working directory

Remarks

The **_chdir** function changes the current working directory to the directory specified by _dirname_. The _dirname_ argument must refer to an existing directory.

This function can change the current working directory on any drive; it cannot be used to change the default drive itself. For example, if A: is the default drive and \BIN is the current working directory, the following call changes the current working directory for drive C:

```
_chdir("c:\\temp");
```

Notice that you must place two backslashes (\\ ) in a C string in order to represent a single backslash (\ ); the backslash is the escape character for C strings and therefore requires special handling.

This function call has no apparent immediate effect. However, when the **_chdrive** function is called to change the default drive to C:, the current working directory becomes C:\TEMP.

With DOS, the new directory set by the program becomes the new current working directory.

Return Value

The **_chdir** function returns a value of 0 if the working directory is successfully changed. A return value of –1 indicates an error, in which case **errno** is set to **ENOENT**, indicating that the specified path name could not be found.

Compatibility	Standards:	UNIX
	16-Bit:	DOS, QWIN, WIN, WIN DLL
	32-Bit:	DOS32X

Use **_chdir** for compatibility with ANSI naming conventions of non-ANSI functions. Use **chdir** and link with OLDNAMES.LIB for UNIX compatibility.

See Also   **_dos_setdrive, _mkdir, _rmdir, system**

Example
```
/* CHGDIR.C: This program uses the _chdir function to verify that a
 * given directory exists. Under real mode that directory also becomes
 * the current directory. Under protected mode, it is only the default
 * directory for the current process.
 */

#include <direct.h>
#include <stdio.h>
#include <stdlib.h>

void main( int argc, char *argv[] )
{
   if( _chdir( argv[1] )   )
      printf( "Unable to locate the directory: %s\n", argv[1] );
   else
      system( "dir *.c" );
}
```

Output
```
[C:\LIBREF] chgdir \tmp

The volume label in drive C is ZEPPELIN.
Directory of C:\TMP

DUP      C       232    4-18-99   11:18a
TEST     C       713    4-07-98    2:49p
      2 File(s)   14155776 bytes free
```

_chdrive

Description   Changes the current working drive.

#include <direct.h>   Required only for function declarations

int _chdrive(int *drive* **);**

drive   Number of new working drive

Remarks   The **_chdrive** function changes the current working drive to the drive specified by *drive*. The *drive* argument uses an integer to specify the new working drive (1=A, 2=B, etc.).

This function changes only the working drive; the **_chdir** function changes the working directory.

With DOS, the new drive set by the program becomes the new working drive.

Return Value   The **_chdrive** function returns a value of 0 if the working drive is successfully changed. A return value of −1 indicates an error.

Compatibility   Standards: None
16-Bit: DOS, QWIN, WIN, WIN DLL
32-Bit: DOS32X

See Also   **_chdir, _dos_setdrive, _fullpath, _getcwd, _getdrive, _mkdir, _rmdir, system**

Example

```
/* GETDRIVE.C illustrates drive functions including:
 *      _getdrive       _chdrive        _getdcwd
 */

#include <stdio.h>
#include <conio.h>
#include <direct.h>
#include <stdlib.h>
```

```
void main( void )
{
    int ch, drive, curdrive;
    static char path[_MAX_PATH];

    /* Save current drive. */
    curdrive = _getdrive();

    printf( "Available drives are: \n" );

    /* If we can switch to the drive, it exists. */
    for( drive = 1; drive <= 26; drive++ )
        if( !_chdrive( drive ) )
            printf( "%c: ", drive + 'A' - 1 );

    while( 1 )
    {
        printf( "\nType drive letter to check or ESC to quit: " );
        ch = _getch();
        if( ch == 27 )
            break;
        if( isalpha( ch ) )
            _putch( ch );
        if( _getdcwd( toupper( ch ) - 'A' + 1, path, _MAX_PATH ) != NULL )
            printf( "\nCurrent directory on that drive is %s\n", path );
    }

    /* Restore original drive. This is only necessary for DOS. Under OS/2
     * the current drive of the calling process is always restored.
     */
    _chdrive( curdrive );
    printf( "\n" );
}
```

Output

```
Available drives are:
A: B: C:
Type drive letter to check or ESC to quit: q
Type drive letter to check or ESC to quit: a
Current directory on that drive is A:\

Type drive letter to check or ESC to quit: c
Current directory on that drive is C:\LIBREF

Type drive letter to check or ESC to quit:
```

_chmod

Description

Changes the file-permission settings.

#include <sys\types.h>

#include <sys\stat.h>

#include <errno.h>

#include <io.h>   Required only for function declarations

int _chmod(char *__filename__, int __pmode__);

filename	Path name of existing file
pmode	Permission setting for file

Remarks

The **_chmod** function changes the permission setting of the file specified by *filename*. The permission setting controls read and write access to the file. The constant expression *pmode* contains one or both of the manifest constants **_S_IWRITE** and **_S_IREAD**, defined in SYS\STAT.H. Any other values for *pmode* are ignored. When both constants are given, they are joined with the bitwise-OR operator (|). The meaning of the *pmode* argument is as follows:

Value	Meaning
_S_IWRITE	Writing permitted
_S_IREAD	Reading permitted
**_S_IREAD	_S_IWRITE**	Reading and writing permitted

If write permission is not given, the file is read-only. Note that all files are always readable; it is not possible to give write-only permission. Thus the modes **_S_IWRITE** and **_S_IREAD | _S_IWRITE** are equivalent.

Return Value

The **_chmod** function returns the value 0 if the permission setting is successfully changed. A return value of −1 indicates an error; in this case, **errno** is set to **ENOENT**, indicating that the specified file could not be found.

Compatibility	Standards: UNIX
	16-Bit: DOS, QWIN, WIN, WIN DLL
	32-Bit: DOS32X

Use **_chmod** for compatibility with ANSI naming conventions of non-ANSI functions. Use **chmod** and link with OLDNAMES.LIB for UNIX compatibility.

See Also   **_access, _creat, _fstat, _open, _stat**

Example

```
/* CHMOD.C: This program uses _chmod to change the mode of a file to
 * read-only. It then attempts to modify the file.
 */

#include <sys\types.h>
#include <sys\stat.h>
#include <io.h>
#include <stdio.h>
#include <stdlib.h>

void main( void )
{
    /* Make file read-only: */
    if( _chmod( "CHMOD.C", _S_IREAD ) == -1 )
        perror( "File not found\n" );
    else
        printf( "Mode changed to read-only\n" );
    system( "echo /* End of file */ >> CHMOD.C" );

    /* Change back to read/write: */
    if( _chmod( "CHMOD.C", _S_IWRITE ) == -1 )
        perror( "File not found\n" );
    else
        printf( "Mode changed to read/write\n" );
}
```

Output

```
Mode changed to read-only
Access denied
Mode changed to read/write
```

_chsize

Description

Changes the file size.

#include <io.h>   Required only for function declarations
#include <errno.h>

int _chsize(int *handle*, **long** *size* **);**

handle   Handle referring to open file
size   New length of file in bytes

Remarks

The **_chsize** function extends or truncates the file associated with *handle* to the length specified by *size*. The file must be open in a mode that permits writing. Null characters (**'\0'**) are appended if the file is extended. If the file is truncated, all data from the end of the shortened file to the original length of the file is lost.

In DOS and Windows, the directory update is done when a file is closed. Consequently, while a program is running, requests to determine the amount of free disk space may receive inaccurate results.

Return Value

The **_chsize** function returns the value 0 if the file size is successfully changed. A return value of –1 indicates an error, and **errno** is set to one of the following values:

Value	Meaning
EACCES	Specified file is locked against access.
EBADF	Specified file is read-only or an invalid file handle.
ENOSPC	No space is left on device.

Compatibility

Standards: UNIX
16-Bit: DOS, QWIN, WIN, WIN DLL
32-Bit: DOS32X

Use **_chsize** for compatibility with ANSI naming conventions of non-ANSI functions. Use **chsize** and link with OLDNAMES.LIB for UNIX compatibility.

See Also

_close, _creat, _open

Example

```
/* CHSIZE.C: This program uses _filelength to report the size of a
 * file before and after modifying it with _chsize.
 */

#include <io.h>
#include <fcntl.h>
#include <sys\types.h>
#include <sys\stat.h>
#include <stdio.h>

void main( void )
{
    int fh, result;
    unsigned int nbytes = BUFSIZ;

    /* Open a file */
    if( (fh = _open( "data", _O_RDWR | _O_CREAT, _S_IREAD | _S_IWRITE )) != -1 )
    {
        printf( "File length before: %ld\n", _filelength( fh ) );
        if( _chsize( fh, 329678 ) == 0 )
            printf( "Size successfully changed\n" );
        else
            printf( "Problem in changing the size\n" );
        printf( "File length after:  %ld\n", _filelength( fh ) );
        _close( fh );
    }
}
```

Output

```
File length before: 0
Size successfully changed
File length after:  329678
```

_clear87

Description

Gets and clears the floating-point status word.

#include <float.h>

unsigned int _clear87(void);

Remarks

The **_clear87** function gets and clears the floating-point status word. The floating-point status word is a combination of the 8087/80287 status word and other conditions detected by the 8087/80287 exception handler, such as floating-point stack overflow and underflow.

Return Value

The bits in the value returned indicate the floating-point status. See the FLOAT.H include file for a complete definition of the bits returned by **_clear87**.

Many of the math library functions modify the 8087/80287 status word, with unpredictable results. Return values from **_clear87** and **_status87** become more reliable as fewer floating-point operations are performed between known states of the floating-point status word.

Compatibility

Standards: None
16-Bit: DOS, QWIN, WIN, WIN DLL
32-Bit: DOS32X

See Also

_control87, _status87

Example

```
/* CLEAR87.C: This program creates various floating-point problems,
 * then uses _clear87 to report on these problems.
 * Compile this program with Optimizations disabled (/Od). Otherwise
 * the optimizer will remove the code associated with the unused
 * floating-point values.
 */

#include <stdio.h>
#include <float.h>
```

```
void main( void )
{
    double a = 1e-40, b;
    float x, y;

    printf( "Status: %.4x - clear\n", _clear87()  );

    /* Store into y is inexact and underflows: */
    y = a;
    printf( "Status: %.4x - inexact, underflow\n", _clear87() );

    /* y is denormal: */
    b = y;
    printf( "Status: %.4x - denormal\n", _clear87() );
}
```

Output

```
Status: 0000 - clear
Status: 0030 - inexact, underflow
Status: 0002 - denormal
```

clearerr

Description

Resets the error indicator for a stream.

#include <stdio.h>

void clearerr(FILE *_stream_);

stream   Pointer to **FILE** structure

Remarks

The **clearerr** function resets the error indicator and end-of-file indicator for _stream_. Error indicators are not automatically cleared; once the error indicator for a specified stream is set, operations on that stream continue to return an error value until **clearerr**, **fseek**, **fsetpos**, or **rewind** is called.

Return Value

None.

Compatibility

Standards: ANSI, UNIX

16-Bit: DOS, QWIN, WIN, WIN DLL

32-Bit: DOS32X

See Also

_eof, feof, ferror, perror

Example

```
/* CLEARERR.C: This program creates an error on the standard input
 * stream, then clears it so that future reads won't fail.
 */

#include <stdio.h>

void main( void )
{
    int c;

    /* Create an error by writing to standard input. */
    putc( 'c', stdin );
    if( ferror( stdin ) )
    {
        perror( "Write error" );
        clearerr( stdin );
    }
```

```
            /* See if read causes an error. */
            printf( "Will input cause an error? " );
            c = getc( stdin );
            if( ferror( stdin ) )
            {
                perror( "Read error" );
                clearerr( stdin );
            }
        }
```

Output   Write error: Error 0
            Will input cause an error? n

_clearscreen

Description   Clears the specified area of the screen.

#include <graph.h>

void __far _clearscreen(short *area*);

area   Target area

Remarks   The _**clearscreen** function erases the target area, filling it with the current background color. The *area* argument can be one of the following manifest constants (defined in GRAPH.H):

Constant	Action
_GCLEARSCREEN	Clears and fills the entire screen
_GVIEWPORT	Clears and fills only within the current view port
_GWINDOW	Clears and fills only within the current text window

Return Value   None.

Compatibility   Standards: None
16-Bit: DOS
32-Bit: None

See Also   _getbkcolor, _setbkcolor

Example
```
/* CLRSCRN.C */
#include <conio.h>
#include <graph.h>
#include <stdlib.h>
```

```
void main( void )
{
   short xhalf, yhalf, xquar, yquar;
   struct _videoconfig vc;

   /* Find a valid graphics mode. */
   if( !_setvideomode( _MAXRESMODE ) )
      exit( 1 );

   _getvideoconfig( &vc );

   xhalf = vc.numxpixels / 2;
   yhalf = vc.numypixels / 2;
   xquar = xhalf / 2;
   yquar = yhalf / 2;

   _setviewport( 0, 0, xhalf - 1, yhalf - 1 );
   _rectangle( _GBORDER, 0,  0, xhalf - 1, yhalf - 1 );
   _ellipse( _GFILLINTERIOR, xquar / 4, yquar / 4,
                      xhalf - (xquar / 4), yhalf - (yquar / 4) );
   _getch();
   _clearscreen( _GVIEWPORT );

   _getch();
   _setvideomode( _DEFAULTMODE );
}
```

clock

Description   Calculates the time used by the calling process.

#include <time.h>

clock_t clock(void);

Remarks   The **clock** function tells how much processor time has been used by the calling process. The time in seconds is approximated by dividing the **clock** return value by the value of the **CLOCKS_PER_SEC** constant.

In other words, the **clock** function returns the number of processor timer ticks that have elapsed. A timer tick is approximately equal to 1/**CLOCKS_PER_SEC** seconds.

In versions of Microsoft C prior to version 6.0, the **CLOCKS_PER_SEC** constant was called **CLK_TCK**.

Return Value   The **clock** function returns the product of the time in seconds and the value of the **CLOCKS_PER_SEC** constant. If the processor time is not available, the function returns the value −1, cast as **clock_t**.

In DOS, **clock** returns the time elapsed since the process started. This may not be equal to the actual processor time used by the process.

Compatibility   Standards: ANSI
                       16-Bit: DOS, QWIN, WIN
                       32-Bit: DOS32X

See Also   **difftime, time**

Example

```
/* CLOCK.C: This example prompts for how long the program is to run and
 * then continuously displays the elapsed time for that period.
 */

#include <stdio.h>
#include <stdlib.h>
#include <time.h>

void sleep( clock_t wait );

void main( void )
{
   long    i = 600000L;
   clock_t start, finish;
   double  duration;

   /* Delay for a specified time. */
   printf( "Delay for three seconds\n" );
   sleep( (clock_t)3 * CLOCKS_PER_SEC );
   printf( "Done!\n" );

   /* Measure the duration of an event. */
   printf( "Time to do %ld empty loops is ", i );
   start = clock();
   while( i-- )
      ;
   finish = clock();
   duration = (double)(finish - start) / CLOCKS_PER_SEC;
   printf( "%2.1f seconds\n", duration );
}

/* Pauses for a specified number of microseconds. */
void sleep( clock_t wait )
{
   clock_t goal;

   goal = wait + clock();
   while( goal > clock() )
      ;
}
```

Output

```
Delay for three seconds
Done!
Time to do 600000 empty loops is 2.0 seconds
```

_close

Description

Closes a file.

#include <io.h> Required only for function declarations

#include <errno.h>

int _close(int *handle* **);**

handle Handle referring to open file

Remarks

The **_close** function closes the file associated with *handle*.

Return Value

The **_close** function returns 0 if the file was successfully closed. A return value of −1 indicates an error, and **errno** is set to **EBADF**, indicating an invalid file-handle argument.

Compatibility

Standards: UNIX

16-Bit: DOS, QWIN, WIN, WIN DLL

32-Bit: DOS32X

Use **_close** for compatibility with ANSI naming conventions of non-ANSI functions. Use **close** and link with OLDNAMES.LIB for UNIX compatibility.

See Also

_chsize, _creat, _dup, _dup2, _open, _unlink

Example

```
/* OPEN.C: This program uses _open to open a file named OPEN.C for input
 * and a file named OPEN.OUT for output. The files are then closed.
 */

#include <fcntl.h>
#include <sys\types.h>
#include <sys\stat.h>
#include <io.h>
#include <stdio.h>
```

```
void main( void )
{
   int fh1, fh2;
   fh1 = _open( "OPEN.C", _O_RDONLY );
   if( fh1 == -1 )
      perror( "open failed on input file" );
   else
   {
      printf( "open succeeded on input file\n" );
      _close( fh1 );
   }

   fh2 = _open( "OPEN.OUT", _O_WRONLY | _O_CREAT, _S_IREAD | _S_IWRITE );
   if( fh2 == -1 )
      perror( "open failed on output file" );
   else
   {
      printf( "open succeeded on output file\n" );
      _close( fh2 );
   }
}
```

Output   open succeeded on input file
open succeeded on output file

_commit

Description   Flushes a file directly to disk.

#include <io.h>   Required only for function declarations
#include <errno.h>

int _commit(int *handle* **);**

handle   Handle referring to open file

Remarks   The **_commit** function forces the operating system to write the file associated with *handle* to disk. This call ensures that the specified file is flushed immediately—not at the operating system's discretion.

Return Value   The **_commit** function returns 0 if the file was successfully flushed to disk. A return value of –1 indicates an error, and **errno** is set to **EBADF**, indicating an invalid file-handle argument.

Compatibility   Standards: None
                       16-Bit: DOS, QWIN, WIN, WIN DLL
                       32-Bit: DOS32X

See Also   **_creat, _open, _read, _write**

Example
```
/* COMMIT.C illustrates low-level file I/O functions including:
 *
 *      _close    _commit    memset    _open    _write
 *
 * This is example code, to keep the code simple and readable
 * return values are not checked.
 */

#include <io.h>
#include <stdio.h>
#include <fcntl.h>

#define MAXBUF 32

int log_receivable( int );
```

```
void main( void )
{
    int fhandle;
    fhandle = _open( "TRANSACT.LOG", _O_APPEND | _O_CREAT |
                                     _O_BINARY | _O_RDWR );
    log_receivable( fhandle );
    _close( fhandle );
}

int log_receivable( int fhandle )
{
/* The log_receivable function prompts for a name and a monetary amount
 * and places both values into a buffer (buf). The _write function
 * writes the values to the operating system and the _commit function
 * ensures that they are written to a disk file.
 */

    int i;
    char  buf[MAXBUF];

    memset( buf, '\0', MAXBUF );
    /* Begin Transaction. */
    printf( "Enter name: " );
    gets( buf );
    for( i = 1; buf[i] != '\0'; i++ );
    /* Write the value as a '\0' terminated string. */
    _write( fhandle, buf, i+1 );
    printf( "\n" );

    memset( buf, '\0', MAXBUF );
    printf( "Enter amount: $" );
    gets( buf );
    for( i = 1; buf[i] != '\0'; i++ );
    /* Write the value as a '\0' terminated string. */
    _write( fhandle, buf, i+1 );
    printf( "\n" );

    return _commit( fhandle );
    /* The _commit function ensures that two important pieces of data are
     * safely written to disk. The return value of the _commit function
     * is returned to the calling function.
     */
}
```

_ control87

Description

Gets and sets the floating-point control word.

#include <float.h>

unsigned int _ control87(unsigned int *new*, **unsigned int** *mask* **);**

new   New control-word bit values

mask   Mask for new control-word bits to set

Remarks

The **_ control87** function gets and sets the floating-point control word. The floating-point control word allows the program to change the precision, rounding, and infinity modes in the floating-point-math package. Floating-point exceptions can also be masked or unmasked using the **_ control87** function.

If the value for *mask* is equal to 0, then **_ control87** gets the floating-point control word. If *mask* is nonzero, then a new value for the control word is set in the following manner: for any bit that is on (equal to 1) in *mask*, the corresponding bit in *new* is used to update the control word. To put it another way,

```
fpcntrl = ((fpcntrl & ~mask) | (new & mask))
```

where `fpcntrl` is the floating-point control word.

The possible values for the mask constant (*mask*) and new control values (*new*) are shown in Table R.1.

Table R.1   Hex Values

Mask	Hex Value	Constant	Hex Value
MCW_EM (Interrupt exception)	0x003F		
		_EM_INVALID	0x0001
		_EM_DENORMAL	0x0002
		_EM_ZERODIVIDE	0x0004
		_EM_OVERFLOW	0x0008
		_EM_UNDERFLOW	0x0010
		_EM_INEXACT	0x0020

Table R.1   Hex Values (*continued*)

Mask	Hex Value	Constant	Hex Value
MCW_IC (Infinity control)	0x1000		
		_IC_AFFINE	0x1000
		_IC_PROJECTIVE	0x0000
MCW_RC (Rounding control)	0x0C00		
		RC_CHOP	0x0C00
		RC_UP	0x0800
		_RC_DOWN	0x0400
		_RC_NEAR	0x0000
MCW_PC (Precision control)	0x0300		
		_PC_24 (24 bits)	0x0000
		_PC_53 (53 bits)	0x0200
		_PC_64 (64 bits)	0x0300

Return Value   The bits in the value returned indicate the floating-point control state. See the FLOAT.H include file for a complete definition of the bits returned by **_control87**.

Compatibility

Standards: None

16-Bit: DOS, QWIN, WIN, WIN DLL

32-Bit: DOS32X

See Also   **_clear87**, **_status87**

Example   /* CNTRL87.C: This program uses _control87 to output the control word,
                * set the precision to 24 bits, and reset the status to the default.
                */

```
#include <stdio.h>
#include <float.h>

void main( void )
{
    double a = 0.1;

    /* Show original control word and do calculation. */
    printf( "Original: 0x%.4x\n", _control87( 0, 0 ) );
    printf( "%1.1f * %1.1f = %.15e\n", a, a, a * a );

    /* Set precision to 24 bits and recalculate. */
    printf( "24-bit:   0x%.4x\n", _control87( _PC_24, MCW_PC ) );
    printf( "%1.1f * %1.1f = %.15e\n", a, a, a * a );

    /* Restore to default and recalculate. */
    printf( "Default: 0x%.4x\n", _control87( CW_DEFAULT, 0xffff ) );
    printf( "%1.1f * %1.1f = %.15e\n", a, a, a * a );
}
```

Output   Original: 0x1332
                0.1 * 0.1 = 1.000000000000000e-002
                24-bit: 0x1332
                0.1 * 0.1 = 9.999999776482582e-003
                Default: 0x1032
                0.1 * 0.1 = 1.000000000000000e-002

cos Functions

Description

Calculate the cosine (**cos** and **_cosl**) or hyperbolic cosine (**cosh** and **_coshl**).

#include <math.h>

double cos(double *x* **);**

double cosh(double *x* **);**

long double _cosl(long double *x* **);**

long double _coshl(long double *x* **);**

x   Angle in radians

Remarks

The **cos** and **cosh** functions return the cosine and hyperbolic cosine, respectively, of *x*.

The **_cosl** and **_coshl** functions are the 80-bit counterparts and use the 80-bit, 10-byte coprocessor form of arguments and return values. See the reference page on the long double functions for more details on this data type.

Return Value

If *x* is large, a partial loss of significance in the result may occur in a call to **cos**, in which case the function generates a **_PLOSS** error. If *x* is so large that significance is completely lost, **cos** prints a **_TLOSS** message to **stderr** and returns 0. In both cases, **errno** is set to **ERANGE**.

If the result is too large in a **cosh** call, the function returns **HUGE_VAL** and sets **errno** to **ERANGE**. This behavior can be changed with **_matherr.**

Compatibility

cos, cosh

Standards: ANSI, UNIX
16-Bit: DOS, QWIN, WIN, WIN DLL
32-Bit: DOS32X

_cosl, _coshl

Standards: None

16-Bit: DOS, QWIN, WIN, WIN DLL

32-Bit: None

See Also   **acos** functions, **asin** functions, **atan** functions, **_matherr**, **sin** functions, **tan** functions

Example
```
/* SINCOS.C: This program displays the sine, hyperbolic sine, cosine,
 * and hyperbolic cosine of pi / 2.
 */

#include <math.h>
#include <stdio.h>

void main( void )
{
    double pi = 3.1415926535;
    double x, y;

    x = pi / 2;
    y = sin( x );
    printf( "sin( %f ) = %f\n", x, y );
    y = sinh( x );
    printf( "sinh( %f ) = %f\n",x, y );
    y = cos( x );
    printf( "cos( %f ) = %f\n", x, y );
    y = cosh( x );
    printf( "cosh( %f ) = %f\n",x, y );
}
```

Output
```
sin( 1.570796 ) = 1.000000
sinh( 1.570796 ) = 2.301299
cos( 1.570796 ) = 0.000000
cosh( 1.570796 ) = 2.509178
```

_cprintf

Description

Formats and prints to the console.

#include <conio.h>   Required only for function declarations

int _cprintf(char *_format_ [[, _argument_]] ...);

format   Format control string

argument   Optional arguments

Remarks

The **_cprintf** function formats and prints a series of characters and values directly to the console, using the **_putch** function to output characters. Each _argument_ (if any) is converted and output according to the corresponding format specification in _format_. The format has the same form and function as the _format_ argument for the **printf** function; see **printf** for a description of the format and arguments.

Note that unlike the **fprintf**, **printf**, and **sprintf** functions, **_cprintf** does not translate line-feed characters into carriage-return–line-feed (CR-LF) combinations on output.

Return Value

The **_cprintf** function returns the number of characters printed.

Compatibility

Standards: None
16-Bit: DOS, QWIN, WIN, WIN DLL
32-Bit: DOS32X

See Also

_cscanf, fprintf, printf, sprintf, vprintf

Example   /* CPRINTF.C: This program displays some variables to the console. */

```
#include <conio.h>

void main( void )
{
    int     i = -16, h = 29;
    unsigned u = 62511;
    char    c = 'A';
    char    s[] = "Test";

    /* Note that console output does not translate \n as
     * standard output does. Use \r\n instead.
     */
    _cprintf( "%d  %.4x  %u  %c %s\r\n", i, h, u, c, s );
}
```

Output   -16 001d 62511 A Test

_cputs

Description

Puts a string to the console.

#include <conio.h>   Required only for function declarations

int _cputs(char *_string_);

string   Output string

Remarks

The **_cputs** function writes the null-terminated string pointed to by _string_ directly to the console. Note that a carriage-return–line-feed (CR-LF) combination is not automatically appended to the string.

Return Value

If successful, **_cputs** returns a 0. If the function fails, it returns a nonzero value.

Compatibility

Standards: None
16-Bit: DOS, QWIN, WIN, WIN DLL
32-Bit: DOS32X

See Also

_putch

Example

```
/* CPUTS.C: This program first displays a string to the console. */

#include <conio.h>

void main( void )
{
    /* String to print at console. Note the \r (return) character. */
    char *buffer = "Hello world (courtesy of _cputs)!\r\n";

    _cputs( buffer );
}
```

Output

```
Hello world (courtesy of _cputs)!
```

_creat

Description

Creates a new file.

#include <sys\types.h>
#include <sys\stat.h>
#include <errno.h>
#include <io.h>   Required only for function declarations

int _creat(char *filename, int pmode);

filename   Path name of new file

pmode   Permission setting

Remarks

The **_creat** function either creates a new file or opens and truncates an existing file. If the file specified by *filename* does not exist, a new file is created with the given permission setting and is opened for writing. If the file already exists and its permission setting allows writing, **_creat** truncates the file to length 0, destroying the previous contents, and opens it for writing.

The permission setting, *pmode*, applies to newly created files only. The new file receives the specified permission setting after it is closed for the first time. The integer expression *pmode* contains one or both of the manifest constants **_S_IWRITE** and **_S_IREAD**, defined in SYS\STAT.H. When both of the constants are given, they are joined with the bitwise-OR operator (|). The *pmode* argument is set to one of the following values:

Value	Meaning
_S_IWRITE	Writing permitted
_S_IREAD	Reading permitted
**_S_IREAD	_S_IWRITE**	Reading and writing permitted

If write permission is not given, the file is read-only. Note that all files are always readable; it is not possible to give write-only permission. Thus, the modes **_S_IWRITE** and **_S_IREAD | _S_IWRITE** are equivalent. With DOS versions 3.0 and later, files opened using **_creat** are always opened in compatibility mode (see **_sopen**). With DOS32X, the files are always opened with **_SH_DENYNO**.

The **_creat** function applies the current file-permission mask to *pmode* before setting the permissions (see **_umask**).

Note that the **_creat** routine is provided primarily for compatibility with previous libraries. A call to **_open** with **_O_CREAT** and **_O_TRUNC** in the *oflag* argument is equivalent to **_creat** and is preferable for new code.

Return Value

If successful, **_creat** returns a handle for the created file. Otherwise, it returns –1 and sets **errno** to one of the following constants:

Value	Meaning
EACCES	Path name specifies an existing read-only file or specifies a directory instead of a file
EMFILE	No more handles available (too many open files)
ENOENT	Path name not found

Compatibility

Standards:	UNIX
16-Bit:	DOS, QWIN, WIN, WIN DLL
32-Bit:	DOS32X

Use **_creat** for compatibility with ANSI naming conventions of non-ANSI functions. Use **creat** and link with OLDNAMES.LIB for UNIX compatibility.

See Also

_chmod, _chsize, _close, _dup, _dup2, _open, _sopen, _umask

Example

```
/* CREAT.C: This program uses _creat to create the file (or truncate the
 * existing file) named data and open it for writing.
 */

#include <sys\types.h>
#include <sys\stat.h>
#include <io.h>
#include <stdio.h>
#include <stdlib.h>
```

```
void main( void )
{
   int fh;

   fh = _creat( "data", _S_IREAD | _S_IWRITE );
   if( fh == -1 )
      perror( "Couldn't create data file" );
   else
   {
      printf( "Created data file.\n" );
      _close( fh );
   }
}
```

Output   Created data file.

_cscanf

Description

Reads formatted data from the console.

#include <conio.h>   Required only for function declarations

int _cscanf(char *_format_ [[, _argument_]] ...);

format   Format-control string
argument   Optional arguments

Remarks

The **_cscanf** function reads data directly from the console into the locations given by _argument_. The **_getche** function is used to read characters. Each optional argument must be a pointer to a variable with a type that corresponds to a type specifier in _format_. The format controls the interpretation of the input fields and has the same form and function as the _format_ argument for the **scanf** function; see **scanf** for a description of _format_.

While **_cscanf** normally echoes the input character, it will not do so if the last call was to **_ungetch**.

Return Value

The **_cscanf** function returns the number of fields that were successfully converted and assigned. The return value does not include fields that were read but not assigned.

The return value is **EOF** for an attempt to read at end-of-file. This may occur when keyboard input is redirected at the operating system command-line level. A return value of 0 means that no fields were assigned.

Compatibility

Standards: None
16-Bit: DOS, QWIN, WIN, WIN DLL
32-Bit: DOS32X

See Also

_cprintf, fscanf, scanf, sscanf

Example   /* CSCANF.C: This program prompts for a string and uses _cscanf to read
               * in the response. Then _cscanf returns the number of items matched,
               * and the program displays that number.
               */

```c
#include <stdio.h>
#include <conio.h>

void main( void )
{
    int    result, i[3];

    _cprintf( "Enter three integers: " );
    result = _cscanf( "%i %i %i", &i[0], &i[1], &i[2] );
    _cprintf( "\r\nYou entered " );
    while( result-- )
        _cprintf( "%i ", i[result] );
    _cprintf( "\r\n" );
}
```

Output   Enter three integers: 34 43 987k
              You entered 987 43 34

ctime

Description

Converts a time stored as a **time_t** value to a character string.

#include <time.h>   Required only for function declarations

char *ctime(const time_t *timer **);**

timer   Pointer to stored time

Remarks

The **ctime** function converts a time stored as a **time_t** value to a character string. The *timer* value is usually obtained from a call to **time**, which returns the number of seconds elapsed since midnight (00:00:00), December 31, 1899, Universal Coordinated Time.

The string result produced by **ctime** contains exactly 26 characters and has the form of the following example:

```
Wed Jan 02 02:03:55 1980\n\0
```

A 24-hour clock is used. All fields have a constant width. The newline character (**\n**) and the null character (**'\0'**) occupy the last two positions of the string.

Calls to the **ctime** function modify the single statically allocated buffer used by the **gmtime** and the **localtime** functions. Each call to one of these routines destroys the result of the previous call. The **ctime** function also shares a static buffer with the **asctime** function. Thus, a call to **ctime** destroys the results of any previous call to **asctime**, **localtime**, or **gmtime**.

Return Value

The **ctime** function returns a pointer to the character string result. If *time* represents a date before midnight, December 31, 1899, Universal Coordinated Time, **ctime** returns **NULL**.

Compatibility

Standards: ANSI, UNIX
16-Bit: DOS, QWIN, WIN, WIN DLL
32-Bit: DOS32X

See Also

asctime, _ftime, gmtime, localtime, time

Example   /* CTIME.C: This program gets the current time in time_t form, then uses
                 * ctime to display the time in string form.
                 */

                #include <time.h>
                #include <stdio.h>

                void main(void)
                {
                    time_t ltime;

                    time(&ltime);
                    printf("The time is %s\n", ctime(&ltime));
                }

Output   The time is Tue Jun 15 16:08:18 1999

_dieeetomsbin, _dmsbintoieee

Description

Convert between IEEE double value and Microsoft (MS) binary double value.

#include <math.h>

int _dieeetomsbin(double *_src8_, double *_dst8_);

int _dmsbintoieee(double *_src8_, double *_dst8_);

src8	Buffer containing value to convert
dst8	Buffer to store converted value

Remarks

The **_dieeetomsbin** routine converts a double-precision number in IEEE (Institute of Electrical and Electronic Engineers) format to Microsoft (MS) binary format. The routine **_dmsbintoieee** converts a double-precision number in MS binary format to IEEE format.

These routines allow C programs (which store floating-point numbers in the IEEE format) to use numeric data in random-access data files created with those versions of Microsoft Basic that store floating-point numbers in MS binary format, and vice versa.

The argument _src8_ is a pointer to the **double** value to be converted. The result is stored at the location given by _dst8_.

These routines do not handle IEEE NANs ("not a number") and infinities. IEEE denormals are treated as 0 in the conversions.

Return Value

These functions return 0 if the conversion is successful and 1 if the conversion causes an overflow.

Compatibility

Standards:	None
16-Bit:	DOS, QWIN, WIN, WIN DLL
32-Bit:	None

See Also

_fieeetomsbin, _fmsbintoieee

difftime

Description   Finds the difference between two times.

#include <time.h>   Required only for function declarations

double difftime(time_t *timer1***, time_t** *timer0* **);**

timer0   Beginning time

timer1   Ending time

Remarks   The **difftime** function computes the difference between the supplied time values,
timer0 and *timer1*.

Return Value   The **difftime** function returns, in seconds, the elapsed time from *timer0* to *timer1*.
The value returned is a double-precision number.

Compatibility   Standards: ANSI, UNIX

16-Bit: DOS, QWIN, WIN, WIN DLL

32-Bit: DOS32X

See Also   **time**

Example   ```
/* DIFFTIME.C: This program calculates the amount of time needed to
 * do a floating-point multiply 50000 times.
 */

#include <stdio.h>
#include <stdlib.h>
#include <time.h>
```
```

```
void main( void )
{
    time_t   start, finish;
    unsigned loop;
    double   result, elapsed_time;

    printf( "This program will do a floating point multiply 50000 times\n" );
    printf( "Working...\n" );

    time( &start );
    for( loop = 0; loop < 50000L; loop++ )
        result = 3.63 * 5.27;
    time( &finish );

    elapsed_time = difftime( finish, start );
    printf( "\nProgram takes %6.2f seconds.\n", elapsed_time );
}
```

Output

```
This program will do a floating point multiply 50000 times
Working...

Program takes   4.00 seconds.
```

_disable

Description

Disables interrupts.

#include <dos.h>

void _disable(void);

Remarks

The **_disable** routine disables interrupts by executing an 8086 **CLI** machine instruction. Use **_disable** before modifying an interrupt vector.

Return Value

None.

Compatibility

Standards: None
16-Bit: DOS, QWIN, WIN, WIN DLL
32-Bit: None

See Also

_enable

_displaycursor

Description   Sets the cursor toggle for graphics functions.

#include <graph.h>

short __far _displaycursor(short *flag* **);**

flag   Cursor state

Remarks   Upon entry into each graphic routine, the screen cursor is turned off. The
_displaycursor function determines whether the cursor will be turned back on
when programs exit graphic routines. If *flag* is set to **_GCURSORON**, the
cursor will be restored on exit. If *flag* is set to **_GCURSOROFF**, the cursor
will be left off.

Return Value   The function returns the previous value of *flag*. There is no error return.

Compatibility   Standards: None
16-Bit: DOS, QWIN, WIN, WIN DLL
32-Bit: None

See Also   **_gettextcursor, _settextcursor**

Example
```
/* DISCURS.C: This program changes the cursor shape using _gettextcursor
 * and _settextcursor, and hides the cursor using _displaycursor.
 */

#include <conio.h>
#include <graph.h>
```

```
void main( void )
{
    short oldcursor;
    short newcursor = 0x007;            /* Full block cursor */

    /* Save old cursor shape and make sure cursor is on */
    oldcursor = _gettextcursor();
    _clearscreen( _GCLEARSCREEN );
    _displaycursor( _GCURSORON );
    _outtext( "\nOld cursor shape: " );
    _getch();

    /* Change cursor shape */
    _outtext( "\nNew cursor shape: " );
    _settextcursor( newcursor );
    _getch();

    /* Restore original cursor shape */
    _outtext( "\n" );
    _settextcursor( oldcursor );
}
```

div

Description

Computes the quotient and the remainder of two integer values.

#include <stdlib.h>

div_t div(int *numer*, **int** *denom* **);**

numer	Numerator
denom	Denominator

Remarks

The **div** function divides *numer* by *denom*, computing the quotient and the remainder. The **div_t** structure contains the following elements:

Element	Description
int quot	Quotient
int rem	Remainder

The sign of the quotient is the same as that of the mathematical quotient. Its absolute value is the largest integer that is less than the absolute value of the mathematical quotient. If the denominator is 0, the program will terminate with an error message.

Return Value

The **div** function returns a structure of type **div_t**, comprising both the quotient and the remainder. The structure is defined in STDLIB.H.

Compatibility

Standards:	ANSI
16-Bit:	DOS, QWIN, WIN, WIN DLL
32-Bit:	DOS32X

See Also

ldiv

Example

```
/* DIV.C: This example takes two integers as command-line arguments and
 * displays the results of the integer division. This program accepts
 * two arguments on the command line following the program name, then
 * calls div to divide the first argument by the second. Finally,
 * it prints the structure members quot and rem.
 */

#include <stdlib.h>
#include <stdio.h>
#include <math.h>

void main( int argc, char *argv[] )
{
    int x,y;
    div_t div_result;

    x = atoi( argv[1] );
    y = atoi( argv[2] );

    printf( "x is %d, y is %d\n", x, y );
    div_result = div( x, y );
    printf( "The quotient is %d, and the remainder is %d\n",
            div_result.quot, div_result.rem );
}
```

Output

```
[C:\LIBREF] div 876 13
x is 876, y is 13
The quotient is 67, and the remainder is 5
```

_dos_allocmem

Description

Allocates a block of memory, using DOS service 0x48.

#include <dos.h>

#include <errno.h>

unsigned _dos_allocmem(unsigned *size*, **unsigned** **seg* **);**

size	Block size to allocate
seg	Return buffer for segment descriptor

Remarks

The **_dos_allocmem** function uses DOS service 0x48 to allocate a block of memory *size* paragraphs long. (A paragraph is 16 bytes.) Allocated blocks are always paragraph aligned. The segment descriptor for the initial segment of the new block is returned in the word that *seg* points to. If the request cannot be satisfied, the maximum possible size (in paragraphs) is returned in this word instead.

Return Value

If successful, the **_dos_allocmem** returns 0. Otherwise, it returns the DOS error code and sets **errno** to **ENOMEM**, indicating insufficient memory or invalid arena (memory area) headers.

Compatibility

Standards: None
16-Bit: DOS
32-Bit: None

See Also

_alloca, **calloc** functions, **_dos_freemem**, **_dos_setblock**, **_halloc**, **malloc** functions

Example

```
/* DALOCMEM.C: This program allocates 20 paragraphs of memory, increases
 * the allocation to 40 paragraphs, and then frees the memory space.
 */

#include <dos.h>
#include <stdio.h>

void main( void )
{
    unsigned segment;
    unsigned maxsize;

    /* Allocate 20 paragraphs */
    if( _dos_allocmem( 20, &segment ) != 0 )
       printf( "allocation failed\n" );
    else
       printf( "allocation successful\n" );

    /* Increase allocation to 40 paragraphs */
    if( _dos_setblock( 40, segment, &maxsize ) != 0 )
       printf( "allocation increase failed\n" );
    else
       printf( "allocation increase successful\n" );

    /* free memory */
    if( _dos_freemem( segment ) != 0 )
       printf( "free memory failed\n" );
    else
       printf( "free memory successful\n" );
}
```

Output

```
allocation successful
allocation increase successful
free memory successful
```

_dos_close

Description

Closes a file using system call 0x3E.

#include <dos.h>
#include <errno.h>

unsigned _dos_close(int *handle* **);**

handle   Target file handle

Remarks

The **_dos_close** function uses system call 0x3E to close the file indicated by *handle*. The file's *handle* argument is returned by the call that created or last opened the file.

Return Value

The function returns 0 if successful. Otherwise, it returns the DOS error code and sets **errno** to **EBADF**, indicating an invalid file handle.

Do not use the DOS interface I/O routines with the console, low-level, or stream I/O routines.

Compatibility

Standards: None
16-Bit: DOS, QWIN, WIN, WIN DLL
32-Bit: None

See Also

_close, _creat, _dos_creat functions, **_dos_open, _dos_read, _dos_write, _dup, _open**

Example

```
/* DOPEN.C: This program uses DOS I/O functions to open and close a file. */

#include <fcntl.h>
#include <stdio.h>
#include <dos.h>
```

```
void main( void )
{
    int fh;

    /* Open file with _dos_open function */
    if( _dos_open( "data1", _O_RDONLY, &fh ) != 0 )
        perror( "Open failed on input file\n" );
    else
        printf( "Open succeeded on input file\n" );

    /* Close file with _dos_close function */
    if( _dos_close( fh ) != 0 )
        perror( "Close failed\n" );
    else
        printf( "File successfully closed\n" );
}
```

Output   Open succeeded on input file
File successfully closed

_dos_commit

Description

Flushes a file to disk using system call 0x68.

#include <dos.h>

#include <errno.h>

unsigned _dos_commit(int *handle* **);**

handle   Target file handle

Remarks

The **_dos_commit** function uses system call 0x68 to flush to disk the DOS buffers associated with the file indicated by *handle*. It also forces an update on the corresponding disk directory and the file allocation table. System call 0x68 ensures that the specified file is flushed directly to disk and not flushed at the operating system's discretion.

The system call used to implement **_dos_commit** is only available in DOS versions 3.3 and later. Using **_dos_commit** in earlier versions of DOS results in undefined behavior.

Do not use the DOS interface I/O routines with the console, low-level, or stream I/O routines.

Return Value

The function returns 0 if successful. Otherwise, it returns the DOS error code and sets **errno** to **EBADF**, indicating an invalid file handle.

Compatibility

Standards: None

16-Bit: DOS, QWIN, WIN, WIN DLL

32-Bit: None

See Also

_close, _creat, _dos_creat functions, **_dos_open, _dos_read, _dos_write, _dup, _open**

Example

```
/* DCOMMIT.C illustrates DOS file I/O functions including:
 *      _dos_commit      _dos_creatnew    _dos_write
 *      _dos_creat       _dos_close
 */
```

```c
#include <dos.h>
#include <errno.h>
#include <conio.h>

void main( void )
{
    char saveit[] = "Straight to disk. ",
        prompt[] = "File exists, overwrite? [y|n] ",
        err[] = "Error occured. ",
        newline[] = "\n\r";
    int hfile, ch;
    unsigned count;

    /* Open file and create, overwriting if necessary. */
    if( _dos_creatnew( "COMMIT.LOG", _A_NORMAL, &hfile ) != 0 )
    {
        if( errno == EEXIST )
        {
            /* Use _dos_write to display prompts. Use bdos to call
             * function 1 to get and echo keystroke.
             */
            _dos_write( 1, prompt, sizeof( prompt ) - 1, &count );
            ch = bdos( 1, 0, 0 ) & 0x00ff;
            if( (ch == 'y') || (ch == 'Y') )
                _dos_creat( "COMMIT.LOG", _A_NORMAL, &hfile );
            _dos_write( 1, newline, sizeof( newline ) - 1, &count );
        }
    }

    /* Write to file; output passes through operating system's buffers. */
    if( _dos_write( hfile, saveit, sizeof( saveit ), &count ) != 0 )
    {
        _dos_write( 1, err, sizeof( err ) - 1, &count );
        _dos_write( 1, newline, sizeof( newline ) - 1, &count );
    }

    /* Write directly to file with no intermediate buffering */
    if( _dos_commit( hfile ) != 0 )
    {
        _dos_write( 1, err, sizeof( err ) - 1, &count );
        _dos_write( 1, newline, sizeof( newline ) - 1, &count );
    }

    /* Close file. */
    if( _dos_close( hfile ) != 0 )
    {
        _dos_write( 1, err, sizeof( err ) - 1, &count );
        _dos_write( 1, newline, sizeof( newline ) - 1, &count );
    }
}
```

_dos_creat Functions

Description

Create a new file.

#include <dos.h>

#include <errno.h>

unsigned _dos_creat(char *filename, unsigned attrib, int *handle);

unsigned _dos_creatnew(char *filename, unsigned attrib, int *handle);

filename	File path name
attrib	File attributes
handle	Handle return buffer

Remarks

The **_dos_creat** and **_dos_creatnew** routines create and open a new file named filename; this new file has the access attributes specified in the attrib argument. The new file's handle is copied into the integer location pointed to by handle. The file is opened for both read and write access. If file sharing is installed, the file is opened in compatibility mode.

The **_dos_creat** routine uses system call 0x3C, and the **_dos_creatnew** routine uses system call 0x5B. If the file already exists, **_dos_creat** erases its contents and leaves its attributes unchanged; however, the **_dos_creatnew** routine fails if the file already exists.

Return Value

If successful, both routines return 0. Otherwise, they return the DOS error code and set **errno** to one of the following values:

Constant	Meaning
EACCES	Access denied because the directory is full or, for **_dos_creat** only, the file exists and cannot be overwritten
EEXIST	File already exists (**_dos_creatnew** only)
EMFILE	Too many open file handles
ENOENT	Path or file not found

Compatibility   Standards: None

16-Bit: DOS, QWIN, WIN, WIN DLL

32-Bit: None

Example

```
/* DCREAT.C: This program creates a file using the _dos_creat function. The
 * program cannot create a new file using the _dos_creatnew function
 * because it already exists.
 */

#include <stdio.h>
#include <stdlib.h>
#include <dos.h>

void main( void )
{
    int fh1, fh2;
    int result;

    if( _dos_creat( "data", _A_NORMAL, &fh1 ) != 0 )
       printf( "Couldn't create data file\n" );
    else
    {
       printf( "Created data file.\n" );

       /* If _dos_creat is successful, the _dos_creatnew call
        * will fail since the file exists
        */
       if( _dos_creatnew( "data", _A_RDONLY, &fh2 ) != 0 )
          printf( "Couldn't create data file\n" );
       else
       {
          printf( "Created data file.\n" );
          _dos_close( fh2 );
       }
       _dos_close( fh1 );
    }
}
```

Output

```
Created data file.
Couldn't create data file
```

_dos_find Functions

Description   Find the file with the specified attributes or find the next file with the specified attributes.

#include <dos.h>

#include <errno.h>

unsigned _dos_findfirst(char *filename*, **unsigned** *attrib*,
    struct _find_t **fileinfo* **);**

unsigned _dos_findnext(struct _find_t **fileinfo* **);**

filename	Target filename
attrib	Target attributes
fileinfo	File-information buffer

Remarks   The **_dos_findfirst** routine uses system call 0x4E to return information about the first instance of a file whose name and attributes match *filename* and *attrib*.

The *filename* argument may use wildcards (* and ?). The *attrib* argument can be any of the following manifest constants:

Constant	Meaning
_A_ARCH	Archive. Set whenever the file is changed, and cleared by the DOS BACKUP command.
_A_HIDDEN	Hidden file. Cannot be found with the DOS DIR command. Returns information about normal files as well as about files with this attribute.
_A_NORMAL	Normal. File can be read or written without restriction.
_A_RDONLY	Read-only. File cannot be opened for writing, and a file with the same name cannot be created. Returns information about normal files as well as about files with this attribute.
_A_SUBDIR	Subdirectory. Returns information about normal files as well as about files with this attribute.

Constant	Meaning
_A_SYSTEM	System file. Cannot be found with the DOS DIR command. Returns information about normal files as well as about files with this attribute.
_A_VOLID	Volume ID. Only one file can have this attribute, and it must be in the root directory.

Multiple constants can be combined (with the OR operator), using the vertical-bar (|) character.

If the *attrib* argument to either of these functions is **_A_RDONLY, _A_HIDDEN, _A_SYSTEM**, or **_A_SUBDIR**, the function also returns any normal attribute files that match the *filename* argument. That is, a normal file does not have a read-only, hidden, system, or directory attribute.

Information is returned in a **_find_t** structure, defined in DOS.H. The **_find_t** structure contains the following elements:

Element	Description
char reserved[21]	Reserved for use by DOS
char attrib	Attribute byte for matched path
unsigned wr_time	Time of last write to file
unsigned wr_date	Date of last write to file
long size	Length of file in bytes
char name[13]	Null-terminated name of matched file/directory, without the path

The formats for the **wr_time** and **wr_date** elements are in DOS format and are not usable by any other C run-time function. The time format is shown below:

Bits	Contents
0–4	Number of 2-second increments (0–29)
5–10	Minutes (0–59)
11–15	Hours (0–23)

The date format is shown below:

Bits	Contents
0–4	Day of month (1–31)
5–8	Month (1–12)
9–15	Year (relative to 1980)

Do not alter the contents of the buffer between a call to **_dos_findfirst** and a subsequent call to the **_dos_findnext** function. Also, the buffer should not be altered between calls to **_dos_findnext**.

The **_dos_findnext** routine uses system call 0x4F to find the next name, if any, that matches the *filename* and *attrib* arguments specified in a prior call to **_dos_findfirst**. The *fileinfo* argument must point to a structure initialized by a previous call to **_dos_findfirst**. The contents of the structure will be altered as described above if a match is found.

Return Value

If successful, both functions return 0. Otherwise, they return the DOS error code and set **errno** to **ENOENT**, indicating that *filename* could not be matched.

Compatibility

Standards: None

16-Bit: DOS, QWIN, WIN, WIN DLL

32-Bit: None

Example

```
/* DFIND.C: This program finds and prints all files in the current directory
 * with the .c extension.
 */

#include <stdio.h>
#include <dos.h>

void main( void )
{
    struct _find_t  c_file;

    /* find first .c file in current directory */
    _dos_findfirst( "*.c", _A_NORMAL, &c_file );

    printf( "Listing of .c files\n\n" );
    printf( "File: %s is %ld bytes\n", c_file.name, c_file.size );

    /* find the rest of the .c files */
    while( _dos_findnext( &c_file ) == 0 )
        printf( "File: %s is %ld bytes\n", c_file.name, c_file.size );
}
```

Output

```
Listing of .c files

File: CHDIR.C is 524 bytes
File: SIGFP.C is 2674 bytes
File: MAX.C is 258 bytes
File: CGETS.C is 577 bytes
File: FWRITE.C is 1123 bytes
```

_dos_freemem

Description

Releases a block of memory (0x49).

#include <dos.h>

#include <errno.h>

unsigned _dos_freemem(unsigned *seg*);

seg   Block to be released

Remarks

The **_dos_freemem** function uses system call 0x49 to release a block of memory previously allocated by **_dos_allocmem**. The *seg* argument is a value returned by a previous call to **_dos_allocmem**. The freed memory may no longer be used by the application program.

Return Value

If successful, **_dos_freemem** returns 0. Otherwise, it returns the DOS error code and sets **errno** to **ENOMEM**, indicating a bad segment value (one that does not correspond to a segment returned by a previous **_dos_allocmem** call) or invalid arena headers.

Compatibility

Standards: None
16-Bit: DOS
32-Bit: None

See Also

_dos_allocmem, **_dos_setblock**, **free** functions

Example

```
/* DALOCMEM.C: This program allocates 20 paragraphs of memory, increases
 * the allocation to 40 paragraphs, and then frees the memory space.
 */

#include <dos.h>
#include <stdio.h>
```

```
void main( void )
{
    unsigned segment;
    unsigned maxsize;

    /* Allocate 20 paragraphs */
    if( _dos_allocmem( 20, &segment ) != 0 )
        printf( "allocation failed\n" );
    else
        printf( "allocation successful\n" );

    /* Increase allocation to 40 paragraphs */
    if( _dos_setblock( 40, segment, &maxsize ) != 0 )
        printf( "allocation increase failed\n" );
    else
        printf( "allocation increase successful\n" );

    /* Free memory */
    if( _dos_freemem( segment ) != 0 )
        printf( "free memory failed\n" );
    else
        printf( "free memory successful\n" );
}
```

Output   allocation successful
allocation increase successful
free memory successful

_dos_getdate

Description

Gets current system date using system call 0x2A.

#include <dos.h>

void _dos_getdate(struct _dosdate_t *date);

date	Current system date

Remarks

The **_dos_getdate** routine uses system call 0x2A to obtain the current system date. The date is returned in a **_dosdate_t** structure, defined in DOS.H.

The **_dosdate_t** structure contains the following elements:

Element	Description
unsigned char day	1–31
unsigned char month	1–12
unsigned int year	1980–2099
unsigned char dayofweek	0–6 (0 = Sunday)

Return Value

None.

Compatibility

Standards:	None
16-Bit:	DOS, QWIN, WIN, WIN DLL
32-Bit:	None

See Also

_dos_gettime, _dos_setdate, _dos_settime, gmtime, localtime, mktime, _strdate, _strtime, time

Example

```
/* DGTIME.C: This program gets and displays current date and time values. */

#include <stdio.h>
#include <dos.h>

void main( void )
{
    struct _dosdate_t date;
    struct _dostime_t time;

    /* Get current date and time values */

    _dos_getdate( &date );
    _dos_gettime( &time );

    printf( "Today's date is %d-%d-%d\n", date.month, date.day, date.year );
    printf( "The time is %02d:%02d\n", time.hour, time.minute );
}
```

Output

```
Today's date is 12-15-1999
The time is 18:07
```

_dos_getdiskfree

Description

Gets disk information using system call 0x36.

#include <dos.h>

#include <errno.h>

unsigned _dos_getdiskfree(unsigned *drive*, **struct _diskfree_t** *diskspace* **);**

drive	Drive number (default is 0)
diskspace	Buffer to hold disk information

Remarks

The **_dos_getdiskfree** routine uses system call 0x36 to obtain information on the disk drive specified by *drive*. The default drive is 0, drive A is 1, drive B is 2, and so on. Information is returned in the **_diskfree_t** structure (defined in DOS.H) pointed to by *diskspace*.

The **struct _diskfree_t** structure contains the following elements:

Element	Description
unsigned total_clusters	Total clusters on disk
unsigned avail_clusters	Available clusters on disk
unsigned sectors_per_cluster	Sectors per cluster
unsigned bytes_per_sector	Bytes per sector

Return Value

If successful, the function returns 0. Otherwise, it returns a nonzero value and sets **errno** to **EINVAL**, indicating that an invalid drive was specified.

Compatibility

Standards:	None
16-Bit:	DOS, QWIN, WIN, WIN DLL
32-Bit:	None

See Also

_dos_getdrive, _dos_setdrive

Example

```
/* DGDISKFR.C: This program displays information about the default disk drive.
 */

#include <stdio.h>
#include <dos.h>

void main( void )
{
    struct _diskfree_t drive;

    /* Get information on default disk drive 0 */

    _dos_getdiskfree( 0, &drive );
    printf( "total clusters: %d\n", drive.total_clusters );
    printf( "available clusters: %d\n", drive.avail_clusters );
    printf( "sectors per cluster: %d\n", drive.sectors_per_cluster );
    printf( "bytes per sector: %d\n", drive.bytes_per_sector );
}
```

Output

```
total clusters: 9013
available clusters: 6030
sectors per cluster: 4
bytes per sector: 512
```

_dos_getdrive

Description   Gets the current disk drive using system call 0x19.

#include <dos.h>

void _dos_getdrive(unsigned *_drive_);

drive   Current-drive return buffer

Remarks   The **_dos_getdrive** routine uses system call 0x19 to obtain the current disk drive. The current drive is returned in the word that _drive_ points to: 1 = drive A, 2 = drive B, and so on.

Return Value   None.

Compatibility
Standards: None
16-Bit: DOS, QWIN, WIN, WIN DLL
32-Bit: None

See Also   **_dos_getdiskfree, _dos_setdrive, _getdrive**

Example

```
/* DGDRIVE.C: This program prints the letter of the current drive,
 * changes the default drive to A, then returns the number of disk drives.
 */

#include <stdio.h>
#include <dos.h>

void main( void )
{
    unsigned olddrive, newdrive;
    unsigned number_of_drives;

    /* Print current default drive information */
    _dos_getdrive( &olddrive );
    printf( "The current drive is: %c\n", 'A' + olddrive - 1 );
```

```
                    /* Set default drive to be drive A */
                    printf( "Changing default drive to A\n");
                    _dos_setdrive( 1, &number_of_drives );

                    /* Get new default drive information and total number of drives */
                    _dos_getdrive( &newdrive );
                    printf( "The current drive is: %c\n", 'A' + newdrive - 1 );
                    printf( "Number of logical drives: %d\n", number_of_drives );

                    /* Restore default drive */
                    _dos_setdrive( olddrive, &number_of_drives );
                }
```

Output   The current drive is: C
                  Changing default drive to A
                  The current drive is: A
                  Number of logical drives: 26

_dos_getfileattr

Description

Gets the current attributes of a file or directory, using system call 0x43.

#include <dos.h>

#include <errno.h>

unsigned _dos_getfileattr(char *pathname, unsigned *attrib);

pathname	Full path of target file/directory
attrib	Word to store attributes in

Remarks

The **_dos_getfileattr** routine uses system call 0x43 to obtain the current attributes of the file or directory pointed to by *pathname*. The attributes are copied to the low-order byte of the *attrib* word. Attributes are represented by manifest constants, as described below:

Constant	Meaning
_A_ARCH	Archive. Set whenever the file is changed, or cleared by the DOS BACKUP command.
_A_HIDDEN	Hidden file. Cannot be found by a directory search.
_A_NORMAL	Normal. File can be read or written without restriction.
_A_RDONLY	Read-only. File cannot be opened for a write, and a file with the same name cannot be created.
_A_SUBDIR	Subdirectory.
_A_SYSTEM	System file. Cannot be found by a directory search.
_A_VOLID	Volume ID. Only one file can have this attribute, and it must be in the root directory.

Return Value

If successful, the function returns 0. Otherwise, it returns the DOS error code and sets **errno** to **ENOENT**, indicating that the target file or directory could not be found.

Compatibility

Standards:	None
16-Bit:	DOS, QWIN, WIN, WIN DLL
32-Bit:	None

See Also

_access, _chmod, _dos_setfileattr, _umask

Example

```
/* DGFILEAT.C: This program creates a file with the specified attributes,
 * then prints this information before changing the file attributes back
 * to normal.
 */

#include <stdio.h>
#include <dos.h>

void main( void )
{
    unsigned oldattrib, newattrib;
    int fh;

    /* Get and display file attribute */
    _dos_getfileattr( "DGFILEAT.C", &oldattrib );
    printf( "Attribute: 0x%.4x\n", oldattrib );
    if( ( oldattrib & _A_RDONLY ) != 0 )
       printf( "Read only file\n" );
    else
       printf( "Not a read only file.\n" );

    /* Reset file attribute to normal file */
    _dos_setfileattr( "DGFILEAT.C", _A_RDONLY );
    _dos_getfileattr( "DGFILEAT.C", &newattrib );
    printf( "Attribute: 0x%.4x\n", newattrib );

    /* Restore file attribute */
    _dos_setfileattr( "DGFILEAT.C", oldattrib );
    _dos_getfileattr( "DGFILEAT.C", &newattrib );
    printf( "Attribute: 0x%.4x\n", newattrib );
}
```

Output

```
Attribute: 0x0020
Not a read only file.
Attribute: 0x0001
Attribute: 0x0020
```

_dos_getftime

Description

Gets the date and time a file was last written, using system call 0x57.

#include <dos.h>

#include <errno.h>

unsigned _dos_getftime(int *handle*, **unsigned** ***date*, **unsigned** ***time*);

handle	Target file
date	Date-return buffer
time	Time-return buffer

Remarks

The **_dos_getftime** routine uses system call 0x57 to get the date and time that the specified file was last written. The file must have been opened with a call to **_dos_open** or **_dos_creat** prior to calling **_dos_getftime**. The date and time are returned in the words pointed to by *date* and *time*. The values appear in the DOS date and time format:

Time Bits	Meaning
0–4	Number of 2-second increments (0–29)
5–10	Minutes (0–59)
11–15	Hours (0–23)

Date Bits	Meaning
0–4	Day (1–31)
5–8	Month (1–12)
9–15	Year (1980–2099)

Return Value

If successful, the function returns 0. Otherwise, it returns the DOS error code and sets **errno** to **EBADF**, indicating that an invalid file handle was passed.

Compatibility

Standards:	None
16-Bit:	DOS, QWIN, WIN, WIN DLL
32-Bit:	None

See Also

_dos_setftime, _fstat, _stat

Example

```
/* DGFTIME.C: This program displays and modifies the date and time
 * fields of a file.
 */

#include <fcntl.h>
#include <stdio.h>
#include <stdlib.h>
#include <dos.h>

void main( void )
{
                                    /* FEDC BA98 7654 3210           */
    unsigned new_date = 0x26cf;     /* 0010 0110 1100 1111  12/15/99 */
    unsigned new_time = 0x48e0;     /* 0100 1000 1110 0000   9:07 AM */
    unsigned old_date, old_time;

    int fh;

    /* Open file with _dos_open function */
    if( _dos_open( "dgftime.obj", _O_RDONLY, &fh ) != 0 )
       exit( 1 );

    /* Get file date and time */
    _dos_getftime( fh, &old_date, &old_time );
    printf( "Old date field: 0x%.4x\n", old_date );
    printf( "Old time field: 0x%.4x\n", old_time );
    system( "dir dgftime.obj" );

    /* Modify file date and time */
    if( !_dos_setftime( fh, new_date, new_time ) )
    {
       _dos_getftime( fh, &new_date, &new_time );
       printf( "New date field: 0x%.4x\n", new_date );
       printf( "New time field: 0x%.4x\n", new_time );
       system( "dir dgftime.obj" );

       /* Restore date and time */
       _dos_setftime( fh, old_date, old_time );
    }
    _dos_close( fh );
}
```

Output

```
Old date field: 0x274f
Old time field: 0x94bb

Volume in drive C is ZEPPELIN
Directory of  C:\LIBREF

DGFTIME  OBJ     3923    6-15-99    6:37p
         1 File(s)  13676544 bytes free

New date field: 0x26cf
New time field: 0x48e0

Volume in drive C is ZEPPELIN
Directory of  C:\LIBREF

DGFTIME  OBJ     3923   12-15-99    9:07a
         1 File(s)  13676544 bytes free
```

_dos_gettime

Description

Gets the current system time, using system call 0x2C.

#include <dos.h>

void _dos_gettime(struct _dostime_t *time);

| time | Current system time |

Remarks

The _dos_gettime routine uses system call 0x2C to obtain the current system time. The time is returned in a _dostime_t structure, defined in DOS.H.

The dostime_t structure contains the following elements:

Element	Description
unsigned char hour	0–23
unsigned char minute	0–59
unsigned char second	0–59
unsigned char hsecond	1/100 second; 0–99

Return Value

None.

Compatibility

Standards:	None
16-Bit:	DOS, QWIN, WIN, WIN DLL
32-Bit:	None

See Also

_dos_getdate, _dos_setdate, _dos_settime, gmtime, localtime, _strtime

Example   ```
/* DGTIME.C: This program gets and displays current date and time values. */

#include <stdio.h>
#include <dos.h>

void main(void)
{
    struct _dosdate_t date;
    struct _dostime_t time;

    /* Get current date and time values */

    _dos_getdate(&date);
    _dos_gettime(&time);

    printf("Today's date is %d-%d-%d\n", date.month, date.day, date.year);
    printf("The time is %02d:%02d\n", time.hour, time.minute);
}
```

**Output**   ```
Today's date is 12-15-1999
The time is 18:07
```

_dos_getvect

Description

Gets the current value of the interrupt vector, using system call 0x35.

#include <dos.h>

void (__cdecl __interrupt __far *_dos_getvect(unsigned *intnum*))( );

intnum   Target interrupt vector

Remarks

The **_dos_getvect** routine uses system call 0x35 to get the current value of the interrupt vector specified by *intnum*.

This routine is typically used in conjunction with the **_dos_setvect** function. To replace an interrupt vector, first save the current vector of the interrupt using **_dos_getvect**. Then set the vector to your own interrupt routine with **_dos_setvect**. The saved vector can later be restored, if necessary, using **_dos_setvect**. The user-defined routine may also need the original vector in order to call that vector or chain to it with **_chain_intr**.

Return Value

The function returns a far pointer for the *intnum* interrupt to the current handler, if there is one.

Compatibility

Standards: None
16-Bit: DOS, QWIN, WIN, WIN DLL
32-Bit: None

See Also

_chain_intr, **_dos_keep**, **_dos_setvect**

_dos_keep

Description

Installs TSR (terminate-and-stay-resident) programs in memory, using system call 0x31.

#include <dos.h>

void _dos_keep(unsigned *retcode*, **unsigned** *memsize* **);**

retcode	Exit status code
memsize	Allocated resident memory (in 16-byte paragraphs)

Remarks

The **_dos_keep** routine installs TSRs (terminate-and-stay-resident programs) in memory, using system call 0x31.

The routine first exits the calling process, leaving it in memory. It then returns the low-order byte of *retcode* to the parent of the calling process. Before returning execution to the parent process, **_dos_keep** sets the allocated memory for the now-resident process to *memsize* 16-byte paragraphs. Any excess memory is returned to the system.

The **_dos_keep** function calls the same internal routines called by **exit**. It therefore takes the following actions:

- Calls any functions that have been registered by **atexit** or **_onexit** calls.
- Flushes all file buffers.
- Restores interrupt vectors replaced by the C startup code. The primary one is interrupt 0 (divide by zero). If the emulator math library is used and there is no coprocessor, interrupts 0x34 through 0x3D are restored. If there is a coprocessor, interrupt 2 is restored.

Do not use the emulator math library in TSRs unless you are familiar with the startup code and the coprocessor. Use the alternate math package if the TSR must do floating-point math.

Do not run programs that use **_dos_keep** from inside the Microsoft Programmer's WorkBench environment, since doing so causes subsequent memory problems. The **_dos_keep** function terminates the program when executed in the Programmer's WorkBench environment.

Return Value	None.
Compatibility	Standards: None
	16-Bit: DOS
	32-Bit: None
See Also	_cexit, _chain_intr, _dos_getvect, _dos_setvect, _exit

_dos_open

Description

Opens a file, using system call 0x3D.

#include <dos.h>
#include <errno.h>
#include <fcntl.h>   Access mode constants
#include <share.h>   Sharing mode constants

unsigned _dos_open(char *_filename_, unsigned _mode_, int *_handle_);

filename	Path to an existing file
mode	Permissions
handle	Pointer to integer

Remarks

The **_dos_open** routine uses system call 0x3D to open the existing file pointed to by _filename_. The handle for the opened file is copied into the integer pointed to by _handle_. The _mode_ argument specifies the file's access, sharing, and inheritance modes by combining (with the OR operator) manifest constants from the three groups shown below. At most, one access mode and one sharing mode can be specified at a time.

Constant	Mode	Meaning
_O_RDONLY	Access	Read-only
_O_WRONLY	Access	Write-only
_O_RDWR	Access	Both read and write
_SH_COMPAT	Sharing	Compatibility
_SH_DENYRW	Sharing	Deny reading and writing
_SH_DENYWR	Sharing	Deny writing
_SH_DENYRD	Sharing	Deny reading
_SH_DENYNO	Sharing	Deny neither
_O_NOINHERIT	Inheritance by the child process	File is not inherited

Do not use the DOS interface I/O routines in conjunction with the console, low-level, or stream I/O routines.

Return Value

If successful, the function returns 0. Otherwise, it returns the DOS error code and sets **errno** to one of the following manifest constants:

Constant	Meaning
EACCES	Access denied (possible reasons include specifying a directory or volume ID for *filename*, or opening a read-only file for write access)
EINVAL	Sharing mode specified when file sharing not installed, or access-mode value is invalid
EMFILE	Too many open file handles
ENOENT	Path or file not found

Compatibility

Standards: None

16-Bit: DOS, QWIN, WIN, WIN DLL

32-Bit: None

See Also

_dos_close, _dos_read, _dos_write

Example

```
/* DOPEN.C: This program uses DOS I/O functions to open and close a file. */

#include <fcntl.h>
#include <stdio.h>
#include <dos.h>

void main( void )
{
   int fh;

   /* Open file with _dos_open function */
   if( _dos_open( "data1", _O_RDONLY, &fh ) != 0 )
      perror( "Open failed on input file\n" );
   else
      printf( "Open succeeded on input file\n" );

   /* Close file with _dos_close function */
   if( _dos_close( fh ) != 0 )
      perror( "Close failed\n" );
   else
      printf( "File successfully closed\n" );
}
```

Output

```
Open succeeded on input file
File successfully closed
```

_dos_read

Description

Reads data from a file, using system call 0x3F.

#include <dos.h>

unsigned _dos_read(int *handle*, void _ _ far **buffer*, unsigned *count*,
    unsigned **numread*);

handle	File to read
buffer	Buffer to write to
count	Number of bytes to read
numread	Number of bytes actually read

Remarks

The **_dos_read** routine uses system call 0x3F to read *count* bytes of data from the file specified by *handle*. The routine then copies the data to the buffer pointed to by *buffer*. The integer pointed to by *numread* will show the number of bytes actually read, which may be less than the number requested in *count*. If the number of bytes actually read is 0, it means the routine tried to read at end-of-file.

Do not use the DOS interface I/O routines in conjunction with the console, low-level, or stream I/O routines.

Return Value

If successful, the function returns 0. Otherwise, it returns the DOS error code and sets **errno** to one of the following constants:

Constant	Meaning
EACCES	Access denied (*handle* is not open for read access)
EBADF	File handle is invalid

Compatibility

Standards:	None
16-Bit:	DOS, QWIN, WIN, WIN DLL
32-Bit:	None

See Also

_dos_close, _dos_open, _dos_write, _read

Example

```
/* DREAD.C: This program uses the DOS I/O operations to read the contents
 * of a file.
 */

#include <fcntl.h>
#include <stdlib.h>
#include <stdio.h>
#include <dos.h>

void main( void )
{
    int fh;
    char buffer[50];
    unsigned number_read;

    /* Open file with _dos_open function */
    if( _dos_open( "dread.c", _O_RDONLY, &fh ) != 0 )
        perror( "Open failed on input file\n" );
    else
        printf( "Open succeeded on input file\n" );

    /* Read data with _dos_read function */
    _dos_read( fh, buffer, 50, &number_read );
    printf( "First 40 characters are: %.40s\n\n", buffer );

    /* Close file with _dos_close function */
    _dos_close( fh );
}
```

Output

```
Open succeeded on input file
First 40 characters are: /* DREAD.C: This program uses the DOS I/
```

_dos_setblock

Description

Changes the size of a memory segment, using system call 0x4A.

#include <dos.h>

unsigned _dos_setblock(unsigned *size***, unsigned** *seg***, unsigned ***maxsize* **);**

size	New segment size
seg	Target segment
maxsize	Maximum-size buffer

Remarks

The **_dos_setblock** routine uses system call 0x4A to change the size of *seg*, previously allocated by **_dos_allocmem**, to *size* paragraphs. If the request cannot be satisfied, the maximum possible segment size is copied to the buffer pointed to by *maxsize*.

Return Value

The function returns 0 if successful. If the call fails, it returns the DOS error code and sets **errno** to **ENOMEM**, indicating a bad segment value was passed. A bad segment value is one that does not correspond to a segment returned from a previous **_dos_allocmem** call, or one that contains invalid arena headers.

Compatibility

Standards: None
16-Bit: DOS
32-Bit: None

See Also

_dos_allocmem, **_dos_freemem**, **realloc** functions

Example

```
/* DALOCMEM.C: This program allocates 20 paragraphs of memory, increases
 * the allocation to 40 paragraphs, and then frees the memory space.
 */

#include <dos.h>
#include <stdio.h>
```

```
void main( void )
{
   unsigned segment;
   unsigned maxsize;

   /* Allocate 20 paragraphs */
   if( _dos_allocmem( 20, &segment ) != 0 )
      printf( "allocation failed\n" );
   else
      printf( "allocation successful\n" );

   /* Increase allocation to 40 paragraphs */
   if( _dos_setblock( 40, segment, &maxsize ) != 0 )
      printf( "allocation increase failed\n" );
   else
      printf( "allocation increase successful\n" );

   /* Free memory */
   if( _dos_freemem( segment ) != 0 )
      printf( "free memory failed\n" );
   else
      printf( "free memory successful\n" );
}
```

Output
```
allocation successful
allocation increase successful
free memory successful
```

_dos_setdate

Description

Sets the current system date, using system call 0x2B.

#include <dos.h>

unsigned _dos_setdate(struct _dosdate_t *date);

date   New system date

Remarks

The **_dos_setdate** routine uses system call 0x2B to set the current system date. The date is stored in the **_dosdate_t** structure pointed to by *date*, defined in DOS.H. The **_dosdate_t** structure contains the following elements:

Element	Description
unsigned char day	1–31
unsigned char month	1–12
unsigned int year	1980–2099
unsigned char dayofweek	0–6 (0 = Sunday)

Return Value

If successful, the function returns 0. Otherwise, it returns a nonzero value and sets **errno** to **EINVAL**, indicating an invalid date was specified.

Compatibility

Standards: None
16-Bit: DOS, QWIN, WIN, WIN DLL
32-Bit: None

See Also

_dos_getdate, _dos_gettime, _dos_settime, gmtime, localtime, mktime, _strdate, _strtime, time

Example   /* DSTIME.C: This program changes the time and date values and displays the
              * new date and time values.
              */

```
#include <dos.h>
#include <conio.h>
#include <stdio.h>
#include <time.h>

void main( void )
{
    struct _dosdate_t olddate, newdate = { { 4 }, { 7 }, { 1999 } };
    struct _dostime_t oldtime, newtime = { { 3 }, { 45 }, { 30 }, { 0 } };
    char    datebuf[40], timebuf[40];

    /* Get current date and time values */
    _dos_getdate( &olddate );
    _dos_gettime( &oldtime );
    printf( "%s    %s\n" , _strdate( datebuf ), _strtime( timebuf ) );

    /* Modify date and time structures */
    _dos_setdate( &newdate );
    _dos_settime( &newtime );
    printf( "%s    %s\n" , _strdate( datebuf ), _strtime( timebuf ) );

    /* Restore old date and time */
    _dos_setdate( &olddate );
    _dos_settime( &oldtime );
}
```

Output   12/15/99   18:26:09
              07/04/99   03:45:30

_dos_setdrive

Description

Sets the default drive, using system call 0x0E.

#include <dos.h>

void _dos_setdrive(unsigned *drive***, unsigned** **numdrives* **);**

drive	New default drive
numdrives	Total drives available

Remarks

The **_dos_setdrive** routine uses system call 0x0E to set the current default drive to the *drive* argument: 1 = drive A, 2 = drive B, and so on. The *numdrives* argument indicates the total number of drives in the system. If this value is 4, for example, it does not mean the drives are designated A, B, C, and D; it means only that four drives are in the system.

Return Value

There is no return value. If an invalid drive number is passed, the function fails without indication. Use the **_dos_getdrive** routine to verify whether the desired drive has been set.

Compatibility

Standards: None
16-Bit: DOS, QWIN, WIN, WIN DLL
32-Bit: None

See Also

_dos_getdiskfree, _dos_getdrive

Example

```
/* DGDRIVE.C: This program prints the letter of the current drive,
 * changes the default drive to A, then returns the number of disk drives.
 */

#include <stdio.h>
#include <dos.h>
```

```
void main( void )
{
    unsigned olddrive, newdrive;
    unsigned number_of_drives;

    /* Print current default drive information */
    _dos_getdrive( &olddrive );
    printf( "The current drive is: %c\n", 'A' + olddrive - 1 );

    /* Set default drive to be drive A */
    printf( "Changing default drive to A\n");
    _dos_setdrive( 1, &number_of_drives );

    /* Get new default drive information and total number of drives */
    _dos_getdrive( &newdrive );
    printf( "The current drive is: %c\n", 'A' + newdrive - 1 );
    printf( "Number of logical drives: %d\n", number_of_drives );

    /* Restore default drive */
    _dos_setdrive( olddrive, &number_of_drives );
}
```

Output

```
The current drive is: C
Changing default drive to A
The current drive is: A
Number of logical drives: 26
```

_dos_setfileattr

Description

Sets the attributes of the file or directory, using system call 0x43.

#include <dos.h>

unsigned _dos_setfileattr(char *_pathname_, unsigned _attrib_);

pathname	Full path of target file/directory
attrib	New attributes

Remarks

The **_dos_setfileattr** routine uses system call 0x43 to set the attributes of the file or directory pointed to by _pathname_. The actual attributes are contained in the low-order byte of the _attrib_ word. Attributes are represented by manifest constants, as described below:

Constant	Meaning
_A_ARCH	Archive. Set whenever the file is changed, or cleared by the DOS BACKUP command.
_A_HIDDEN	Hidden file. Cannot be found by a directory search.
_A_NORMAL	Normal. File can be read or written to without restriction.
_A_RDONLY	Read-only. File cannot be opened for writing, and a file with the same name cannot be created.
_A_SUBDIR	Subdirectory.
_A_SYSTEM	System file. Cannot be found by a directory search.
_A_VOLID	Volume ID. Only one file can have this attribute, and it must be in the root directory.

Return Value

The function returns 0 if successful. Otherwise, it returns the DOS error code and sets **errno** to one of the following:

Constant	Meaning
EACCES	Access denied; cannot change the volume ID or the subdirectory.
ENOENT	No file or directory matching the target was found.

Compatibility   Standards: None

16-Bit: DOS, QWIN, WIN, WIN DLL

32-Bit: None

See Also   **_dos_getfileattr**

Example
```
/* DGFILEAT.C: This program creates a file with the specified attributes,
 * then prints this information before changing the file attributes back
 * to normal.
 */

#include <stdio.h>
#include <dos.h>

void main( void )
{
    unsigned oldattrib, newattrib;
    int fh;

    /* Get and display file attribute */
    _dos_getfileattr( "DGFILEAT.C", &oldattrib );
    printf( "Attribute: 0x%.4x\n", oldattrib );
    if( ( oldattrib & _A_RDONLY ) != 0 )
       printf( "Read only file\n" );
    else
       printf( "Not a read only file.\n" );

    /* Reset file attribute to normal file */
    _dos_setfileattr( "DGFILEAT.C", _A_RDONLY );
    _dos_getfileattr( "DGFILEAT.C", &newattrib );
    printf( "Attribute: 0x%.4x\n", newattrib );

    /* Restore file attribute */
    _dos_setfileattr( "DGFILEAT.C", oldattrib );
    _dos_getfileattr( "DGFILEAT.C", &newattrib );
    printf( "Attribute: 0x%.4x\n", newattrib );
}
```

Output
```
Attribute: 0x0020
Not a read only file.
Attribute: 0x0001
Attribute: 0x0020
```

_dos_setftime

Description

Sets the date and time for a file, using system call 0x57.

#include <dos.h>

unsigned _dos_setftime(int *handle*, unsigned *date*, unsigned *time*);

handle	Target file
date	Date of last write
time	Time of last write

Remarks

The **_dos_setftime** routine uses system call 0x57 to set the *date* and *time* at which the file identified by *handle* was last written to. These values appear in the DOS date and time format, described in the following lists:

Time Bits	Meaning
0–4	Number of two-second increments (0–29)
5–10	Minutes (0–59)
11–15	Hours (0–23)

Date Bits	Meaning
0–4	Day (1–31)
5–8	Month (1–12)
9–15	Year since 1980 (for example, 1999 is stored as 9)

Return Value

If successful, the function returns 0. Otherwise, it returns the DOS error code and sets **errno** to **EBADF**, indicating that an invalid file handle was passed.

Compatibility

Standards:	None
16-Bit:	DOS, QWIN, WIN, WIN DLL
32-Bit:	None

See Also   **_dos_getftime**, **_fstat**, **_stat**

Example

```c
/* DGFTIME.C: This program displays and modifies the date and time
 * fields of a file.
 */

#include <fcntl.h>
#include <stdio.h>
#include <stdlib.h>
#include <dos.h>

void main( void )
{
                                    /* FEDC BA98 7654 3210           */
    unsigned new_date = 0x26cf;     /* 0010 0110 1100 1111  12/15/99 */
    unsigned new_time = 0x48e0;     /* 0100 1000 1110 0000   9:07 AM */
    unsigned old_date, old_time;

    int fh;

    /* Open file with _dos_open function */
    if( _dos_open( "dgftime.obj", _O_RDONLY, &fh ) != 0 )
        exit( 1 );

    /* Get file date and time */
    _dos_getftime( fh, &old_date, &old_time );
    printf( "Old date field: 0x%.4x\n", old_date );
    printf( "Old time field: 0x%.4x\n", old_time );
    system( "dir dgftime.obj" );

    /* Modify file date and time */
    if( !_dos_setftime( fh, new_date, new_time ) )
    {
        _dos_getftime( fh, &new_date, &new_time );
        printf( "New date field: 0x%.4x\n", new_date );
        printf( "New time field: 0x%.4x\n", new_time );
        system( "dir dgftime.obj" );

        /* Restore date and time */
        _dos_setftime( fh, old_date, old_time );
    }
    _dos_close( fh );
}
```

Output

```
Old date field: 0x274f
Old time field: 0x94bb

 Volume in drive C is ZEPPELIN
 Directory of  C:\LIBREF

DGFTIME  OBJ    3923   6-15-99   6:37p
        1 File(s)  13676544 bytes free

New date field: 0x26cf
New time field: 0x48e0

 Volume in drive C is ZEPPELIN
 Directory of  C:\LIBREF

DGFTIME  OBJ    3923   12-15-99   9:07a
        1 File(s)  13676544 bytes free
```

_dos_settime

Description

Sets the current system time, using system call 0x2D.

#include <dos.h>

unsigned _dos_settime(struct _dostime_t *_time_);

time   New system time

Remarks

The **_dos_settime** routine uses system call 0x2D to set the current system time to the value stored in the **_dostime_t** structure that _time_ points to, as defined in DOS.H. The **_dostime_t** structure contains the following elements:

Element	Description
unsigned char hour	0–23
unsigned char minute	0–59
unsigned char second	0–59
unsigned char hsecond	Hundredths of a second; 0–99

Return Value

If successful, the function returns 0. Otherwise, it returns a nonzero value and sets **errno** to **EINVAL**, indicating an invalid time was specified.

Compatibility

Standards: None
16-Bit: DOS, QWIN, WIN, WIN DLL
32-Bit: None

See Also

_dos_getdate, _dos_gettime, _dos_setdate, gmtime, localtime, mktime, _strdate, _strtime

Example   /* DSTIME.C: This program changes the time and date values and displays the
                 * new date and time values.
                 */

```
#include <dos.h>
#include <conio.h>
#include <stdio.h>
#include <time.h>

void main( void )
{
    struct _dosdate_t olddate, newdate = { { 4 }, { 7 }, { 1999 } };
    struct _dostime_t oldtime, newtime = { { 3 }, { 45 }, { 30 }, { 0 } };
    char    datebuf[40], timebuf[40];

    /* Get current date and time values */
    _dos_getdate( &olddate );
    _dos_gettime( &oldtime );
    printf( "%s    %s\n" , _strdate( datebuf ), _strtime( timebuf ) );

    /* Modify date and time structures */
    _dos_setdate( &newdate );
    _dos_settime( &newtime );
    printf( "%s    %s\n" , _strdate( datebuf ), _strtime( timebuf ) );

    /* Restore old date and time */
    _dos_setdate( &olddate );
    _dos_settime( &oldtime );
}
```

Output   12/15/99   18:26:09
                07/04/99   03:45:30

_dos_setvect

Description

Sets the current value of the interrupt vector, using system call 0x25.

#include <dos.h>

void _dos_setvect(unsigned *intnum*,
   void(__cdecl __interrupt __far **handler*)());

intnum	Target-interrupt vector
handler	Interrupt handler for which to assign *intnum*

Remarks

The **_dos_setvect** routine uses system call 0x25 to set the current value of the interrupt vector *intnum* to the function pointed to by *handler*. Subsequently, whenever the *intnum* interrupt is generated, the *handler* routine will be called. If *handler* is a C function, it must have been previously declared with the **interrupt** attribute. Otherwise, you must make sure that the function satisfies the requirements for an interrupt-handling routine. For example, if *handler* is an assembler function, it must be a **far** routine that returns with an **IRET** instead of a **RET**.

The **interrupt** attribute indicates that the function is an interrupt handler. The compiler generates appropriate entry and exit sequences for the interrupt-handling function, including saving and restoring all registers and executing an **IRET** instruction to return.

The **_dos_setvect** routine is generally used with the **_dos_getvect** function. To replace an interrupt vector, first save the current vector of the interrupt using **_dos_getvect**. Then set the vector to your own interrupt routine with **_dos_setvect**. The saved vector can later be restored, if necessary, using **_dos_setvect**. The user-defined routine may also need the original vector in order to call it or to chain to it with **_chain_intr**.

Registers and Interrupt Functions

When you call an interrupt function, the DS register is initialized to the C data segment. This allows you to access global variables from within an interrupt function.

In addition, all registers except SS are saved on the stack. You can access these registers within the function if you declare a function parameter list containing a formal parameter for each saved register. The following example illustrates such a declaration:

```
void __interrupt __far int_handler( unsigned _es, unsigned _ds,
                                     unsigned _di, unsigned _si,
                                     unsigned _bp, unsigned _sp,
                                     unsigned _bx, unsigned _dx,
                                     unsigned _cx, unsigned _ax,
                                     unsigned _ip, unsigned _cs,
                                     unsigned _flags )
{
    .
    .
    .
}
```

The formal parameters must appear in the opposite order from which they are pushed onto the stack. You can omit parameters from the end of the list in a declaration, but not from the beginning. For example, if your handler needs to use only DI and SI, you must still provide ES and DS, but not necessarily BX or DX.

You can pass additional arguments if your interrupt handler will be called directly from C rather than by an INT instruction. To do this, you must declare all register parameters and then declare your parameter at the end of the list.

The compiler always saves and restores registers in the same, fixed order. Thus, no matter what names you use in the formal parameter list, the first parameter in the list refers to ES, the second refers to DS, and so on. If your interrupt routines will use inline assembler, you should distinguish the parameter names so that they will not be the same as the real register names.

If you change any of the register parameters of an interrupt function while the function is executing, the corresponding register contains the changed value when the function returns. For example:

```
void __interrupt __far int_handler( unsigned _es, unsigned _ds,
                                     unsigned _di, unsigned _si )
{
    _di = -1;
}
```

This code causes the DI register to contain −1 when the *handler* function returns. It is not a good idea to modify the values of the parameters representing the IP and CS registers in interrupt functions. If you must modify a particular flag (such as the carry flag for certain DOS and BIOS interrupt routines), use the OR operator (|) so that other bits in the flag register are not changed.

When an interrupt function is called by an INT instruction, the interrupt-enable flag is cleared. If your interrupt function needs to do significant processing, you should use the **_enable** function to set the interrupt flag so that interrupts can be handled.

Precautions for Interrupt Functions

Since DOS is not reentrant (a DOS interrupt cannot be called from inside a DOS interrupt), it is usually not safe to call from inside an interrupt function any standard library function that calls DOS INT 21H. Similar precautions apply to many BIOS functions. Functions that rely on INT 21H calls include I/O functions and the **_dos** family of functions. Functions that rely on the machine's BIOS include graphics functions and the **_bios** family of functions. It is usually safe to use functions that do not rely on INT 21H or BIOS, such as string-handling functions. Before using a standard library function in an interrupt function, be sure that you are familiar with the action of the library function.

Return Value   None.

Compatibility

Standards:	None
16-Bit:	DOS
32-Bit:	None

See Also   **_chain_intr**, **_dos_getvect**, **_dos_keep**

_dos_write

Description

Writes a buffer to a file, using system call 0x40.

#include <dos.h>

unsigned _dos_write(int *handle*, void __far *buffer*, unsigned *count*,
   unsigned *numwrt*);

handle	File to write to
buffer	Buffer to write from
count	Number of bytes to write
numwrt	Number of bytes actually written

Remarks

The **_dos_write** routine uses system call 0x40 to write data to the file that *handle* references; *count* bytes of data from the buffer to which *buffer* points are written to the file. The integer pointed to by *numwrt* will be the number of bytes actually written, which may be less than the number requested.

Do not use the DOS interface routines with the console, low-level, or stream I/O routines.

Return Value

If successful, the function returns 0. Otherwise, it returns the DOS error code and sets **errno** to one of the following manifest constants:

Constant	Meaning
EACCES	Access denied (*handle* references a file not open for write access)
EBADF	Invalid file handle

Compatibility

Standards: None
16-Bit: DOS, QWIN, WIN, WIN DLL
32-Bit: None

See Also

_dos_close, _dos_open, _dos_read, _write

Example

```
/* DWRITE.C: This program uses DOS I/O functions to write to a file. */

#include <fcntl.h>
#include <stdio.h>
#include <stdlib.h>
#include <dos.h>

void main( void )
{
   char out_buffer[] = "Hello";
   int   fh;
   unsigned n_written;

   /* Open file with _dos_creat function */
   if( _dos_creat( "data", _A_NORMAL, &fh ) == 0 )
   {
      /* Write data with _dos_write function */
      _dos_write( fh, out_buffer, 5, &n_written );
      printf( "Number of characters written: %d\n", n_written );

      _dos_close( fh );
      printf( "Contents of file are:\n" );
      system( "type data" );
   }
}
```

Output

```
Number of characters written: 5
Contents of file are:
Hello
```

_dosexterr

Description

Gets register values returned by 0x59.

#include <dos.h>

int _dosexterr(struct _DOSERROR *errorinfo);

errorinfo   Extended DOS error information

Remarks

The **_dosexterr** function obtains the extended error information returned by DOS system call 0x59 and stores the values in the structure pointed to by *errorinfo*. This function is useful when making system calls with DOS versions 3.0 or later, which offer extended error handling.

The structure type **_DOSERROR** is defined in DOS.H. The **_DOSERROR** structure contains the following elements:

Element	Description
int exterror	AX register contents
char errclass	BH register contents
char action	BL register contents
char locus	CH register contents

Giving a **NULL** pointer argument causes **_dosexterr** to return the value in AX without filling in the structure fields. See *MS-DOS Encyclopedia* (Duncan, ed.; Redmond, WA: Microsoft Press, 1988) or *Programmer's PC Sourcebook* 2nd ed. (Hogan; Redmond, WA: Microsoft Press, 1991) for more information on the register contents.

Return Value

The **_dosexterr** function returns the value in the AX register (identical to the value in the **exterror** structure field).

Compatibility

Standards: None
16-Bit: DOS, QWIN, WIN, WIN DLL
32-Bit: None

The **_dosexterr** function should be used only with DOS versions 3.0 or later.

See Also   **perror**

Example
```
/* DOSEXERR.C: This program tries to open the file test.dat.
 * If the attempted open operation fails, the program uses
 * _dosexterr to display extended error information.
 */

#include <dos.h>
#include <io.h>
#include <fcntl.h>
#include <stdio.h>

void main( void )
{
    struct _DOSERROR doserror;
    int fd;

    /* Attempt to open a non-existent file */
    if( (fd = _open( "NOSUCHF.ILE", _O_RDONLY )) == -1 )
    {
        _dosexterr( &doserror );
        printf( "Error: %d  Errclass: %d  Action: %d  Locus: %d\n",
                doserror.exterror, doserror.errclass,
                doserror.action,   doserror.locus );
    }
    else
    {
        printf( "Open succeeded so no extended information printed\n" );
        _close( fd );
    }
}
```

Output
```
Error: 2  Errclass: 8  Action: 3  Locus: 2
```

_dup, _dup2

Description   Create a second handle for an open file (**_dup**), or reassign a file handle (**_dup2**).

#include <io.h>   Required only for function declarations

int _dup(int *handle* **);**

int _dup2(int *handle1*, **int** *handle2* **);**

handle, handle1	Handle referring to open file
handle2	Any handle value

Remarks   The **_dup** and **_dup2** functions cause a second file handle to be associated with a currently open file. Operations on the file can be carried out using either file handle. The type of access allowed for the file is unaffected by the creation of a new handle.

The **_dup** function returns the next available file handle for the given file. The **_dup2** function forces *handle2* to refer to the same file as *handle1*. If *handle2* is associated with an open file at the time of the call, that file is closed.

Note that in a QuickWin application you cannot use the **_dup** and **_dup2** functions on **stdin**, **stdout**, or **stderr** (defined in STDIO.H). You can, however, use the **_dup** and **_dup2** functions on other handles.

Return Value   The **_dup** function returns a new file handle. The **_dup2** function returns 0 to indicate success. Both functions return –1 if an error occurs and set **errno** to one of the following values:

Value	Meaning
EBADF	Invalid file handle
EMFILE	No more file handles available (too many open files)

Compatibility	Standards: UNIX
	16-Bit: DOS, QWIN, WIN, WIN DLL
	32-Bit: DOS32X

Use **_dup** and **_dup2** for compatibility with ANSI naming conventions of non-ANSI functions. Use **dup** and **dup2** and link with OLDNAMES.LIB for UNIX compatibility.

See Also   **_close, _creat, _open**

Example

```
/* DUP.C: This program uses the variable old to save the original stdout.
 * It then opens a new file named new and forces stdout to refer
 * to it. Finally, it restores stdout to its original state.
 */

#include <io.h>
#include <stdlib.h>
#include <stdio.h>

void main( void )
{
   int old;
   FILE *new;

   old = _dup( 1 );    /* "old" now refers to "stdout" */
                       /* Note:  file handle 1 == "stdout" */
   if( old == -1 )
   {
      perror( "_dup( 1 ) failure" );
      exit( 1 );
   }
   write( old, "This goes to stdout first\r\n", 27 );
   if( ( new = fopen( "data", "w" ) ) == NULL )
   {
      puts( "Can't open file 'data'\n" );
      exit( 1 );
   }

   /* stdout now refers to file "data" */
   if( -1 == _dup2( _fileno( new ), 1 ) )
   {
      perror( "Can't _dup2 stdout" );
      exit( 1 );
   }
   puts( "This goes to file 'data'\r\n" );

   /* Flush stdout stream buffer so it goes to correct file */
   fflush( stdout );
   fclose( new );
```

```
        /* Restore original stdout */
        _dup2( old, 1 );
        puts( "This goes to stdout\n" );
        puts( "The file 'data' contains:" );
        system( "type data" );
}
```

Output   This goes to stdout first
                This goes to stdout

                The file 'data' contains:
                This goes to file 'data'

_ecvt

Description

Converts a **double** number to a string.

#include <stdlib.h>   Required only for function declarations

char *_ecvt(double *value***, int** *count***, int ****dec***, int ****sign* **);**

value	Number to be converted
count	Number of digits stored
dec	Stored decimal-point position
sign	Sign of converted number

Remarks

The **_ecvt** function converts a floating-point number to a character string. The *value* argument is the floating-point number to be converted. The **_ecvt** function stores up to *count* digits of *value* as a string and appends a null character (**'\0'**). If the number of digits in *value* exceeds *count,* the low-order digit is rounded. If there are fewer than *count* digits, the string is padded with zeros.

Only digits are stored in the string. The position of the decimal point and the sign of *value* can be obtained from *dec* and *sign* after the call. The *dec* argument points to an integer value giving the position of the decimal point with respect to the beginning of the string. A 0 or negative integer value indicates that the decimal point lies to the left of the first digit. The *sign* argument points to an integer indicating the sign of the converted number. If the integer value is 0, the number is positive. Otherwise, the number is negative.

The **_ecvt** and **_fcvt** functions use a single statically allocated buffer for the conversion. Each call to one of these routines destroys the result of the previous call.

Return Value

The **_ecvt** function returns a pointer to the string of digits. There is no error return.

Compatibility

Standards:	UNIX
16-Bit:	DOS, QWIN, WIN, WIN DLL
32-Bit:	DOS32X

Use **_ecvt** for compatibility with ANSI naming conventions of non-ANSI functions. Use **ecvt** and link with OLDNAMES.LIB for UNIX compatibility.

See Also

atof, atoi, atol, _fcvt, _gcvt

Example   /* ECVT.C: This program uses _ecvt to convert a floating-point
                 * number to a character string.
                 */

```c
#include <stdlib.h>
#include <stdio.h>

void main( void )
{
    int     decimal, sign;
    char    *buffer;
    int     precision = 10;
    double  source = 3.1415926535;

    buffer = _ecvt( source, precision, &decimal, &sign );
    printf( "source: %2.10f   buffer: '%s'  decimal: %d   sign: %d\n",
            source, buffer, decimal, sign );
}
```

Output   source: 3.1415926535   buffer: '3141592654' decimal: 1   sign: 0

_ellipse Functions

Description

Draw ellipses.

#include <graph.h>

short __far _ellipse(short *control*, short *x1*, short *y1*, short *x2*, short *y2*);

short __far _ellipse_w(short *control*, double *wx1*, double *wy1*, double *wx2*, double *wy2*);

short __far _ellipse_wxy(short *control*, struct _wxycoord __far *pwxy1*, struct _wxycoord __far *pwxy2*);

control	Fill flag
x1, *y1*	Upper-left corner of bounding rectangle
x2, *y2*	Lower-right corner of bounding rectangle
wx1, *wy1*	Upper-left corner of bounding rectangle
wx2, *wy2*	Lower-right corner of bounding rectangle
pwxy1	Upper-left corner of bounding rectangle
pwxy2	Lower-right corner of bounding rectangle

Remarks

The **_ellipse** functions draw ellipses or circles. The borders are drawn in the current color. In the **_ellipse** function, the center of the ellipse is the center of the bounding rectangle defined by the view-coordinate points (*x1*, *y1*) and (*x2*, *y2*).

In the **_ellipse_w** function, the center of the ellipse is the center of the bounding rectangle defined by the window-coordinate points (*wx1*, *wy1*) and (*wx2*, *wy2*).

In the **_ellipse_wxy** function, the center of the ellipse is the center of the bounding rectangle defined by the window-coordinate points (*pwxy1*) and (*pwxy2*).

If the bounding-rectangle arguments define a point or a vertical or horizontal line, no figure is drawn.

The *control* argument can be one of the following manifest constants:

Constant	Action
_GFILLINTERIOR	Uses **_floodfill** to fill the ellipse using the current fill mask
_GBORDER	Does not fill the ellipse

The control option given by **_GFILLINTERIOR** is equivalent to a subsequent call to the **_floodfill** function, using the center of the ellipse as the starting point and the current color (set by **_setcolor**) as the boundary color.

Return Value

The **_ellipse** functions return a nonzero value if the ellipse is drawn successfully; otherwise, they return 0.

Compatibility

Standards: None

16-Bit: DOS

32-Bit: None

See Also

_arc functions, **_floodfill**, **_grstatus**, **_lineto** functions, **_pie** functions, **_polygon** functions, **_rectangle** functions, **_setcolor**, **_setfillmask**

Example

```
/* ELLIPSE.C: This program draws a simple ellipse. */

#include <conio.h>
#include <stdlib.h>
#include <graph.h>

void main( void )
{
    /* Find a valid graphics mode. */
    if( !_setvideomode( _MAXRESMODE ) )
        exit( 1 );

    _ellipse( _GFILLINTERIOR, 80, 50, 240, 150 );

    /* Strike any key to clear screen. */
    _getch();
    _setvideomode( _DEFAULTMODE );
}
```

_enable

Description

Enables interrupts.

#include <dos.h>

void _enable(void);

Remarks

The **_enable** routine enables interrupts by executing an 8086 **STI** machine instruction.

Return Value

None.

Compatibility

Standards: None
16-Bit: DOS, QWIN, WIN, WIN DLL
32-Bit: None

See Also

_disable

_eof

Description   Tests for end-of-file.

#include <io.h>   Required only for function declarations

int _eof(int *handle* **);**

handle   Handle referring to open file

Remarks   The **_eof** function determines whether the end of the file associated with *handle* has been reached.

Return Value   The **_eof** function returns the value 1 if the current position is end-of-file, or 0 if it is not. A return value of –1 indicates an error; in this case, **errno** is set to **EBADF**, indicating an invalid file handle.

Compatibility   Standards: None
16-Bit: DOS, QWIN, WIN, WIN DLL
32-Bit: DOS32X

See Also   **clearerr, feof, ferror, perror**

Example
```
/* EOF.C: This program reads data from a file ten bytes at a time
 * until the end of the file is reached or an error is encountered.
 */

#include <io.h>
#include <fcntl.h>
#include <stdio.h>
#include <stdlib.h>
```

```
void main( void )
{
    int  fh, count, total = 0;
    char buf[10];

    if( (fh = _open( "_eof.c", _O_RDONLY )) == - 1 )
        exit( 1 );
    /* Cycle until end of file reached: */
    while( !_eof( fh ) )
    {
        /* Attempt to read in 10 bytes: */
        if( (count = _read( fh, buf, 10 )) == -1 )
        {
            perror( "Read error" );
            break;
        }

        /* Total up actual bytes read */
        total += count;
    }
    printf( "Number of bytes read = %d\n", total );
    _close( fh );
}
```

Output   Number of bytes read = 715

_exec Functions

Description

Load and execute new child processes.

#include <process.h>   Required only for function declarations

int _execl(char *cmdname, char *arg0, ... char *argn, NULL);

int _execle(char *cmdname, char *arg0, ... char *argn, NULL, char **envp);

int _execlp(char *cmdname, char *arg0, ... char *argn, NULL);

int _execlpe(char *cmdname, char *arg0, ... char *argn, NULL, char **envp);

int _execv(char *cmdname, char **argv);

int _execve(char *cmdname, char **argv, char **envp);

int _execvp(char *cmdname, char **argv);

int _execvpe(char *cmdname, char **argv, char **envp);

cmdname	Path name of file to be executed
arg0, ... argn	List of pointers to arguments
argv	Array of pointers to arguments
envp	Array of pointers to environment settings

Remarks

The _exec functions load and execute new child processes. When the call is successful in DOS, the child process is placed in the memory previously occupied by the calling process. Sufficient memory must be available for loading and executing the child process.

All of the _exec functions use the same operating system function. The letter(s) at the end of the function name determine the specific variation, as shown in the following list:

Letter	Variation
e	An array of pointers to environment arguments is explicitly passed to the child process.
l	Command-line arguments are passed individually to the _**exec** function.
p	Uses the PATH environment variable to find the file to be executed.
v	Command-line arguments are passed to the _**exec** function as an array of pointers.

The *cmdname* argument specifies the file to be executed as the child process. It can specify a full path (from the root), a partial path (from the current working directory), or just a filename. If *cmdname* does not have a filename extension or does not end with a period (.), the _**exec** function searches for the named file; if the search is unsuccessful, it tries the same base name, first with the extension .COM, then with the extension .EXE. If *cmdname* has an extension, only that extension is used in the search. If *cmdname* ends with a period, the _**exec** calls search for *cmdname* with no extension. The _**execlp**, _**execlpe**, _**execvp**, and _**execvpe** routines search for *cmdname* (using the same procedures) in the directories specified by the PATH environment variable.

If *cmdname* contains a drive specifier or any slashes (that is, if it is a relative path name), the _**exec** call searches only for the specified file; the path is not searched. Note that the DOS APPEND command cannot be used with the _**exec** functions.

Arguments are passed to the new process by giving one or more pointers to character strings as arguments in the _**exec** call. These character strings form the argument list for the child process. The combined length of the strings forming the argument list for the new process must not exceed 128 bytes (in real mode only). The terminating null character ('\0') for each string is not included in the count, but space characters (inserted automatically to separate the arguments) are counted.

The argument pointers can be passed as separate arguments (_**execl**, _**execle**, _**execlp**, and _**execlpe**) or as an array of pointers (_**execv**, _**execve**, _**execvp**, and _**execvpe**). At least one argument, *arg0*, must be passed to the child process; this argument is *argv*[0] of the child process. Usually, this argument is a copy of the *cmdname* argument. (A different value will not produce an error.) Under versions of DOS earlier than 3.0, the passed value of *arg0* is not available for use in the child process. However, with DOS versions 3.0 and later, *cmdname* is available as *arg0*.

The _**execl**, _**execle**, _**execlp**, and _**execlpe** calls are typically used when the number of arguments is known in advance. The argument *arg0* is usually a pointer to *cmdname*. The arguments *arg1* through *argn* point to the character strings forming the new argument list. A null pointer must follow *argn* to mark the end of the argument list.

The _**execv**, _**execve**, _**execvp**, and _**execvpe** calls are useful when the number of arguments to the new process is variable. Pointers to the arguments are passed as an array, *argv*. The argument *argv*[0] is usually a pointer to *cmdname*. The arguments *argv*[1] through *argv*[*n*] point to the character strings forming the new argument list. The argument *argv*[*n*+1] must be a **NULL** pointer to mark the end of the argument list.

Files that are open when an _**exec** call is made remain open in the new process. In the _**execl**, _**execlp**, _**execv**, and _**execvp** calls, the child process inherits the environment of the parent. The _**execle**, _**execlpe**, _**execve**, and _**execvpe** calls allow the user to alter the environment for the child process by passing a list of environment settings through the *envp* argument. The argument *envp* is an array of character pointers, each element of which (except for the final element) points to a null-terminated string defining an environment variable. Such a string usually has the form

NAME=*value*

where NAME is the name of an environment variable and *value* is the string value to which that variable is set. (Note that *value* is not enclosed in double quotation marks.) The final element of the *envp* array should be **NULL**. When *envp* itself is **NULL**, the child process inherits the environment settings of the parent process.

A program executed with one of the _**exec** family of functions is always loaded into memory as if the "maximum allocation" field in the program's .EXE file header is set to the default value of 0xFFFFH. You can use the EXEHDR utility to change the maximum allocation field of a program; however, such a program invoked with one of the _**exec** functions may behave differently from a program invoked directly from the operating-system command line or with one of the _**spawn** functions.

Note that COMMAND.COM checks the first two bytes of a file to determine whether it is an .EXE file or a .COM file—you can execute a file named by any extension, as long as its content is truly executable.

The _**exec** calls do not preserve the translation modes of open files. If the child process must use files inherited from the parent, the _**setmode** routine should be used to set the translation mode of these files to the desired mode.

You must explicitly flush (using **fflush** or _**flushall**) or close any stream prior to the _**exec** function call.

Signal settings are not preserved in child processes that are created by calls to _**exec** routines. The signal settings are reset to the default in the child process.

Return Value   The **_exec** functions do not normally return to the calling process. If an **_exec** function returns, an error has occurred and the return value is –1. The **errno** variable is set to one of the following values:

Value	Meaning
E2BIG	The argument list exceeds 128 bytes, or the space required for the environment information exceeds 32K.
EACCES	The specified file has a locking or sharing violation (DOS version 3.0 or later).
EMFILE	Too many files open (the specified file must be opened to determine whether it is executable).
ENOENT	File or path name not found.
ENOEXEC	The specified file is not executable or has an invalid executable-file format.
ENOMEM	Not enough memory is available to execute the child process; or the available memory has been corrupted; or an invalid block exists, indicating that the parent process was not allocated properly.

Compatibility   Standards: UNIX

16-Bit: DOS

32-Bit: DOS32X

Use **_exec** for compatibility with ANSI naming conventions of non-ANSI functions. Use **exec** and link with OLDNAMES.LIB for UNIX compatibility.

Because of differences in DOS versions 2.0 and 2.1, child processes generated by the **_exec** family of functions (or by the equivalent **_spawn** functions with the **_P_OVERLAY** argument) may cause fatal system errors when they exit. If you are running DOS 2.0 or 2.1, you must upgrade to DOS version 3.0 or later to use these functions.

Bound programs cannot use the **_exec** family of functions in real mode.

See Also   **abort, atexit, exit, _exit, _onexit, _spawn** functions, **system**

Example
```
/* EXEC.C: This program accepts a number in the range 1 through 8 from the
 * command line. Based on the number it receives, it executes one of the
 * eight different procedures that spawn the process named child. For
 * some of these procedures, the child.exe file must be in the same
 * directory; for others, it need only be in the same path.
 */

#include <stdio.h>
#include <process.h>
```

```
            char *my_env[] = {
                        "THIS=environment will be",
                        "PASSED=to child.exe by the",
                        "_EXECLE=and",
                        "_EXECLPE=and",
                        "_EXECVE=and",
                        "_EXECVPE=functions",
                        NULL
                        };

        void main( int argc, char *argv[] )
        {
            char *args[4];
            int result;

            args[0] = "child";        /* Set up parameters to send */
            args[1] = "_execv??";
            args[2] = "two";
            args[3] = NULL;

            switch( argv[1][0] )    /* Based on first letter of argument */
            {
                case '1':
                    _execl( argv[2], argv[2], "_execl", "two", NULL );
                    break;
                case '2':
                    _execle( argv[2], argv[2], "_execle", "two", NULL, my_env );
                    break;
                case '3':
                    _execlp( argv[2], argv[2], "_execlp", "two", NULL );
                    break;
                case '4':
                    _execlpe( argv[2], argv[2], "_execlpe", "two", NULL, my_env );
                    break;
                case '5':
                    _execv( argv[2], args );
                    break;
                case '6':
                    _execve( argv[2], args, my_env );
                    break;
                case '7':
                    _execvp( argv[2], args );
                    break;
                case '8':
                    _execvpe( argv[2], args, my_env );
                    break;
                default:
                    printf( "SYNTAX: EXEC <1-8> <childprogram>\n" );
                    exit( 1 );
            }
            printf( "Process was not spawned.\n" );
            printf( "Program 'child' was not found." );
        }
```

exit, _exit

Description

Terminate the calling process after cleanup (**exit**) or immediately (**_exit**).

#include <process.h>   Required only for function declarations
#include <stdlib.h>   Use either PROCESS.H or STDLIB.H

void exit(int *status* **);**

void _exit(int *status* **);**

status   Exit status

Remarks

The **exit** and **_exit** functions terminate the calling process. The **exit** function first calls, in LIFO (last-in–first-out) order, the functions registered by **atexit** and **_onexit**, then flushes all file buffers before terminating the process. The **_exit** function terminates the process without processing **atexit** or **_onexit** functions or flushing stream buffers. The *status* value is typically set to 0 to indicate a normal exit and set to some other value to indicate an error.

Although the **exit** and **_exit** calls do not return a value, the low-order byte of *status* is made available to the waiting parent process, if one exists, after the calling process exits. The *status* value is available to the operating-system batch command ERRORLEVEL.

The behavior of the **exit**, **_exit**, **_cexit**, and **_c_exit** functions is as follows:

Function	Action
exit	Performs complete C library termination procedures, terminates the process, and exits with the supplied status code.
_exit	Performs "quick" C library termination procedures, terminates the process, and exits with the supplied status code.
_cexit	Performs complete C library termination procedures and returns to caller, but does not terminate the process.
_c_exit	Performs "quick" C library termination procedures and returns to caller, but does not terminate the process.

Return Value   None.

Compatibility

exit

Standards:	ANSI, UNIX
16-Bit:	DOS, QWIN, WIN
32-Bit:	DOS32X

_exit

Standards:	None
16-Bit:	DOS, QWIN, WIN
32-Bit:	DOS32X

See Also   **abort**, **atexit**, **_cexit**, **_exec** functions, **_onexit**, **_spawn** functions, **system**

Example
```
/* EXITER.C: This program prompts the user for a yes or no and returns
 * a DOS error code of 1 if the user answers Y or y; otherwise it
 * returns 0. The error code could be tested in a batch file.
 */

#include <conio.h>
#include <stdlib.h>

void main( void )
{
    char   ch;

    _cputs( "Yes or no? " );
    ch = _getch();
    _cputs( "\r\n" );
    if( toupper( ch ) == 'Y' )
       exit( 1 );
    else
       exit( 0 );
}
```

exp, _expl

Description

Calculate the exponential.

#include <math.h>

double exp(double *x*);

long double _expl(long double *x*);

x   Floating-point value

Remarks

The **exp** and **_expl** functions return the exponential function of their floating-point arguments (*x*).

The **_expl** function is the 80-bit counterpart; it uses an 80-bit, 10-byte coprocessor form of arguments and return values. See the reference page on the long double functions for more details on this data type.

Return Value

These functions return e^x. The functions return **HUGE_VAL** on overflow and set **errno** to **ERANGE**; on underflow, they return 0 but do not set **errno**. This behavior can be changed with the **_matherr** function.

Compatibility

exp

Standards:	ANSI, UNIX
16-Bit:	DOS, QWIN, WIN, WIN DLL
32-Bit:	DOS32X

_expl

Standards:	None
16-Bit:	DOS, QWIN, WIN, WIN DLL
32-Bit:	None

See Also

log functions

Example

```
/* EXP.C */
#include <math.h>
#include <stdio.h>

void main( void )
{
    double x = 2.302585093, y;

    y = exp( x );
    printf( "exp( %f ) = %f\n", x, y );
}
```

Output

```
exp( 2.302585 ) = 10.000000
```

_expand Functions

Description

Change the size of a memory block.

#include <malloc.h>   Required only for function declarations

void *_expand(void *_memblock_, **size_t** _size_);

void __based(void) *_bexpand(__segment _seg_,
    void __based(void) *_memblock_, **size_t** _size_);

void __far *_fexpand(void __far *_memblock_, **size_t** _size_);

void __near *_nexpand(void __near *_memblock_, **size_t** _size_);

memblock	Pointer to previously allocated memory block
size	New size in bytes
seg	Value of base segment

Remarks

The **_expand** family of functions changes the size of a previously allocated memory block by attempting to expand or contract the block without moving its location in the heap. The _memblock_ argument points to the beginning of the block. The _size_ argument gives the new size of the block, in bytes. The contents of the block are unchanged up to the shorter of the new and old sizes.

The _memblock_ argument can also point to a block that has been freed, as long as there has been no intervening call to **calloc**, **_expand**, **malloc**, or **realloc**. If _memblock_ points to a freed block, the block remains free after a call to one of the **_expand** functions.

The _seg_ argument is the segment address of the **__based** heap.

In large data models (compact-, large-, and huge-model programs), **_expand** maps to **_fexpand**. In small data models (tiny-, small-, and medium-model programs), **_expand** maps to **_nexpand**.

The various **_expand** functions change the size of the storage block in the data segments shown in the list below:

Function	Data Segment
_expand	Depends on data model of program
_bexpand	Based heap specified by *seg*, or in all based heaps if *seg* is zero
_fexpand	Far heap (outside default data segment)
_nexpand	Near heap (inside default data segment)

Return Value

The **_expand** family of functions returns a **void** pointer to the reallocated memory block. Unlike **realloc**, **_expand** cannot move a block to change its size. This means the *memblock* argument to **_expand** is the same as the return value if there is sufficient memory available to expand the block without moving it.

With the exception of the **_bexpand** function, these functions return **NULL** if there is insufficient memory available to expand the block to the given size without moving it. The **_bexpand** function returns **_NULLOFF** if insufficient memory is available. The item pointed to by *memblock* will have been expanded as much as possible in its current location.

The storage space pointed to by the return value is guaranteed to be suitably aligned for storage of any type of object. The new size of the item can be checked with one of the **_msize** functions. To get a pointer to a type other than **void**, use a type cast on the return value.

Compatibility

_expand

Standards:	None
16-Bit:	DOS, QWIN, WIN, WIN DLL
32-Bit:	DOS32X

_bexpand, _fexpand, _nexpand

Standards:	None
16-Bit:	DOS, QWIN, WIN, WIN DLL
32-Bit:	None

See Also

calloc functions, **free** functions, **malloc** functions, **_msize** functions, **realloc** functions

Example

```
/* EXPAND.C */
#include <stdio.h>
#include <malloc.h>
#include <stdlib.h>

void main( void )
{
    char *bufchar;

    printf( "Allocate a 512 element buffer\n" );
    if( (bufchar = (char *)calloc( 512, sizeof( char ) )) == NULL )
        exit( 1 );
    printf( "Allocated %d bytes at %Fp\n",
            _msize( bufchar ), (void __far *)bufchar );

    if( (bufchar = (char *)_expand( bufchar, 1024 )) == NULL )
        printf( "Can't expand" );
    else
        printf( "Expanded block to %d bytes at %Fp\n",
                _msize( bufchar ), (void __far *)bufchar );

    /* Free memory */
    free( bufchar );
    exit( 0 );
}
```

Output

```
Allocate a 512 element buffer
Allocated 512 bytes at 0067:142A
Expanded block to 1024 bytes at 0067:142A
```

fabs, _fabsl

Description   Calculate the absolute value of their floating-point arguments.

#include <math.h>

double fabs(double *x* **);**

long double _fabsl(long double *x* **);**

x   Floating-point value

Remarks   The **fabs** and **_fabsl** functions calculate the absolute value of their floating-point arguments.

The **_fabsl** function is the 80-bit counterpart; it uses an 80-bit, 10-byte coprocessor form of arguments and return values. See the reference page on the long double functions for more details on this data type.

Return Value   These functions return the absolute value of their arguments. There is no error return.

Compatibility   **fabs**

Standards: ANSI, UNIX
16-Bit: DOS, QWIN, WIN, WIN DLL
32-Bit: DOS32X

_fabsl

Standards: None
16-Bit: DOS, QWIN, WIN, WIN DLL
32-Bit: None

See Also   **abs, _cabs, labs**

Example

```
/* ABS.C: This program computes and displays the absolute values of
 * several numbers.
 */

#include <stdio.h>
#include <math.h>
#include <stdlib.h>

void main( void )
{
    int    ix = -4, iy;
    long   lx = -41567L, ly;
    double dx = -3.141593, dy;

    iy = abs( ix );
    printf( "The absolute value of %d is %d\n", ix, iy);

    ly = labs( lx );
    printf( "The absolute value of %ld is %ld\n", lx, ly);

    dy = fabs( dx );
    printf( "The absolute value of %f is %f\n", dx, dy );
}
```

Output

```
The absolute value of -4 is 4
The absolute value of -41567 is 41567
The absolute value of -3.141593 is 3.141593
```

fclose, _fcloseall

Description

Closes a stream (**fclose**) or closes all open streams (**_fcloseall**).

#include <stdio.h>

int fclose(FILE * *stream* **);**

int _fcloseall(void);

stream   Pointer to **FILE** structure

Remarks

The **fclose** function closes *stream*. The **_fcloseall** function closes all open streams except **stdin**, **stdout**, **stderr** (and in DOS, **stdaux** and **stdprn**). It also closes and deletes any temporary files created by **tmpfile**.

In both functions, all buffers associated with the stream are flushed prior to closing. System-allocated buffers are released when the stream is closed. Buffers assigned by the user with **setbuf** and **setvbuf** are not automatically released.

Return Value

The **fclose** function returns 0 if the stream is successfully closed. The **_fcloseall** function returns the total number of streams closed. Both functions return **EOF** to indicate an error.

Compatibility

fclose

Standards:	ANSI, UNIX
16-Bit:	DOS, QWIN, WIN, WIN DLL
32-Bit:	DOS32X

_fcloseall

Standards:	None
16-Bit:	DOS, QWIN, WIN, WIN DLL
32-Bit:	DOS32X

See Also

_close, _fdopen, fflush, fopen, freopen

Example

```
/* FOPEN.C: This program opens files named "data" and "data2". It uses
 * fclose to close "data" and _fcloseall to close all remaining files.
 */

#include <stdio.h>

FILE *stream, *stream2;

void main( void )
{
   int numclosed;

   /* Open for read (will fail if 'data does not exist) */
   if( (stream = fopen( "data", "r" )) == NULL )
      printf( "The file 'data' was not opened\n" );
   else
      printf( "The file 'data' was opened\n" );

   /* Open for write */
   if( (stream2 = fopen( "data2", "w+" )) == NULL )
      printf( "The file 'data2' was not opened\n" );
   else
      printf( "The file 'data2' was opened\n" );

   /* Close stream */
   if( fclose( stream ) )
      printf( "The file 'data' was not closed\n" );

   /* All other files are closed: */
   numclosed = _fcloseall( );
   printf( "Number of files closed by _fcloseall: %u\n", numclosed );
}
```

Output

```
The file 'data' was opened
The file 'data2' was opened
Number of files closed by _fcloseall: 1
```

_fcvt

Description

Converts a floating-point number to a string.

#include <stdlib.h>   Required only for function declarations

char *_fcvt(double *value*, **int** *count*, **int** *dec, **int** *sign **);**

value	Number to be converted
count	Number of digits after decimal point
dec	Pointer to stored decimal-point position
sign	Pointer to stored sign indicator

Remarks

The **_fcvt** function converts a floating-point number to a null-terminated character string. The *value* argument is the floating-point number to be converted. The **_fcvt** function stores the digits of *value* as a string and appends a null character ('\0'). The *count* argument specifies the number of digits to be stored after the decimal point. Excess digits are rounded off to *count* places. If there are fewer than *count* digits of precision, the string is padded with zeros.

Only digits are stored in the string. The position of the decimal point and the sign of *value* can be obtained from *dec* and *sign* after the call. The *dec* argument points to an integer value; this integer value gives the position of the decimal point with respect to the beginning of the string. A zero or negative integer value indicates that the decimal point lies to the left of the first digit. The argument *sign* points to an integer indicating the sign of *value*. The integer is set to 0 if *value* is positive and is set to a nonzero number if *value* is negative.

The **_ecvt** and **_fcvt** functions use a single statically allocated buffer for the conversion. Each call to one of these routines destroys the results of the previous call.

Return Value

The **_fcvt** function returns a pointer to the string of digits. There is no error return.

Compatibility

Standards:	UNIX
16-Bit:	DOS, QWIN, WIN, WIN DLL
32-Bit:	DOS32X

Use **_fcvt** for compatibility with ANSI naming conventions of non-ANSI functions. Use **fcvt** and link with OLDNAMES.LIB for UNIX compatibility.

See Also   atof, atoi, atol, _ecvt, _gcvt

Example

```
/* FCVT.C: This program converts the constant 3.1415926535 to a string and
 * sets the pointer *buffer to point to that string.
 */

#include <stdlib.h>
#include <stdio.h>

void main( void )
{
    int  decimal, sign;
    char *buffer;
    double source = 3.1415926535;

    buffer = _fcvt( source, 7, &decimal, &sign );
    printf( "source: %2.10f   buffer: '%s'   decimal: %d   sign: %d\n",
            source, buffer, decimal, sign );
}
```

Output

```
source: 3.1415926535   buffer: '31415927'   decimal: 1   sign: 0
```

_fdopen

Description

Associates a stream with a file that was previously opened for low-level I/O.

#include <stdio.h>

FILE *_fdopen(int *handle*, char **mode*);

| *handle* | Handle referring to open file |
| *mode* | Type of access permitted |

Remarks

The **_fdopen** function associates an input/output stream with the file identified by *handle*, thus allowing a file opened for low-level I/O to be buffered and formatted. (For an explanation of stream I/O and low-level I/O see "Input and Output" on page 31.) The *mode* character string specifies the type of access requested for the file, as shown below. The following list gives the *mode* string used in the **fopen** and **_fdopen** functions and the corresponding *oflag* arguments used in the **_open** and **_sopen** functions. A complete description of the *mode* string argument is given in the remarks section of the **fopen** function.

Type String	Equivalent Value for _open/_sopen
"r"	**_O_RDONLY**
"w"	**_O_WRONLY** (usually **_O_WRONLY** | **_O_CREAT** | **_O_TRUNC**)
"a"	**_O_WRONLY** | **_O_APPEND** (usually **_O_WRONLY** | **_O_CREAT** | **_O_APPEND**)
"r+"	**_O_RDWR**
"w+"	**_O_RDWR** (usually **_O_RDWR** | **_O_CREAT** | **_O_TRUNC**)
"a+"	**_O_RDWR** | **_O_APPEND** (usually **_O_RDWR** | **_O_APPEND** | **_O_CREAT**)

In addition to the values listed above, one of the following characters can be included in the *mode* string to specify the translation mode for new lines. These characters correspond to the constants used in the **_open** and **_sopen** functions, as shown below:

Mode	Equivalent Value for _open/_sopen
t	**_O_TEXT**
b	**_O_BINARY**

If **t** or **b** is not given in the *mode* string, the translation mode is defined by the default-mode variable **_fmode**.

In addition to the file attribute and the text or binary mode listed above, the *mode* string accepts either **c** or **n** to specify commit to disk, or do not commit to disk, respectively. These characters have no correspondence to constants used in the **_open** and **_sopen** functions. For more information on the commit feature, see "Committing Buffer Contents to Disk" on page 3737.

Mode	Description
c	Commit to disk, no **_open/_sopen** equivalent.
n	No commit, no **_open/_sopen** equivalent. Default.

If **c** or **n** is not given in the *mode* string, **n** is the default mode.

Return Value

The **_fdopen** function returns a pointer to the open stream. A null pointer value indicates an error.

Compatibility

Standards: UNIX

16-Bit: DOS, QWIN, WIN, WIN DLL

32-Bit: DOS32X

Use **_fdopen** for compatibility with ANSI naming conventions of non-ANSI functions. Use **fdopen** and link with OLDNAMES.LIB for UNIX compatibility.

The **t**, **c**, and **n** options are not part of the ANSI standard for **fopen** and **_fdopen**, but are instead Microsoft extensions and should not be used where ANSI portability is desired.

See Also

_dup, **_dup2**, **fclose**, **_fcloseall**, **fopen**, **freopen**, **_open**

Example

```
/* _FDOPEN.C: This program opens a file using low-level I/O, then uses
 * _fdopen to switch to stream access. It counts the lines in the file.
 */

#include <stdlib.h>
#include <stdio.h>
#include <fcntl.h>
#include <io.h>
```

```
        void main( void )
        {
            FILE *stream;
            int  fh, count = 0;
            char inbuf[128];

            /* Open a file handle. */
            if( (fh = _open( "_fdopen.c", _O_RDONLY )) == -1 )
                exit( 1 );

            /* Change handle access to stream access. */
            if( (stream = _fdopen( fh, "r" )) == NULL )
                exit( 1 );

            while( fgets( inbuf, 128, stream ) != NULL )
                count++;

            /* After _fdopen, close with fclose, not _close. */
            fclose( stream );

            printf( "Lines in file: %d\n", count );
        }
```

Output   Lines in file: 31

feof

Description

Tests for end-of-file on a stream.

#include <stdio.h>

int feof(FILE *stream);

stream   Pointer to **FILE** structure

Remarks

The **feof** routine (implemented both as a function and as a macro) determines whether the end of *stream* has been reached. Once the end of the file is reached, read operations return an end-of-file indicator until the stream is closed or until **rewind**, **fsetpos**, **fseek**, or **clearerr** is called against it.

Return Value

The **feof** function returns a nonzero value after the first read operation that attempts to read past the end of the file. It returns 0 if the current position is not end-of-file. There is no error return.

Compatibility

Standards: ANSI, UNIX
16-Bit: DOS, QWIN, WIN, WIN DLL
32-Bit: DOS32X

See Also

clearerr, _eof, ferror, perror

Example

```
/* FEOF.C: This program uses feof to indicate when it reaches the end
 * of the file FEOF.C. It also checks for errors with ferror.
 */

#include <stdio.h>
#include <stdlib.h>
```

```
void main( void )
{
    int   count, total = 0;
    char buffer[100];
    FILE *stream;

    if( (stream = fopen( "feof.c", "r" )) == NULL )
        exit( 1 );

    /* Cycle until end of file reached: */
    while( !feof( stream ) )
    {
        /* Attempt to read in 10 bytes: */
        count = fread( buffer, sizeof( char ), 100, stream );
        if( ferror( stream ) )
        {
            perror( "Read error" );
            break;
        }

        /* Total up actual bytes read */
        total += count;
    }
    printf( "Number of bytes read = %d\n", total );
    fclose( stream );
}
```

Output   Number of bytes read = 697

ferror

Description   Tests for an error on a stream.

#include <stdio.h>

int ferror(FILE *stream **);**

stream   Pointer to **FILE** structure

Remarks   The **ferror** routine (implemented both as a function and as a macro) tests for a reading or writing error on the file associated with *stream*. If an error has occurred, the error indicator for the stream remains set until the stream is closed or rewound, or until **clearerr** is called against it.

Return Value   If no error has occurred on *stream*, **ferror** returns 0. Otherwise, it returns a non-zero value.

Compatibility   Standards: ANSI, UNIX
16-Bit: DOS, QWIN, WIN, WIN DLL
32-Bit: DOS32X

See Also   **clearerr, _eof, feof, fopen, perror**

Example
```
/* FEOF.C: This program uses feof to indicate when it reaches the end
 * of the file FEOF.C. It also checks for errors with ferror.
 */

#include <stdio.h>
#include <stdlib.h>
```

```
void main( void )
{
   int  count, total = 0;
   char buffer[100];
   FILE *stream;

   if( (stream = fopen( "feof.c", "r" )) == NULL )
      exit( 1 );

   /* Cycle until end of file reached: */
   while( !feof( stream ) )
   {
      /* Attempt to read in 10 bytes: */
      count = fread( buffer, sizeof( char ), 100, stream );
      if( ferror( stream ) )
      {
         perror( "Read error" );
         break;
      }

      /* Total up actual bytes read */
      total += count;
   }
   printf( "Number of bytes read = %d\n", total );
   fclose( stream );
}
```

Output   Number of bytes read = 697

fflush

Description   Flushes a stream.

#include <stdio.h>

int fflush(FILE *stream);

stream   Pointer to FILE structure

Remarks   If the file associated with stream is open for output, **fflush** writes to that file the contents of the buffer associated with the stream. If the stream is open for input, **fflush** clears the contents of the buffer. The **fflush** function negates the effect of any prior call to **ungetc** against stream.

Buffers are automatically flushed when they are full, when the stream is closed, or when a program terminates normally without closing the stream. Also, **fflush(NULL)** flushes all streams opened for output.

The stream remains open after the call. The **fflush** function has no effect on an un-buffered stream.

Return Value   The **fflush** function returns the value 0 if the buffer was successfully flushed. The value 0 is also returned in cases in which the specified stream has no buffer or is open for reading only. A return value of **EOF** indicates an error.

Note If **fflush** returns **EOF**, data may have been lost because of a failed write. When setting up a critical error handler, it is safest to turn buffering off with the **setvbuf** function or to use low-level I/O routines such as **_open**, **_close**, and **_write** instead of the stream I/O functions.

Compatibility   Standards: ANSI, UNIX
                      16-Bit: DOS, QWIN, WIN, WIN DLL
                      32-Bit: DOS32X

See Also   fclose, _flushall, setbuf

Example

```
/* FFLUSH.C */
#include <stdio.h>
#include <conio.h>

void main( void )
{
    int integer;
    char string[81];

    /* Read each word as a string. */
    printf( "Enter a sentence of four words with scanf: " );
    for( integer = 0; integer < 4; integer++ )
    {
        scanf( "%s", string );
        printf( "%s\n", string );
    }

    /* You must flush the input buffer before using gets. */
    fflush( stdin );
    printf( "Enter the same sentence with gets: " );
    gets( string );
    printf( "%s\n", string );
}
```

Output

```
Enter a sentence of four words with scanf: This is a test
This
is
a
test
Enter the same sentence with gets: This is a test
This is a test
```

fgetc, _fgetchar

Description   Read a character from a stream (**fgetc**) or **stdin** (**_fgetchar**).

#include <stdio.h>

int fgetc(FILE ***stream** **);**

int _fgetchar(void);

stream   Pointer to **FILE** structure

Remarks   The **fgetc** function reads a single character from the current position of the file as-sociated with *stream*. The character is converted and returned as an **int**. The func-tion then increments the associated file pointer (if any) to point to the next character. The **_fgetchar** function is equivalent to **fgetc(stdin)**.

The **fgetc** and **_fgetchar** routines are identical to **getc** and **getchar**, but they are functions rather than macros.

Return Value   The **fgetc** and **_fgetchar** functions return the character read. They return **EOF** to indicate an error or end-of-file. Use **feof** or **ferror** to distinguish between an error and an end-of-file condition.

Compatibility   **fgetc**

Standards: ANSI, UNIX
16-Bit: DOS, QWIN, WIN, WIN DLL
32-Bit: DOS32X

_fgetchar

Standards: None
16-Bit: DOS, QWIN
32-Bit: DOS32X

See Also   **fputc, _fputchar, getc, getchar**

Example
```
/* FGETC.C: This program uses getc to read the first 80 input characters
 * (or until the end of input) and place them into a string named buffer.
 */

#include <stdio.h>
#include <stdlib.h>

void main( void )
{
    FILE *stream;
    char buffer[81];
    int  i, ch;

    /* Open file to read line from: */
    if( (stream = fopen( "fgetc.c", "r" )) == NULL )
        exit( 0 );

    /* Read in first 80 characters and place them in "buffer": */
    ch = fgetc( stream );
    for( i=0; (i < 80 ) && ( feof( stream ) == 0 ); i++ )
    {
        buffer[i] = ch;
        ch = fgetc( stream );
    }
    /* Add null to end string */
    buffer[i] = '\0';
    printf( "%s\n", buffer );
    fclose( stream );
}
```

Output
```
/* FGETC.C: This program uses getc to read the first 80 input characters
/* (or
```

fgetpos

Description

Gets a stream's file-position indicator.

#include <stdio.h>

int fgetpos(FILE *stream, fpos_t *pos);

stream	Target stream
pos	Position-indicator storage

Remarks

The **fgetpos** function gets the current value of the *stream* argument's file-position indicator and stores it in the object pointed to by *pos*. The **fsetpos** function can later use information stored in *pos* to reset the *stream* argument's pointer to its position at the time **fgetpos** was called.

The *pos* value is stored in an internal format and is intended for use only by the **fgetpos** and **fsetpos** functions.

Return Value

If successful, the **fgetpos** function returns 0. On failure, it returns a nonzero value and sets **errno** to one of the following manifest constants (defined in STDIO.H):

Constant	Meaning
EBADF	The specified stream is not a valid file handle or is not accessible.
EINVAL	The *stream* value is invalid.

Compatibility

Standards:	ANSI
16-Bit:	DOS, QWIN, WIN, WIN DLL
32-Bit:	DOS32X

See Also

fsetpos

Example
```
/* FGETPOS.C: This program opens a file and reads bytes at several
 * different locations.
 */

#include <stdio.h>

void main( void )
{
   FILE    *stream;
   fpos_t pos;
   int     val;
   char    buffer[20];

   if( (stream = fopen( "fgetpos.c", "rb" )) == NULL )
      printf( "Trouble opening file\n" );
   else
   {
      /* Read some data and then check the position. */
      fread( buffer, sizeof( char ), 10, stream );
      if( fgetpos( stream, &pos ) != 0 )
         perror( "fgetpos error" );
      else
      {
         fread( buffer, sizeof( char ), 10, stream );
         printf( "10 bytes at byte %ld: %.10s\n", pos, buffer );
      }

      /* Set a new position and read more data */
      pos = 140;
      if( fsetpos( stream, &pos ) != 0 )
         perror( "fsetpos error" );

      fread( buffer, sizeof( char ), 10, stream );
         printf( "10 bytes at byte %ld: %.10s\n", pos, buffer );

      fclose( stream );
   }
}
```

Output
```
10 bytes at byte 10: .C: This p
10 bytes at byte 140:   FILE   *
```

fgets

Description

Gets a string from a stream.

#include <stdio.h>

char *fgets(char **string***, int** *n***, FILE ****stream* **);**

string	Storage location for data
n	Number of characters stored
stream	Pointer to **FILE** structure

Remarks

The **fgets** function reads a string from the input *stream* argument and stores it in *string*. Characters are read from the current stream position up to and including the first newline character (**'\n'**), up to the end of the stream, or until the number of characters read is equal to *n* – 1, whichever comes first. The result is stored in *string*, and a null character (**'\0'**) is appended. The newline character, if read, is included in the string. If *n* is equal to 1, *string* is empty (""). The **fgets** function is similar to the **gets** function; however, **gets** replaces the newline character with **NULL**.

Return Value

If successful, the **fgets** function returns *string*. It returns **NULL** to indicate either an error or end-of-file condition. Use **feof** or **ferror** to determine whether an error occurred.

Compatibility

Standards:	ANSI, UNIX
16-Bit:	DOS, QWIN, WIN, WIN DLL
32-Bit:	DOS32X

See Also

fputs, gets, puts

Example   /* FGETS.C: This program uses fgets to display a line from a file on the
                 * screen.
                 */

```c
#include <stdio.h>

FILE *stream;

void main( void )
{
    char line[100], *result;

    if( (stream = fopen( "fgets.c", "r" )) != NULL )
    {
        if( fgets( line, 100, stream ) == NULL)
            printf( "fgets error\n" );
        else
            printf( "%s", line);
        fclose( stream );
    }
}
```

Output   /* FGETS.C: This program uses fgets to display a line from a file on the

_fieeetomsbin, _fmsbintoieee

Description

Convert floating-point numbers between IEEE and Microsoft binary formats.

#include <math.h>

int _fieeetomsbin(float *_src4_, float *_dst4_);

int _fmsbintoieee(float *_src4_, float *_dst4_);

scr4	Value to be converted
dst4	Converted value

Remarks

The **_fieeetomsbin** routine converts a single-precision floating-point number in IEEE (Institute of Electrical and Electronic Engineers) format to Microsoft (MS) binary format.

The **_fmsbintoieee** routine converts a floating-point number in Microsoft binary format to IEEE format.

These routines allow C programs (which store floating-point numbers in the IEEE format) to use numeric data in random-access data files created with Microsoft Basic (which stores floating-point numbers in the Microsoft binary format), and vice versa.

The argument _src4_ points to the **float** value to be converted. The result is stored at the location given by _dst4_.

These routines do not handle IEEE NANs ("not a number") and infinities. IEEE denormals are treated as 0 in the conversions.

Return Value

These functions return 0 if the conversion is successful and 1 if the conversion causes an overflow.

Compatibility

Standards:	None
16-Bit:	DOS, QWIN, WIN, WIN DLL
32-Bit:	DOS32X

See Also

_dieeetomsbin, _dmsbintoieee

_filelength

Description

Gets the length of a file.

#include <io.h>   Required only for function declarations

long _filelength(int *handle* **);**

handle   Target file handle

Remarks

The **_filelength** function returns the length, in bytes, of the target file associated with *handle*.

Return Value

The **_filelength** function returns the file length in bytes. A return value of –1L indicates an error, and an invalid handle sets **errno** to **EBADF**.

Compatibility

Standards: None
16-Bit: DOS, QWIN, WIN, WIN DLL
32-Bit: DOS32X

See Also

_chsize, _fileno, _fstat, _stat

Example

```
/* CHSIZE.C: This program uses _filelength to report the size of a
 * file before and after modifying it with _chsize.
 */

#include <io.h>
#include <fcntl.h>
#include <sys\types.h>
#include <sys\stat.h>
#include <stdio.h>
```

```
void main( void )
{
    int fh, result;
    unsigned int nbytes = BUFSIZ;

    /* Open a file */
    if( (fh = _open( "data", _O_RDWR | _O_CREAT,
                            _S_IREAD | _S_IWRITE )) != -1 )
    {
        printf( "File length before: %ld\n", _filelength( fh ) );
        if( _chsize( fh, 329678 ) == 0 )
            printf( "Size successfully changed\n" );
        else
            printf( "Problem in changing the size\n" );
        printf( "File length after:  %ld\n", _filelength( fh ) );
        _close( fh );
    }
}
```

Output

```
File length before: 0
Size successfully changed
File length after:  329678
```

_fileno

Description

Gets the file handle associated with a stream.

#include <stdio.h>

int _fileno(FILE *stream);

stream   Pointer to **FILE** structure

Remarks

The **_fileno** routine returns the file handle currently associated with *stream*. This routine is implemented both as a function and as a macro.

Return Value

The **_fileno** routine returns the file handle. There is no error return. The result is undefined if *stream* does not specify an open file.

Compatibility

Standards: UNIX
16-Bit: DOS, QWIN, WIN, WIN DLL
32-Bit: DOS32X

Use **_fileno** for compatibility with ANSI naming conventions of non-ANSI functions. Use **fileno** and link with OLDNAMES.LIB for UNIX compatibility.

See Also

_fdopen, _filelength, fopen, freopen

Example

```
/* FILENO.C: This program uses _fileno to obtain the file handle for
 * some standard C streams.
 */

#include <stdio.h>

void main( void )
{
    printf( "The file handle for stdin is %d\n", _fileno( stdin ) );
    printf( "The file handle for stdout is %d\n", _fileno( stdout ) );
    printf( "The file handle for stderr is %d\n", _fileno( stderr ) );
}
```

Output

```
The file handle for stdin is 0
The file handle for stdout is 1
The file handle for stderr is 2
```

_floodfill, _floodfill_w

Description

Fill an area of a display using the current color and fill mask.

#include <graph.h>

short __far _floodfill(short *x*, short *y*, short *boundary*);

short __far _floodfill_w(double *wx*, double *wy*, short *boundary*);

x, *y*	Start point
wx, *wy*	Start point
boundary	Boundary color of area to be filled

Remarks

The functions in the **_floodfill** family fill an area of the display, using the current color and fill mask. The **_floodfill** routine begins filling at the view-coordinate point (x, y). The **_floodfill_w** routine begins filling at the window-coordinate point (wx, wy).

If this point lies inside the figure, the interior is filled; if it lies outside the figure, the background is filled. The point must be inside or outside the figure to be filled, not on the figure boundary itself. Filling occurs in all directions, stopping at the color of *boundary*.

Return Value

The **_floodfill** functions return a nonzero value if the fill is successful. They return 0 if the fill could not be completed, the starting point lies on the *boundary* color, or the start point lies outside the clipping region.

Compatibility

Standards:	None
16-Bit:	DOS
32-Bit:	None

See Also

_ellipse functions, **_getcolor**, **_getfillmask**, **_grstatus**, **_pie** functions, **_setfillmask**, **_setcliprgn**, **_setcolor**

Example

```
/* FLOODFIL.C: This program draws a series of nested rectangles in
 * different colors, constantly changing the background color.
 */

#include <conio.h>
#include <stdlib.h>
#include <graph.h>

void main( void )
{
    int loop;
    int xvar, yvar;

    /* find a valid graphics mode */
    if( !_setvideomode( _MAXCOLORMODE ) )
        exit( 1 );

    for( xvar = 163, loop = 0; xvar < 320; loop++, xvar += 3 )
    {
        _setcolor( loop % 16 );
        yvar = xvar * 5 / 8;
        _rectangle( _GBORDER, 320-xvar, 200-yvar, xvar, yvar );
        _setcolor( rand() % 16 );
        _floodfill( 0, 0, loop % 16 );
    }
    _getch();
    _setvideomode( _DEFAULTMODE );
}
```

floor, _floorl

Description

Calculate the floor of a value.

#include <math.h>

double floor(double *x* **);**

long double _floorl(long double *x* **);**

x   Floating-point value

Remarks

The **floor** and **_floorl** functions return a floating-point value representing the largest integer that is less than or equal to *x*.

The **_floorl** function is the 80-bit counterpart, and it uses the 80-bit, 10-byte co-processor form of arguments and return values. See the reference page on the long double functions for more details on this data type.

Return Value

These functions return the floating-point result. There is no error return.

Compatibility

floor

Standards:	ANSI, UNIX
16-Bit:	DOS, QWIN, WIN, WIN DLL
32-Bit:	DOS32X

_floorl

Standards:	None
16-Bit:	DOS, QWIN, WIN, WIN DLL
32-Bit:	None

See Also

ceil, fmod

Example   ```
/* FLOOR.C: This example displays the largest integers less than or equal
 * to the floating-point values 2.8 and -2.8. It then shows the smallest
 * integers greater than or equal to 2.8 and -2.8.
 */

#include <math.h>
#include <stdio.h>

void main(void)
{
    double y;

    y = floor(2.8);
    printf("The floor of 2.8 is %f\n", y);
    y = floor(-2.8);
    printf("The floor of -2.8 is %f\n", y);

    y = ceil(2.8);
    printf("The ceil of 2.8 is %f\n", y);
    y = ceil(-2.8);
    printf("The ceil of -2.8 is %f\n", y);
}
```

**Output**    ```
The floor of 2.8 is 2.000000
The floor of -2.8 is -3.000000
The ceil of 2.8 is 3.000000
The ceil of -2.8 is -2.000000
```

_flushall

Description

Flushes all streams; clears all buffers.

#include <stdio.h>

int _flushall(void);

Remarks

The **_flushall** function writes to its associated files the contents of all buffers associated with open output streams. All buffers associated with open input streams are cleared of their current contents. The next read operation (if there is one) then reads new data from the input files into the buffers.

Buffers are automatically flushed when they are full, when streams are closed, or when a program terminates normally without closing streams.

All streams remain open after the call to **_flushall**.

Return Value

The **_flushall** function returns the number of open streams (input and output). There is no error return.

Compatibility

Standards: None
16-Bit: DOS, QWIN, WIN, WIN DLL
32-Bit: DOS32X

See Also

fflush

Example

```
/* FLUSHALL.C: This program uses _flushall to flush all open buffers. */

#include <stdio.h>

void main( void )
{
    int numflushed;

    numflushed = _flushall();
    printf( "There were %d streams flushed\n", numflushed );
}
```

Output

```
There were 3 streams flushed
```

fmod, _fmodl

Description
Calculate the floating-point remainder.

#include <math.h>

double fmod(double *x*, **double** *y* **);**

long double _fmodl(long double *x*, **long double** *y* **);**

x, y   Floating-point values

Remarks
The **fmod** and **_fmodl** functions calculate the floating-point remainder f of x / y such that $x = i * y + f$, where i is an integer, f has the same sign as x, and the absolute value of f is less than the absolute value of y.

The **_fmodl** function is the 80-bit counterpart; it uses the 80-bit, 10-byte coprocessor form of arguments and return values. See the discussion of the long double functions for more details on this data type.

Return Value
These functions return the floating-point remainder. If y is 0, the function returns 0.

Compatibility
fmod

Standards:	ANSI, UNIX
16-Bit:	DOS, QWIN, WIN, WIN DLL
32-Bit:	DOS32X

_fmodl

Standards:	None
16-Bit:	DOS, QWIN, WIN, WIN DLL
32-Bit:	None

See Also
ceil, fabs, floor

Example   `/* FMOD.C: This program displays a floating-point remainder. */`

```
#include <math.h>
#include <stdio.h>

void main( void )
{
    double x = -10.0, y = 3.0, z;

    z = fmod( x, y );
    printf( "The remainder of %.2f / %.2f is %f\n", x, y, z );
}
```

Output   `The remainder of -10.00 / 3.00 is -1.000000`

fopen

Description   Opens a file.

#include <stdio.h>

FILE *fopen(const char *filename, const char *mode);

| filename | Path name of file |
| mode | Type of access permitted |

Remarks   The **fopen** function opens the file specified by filename. The character string mode specifies the type of access requested for the file, as follows:

Type	Description
"r"	Opens for reading. If the file does not exist or cannot be found, the **fopen** call will fail.
"w"	Opens an empty file for writing. If the given file exists, its contents are destroyed.
"a"	Opens for writing at the end of the file (appending); creates the file first if it doesn't exist.
"r+"	Opens for both reading and writing. (The file must exist.)
"w+"	Opens an empty file for both reading and writing. If the given file exists, its contents are destroyed.
"a+"	Opens for reading and appending; creates the file first if it doesn't exist.

When a file is opened with the **"a"** or **"a+"** access type, all write operations occur at the end of the file. Although the file pointer can be repositioned using **fseek** or **rewind**, the file pointer is always moved back to the end of the file before any write operation is carried out. Thus, existing data cannot be overwritten.

When the **"r+"**, **"w+"**, or **"a+"** access type is specified, both reading and writing are allowed (the file is said to be open for "update"). However, when you switch between reading and writing, there must be an intervening **fsetpos**, **fseek**, or **rewind** operation. The current position can be specified for the **fsetpos** or **fseek** operation, if desired.

In addition to the values listed above, the following characters can be included in *mode* to specify the translation mode for newline characters:

Mode	Meaning
t	Open in text (translated) mode. In this mode, carriage-return–line-feed (CR-LF) combinations are translated into single line feeds (LF) on input and LF characters are translated to CR-LF combinations on output. Also, CTRL+Z is interpreted as an end-of-file character on input. In files opened for reading or for reading/writing, **fopen** checks for a CTRL+Z at the end of the file and removes it, if possible. This is done because using the **fseek** and **ftell** functions to move within a file that ends with a CTRL+Z may cause **fseek** to behave improperly near the end of the file.
b	Open in binary (untranslated) mode; the above translations are suppressed.
c	Enable the commit flag for the associated *filename* so that the contents of the file buffer are written directly to disk if either **fflush** or **_flushall** is called.
n	Reset the commit flag for the associated *filename* to "no-commit". This is the default. It will also override the global commit flag if you have linked your program with COMMODE.OBJ. The global commit flag default is "no-commit" unless you explicitly link your program with COMMODE.OBJ.

If **t** or **b** is not given in *mode*, the translation mode is defined by the default-mode variable **_fmode**. If **t** or **b** is prefixed to the argument, the function will fail and return **NULL**.

For a discussion of text and binary modes see "Input and Output" on page 31.

Return Value

The **fopen** function returns a pointer to the open file. A null pointer value indicates an error.

Compatibility

Standards:	ANSI, UNIX
16-Bit:	DOS, QWIN, WIN, WIN DLL
32-Bit:	DOS32X

Note that the **c**, **n**, and **t** options are not part of the ANSI standard for **fopen**; they are Microsoft extensions and should not be used where ANSI portability is desired.

See Also

fclose, _fcloseall, _fdopen, ferror, _fileno, freopen, _open, _setmode

Example

```
/* FOPEN.C: This program opens files named "data" and "data2". It uses
 * fclose to _close "data" and _fcloseall to close all remaining files.
 */

#include <stdio.h>

FILE *stream, *stream2;

void main( void )
{
   int numclosed;

   /* Open for read (will fail if 'data' does not exist) */
   if( (stream  = fopen( "data", "r" )) == NULL )
      printf( "The file 'data' was not opened\n" );
   else
      printf( "The file 'data' was opened\n" );

   /* Open for write */
   if( (stream2 = fopen( "data2", "w+" )) == NULL )
      printf( "The file 'data2' was not opened\n" );
   else
      printf( "The file 'data2' was opened\n" );

   /* Close stream */
   if( fclose( stream ) )
      printf( "The file 'data' was not closed\n" );

   /* All other files are closed: */
   numclosed = _fcloseall( );
   printf( "Number of files closed by _fcloseall: %u\n", numclosed );
}
```

Output

```
The file 'data' was opened
The file 'data2' was opened
Number of files closed by _fcloseall: 1
```

_FP_OFF, _FP_SEG

Description   Get or set a far-pointer offset (**_FP_OFF**) or a far-pointer segment (**_FP_SEG**).

#include <dos.h>

unsigned _FP_OFF(void __far **address**);

unsigned _FP_SEG(void __far **address**);

address   Far pointer to memory address

Remarks   The **_FP_OFF** and **_FP_SEG** macros can be used to set or get the offset and segment, respectively, of the far pointer at *address*.

Return Value   The **_FP_OFF** macro returns an offset. The **_FP_SEG** macro returns a segment address.

Compatibility   Standards: None
16-Bit: DOS, QWIN, WIN, WIN DLL
32-Bit: None

Example
```
/* _FP_SEG.C: This program uses _FP_SEG and _FP_OFF to obtain
 * the segment and offset of the long pointer p.
 */

#include <dos.h>
#include <malloc.h>
#include <stdio.h>

void main( void )
{
    void __far *p;
    unsigned int seg_val;
    unsigned int off_val;

    p = _fmalloc( 100 );         /* Points pointer at something */

    seg_val = _FP_SEG( p );      /* Gets address pointed to */
    off_val = _FP_OFF( p );

    printf( "Segment is %.4X; Offset is %.4X\n", seg_val, off_val );
}
```

Output   Segment is 00C7; Offset is 0016

_fpreset

Description

Resets the floating-point package.

#include <float.h>

void _fpreset(void);

Remarks

The **_fpreset** function reinitializes the floating-point-math package. This function is usually used in conjunction with **signal**, **system**, or the **_exec** or **_spawn** functions.

If a program traps floating-point error signals (**SIGFPE**) with **signal**, it can safely recover from floating-point errors by invoking **_fpreset** and using **longjmp**.

In DOS versions prior to 3.0, a child process executed by **_exec**, **_spawn**, or **system** may affect the floating-point state of the parent process if an 8087, 80287, or 80387 coprocessor is used. If you are using either coprocessor, the following precautions are recommended:

- The **_exec**, **_spawn**, and **system** functions should not be called during the evaluation of a floating-point expression.
- The **_fpreset** function should be called after these routines if there is a possibility of the child process performing any floating-point operations.

Return Value

None.

Compatibility

Standards: None
16-Bit: DOS, QWIN, WIN, WIN DLL
32-Bit: DOS32X

See Also

_exec functions, **signal**, **_spawn** functions

Example

```
/* FPRESET.C: This program uses signal to set up a routine for handling
 * floating-point errors.
 */

#include <stdio.h>
#include <signal.h>
#include <setjmp.h>
#include <stdlib.h>
#include <float.h>
#include <math.h>
#include <string.h>

jmp_buf mark;                   /* Address for long jump to jump to */
int  fperr;                     /* Global error number */

void fphandler( int sig, int num ); /* Prototypes */
void fpcheck( void );

void main( void )
{
    double n1, n2, r;
    int jmpret;

    /* Set up floating-point error handler. The compiler
     * will generate a warning because it expects
     * signal-handling functions to take only one argument.
     */
    if( signal( SIGFPE, fphandler ) == SIG_ERR )
    {
        fprintf( stderr, "Couldn't set SIGFPE\n" );
        abort();
    }

    /* Save stack environment for return in case of error. First time
     * through, jmpret is 0, so true conditional is executed. If an
     * error occurs, jmpret will be set to -1 and false conditional
     * will be executed.
     */
    jmpret = setjmp( mark );
    if( jmpret == 0 )
    {
        printf( "Test for invalid operation - " );
        printf( "enter two numbers: " );
        scanf( "%lf %lf", &n1, &n2 );

        r = n1 / n2;
        /* This won't be reached if error occurs. */
        printf( "\n\n%4.3g / %4.3g = %4.3g\n", n1, n2, r );
```

```
            r = n1 * n2;
            /* This won't be reached if error occurs. */
            printf( "\n\n%4.3g * %4.3g = %4.3g\n", n1, n2, r );
        }
    else
        fpcheck();
}

/* fphandler handles SIGFPE (floating-point error) interrupt. Note
 * that this prototype accepts two arguments and that the prototype
 * for signal in the run-time library expects a signal handler to
 * have only one argument.
 *
 * The second argument in this signal handler allows processing of
 * _FPE_INVALID, _FPE_OVERFLOW, _FPE_UNDERFLOW, and _FPE_ZERODIVIDE
 * all of which are Microsoft-specific symbols that augment the
 * information provided by SIGFPE. The compiler will generate a
 * warning, which is harmless and expected.
 */
void fphandler( int sig, int num )
{
    /* Set global for outside check since we don't want
     * to do I/O in the handler.
     */
    fperr = num;

    /* Initialize floating-point package. */
    _fpreset();

    /* Restore calling environment and jump back to setjmp. Return -1
     * so that setjmp will return false for conditional test.
     */
    longjmp( mark, -1 );
}

void fpcheck( void )
{
    char fpstr[30];

    switch( fperr )
    {
        case _FPE_INVALID:
            strcpy( fpstr, "Invalid number" );
            break;

        case _FPE_OVERFLOW:
            strcpy( fpstr, "Overflow" );
            break;

        case _FPE_UNDERFLOW:
            strcpy( fpstr, "Underflow" );
            break;
```

```
            case _FPE_ZERODIVIDE:
                strcpy( fpstr, "Divide by zero" );
                break;

            default:
                strcpy( fpstr, "Other floating point error" );
                break;
        }
        printf( "Error %d: %s\n", fperr, fpstr );
    }
```

Output   Test for invalid operation - enter two numbers: 5 0
Error 131: Divide by zero

fprintf

Description

Prints formatted data to a stream.

#include <stdio.h>

int fprintf(FILE *_stream_, const char *_format_ [[, _argument_]]...);

stream	Pointer to **FILE** structure
format	Format-control string
argument	Optional arguments

Remarks

The **fprintf** function formats and prints a series of characters and values to the output _stream_. Each _argument_ (if any) is converted and output according to the corresponding format specification in _format_.

The _format_ argument has the same form and function that it does for the **printf** function; see the Remarks section for the **printf** function for more information on _format_ and _argument_.

Return Value

The **fprintf** function returns the number of characters printed, or a negative value in the case of an output error.

Compatibility

Standards: ANSI, UNIX

16-Bit: DOS, QWIN, WIN

32-Bit: DOS32X

See Also

_cprintf, fscanf, printf, sprintf

Example

```
/* FPRINTF.C: This program uses fprintf to format various data and
 * print them to the file named FPRINTF.OUT. It then displays
 * FPRINTF.OUT on the screen using the system function to invoke
 * the DOS TYPE command.
 */

#include <stdio.h>
#include <process.h>

FILE *stream;

void main( void )
{
    int    i = 10;
    double fp = 1.5;
    char   s[] = "this is a string";
    char   c = '\n';

    stream = fopen( "fprintf.out", "w" );
    fprintf( stream, "%s%c", s, c );
    fprintf( stream, "%d\n", i );
    fprintf( stream, "%f\n", fp );
    fclose( stream );
    system( "type fprintf.out" );
}
```

Output

```
this is a string
10
1.500000
```

fputc, _fputchar

Description

Write a character to a stream (**fputc**) or to stdout (**_fputchar**).

#include <stdio.h>

int fputc(int *c*, **FILE ***stream* **);**

int _fputchar(int *c* **);**

c	Character to be written
stream	Pointer to **FILE** structure

Remarks

The **fputc** function writes the single character *c* to the output *stream* at the current position. The **_fputchar** function is equivalent to **fputc**(*c*, **stdout**).

The **fputc** and **_fputchar** routines are similar to **putc** and **putchar**, but are functions rather than macros.

Return Value

The **fputc** and **_fputchar** functions return the character written. A return value of **EOF** indicates an error.

Compatibility

fputc

Standards:	ANSI, UNIX
16-Bit:	DOS, QWIN, WIN, WIN DLL
32-Bit:	DOS32X

_fputchar

Standards:	None
16-Bit:	DOS, QWIN
32-Bit:	DOS32X

See Also

fgetc, _fgetchar, putc, putchar

Example   /* FPUTC.C: This program uses fputc and _fputchar to send a character
                 * array to stdout.
                 */

```
#include <stdio.h>

void main( void )
{
    char strptr1[] = "This is a test of fputc!!\n";
    char strptr2[] = "This is a test of _fputchar!!\n";
    char *p;

    /* Print line to stream using fputc. */
    p = strptr1;
    while( (*p != '\0') && fputc( *(p++), stdout ) != EOF )
        ;

    /* Print line to stream using _fputchar. */
    p = strptr2;
    while( (*p != '\0') && _fputchar( *(p++) ) != EOF )
        ;
}
```

Output   This is a test of fputc!!
                This is a test of _fputchar!!

fputs

Description   Writes a string to a stream.

#include <stdio.h>

int fputs(const char **string***, FILE ****stream***);**

string	String to be output
stream	Pointer to **FILE** structure

Remarks   The **fputs** function copies *string* to the output *stream* at the current position. The terminating null character ('**\0**') is not copied.

Return Value   The **fputs** function returns a nonnegative value if it is successful. If an error occurs, it returns **EOF**.

Compatibility   Standards: ANSI, UNIX
16-Bit: DOS, QWIN, WIN, WIN DLL
32-Bit: DOS32X

See Also   **fgets, gets, puts**

Example
```
/* FPUTS.C: This program uses fputs to write a single line to the
 * stdout stream.
 */

#include <stdio.h>

void main( void )
{
    fputs( "Hello world from fputs.\n", stdout );
}
```

Output   Hello world from fputs.

fread

Description

Reads data from a stream.

#include <stdio.h>

size_t fread(void ***buffer*, size_t** *size***, size_t** *count***, FILE ***stream* **);**

buffer	Storage location for data
size	Item size in bytes
count	Maximum number of items to be read
stream	Pointer to **FILE** structure

Remarks

The **fread** function reads up to *count* items of *size* bytes from the input *stream* and stores them in *buffer*. The file pointer associated with *stream* (if there is one) is increased by the number of bytes actually read.

If the given stream is opened in text mode, carriage-return–line-feed pairs are replaced with single line-feed characters. The replacement has no effect on the file pointer or the return value.

The file-pointer position is indeterminate if an error occurs. The value of a partially read item cannot be determined.

Return Value

The **fread** function returns the number of full items actually read, which may be less than *count* if an error occurs or if the file end is encountered before reaching *count*.

The **feof** or **ferror** function should be used to distinguish a read error from an end-of-file condition. If *size* or *count* is 0, **fread** returns 0 and the buffer contents are unchanged.

Compatibility

Standards:	ANSI, UNIX
16-Bit:	DOS, QWIN, WIN, WIN DLL
32-Bit:	DOS32X

See Also

fwrite, _read

Example

```
/* FREAD.C: This program opens a file named FREAD.OUT and writes 25
 * characters to the file. It then tries to open FREAD.OUT and
 * read in 25 characters. If the attempt succeeds, the program
 * displays the number of actual items read.
 */

#include <stdio.h>

void main( void )
{
    FILE *stream;
    char list[30];
    int  i, numread, numwritten;

    /* Open file in text mode: */
    if( (stream = fopen( "fread.out", "w+t" )) != NULL )
    {
        for ( i = 0; i < 25; i++ )
            list[i] = 'z' - i;
        /* Write 25 characters to stream */
        numwritten = fwrite( list, sizeof( char ), 25, stream );
        printf( "Wrote %d items\n", numwritten );
        fclose( stream );
    }
    else
        printf( "Problem opening the file\n" );

    if( (stream = fopen( "fread.out", "r+t" )) != NULL )
    {
        /* Attempt to read in 25 characters */
        numread = fread( list, sizeof( char ), 25, stream );
        printf( "Number of items read = %d\n", numread );
        printf( "Contents of buffer = %.25s\n", list );
        fclose( stream );
    }
    else
        printf( "Was not able to open the file\n" );
}
```

Output

```
Wrote 25 items
Number of items read = 25
Contents of buffer = zyxwvutsrqponmlkjihgfedcb
```

free Functions

Description   Deallocate a memory block.

    #include <stdlib.h>   For ANSI compatibility (**free** only)

    #include <malloc.h>   Required only for function declarations

    void free(void *memblock* **);**

    void _bfree(__segment *seg*, **void __based(void) *** *memblock* **);**

    void _ffree(void __far * *memblock* **);**

    void _nfree(void __near * *memblock* **);**

    memblock   Allocated memory block

    seg   Based-heap segment selector

Remarks   The **free** family of functions deallocates a memory block. The argument
memblock points to a memory block previously allocated through a call to **calloc**,
malloc, or **realloc**. The number of bytes freed is the number of bytes specified
when the block was allocated (or reallocated, in the case of **realloc**). After the call,
the freed block is available for allocation.

The *seg* argument specifies the based heap containing the memory block to be
freed by the **_bfree** function.

Attempting to free an invalid pointer may affect subsequent allocation and cause
errors. An invalid pointer is one not allocated with the appropriate call.

The following restrictions apply to use of the **free**, **_bfree**, **_ffree**, and **_nfree**
functions:

Blocks allocated with:	Should be freed with:
calloc, malloc, realloc	**free**
_bcalloc, _bmalloc, _brealloc	**_bfree**
_fcalloc, _fmalloc, _frealloc	**_ffree**
_ncalloc, _nmalloc, _nrealloc	**_nfree**

A **NULL** pointer argument is ignored.

In large data models (compact-, large-, and huge-model programs), **free** maps to **_ffree**. In small data models (tiny-, small-, and medium-model programs), **free** maps to **_nfree**.

The various **free** functions deallocate a memory block in the segments shown in the list below:

Function	Data Segment
free	Depends on data model of program
_bfree	Based heap specified by *seg* value
_ffree	Far heap (outside default data segment)
_nfree	Near heap (inside default data segment)

Return Value   None.

Compatibility   **free**

Standards: ANSI, UNIX

16-Bit: DOS, QWIN, WIN, WIN DLL

32-Bit: DOS32X

_bfree, _ffree, _nfree

Standards: None

16-Bit: DOS, WIN, WIN DLL

32-Bit: None

See Also   **calloc** functions, **malloc** functions, **realloc** functions

Example

```
/* MALLOC.C: This program allocates memory with malloc, then frees
 * the memory with free.
 */

#include <stdlib.h>        /* Definition of _MAX_PATH */
#include <stdio.h>
#include <malloc.h>
```

```
void main( void )
{
    char *string;

    /* Allocate space for a path name */
    string = malloc( _MAX_PATH );
    if( string == NULL )
        printf( "Insufficient memory available\n" );
    else
        printf( "Memory space allocated for path name\n" );
    free( string );
    printf( "Memory freed\n" );
}
```

Output   Memory space allocated for path name
Memory freed

_freect

Description

Returns the amount of memory available for memory allocation.

#include <malloc.h>   Required only for function declarations

unsigned int _freect(size_t *size* **);**

size   Item size in bytes

Remarks

The **_freect** function tells you how much memory is available for dynamic memory allocation in the near heap. It does so by returning the approximate number of times your program can call **_nmalloc** (or **malloc** in small data models) to allocate an item *size* bytes long in the near heap (default data segment).

Return Value

The **_freect** function returns the number of calls as an unsigned integer.

Compatibility

Standards: None
16-Bit: DOS, QWIN, WIN, WIN DLL
32-Bit: None

See Also

calloc functions, **_expand** functions, **malloc** functions, **_memavl**, **_msize** functions, **realloc** functions

Example

```
/* FREECT.C: This program determines how much free space is available for
 * integers in the default data segment. Then it allocates space for
 * 1,000 integers and checks the space again, using _freect.
 */

#include <malloc.h>
#include <stdio.h>
```

```
void main( void )
{
    int i;

    /* First report on the free space: */
    printf( "Integers (approximate) available on heap: %u\n\n",
            _freect( sizeof( int ) ) );

    /* Allocate space for 1000 integers: */
    for( i = 0; i < 1000; ++i )
        malloc( sizeof( int ) );

    /* Report again on the free space: */
    printf( "After allocating space for 1000 integers:\n" );
    printf( "Integers (approximate) available on heap: %u\n\n",
            _freect( sizeof( int ) ) );
}
```

Output

```
Integers (approximate) available on heap: 15212

After allocating space for 1000 integers:
Integers (approximate) available on heap: 14084
```

freopen

Description   Reassigns a file pointer.

#include <stdio.h>

FILE *freopen(const char **filename***, const char** **mode***, FILE** **stream* **);**

filename	Path name of new file
mode	Type of access permitted
stream	Pointer to **FILE** structure

Remarks   The **freopen** function closes the file currently associated with *stream* and reassigns *stream* to the file specified by *filename*. The **freopen** function is typically used to redirect the pre-opened files **stdin**, **stdout**, and **stderr** to files specified by the user. The new file associated with *stream* is opened with *mode*, which is a character string specifying the type of access requested for the file, as follows:

Type	Description
"r"	Opens for reading. If the file does not exist or cannot be found, the **freopen** call fails.
"w"	Opens an empty file for writing. If the given file exists, its contents are destroyed.
"a"	Opens for writing at the end of the file (appending); creates the file first if it does not exist.
"r+"	Opens for both reading and writing. (The file must exist.)
"w+"	Opens an empty file for both reading and writing. If the given file exists, its contents are destroyed.
"a+"	Opens for reading and appending; creates the file first if it does not exist.

Use the **"w"** and **"w+"** types with care, as they can destroy existing files.

When a file is opened with the **"a"** or **"a+"** access type, all write operations take place at the end of the file. Although the file pointer can be repositioned using **fseek** or **rewind**, the file pointer is always moved back to the end of the file before any write operation is carried out. Thus, existing data cannot be overwritten.

When the **"r+"**, **"w+"**, or **"a+"** access type is specified, both reading and writing are allowed (the file is said to be open for "update"). However, when you switch between reading and writing, there must be an intervening **fsetpos**, **fseek**, or **rewind** operation. The current position can be specified for the **fsetpos** or **fseek** operation, if desired.

In addition to the values listed above, one of the following characters may be included in the *mode* string to specify the translation mode for new lines.

Mode	Meaning
t	Open in text (translated) mode; carriage-return–line-feed (CR-LF) combinations are translated into single line-feed (LF) characters on input; LF characters are translated to CR-LF combinations on output. Also, CTRL+Z is interpreted as an end-of-file character on input. In files opened for reading, or writing and reading, the run-time library checks for a CTRL+Z at the end of the file and removes it, if possible. This is done because using the **fseek** and **ftell** functions to move within a file may cause **fseek** to behave improperly near the end of the file.
b	Open in binary (untranslated) mode; the above translations are suppressed.

If **t** or **b** is not given in the *mode* string, the translation mode is defined by the default mode variable **_fmode**.

See "Input and Output" on page 31 for a discussion of text and binary modes.

Return Value

The **freopen** function returns a pointer to the newly opened file. If an error occurs, the original file is closed and the function returns a **NULL** pointer value.

Compatibility

Standards: ANSI, UNIX

16-Bit: DOS, QWIN, WIN, WIN DLL

32-Bit: DOS32X

The **t** option is not part of the ANSI standard for **freopen**; it is a Microsoft extension that should not be used where ANSI portability is desired.

See Also

fclose, _fcloseall, _fdopen, _fileno, fopen, _open, _setmode

Example

```
/* FREOPEN.C: This program reassigns stdaux to the file
 * named FREOPEN.OUT and writes a line to that file.
 */

#include <stdio.h>
#include <stdlib.h>

FILE *stream;

void main( void )
{
   /* Reassign "stdaux" to "freopen.out": */
   stream = freopen( "freopen.out", "w", stdaux );

   if( stream == NULL )
      fprintf( stdout, "error on freopen\n" );
   else
   {
      fprintf( stream, "This will go to the file 'freopen.out'\n" );
      fprintf( stdout, "successfully reassigned\n" );
      fclose( stream );
   }
   system( "type freopen.out" );
}
```

Output

```
successfully reassigned
This will go to the file 'freopen.out'
```

frexp, _frexpl

Description

Get the mantissa and exponent of a floating-point number.

#include <math.h>

double frexp(double *x*, **int** **expptr* **);**

long double _frexpl(long double *x*, **int** **expptr* **);**

x	Floating-point value
expptr	Pointer to stored integer exponent

Remarks

The **frexp** and **_frexpl** functions break down the floating-point value (*x*) into a mantissa (*m*) and an exponent (*n*), such that the absolute value of *m* is greater than or equal to 0.5 and less than 1.0, and $x = m*2^n$. The integer exponent *n* is stored at the location pointed to by *expptr*.

The **_frexpl** function is the 80-bit counterpart and uses an 80-bit, 10-byte co-processor form of arguments and return values. See the reference page on the long double functions for more details on this data type.

Return Value

These functions return the mantissa. If *x* is 0, the function returns 0 for both the mantissa and the exponent. There is no error return.

Compatibility

frexp

Standards:	ANSI, UNIX
16-Bit:	DOS, QWIN, WIN, WIN DLL
32-Bit:	DOS32X

_frexpl

Standards:	None
16-Bit:	DOS, QWIN, WIN, WIN DLL
32-Bit:	None

See Also

ldexp functions, **modf**

Example

```
/* FREXP.C: This program calculates frexp( 16.4, &n ), then displays y
 * and n.
 */

#include <math.h>
#include <stdio.h>

void main( void )
{
    double x, y;
    int n;

    x = 16.4;
    y = frexp( x, &n );
    printf( "frexp( %f, &n ) = %f, n = %d\n", x, y, n );
}
```

Output

```
frexp( 16.400000, &n ) = 0.512500, n = 5
```

fscanf

Description   Reads formatted data from a stream.

#include <stdio.h>

int fscanf(FILE *stream, const char *format [[, argument]]...);

stream	Pointer to **FILE** structure
format	Format-control string
argument	Optional arguments

Remarks   The **fscanf** function reads data from the current position of *stream* into the locations given by *argument* (if any). Each argument must be a pointer to a variable with a type that corresponds to a type specifier in *format*. The format controls the interpretation of the input fields and has the same form and function as the *format* argument for the **scanf** function; see **scanf** for a description of *format*.

Return Value   The **fscanf** function returns the number of fields that were successfully converted and assigned. The return value does not include fields that were read but not assigned.

The return value is **EOF** for an error or end-of-file on *stream* before the first conversion. A return value of 0 means that no fields were assigned.

Compatibility   Standards: ANSI, UNIX
16-Bit: DOS, QWIN, WIN
32-Bit: DOS32X

See Also   _ cscanf, fprintf, scanf, sscanf

Example

```
/* FSCANF.C: This program writes formatted data to a file. It
 * then uses fscanf to read the various data back from the file.
 */

#include <stdio.h>

FILE *stream;

void main( void )
{
    long l;
    float fp;
    char s[81];
    char c;
    int result;

    stream = fopen( "fscanf.out", "w+" );
    if( stream == NULL )
        printf( "The file fscanf.out was not opened\n" );
    else
    {
        fprintf( stream, "%s %ld %f%c", "a-string", 65000, 3.14159, 'x' );

        /* Set pointer to beginning of file: */
        fseek( stream, 0L, SEEK_SET );

        /* Read data back from file: */
        fscanf( stream, "%s", s );
        fscanf( stream, "%ld", &l );
        fscanf( stream, "%f", &fp );
        fscanf( stream, "%c", &c );

        /* Output data read: */
        printf( "%s\n", s );
        printf( "%ld\n", l );
        printf( "%f\n", fp );
        printf( "%c\n", c );

        fclose( stream );
    }
}
```

Output

```
a-string
65000
3.141590
x
```

fseek

Description

Moves the file pointer to a specified location.

#include <stdio.h>

int fseek(FILE *stream, long offset, int origin);

stream	Pointer to **FILE** structure
offset	Number of bytes from *origin*
origin	Initial position

Remarks

The **fseek** function moves the file pointer (if any) associated with *stream* to a new location that is *offset* bytes from *origin*. The next operation on the stream takes place at the new location. On a stream open for update, the next operation can be either a read or a write.

The argument *origin* must be one of the following constants defined in STDIO.H:

Origin	Definition
SEEK_CUR	Current position of file pointer
SEEK_END	End of file
SEEK_SET	Beginning of file

The **fseek** function can be used to reposition the pointer anywhere in a file. The pointer can also be positioned beyond the end of the file. However, an attempt to position the pointer in front of the beginning of the file causes an error.

The **fseek** function clears the end-of-file indicator and negates the effect of any prior **ungetc** calls against *stream*.

When a file is opened for appending data, the current file position is determined by the last I/O operation, not by where the next write would occur. If no I/O operation has yet occurred on a file opened for appending, the file position is the start of the file.

For streams opened in text mode, **fseek** has limited use because carriage-return–line-feed translations can cause **fseek** to produce unexpected results. The only **fseek** operations guaranteed to work on streams opened in text mode are

- Seeking with an offset of 0 relative to any of the *origin* values

- Seeking from the beginning of the file with an offset value returned from a call to **ftell**

Return Value

If successful, **fseek** returns 0. Otherwise, it returns a nonzero value. On devices incapable of seeking, the return value is undefined.

Compatibility

Standards:	ANSI, UNIX
16-Bit:	DOS, QWIN, WIN, WIN DLL
32-Bit:	DOS32X

See Also

ftell, _lseek, rewind

Example

```
/* FSEEK.C: This program opens the file FSEEK.OUT and
 * moves the pointer to the file's beginning.
 */
#include <stdio.h>

void main( void )
{
   FILE *stream;
   char line[81];
   int  result;

   stream = fopen( "fseek.out", "w+" );
   if( stream == NULL )
      printf( "The file fseek.out was not opened\n" );
   else
   {
      fprintf( stream, "The fseek begins here: "
                       "This is the file 'fseek.out'.\n" );
      result = fseek( stream, 23L, SEEK_SET);
      if( result )
         perror( "Fseek failed" );
      else
      {
         printf( "File pointer is set to middle of first line.\n" );
         fgets( line, 80, stream );
         printf( "%s", line );
      }
      fclose( stream );
   }
}
```

Output   File pointer is set to middle of first line.
              This is the file 'fseek.out'.

fsetpos

Description

Sets the stream-position indicator.

#include <stdio.h>

int fsetpos(FILE *stream, const fpos_t *pos) ;

stream	Target stream
pos	Position-indicator storage

Remarks

The **fsetpos** function sets the file-position indicator for *stream* to the value of *pos*, which is obtained in a prior call to **fgetpos** against *stream*.

The function clears the end-of-file indicator and undoes any effects of the **ungetc** function on *stream*. After calling **fsetpos**, the next operation on *stream* may be either input or output.

Return Value

If successful, the **fsetpos** function returns 0. On failure, the function returns a non-zero value and sets **errno** to one of the following manifest constants (defined in ERRNO.H):

Constant	Meaning
EBADF	The object that *stream* points to is not a valid file handle, or the file is not accessible.
EINVAL	An invalid *stream* value was passed.

Compatibility

Standards:	ANSI
16-Bit:	DOS, QWIN, WIN, WIN DLL
32-Bit:	DOS32X

See Also

fgetpos

Example

```
/* FGETPOS.C: This program opens a file and reads bytes at several
 * different locations.
 */

#include <stdio.h>

void main( void )
{
    FILE   *stream;
    fpos_t pos;
    int    val;
    char   buffer[20];

    if( (stream = fopen( "fgetpos.c", "rb" )) == NULL )
      printf( "Trouble opening file\n" );
    else
    {
        /* Read some data and then check the position. */
        fread( buffer, sizeof( char ), 10, stream );
        if( fgetpos( stream, &pos ) != 0 )
           perror( "fgetpos error" );
        else
        {
            fread( buffer, sizeof( char ), 10, stream );
            printf( "10 bytes at byte %ld: %.10s\n", pos, buffer );
        }

        /* Set a new position and read more data. */
        pos = 140;
        if( fsetpos( stream, &pos ) != 0 )
           perror( "fsetpos error" );

        fread( buffer, sizeof( char ), 10, stream );
           printf( "10 bytes at byte %ld: %.10s\n", pos, buffer );

        fclose( stream );
    }
}
```

Output

```
10 bytes at byte 10: .C: This p
10 bytes at byte 140:    FILE   *
```

_fsopen

Description

Opens a stream with file sharing.

#include <stdio.h>

#include <share.h>   *shflag* constants

FILE *_fsopen(const char **filename***, const char ****mode***, int** *shflag* **);**

filename	Filename to open
mode	Type of access permitted
shflag	Type of sharing allowed

Remarks

The **_fsopen** function opens the file specified by *filename* as a stream and pre-pares the file for subsequent shared reading or writing, as defined by the *mode* and *shflag* arguments.

The character string *mode* specifies the type of access requested for the file, as follows:

Type	Description
"r"	Opens for reading. If the file does not exist or cannot be found, the **_fsopen** call will fail.
"w"	Opens an empty file for writing. If the given file exists, its contents are destroyed.
"a"	Opens for writing at the end of the file (appending); creates the file first if it does not exist.
"r+"	Opens for both reading and writing. (The file must exist.)
"w+"	Opens an empty file for both reading and writing. If the given file exists, its contents are destroyed.
"a+"	Opens for reading and appending; creates the file first if it does not exist.

Use the **"w"** and **"w+"** types with care, as they can destroy existing files.

When a file is opened with the **"a"** or **"a+"** access type, all write operations occur at the end of the file. Although the file pointer can be repositioned using **fseek** or **rewind**, the file pointer is always moved back to the end of the file before any write operation is carried out. Thus, existing data cannot be overwritten.

When the **"r+"**, **"w+"**, or **"a+"** access type is specified, both reading and writing are allowed (the file is said to be open for "update"). However, when switching between reading and writing, there must be an intervening **fsetpos**, **fseek**, or **rewind** operation. The current position can be specified for the **fsetpos** or **fseek** operation, if desired.

In addition to the values listed above, one of the following characters can be included in *mode* to specify the translation mode for new lines:

Mode	Meaning
t	Open in text (translated) mode. In this mode, carriage-return–line-feed (CR-LF) combinations are translated into single line feeds (LF) on input and LF characters are translated to CR-LF combinations on output. Also, CTRL+Z is interpreted as an end-of-file character on input. In files opened for reading or reading/writing, **_fsopen** checks for a CTRL+Z at the end of the file and removes it, if possible. This is done because using the **fseek** and **ftell** functions to move within a file that ends with a CTRL+Z may cause **fseek** to behave improperly near the end of the file.
b	Open in binary (untranslated) mode; the above translations are suppressed.

If **t** or **b** is not given in *mode*, the translation mode is defined by the default-mode variable **_fmode**. If **t** or **b** is prefixed to the argument, the function will fail and will return **NULL**.

See "Input and Output" on page 31 for a discussion of text and binary modes.

The argument *shflag* is a constant expression consisting of one of the following manifest constants, defined in SHARE.H. If SHARE.COM—or SHARE.EXE for some versions of DOS—is not installed, DOS ignores the sharing mode. (See your system documentation for detailed information about sharing modes.)

Constant	Meaning
_SH_COMPAT	Sets compatibility mode
_SH_DENYNO	Permits read and write access
_SH_DENYRD	Denies read access to file
_SH_DENYRW	Denies read and write access to file
_SH_DENYWR	Denies write access to file

The **_fsopen** function should be used only under DOS versions 3.0 and later. Under earlier versions of DOS, the *shflag* argument is ignored.

Return Value

The **_fsopen** function returns a pointer to the stream. A **NULL** pointer value indicates an error.

Compatibility	Standards:	None
	16-Bit:	DOS, QWIN, WIN, WIN DLL
	32-Bit:	DOS32X

See Also **fclose**, **_fcloseall**, **_fdopen**, **ferror**, **_fileno**, **fopen**, **freopen**, **_open**, **_setmode**, **_sopen**

Example

```
/* FSOPEN.C: This program opens files named "data" and "data2". It uses
 * fclose to close "data" and _fcloseall to close all remaining files.
 */

#include <stdio.h>
#include <share.h>

FILE *stream;

void main( void )
{
   FILE *stream;

   /* Open output file for writing. Using _fsopen allows us to ensure
    * that no one else writes to the file while we are writing to it.
    */
   if( (stream = _fsopen( "outfile", "wt", _SH_DENYWR )) != NULL )
   {
      fprintf( stream, "No one else in the network can write "
                       "to this file until we are done.\n" );
      fclose( stream );
   }
   /* Now others can write to the file while we read it. */
   system( "type outfile" );
}
```

Output

```
No one else in the network can write to this file until we are done.
```

_fstat

Description

Gets information about an open file.

#include <sys\types.h>

#include <sys\stat.h>

int _fstat(int *handle*, struct _stat **buffer*);

handle	Handle of open file
buffer	Pointer to structure to store results

Remarks

The **_fstat** function obtains information about the open file associated with *handle* and stores it in the structure pointed to by *buffer*. The structure, whose type **_stat** is defined in SYS\STAT.H, contains the following fields:

Field	Value
st_atime	Time of last access of file.
st_ctime	Time of creation of file.
st_dev	Either the drive number of the disk containing the file, or *handle* in the case of a device (same as **st_rdev**).
st_mode	Bit mask for file-mode information. The **_S_IFCHR** bit is set if *handle* refers to a device. The **_S_IFREG** bit is set if *handle* refers to an ordinary file. The read/write bits are set according to the file's permission mode. (**_S_IFCHR** and other constants are defined in SYS\ STAT.H.)
st_mtime	Time of last modification of file.
st_nlink	Always 1.
st_rdev	Either the drive number of the disk containing the file, or *handle* in the case of a device (same as **st_dev**).
st_size	Size of the file in bytes.

If *handle* refers to a device, the size and time fields in the **_stat** structure are not meaningful.

Return Value

The **_fstat** function returns the value 0 if the file-status information is obtained. A return value of –1 indicates an error; in this case, **errno** is set to **EBADF**, indicating an invalid file handle.

Compatibility	Standards:	UNIX
	16-Bit:	DOS, QWIN, WIN, WIN DLL
	32-Bit:	DOS32X

Use **_fstat** for compatibility with ANSI naming conventions of non-ANSI functions. Use **fstat** and link with OLDNAMES.LIB for UNIX compatibility.

See Also   **_access, _chmod, _filelength, _stat**

Example

```
/* FSTAT.C: This program uses _fstat to report the size of a file
 * named FSTAT.OUT.
 */

#include <io.h>
#include <fcntl.h>
#include <time.h>
#include <sys\types.h>
#include <sys\stat.h>
#include <stdio.h>
#include <stdlib.h>
#include <string.h>

void main( void )
{
    struct _stat buf;
    int fh, result;
    char buffer[] = "A line to output";

    if( (fh = _open( "f_stat.out", _O_CREAT | _O_WRONLY | _O_TRUNC )) == -1 )
        exit( 1 );
    _write( fh, buffer, strlen( buffer ) );

    /* Get data associated with "fh": */

    result = _fstat( fh, &buf );

    /* Check if statistics are valid: */
    if( result != 0 )
        printf( "Bad file handle\n" );
    else
    {
        printf( "File size     : %ld\n", buf.st_size );
        printf( "Drive number  : %d\n", buf.st_dev );
        printf( "Time modified : %s", ctime( &buf.st_atime ) );
    }
    _close( fh );
}
```

Output   File size   : 16
Drive number : 0
Time modified : Tue Jun 15 21:38:46 1999

ftell

Description   Gets the current position of a file pointer.

#include <stdio.h>

long ftell(FILE *stream);

stream   Target **FILE** structure

Remarks   The **ftell** function gets the current position of the file pointer (if any) associated with *stream*. The position is expressed as an offset relative to the beginning of the stream.

Note that when a file is opened for appending data, the current file position is determined by the last I/O operation, not by where the next write would occur. For example, if a file is opened for an append and the last operation was a read, the file position is the point where the next read operation would start, not where the next write would start. (When a file is opened for appending, the file position is moved to end-of-file before any write operation.) If no I/O operation has yet occurred on a file opened for appending, the file position is the beginning of the file.

Return Value   The **ftell** function returns the current file position. The value returned by **ftell** may not reflect the physical byte offset for streams opened in text mode, since text mode causes carriage-return–line-feed translation. Use **ftell** in conjunction with the **fseek** function to return to file locations correctly. On error, the function returns −1L and **errno** is set to one of the following constants, defined in ERRNO.H:

Constant	Description
EBADF	Bad file number. The *stream* argument is not a valid file-handle value or does not refer to an open file.
EINVAL	Invalid argument. An invalid *stream* argument was passed to the function.

On devices incapable of seeking (such as terminals and printers), or when *stream* does not refer to an open file, the return value is undefined.

Compatibility	Standards:	ANSI, UNIX
	16-Bit:	DOS, QWIN, WIN, WIN DLL
	32-Bit:	DOS32X

See Also   **fgetpos, fseek, _lseek, _tell**

Example
```c
/* FTELL.C: This program opens a file named FTELL.C for reading and
 * tries to read 100 characters. It then uses ftell to determine the
 * position of the file pointer and displays this position.
 */

#include <stdio.h>

FILE *stream;

void main( void )
{
    long position;
    char list[100];

    if( (stream = fopen( "ftell.c", "rb" )) != NULL )
    {
        /* Move the pointer by reading data: */
        fread( list, sizeof( char ), 100, stream );

        /* Get position after read: */
        position = ftell( stream );
        printf( "Position after trying to read 100 bytes: %ld\n", position );
        fclose( stream );
    }
}
```

Output   Position after trying to read 100 bytes: 100

_ftime

Description

Gets the current time.

#include <sys\types.h>

#include <sys\timeb.h>

void _ftime(struct _timeb *_timeptr_);

timeptr   Pointer to structure defined in SYS\TIMEB.H

Remarks

The **_ftime** function gets the current time and stores it in the structure pointed to by _timeptr_. The **_timeb** structure is defined in SYS\TIMEB.H. It contains four fields (**dstflag**, **millitm**, **time**, and **timezone**), which have the following values:

Field	Value
dstflag	Nonzero if daylight saving time is currently in effect for the local time zone. (See **_tzset** for an explanation of how daylight saving time is determined.)
millitm	Fraction of a second in milliseconds. The last digit is always 0 since **millitm** is incremented to the nearest one-hundredth of a second.
time	Time in seconds since midnight (00:00:00), December 31, 1899.
timezone	Difference in minutes, moving westward, between Universal Coordinated Time and local time. The value of **timezone** is set from the value of the global variable **_timezone** (see **_tzset**).

Return Value

The **_ftime** function gives values to the fields in the structure pointed to by _timeptr_. It does not return a value.

Compatibility

Standards: None

16-Bit: DOS, QWIN, WIN, WIN DLL

32-Bit: DOS32X

See Also

asctime, ctime, gmtime, localtime, time, _tzset

Example
```
/* FTIME.C: This program uses _ftime to obtain the current time
 * and then stores this time in timebuffer.
 */

#include <stdio.h>
#include <sys\timeb.h>
#include <time.h>

void main( void )
{
   struct _timeb timebuffer;
   char *timeline;

   _ftime( &timebuffer );
   timeline = ctime( & ( timebuffer.time ) );

   printf( "The time is %.19s.%hu %s",
           timeline, timebuffer.millitm, &timeline[20] );
}
```

Output
```
The time is Tue Jun 15 21:40:34.870 1999
```

_fullpath

Description

Makes an absolute path name from a relative path name.

#include <stdlib.h>

char *_fullpath(char *_buffer_, const char *_pathname_, size_t _maxlen_);

buffer	Full path-name buffer
pathname	Relative path name
maxlen	Length of the buffer pointed to by _buffer_

Remarks

The **_fullpath** routine converts the partial path stored in _pathname_ to a fully qualified path that is stored in _buffer_. Unlike **_makepath**, the **_fullpath** routine can be used with .\ and ..\ in the path.

If the length of the fully qualified path is greater than the value of _maxlen_, then **NULL** is returned; otherwise, the address of _buffer_ is returned.

If the _buffer_ is **NULL**, **_fullpath** will allocate a buffer of **_MAX_PATH** size using **malloc** and the _maxlen_ argument is ignored. It is the caller's responsibility to deallocate this buffer (using **free**) as appropriate.

If the _pathname_ argument specifies a disk drive, the current directory of this drive is combined with the path. If the drive is not valid, **_fullpath** returns **NULL**.

Return Value

The **_fullpath** function returns a pointer to the buffer containing the absolute path (_buffer_). If there is an error, **_fullpath** returns **NULL**.

Compatibility

Standards: None
16-Bit: DOS, QWIN, WIN, WIN DLL
32-Bit: DOS32X

See Also

_getcwd, _getdcwd, _makepath, _splitpath

Example

```
/* FULLPATH.C: This program demonstrates how _fullpath creates a full
 * path from a partial path.
 */

#include <stdio.h>
#include <conio.h>
#include <stdlib.h>
#include <direct.h>

char full[_MAX_PATH], part[_MAX_PATH];

void main( void )
{
    while( 1 )
    {
        printf( "Enter partial path or ENTER to quit: " );
        gets( part );
        if( part[0] == 0 )
            break;

        if( _fullpath( full, part, _MAX_PATH ) != NULL )
            printf( "Full path is: %s\n", full );
        else
            printf( "Invalid path\n" );
    }
}
```

Output

```
Enter partial path or ENTER to quit: ..
Full path is: C:\
Enter partial path or ENTER to quit: ..\include
Full path is: C:\include
Enter partial path or ENTER to quit: p:
Full path is: P:\
Enter partial path or ENTER to quit: fullpath.c
Full path is: C:\LIBREF\fullpath.c
Enter partial path or ENTER to quit:
```

_fwopen

Description

Opens a new file stream for a QuickWin window.

#include <stdio.h>

FILE * _fwopen(struct _wopeninfo **wopeninfo,*
struct _wsizeinfo **wsizeinfo,* **char *** *mode* **);**

wopeninfo	Pointer to a **_wopeninfo** structure
wsizeinfo	Pointer to a **_wsizeinfo** structure
mode	Type of access permitted

Remarks

The **_fwopen** function is a high-level call that opens a new QuickWin window, re-turning a file-stream pointer. This routine is used only in QuickWin programs; it is not part of the Windows API. For full details about QuickWin, see Chapter 8 of *Programming Techniques* (in the Microsoft C/C++ version 7.0 documentation set).

The **_wopeninfo** and **_wsizeinfo** structures, declared in STDIO.H, are used to pass window initialization information, including the window's initial size and position on the screen. You can pass **NULL** for these arguments to accept Quick-Win defaults or declare variables of these two structure types and fill in their fields.

If you declare **_wopeninfo** and **_wsizeinfo** variables, assign the **_WINVER** macro to the **_version** field. **_WINVER** is the current QuickWin version, defined in STDIO.H.

For the **_wopeninfo** variable, assign a null-terminated string to the **_title** field con-taining the desired window title. You can also optionally set the size of the win-dow's screen buffer in the **_wbufsize** field. The default is 2,048 bytes, but you can pass some other number or the value **_WINBUFINF**. This causes the buffer to be reallocated continually so that all window output is retained for scrolling.

For the **_wsizeinfo** variable, assign one of the following values to the **_type** field:

Value	Meaning
_WINSIZEMIN	Minimize the window
_WINSIZEMAX	Maximize the window
_WINSIZECHAR	Use character coordinates for the window size

If the type is **_WINSIZECHAR**, you must supply the **_x**, **_y**, **_h**, and **_w** values in the remainder of the structure. They specify the upper-left corner and the height and width of the window (in characters).

The *mode* parameter is a pointer to the stream I/O mode. The **_fwopen** function accepts the same mode values as the STDIO.H **fopen** function:

Type	Description
"**r**"	Opens for reading
"**w**"	Opens for writing
"**r+**"	Opens for both reading and writing
"**w+**"	Opens for both reading and writing

In addition to the values listed above, one of the following characters can be included in *mode* to specify the translation mode for newline characters:

Mode	Meaning
t	Open in text (translated) mode
b	Open in binary (untranslated) mode

If **t** or **b** is not given in *mode*, the translation mode is defined by the default-mode variable **_fmode**. If **t** or **b** is prefixed to the argument, the function fails and returns **NULL**. See "Input and Output" on page 31 for a discussion of text and binary modes.

If **_fwopen** is successful, the returned stream can be passed to standard STDIO.H functions such as **fread**, **fwrite**, and **fprintf**. If you write to a stream and then read from it, or if you read from a stream and then write to it, call the STDIO.H **rewind** function between the I/O calls. To close an open window stream, call the STDIO.H function **fclose**. If you have opened a window with **_fwopen**, you can use the **_fileno** macro to obtain a file handle, which you can then pass to other QuickWin calls, such as **_wsetscreenbuf** or **_wsetsize**.

Return Value

If successful, the **_fwopen** function returns a stream pointer (**FILE ***) to the new window. A return value of **NULL** indicates an error.

Compatibility

Standards:	None
16-Bit:	QWIN
32-Bit:	None

See Also

fclose, _fileno, _wabout, _wclose, _wgetfocus, _wgetscreenbuf, _wgetsize, _wmenuclick, _wopen, _wsetfocus, _wsetscreenbuf, _wsetsize, _wyield

Example

```
/* FOWPEN.C - Demonstrate opening QuickWin windows with _fwopen */

#include <io.h>
#include <stdio.h>

#define OPENFLAGS "w"                        /* Access permission */

void main( void )
{
    struct _wopeninfo wininfo;          /* Open information */
    char wintitle[32] = "QuickWin ";    /* Title for window */
    FILE *wp;                           /* FILE ptr to window */
    int nRes;                           /* I/O result */

    /* Set up window info structure for _fwopen */
    wininfo._version = _WINVER;
    wininfo._title = wintitle;
    wininfo._wbufsize = _WINBUFDEF;

    /* Create a new window */
    /* NULL second argument accepts default size/position */
    wp = _fwopen( &wininfo, NULL, OPENFLAGS );
    if( wp == NULL )
    {
        printf( "***ERROR: _fwopen\n" );
        exit( -1 );
    }

    /* Write in the window */
    nRes = fprintf( wp, "Hello, QuickWin!\n" );

    /* Close the window */
    nRes = fclose( wp );

    exit( 0 );
}
```

fwrite

Description

Writes data to a stream.

#include <stdio.h>

size_t fwrite(const void *buffer, size_t size, size_t count, FILE *stream);

buffer	Pointer to data to be written
size	Item size in bytes
count	Maximum number of items to be written
stream	Pointer to **FILE** structure

Remarks

The **fwrite** function writes up to *count* items, of length *size* each, from *buffer* to the output *stream*. The file pointer associated with *stream* (if there is one) is incremented by the number of bytes actually written.

If *stream* is opened in text mode, each carriage return is replaced with a carriage-return–line-feed pair. The replacement has no effect on the return value.

Return Value

The **fwrite** function returns the number of full items actually written, which may be less than *count* if an error occurs. Also, if an error occurs, the file-position indicator cannot be determined.

Compatibility

Standards:	ANSI, UNIX
16-Bit:	DOS, QWIN, WIN, WIN DLL
32-Bit:	DOS32X

See Also

fread, _write

Example

```
/* FREAD.C: This program opens a file named FREAD.OUT and writes 25
 * characters to the file. It then tries to open FREAD.OUT and
 * read in 25 characters. If the attempt succeeds, the program
 * displays the number of actual items read.
 */

#include <stdio.h>

void main( void )
{
    FILE *stream;
    char list[30];
    int  i, numread, numwritten;

    /* Open file in text mode: */
    if( (stream = fopen( "fread.out", "w+t" )) != NULL )
    {
        for ( i = 0; i < 25; i++ )
            list[i] = 'z' - i;
        /* Write 25 characters to stream */
        numwritten = fwrite( list, sizeof( char ), 25, stream );
        printf( "Wrote %d items\n", numwritten );
        fclose( stream );
    }
    else
        printf( "Problem opening the file\n" );

    if( (stream = fopen( "fread.out", "r+t" )) != NULL )
    {
        /* Attempt to read in 25 characters */
        numread = fread( list, sizeof( char ), 25, stream );
        printf( "Number of items read = %d\n", numread );
        printf( "Contents of buffer = %.25s\n", list );
        fclose( stream );
    }
    else
        printf( "Was not able to open the file\n" );
}
```

Output

```
Wrote 25 items
Number of items read = 25
Contents of buffer = zyxwvutsrqponmlkjihgfedcb
```

_gcvt

Description

Converts a floating-point value to a string, which it stores in a buffer.

#include <stdlib.h>   Required only for function declarations

char *_gcvt(double *value*, **int** *digits*, **char** *buffer **);**

value	Value to be converted
digits	Number of significant digits stored
buffer	Storage location for result

Remarks

The **_gcvt** function converts a floating-point *value* to a character string (which includes a decimal point and a possible sign byte) and stores the string in *buffer*. The *buffer* should be large enough to accommodate the converted value plus a terminating null character ('**\0**'), which is appended automatically. If a buffer size of significant digits + 1 is used, the function will overwrite the end of the buffer. This is because the converted string includes a decimal point and can contain sign and exponent information. There is no provision for overflow.

The **_gcvt** function attempts to produce *digits* significant digits in decimal format. If this is not possible, it produces *digits* significant digits in exponential format. Trailing zeros may be suppressed in the conversion.

Return Value

The **_gcvt** function returns a pointer to the string of digits. There is no error return.

Compatibility

Standards:	UNIX
16-Bit:	DOS, QWIN, WIN
32-Bit:	DOS32X

Use **_gcvt** for compatibility with ANSI naming conventions of non-ANSI functions. Use **gcvt** and link with OLDNAMES.LIB for UNIX compatibility.

See Also

atof, atoi, atol, _ecvt, _fcvt

Example   `/* _GCVT.C: This program converts -3.1415e5 to its string representation. */`

```
#include <stdlib.h>
#include <stdio.h>

void main( void )
{
   char buffer[50];
   double source = -3.1415e5;

   _gcvt( source, 7, buffer );
   printf( "source: %f  buffer: '%s'\n", source, buffer );

   _gcvt( source, 7, buffer );
   printf( "source: %e  buffer: '%s'\n", source, buffer );
}
```

Output
```
source: -314150.000000  buffer: '-314150.'
source: -3.141500e+005  buffer: '-314150.'
```

_getactivepage

Description   Gets the current active page number.

#include <graph.h>

short __far _getactivepage(void);

Remarks   The **_getactivepage** function returns the number of the current active page.

Return Value   The function returns the number of the current active video page. All hardware combinations support at least one page (page number 0).

Compatibility   Standards: None
16-Bit: DOS
32-Bit: None

See Also   **_getvideoconfig**, **_getvisualpage**, **_grstatus**, **_setactivepage**, **_setvideomode**, **_setvisualpage**

Example
```
/* PAGE.C illustrates video page functions including:
 *      _getactivepage  _getvisualpage  _setactivepage  _setvisualpage
 */

#include <conio.h>
#include <graph.h>
#include <stdlib.h>

void main( void )
{
    short  oldvpage, oldapage, page, row, col, line;
    struct _videoconfig vc;
    char    buf[80];

    _getvideoconfig( &vc );
    if( vc.numvideopages < 4 )
        exit( 1 );              /* Fail for or monochrome. */
    oldapage = _getactivepage();
    oldvpage = _getvisualpage();
    _displaycursor( _GCURSOROFF );
```

```
    /* Draw arrows in different place on each page. */
    for( page = 1; page < 4; page++ )
    {
        _setactivepage( page );
        _settextposition( 12, 16 * page );
        _outtext( ">>>>>>>>" );
    }

    while( !_kbhit() )
        /* Cycle through pages 1 to 3 to show moving image. */
        for( page = 1; page < 4; page++ )
            _setvisualpage( page );
    _getch();

    /* Restore original page (normally 0) to restore screen. */
    _setactivepage( oldapage );
    _setvisualpage( oldvpage );
    _displaycursor( _GCURSORON );
}
```

_getarcinfo

Description

Determines the endpoints in viewport coordinates of the most recently drawn arc or pie.

#include <graph.h>

short __far _getarcinfo(struct _xycoord __far *start,
    struct _xycoord __far *end, struct _xycoord __far *fillpoint);

start	Starting point of arc
end	Ending point of arc
fillpoint	Point at which pie fill will begin

Remarks

The **_getarcinfo** function determines the endpoints in viewport coordinates of the most recently drawn arc or pie.

If successful, the **_getarcinfo** function updates the *start* and *end* **_xycoord** structures to contain the endpoints (in viewport coordinates) of the arc drawn by the most recent call to one of the **_arc** or **_pie** functions.

In addition, *fillpoint* specifies a point from which a pie can be filled. This is useful for filling a pie in a color different from the border color. After a call to **_getarcinfo**, change colors using the **_setcolor** function. Use the color, along with the coordinates in *fillpoint*, as arguments for the **_floodfill** function.

Return Value

The **_getarcinfo** function returns a nonzero value if successful. If neither the **_arc** nor the **_pie** function has been successfully called since the last time the screen was cleared or a new graphics mode or viewport was selected, the **_getarcinfo** function returns 0.

Compatibility

Standards: None
16-Bit: DOS
32-Bit: None

See Also

_arc functions, **_floodfill**, **_getvideoconfig**, **_grstatus**, **_pie** functions

Example

See the example for **_arc**.

_getbkcolor

Description

Gets the current background color.

#include <graph.h>

long __far _getbkcolor(void);

Remarks

The **_getbkcolor** function returns the current background color. The default is 0.

In a color text mode such as **_TEXTC80**, **_setbkcolor** accepts, and **_getbkcolor** returns, a color index. For example, **_setbkcolor(2L)** sets the background color to color index 2. The actual color displayed depends on the palette mapping for color index 2. The default for color index 2 is green in a color text mode.

In a color graphics mode such as **_ERESCOLOR**, **_setbkcolor** accepts, and **_getbkcolor** returns, a color value (as used in **_remappalette**). The value for the simplest background colors is given by the manifest constants defined in the GRAPH.H include file. For example, **_setbkcolor(_GREEN)** sets the background color in a graphics mode to green. These manifest constants are provided as a convenience in defining and manipulating the most common colors. In general, the actual range of colors is much greater.

In most cases, whenever a color argument is long, it refers to a color value, and whenever it is short, it refers to a color index. The two exceptions are **_setbkcolor** and **_getbkcolor**, described above. For a more complete discussion of colors, see **_remappalette**.

Return Value

The function returns the current background color. There is no error return.

Compatibility

Standards:	None
16-Bit:	DOS
32-Bit:	None

See Also

_remappalette, **_setbkcolor**

Example

See the example for **_getcolor**.

getc, getchar

Description

Reads a character from a stream (**getc**), or gets a character from **stdin** (**getchar**).

#include <stdio.h>

int getc(FILE *****stream **);**

int getchar(void);

stream   Current stream

Remarks

The **getc** routine reads a single character from the *stream* position and increments the associated file pointer (if there is one) to point to the next character. The **getchar** routine is identical to **getc(stdin)**.

The **getc** and **getchar** routines are similar to **fgetc** and **_fgetchar**, respectively, but are implemented both as macros and functions.

Return Value

Both **getc** and **getchar** return the character read. A return value of **EOF** indicates an error or end-of-file condition. Use **ferror** or **feof** to determine whether an error or end-of-file occurred.

Compatibility

getc

Standards:	ANSI, UNIX
16-Bit:	DOS, QWIN, WIN, WIN DLL
32-Bit:	DOS32X

getchar

Standards:	ANSI, UNIX
16-Bit:	DOS, QWIN
32-Bit:	DOS32X

See Also

fgetc, _fgetchar, _getch, _getche, putc, putchar, ungetc

Example

```
/* GETC.C: This program uses getchar to read a single line of input
 * from stdin, places this input in buffer, then terminates the
 * string before printing it to the screen.
 */

#include <stdio.h>

void main( void )
{
   char buffer[81];
   int i, ch;

   printf( "Enter a line: " );

   /* Read in single line from "stdin": */
   for( i = 0; (i < 80) &&  ((ch = getchar()) != EOF) && (ch != '\n'); i++ )
      buffer[i] = ch;

   /* Terminate string with null character: */
   buffer[i] = '\0';
   printf( "%s\n", buffer );
}
```

Output

```
Enter a line: This is a line of text.
This is a line of text.
```

_getch, _getche

Description   Get a character from the console without echo (_getch) or with echo (_getche).

#include <conio.h>   Required only for function declarations

int _getch(void);

int _getche(void);

Remarks   The _getch function reads a single character from the console without echoing. The _getche function reads a single character from the console and echoes the character read. Neither function can be used to read CTRL+C.

When reading a function key or cursor-moving key, the _getch and _getche functions must be called twice; the first call returns 0 or 0xE0, and the second call returns the actual key code.

Return Value   Both the _getch and _getche functions return the character read. There is no error return.

Compatibility

Standards:	None
16-Bit:	DOS, QWIN, WIN, WIN DLL
32-Bit:	DOS32X

See Also   _cgets, getchar, _ungetch

Example
```
/* GETCH.C: This program reads characters from the keyboard until it
 * receives a 'Y' or 'y'.
 */

#include <conio.h>
#include <ctype.h>
```

```
void main( void )
{
    int ch;

    _cputs( "Type 'Y' when finished typing keys: " );
    do
    {
        ch = _getch();
        ch = toupper( ch );
    } while( ch != 'Y' );

    _putch( ch );
    _putch( '\r' );     /* Carriage return */
    _putch( '\n' );     /* Line feed       */
}
```

Output   Type 'Y' when finished typing keys: Y

_getcolor

Description

Gets the current color.

#include <graph.h>

short __far _getcolor(void);

Remarks

The **_getcolor** function returns the current graphics color index. The default is the highest legal index in the current palette.

Return Value

The **_getcolor** function returns the current color index.

Compatibility

Standards: None
16-Bit: DOS
32-Bit: None

See Also

_setcolor

Example

```
/* OUTTXT.C: This example illustrates text output functions:
 *    _gettextcolor   _getbkcolor   _gettextposition   _outtext
 *    _settextcolor   _setbkcolor   _settextposition
 */

#include <conio.h>
#include <stdio.h>
#include <graph.h>

char buffer [80];

void main( void )
{
    /* Save original foreground, background, and text position. */
    short blink, fgd, oldfgd;
    long  bgd, oldbgd;
    struct _rccoord oldpos;

    /* Save original foreground, background, and text position. */
    oldfgd = _gettextcolor();
    oldbgd = _getbkcolor();
    oldpos = _gettextposition();
    _clearscreen( _GCLEARSCREEN );
```

```
    /* First time no blink, second time blinking. */
    for( blink = 0; blink <= 16; blink += 16 )
    {
        /* Loop through 8 background colors. */
        for( bgd = 0; bgd < 8; bgd++ )
        {
            _setbkcolor( bgd );
            _settextposition( (short)bgd + ((blink / 16) * 9) + 3, 1 );
            _settextcolor( 7 );
            sprintf(buffer, "Back: %d Fore:", bgd );
            _outtext( buffer );

            /* Loop through 16 foreground colors. */
            for( fgd = 0; fgd < 16; fgd++ )
            {
                _settextcolor( fgd + blink );
                sprintf( buffer, " %2d ", fgd + blink );
                _outtext( buffer );
            }
        }
    }
    _getch();

    /* Restore original foreground, background, and text position. */
    _settextcolor( oldfgd );
    _setbkcolor( oldbgd );
    _clearscreen( _GCLEARSCREEN );
    _settextposition( oldpos.row, oldpos.col );
}
```

_getcurrentposition Functions

Description   Get the current position and return it as a structure.

#include <graph.h>

struct _xycoord __far _getcurrentposition(void);

struct _wxycoord __far _getcurrentposition_w(void);

Remarks   The _getcurrentposition functions return the coordinates of the current graphics output position. The _getcurrentposition function returns the position as an _xycoord structure, defined in GRAPH.H.

The _xycoord structure contains the following elements:

Element	Description
short xcoord	*x* coordinate
short ycoord	*y* coordinate

The _getcurrentposition_w function returns the position as a _wxycoord structure, defined in GRAPH.H.

The _wxycoord structure contains the following elements:

Element	Description
double wx	window *x* coordinate
double wy	window *y* coordinate

The current position can be changed by the _lineto, _moveto, and _outgtext functions.

The default position, set by _setvideomode, _setvideomoderows, or _setviewport, is the center of the viewport.

Only graphics output starts at the current position; these functions do not affect text output, which begins at the current text position. (See _settextposition for more information.)

Return Value   The _getcurrentposition functions return the coordinates of the current graphics output position. There is no error return.

Compatibility   Standards: None
16-Bit: DOS
32-Bit: None

See Also   **_grstatus**, **_lineto** functions, **_moveto** functions, **_outgtext**

Example

```
/* GCURPOS.C: This program sets a random current location, then gets that
 * location with _getcurrentposition.
 */

#include <stdio.h>
#include <stdlib.h>
#include <conio.h>
#include <graph.h>

char    buffer[255];

void main( void )
{
    struct _videoconfig vc;
    struct _xycoord position;

    /* Find a valid graphics mode. */
    if( !_setvideomode( _MAXRESMODE ) )
      exit( 1 );
    _getvideoconfig( &vc );

    /* Move to random location and report that location. */
    _moveto( rand() % vc.numxpixels, rand() % vc.numypixels );
    position = _getcurrentposition();
    sprintf( buffer, "x = %d, y = %d", position.xcoord, position.ycoord );
    _settextposition( 1, 1 );
    _outtext( buffer );

    _getch();
    _setvideomode( _DEFAULTMODE );
}
```

_getcwd

Description

Gets the current working directory.

#include <direct.h>   Required only for function declarations

char *_getcwd(char *_buffer_, int _maxlen_);

buffer	Storage location for path name
maxlen	Maximum length of path name

Remarks

The **_getcwd** function gets the full path name of the current working directory for the default drive and stores it at _buffer_. The integer argument _maxlen_ specifies the maximum length for the path name. An error occurs if the length of the path name (including the terminating null character) exceeds _maxlen_.

The _buffer_ argument can be **NULL**; a buffer of at least size _maxlen_ (more only if necessary) will automatically be allocated, using **malloc**, to store the path name. This buffer can later be freed by calling **free** and passing it the **_getcwd** return value (a pointer to the allocated buffer).

Note that **_getcwd** returns a string that represents the path name of the current working directory. If the current working directory is set to the root, the string will end with a backslash (\). If the current working directory is set to a directory other than the root, the string will end with the name of the directory and not with a backslash.

Return Value

The **_getcwd** function returns a pointer to _buffer_. A **NULL** return value indicates an error, and **errno** is set to one of the following values:

Value	Meaning
ENOMEM	Insufficient memory to allocate _maxlen_ bytes (when a **NULL** argument is given as _buffer_)
ERANGE	Path name longer than _maxlen_ characters

Compatibility

Standards: UNIX

16-Bit: DOS, QWIN, WIN, WIN DLL

32-Bit: DOS32X

Use **_getcwd** for compatibility with ANSI naming conventions of non-ANSI functions. Use **getcwd** and link with OLDNAMES.LIB for UNIX compatibility.

See Also   **_chdir, _mkdir, _rmdir**

Example

```
/* This program places the name of the current directory in the buffer
 * array, then displays the name of the current directory on the screen.
 * Specifying a length of _MAX_DIR leaves room for the longest legal
 * directory name.
 */

#include <direct.h>
#include <stdlib.h>
#include <stdio.h>

void main( void )
{
   char buffer[_MAX_DIR];

   /* Get the current working directory: */
   if( _getcwd( buffer, _MAX_DIR ) == NULL )
     perror( "_getcwd error" );
   else
     printf( "%s\n", buffer );
}
```

Output   C:\LIBREF

_getdcwd

Description   Gets full path name of current working directory on the specified drive.

#include <direct.h>   Required only for function declarations

char *_getdcwd(int *drive*, **char ****buffer*, **int** *maxlen* **);**

drive	Disk drive
buffer	Storage location for path name
maxlen	Maximum length of path name

Remarks   The **_getdcwd** function gets the full path name of the current working directory on the specified drive and stores it at *buffer*. The argument *maxlen* specifies the maximum length for the path name. An error occurs if the length of the path name (including the terminating null character) exceeds *maxlen*.

The *drive* argument specifies the drive (0 = default drive, 1=A, 2=B, etc.). The *buffer* argument can be **NULL**; a buffer of at least size *maxlen* (more only if necessary) will automatically be allocated, using **malloc**, to store the path name. This buffer can later be freed by calling **free** and passing it the **_getdcwd** return value (a pointer to the allocated buffer).

Note that **_getdcwd** returns a string that represents the path name of the current working directory. If the current working directory is set to the root, the string will end with a backslash (\). If the current working directory is set to a directory other than the root, the string will end with the name of the directory and not with a backslash.

Return Value   The **_getdcwd** function returns *buffer*. A **NULL** return value indicates an error, and **errno** is set to one of the following values:

Value	Meaning
ENOMEM	Insufficient memory to allocate *maxlen* bytes (when a **NULL** argument is given as *buffer*)
ERANGE	Path name longer than *maxlen* characters

Compatibility   Standards: None
                           16-Bit: DOS, QWIN, WIN, WIN DLL
                           32-Bit: DOS32X

See Also   **_chdir, _getcwd, _getdrive, _mkdir, _rmdir**

Example
```c
/* GETDRIVE.C illustrates drive functions including:
 *      _getdrive       _chdrive        _getdcwd
 */

#include <stdio.h>
#include <conio.h>
#include <direct.h>
#include <stdlib.h>

void main( void )
{
   int ch, drive, curdrive;
   static char path[_MAX_PATH];

   /* Save current drive. */
   curdrive = _getdrive();

   printf( "Available drives are: \n" );

   /* If we can switch to the drive, it exists. */
   for( drive = 1; drive <= 26; drive++ )
      if( !_chdrive( drive ) )
         printf( "%c: ", drive + 'A' - 1 );

   while( 1 )
   {
      printf( "\nType drive letter to check or ESC to quit: " );
      ch = _getch();
      if( ch == 27 )
         break;
      if( isalpha( ch ) )
         _putch( ch );
      if( _getdcwd( toupper( ch ) - 'A' + 1, path, _MAX_PATH ) != NULL )
         printf( "\nCurrent directory on that drive is %s\n", path );
   }

   /* Restore original drive. This is only necessary for DOS.*/
   _chdrive( curdrive );
   printf( "\n" );
}
```

Output
```
Available drives are:
A: B: C:
Type drive letter to check or ESC to quit: q
Type drive letter to check or ESC to quit: a
Current directory on that drive is A:\

Type drive letter to check or ESC to quit: c
Current directory on that drive is C:\LIBREF

Type drive letter to check or ESC to quit:
```

_getdrive

Description

Gets the current disk drive.

#include <direct.h>

int _getdrive(void);

Remarks

The **_getdrive** function returns the current (default) drive (1=A, 2=B, etc.).

Return Value

The return value is stated above. There is no error return.

Compatibility

Standards:	None
16-Bit:	DOS, QWIN, WIN, WIN DLL
32-Bit:	DOS32X

See Also

_chdrive, _dos_getdrive, _dos_setdrive, _getcwd, _getdcwd

Example

See the example for **_getdcwd**.

getenv

Description

Gets a value from the current environment.

#include <stdlib.h>   Required only for function declarations

char *getenv(const char *varname **);**

varname   Name of environment variable

Remarks

The **getenv** function searches the list of environment variables for an entry corresponding to *varname*. Environment variables define the environment in which a process executes. (For example, the LIB environment variable defines the default search path for libraries to be linked with a program.) Because the **getenv** function is case sensitive, the *varname* variable should match the case of the environment variable.

The **getenv** function returns a pointer to an entry in the environment table. It is, however, only safe to retrieve the value of the environment variable using the returned pointer. To modify the value of an environmental variable, use the **_putenv** function.

The **getenv** and **_putenv** functions use the copy of the environment contained in the global variable **environ** to access the environment. Programs that use the *envp* argument to **main** and the **_putenv** function may retrieve invalid information. The safest programming practice is to use **getenv** and **_putenv**.

The **getenv** function operates only on the data structures accessible to the run-time library and not on the environment "segment" created for the process by the operating system.

Return Value

The **getenv** function returns a pointer to the environment table entry containing the current string value of *varname*. The return value is **NULL** if the given variable is not currently defined.

Compatibility

Standards: ANSI, UNIX
16-Bit: DOS, QWIN, WIN, WIN DLL
32-Bit: DOS32X

See Also

_putenv

Example

```
/* GETENV.C: This program uses getenv to retrieve the LIB environment
 * variable and then uses _putenv to change it to a new value.
 */

#include <stdlib.h>
#include <stdio.h>

void main( void )
{
    char *libvar;

    /* Get the value of the LIB environment variable. */
    libvar = getenv( "LIB" );
    if( libvar != NULL )
       printf( "Original LIB variable is: %s\n", libvar );

    /* Attempt to change path. Note that this only affects the environment
     * variable of the current process. The command processor's environment
     * is not changed.
     */
    _putenv( "LIB=c:\\mylib;c:\\yourlib" );

    /* Get new value. */
    libvar = getenv( "LIB" );
    if( libvar != NULL )
       printf( "New LIB variable is: %s\n", libvar );
}
```

Output

```
Original LIB variable is: C:\LIB
New LIB variable is: c:\mylib;c:\yourlib
```

_getfillmask

Description

Gets the current fill mask for some graphics routines.

#include <graph.h>

unsigned char __far * __far _getfillmask(unsigned char __far *_mask_);

mask	Mask array

Remarks

Some graphics routines (**_ellipse**, **_floodfill**, **_pie**, **_polygon**, and **_rectangle**) can fill part or all of the screen with the current color. The fill mask controls the pattern used for filling.

The **_getfillmask** function returns the current fill mask. The mask is an 8-by-8-bit array, in which each bit represents a pixel. If the bit is 1, the corresponding pixel is set to the current color; if the bit is 0, the pixel is left unchanged. The mask is repeated over the entire fill area. If no fill mask is set, or if *mask* is **NULL**, a solid (unpatterned) fill is performed using the current color.

Return Value

If no mask is set, the function returns **NULL**. Otherwise, it returns the current fill mask.

Compatibility

Standards:	None
16-Bit:	DOS
32-Bit:	None

See Also

_ellipse functions, **_floodfill**, **_pie** functions, **_polygon** functions, **_rectangle** functions, **_setfillmask**

Example

```
/* GFILLMSK.C: This program illustrates _getfillmask and _setfillmask. */

#include <conio.h>
#include <stdlib.h>
#include <graph.h>

void ellipsemask( short x1, short y1, short x2, short y2, char __far *newmask );

unsigned char mask1[8] = { 0x43, 0x23, 0x7c, 0xf7, 0x8a, 0x4d, 0x78, 0x39 };
unsigned char mask2[8] = { 0x18, 0xad, 0xc0, 0x79, 0xf6, 0xc4, 0xa8, 0x23 };
char oldmask[8];

void main( void )
{
    int loop;

    /* Find a valid graphics mode. */
    if( !_setvideomode( _MAXRESMODE ) )
        exit( 1 );

    /* Set first fill mask and draw rectangle. */
    _setfillmask( mask1 );
    _rectangle( _GFILLINTERIOR, 20, 20, 100, 100 );
    _getch();

    /* Call routine that saves and restores mask. */
    ellipsemask( 60, 60, 150, 150, mask2 );
    _getch();

    /* Back to original mask. */
    _rectangle( _GFILLINTERIOR, 120, 120, 190, 190 );
    _getch();

    _setvideomode( _DEFAULTMODE );
    exit( 0 );
}

/* Draw an ellipse with a specified fill mask. */
void ellipsemask( short x1, short y1, short x2, short y2, char __far *newmask )
{
    unsigned char savemask[8];

    _getfillmask( savemask );                           /* Save mask       */
    _setfillmask( newmask );                            /* Set new mask    */
    _ellipse( _GFILLINTERIOR, x1, y1, x2, y2 );         /* Use new mask    */
    _setfillmask( savemask );                           /* Restore original */
}
```

_getfontinfo

Description   Gets the current font characteristics.

#include <graph.h>

short __far _getfontinfo(struct _fontinfo __far *__*fontbuffer*__);

fontbuffer   Buffer to hold font information

Remarks   The **_getfontinfo** function gets the current font characteristics and stores them in a **_fontinfo** structure, defined in GRAPH.H.

The **_fontinfo** structure contains the following elements:

Element	Contents
int type	Specifies vector (1) or bitmapped (0) font
int ascent	Specifies pixel distance from top to baseline
int pixwidth	Specifies the character width in pixels; 0 indicates a proportional font
int pixheight	Specifies the character height in pixels
int avgwidth	Specifies the average character width in pixels
char filename [81]	Specifies the filename, including the path
char facename [32]	Specifies the font name

Return Value   The **_getfontinfo** function returns a negative number if a font has not been registered or loaded.

Compatibility   Standards: None

16-Bit: DOS

32-Bit: None

See Also   **_getgtextextent, _outgtext, _registerfonts, _setfont, _setgtextvector, _unregisterfonts**

Example   See the example for **_outgtext**.

_getgtextextent

Description   Gets the width in pixels of font-based text.

#include <graph.h>

short __far _getgtextextent(const char __far *_text_);

text   Text to be analyzed

Remarks   The **_getgtextextent** function returns the width in pixels that would be required to print the _text_ string using **_outgtext** with the current font.

This function is particularly useful for determining the size of text that uses proportionally spaced fonts.

Return Value   The **_getgtextextent** function returns the width in pixels. It returns –1 if a font has not been registered.

Compatibility   Standards: None
16-Bit: DOS
32-Bit: None

See Also   **_getfontinfo, _outgtext, _registerfonts, _setfont, _unregisterfonts**

Example   See the example for **_outgtext**.

_getgtextvector

Description

Changes the orientation of font text output.

#include <graph.h>

struct _xycoord __far _getgtextvector(void);

Remarks

The **_getgtextvector** function gets the current orientation for font text output. The current orientation is used in calls to the **_outgtext** function.

The text-orientation vector, which determines the direction of font-text rotation on the screen, is returned in a structure of type **_xycoord**. The *xcoord* and *ycoord* members of the structure describe the vector. The text-rotation options are shown below:

(x, y)	Text Orientation
(1,0)	Horizontal text (default)
(0,1)	Rotated 90 degrees counterclockwise
(-1,0)	Rotated 180 degrees
(0,-1)	Rotated 270 degrees counterclockwise

Return Value

The **_getgtextvector** function returns the current text-orientation vector in a structure of type **_xycoord**.

Compatibility

Standards: None
16-Bit: DOS
32-Bit: None

See Also

_getgtextextent, _grstatus, _outgtext, _setfont, _setgtextvector

_getimage Functions

Description

Store images in buffers.

#include <graph.h>

void __far _getimage(short *x1*, short *y1*, short *x2*, short *y2*, char __huge **image*);

void __far _getimage_w(double *wx1*, double *wy1*, double *wx2*, double *wy2*, char __huge **image*);

void __far _getimage_wxy(struct_wxycoord __far **pwxy1*, struct_wxycoord __far **pwxy2*, char __huge **image*);

x1, y1	Upper-left corner of bounding rectangle
x2, y2	Lower-right corner of bounding rectangle
wx1, wy1	Upper-left corner of bounding rectangle
wx2, wy2	Lower-right corner of bounding rectangle
pwxy1	Upper-left corner of bounding rectangle
pwxy2	Lower-right corner of bounding rectangle
image	Storage buffer for screen image

Remarks

The **_getimage** functions store the screen image defined by a specified bounding rectangle into the buffer pointed to by *image*.

The **_getimage** function defines the bounding rectangle with the view coordinates (*x1, y1*) and (*x2, y2*).

The **_getimage_w** function defines the bounding rectangle with the window coordinates (*wx1, wy1*) and (*wx2, wy2*).

The **_getimage_wxy** function defines the bounding rectangle with the window-coordinate pairs *pwxy1* and *pwxy2*.

The buffer must be large enough to hold the image. You can determine the size by calling the appropriate **_imagesize** function at run time, or by using the formula described on the **_imagesize** reference page.

Return Value

None. Use **_grstatus** to check success.

Compatibility

Standards:	None
16-Bit:	DOS
32-Bit:	None

See Also   _grstatus, _imagesize functions, _putimage functions

Example

```
/* GIMAGE.C: This example illustrates animation routines including:
 *              _imagesize      _getimage       _putimage
 */

#include <conio.h>
#include <stddef.h>
#include <stdlib.h>
#include <malloc.h>
#include <graph.h>

short action[5]  = { _GPSET,   _GPRESET, _GXOR,    _GOR,     _GAND      };
char *descrip[5] = {  "PSET ", "PRESET", "XOR ",   "OR  ",  "AND   " };

void exitfree( char __huge *buffer );

void main( void )
{
    char __huge *buffer;    /* Far pointer (with _fmalloc) could be used. */
    long  imsize;
    short i, x, y = 30;

    if( !_setvideomode( _MAXRESMODE ) )
        exit( 1 );

    /* Measure the image to be drawn and allocate memory for it. */
    imsize = (size_t)_imagesize( -16, -16, +16, +16 );
    buffer = _halloc( imsize, sizeof( char ) );
    if ( buffer == (char __far *)NULL )
        exit( 1 );

    _setcolor( 3 );
    for ( i = 0; i < 5; i++ )
    {
        /* Draw ellipse at new position and get a copy of it. */
        x = 50; y += 40;
        _ellipse( _GFILLINTERIOR, x - 15, y - 15, x + 15, y + 15 );
        _getimage( x - 16, y - 16, x + 16, y + 16, buffer );
        if( _grstatus() )
            exitfree( buffer );              /* Quit on error */
```

```
        /* Display action type and copy a row of ellipses with that type. */
        _settextposition( 1, 1 );
        _outtext( descrip[i] );
        while( x < 260 )
        {
            x += 5;
            _putimage( x - 16, y - 16, buffer, action[i] );
            if( _grstatus() < 0 )        /* Ignore warnings, quit on errors. */
                exitfree( buffer );
        }
        _getch();
    }
    exitfree( buffer );
}

void exitfree( char __huge *buffer )
{
    _hfree( buffer );
    exit( !_setvideomode( _DEFAULTMODE ) );
}
```

_getlinestyle

Description
Gets the current line style.

#include <graph.h>

unsigned short __far _getlinestyle(void);

Remarks
Some graphics routines (_**lineto**, _**polygon**, and _**rectangle**) output straight lines to the screen. The type of line can be controlled with the current line-style mask.

The _**getlinestyle** function returns the current line-style mask. The mask is a 16-bit array in which each bit represents a pixel in the line being drawn. If the bit is 1, the corresponding pixel is set to the color of the line (the current color). If the bit is 0, the corresponding pixel is left unchanged. The mask is repeated over the length of the line. The default mask is 0xFFFF (a solid line).

Return Value
If no mask has been set, _**getlinestyle** returns the default mask.

Compatibility

Standards:	None
16-Bit:	DOS
32-Bit:	None

See Also
_**lineto** functions, _**polygon** functions, _**rectangle** functions, _**setlinestyle**, _**setwritemode**

Example
```
/* GLINESTY.C: This program illustrates _setlinestyle and _getlinestyle. */

#include <conio.h>
#include <stdlib.h>
#include <graph.h>

void zigzag( short x1, short y1, short size );
```

```
void main( void )
{
    /* Find a valid graphics mode. */
    if( !_setvideomode( _MAXCOLORMODE ) )
        exit( 1 );

    /* Set line style and draw rectangle. */
    _setlinestyle( 0x4d );
    _rectangle( _GBORDER, 10, 10, 60, 60 );
    _getch();

    /* Draw figure with function that changes and restores line style. */
    zigzag( 100, 100, 90 );
    _getch();

    /* Original style reused. */
    _rectangle( _GBORDER, 190, 190, 130, 130 );
    _getch();

    _setvideomode( _DEFAULTMODE );
}

/* Draw box with changing line styles. Restore original style. */
void zigzag( short x1, short y1, short size )
{
    short x, y, oldcolor;
    unsigned short oldstyle;
    unsigned short style[16] = { 0x0001, 0x0003, 0x0007, 0x000f,
                                 0x001f, 0x003f, 0x007f, 0x00ff,
                                 0x01ff, 0x03ff, 0x07ff, 0x0fff,
                                 0x1fff, 0x3fff, 0x7fff, 0xffff };

    oldcolor = _getcolor();
    oldstyle = _getlinestyle();              /* Save old line style.    */
    for( x = 3, y = 3; x < size; x += 3, y += 3 )
    {
        _setcolor( x % 16 );
        _setlinestyle( style[x % 16] );      /* Set and use new line styles */
        _rectangle( _GBORDER, x1 - x, y1 - y, x1 + x, y1 + y );
    }
    _setlinestyle( oldstyle );               /* Restore old line style. */
    _setcolor( oldcolor );
}
```

_getphyscoord

Description   Gets physical coordinates.

#include <graph.h>

struct _xycoord __far _getphyscoord(short *x*, short *y*);

x, y   View coordinates to translate

Remarks   The **_getphyscoord** function translates the view coordinates (*x, y*) to physical coordinates and returns them in an **_xycoord** structure, defined in GRAPH.H.

The **_xycoord** structure contains the following elements:

Element	Description
short xcoord	*x* coordinate
short ycoord	*y* coordinate

Return Value   None.

Compatibility

Standards: None
16-Bit: DOS
32-Bit: None

See Also   **_getviewcoord** functions, **_grstatus**, **_setvieworg**, **_setviewport**

Example   See the example for **_setwindow**.

_getpid

Description   Gets the process identification.

#include <process.h>   Required only for function declarations

int _getpid(void);

Remarks   The **_getpid** function returns the process ID, an integer that uniquely identifies the calling process.

Return Value   The **_getpid** function returns the process ID. There is no error return.

Compatibility   Standards: UNIX
16-Bit: DOS, QWIN, WIN, WIN DLL
32-Bit: DOS32X

Use **_getpid** for compatibility with ANSI naming conventions of non-ANSI functions. Use **getpid** and link with OLDNAMES.LIB for UNIX compatibility.

See Also   **_mktemp**

Example
```
/* GETPID.C: This program uses _getpid to obtain the process ID and
 * then prints the ID.
 */

#include <stdio.h>
#include <process.h>

void main( void )
{
    /* If run from DOS, shows different ID for DOS than for DOS shell.
     * If execed or spawned, shows ID of parent.
     */
    printf( "\nProcess id of parent: %d\n", _getpid() );
}
```

Output   Process id of parent: 828

_getpixel Functions

Description   Get pixel values.

#include <graph.h>

short __far _getpixel(short *x*, short *y*);

short __far _getpixel_w(double *wx*, double *wy*);

x, *y*	Pixel position
wx, *wy*	Pixel position

Remarks   The functions in the **_getpixel** family return the pixel value (a color index) at a specified location. The **_getpixel** function uses the view coordinate (*x*, *y*). The **_getpixel_w** function uses the window coordinate (*wx*, *wy*). The range of possible pixel values is determined by the current video mode. The color translation of pixel values is determined by the current palette.

Return Value   If successful, the function returns the color index. If the function fails (for example, the point lies outside the clipping region, or the program is in a text mode), it returns −1.

Compatibility   Standards: None
16-Bit: DOS
32-Bit: None

See Also   _getvideoconfig, _grstatus, _remapallpalette, _remappalette, _selectpalette, _setpixel functions, _setvideomode

Example

```
/* GPIXEL.C: This program assigns different colors to randomly
 * selected pixels.
 */

#include <conio.h>
#include <stdlib.h>
#include <graph.h>

void main( void )
{
    short xvar, yvar;
    struct _videoconfig vc;

    /* Find a valid graphics mode. */
    if( !_setvideomode( _MAXCOLORMODE ) )
        exit( 1 );
    _getvideoconfig( &vc );

    /* Draw filled ellipse to turn on certain pixels. */
    _ellipse( _GFILLINTERIOR, vc.numxpixels / 6, vc.numypixels / 6,
                             vc.numxpixels / 6 * 5, vc.numypixels / 6 * 5 );

    /* Draw random pixels in random colors... */
    while( !_kbhit() )
    {
        /* ...but only if they are already on (inside the ellipse). */
        xvar = rand() % vc.numxpixels;
        yvar = rand() % vc.numypixels;
        if( _getpixel( xvar, yvar ) != 0 )
        {
            _setcolor( rand() % 16 );
            _setpixel( xvar, yvar );
        }
    }

    _getch();              /* Throw away the keystroke. */
    _setvideomode( _DEFAULTMODE );
    exit( 0 );
}
```

gets

Description

Gets a line from the **stdin** stream.

#include <stdio.h>

char *gets(char **buffer***);**

buffer   Storage location for input string

Remarks

The **gets** function reads a line from the standard input stream **stdin** and stores it in *buffer*. The line consists of all characters up to and including the first newline character (**\n**). The **gets** function then replaces the newline character with a null character ('**\0**') before returning the line. In contrast, the **fgets** function retains the newline character.

Return Value

If successful, the **gets** function returns its argument. A **NULL** pointer indicates an error or end-of-file condition. Use **ferror** or **feof** to determine which one has occurred.

Compatibility

Standards: ANSI, UNIX
16-Bit: DOS, QWIN
32-Bit: DOS32X

See Also

fgets, fputs, puts

Example

```
/* GETS.C */

#include <stdio.h>

void main( void )
{
    char line[81];

    printf( "Input a string: " );
    gets( line );
    printf( "The line entered was: %s\n", line );
}
```

Output   Input a string: This is a string
The line entered was: This is a string

_gettextcolor

Description

Gets the current text color.

#include <graph.h>

short __far _gettextcolor(void);

Remarks

The _gettextcolor function returns the color index of the current text color. The text color is set by the _settextcolor function and affects text output with the _outtext and _outmem functions only. The _setcolor function sets the color for font text output using the _outgtext function.

The default is 7 in text modes; it is the highest legal color index of the current palette in graphics modes.

Return Value

The _gettextcolor function returns the color index of the current text color.

Compatibility

Standards: None
16-Bit: DOS
32-Bit: None

See Also

_getvideoconfig, _outmem, _outtext, _remappalette, _selectpalette, _setcolor, _settextcolor

Example

See the example for _gettextposition.

_gettextcursor

Description

Gets the current cursor attribute.

#include <graph.h>

short __far _gettextcursor(void);

Remarks

The **_gettextcursor** function returns the current cursor attribute (i.e., the shape). This function works only in text video modes.

Return Value

The function returns the current cursor attribute, or –1 if an error occurs (such as a call to the function in a graphics mode).

Compatibility

Standards: None
16-Bit: DOS
32-Bit: None

See Also

_displaycursor, _grstatus, _settextcursor

Example

See the example for **_settextcursor**.

_gettextposition

Description   Gets the current text position.

#include <graph.h>

struct _rccoord __far _gettextposition(void);

Remarks   The **_gettextposition** function returns the current text position as an **_rccoord** structure, defined in GRAPH.H.

The **_rccoord** structure contains the following elements:

Element	Description
short row	Row coordinate
short col	Column coordinate

The text position given by the coordinates (1,1) is defined as the upper-left corner of the text window.

Text output from the **_outtext** and **_outmem** functions begins at the current text position. Font text is not affected by the current text position. Font text output begins at the current graphics output position, which is a separate position. Use the **_moveto** function to set the graphics output position.

Return Value   None.

Compatibility   Standards: None
16-Bit: DOS
32-Bit: None

See Also   **_getcurrentposition** functions, **_moveto** functions, **_outmem**, **_outtext**, **_settextposition**, **_settextwindow**, **_wrapon**

Example
```
/* OUTTXT.C: This example illustrates text output functions:
 *     _gettextcolor    _getbkcolor    _gettextposition    _outtext
 *     _settextcolor    _setbkcolor    _settextposition
 */
```

```
#include <conio.h>
#include <stdio.h>
#include <graph.h>

char buffer [80];

void main( void )
{
    /* Save original foreground, background, and text position. */
    short blink, fgd, oldfgd;
    long  bgd, oldbgd;
    struct _rccoord oldpos;

    /* Save original foreground, background, and text position. */
    oldfgd = _gettextcolor();
    oldbgd = _getbkcolor();
    oldpos = _gettextposition();
    _clearscreen( _GCLEARSCREEN );

    /* First time no blink, second time blinking. */
    for( blink = 0; blink <= 16; blink += 16 )
    {
        /* Loop through 8 background colors. */
        for( bgd = 0; bgd < 8; bgd++ )
        {
            _setbkcolor( bgd );
            _settextposition( (short)bgd + ((blink / 16) * 9) + 3, 1 );
            _settextcolor( 7 );
            sprintf(buffer, "Back: %d Fore:", bgd );
            _outtext( buffer );

            /* Loop through 16 foreground colors. */
            for( fgd = 0; fgd < 16; fgd++ )
            {
                _settextcolor( fgd + blink );
                sprintf( buffer, " %2d ", fgd + blink );
                _outtext( buffer );
            }
        }
    }
    _getch();

    /* Restore original foreground, background, and text position. */
    _settextcolor( oldfgd );
    _setbkcolor( oldbgd );
    _clearscreen( _GCLEARSCREEN );
    _settextposition( oldpos.row, oldpos.col );
}
```

_gettextwindow

Description   Gets the boundaries of the current text window.

#include <graph.h>

void __far _gettextwindow(short __far *r1, short __far *c1,
   short __far *r2, short __far *c2);

r1   Top row of current text window

c1   Leftmost column of current text window

r2   Bottom row of current text window

c2   Rightmost column of current text window

Remarks   The **_gettextwindow** function finds the boundaries of the current text window. The text window is the region of the screen to which output from the **_outtext** and **_outmem** functions is limited. By default, this is the entire screen, unless it has been redefined by the **_settextwindow** function.

The window defined by **_settextwindow** has no effect on output from the **_outgtext** function. Text displayed with **_outgtext** is limited to the current viewport.

Return Value   None.

Compatibility
Standards: None
16-Bit: DOS
32-Bit: None

See Also   **_gettextposition, _outmem, _outtext, _scrolltextwindow, _settextposition, _settextwindow, _wrapon**

Example   See the example for **_scrolltextwindow**.

_getvideoconfig

Description

Gets graphics video configuration information.

#include <graph.h>

struct _videoconfig __far * __far _getvideoconfig(struct _videoconfig __far * *config* **);**

config   Configuration information

Remarks

The **_getvideoconfig** function returns the current graphics environment configuration in a **_videoconfig** structure, defined in GRAPH.H.

The values returned reflect the currently active video adapter and monitor, as well as the current video mode.

The **_videoconfig** structure contains the following members, each of which is of type **short**:

Member	Contents
numxpixels	Number of pixels on the x axis
numypixels	Number of pixels on the y axis
numtextcols	Number of text columns available
numtextrows	Number of text rows available
numcolors	Number of color indices
bitsperpixel	Number of bits per pixel
numvideopages	Number of available video pages
adapter	Active display adapter
mode	Current video mode
monitor	Active display monitor
memory	Adapter video memory in kilobytes

The values for the **adapter** member of the **_videoconfig** structure are given by the manifest constants shown in the list below. For any applicable adapter (**_CGA**, **_EGA**, or **_VGA**), the corresponding Olivetti adapter (**_OCGA**, **_OEGA**, or **_OVGA**) represents a superset of graphics capabilities.

Adapter Constant	Meaning
_CGA	Color Graphics Adapter
_EGA	Enhanced Graphics Adapter
_HGC	Hercules Graphics Card
_MCGA	Multicolor Graphics Array
_MDPA	Monochrome Display Printer Adapter
_OCGA	Olivetti (AT&T) Color Graphics Adapter
_OEGA	Olivetti (AT&T) Enhanced Graphics Adapter
_OVGA	Olivetti (AT&T) Video Graphics Array
_VGA	Video Graphics Array
_SVGA	Super Video Graphics Array (VESA)

The values for the **monitor** member of the **_videoconfig** structure are given by the manifest constants listed below:

Monitor Constant	Meaning
_ANALOG	Analog monochrome and color
_ANALOGCOLOR	Analog color only
_ANALOGMONO	Analog monochrome only
_COLOR	Color (or enhanced monitor emulating a color monitor)
_ENHCOLOR	Enhanced color
_MONO	Monochrome monitor

In every text mode, including monochrome, the **_getvideoconfig** function returns the value 32 for the number of available colors. The value 32 indicates the range of values (0–31) accepted by the **_settextcolor** function. This includes 16 normal colors (0–15) and 16 blinking colors (16–31). Blinking is selected by adding 16 to the normal color index. Because monochrome text mode has fewer unique display attributes, some color indices are redundant. However, because blinking is selected in the same manner, monochrome text mode has the same range (0–31) as other text modes.

Return Value   The **_getvideoconfig** function returns the video configuration information in a structure, as noted above. There is no error return.

Compatibility	Standards:	None
	16-Bit:	DOS
	32-Bit:	None

See Also   **_setvideomode**, **_setvideomoderows**

Example

```
/* GVIDCFG.C: This program displays information about the current
 * video configuration.
 */

#include <stdio.h>
#include <graph.h>

void main( void )
{
    struct _videoconfig vc;
    short  c;
    char   b[500];                           /* Buffer for string */

    _getvideoconfig( &vc );

    /* Write all information to a string, then output string. */
    c  = sprintf( b,     "X pixels:     %d\n", vc.numxpixels );
    c += sprintf( b + c, "Y pixels:     %d\n", vc.numypixels );
    c += sprintf( b + c, "Text columns: %d\n", vc.numtextcols );
    c += sprintf( b + c, "Text rows:    %d\n", vc.numtextrows );
    c += sprintf( b + c, "Colors:       %d\n", vc.numcolors );
    c += sprintf( b + c, "Bits/pixel:   %d\n", vc.bitsperpixel );
    c += sprintf( b + c, "Video pages:  %d\n", vc.numvideopages );
    c += sprintf( b + c, "Mode:         %d\n", vc.mode );
    c += sprintf( b + c, "Adapter:      %d\n", vc.adapter );
    c += sprintf( b + c, "Monitor:      %d\n", vc.monitor );
    c += sprintf( b + c, "Memory:       %d\n", vc.memory );
    _outtext( b );
}
```

Output

```
X pixels:     0
Y pixels:     0
Text columns: 80
Text rows:    25
Colors:       32
Bits/pixel:   0
Video pages:  1
Mode:         3
Adapter:      8
Monitor:      24
Memory:       256
```

_getviewcoord Functions

Description   Translate coordinates to view coordinates.

#include <graph.h>

struct _xycoord __far _getviewcoord(short *x*, short *y*);

struct _xycoord __far _getviewcoord_w(double *wx*, double *wy*);

struct _xycoord __far _getviewcoord_wxy(struct _wxycoord
   __far *pwxy1*);

x, y	Physical point to translate
wx, wy	Window point to translate
pwxy1	Window point to translate

Remarks   The **_getviewcoord** routines translate the specified coordinates (x, y) from one coordinate system to view coordinates and then return them in an **_xycoord** structure, defined in GRAPH.H. The **_xycoord** structure contains the following elements:

Element	Description
short xcoord	*x* coordinate
short ycoord	*y* coordinate

The various **_getviewcoord** routines translate in the following manner:

Routine	Translation
_getviewcoord	Physical coordinates (x, y) to view coordinates
_getviewcoord_w	Window coordinates (wx, wy) to view coordinates
_getviewcoord_wxy	Window coordinates structure $(pwxy1)$ to view coordinates

In Microsoft C version 5.1, the function **_getviewcoord** was called **_getlogcoord**.

Return Value   The **_getviewcoord** function returns the coordinates as noted above. There is no error return.

Compatibility

Standards:	None
16-Bit:	DOS
32-Bit:	None

See Also   _getphyscoord, _getwindowcoord, _grstatus

Example   See the example for _setwindow.

_getvisualpage

Description

Gets the current visual page number.

#include <graph.h>

short __far _getvisualpage(void);

Remarks

The _getvisualpage function returns the current visual page number.

Return Value

The function returns the number of the current visual page. All hardware combinations support at least one page (page number 0).

Compatibility

Standards: None
16-Bit: DOS
32-Bit: None

See Also

_getactivepage, _gettextcolor, _gettextposition, _outtext, _setactivepage, _settextcolor, _settextposition, _settextwindow, _setvideomode, _setvisualpage, _wrapon

Example

See the example for _getactivepage.

_getw

Description

Gets an integer from a stream.

#include <stdio.h>

int _getw(FILE *_stream_);

stream   Pointer to **FILE** structure

Remarks

The **_getw** function reads the next binary value of type **int** from the file associated with _stream_ and increments the associated file pointer (if there is one) to point to the next unread character. The **_getw** function does not assume any special alignment of items in the stream.

Return Value

The **_getw** function returns the integer value read. A return value of **EOF** may indicate an error or end-of-file. However, since the **EOF** value is also a legitimate integer value, **feof** or **ferror** should be used to verify an end-of-file or error condition.

Compatibility

Standards: UNIX
16-Bit: DOS, QWIN, WIN, WIN DLL
32-Bit: DOS32X

Use **_getw** for compatibility with ANSI naming conventions of non-ANSI functions. Use **getw** and link with OLDNAMES.LIB for UNIX compatibility.

The **_getw** function is provided primarily for compatibility with previous libraries. Note that portability problems may occur with **_getw**, since the size of the **int** type and the ordering of bytes within the **int** type differ across systems.

See Also

_putw

Example

```
/* GETW.C: This program uses _getw to read a word from a stream,
 * then performs an error check.
 */

#include <stdio.h>
#include <stdlib.h>

void main( void )
{
    FILE *stream;
    int i;

    if( (stream = fopen( "_getw.c", "rb" )) == NULL )
        printf( "Couldn't open file\n" );
    else
    {
        /* Read a word from the stream: */
        i = _getw( stream );

        /* If there is an error... */
        if( ferror( stream ) )
        {
            printf( "_getw failed\n" );
            clearerr( stream );
        }
        else
            printf( "First data word in file: 0x%.4x\n", i );
        fclose( stream );
    }
}
```

Output

```
First data word in file: 0x2a2f
```

_getwindowcoord

Description

Translates view coordinates to window coordinates.

#include <graph.h>

struct _wxycoord __far _getwindowcoord(short *x*, **short** *y* **);**

x, y   Viewport coordinate to translate

Remarks

The **_getwindowcoord** function translates the view coordinates (*x, y*) to window coordinates and returns them in the **_wxycoord** structure, defined in GRAPH.H.

The **_wxycoord** structure contains the following elements:

Element	Description
double wx	*x* coordinate
double wy	*y* coordinate

Return Value

The function returns the coordinates in the **_wxycoord** structure. There is no error return.

Compatibility

Standards: None
16-Bit: DOS
32-Bit: None

See Also

_getphyscoord, **_getviewcoord** functions, **_moveto** functions, **_setwindow**

Example

See the example for **_setwindow**.

_getwritemode

Description   Gets the current logical mode for line drawing.

#include <graph.h>

short __far _getwritemode(void);

Remarks   The **_getwritemode** function returns the current logical write mode, which is used when drawing lines with the **_lineto**, **_polygon**, and **_rectangle** functions.

The default value is **_GPSET**, which causes lines to be drawn in the current graphics color. The other possible return values are **_GXOR**, **_GAND**, **_GOR**, and **_GPRESET**. See **_putimage** for more details on these manifest constants.

Return Value   The **_getwritemode** function returns the current logical write mode, or –1 if not in graphics mode.

Compatibility   Standards: None
16-Bit: DOS
32-Bit: None

See Also   **_grstatus**, **_lineto** functions, **_putimage** functions, **_rectangle** functions, **_setcolor**, **_setlinestyle**, **_setwritemode**

Example
```
/* GWRMODE.C: This program illustrates _getwritemode and _setwritemode. */

#include <conio.h>
#include <stdlib.h>
#include <graph.h>

short wmodes[5]  = { _GPSET,   _GPRESET, _GXOR,    _GOR,    _GAND   };
char *wmstr[5]   = { "PSET  ", "PRESET", "XOR   ", "OR   ", "AND   " };

void box( short x, short y, short size, short writemode, short fillmode );
```

```
void main( void )
{
   short i, x, y;

   /* Find a valid graphics mode. */
   if( !_setvideomode( _MAXCOLORMODE ) )
      exit( 1 );

   x = y = 70;
   box( x, y, 50, _GPSET, _GFILLINTERIOR );
   _setcolor( 2 );
   box( x, y, 40, _GPSET, _GFILLINTERIOR );
   for( i = 0; i < 5; i++ )
   {
      _settextposition( 1, 1 );
      _outtext( wmstr[i] );
      box( x += 12, y += 12, 50, wmodes[i], _GBORDER );
      _getch();
   }
   _setvideomode( _DEFAULTMODE );
   exit( 0 );
}

void box( short x, short y, short size, short writemode, short fillmode )
{
   short wm, side;

   wm = _getwritemode();           /* Save write mode and set new. */
   _setwritemode( writemode );
   _rectangle( fillmode, x - size, y - size, x + size, y + size );
   _setwritemode( wm );            /* Restore original write mode. */
}
```

gmtime

Description

Converts a time value to a structure.

#include <time.h>

struct tm *gmtime(const time_t *time**);**

timer   Pointer to stored time

Remarks

The **gmtime** function converts the *timer* value to a structure. The *timer* argument represents the seconds elapsed since midnight (00:00:00), December 31, 1899, Universal Coordinated Time. This value is usually obtained from a call to the **time** function.

The **gmtime** function breaks down the *timer* value and stores it in a structure of type **tm**, defined in TIME.H. The structure result reflects Universal Coordinated Time, not local time.

The fields of the structure type **tm** store the following values, each of which is an **int**:

Field	Value Stored
tm_sec	Seconds
tm_min	Minutes
tm_hour	Hours (0–24)
tm_mday	Day of month (1–31)
tm_mon	Month (0–11; January = 0)
tm_year	Year (current year minus 1900)
tm_wday	Day of week (0–6; Sunday = 0)
tm_yday	Day of year (0–365; January 1 = 0)
tm_isdst	Always 0 for **gmtime**

The **gmtime, mktime,** and **localtime** functions use a single statically allocated structure to hold the result. Each call to one of these routines destroys the result of any previous call.

If *timer* represents a date before midnight, December 31, 1899, **gmtime** returns **NULL**.

Return Value   The **gmtime** function returns a pointer to the structure result. There is no error return.

Compatibility   Standards: ANSI, UNIX

16-Bit: DOS, QWIN, WIN, WIN DLL

32-Bit: DOS32X

See Also   **asctime, ctime, _ftime, localtime, time**

Example
```
/* GMTIME.C: This program uses gmtime to convert a long-integer
 * representation of Universal Coordinated Time to a structure named newtime,
 * then uses asctime to convert this structure to an output string.
 */

#include <time.h>
#include <stdio.h>

void main( void )
{
    struct tm *newtime;
    long ltime;

    time( &ltime );

    /* Obtain Universal Coordinated Time: */
    newtime = gmtime( &ltime );
    printf( "Universal Coordinated Time is %s\n", asctime( newtime ) );
}
```

Output   Universal Coordinated Time is Wed Jun 16 16:37:53 1999

_grstatus

Description

Returns the status of the most recent graphics function call.

#include <graph.h>

short __far _grstatus(void);

Remarks

The **_grstatus** function returns the status of the most recently used graphics function. The **_grstatus** function can be used immediately following a call to a graphics routine to determine if errors or warnings were generated. Return values less than 0 are errors, and values greater than 0 are warnings.

The following manifest constants are defined in the GRAPH.H header file for use with the **_grstatus** function:

Value	Constant	Meaning
0	**_GROK**	Success.
−1	**_GRERROR**	Graphics error.
−2	**_GRMODENOTSUPPORTED**	Requested video mode not supported.
−3	**_GRNOTINPROPERMODE**	Requested routine only works in certain video modes.
−4	**_GRINVALIDPARAMETER**	One or more parameters invalid.
−5	**_GRFONTFILENOTFOUND**	No matching font file found.
−6	**_GRINVALIDFONTFILE**	One or more font files invalid.
−7	**_GRCORRUPTEDFONTFILE**	One or more font files inconsistent.
−8	**_GRINSUFFICIENTMEMORY**	Not enough memory to allocate buffer or to complete a **_floodfill** operation.
−9	**_GRINVALIDIMAGEBUFFER**	Image buffer data inconsistent.
1	**_GRNOOUTPUT**	Nothing drawn.
2	**_GRCLIPPED**	Output was clipped to viewport.
3	**_GRPARAMETERALTERED**	One or more input parameters was altered to be within range, or pairs of parameters were interchanged to be in the proper order.

After a graphics call, use an **if** statement to compare the return value of **_grstatus** to **_GROK**. For example:

```
if( _grstatus < _GROK )
    /*handle graphics error*/ ;
```

The functions listed below cannot cause errors, and they all set **_grstatus** to **_GROK**:

_displaycursor	**_gettextposition**	**_outtext**
_getactivepage	**_gettextwindow**	**_unregisterfonts**
_getbkcolor	**_getvideoconfig**	**_wrapon**
_getgtextvector	**_getvisualpage**	
_gettextcolor	**_outmem**	

See the list below for the graphics functions that affect **_grstatus**. The list shows error or warning messages that can be set by the graphics function. In addition to the error codes listed, any of these functions can produce the **_GRERROR** error code.

Function	Possible _grstatus Error Codes	Possible _grstatus Warning Codes
_arc functions	**_GRNOTINPROPERMODE,** **_GRINVALIDPARAMETER**	**_GRNOOUTPUT,** **_GRCLIPPED**
_clearscreen	**_GRNOTINPROPERMODE,** **_GRINVALIDPARAMETER**	
_ellipse functions	**_GRNOTINPROPERMODE,** **_GRINVALIDPARAMETER,** **_GRINSUFFICIENTMEMORY**	**_GRNOOUTPUT,** **_GRCLIPPED**
_floodfill functions	**_GRNOTINPROPERMODE,** **_GRINVALIDPARAMETER,** **_GRINSUFFICIENTMEMORY**	**_GRNOOUTPUT**
_getarcinfo	**_GRNOTINPROPERMODE**	
_getcurrentposition functions	**_GRNOTINPROPERMODE**	
_getfontinfo	(**_GRERROR** only)	
_getgtextextent	(**_GRERROR** only)	
_getgtextvector	**_GRPARAMETERALTERED**	
_getimage functions	**_GRNOTINPROPERMODE**	**_GRPARAMETERALTERED**
_getphyscoord	**_GRNOTINPROPERMODE**	
_getpixel functions	**_GRNOTINPROPERMODE**	
_gettextcursor	**_GRNOTINPROPERMODE**	
_getviewcoord functions	**_GRNOTINPROPERMODE**	
_getwindowcoord	**_GRNOTINPROPERMODE**	

Function	Possible _grstatus Error Codes	Possible _grstatus Warning Codes
_getwritemode	_GRNOTINPROPERMODE	
_imagesize functions	_GRNOTINPROPERMODE	
_lineto functions	_GRNOTINPROPERMODE	_GRNOOUTPUT, _GRCLIPPED
_moveto functions	_GRNOTINPROPERMODE	
_outgtext	_GRNOTINPROPERMODE	_GRCLIPPED, _GRNOOUTPUT
_pie functions	_GRNOTINPROPERMODE, _GRINVALIDPARAMETER, _GRINSUFFICIENTMEMORY	_GRNOOUTPUT, _GRCLIPPED
_polygon functions	_GRNOTINPROPERMODE, _GRINVALIDPARAMETER, _GRINSUFFICIENTMEMORY	_GRNOOUTPUT, _GRCLIPPED
_putimage functions	_GRERROR, _GRNOTINPROPERMODE, _GRINVALIDPARAMETER, _GRINVALIDIMAGEBUFFER	_GRPARAMETERALTERED, _GRNOOUTPUT
_rectangle functions	_GRNOTINPROPERMODE, _GRINVALIDPARAMETER, _GRINSUFFICIENTMEMORY	_GRNOOUTPUT, _GRCLIPPED
_registerfonts	_GRCORRUPTEDFONTFILE, _GRFONTFILENOTFOUND, _GRINSUFFICIENTMEMORY, _GRINVALIDFONTFILE	
_remappalette	_GRERROR, _GRINVALIDPARAMETER	
_remapallpalette	_GRERROR, _GRINVALIDPARAMETER	
_scrolltextwindow		_GRNOOUTPUT
_selectpalette	_GRNOTINPROPERMODE, _GRINVALIDPARAMETER	
_setactivepage	_GRINVALIDPARAMETER	
_setbkcolor	_GRINVALIDPARAMETER	_GRPARAMETERALTERED
_setcliprgn	_GRNOTINPROPERMODE	_GRPARAMETERALTERED
_setcolor	_GRNOTINPROPERMODE	_GRPARAMETERALTERED
_setfont	_GRERROR, _GRFONTFILENOTFOUND, _GRINSUFFICIENTMEMORY, _GRPARAMETERALTERED	
_setgtextvector	_GRPARAMETERALTERED	
_setpixel	_GRNOTINPROPERMODE	_GRNOOUTPUT

Function	Possible _grstatus Error Codes	Possible _grstatus Warning Codes
_settextcolor		_GRPARAMETERALTERED
_settextcursor	_GRNOTINPROPERMODE	
_settextposition		_GRPARAMETERALTERED
_settextrows	_GRINVALIDPARAMETER	_GRPARAMETERALTERED
_settextwindow		_GRPARAMETERALTERED
_setvideomode	_GRERROR, _GRMODENOTSUPPORTED, _GRINVALIDPARAMETER	
_setvideomoderows	_GRERROR, _GRMODENOTSUPPORTED, _GRINVALIDPARAMETER	
_setvieworg	_GRNOTINPROPERMODE	
_setviewport	_GRNOTINPROPERMODE	_GRPARAMETERALTERED
_setvisualpage	_GRINVALIDPARAMETER	
_setwindow	_GRNOTINPROPERMODE, _GRINVALIDPARAMETER	_GRPARAMETERALTERED
_setwritemode	_GRNOTINPROPERMODE, _GRINVALIDPARAMETER	

Return Value   The **_grstatus** function returns the status of the most recently used graphics function.

See Also   **_arc** functions, **_ellipse** functions, **_floodfill** functions, **_lineto** functions, **_pie** functions, **_remapallpalette**, **_setactivepage**, **_setbkcolor**, **_setcolor**, **_setpixel** functions, **_settextcolor**, **_settextcursor**, **_setvisualpage**, **_setwindow**, **_setwritemode**

Compatibility
Standards:	None
16-Bit:	DOS
32-Bit:	None

_halloc

Description

Allocates a huge memory block.

#include <malloc.h>   Required only for function declarations

void __huge *_halloc(long *num*, **size_t** *size* **);**

num	Number of elements
size	Length in bytes of each element

Remarks

The **_halloc** function allocates a huge array from the operating system consisting of *num* elements, each of which is *size* bytes long. Each element is initialized to 0. If the size of the array is greater than 128K (131,072 bytes), the size of an array element must then be a power of 2.

Use the **_hfree** function to deallocate a block of memory returned by **halloc**.

Return Value

The **_halloc** function returns a **void** huge pointer to the allocated space, which is guaranteed to be suitably aligned for storage of any type of object. To get a pointer to a type other than **void** huge, use a type cast on the return value. If the request cannot be satisfied, the return value is **NULL**.

Compatibility

Standards: None
16-Bit: DOS, QWIN, WIN, WIN DLL
32-Bit: None

See Also

calloc functions, **free** functions, **_hfree**, **malloc** functions

Example
```
/* HALLOC.C: This program uses _halloc to allocate space for 30,000 long
 * integers, then uses _hfree to deallocate the memory.
 */

#include <stdio.h>
#include <stdlib.h>
#include <malloc.h>

void main( void )
{
    long __huge *hbuf;

    /* Allocate huge buffer */
    hbuf = (long __huge *)_halloc( 30000L, sizeof( long ) );
    if ( hbuf == NULL )
        printf( "Insufficient memory available\n" );
    else
        printf( "Memory successfully allocated\n" );

    /* Free huge buffer */
    _hfree( hbuf );
}
```

Output   Memory successfully allocated

_hard Functions

Description

Handle critical error conditions.

#include <dos.h>

void _harderr(void(__far *_handler_)( ));

void _hardresume(int _result_);

void _hardretn(int _error_);

handler ( )	New INT 0x24 handler
result	Handler return parameter
error	Error to return from

Remarks

These three functions are used to handle critical error conditions that use DOS interrupt 0x24. The **_harderr** function installs a new critical-error handler for interrupt 0x24.

When a critical error occurs, control is passed to the function specified in the **_harderr** call. The **_hardresume** and **_hardretn** functions control how the program will return from the critical error handler.

The **_hardresume** function returns to DOS the code that encountered the critical error.

The **_hardretn** function returns directly to the application program that issued the INT 0x21 DOS system call, which, in turn, encountered the critical error.

The **_harderr** function does not directly install the handler pointed to by _handler_; instead, **_harderr** installs a handler that calls the function referenced by _handler_. The handler calls the function with the following parameters:

handler(unsigned _deverror_, unsigned _errcode_, unsigned __far *_devhdr_);

The _deverror_ argument is the device error code. It contains the AX register value passed by DOS to the INT 0x24 handler. The _errcode_ argument is the DI register value that DOS passes to the handler. The low-order byte of *errcode* can be one of the following values:

Code	Meaning
0	Attempt to write to a write-protected disk
1	Unknown unit
2	Drive not ready
3	Unknown command
4	Cyclic-redundancy-check error in data
5	Bad drive-request structure length
6	Seek error
7	Unknown media type
8	Sector not found
9	Printer out of paper
10	Write fault
11	Read fault
12	General failure

The *devhdr* argument is a far pointer to a device header that contains descriptive information about the device on which the error occurred. The user-defined handler must not change the information in the device-header control block.

Errors on Disk Devices

If the error occurred on a disk device, the high-order bit (bit 15) of the *deverror* argument will be set to 0, and the *deverror* argument will indicate the following:

Bit	Meaning
15	Disk error if false (0).
14	Not used.
13	"Ignore" response not allowed if false (0).
12	"Retry" response not allowed if false (0).
11	"Fail" response not allowed if false (0). Note that DOS changes "fail" to "abort".
10, 9	

Code	Location
00	DOS
01	File allocation table
10	Directory
11	Data area

Bit	Meaning
8	Read error if false; write error if true.

The low-order byte of *deverror* indicates the drive in which the error occurred (0 = drive A, 1 = drive B, etc.).

Errors on Other Devices

If the error occurs on a device other than a disk drive, the high-order bit (bit 15) of the *deverror* argument is 1. The attribute word located at offset 4 in the device-header block indicates the type of device that had the error. If bit 15 of the attribute word is 0, the error is a bad memory image of the file allocation table. If the bit is 1, the error occurred on a character device and bits 0–3 of the attribute word indicate the type of device, as shown in the following list:

Bit	Meaning
0	Current standard input
1	Current standard output
2	Current null device
3	Current clock device

Restrictions on Handler Functions

The user-defined handler function can issue only system calls 0x01 through 0x0C, or 0x59. Thus, many of the standard C run-time functions (such as the I/O and **_heap** functions) cannot be used in a hardware error handler. System call 0x59 can be used to obtain further information about the error that occurred.

Using _hardresume and _harderr

If the handler returns, it can do so in several different ways:

- Via the **return** statement
- By calling the **_hardresume** function
- By calling the **_hardretn** function

If the handler returns from **_hardresume** or from a **return** statement, control returns to DOS.

The **_hardresume** function should be called only from within the user-defined hardware error-handler function. The result supplied to **_hardresume** must be one of the following constants:

Constant	Action
_HARDERR_ABORT	Aborts the program by issuing INT 0x24
_HARDERR_FAIL	Fails the system call that is in progress (this is not supported on DOS 2.x)
_HARDERR_IGNORE	Ignores the error
_HARDERR_RETRY	Retries the operation

The **_hardretn** function allows the user-defined hardware error handler to return directly to the application program rather than returning to DOS. The application resumes at the point just after the failing I/O function request. The **_hardretn** function should be called only from within a user-defined hardware error-handler function.

The error parameter of **_hardretn** should be a DOS error code, as opposed to the XENIX-style error code that is available in **errno**. Refer to *MS-DOS Encyclopedia* (Duncan, ed.; Redmond, Wa.: Microsoft Press, 1988) or *Programmer's PC Sourcebook* 2nd ed. (Hogan; Redmond, Wa.: Microsoft Press, 1991) for information about the DOS error codes that may be returned by a given DOS function call.

If the failing I/O function request is an INT 0x21 function greater than or equal to function 0x38, **_hardretn** will then return to the application with the carry flag set and the AX register set to the **_hardretn** *error* parameter. If the failing INT 0x21 function request is less than function 0x38 and the function can return an error, the AL register will be set to 0xFF on return to the application. If the failing INT 0x21 does not have a way of returning an error condition (which is true of certain INT 0x21 functions below 0x38), the error parameter of **_hardretn** is not used, and no error code is returned to the application.

Return Value   None.

Compatibility   Standards: None
                       16-Bit: DOS
                       32-Bit: None

See Also   **_chain_intr**, **_dos_getvect**, **_dos_setvect**

_ heapadd Functions

Description   Add memory to the heap (**_ heapadd**) or to the based heap (**_ bheapadd**).

#include <malloc.h>   Required only for function declarations

int _ heapadd(void _ _ far **memblock***, size_ t** *size* **);**

int _ bheapadd(_ _ segment *seg***, void _ _ based (void) ****memblock***, size_ t** *size* **);**

seg	Based-heap segment selector
buffer	Pointer to heap memory
size	Size in bytes of memory to add

Remarks   The **_ heapadd** and **_ bheapadd** functions add an unused piece of memory to the heap. The **_ bheapadd** function adds the memory to the based heap specified by *seg*. The **_ heapadd** function looks at the segment value and, if it is DGROUP, adds the memory to the near heap. Otherwise, **_ heapadd** adds the memory to the far heap.

Return Value   These functions return 0 if successful, or –1 if an error occurred.

Compatibility   **_ headadd**

Standards:	None
16-Bit:	DOS
32-Bit:	DOS32X

_ bheadadd

Standards:	None
16-Bit:	DOS, QWIN, WIN, WIN DLL
32-Bit:	None

See Also   **free** functions, **_ halloc**, **_ hfree**, **malloc** functions, **realloc** functions

Example

```c
/* HEAPMIN.C: This program illustrates heap management using
 * _heapadd and _heapmin.
 */

#include <stdio.h>
#include <conio.h>
#include <process.h>
#include <malloc.h>

void heapdump( char *msg );      /* Prototype */

char s1[] = { "Here are some strings that we use at first, then don't\n" };
char s2[] = { "need any more. We'll give their space to the heap.\n" };

void main( void )
{
    int *p[3], i;

    printf( "%s%s", s1, s2 );
    heapdump( "Initial heap" );

    /* Give space of used strings to heap. */
    if ( _heapadd( s1, sizeof( s1 )) == -1 )
        printf("Error.\n");
    if ( _heapadd( s2, sizeof( s2 )) == -1 )
        printf("Error.\n");
    heapdump( "After adding used strings" );

    /* Allocate some blocks. Some may use string blocks from _heapadd. */
    for( i = 0; i < 2; i++ )
        if( (p[i] = (int *)calloc( 10 * (i + 1), sizeof( int ) )) == NULL )
        {
            --i;
            break;
        }
    heapdump( "After allocating memory" );

    /* Free some of the blocks. */
    free( p[1] );
    free( p[2] );
    heapdump( "After freeing memory" );

    /* Minimize heap. */
    _heapmin();
    heapdump( "After compacting heap" );
}
```

```
/* Walk through heap entries, displaying information about each block. */
void heapdump( char *msg )
{
    _HEAPINFO hi;

    printf( "%s\n", msg );
    hi._pentry = NULL;
    while( _heapwalk( &hi ) == _HEAPOK )
        printf( "\t%s block at %Fp of size %u\t\n",
                hi._useflag == _USEDENTRY ? "USED" : "FREE",
                hi._pentry,
                hi._size );
    printf("Press any key.\n");
    _getch();
}
```

Output   Here are some strings that we use at first, then don't
need any more. We'll give their space to the heap.
```
Initial heap
    USED block at 2D39:0E9C of size 364
    USED block at 2D39:100A of size 36
    USED block at 2D39:1030 of size 512
    FREE block at 2D39:1232 of size 460
After adding used strings
    FREE block at 2D39:0044 of size 52
    FREE block at 2D39:007A of size 50
    USED block at 2D39:00AE of size 3564
    USED block at 2D39:0E9C of size 364
    USED block at 2D39:100A of size 36
    USED block at 2D39:1030 of size 512
    FREE block at 2D39:1232 of size 460
After allocating memory
    USED block at 2D39:0044 of size 20
    USED block at 2D39:005A of size 40
    FREE block at 2D39:0084 of size 40
    USED block at 2D39:00AE of size 3564
    USED block at 2D39:0E9C of size 364
    USED block at 2D39:100A of size 36
    USED block at 2D39:1030 of size 512
    FREE block at 2D39:1232 of size 460
After freeing memory
    USED block at 2D39:0044 of size 20
    FREE block at 2D39:005A of size 40
    FREE block at 2D39:0084 of size 40
    USED block at 2D39:00AE of size 3564
    USED block at 2D39:0E9C of size 364
    USED block at 2D39:100A of size 36
    USED block at 2D39:1030 of size 512
    FREE block at 2D39:1232 of size 460
```

```
After compacting heap
    USED block at 2D39:0044 of size 20
    FREE block at 2D39:005A of size 82
    USED block at 2D39:00AE of size 3564
    USED block at 2D39:0E9C of size 364
    USED block at 2D39:100A of size 36
    USED block at 2D39:1030 of size 512
    FREE block at 2D39:1232 of size 12
```

_heapchk Functions

Description

Run consistency checks on the heap.

#include <malloc.h>

int _heapchk(void);

int _bheapchk(__segment *seg*);

int _fheapchk(void);

int _nheapchk(void);

seg   Specified base heap

Remarks

The **_heapchk** routines help to debug heap-related problems by checking for mini-mal consistency of the heap. Each function checks a particular heap, as listed below:

Function	Heap Checked
_heapchk	Depends on data model of program
_bheapchk	Based heap specified by *seg* value
_fheapchk	Far heap (outside the default data segment)
_nheapchk	Near heap (inside the default data segment)

In large data models (that is, compact-, large-, and huge-model programs), **_heapchk** maps to **_fheapchk**. In small data models (tiny-, small-, and medium-model programs), **_heapchk** maps to **_nheapchk**.

For **_heapchk**, if the *seg* value is **_NULLSEG**, all based heap segments are checked; otherwise, only the specified one is checked.

Return Value	All four routines return an integer value that is one of the following manifest constants (defined in MALLOC.H):

Constant	Meaning
_HEAPBADBEGIN	Initial header information cannot be found, or it is bad.
_HEAPBADNODE	Bad node has been found, or the heap is damaged.
_HEAPEMPTY	Heap has not been initialized.
_HEAPOK	Heap appears to be consistent.

Compatibility

_heapchk

Standards:	None
16-Bit:	DOS
32-Bit:	DOS32X

_bheapchk, _fheapchk

Standards:	None
16-Bit:	DOS, QWIN, WIN, WIN DLL
32-Bit:	None

_nheapchk

Standards:	None
16-Bit:	DOS
32-Bit:	None

See Also

_heapset functions, **_heapwalk** functions

Example

```
/* HEAPCHK.C: This program checks the heap for consistency
 * and prints an appropriate message.
 */

#include <malloc.h>
#include <stdio.h>
```

```
void main( void )
{
   int  heapstatus;
   char *buffer;

   /* Allocate and deallocate some memory */
   if( (buffer = (char *)malloc( 100 )) != NULL )
      free( buffer );

   /* Check heap status */
   heapstatus = _heapchk();
   switch( heapstatus )
   {
      case _HEAPOK:
         printf(" OK - heap is fine\n" );
         break;
      case _HEAPEMPTY:
         printf(" OK - heap is empty\n" );
         break;
      case _HEAPBADBEGIN:
         printf( "ERROR - bad start of heap\n" );
         break;
      case _HEAPBADNODE:
         printf( "ERROR - bad node in heap\n" );
         break;
   }
}
```

Output   OK - heap is fine

_heapmin Functions

Description

Release unused heap memory to the operating system.

#include <malloc.h>

int _heapmin(void);

int _bheapmin(__segment *seg* **)**

int _fheapmin(void);

int _nheapmin(void);

seg   Specified based-heap selector

Remarks

The **_heapmin** functions minimize the heap by releasing unused heap memory to the operating system.

The various **_heapmin** functions release unused memory in these heaps:

Function	Heap Minimized
_heapmin	Depends on data model of program.
_bheapmin	Based heap specified by *seg* value; **_NULLSEG** specifies all based heaps.
_fheapmin	Far heap (outside default data segment).
_nheapmin	Near heap (inside default data segment).

In large data models (that is, compact-, large-, and huge-model programs), **_heapmin** maps to **_fheapmin**. In small data models (tiny-, small-, and medium-model programs), **_heapmin** maps to **_nheapmin**.

For **_heapmin**, if the supplied *seg* value is **_NULLSEG**, all based heap segments are minimized; otherwise, only the specified one is minimized.

Based-heap segments are never freed (i.e., unlinked from the based heap list and released back to the operating system) by the **_bheapmin** function. The **_bfreeseg** function is used for that purpose.

Return Value

The **_heapmin** functions return 0 if the function completed successfully, or –1 in the case of an error.

Compatibility

_heapmin

Standards:	None
16-Bit:	DOS, QWIN, WIN, WIN DLL
32-Bit:	DOS32X

_bheapmin, _fheapmin, _nheapmin

Standards:	None
16-Bit:	DOS, QWIN, WIN, WIN DLL
32-Bit:	None

See Also

_bfreeseg, **free** functions, **malloc** functions

_heapset Functions

Description

Check heaps for minimal consistency and set the free entries to a specified value.

#include <malloc.h>

int _heapset(unsigned int *fill* **);**

int _bheapset(__ segment *seg*, **unsigned int** *fill* **);**

int _fheapset(unsigned int *fill* **);**

int _nheapset(unsigned int *fill* **);**

fill	Fill character
seg	Specified based-heap segment selector

Remarks

The **_heapset** family of routines helps debug heap-related problems in programs by showing free memory locations or nodes unintentionally overwritten.

The **_heapset** routines first check for minimal consistency on the heap in a manner identical to that of the **_heapchk** functions. In addition, the **_heapset** functions set each byte of the heap's free entries to the *fill* value. This known value shows which memory locations of the heap contain free nodes and which locations contain data that were unintentionally written to freed memory.

The various **_heapset** functions check and fill these heaps:

Function	Heap Filled
_heapset	Depends on data model of program.
_bheapset	Based heap specified by *seg* value; **_NULLSEG** specifies all based heaps.
_fheapset	Far heap (outside default data segment).
_nheapset	Near heap (inside default data segment).

In large data models (that is, compact-, large-, and huge-model programs), **_heapset** maps to **_fheapset**. In small data models (tiny-, small-, and medium-model programs), **_heapset** maps to **_nheapset**.

For **_heapset**, if the *seg* value is **_NULLSEG**, all based heap segments are checked; otherwise, only the specified one is checked.

Return Value   All four routines return an **int** whose value is one of the following manifest constants (defined in MALLOC.H):

Constant	Meaning
_HEAPBADBEGIN	Initial header information cannot be found, or it is invalid.
_HEAPBADNODE	Bad node has been found, or the heap is damaged.
_HEAPEMPTY	Heap has not been initialized.
_HEAPOK	Heap appears to be consistent.

Compatibility   **_heapset**

Standards:	None
16-Bit:	DOS
32-Bit:	DOS32X

_bheapset, _fheapset

Standards:	None
16-Bit:	DOS, QWIN, WIN, WIN DLL
32-Bit:	None

_nheapset

Standards:	None
16-Bit:	DOS
32-Bit:	None

See Also   **_heapchk** functions, **_heapwalk** functions

Example
```
/* HEAPSET.C: This program checks the heap and fills in free entries
 * with the character 'Z'.
 */

#include <malloc.h>
#include <stdio.h>
#include <stdlib.h>
```

```
void main( void )
{
    int heapstatus;
    char *buffer;

    if( (buffer = malloc( 1 )) == NULL )   /* Make sure heap is initialized */
        exit( 0 );
    heapstatus = _heapset( 'Z' );          /* Fill in free entries */
    switch( heapstatus )
    {
        case _HEAPOK:
            printf( "OK - heap is fine\n" );
            break;
        case _HEAPEMPTY:
            printf( "OK - heap is empty\n" );
            break;
        case _HEAPBADBEGIN:
            printf( "ERROR - bad start of heap\n" );
            break;
        case _HEAPBADNODE:
            printf( "ERROR - bad node in heap\n" );
            break;
    }
    free( buffer );
}
```

Output   OK - heap is fine

_heapwalk Functions

Description   Traverse the heap and return information about the next entry.

include <malloc.h>

int **_heapwalk**(_HEAPINFO *entryinfo*);

int **_bheapwalk**(__segment *seg*, _HEAPINFO *entryinfo*);

int **_fheapwalk**(_HEAPINFO *entryinfo*);

int **_nheapwalk**(_HEAPINFO *entryinfo*);

entryinfo	Buffer to contain heap information
seg	Based-heap segment selector

Remarks   The **_heapwalk** family of routines helps debug heap-related problems in programs.

The **_heapwalk** routines walk through the heap, traversing one entry per call, and return a pointer to a structure of type **_HEAPINFO** that contains information about the next heap entry. The **_HEAPINFO** type, defined in MALLOC.H, contains the following elements:

Element	Description
int far *_pentry	Heap entry pointer
size_t _size	Size of heap entry
int _useflag	Entry "in use" flag

A call to **_heapwalk** that returns **_HEAPOK** stores the size of the entry in the **_size** field and sets the **_useflag** field to either **_FREEENTRY** or **_USEDENTRY** (both are constants defined in MALLOC.H). To obtain this information about the first entry in the heap, pass the **_heapwalk** routine a pointer to a **_HEAPINFO** structure whose **_pentry** member is **NULL**.

The various **_heapwalk** functions walk through and gather information on these heaps:

Function	Heap Walked
_heapwalk	Depends on data model of program.
_bheapwalk	Based heap specified by *seg* value; **_NULLSEG** specifies all based heaps.
_fheapwalk	Far heap (outside default data segment).
_nheapwalk	Near heap (inside default data segment).

In large data models (that is, compact-, large-, and huge-model programs), **_heapwalk** maps to **_fheapwalk**. In small data models (tiny-, small-, and medium-model programs), **_heapwalk** maps to **_nheapwalk**.

For **_heapwalk**, if the *seg* value is **_NULLSEG**, all based heap segments will be traversed; otherwise, only the specified based heap is walked.

Return Value

All three routines return one of the following manifest constants (defined in MALLOC.H):

Constant	Meaning
_HEAPBADBEGIN	The initial header information cannot be found, or it is invalid.
_HEAPBADNODE	A bad node has been found, or the heap is damaged.
_HEAPBADPTR	The **_pentry** field of the **_HEAPINFO** structure does not contain a valid pointer into the heap.
_HEAPEND	The end of the heap has been reached successfully.
_HEAPEMPTY	The heap has not been initialized.
_HEAPOK	No errors so far; the **_HEAPINFO** structure contains information about the next entry.

Compatibility

_heapwalk

Standards:	None
16-Bit:	DOS
32-Bit:	DOS32X

_bheapwalk, _fheapwalk

Standards:	None
16-Bit:	DOS, QWIN, WIN, WIN DLL
32-Bit:	None

_nheapwalk

Standards: None

16-Bit: DOS

32-Bit: None

See Also   **_heapchk** functions, **_heapset** functions

Example
```
/* HEAPWALK.C: This program "walks" the heap, starting at the beginning
 * (_pentry = NULL). It prints out each heap entry's use, location,
 * and size. It also prints out information about the overall state
 * of the heap as soon as _heapwalk returns a value other than _HEAPOK.
 */

#include <stdio.h>
#include <malloc.h>

void heapdump( void );

void main( void )
{
    char *buffer;

    heapdump();
    if( (buffer = malloc( 59 )) != NULL )
    {
        heapdump();
        free( buffer );
    }
    heapdump();
}

void heapdump( void )
{
    _HEAPINFO hinfo;
    int heapstatus;

    hinfo._pentry = NULL;
    while( ( heapstatus = _heapwalk( &hinfo ) ) == _HEAPOK )
    {
        printf( "%6s block at %Fp of size %4.4X\n",
            ( hinfo._useflag == _USEDENTRY ? "USED" : "FREE" ),
            hinfo._pentry, hinfo._size );
    }
```

```
switch( heapstatus )
{
    case _HEAPEMPTY:
        printf( "OK - empty heap\n" );
        break;
    case _HEAPEND:
        printf( "OK - end of heap\n" );
        break;
    case _HEAPBADPTR:
        printf( "ERROR - bad pointer to heap\n" );
        break;
    case _HEAPBADBEGIN:
        printf( "ERROR - bad start of heap\n" );
        break;
    case _HEAPBADNODE:
        printf( "ERROR - bad node in heap\n" );
        break;
}
}
```

Output
```
  USED block at 0067:103E of size 000E
  USED block at 0067:104E of size 01F4
  USED block at 0067:1244 of size 0026
  USED block at 0067:126C of size 0200
  FREE block at 0067:146E of size 0B90
OK - end of heap
  USED block at 0067:103E of size 000E
  USED block at 0067:104E of size 01F4
  USED block at 0067:1244 of size 0026
  USED block at 0067:126C of size 0200
  USED block at 0067:146E of size 003C
  FREE block at 0067:14AC of size 0B52
OK - end of heap
  USED block at 0067:103E of size 000E
  USED block at 0067:104E of size 01F4
  USED block at 0067:1244 of size 0026
  USED block at 0067:126C of size 0200
  FREE block at 0067:146E of size 003C
  FREE block at 0067:14AC of size 0B52
OK - end of heap
```

_hfree

Description

Frees a huge memory block.

#include <malloc.h>   Required only for function declarations

void _hfree(void _ _huge *memblock* **);**

memblock   Pointer to allocated memory block

Remarks

The **_hfree** function deallocates a memory block; the freed memory is returned to the operating system. The *memblock* argument points to a memory block previously allocated through a call to **_halloc**. The number of bytes freed is the number of bytes specified when the block was allocated.

Note that attempting to free an invalid *memblock* argument (one not allocated with **_halloc**) may affect subsequent allocation and cause errors.

Return Value

None.

Compatibility

Standards: None
16-Bit: DOS, QWIN, WIN, WIN DLL
32-Bit: None

See Also

_halloc

Example

```
/* HALLOC.C: This program uses _halloc to allocate space for 30,000 long
 * integers, then uses _hfree to deallocate the memory.
 */

#include <stdio.h>
#include <stdlib.h>
#include <malloc.h>
```

```
void main( void )
{
   long __huge *hbuf;

   /* Allocate huge buffer */
   hbuf = (long __huge *)_halloc( 30000L, sizeof( long ) );
   if ( hbuf == NULL )
      printf( "Insufficient memory available\n" );
   else
      printf( "Memory successfully allocated\n" );

   /* Free huge buffer */
   _hfree( hbuf );
}
```

Output   Memory successfully allocated

_hypot, _hypotl

Description

Calculate the hypotenuse.

#include <math.h>

double _hypot(double *x*, double *y*);

long double _hypotl(long double *x*, long double *y*);

x, y   Floating-point values

Remarks

The **_hypot** and **_hypotl** functions calculate the length of the hypotenuse of a right triangle, given the length of the two sides *x* and *y* (or *xl* and *yl*). A call to **_hypot** is equivalent to $\sqrt{x^2 + y^2}$.

The **_hypotl** function uses the 80-bit, 10-byte coprocessor form of arguments and return values. See the reference page on the long double functions for more details on this data type.

Return Value

The functions return the length of the hypotenuse. If an overflow results, the functions return **HUGE_VAL** and set **errno** to **ERANGE.**

Compatibility

_hypot

Standards:	UNIX
16-Bit:	DOS, QWIN, WIN, WIN DLL
32-Bit:	DOS32X

Use **_hypot** for compatibility with ANSI naming conventions of non-ANSI functions. Use **hypot** and link with OLDNAMES.LIB for UNIX compatibility.

_hypotl

Standards:	None
16-Bit:	DOS, QWIN, WIN, WIN DLL
32-Bit:	None

See Also

_cabs

Example   /* HYPOT.C: This program prints the hypotenuse of a right triangle. */

```
#include <math.h>
#include <stdio.h>

void main( void )
{
    double x = 3.0, y = 4.0;

    printf( "If a right triangle has sides %2.1f and %2.1f, "
            "its hypotenuse is %2.1f\n", x, y, _hypot( x, y ) );
}
```

Output   If a right triangle has sides 3.0 and 4.0, its hypotenuse is 5.0

_imagesize Functions

Description   Get amount of memory required to store graphics images.

#include <graph.h>

long __far _imagesize(short *x1*, short *y1*, short *x2*, short *y2*);

long __far _imagesize_w(double *wx1*, double *wy1*, double *wx2*, double *wy2*);

long __far _imagesize_wxy(struct _wxycoord __far *pwxy1*,
   struct _wxycoord __far *pwxy2*);

x1, *y1*	Upper-left corner of bounding rectangle
x2, *y2*	Lower-right corner of bounding rectangle
wx1, *wy1*	Upper-left corner of bounding rectangle
wx2, *wy2*	Lower-right corner of bounding rectangle
pwxy1	Upper-left corner of bounding rectangle
pwxy2	Lower-right corner of bounding rectangle

Remarks   The functions in the **_imagesize** family return the number of bytes needed to store the image defined by the bounding rectangle and specified by the coordinates given in the function call.

The **_imagesize** function defines the bounding rectangle in terms of view-coordinate points (*x1*, *y1*) and (*x2*, *y2*).

The **_imagesize_w** function defines the bounding rectangle in terms of window-coordinate points (*x1*, *y1*) and (*x2*, *y2*).

The **_imagesize_wxy** function defines the bounding rectangle in terms of the window-coordinate pairs *pwxy1* and *pwxy2*.

Return Value   The function returns the storage size of the image in bytes. There is no error return.

Compatibility	Standards:	None
	16-Bit:	DOS
	32-Bit:	None

See Also   **_getimage** functions, **_getvideoconfig**, **_putimage** functions

Example   See the example for **_getimage**.

_inp, _inpw

Description

Input a byte (**_inp**) or a word (**_inpw**) from a port.

#include <conio.h>   Required only for function declarations

int _inp(unsigned *port* **);**

unsigned _inpw(unsigned *port* **);**

port   Port number

Remarks

The **_inp** and **_inpw** functions read a byte and a word, respectively, from the specified input port. The input value can be any unsigned integer in the range 0 – 65,535.

Return Value

The functions return the byte or word read from *port*. There is no error return.

Compatibility

Standards: None
16-Bit: DOS
32-Bit: None

See Also

_outp, _outpw

Example

See the example for **_outp**.

_int86

Description

Executes an 8086 interrupt.

#include <dos.h>

int _int86(int *intnum***, union _REGS** **inregs***, union _REGS** **outregs* **);**

intnum	Interrupt number
inregs	Register values on call
outregs	Register values on return

Remarks

The **_int86** function executes the 8086-processor-family interrupt specified by the interrupt number *intnum*. Before executing the interrupt, **_int86** copies the contents of *inregs* to the corresponding registers. After the interrupt returns, the function copies the current register values to *outregs*. It also copies the status of the system carry flag to the **cflag** field in the *outregs* argument. The *inregs* and *outregs* arguments are unions of type **_REGS**. The union type is defined in the include file DOS.H.

Do not use the **_int86** function to call interrupts that modify the DS register. Instead, use the **_int86x** function. (The **_int86x** function loads the DS and ES registers from the *segregs* parameter and also stores the DS and ES registers into *segregs* after the function call.)

The **_REGS** type is defined in the include file DOS.H.

Return Value

The return value is the value in the AX register after the interrupt returns. If the **cflag** field in *outregs* is nonzero, an error has occurred; in such cases, the **_doserrno** variable is also set to the corresponding error code.

Compatibility

Standards:	None
16-Bit:	DOS, QWIN, WIN, WIN DLL
32-Bit:	None

See Also

_bdos, _int86x, _intdos, _intdosx

Example

```
/* INT86.C: This program uses _int86 to call the BIOS video service
 * (INT 10H) to get information about the cursor.
 */

#include <dos.h>
#include <stdio.h>

void main( void )
{
    union _REGS inregs, outregs;

    /* Set up to get cursor information. */
    inregs.h.ah = 3;        /* Get Cursor Position function */
    inregs.h.bh = 0;        /* Page 0 */

    /* Execute video interrupt: */
    _int86( 0x10, &inregs, &outregs );

    /* Display results. */
    printf( "Cursor position\n\tRow: %d\n\tColumn: %d\n",
            outregs.h.dh, outregs.h.dl );
    printf( "Cursor shape\n\tStart: %d\n\tEnd: %d\n",
            outregs.h.ch, outregs.h.cl );
}
```

Output

```
Cursor position
        Row: 2
        Column: 0
Cursor shape
        Start: 6
        End: 7
```

_int86x

Description

Executes an 8086 interrupt; accepts segment-register values.

#include <dos.h>

int _int86x(int *intnum*, union _REGS **inregs*, union _REGS **outregs*,
    struct _SREGS **segregs*);

intnum	Interrupt number
inregs	Register values on call
outregs	Register values on return
segregs	Segment-register values on call

Remarks

The **_int86x** function executes the 8086-processor-family interrupt specified by the interrupt number *intnum*. Unlike the **_int86** function, **_int86x** accepts segment-register values in *segregs*, enabling programs that use large-model data segments or far pointers to specify which segment or pointer should be used during the system call.

Before executing the specified interrupt, **_int86x** copies the contents of *inregs* and *segregs* to the corresponding registers. Only the DS and ES register values in *segregs* are used. After the interrupt returns, the function copies the current register values to *outregs*, copies the current ES and DS values to *segregs*, and restores DS. It also copies the status of the system carry flag to the **cflag** field in *outregs*.

The **_REGS** and **_SREGS** types are defined in the include file DOS.H.

Segment values for the *segregs* argument can be obtained by using either the **_segread** function or the **_FP_SEG** macro.

Return Value

The return value is the value in the AX register after the interrupt returns. If the **cflag** field in *outregs* is nonzero, an error has occurred; in such cases, the **_doserrno** variable is also set to the corresponding error code.

Compatibility

Standards:	None
16-Bit:	DOS, QWIN, WIN, WIN DLL
32-Bit:	None

See Also

_bdos, _FP_SEG, _int86, _intdos, _intdosx, _segread

Example

```
/* INT86X.C: In this program, _int86x executes an INT 21H instruction
 * to invoke DOS system call 43H (change file attributes). The program
 * uses _int86x because the file, which is referenced with a far pointer,
 * may be in a segment other than the default data segment. Thus, the
 * program must explicitly set the DS register with the _SREGS structure.
 */

#include <signal.h>
#include <dos.h>
#include <stdio.h>
#include <process.h>

char __far *filename = "_int86x.c";

void main( void )
{
    union  _REGS inregs, outregs;
    struct _SREGS segregs;
    int    result;

    inregs.h.ah = 0x43;        /* DOS function to change attributes  */
    inregs.h.al = 0;           /* Subfunction 0 to get attributes)   */
    inregs.x.dx = _FP_OFF( filename );  /* DS:DX points to file name */
    segregs.ds  = _FP_SEG( filename );
    result = _int86x( 0x21, &inregs, &outregs, &segregs );
    if( outregs.x.cflag )
        printf( "Can't get file attributes; error no. %d\n", result);
    else
        printf( "Attribs = 0x%.4x\n", outregs.x.cx );
}
```

Output   `Attribs = 0x0020`

_intdos

Description

Executes a DOS system call.

#include <dos.h>

int _intdos(union _REGS *_inregs_, union _REGS *_outregs_);

inregs	Register values on call
outregs	Register values on return

Remarks

The **_intdos** function invokes the DOS system call specified by register values defined in _inregs_ and returns the effect of the system call in _outregs_. The _inregs_ and _outregs_ arguments are unions of type **_REGS**. The **_REGS** type is defined in the include file DOS.H.

To invoke a system call, **_intdos** executes an INT 21H instruction. Before executing the instruction, the function copies the contents of _inregs_ to the corresponding registers. After the INT instruction returns, **_intdos** copies the current register values to _outregs_. It also copies the status of the system carry flag to the **cflag** field in _outregs_. A nonzero **cflag** field indicates the flag was set by the system call and also indicates an error condition.

The **_intdos** function is used to invoke DOS system calls that take arguments for input or output in registers other than DX (DH/DL) and AL. The **_intdos** function is also used to invoke system calls that indicate errors by setting the carry flag. Under any other conditions, the **_bdos** function can be used.

Do not use the **_intdos** function to call interrupts that modify the DS register. Instead, use the **_intdosx** or **_int86x** function.

Return Value

The **_intdos** function returns the value of the AX register after the system call is completed. If the **cflag** field in _outregs_ is nonzero, an error has occurred and **_doserrno** is also set to the corresponding error code.

Compatibility

Standards:	None
16-Bit:	DOS, QWIN, WIN, WIN DLL
32-Bit:	None

See Also

_bdos, _intdosx

Example   /* INTDOS.C: This program uses _intdos to invoke DOS system call 2AH
               * (gets the current date).
               */

               #include <dos.h>
               #include <stdio.h>

               void main(void)
               {
                   union _REGS inregs, outregs;

                   inregs.h.ah = 0x2a;   /* DOS Get Date function: */
                   _intdos(&inregs, &outregs);
                   printf("Date: %d/%d/%d\n", outregs.h.dh, outregs.h.dl, outregs.x.cx);
               }

Output   Date: 6/16/1999

_intdosx

Description

Executes a DOS system call; accepts segment-register values.

#include <dos.h>

int _intdosx(union _REGS *inregs***, union _REGS** *outregs***,
    struct _SREGS** *segregs* **);**

inregs	Register values on call
outregs	Register values on return
segregs	Segment-register values on call

Remarks

The **_intdosx** function invokes the DOS system call specified by register values defined in *inregs* and returns the results of the system call in *outregs*. Unlike the **_intdos** function, **_intdosx** accepts segment-register values in *segregs*, enabling programs that use large-model data segments or far pointers to specify which segment or pointer should be used during the system call. The **_REGS** and **_SREGS** types are defined in the include file DOS.H.

To invoke a system call, **_intdosx** executes an INT 21H instruction. Before executing the instruction, the function copies the contents of *inregs* and *segregs* to the corresponding registers. Only the DS and ES register values in *segregs* are used. After the INT instruction returns, **_intdosx** copies the current register values to *outregs* and restores DS. It also copies the status of the system carry flag to the **cflag** field in *outregs*. A nonzero **cflag** field indicates the flag was set by the system call and also indicates an error condition.

The **_intdosx** function is used to invoke DOS system calls that take an argument in the ES register or that take a DS register value different from the default data segment.

Segment values for the *segregs* argument can be obtained by using either the **_segread** function or the **_FP_SEG** macro.

Return Value

The **_intdosx** function returns the value of the AX register after the system call is completed. If the **cflag** field in *outregs* is nonzero, an error has occurred; in such cases, **_doserrno** is also set to the corresponding error code.

Compatibility   Standards: None
                      16-Bit: DOS, QWIN, WIN, WIN DLL
                      32-Bit: None

See Also   **_bdos, _FP_SEG, _intdos, _segread**

Example   `/* INTDOSX.C Sends a $-terminated string to the standard output device */`

```
#include <dos.h>
#include <stdio.h>

char __far *buffer = "Dollar-sign terminated string\n\r\n\r$";

void main( void )
{
   union  _REGS inregs, outregs;
   struct _SREGS segregs;

   /* Print a $-terminated string on the screen using DOS function 0x09. */
   inregs.h.ah = 0x9;
   inregs.x.dx = _FP_OFF( buffer );
   segregs.ds  = _FP_SEG( buffer );
   _intdosx( &inregs, &outregs, &segregs );
}
```

Output   `Dollar-sign terminated string`

is Functions

Description

Test characters for specified conditions.

#include <ctype.h>

int isalnum(int *c* **);**

int isalpha(int *c* **);**

int __isascii(int *c* **);**

int iscntrl(int *c* **);**

int __iscsym(int *c* **);**

int __iscsymf(int *c* **);**

int isdigit(int *c* **);**

int isgraph(int *c* **);**

int islower(int *c* **);**

int isprint(int *c* **);**

int ispunct(int *c* **);**

int isspace(int *c* **);**

int isupper(int *c* **);**

int isxdigit(int *c* **);**

c	Integer to be tested

Remarks

Each function in the **is** family tests a given integer value, returning a nonzero value if the integer satisfies the test condition and 0 if it does not. The ASCII character set is assumed.

The **is** functions and their test conditions are listed below:

Function	Test Condition
isalnum	Alphanumeric ('A'–'Z', 'a'–'z', or '0'–'9')
isalpha	Letter ('A'–'Z' or 'a'–'z')
__isascii	ASCII character (0x00 – 0x7F)
iscntrl	Control character (0x00 – 0x1F or 0x7F)
__iscsym	Letter, underscore, or digit
__iscsymf	Letter or underscore
isdigit	Digit ('0'–'9')
isgraph	Printable character except space (' ')
islower	Lowercase letter ('a'–'z')
isprint	Printable character (0x20 – 0x7E)
ispunct	Punctuation character
isspace	White-space character (0x09 – 0x0D or 0x20)
isupper	Uppercase letter ('A'–'Z')
isxdigit	Hexadecimal digit ('A'–'F','a'–'f', or '0'–'9')

The **__isascii** routine produces meaningful results for all integer values. However, the remaining routines produce a defined result only for integer values corresponding to the ASCII character set (that is, only where **__isascii** holds true) or for the non-ASCII value **EOF** (defined in STDIO.H).

These routines are implemented both as functions and as macros. For details on choosing a function or a macro implementation, see "Choosing Between Functions and Macros" on page 9.

Return Value   These routines return a nonzero value if the integer satisfies the test condition and 0 if it does not.

Compatibility   **isalnum, isalpha, iscntrl, isdigit, isgraph, islower, isprint, ispunct, isspace, isupper, isxdigit**

Standards:	ANSI, UNIX
16-Bit:	DOS, QWIN, WIN, WIN DLL
32-Bit:	DOS32X

__isascii

Standards: UNIX

16-Bit: DOS, QWIN, WIN, WIN DLL

32-Bit: DOS32X

Use __isascii for compatibility with ANSI naming conventions of non-ANSI functions. Use isascii and link with OLDNAMES.LIB for UNIX compatibility.

__iscsym, __iscsymf

Standards: None

16-Bit: DOS, QWIN, WIN, WIN DLL

32-Bit: DOS32X

See Also   __toascii, tolower, toupper functions

Example

```
/* ISFAM.C: This program tests all characters between 0x0 and 0x7F,
 * then displays each character with abbreviations for the character-type
 * codes that apply.
 */

#include <stdio.h>
#include <ctype.h>

void main( void )
{
    int ch;
    for( ch = 0; ch <= 0x7F; ch++ )
    {
        printf( "%.2x  ", ch );
        printf( " %c", isprint( ch ) ? ch   : '\0' );
        printf( "%4s", isalnum( ch )  ? "AN" : "" );
        printf( "%3s", isalpha( ch )  ? "A"  : "" );
        printf( "%3s", __isascii( ch )  ? "AS" : "" );
        printf( "%3s", iscntrl( ch )  ? "C"  : "" );
        printf( "%3s", __iscsym( ch )   ? "CS " : "" );
        printf( "%3s", __iscsymf( ch )  ? "CSF" : "" );
        printf( "%3s", isdigit( ch )  ? "D"  : "" );
        printf( "%3s", isgraph( ch )  ? "G"  : "" );
        printf( "%3s", islower( ch )  ? "L"  : "" );
        printf( "%3s", ispunct( ch )  ? "PU" : "" );
        printf( "%3s", isspace( ch )  ? "S"  : "" );
        printf( "%3s", isprint( ch )  ? "PR" : "" );
        printf( "%3s", isupper( ch )  ? "U"  : "" );
        printf( "%3s", isxdigit( ch ) ? "X"  : "" );
        printf( "\n" );
    }
}
```

Output

```
00          AS  C
01          AS  C
02          AS  C
 .
 .
 .
38  8  AN    AS    CS        D  G          PR      X
39  9  AN    AS    CS        D  G          PR      X
3a  :        AS                  G    PU   PR
3b  ;        AS                  G    PU   PR
3c  <        AS                  G    PU   PR
3d  =        AS                  G    PU   PR
3e  >        AS                  G    PU   PR
3f  ?        AS                  G    PU   PR
40  @        AS                  G    PU   PR
41  A  AN  A AS    CS CSF     G          PR  U  X
42  B  AN  A AS    CS CSF     G          PR  U  X
 .
 .
 .
```

_isatty

Description

Checks for a character device.

#include <io.h>   Required only for function declarations

int _isatty(int *handle* **);**

handle   Handle referring to device to be tested

Remarks

The **_isatty** function determines whether *handle* is associated with a character device (a terminal, console, printer, or serial port).

Return Value

The **_isatty** function returns a nonzero value if the device is a character device. Otherwise, the return value is 0.

Compatibility

Standards: UNIX
16-Bit: DOS, QWIN, WIN, WIN DLL
32-Bit: DOS32X

Use **_isatty** for compatibility with ANSI naming conventions of non-ANSI functions. Use **isatty** and link with OLDNAMES.LIB for UNIX compatibility.

Example

```
/* ISATTY.C: This program checks to see whether stdout has been
 * redirected to a file.
 */

#include <stdio.h>
#include <io.h>

void main( void )
{
   if( _isatty( _fileno( stdout ) ) )
      printf( "stdout has not been redirected to a file\n" );
   else
      printf( "stdout has been redirected to a file\n");
}
```

Output

```
stdout has not been redirected to a file
```

_itoa

Description

Converts an integer to a string.

#include <stdlib.h>   Required only for function declarations

char *_itoa(int *value***, char ****string***, int** *radix* **);**

value	Number to be converted
string	String result
radix	Base of *value*

Remarks

The **_itoa** function converts the digits of the given *value* argument to a null-terminated character string and stores the result (up to 17 bytes) in *string*. The *radix* argument specifies the base of *value*; it must be in the range 2–36. If *radix* equals 10 and *value* is negative, the first character of the stored string is the minus sign (–).

Return Value

The **_itoa** function returns a pointer to *string*. There is no error return.

Compatibility

Standards: None
16-Bit: DOS, QWIN, WIN, WIN DLL
32-Bit: DOS32X

See Also

_ltoa, _ultoa

Example

```
/* ITOA.C: This program converts integers of various sizes to strings
 * in various radixes.
 */

#include <stdlib.h>
#include <stdio.h>
```

```
void main( void )
{
    char buffer[20];
    int  i = 3445;
    long l = -344115L;
    unsigned long ul = 1234567890UL;

    _itoa( i, buffer, 10 );
    printf( "String of integer %d (radix 10): %s\n", i, buffer );
    _itoa( i, buffer, 16 );
    printf( "String of integer %d (radix 16): 0x%s\n", i, buffer );
    _itoa( i, buffer, 2  );
    printf( "String of integer %d (radix 2): %s\n", i, buffer );

    _ltoa( l, buffer, 16 );
    printf( "String of long int %ld (radix 16): 0x%s\n", l, buffer );

    _ultoa( ul, buffer, 16 );
    printf( "String of unsigned long %lu (radix 16): 0x%s\n", ul, buffer );
}
```

Output

```
String of integer 3445 (radix 10): 3445
String of integer 3445 (radix 16): 0xd75
String of integer 3445 (radix 2): 110101110101
String of long int -344115 (radix 16): 0xfffabfcd
String of unsigned long 1234567890 (radix 16): 0x499602d2
```

_kbhit

Description

Checks the console for keyboard input.

#include <conio.h>   Required only for function declarations

int _kbhit(void);

Remarks

The **_kbhit** function checks the console for a recent keystroke. If the function returns a nonzero value, a keystroke is waiting in the buffer. The program can then call **_getch** or **_getche** to get the keystroke.

Return Value

The **_kbhit** function returns a nonzero value if a key has been pressed. Otherwise, it returns 0.

Compatibility

Standards: None
16-Bit: DOS, QWIN, WIN, WIN DLL
32-Bit: DOS32X

Example

```
/* KBHIT.C: This program loops until the user presses a key.
 * If _kbhit returns nonzero, a keystroke is waiting in the buffer.
 * The program can call _getch or _getche to get the keystroke.
 */

#include <conio.h>
#include <stdio.h>

void main( void )
{
    /* Display message until key is pressed. */
    while( !_kbhit() )
        _cputs( "Hit me!! " );

    /* Use _getch to throw key away. */
    printf( "\nKey struck was '%c'\n", _getch() );
    _getch();
}
```

Output

```
Hit me!! Hit me!! Hit me!! Hit me!! Hit me!! Hit me!! Hit me!!
Key struck was 'k'
```

labs

Description

Calculates the absolute value of a long integer.

#include <stdlib.h>   Required only for function declarations
#include <math.h>

long labs(long *n*);

n   Long-integer value

Remarks

The **labs** function produces the absolute value of its long-integer argument *n*.

Return Value

The **labs** function returns the absolute value of its argument. There is no error return.

Compatibility

Standards: ANSI
16-Bit: DOS, QWIN, WIN, WIN DLL
32-Bit: DOS32X

See Also

abs, _cabs, fabs

Example

```
/* ABS.C: This program computes and displays the absolute values of
 * several numbers.
 */

#include <stdio.h>
#include <math.h>
#include <stdlib.h>
```

```
void main( void )
{
    int    ix = -4, iy;
    long   lx = -41567L, ly;
    double dx = -3.141593, dy;

    iy = abs( ix );
    printf( "The absolute value of %d is %d\n", ix, iy);

    ly = labs( lx );
    printf( "The absolute value of %ld is %ld\n", lx, ly);

    dy = fabs( dx );
    printf( "The absolute value of %f is %f\n", dx, dy );
}
```

Output   The absolute value of -4 is 4
                The absolute value of -41567 is 41567
                The absolute value of -3.141593 is 3.141593

ldexp, _ldexpl

Description

Compute a real number from the mantissa and exponent.

#include <math.h>

double ldexp(double *x*, **int** *exp* **);**

long double _ldexpl(long double *x*, **int** *exp* **);**

x	Floating-point value
exp	Integer exponent

Remarks

The **ldexp** and **_ldexpl** functions calculate the value of $x * 2^{exp}$.

Return Value

The **ldexp** and **_ldexpl** functions return $x * 2^{exp}$. If an overflow results, the functions return $\pm$ **HUGE_VAL** (depending on the sign of *x*) and set **errno** to **ERANGE**.

The **_ldexpl** function uses the 80-bit, 10-byte coprocessor form of arguments and return values. See the reference page on the long double functions for more details on this data type.

Compatibility

ldexp

Standards:	ANSI, UNIX
16-Bit:	DOS, QWIN, WIN, WIN DLL
32-Bit:	DOS32X

_ldexpl

Standards:	None
16-Bit:	DOS, QWIN, WIN, WIN DLL
32-Bit:	None

See Also

frexp, modf

Example

```
/* LDEXP.C */
#include <math.h>
#include <stdio.h>

void main( void )
{
    double x = 4.0, y;
    int p = 3;

    y = ldexp( x, p );
    printf( "%2.1f times two to the power of %d is %2.1f\n", x, p, y );
}
```

Output

```
4.0 times two to the power of 3 is 32.0
```

ldiv

Description

Computes the quotient and remainder of a long integer.

#include <stdlib.h>

ldiv_t ldiv (long int *numer*, **long int** *denom* **);**

numer	Numerator
denom	Denominator

Remarks

The **ldiv** function divides *numer* by *denom*, computing the quotient and the remainder. The sign of the quotient is the same as that of the mathematical quotient. Its absolute value is the largest integer that is less than the absolute value of the mathematical quotient. If the denominator is 0, the program will terminate with an error message.

The **ldiv** function is similar to the **div** function, with the difference being that the arguments and the members of the returned structure are all of type **long int**.

The **ldiv_t** structure, defined in STDLIB.H, contains the following elements:

Element	Description
long int quot	Quotient
long int rem	Remainder

Return Value

The **ldiv** function returns a structure of type **ldiv_t**, comprising both the quotient and the remainder.

Compatibility

Standards:	ANSI
16-Bit:	DOS, QWIN, WIN, WIN DLL
32-Bit:	DOS32X

See Also

div

Example

```
/* LDIV.C: This program takes two long integers as command-line
 * arguments and displays the results of the integer division.
 */

#include <stdlib.h>
#include <math.h>
#include <stdio.h>

void main( void )
{
    long x = 5149627, y = 234879;
    ldiv_t div_result;

    div_result = ldiv( x, y );
    printf( "For %ld / %ld, the quotient is ", x, y );
    printf( "%ld, and the remainder is %ld\n",
            div_result.quot, div_result.rem );
}
```

Output

```
For 5149627 / 234879, the quotient is 21, and the remainder is 217168
```

_lfind

Description

Performs a linear search for the specified key.

#include <search.h>   Required only for function declarations

void *_lfind(const void **key***, const void ****base***, unsigned int ****num***,
   unsigned int** *width***, int (__cdecl ****compare* **)(const void ****elem1***,
   const void ****elem2* **));**

key	Object to search for
base	Pointer to base of search data
num	Number of array elements
width	Width of array elements
compare( )	Pointer to comparison routine
elem1	Pointer to the key for the search
elem2	Pointer to the array element to be compared with the key

Remarks

The **_lfind** function performs a linear search for the value *key* in an array of *num* elements; each element is *width* bytes in size. (Unlike **bsearch**, **_lfind** does not require the array to be sorted.) The *base* argument is a pointer to the base of the array to be searched.

The *compare* argument is a pointer to a user-supplied routine that compares two array elements and then returns a value specifying their relationship. The **_lfind** function calls the *compare* routine one or more times during the search, passing pointers to two array elements on each call. This routine must compare the elements, then return one of the following values:

Value	Meaning
Nonzero	Elements are different
0	Elements are identical

Return Value

If the key is found, **_lfind** returns a pointer to the element of the array at *base* that matches *key*. If the key is not found, **_lfind** returns **NULL**.

Compatibility

Standards: UNIX

16-Bit: DOS, QWIN, WIN, WIN DLL

32-Bit: DOS32X

Use **_lfind** for compatibility with ANSI naming conventions of non-ANSI functions. Use **lfind** and link with OLDNAMES.LIB for UNIX compatibility.

See Also

bsearch, _lsearch, qsort

Example

```
/* LFIND.C: This program uses _lfind to search for the word "hello"
 * in the command-line arguments.
 */

#include <search.h>
#include <string.h>
#include <stdio.h>

int compare( void *arg1, void *arg2 );

void main( int argc, char **argv )
{
    char **result;
    char *key = "hello";

    result = (char **)_lfind( &key, argv,
                            &argc, sizeof( char * ), compare );
    if( result )
        printf( "%s found\n", *result );
    else
        printf( "hello not found!\n" );
}

int compare(void *arg1, void *arg2 )
{
    return( _stricmp ( * ( char** ) arg1, * ( char** ) arg2 );
}
```

Output

```
[C:\LIBREF] _lfind What if I said Hello world
Hello found
```

_lineto Functions

Description

Draw lines to specified points.

#include <graph.h>

short __far _lineto(short *x*, **short** *y* **);**

short __far _lineto_w(double *wx*, **double** *wy* **);**

x, y	End point
wx, wy	End point

Remarks

The functions in the **_lineto** family draw a line from the current graphics position up to and including the destination point. The destination point for the **_lineto** function is given by the view-coordinate point (*x, y*). The destination point for the **_lineto_w** function is given by the window-coordinate point (*wx, wy*).

The line is drawn using the current color, logical write mode, and line style. If no error occurs, **_lineto** sets the current graphics position to the view-coordinate point (*x, y*); **_lineto_w** sets the current position to the window-coordinate point (*wx, wy*).

If you use **_floodfill** to fill in a closed figure drawn with **_lineto** calls, the figure must be drawn with a solid line-style pattern.

Return Value

The **_lineto** and **_lineto_w** routines return a nonzero value if anything is drawn; otherwise, they return 0.

Compatibility

Standards:	None
16-Bit:	DOS
32-Bit:	None

See Also

_getcurrentposition functions, **_moveto** functions, **_setlinestyle**

Example   /* MOVETO.C: This program draws line segments of different colors. */

```
#include <graph.h>
#include <stdlib.h>
#include <conio.h>

void main( void )
{
    short x, y, xinc, yinc, color = 1;
    struct _videoconfig v;

    /* Find a valid graphics mode. */
    if( !_setvideomode( _MAXCOLORMODE ) )
        exit( 1 );
    _getvideoconfig( &v );
    xinc = v.numxpixels / 50;
    yinc = v.numypixels / 50;

    for( x = 0, y = v.numypixels - 1; x < v.numxpixels; x += xinc, y -= yinc )
    {
        _setcolor( color++ % 16 );
        _moveto( x, 0 );
        _lineto( 0, y );
    }
    _getch();

    _setvideomode( _DEFAULTMODE );
    exit( 0 );
}
```

localeconv

Description

Gets detailed information on locale settings.

#include <locale.h>

struct lconv *localeconv(void);

Remarks

The **localeconv** function gets detailed information on the locale-specific settings for numeric formatting of the program's current locale. This information is stored in a structure of type **lconv**.

The **lconv** structure, defined in LOCALE.H, contains the following members:

Member	Description
char *decimal_point	Decimal-point character for nonmonetary quantities.
char *thousands_sep	Character used to separate groups of digits to the left of the decimal point for nonmonetary quantities.
char *grouping	Size of each group of digits in nonmonetary quantities.
char *int_curr_symbol	International currency symbol for the current locale. The first three characters specify the alphabetic international currency symbol as defined in the *ISO 4217 Codes for the Representation of Currency and Funds* standard. The fourth character (immediately preceding the null character) is used to separate the international currency symbol from the monetary quantity.
char *currency_symbol	Local currency symbol for the current locale.
char *mon_decimal_point	Decimal-point character for monetary quantities.
char *mon_thousands_sep	Separator for groups of digits to the left of the decimal place in monetary quantities.
char *mon_grouping	Size of each group of digits in monetary quantities.
char *positive_sign	String denoting sign for nonnegative monetary quantities.
char *negative_sign	String denoting sign for negative monetary quantities.
char int_frac_digits	Number of digits to the right of the decimal point in internationally formatted monetary quantities.
char frac_digits	Number of digits to the right of the decimal point in formatted monetary quantities.

Member	Description
char p_cs_precedes	Set to 1 if the currency symbol precedes the value for a nonnegative formatted monetary quantity. Set to 0 if the symbol follows the value.
char p_sep_by_space	Set to 1 if the currency symbol is separated by a space from the value for a nonnegative formatted monetary quantity. Set to 0 if there is no space separation.
char n_cs_precedes	Set to 1 if the currency symbol precedes the value for a negative formatted monetary quantity. Set to 0 if the symbol succeeds the value.
char n_sep_by_space	Set to 1 if the currency symbol is separated by a space from the value for a negative formatted monetary quantity. Set to 0 if there is no space separation.
char p_sign_posn	Position of positive sign in nonnegative formatted monetary quantities.
char n_sign_posn	Position of positive sign in negative formatted monetary quantities.

The **char *** members of the struct are pointers to strings. Any of these (other than **char *decimal_point**) that equals "" is either of zero length or is not supported in the current locale. The **char** members of the struct are nonnegative numbers. Any of these that equals **CHAR_MAX** is not supported in the current locale.

The elements of **grouping** and **mon_grouping** are interpreted according to the following rules:

Value	Interpretation
CHAR_MAX	No further grouping is to be performed.
0	The previous element is to be repeatedly used for the remainder of the digits.
n	The integer value *n* is the number of digits that make up the current group. The next element is examined to determine the size of the next group of digits before the current group.

The values for **p_sign_posn** and **n_sign_posn** are interpreted according to the following rules:

Value	Interpretation
0	Parentheses surround the quantity and currency symbol
1	Sign string precedes the quantity and currency symbol
2	Sign string follows the quantity and currency symbol
3	Sign string immediately precedes the currency symbol
4	Sign string immediately follows the currency symbol

Return Value   The **localeconv** function returns a pointer to a filled in object of type **struct lconv**. The values contained in the object can be overwritten by susequent calls to **localeconv** and do not directly modify the object. Calls to the **setlocale** function with *category* values of **LC_ALL**, **LC_MONETARY**, or **LC_NUMERIC** will overwrite the contents of the structure.

Compatibility   Standards: ANSI
16-Bit: DOS, QWIN, WIN, WIN DLL
32-Bit: DOS32X

See Also   **setlocale, strcoll, strftime, strxfrm**

localtime

Description

Converts a time value and corrects for the local time zone.

#include <time.h>

struct tm *localtime(const time_t *timer);

timer   Pointer to stored time

Remarks

The **localtime** function converts a time stored as a **time_t** value and stores the result in a structure of type **tm**. The **long** value *timer* represents the seconds elapsed since midnight (00:00:00), December 31, 1899, Universal Coordinated Time. This value is usually obtained from the **time** function.

The fields of the structure type **tm** store the following values:

Element	Value Stored
int tm_sec	Seconds
int tm_min	Minutes
int tm_hour	Hours (0–24)
int tm_mday	Day of month (1–31)
int tm_mon	Month (0–11; January = 0)
int tm_year	Year (current year minus 1900)
int tm_wday	Day of week (0–6; Sunday = 0)
int tm_yday	Day of year (0–365; January 1 = 0)
int tm_isdst	Nonzero if daylight saving time is in effect, otherwise 0

Note that the **gmtime, mktime,** and **localtime** functions use a single statically allocated **tm** structure for the conversion. Each call to one of these routines destroys the result of the previous call.

The **localtime** function makes corrections for the local time zone if the user first sets the environment variable TZ. When TZ is set, three other environment variables (**_timezone, _daylight,** and **_tzname**) are automatically set as well. See **_tzset** for a description of these variables.

The TZ variable is not part of the ANSI standard definition of **localtime** but is a Microsoft extension.

Return Value   The **localtime** function returns a pointer to the structure result. If the value in *timer* represents a date before midnight, December 31, 1899, the function returns **NULL**.

Compatibility

Standards: ANSI, UNIX

16-Bit: DOS, QWIN, WIN, WIN DLL

32-Bit: DOS32X

See Also   **asctime, ctime, _ftime, gmtime, time, _tzset**

Example

```
/* LOCALTIM.C: This program uses time to get the current time and
 * then uses localtime to convert this time to a structure representing
 * the local time. The program converts the result from a 24-hour clock
 * to a 12-hour clock and determines the proper extension (AM or PM).
 */

#include <stdio.h>
#include <string.h>
#include <time.h>

void main( void )
{
    struct tm *newtime;
    char   am_pm[] = "AM";
    time_t long_time;

    time( &long_time );                  /* Get time as long integer. */
    newtime = localtime( &long_time );   /* Convert to local time. */

    if( newtime->tm_hour < 12 )          /* Set up extension. */
        strcpy( am_pm, "AM" );
    if( newtime->tm_hour > 12 )          /* Convert from 24-hour */
        newtime->tm_hour -=12;           /*   to 12-hour clock.  */

    printf( "%.19s %s\n", asctime( newtime ), am_pm );
}
```

Output   Fri Jun 16 06:27:02 AM

_locking

Description

Locks or unlocks bytes of a file.

#include <sys\locking.h>

#include <io.h>   Required only for function declarations

int _locking(int *handle,* **int** *mode,* **long** *nbytes* **);**

handle	File handle
mode	File-locking mode
nbytes	Number of bytes to lock

Remarks

The **_locking** function locks or unlocks *nbytes* bytes of the file specified by *handle.* Locking bytes in a file prevents access to those bytes by other processes. All locking or unlocking begins at the current position of the file pointer and proceeds for the next *nbytes* bytes. It is possible to lock bytes past the end of the file.

The *mode* argument specifies the locking action to be performed. It must be one of the following manifest constants:

Constant	Action
_LK_LOCK	Locks the specified bytes. If the bytes cannot be locked, immediately tries again after 1 second. If, after 10 attempts, the bytes cannot be locked, returns an error.
_LK_NBLCK	Locks the specified bytes. If bytes cannot be locked, returns an error.
_LK_NBRLCK	Same as **_LK_NBLCK.**
_LK_RLCK	Same as **_LK_LOCK.**
_LK_UNLCK	Unlocks the specified bytes. (The bytes must have been previously locked.)

More than one region of a file can be locked, but no overlapping regions are allowed.

When a region of a file is being unlocked, it must correspond to a region that was previously locked. The **_locking** function does not merge adjacent regions; if two locked regions are adjacent, each region must be unlocked separately.

Regions should be locked only briefly and should be unlocked before closing a file or exiting the program.

The **_locking** function should be used only with DOS versions 3.0 and later; it has no effect under earlier versions of DOS. Also, file sharing must be loaded to use the **_locking** function. Note that with DOS versions 3.0 and 3.1, the files locked by parent processes may become unlocked when child processes exit.

Return Value

The **_locking** function returns 0 if successful. A return value of –1 indicates failure, and **errno** is set to one of the following values:

Value	Meaning
EACCES	Locking violation (file already locked or unlocked).
EBADF	Invalid file handle.
EDEADLOCK	Locking violation. This is returned when the **_LK_LOCK** or **_LK_RLCK** flag is specified and the file cannot be locked after 10 attempts.
EINVAL	An invalid argument was given to the function.

Compatibility

Standards: UNIX

16-Bit: DOS, QWIN, WIN, WIN DLL

32-Bit: DOS32X

Use **_locking** for compatibility with ANSI naming conventions of non-ANSI functions. Use **locking** and link with OLDNAMES.LIB for UNIX compatibility.

See Also

_creat, _open

Example

```
/* LOCKING.C: This program opens a file with sharing. It locks some
 * bytes before reading them, then unlocks them. Note that the program
 * works correctly only if the following conditions are met:
 *      - The file exists
 *      - The program is run with DOS version 3.0 or later
 *        with file sharing installed (SHARE.COM or SHARE.EXE), or
 *        if a Microsoft Networks compatible network is running
 */

#include <io.h>
#include <sys\types.h>
#include <sys\stat.h>
#include <sys\locking.h>
#include <share.h>
#include <fcntl.h>
#include <stdio.h>
#include <stdlib.h>
```

```
void main( void )
{
    int  fh, numread;
    long pos, result;
    char buffer[40];

    /* Quit if can't open file or DOS version doesn't support sharing. */
    fh = _sopen( "locking.c", _O_RDWR, _SH_DENYNO, _S_IREAD | _S_IWRITE );
    if( (fh == -1) || (_osmajor < 3) )
        exit( 1 );

    /* Lock some bytes and read them. Then unlock. */
    if( _locking( fh, LK_NBLCK, 30L ) != -1 )
    {
        printf( "No one can change these bytes while I'm reading them\n" );
        numread = _read( fh, buffer, 30 );
        printf( "%d bytes read: %.30s\n", numread, buffer );
        _locking( fh, LK_UNLCK, 30L );
        printf( "Now I'm done. Do what you will with them\n" );
    }
    else
        perror( "Locking failed\n" );

    _close( fh );
}
```

Output

```
No one can change these bytes while I'm reading them
30 bytes read: /* LOCKING.C: This program open
Now I'm done. Do what you will with them
```

log Functions

Description

Calculate logarithms.

#include <math.h>

double log(double x **);**

double log10(double x **);**

long double _logl(long double x **);**

long double _log10l(long double x **);**

x Value whose logarithm is to be found

Remarks

The **log** and **log10** functions calculate the natural logarithm and the base-10 logarithm, respectively, of x. The **_logl** and **_log10l** functions are the 80-bit counterparts and use the 80-bit, 10-byte coprocessor form of arguments and return values. See the reference page on the long double functions for more details on this data type.

Return Value

The **log** functions return the logarithm of the argument x. If x is negative, the functions print a **_DOMAIN** error message to **stderr**, return the value **–HUGE_VAL**, and set **errno** to **EDOM**. If x is 0, the functions print a **_SING** error message to **stderr**, return the value **–HUGE_VAL**, and set **errno** to **ERANGE.**

Error handling can be modified by using the **_matherr** or **_matherrl** routine.

Compatibility

log, log10

Standards:	ANSI, UNIX
16-Bit:	DOS, QWIN, WIN, WIN DLL
32-Bit:	DOS32X

_logl, _log10l

Standards: None

16-Bit: DOS, QWIN, WIN, WIN DLL

32-Bit: None

See Also

exp, _matherr, pow functions

Example

```
/* LOG.C: This program uses log and log10 to calculate the natural
 * logarithm and the base-10 logarithm of 9,000.
 */

#include <math.h>
#include <stdio.h>

void main( void )
{
    double x = 9000.0;
    double y;

    y = log( x );
    printf( "log( %.2f ) = %f\n", x, y );
    y = log10( x );
    printf( "log10( %.2f ) = %f\n", x, y );
}
```

Output

```
log( 9000.00 ) = 9.104980
log10( 9000.00 ) = 3.954243
```

long double Functions

The 8087 family of numeric coprocessor chips supports the 80-bit precision floating-point data type. Beginning with Microsoft C version 6.0, the long double functions, whose names end with **l**, map the C **long double** type into this 80-bit, 10-byte form. Unlike the regular floating-point functions (such as **acos**), which return values of type **double**, these long double functions (such as **_acosl**) return values of type **long double**. The long double functions also return their values on the coprocessor stack for all calling conventions.

The long double type is also supported by the addition of the "L" prefix for a floating-point format specification in the **printf** and **scanf** family of functions.

The long double versions are described on the reference pages for their regular counterparts. These are the regular run-time math functions with corresponding long double equivalents:

Function	Long Double Form	Function	Long Double Form
acos	_acosl	frexp	_frexpl
asin	_asinl	_hypot	_hypotl
atan	_atanl	ldexp	_ldexpl
atan2	_atan2l	log	_logl
atof	_atold	log10	_log10l
_cabs	_cabsl	_matherr	_matherrl
ceil	_ceill	modf	_modfl
cos	_cosl	pow	_powl
cosh	_coshl	sin	_sinl
exp	_expl	sinh	_sinhl
fabs	_fabsl	sqrt	_sqrtl
floor	_floorl	tan	_tanl
fmod	_fmodl	tanh	_tanhl

longjmp

Description

Restores stack environment and execution locale.

#include <setjmp.h>

void longjmp(jmp_buf *env*, **int** *value* **);**

env	Variable in which environment is stored
value	Value to be returned to **setjmp** call

Remarks

The **longjmp** function restores a stack environment and execution locale previously saved in *env* by **setjmp**. The **setjmp** and **longjmp** functions provide a way to execute a nonlocal **goto**; they are typically used to pass execution control to error handling or recovery code in a previously called routine without using the normal call and return conventions.

A call to **setjmp** causes the current stack environment to be saved in *env*. A subsequent call to **longjmp** restores the saved environment and returns control to the point immediately following the corresponding **setjmp** call. Execution resumes as if *value* had just been returned by the **setjmp** call. The values of all variables (except register variables) that are accessible to the routine receiving control contain the values they had when **longjmp** was called. The values of register variables are unpredictable.

The **longjmp** function must be called before the function that called **setjmp** returns. If **longjmp** is called after the function calling **setjmp** returns, unpredictable program behavior results.

The value returned by **setjmp** must be nonzero. If *value* is passed as 0, the value 1 is substituted in the actual return.

Observe the following four restrictions when using **longjmp**:

- Do not assume that the values of the register variables will remain the same. The values of register variables in the routine calling **setjmp** may not be restored to the proper values after **longjmp** is executed. Do not use **longjmp** with the global register allocation (/Oe) option to the CL driver.

- Do not use **longjmp** to transfer control from within one overlay to within another. The overlay manager keeps the overlay in memory after a call to **longjmp**.

- Do not use **longjmp** to transfer control out of an interrupt-handling routine unless the interrupt is caused by a floating-point exception. In this case, a program may return from an interrupt handler via **longjmp** if it first reinitializes the floating-point math package by calling **_fpreset**.

- Do not use **longjmp** or **setjmp** from a C++ program.

Return Value   None.

Compatibility

Standards:	ANSI, UNIX
16-Bit:	DOS, QWIN, WIN, WIN DLL
32-Bit:	DOS32X

See Also   **setjmp**

Example   See the example for **_fpreset**.

_lrotl, _lrotr

Description

Rotate bits to the left (**_lrotl**) or right (**_lrotr**).

#include <stdlib.h>

unsigned long _lrotl(unsigned long *value***, int** *shift* **);**

unsigned long _lrotr(unsigned long *value***, int** *shift* **);**

value	Value to be rotated
shift	Number of bits to shift

Remarks

The **_lrotl** and **_lrotr** functions rotate *value* by *shift* bits. The **_lrotl** function rotates the value left. The **_lrotr** function rotates the value right. Both functions "wrap" bits rotated off one end of *value* to the other end.

Return Value

Both functions return the rotated value. There is no error return.

Compatibility

Standards: None
16-Bit: DOS, QWIN, WIN, WIN DLL
32-Bit: DOS32X

See Also

_rotl, _rotr

Example

```
/* LROT.C */
#include <stdlib.h>
#include <stdio.h>

void main( void )
{
    unsigned long val = 0x0fac35791;

    printf( "0x%8.8lx rotated left eight times is 0x%8.8lx\n",
            val, _lrotl( val, 8 ) );
    printf( "0x%8.8lx rotated right four times is 0x%8.8lx\n",
            val, _lrotr( val, 4 ) );
}
```

Output

```
xfac35791 rotated left eight times is 0xc35791fa
0xfac35791 rotated right four times is 0x1fac3579
```

_lsearch

Description

Performs a linear search for a value; adds to end of list if not found.

#include <search.h>   Required only for function declarations

void *_lsearch(const void *key**, const void ***base**, unsigned int ***num**, unsigned int** width**, int (__cdecl ***compare**)(const void ***elem1**, const void ***elem2**));**

key	Object to search for
base	Pointer to base of search data
num	Number of elements
width	Width of elements
compare	Pointer to comparison routine
elem1	Pointer to the key for the search
elem2	Pointer to the array element to be compared with the key

Remarks

The **_lsearch** function performs a linear search for the value *key* in an array of *num* elements, each of *width* bytes in size. (Unlike **bsearch**, **_lsearch** does not require the array to be sorted.) The *base* argument is a pointer to the base of the array to be searched.

If *key* is not found, **_lsearch** adds it to the end of the array.

The *compare* argument is a pointer to a user-supplied routine that compares two array elements and returns a value specifying their relationship. The **_lsearch** function calls the *compare* routine one or more times during the search, passing pointers to two array elements on each call. This routine must compare the elements, then return one of the following values:

Value	Meaning
Nonzero	Elements are different
0	Elements are identical

Return Value

If the key is found, **_lsearch** returns a pointer to the element of the array at *base* that matches *key*. If the key is not found, **_lsearch** returns a pointer to the newly added item at the end of the array.

Compatibility

Standards: UNIX

16-Bit: DOS, QWIN, WIN, WIN DLL

32-Bit: DOS32X

Use **_lsearch** for compatibility with ANSI naming conventions of non-ANSI functions. Use **lsearch** and link with OLDNAMES.LIB for UNIX compatibility.

See Also   **bsearch, _lfind**

Example   See the example for **_lfind**.

_lseek

Description

Moves a file pointer to the specified location.

#include <io.h>   Required only for function declarations

#include <stdio.h>

long _lseek(int *handle*, **long** *offset*, **int** *origin* **);**

handle	Handle referring to open file
offset	Number of bytes from *origin*
origin	Initial position

Remarks

The **_lseek** function moves the file pointer associated with *handle* to a new location that is *offset* bytes from *origin*. The next operation on the file occurs at the new location. The *origin* argument must be one of the following constants, which are defined in STDIO.H:

Origin	Definition
SEEK_SET	Beginning of file
SEEK_CUR	Current position of file pointer
SEEK_END	End of file

The **_lseek** function can be used to reposition the pointer anywhere in a file. The pointer can also be positioned beyond the end of the file. However, an attempt to position the pointer before the beginning of the file causes an error.

Return Value

The **_lseek** function returns the offset, in bytes, of the new position from the beginning of the file. The function returns −1L to indicate an error and sets **errno** to one of the following values:

Value	Meaning
EBADF	Invalid file handle
EINVAL	Invalid value for *origin*, or position specified by *offset* is before the beginning of the file

On devices incapable of seeking (such as terminals and printers), the return value is undefined.

Compatibility

Standards: UNIX

16-Bit: DOS, QWIN, WIN, WIN DLL

32-Bit: DOS32X

Use **_lseek** for compatibility with ANSI naming conventions of non-ANSI functions. Use **lseek** and link with OLDNAMES.LIB for UNIX compatibility.

See Also   fseek, **_tell**

Example

```
/* LSEEK.C: This program first opens a file named LSEEK.C.
 * It then uses _lseek to find the beginning of the file,
 * to find the current position in the file, and to find
 * the end of the file.
 */

#include <io.h>
#include <fcntl.h>
#include <stdlib.h>
#include <stdio.h>

void main( void )
{
    int fh;
    long pos;                    /* Position of file pointer */
    char buffer[10];

    fh = _open( "lseek.c", _O_RDONLY );

    /* Seek the beginning of the file: */
    pos = _lseek( fh, 0L, SEEK_SET );
    if( pos == -1L )
       perror( "_lseek to beginning failed" );
    else
       printf( "Position for beginning of file seek = %ld\n", pos );

    /* Move file pointer a little */
    _read( fh, buffer, 10 );

    /* Find current position: */
    pos = _lseek( fh, 0L, SEEK_CUR );
    if( pos == -1L )
       perror( "_lseek to current position failed" );
    else
       printf( "Position for current position seek = %ld\n", pos );
```

```
              /* Set the end of the file: */
              pos = _lseek( fh, 0L, SEEK_END );
              if( pos == -1L )
                 perror( "_lseek to end failed" );
              else
                 printf( "Position for end of file seek = %ld\n", pos );

              _close( fh );
          }
```

Output   Position for beginning of file seek = 0
              Position for current position seek = 10
              Position for end of file seek = 1183

_ltoa

Description

Converts a long integer to a string.

#include <stdlib.h>   Required only for function declarations

char *_ltoa(long *value*, **char** *string, **int** *radix* **);**

value	Number to be converted
string	String result
radix	Base of *value*

Remarks

The **_ltoa** function converts the digits of *value* to a null-terminated character string and stores the result (up to 33 bytes) in *string*. The *radix* argument specifies the base of *value*, which must be in the range 2–36. If *radix* equals 10 and *value* is negative, the first character of the stored string is the minus sign (–).

Return Value

The **_ltoa** function returns a pointer to *string*. There is no error return.

Compatibility

Standards: None
16-Bit: DOS, QWIN, WIN, WIN DLL
32-Bit: DOS32X

See Also

_itoa, _ultoa

Example

```
/* ITOA.C: This program converts integers of various sizes to strings
 * in various radixes.
 */

#include <stdlib.h>
#include <stdio.h>
```

```
void main( void )
{
    char buffer[20];
    int   i = 3445;
    long l = -344115L;
    unsigned long ul = 1234567890UL;

    _itoa( i, buffer, 10 );
    printf( "String of integer %d (radix 10): %s\n", i, buffer );
    _itoa( i, buffer, 16 );
    printf( "String of integer %d (radix 16): 0x%s\n", i, buffer );
    _itoa( i, buffer, 2  );
    printf( "String of integer %d (radix 2): %s\n", i, buffer );

    _ltoa( l, buffer, 16 );
    printf( "String of long int %ld (radix 16): 0x%s\n", l, buffer );

    _ultoa( ul, buffer, 16 );
    printf( "String of unsigned long %lu (radix 16): 0x%s\n", ul, buffer );
}
```

Output

```
String of integer 3445 (radix 10): 3445
String of integer 3445 (radix 16): 0xd75
String of integer 3445 (radix 2): 110101110101
String of long int -344115 (radix 16): 0xfffabfcd
String of unsigned long 1234567890 (radix 16): 0x499602d2
```

_makepath

Description

Creates a path name from components.

#include <stdlib.h>

void _makepath(char *path, char *drive, char *dir, char *fname, char *ext);

path	Full path-name buffer
drive	Drive letter
dir	Directory path
fname	Filename
ext	File extension

Remarks

The **_makepath** routine creates a single path name, composed of a drive letter, directory path, filename, and filename extension. The *path* argument should point to an empty buffer large enough to hold the complete path name. The constant **_MAX_PATH**, defined in STDLIB.H, specifies the maximum size *path* that the **_makepath** function can handle. The other arguments point to buffers containing the path-name elements:

Buffer	Description
drive	The *drive* argument contains a letter (A, B, etc.) corresponding to the desired drive and an optional trailing colon. The **_makepath** routine will insert the colon automatically in the composite path name if it is missing. If *drive* is a null character or an empty string, no drive letter and colon will appear in the composite *path* string.
dir	The *dir* argument contains the path of directories, not including the drive designator or the actual filename. The trailing slash is optional, and either forward slashes (\ ) or backslashes (\ ) or both may be used in a single *dir* argument. If a trailing slash (/ or \ ) is not specified, it will be inserted automatically. If *dir* is a null character or an empty string, no slash is inserted in the composite *path* string.
fname	The *fname* argument contains the base filename without any extensions. If *fname* is **NULL** or points to an empty string, no filename is inserted in the composite *path* string.

Buffer	Description
ext	The *ext* argument contains the actual filename extension, with or without a leading period (.). The **_makepath** routine will insert the period automatically if it does not appear in *ext*. If *ext* is a null character or an empty string, no period is inserted in the composite *path* string.

There are no size limits on any of the above four fields. However, the composite path must be no larger than the **_MAX_PATH** constant. The **_MAX_PATH** limit permits a path name much larger than current operating-system versions will handle.

Return Value

None.

Compatibility

Standards:　None

16-Bit:　　DOS, QWIN, WIN, WIN DLL

32-Bit:　　DOS32X

See Also

_fullpath, **_splitpath**

Example

```
/* MAKEPATH.C */
#include <stdlib.h>
#include <stdio.h>

void main( void )
{
    char path_buffer[_MAX_PATH];
    char drive[_MAX_DRIVE];
    char dir[_MAX_DIR];
    char fname[_MAX_FNAME];
    char ext[_MAX_EXT];

    _makepath( path_buffer, "c", "\\c60\\clibref\\", "makepath", "c" );
    printf( "Path created with _makepath: %s\n\n", path_buffer );
    _splitpath( path_buffer, drive, dir, fname, ext );
    printf( "Path extracted with _splitpath:\n" );
    printf( "  Drive: %s\n", drive );
    printf( "  Dir: %s\n", dir );
    printf( "  Filename: %s\n", fname );
    printf( "  Ext: %s\n", ext );
}
```

Output

```
Path created with _makepath: c:\c60\clibref\makepath.c

Path extracted with _splitpath:
  Drive: c:
  Dir: \c60\clibref\
  Filename: makepath
  Ext: .c
```

malloc Functions

Description

Allocate memory blocks.

#include <stdlib.h>	For ANSI compatibility (**malloc** only)
#include <malloc.h>	Required only for function declarations

void *malloc(size_t *size* **);**

void __ based(void) *_bmalloc(__ segment *seg***, size_t** *size* **);**

void __ far *_fmalloc(size_t *size* **);**

void __ near *_nmalloc(size_t *size* **);**

size	Bytes to allocate
seg	Based heap segment selector

Remarks

Functions in the **malloc** family allocate a memory block of at least *size* bytes. The block may be larger than *size* bytes because of space required for alignment and maintenance information. If *size* is 0, each of these functions allocates a zero-length item in the heap and returns a valid pointer to that item.

The storage space pointed to by the return value is guaranteed to be suitably aligned for storage of any type of object. To get a pointer to a type other than **void**, use a type cast on the return value.

In large data models (compact-, large-, and huge-model programs), **malloc** maps to **_fmalloc**. In small data models (tiny-, small-, and medium-model programs), **malloc** maps to **_nmalloc**. The **_fmalloc** function allocates a memory block of at least *size* bytes in the far heap, which is outside the default data segment.

The **_bmalloc** function allocates a memory block of at least *size* bytes in the based heap segment specified by the segment selector *seg*.

The **malloc** functions allocate memory in the heap segment specified below:

Function	Heap Segment
malloc	Depends on data model of program
_bmalloc	Based heap segment specified by *seg* value
_fmalloc	Far heap (outside default data segment)
_nmalloc	Near heap (within default data segment)

The functions listed below call the **malloc** family of routines. In addition, the startup code uses **malloc** to allocate storage for the **environ/envp** and **argv** strings and arrays.

The following routines call **malloc**:

calloc	**fseek**	**_spawnv**
_execv	**fsetpos**	**_spawnve**
_execve	**_fullpath**	**_spawnvp**
_execvp	**fwrite**	**_spawnvpe**
_execvpe	**getc**	**_spawnl**
_execl	**getchar**	**_spawnle**
_execle	**_getcwd**	**_spawnlp**
_execlp	**_getdcwd**	**_spawnlpe**
_execlpe	**gets**	**_strdup**
fgetc	**_getw**	**system**
_fgetchar	**_popen**	**scanf**
fgets	**printf**	**setvbuf**
fprintf	**putc**	**_tempnam**
fputc	**putchar**	**ungetc**
_fputchar	**_putenv**	**vfprintf**
fputs	**puts**	**vprintf**
fread	**_putw**	
fscanf	**_searchenv**	

The following routines call **_nmalloc**:

_nrealloc
_ncalloc
_nstrdup
realloc (in small data models)

The following routines call **_fmalloc**:

_frealloc
_fcalloc
_fstrdup
realloc (in large data models)

In Microsoft C version 5.1, the **_fmalloc** function would retry allocating within the default data segment (i.e., in the near heap) if sufficient memory was not available outside the default data segment. Since version 6.0, **_fmalloc** returns **NULL** under these conditions.

The **_freect**, **_memavl**, and **_memmax** functions called **malloc** in Microsoft C version 5.1 but do not do so in versions 6.0 and 7.0.

Return Value

The **malloc** function returns a **void** pointer to the allocated space. The **_nmalloc** function returns a (**void** **__near** *****) and **_fmalloc** returns a (**void** **__far** *****). The **_bmalloc** function returns a (**void** **__based**(**void**) *****).

The **_malloc**, **_fmalloc**, and **_nmalloc** functions return **NULL** if there is insufficient memory available. The **_bmalloc** function returns **_NULLOFF** if there is insufficient memory available.

Always check the return from the **malloc** function, even if the amount of memory requested is small.

Compatibility

malloc

Standards:	ANSI, UNIX
16-Bit:	DOS, QWIN, WIN, WIN DLL
32-Bit:	DOS32X

_bmalloc, _fmalloc, _nmalloc

Standards:	None
16-Bit:	DOS, QWIN, WIN, WIN DLL
32-Bit:	None

See Also

calloc functions, **free** functions, **realloc** functions

Example   /* MALLOC.C: This program allocates memory with malloc, then frees
               * the memory with free.
               */

```
#include <stdlib.h>              /* Definition of _MAX_PATH */
#include <stdio.h>
#include <malloc.h>

void main( void )
{
   char *string;

   /* Allocate space for a path name */
   string = malloc( _MAX_PATH );
   if( string == NULL )
      printf( "Insufficient memory available\n" );
   else
      printf( "Memory space allocated for pathname\n" );
   free( string );
   printf( "Memory freed\n" );
}
```

Output   Memory space allocated for pathname
              Memory freed

_matherr, _matherrl

Description

Handle math errors.

#include <math.h>

int _matherr(struct _exception *_except_);

int _matherrl(struct _exceptionl *_except_);

except   Pointer to structure containing error information

Remarks

The **_matherr** functions process errors generated by the functions of the math library. The math functions call the appropriate **_matherr** routine whenever an error is detected. The **_matherrl** function uses the 80-bit, 10-byte coprocessor form of arguments and return values. See the reference page on the long double functions for more details on this data type.

The user can provide a different definition of the **_matherr** or **_matherrl** function to carry out special error handling.

When an error occurs in a math routine, **_matherr** is called with a pointer to an **_exception** type structure (defined in MATH.H) as an argument.

The **_exception** structure contains the following elements:

Element	Description
int type	Exception type
char *name	Name of function where error occurred
double arg1, arg2	First and second (if any) argument to function
double retval	Value to be returned by function

The **type** specifies the type of math error. It is one of the following values, defined in MATH.H:

Value	Meaning
_DOMAIN	Argument domain error
_SING	Argument singularity
_OVERFLOW	Overflow range error
_PLOSS	Partial loss of significance

Value	Meaning
_TLOSS	Total loss of significance
_UNDERFLOW	Underflow range error

The structure member **name** is a pointer to a null-terminated string containing the name of the function that caused the error. The structure members **arg1** and **arg2** specify the values that caused the error. (If only one argument is given, it is stored in **arg1**.)

The default return value for the given error is **retval**. If you change the return value, remember that the return value must specify whether an error actually occurred. If the **_matherr** function returns 0, an error message can be displayed and **errno** is set to an appropriate error value. If **_matherr** returns a nonzero value, no error message is displayed, and **errno** remains unchanged.

Return Value

The **_matherr** functions should return 0 to indicate an error, and a nonzero value to indicate successful corrective action.

Compatibility

_matherr

Standards:	UNIX
16-Bit:	DOS, QWIN, WIN, WIN DLL
32-Bit:	DOS32X

Use **_matherr** for compatibility with ANSI naming conventions of non-ANSI functions. Use **matherr** and link with OLDNAMES.LIB for UNIX compatibility.

_matherrl

Standards:	None
16-Bit:	DOS, QWIN, WIN, WIN DLL
32-Bit:	None

See Also

acos functions, **asin** functions, **atan** functions, **bessel** functions, **_cabs**, **cos** functions, **exp**, **_hypot**, **log** functions, **pow**, **sin** functions, **sqrt**, **tan** functions

Example

```
/* MATHERR.C: To use _matherr, you must turn off the Extended Dictionary
 * flag within the Microsoft Programmer's WorkBench environment, or use the
 * /NOE linker option outside the environment. For example:
 *    CL _matherr.c /link /NOE
 */

#include <math.h>
#include <string.h>
#include <stdio.h>
```

```
void main( void )
{
    /* Do several math operations that cause errors. The _matherr
     * routine handles _DOMAIN errors, but lets the system handle
     * other errors normally.
     */
    printf( "log( -2.0 ) = %e\n", log( -2.0 ) );
    printf( "log10( -5.0 ) = %e\n", log10( -5.0 ) );
    printf( "log( 0.0 ) = %e\n", log( 0.0 ) );
}


/* Handle several math errors caused by passing a negative argument
 * to log or log10 (_DOMAIN errors). When this happens, _matherr returns
 * the natural or base-10 logarithm of the absolute value of the
 * argument and suppresses the usual error message.
 */
int _matherr( struct _exception *except )
{
    /* Handle _DOMAIN errors for log or log10. */
    if( except->type == _DOMAIN )
    {
        if( strcmp( except->name, "log" ) == 0 )
        {
            except->retval = log( -(except->arg1) );
            printf( "Special: using absolute value: %s: _DOMAIN error\n",
                    except->name );
            return 1;
        }
        else if( strcmp( except->name, "log10" ) == 0 )
        {
            except->retval = log10( -(except->arg1) );
            printf( "Special: using absolute value: %s: _DOMAIN error\n",
                    except->name );
            return 1;
        }
    }
    else
    {
        printf( "Normal: " );
        return 0;    /* Else use the default actions */
    }
}
```

Output

```
Special: using absolute value: log: _DOMAIN error
log( -2.0 ) = 6.931472e-001
Special: using absolute value: log10: _DOMAIN error
log10( -5.0 ) = 6.989700e-001
Normal: log: _SING error
log( 0.0 ) = -1.797693e+308
```

__max

Description   Returns the larger of two values.

#include <stdlib.h>

type __**max**(*type a, type b*);

type	Any numeric data type
a, b	Values of any numeric type to be compared

Remarks   The __**max** macro compares two values and returns the value of the larger one. The arguments can be of any numeric data type, signed or unsigned. Both arguments and the return value must be of the same data type.

Return Value   The macro returns the larger of the two arguments.

Compatibility   Standards: None
16-Bit: DOS, QWIN, WIN, WIN DLL
32-Bit: DOS32X

See Also   __**min**

Example
```
/* MINMAX.C */
#include <stdlib.h>
#include <stdio.h>

void main( void )
{
    int a = 10;
    int b = 21;

    printf( "The larger of %d and %d is %d\n",  a, b, __max( a, b ) );
    printf( "The smaller of %d and %d is %d\n", a, b, __min( a, b ) );
}
```

Output   The larger of 10 and 21 is 21
The smaller of 10 and 21 is 10

mblen, _fmblen

Description

Get the length and determine the validity of a multibyte character.

#include <stdlib.h>

int mblen(const char **mbstr***, size_t *count*);**

int __far _fmblen(const char __far **mbstr***, size_t *count*);**

mbstr	The address of a sequence of bytes (a multibyte character)
count	The number of bytes to check

Remarks

The **mblen** function returns the length in bytes of a valid multibyte character. It examines *count* or fewer bytes contained in *mbstr*. It will not examine more than **MB_CUR_MAX** bytes.

The **_fmblen** function is a model-independent (large-model) form of the **mblen** function.

Return Value

If *mbstr* is not **NULL**, both **mblen** and **_fmblen** return the length, in bytes, of the multibyte character. If *mbstr* is **NULL**, or the object that it points to is the wide-character null character (**L'\0'**), both functions return 0. If the object that *mbstr* points to does not form a valid multibyte character within the first *count* characters, both functions return –1.

Compatibility

mblen

Standards:	ANSI
16-Bit:	DOS, QWIN, WIN, WIN DLL
32-Bit:	DOS32X

_fmblen

Standards:	None
16-Bit:	DOS, QWIN, WIN, WIN DLL
32-Bit:	None

See Also

mbstowcs, mbtowc, wcstombs, wctomb, MB_CUR_MAX, MB_LEN_MAX

Example   /* MBLEN.CPP illustrates the behavior of the mblen function. */

```
#include <stdlib.h>
#include <stdio.h>

void main( void )
{
    int      i;
    char     *pmbc = (char *)malloc( sizeof( char ) );
    wchar_t  wc   = L'a';

    printf( "Convert a wide character to multibyte character:\n" );
    i = wctomb( pmbc, wc );
    printf( "\tCharacters converted: %u\n", i );
    printf( "\tMultibyte character: %x\n\n", pmbc );

    printf( "Find length--in bytes--of multibyte character:\n" );
    i = mblen( pmbc, MB_CUR_MAX );
    printf( "\tLength--in bytes--of multibyte character: %u\n", i );
    printf( "\tWide character: %x\n\n", pmbc );

    printf( "Attempt to find length of a NULL pointer:\n" );
    pmbc = NULL;
    i = mblen( pmbc, MB_CUR_MAX );
    printf( "\tLength--in bytes--of multibyte character: %u\n", i );
    printf( "\tWide character: %x\n\n", pmbc );

    printf( "Attempt to find length of a wide-character NULL:\n" );
    wc = L'\0';
    wctomb( pmbc, wc );
    i = mblen( pmbc, MB_CUR_MAX );
    printf( "\tLength--in bytes--of multibyte character: %u\n", i );
    printf( "\tWide character: %x\n", pmbc );
}
```

Output
```
Convert a wide character to multibyte character:
    Characters converted: 1
    Multibyte character: e56

Find length--in bytes--of multibyte character:
    Length--in bytes--of multibyte character: 1
    Wide character: e56

Attempt to find length of a NULL pointer:
    Length--in bytes--of multibyte character: 0
    Wide character: 0

Attempt to find length of a wide-character NULL:
    Length--in bytes--of multibyte character: 0
    Wide character: 0
```

mbstowcs, _fmbstowcs

Description

Convert a sequence of multibyte characters to a corresponding sequence of wide characters.

#include <stdlib.h>

size_t mbstowcs(wchar_t **wcstr***, const char ****mbstr***, size_t** *count* **);**

size_t _ _far _fmbstowcs(wchar_t _ _far **wcstr***, const char _ _far ****mbstr***, size_t** *count* **);**

wcstr	The address of a sequence of wide characters
mbstr	The address of a sequence of multibyte characters
count	The number of multibyte characters to convert

Remarks

The **mbstowcs** function converts *count* or fewer multibyte characters pointed to by *mbstr* to a string of corresponding wide characters that are determined by the current locale. It stores the resulting wide-character string at the address represented by *wcstr*. The result is similiar to a series of calls to the **mbtowc** function.

If **mbstowcs** encounters the null character (**'\0'**) either before or when *count* occurs, it converts the null character to a wide-character null character (**L'\0'**) and stops. Thus, the wide-character string at *wcstr* is null-terminated only if a null character is encountered during conversion. If the sequences pointed to by *wcstr* and *mbstr* overlap, the behavior is undefined.

The **_fmbstowcs** function is a model-independent (large-model) form of the **mbstowcs** function. It can be called from any point in any program.

Return Value

If **mbstowcs** or (**_fmbstowcs**) successfully converts the *source* string, it returns the number of converted multibyte characters. If either function encounters an invalid multibyte character, it returns –1. If the return value is *count*, the wide-character string is not null-terminated.

Compatibility   **mbstowcs**

Standards: ANSI

16-Bit: DOS, QWIN, WIN, WIN DLL

32-Bit: DOS32X

_fmbstowcs

Standards: None

16-Bit: DOS, QWIN, WIN, WIN DLL

32-Bit: None

See Also   **mblen, mbtowc, wcstombs, wctomb, MB_CUR_MAX, MB_LEN_MAX**

Example
```
/* MBSTOWCS.CPP illustrates the behavior of the mbstowcs function. */

#include <stdlib.h>
#include <stdio.h>

void main( void )
{
    int i;
    char    *pmbhello = (char *)malloc( MB_CUR_MAX );
    wchar_t *pwchello = L"Hi";
    wchar_t *pwc      = (wchar_t *)malloc( sizeof( wchar_t ));

    printf( "Convert to multibyte string:\n" );
    i = wcstombs( pmbhello, pwchello, MB_CUR_MAX );
    printf( "\tCharacters converted: %u\n", i );
    printf( "\tHex value of first" );
    printf( " multibyte character: %#.4x\n\n", pmbhello );

    printf( "Convert back to wide-character string:\n" );
    i = mbstowcs( pwc, pmbhello, MB_CUR_MAX );
    printf( "\tCharacters converted: %u\n", i );
    printf( "\tHex value of first" );
    printf( " wide character: %#.4x\n\n", pwc );
}
```

Output
```
Convert to multibyte string:
        Characters converted: 1
        Hex value of first multibyte character: 0x0e26

Convert back to wide-character string:
        Characters converted: 1
        Hex value of first wide character: 0x0e2a
```

mbtowc, _fmbtowc

Description

Convert a multibyte character to a corresponding wide character.

#include <stdlib.h>

int mbtowc(wchar_t *__wchar__, const char *__mbchar__, size_t __count__);

**int __far _fmbtowc(wchar_t __far *__wchar__, const char __far *__mbchar__,
size_t __count__);**

wchar	The address of a wide character (type **wchar_t**)
mbchar	The address of a sequence of bytes (a multibyte character)
count	The number of bytes to check

Remarks

The **mbtowc** function converts *count* or fewer bytes pointed to by *mbchar*, if *mbchar* is not **NULL**, to a corresponding wide character that is determined by the current locale. It stores the resulting wide character at *wchar*, if *wchar* is not **NULL**. It will not examine more than **MB_CUR_MAX** bytes.

The **_fmbtowc** function is a model-independent (large-model) form of the **mbtowc** function.

Return Value

If *mbchar* is not **NULL** and if the object that *mbchar* points to forms a valid multibyte character, both **mbtowc** and **_fmbtowc** return the length in bytes of the multibyte character.

If *mbchar* is **NULL** or the object that it points to is a wide-character null character (**L'\0'**), both functions return 0. If the object that *mbchar* points to does not form a valid multibyte character within the first *count* characters, they return –1.

Compatibility

mbtowc

Standards:	ANSI
16-Bit:	DOS, QWIN, WIN, WIN DLL
32-Bit:	DOS32X

_fmbtowc

Standards:	None
16-Bit:	DOS, QWIN, WIN, WIN DLL
32-Bit:	None

See Also   **mblen, mbtowc, wcstombs, wctomb, MB_CUR_MAX, MB_LEN_MAX**

Example
```
/* MBTOWC.CPP illustrates the behavior of the mbtowc function. */

#include <stdlib.h>
#include <stdio.h>

void main( void )
{
    int     i;
    char    *pmbc    = (char *)malloc( sizeof( char ) );
    wchar_t wc       = L'a';
    wchar_t *pwcnull = NULL;
    wchar_t *pwc     = (wchar_t *)malloc( sizeof( wchar_t ) );

    printf( "Convert a wide character to multibyte character:\n" );
    i = wctomb( pmbc, wc );
    printf( "\tCharacters converted: %u\n", i );
    printf( "\tMultibyte character: %x\n\n", pmbc );

    printf( "Convert multibyte character back to a wide character:\n" );
    i = mbtowc( pwc, pmbc, MB_CUR_MAX );
    printf( "\tBytes converted: %u\n", i );
    printf( "\tWide character: %x\n\n", pwc );

    printf( "Attempt to convert when target is NULL\n" );
    printf( "  returns the length of the multibyte character:\n" );
    i = mbtowc( pwcnull, pmbc, MB_CUR_MAX );
    printf( "\tLength of multibyte character: %u\n\n", i );

    printf( "Attempt to convert a NULL pointer to a" );
    printf( " wide character:\n" );
    pmbc = NULL;
    i = mbtowc( pwc, pmbc, MB_CUR_MAX );
    printf( "\tBytes converted: %u\n", i );
}
```

Output
```
Convert a wide character to multibyte character:
     Characters converted: 1
     Multibyte character: e36

Convert multibyte character back to a wide character:
     Bytes converted: 1
     Wide character: e3a

Attempt to convert when target is NULL
   returns the length of the multibyte character:
     Length of multibyte character: 1

Attempt to convert a NULL pointer to a wide character:
     Bytes converted: 0
```

_memavl

Description

Returns the size of memory available.

#include <malloc.h>   Required only for function declarations

size_t _memavl(void);

Remarks

The **_memavl** function returns the approximate size, in bytes, of the memory available for dynamic memory allocation in the near heap (default data segment). The **_memavl** function can be used with **calloc**, **malloc**, or **realloc** in tiny, small, and medium memory models and with **_ncalloc, _nmalloc** or **_nrealloc** in any memory model.

The number returned by the **_memavl** function may not be the number of contiguous bytes. Consequently, a call to **malloc** requesting allocation of the size returned by **_memavl** may not succeed. Use the **_memmax** function to find the size of the largest available contiguous block of memory.

Return Value

The **_memavl** function returns the size in bytes as an unsigned integer.

Compatibility

Standards: None
16-Bit: DOS, QWIN, WIN, WIN DLL
32-Bit: None

See Also

calloc functions, **_freect, malloc** functions, **_memmax, realloc** functions

Example

```
/* MEMAVL.C: This program uses _memavl to determine the amount of
 * memory available for dynamic allocation. It then uses malloc to
 * allocate space for 5,000 long integers and uses _memavl again to
 * determine the new amount of available memory.
 */

#include <malloc.h>
#include <stdio.h>
```

```
void main( void )
{
   long *longptr;

   printf( "Memory available before _nmalloc = %u\n", _memavl() );
   if( (longptr = _nmalloc( 5000 * sizeof( long ) )) != NULL )
   {
      printf( "Memory available after _nmalloc = %u\n", _memavl() );
      _nfree( longptr );
   }
}
```

Output
```
Memory available before _nmalloc = 60906
Memory available after _nmalloc = 40390
```

_memccpy, _fmemccpy

Description

Copy characters from a buffer.

#include <memory.h>   Required only for function declarations

#include <string.h>   Use either STRING.H or MEMORY.H

void *_memccpy(void *dest, void *src, int c, unsigned int count);

void __far * __far _fmemccpy(void __far *dest, void __far *src, int c, unsigned int count);

dest	Pointer to destination
src	Pointer to source
c	Last character to copy
count	Number of characters

Remarks

The **_memccpy** and **_fmemccpy** functions copy 0 or more bytes of *src* to *dest*, halting when the character *c* has been copied or when *count* bytes have been copied, whichever comes first.

The **_fmemccpy** function is a model-independent (large-model) form of the **_memccpy** function. It can be called from any point in any program.

Return Value

If the character *c* is copied, **_memccpy** or **_fmemccpy** returns a pointer (or far pointer) to the byte in *dest* that immediately follows the character. If *c* is not copied, both return **NULL**.

Compatibility

_memccpy

Standards: UNIX

16-Bit: DOS, QWIN, WIN, WIN DLL

32-Bit: DOS32X

Use **_memccpy** for compatibility with ANSI naming conventions of non-ANSI functions. Use **memccpy** and link with OLDNAMES.LIB for UNIX compatibility.

_fmemccpy

Standards: None

16-Bit: DOS, QWIN, WIN, WIN DLL

32-Bit: None

See Also   **memchr, memcmp, memcpy, memset**

Example
```
/* MEMCCPY.C */
#include <memory.h>
#include <stdio.h>
#include <string.h>

char string1[60] = "The quick brown dog jumps over the lazy fox";

void main( void )
{
    char buffer[61];
    char *pdest;

    printf( "Function:\t_memccpy 60 characters or to character 's'\n" );
    printf( "Source:\t\t%s\n", string1 );
    pdest = _memccpy( buffer, string1, 's', 60 );
    *pdest = '\0';
    printf( "Result:\t\t%s\n", buffer );
    printf( "Length:\t\t%d characters\n\n", strlen( buffer ) );
}
```

Output
```
Function:       _memccpy 60 characters or to character 's'
Source:         The quick brown dog jumps over the lazy fox
Result:         The quick brown dog jumps
Length:         25 characters
```

memchr, _fmemchr

Description   Find characters in a buffer.

#include <memory.h>   Required only for function declarations

#include <string.h>   Use either STRING.H (for ANSI compatibility) or MEMORY.H

void *memchr(const void **buf***, int** *c***, size_t** *count* **);**

void __far * __far _fmemchr(const void __far **buf***, int** *c***, size_t** *count* **);**

buf	Pointer to buffer
c	Character to look for
count	Number of characters

Remarks   The **memchr** and **_fmemchr** functions look for the first occurrence of *c* in the first *count* bytes of *buf*. They stop when they find *c* or when they have checked the first *count* bytes.

The **_fmemchr** function is a model-independent (large-model) form of the **memchr** function. It can be called from any point in any program.

Return Value   If successful, **memchr** or **_fmemchr** returns a pointer (or a far pointer) to the first location of *c* in *buf*. Otherwise, they return **NULL**.

Compatibility   **memchr**

Standards:	ANSI, UNIX
16-Bit:	DOS, QWIN, WIN, WIN DLL
32-Bit:	DOS32X

_fmemchr

Standards:	None
16-Bit:	DOS, QWIN, WIN, WIN DLL
32-Bit:	None

See Also   **_memccpy, memcmp, memcpy, memset, strchr**

Example

```
/* MEMCHR.C */
#include <memory.h>
#include <stdio.h>

int  ch = 'r';
char str[] =     "lazy";
char string[] = "The quick brown dog jumps over the lazy fox";
char fmt1[] =     "         1         2         3         4         5";
char fmt2[] =     "12345678901234567890123456789012345678901234567890";

void main( void )
{
   char *pdest;
   int result;

   printf( "String to be searched:\n\t\t%s\n", string );
   printf( "\t\t%s\n\t\t%s\n\n", fmt1, fmt2 );

   printf( "Search char:\t%c\n", ch );
   pdest = memchr( string, ch, sizeof( string ) );
   result = pdest - string + 1;
   if( pdest != NULL )
      printf( "Result:\t\t%c found at position %d\n\n", ch, result );
   else
      printf( "Result:\t\t%c not found\n" );
}
```

Output

```
String to be searched:
                The quick brown dog jumps over the lazy fox
                         1         2         3         4         5
                12345678901234567890123456789012345678901234567890

Search char:    r
Result:         r found at position 12
```

memcmp, _fmemcmp

Description

Compare characters in two buffers.

#include <memory.h>   Required only for function declarations

#include <string.h>   Use either STRING.H (for ANSI compatibility) or MEMORY.H

int memcmp(const void *_buf1_, const void *_buf2_, size_t _count_);

**int __far _fmemcmp(const void __far *_buf1_, const void __far *_buf2_,
  size_t _count_);**

buf1	First buffer
buf2	Second buffer
count	Number of characters

Remarks

The **memcmp** and **_fmemcmp** functions compare the first _count_ bytes of _buf1_ and _buf2_ and return a value indicating their relationship, as follows:

Value	Meaning
< 0	_buf1_ less than _buf2_
= 0	_buf1_ identical to _buf2_
> 0	_buf1_ greater than _buf2_

The **_fmemcmp** function is a model-independent (large-model) form of the **memcmp** function. It can be called from any point in a program.

There is a semantic difference between the function version of **memcmp** and its intrinsic version. The function version supports huge pointers in compact-, large-, and huge-model programs, but the intrinsic version does not.

Return Value

The **memcmp** and **_fmemcmp** functions return an integer value, as described above.

Compatibility	**memcmp**	
	Standards:	ANSI, UNIX
	16-Bit:	DOS, QWIN, WIN, WIN DLL
	32-Bit:	DOS32X

_fmemcmp

	Standards:	None
	16-Bit:	DOS, QWIN, WIN, WIN DLL
	32-Bit:	None

See Also _memccpy, memchr, memcpy, memset, strcmp, strncmp

Example

```
/* MEMCMP.C: This program uses memcmp to compare the strings named
 * first and second. If the first 19 bytes of the strings are
 * equal, the program considers the strings to be equal.
 */

#include <string.h>
#include <stdio.h>

void main( void )
{
   char first[]  = "12345678901234567890";
   char second[] = "12345678901234567891";
   int result;

   printf( "Compare '%.19s' to '%.19s':\n", first, second );
   result = memcmp( first, second, 19 );
   if( result < 0 )
      printf( "First is less than second.\n" );
   else if( result == 0 )
      printf( "First is equal to second.\n" );
   else if( result > 0 )
      printf( "First is greater than second.\n" );
   printf( "Compare '%.20s' to '%.20s':\n", first, second );
   result = memcmp( first, second, 20 );
   if( result < 0 )
      printf( "First is less than second.\n" );
   else if( result == 0 )
      printf( "First is equal to second.\n" );
   else if( result > 0 )
      printf( "First is greater than second.\n" );
}
```

Output   Compare '1234567890123456789' to '1234567890123456789':
First is equal to second.
Compare '12345678901234567890' to '12345678901234567891':
First is less than second.

memcpy, _fmemcpy

Description   Copy characters between buffers.

#include <memory.h>   Required only for function declarations

#include <string.h>   Use either STRING.H (for ANSI compatibility) or MEMORY.H

void *memcpy(void *dest*, const void ***src*, size_t *count*);**

void __far * __far _fmemcpy(void __far *dest*, const void __far ***src*,
    size_t *count*);**

dest	New buffer
src	Buffer to copy from
count	Number of characters to copy

Remarks   The **memcpy** and **_fmemcpy** functions copy *count* bytes of *src* to *dest*. If the source and destination overlap, these functions do not ensure that the original source bytes in the overlapping region are copied before being overwritten. Use **memmove** to handle overlapping regions.

The **_fmemcpy** function is a model-independent (large-model) form of the **memcpy** function. It can be called from any point in any program.

There is a semantic difference between the function version of **memcpy** and its intrinsic version. The function version supports huge pointers in compact-, large-, and huge-model programs, but the intrinsic version does not.

Return Value   The **memcpy** and **_fmemcpy** functions return the value of *dest*.

Compatibility   **memcpy**

Standards: ANSI, UNIX

16-Bit: DOS, QWIN, WIN, WIN DLL

32-Bit: DOS32X

_fmemcpy

Standards:	None
16-Bit:	DOS, QWIN, WIN, WIN DLL
32-Bit:	None

See Also   **_memccpy, memchr, memcmp, memmove, memset, strcpy, strncpy**

Example

```
/* MEMCPY.C. Illustrate overlapping copy: memmove handles it
 * correctly; memcpy does not.
 */

#include <memory.h>
#include <string.h>
#include <stdio.h>

char string1[60] = "The quick brown dog jumps over the lazy fox";
char string2[60] = "The quick brown fox jumps over the lazy dog";
/*                         1         2         3         4         5
 *               12345678901234567890123456789012345678901234567890
 */

void main( void )
{
    printf( "Function:\tmemcpy without overlap\n" );
    printf( "Source:\t\t%s\n", string1 + 40 );
    printf( "Destination:\t%s\n", string1 + 16 );
    memcpy( string1 + 16, string1 + 40, 3 );
    printf( "Result:\t\t%s\n", string1 );
    printf( "Length:\t\t%d characters\n\n", strlen( string1 ) );

    /* Restore string1 to original contents */
    memcpy( string1 + 16, string2 + 40, 3 );

    printf( "Function:\tmemmove with overlap\n" );
    printf( "Source:\t\t%s\n", string2 + 4 );
    printf( "Destination:\t%s\n", string2 + 10 );
    memmove( string2 + 10, string2 + 4, 40 );
    printf( "Result:\t\t%s\n", string2 );
    printf( "Length:\t\t%d characters\n\n", strlen( string2 ) );

    printf( "Function:\tmemcpy with overlap\n" );
    printf( "Source:\t\t%s\n", string1 + 4 );
    printf( "Destination:\t%s\n", string1 + 10 );
    memcpy( string1 + 10, string1 + 4, 40 );
    printf( "Result:\t\t%s\n", string1 );
    printf( "Length:\t\t%d characters\n\n", strlen( string1 ) );
}
```

Output

    Function: memcpy without overlap
    Source: fox
    Destination: dog jumps over the lazy fox
    Result: The quick brown fox jumps over the lazy fox
    Length: 43 characters

    Function: memmove with overlap
    Source: quick brown fox jumps over the lazy dog
    Destination: brown fox jumps over the lazy dog
    Result: The quick quick brown fox jumps over the lazy dog
    Length: 49 characters

    Function: memcpy with overlap
    Source: quick brown dog jumps over the lazy fox
    Destination: brown dog jumps over the lazy fox
    Result: The quick quick quick quick quick quick quick quick
    Length: 50 characters

_memicmp, _fmemicmp

Description   Compare characters in two buffers (case-insensitive).

#include <memory.h>   Required only for function declarations

#include <string.h>   Use either STRING.H or MEMORY.H

int _memicmp(void **buf1*, **void** **buf2*, **unsigned int** *count* **);**

int __far _fmemicmp(void __far **buf1*, **void __far** **buf2*,
   unsigned int *count* **);**

buf1	First buffer
buf2	Second buffer
count	Number of characters

Remarks   The **_memicmp** and **_fmemicmp** functions compare the first *count* characters of the two buffers *buf1* and *buf2* byte-by-byte. The comparison is made without regard to the case of letters in the two buffers; that is, uppercase and lowercase letters are considered equivalent. The **_memicmp** and **_fmemicmp** functions return a value indicating the relationship of the two buffers, as follows:

Value	Meaning
< 0	*buf1* less than *buf2*
= 0	*buf1* identical to *buf2*
> 0	*buf1* greater than *buf2*

The **_fmemicmp** function is a model-independent (large-model) form of the **_memicmp** function. It can be called from any point in any program.

Return Value   The **_memicmp** and **_fmemicmp** functions return an integer value, as described above.

Compatibility	**_memicmp**

Standards: UNIX

16-Bit: DOS, QWIN, WIN, WIN DLL

32-Bit: DOS32X

Use **_memicmp** for compatibility with ANSI naming conventions of non-ANSI functions. Use **memicmp** and link with OLDNAMES.LIB for UNIX compatibility.

_fmemicmp

Standards: None

16-Bit: DOS, QWIN, WIN, WIN DLL

32-Bit: None

See Also   **_memccpy, memchr, memcmp, memcpy, memset, _stricmp, _strnicmp**

Example
```c
/* MEMICMP.C: This program uses _memicmp to compare the first
 * 29 letters of the strings named first and second without
 * regard to the case of the letters.
 */

#include <memory.h>
#include <stdio.h>
#include <string.h>

void main( void )
{
   int result;
   char first[]  = "Those Who Will Not Learn from History";
   char second[] = "THOSE WHO WILL NOT LEARN FROM their mistakes";
   /* Note that the 29th character is right here ^ */

   printf( "Compare '%.29s' to '%.29s'\n", first, second );
   result = _memicmp( first, second, 29 );
   if( result < 0 )
      printf( "First is less than second.\n" );
   else if( result == 0 )
      printf( "First is equal to second.\n" );
   else if( result > 0 )
      printf( "First is greater than second.\n" );
}
```

Output
```
Compare 'Those Who Will Not Learn from' to 'THOSE WHO WILL NOT LEARN FROM'
First is equal to second.
```

_memmax

Description

Finds the size of the largest contiguous memory block.

#include <malloc.h>

size_t _memmax(void);

Remarks

The **_memmax** function returns the size (in bytes) of the largest contiguous block of memory that can be allocated from the near heap (i.e., the default data segment). Calling **_nmalloc** with the value returned by the **_memmax** function will succeed as long as **_memmax** returns a nonzero value.

Return Value

The function returns the block size, if successful. Otherwise, it returns 0, indicating that nothing more can be allocated from the near heap.

Compatibility

Standards: None
16-Bit: DOS, QWIN, WIN, WIN DLL
32-Bit: None

See Also

malloc functions, **_msize** functions

Example

```
/* MEMMAX.C: This program uses _memmax and _nmalloc to allocate
 * the largest block of memory available in the near heap.
 */

#include <stddef.h>
#include <malloc.h>
#include <stdio.h>

void main( void )
{
    size_t contig;
    char *p;
```

```
      /* Determine contiguous memory size */
      contig = _memmax();
      printf( "Largest block of available memory is %u bytes long\n", contig );
      if( contig )
      {
         p = _nmalloc( contig * sizeof( int ) );
         if( p == NULL )
            printf( "Error with malloc (should never occur)\n" );
         else
         {
            printf( "Maximum allocation succeeded\n" );
            free( p );
         }
      }
      else
         printf( "Near heap is already full\n" );
   }
```

Output

```
Largest block of available memory is 60844 bytes long
Maximum allocation succeeded
```

memmove, _fmemmove

Description   Move one buffer to another.

#include <string.h>

void *memmove(void *dest**, const void *src, size_t** count **);**

void __far * __far _fmemmove(void __far *dest**, const void __far *src,**
  size_t count **);**

dest	Destination object
src	Source object
count	Number of characters to copy

Remarks   The **memmove** and **_fmemmove** functions copy count characters from the source (src) to the destination (dest). If some regions of the source area and the destination overlap, the **memmove** and **_fmemmove** functions ensure that the original source bytes in the overlapping region are copied before being overwritten.

The **_fmemmove** function is a model-independent (large-model) form of the **memmove** function. It can be called from any point in any program.

Return Value   The **memmove** and **_fmemmove** functions return the value of dest.

Compatibility   **memmove**

Standards:	ANSI
16-Bit:	DOS, QWIN, WIN, WIN DLL
32-Bit:	DOS32X

_fmemmove

Standards:	None
16-Bit:	DOS, QWIN, WIN, WIN DLL
32-Bit:	None

See Also   **_memccpy, memcpy, strcpy, strncpy**

Example
```
/* MEMCPY.C. Illustrate overlapping copy: memmove handles it
 * correctly; memcpy does not.
 */

#include <memory.h>
#include <string.h>
#include <stdio.h>

char string1[60] = "The quick brown dog jumps over the lazy fox";
char string2[60] = "The quick brown fox jumps over the lazy dog";
/*                            1         2         3         4         5
 *                   12345678901234567890123456789012345678901234567890
 */

void main( void )
{
    printf( "Function:\tmemcpy without overlap\n" );
    printf( "Source:\t\t%s\n", string1 + 40 );
    printf( "Destination:\t%s\n", string1 + 16 );
    memcpy( string1 + 16, string1 + 40, 3 );
    printf( "Result:\t\t%s\n", string1 );
    printf( "Length:\t\t%d characters\n\n", strlen( string1 ) );

    /* Restore string1 to original contents */
    memcpy( string1 + 16, string2 + 40, 3 );

    printf( "Function:\tmemmove with overlap\n" );
    printf( "Source:\t\t%s\n", string2 + 4 );
    printf( "Destination:\t%s\n", string2 + 10 );
    memmove( string2 + 10, string2 + 4, 40 );
    printf( "Result:\t\t%s\n", string2 );
    printf( "Length:\t\t%d characters\n\n", strlen( string2 ) );

    printf( "Function:\tmemcpy with overlap\n" );
    printf( "Source:\t\t%s\n", string1 + 4 );
    printf( "Destination:\t%s\n", string1 + 10 );
    memcpy( string1 + 10, string1 + 4, 40 );
    printf( "Result:\t\t%s\n", string1 );
    printf( "Length:\t\t%d characters\n\n", strlen( string1 ) );
}
```

Output

```
Function:      memcpy without overlap
Source:        fox
Destination:   dog jumps over the lazy fox
Result:        The quick brown fox jumps over the lazy fox
Length:        43 characters

Function:      memmove with overlap
Source:        quick brown fox jumps over the lazy dog
Destination:   brown fox jumps over the lazy dog
Result:        The quick quick brown fox jumps over the lazy dog
Length:        49 characters

Function:      memcpy with overlap
Source:        quick brown dog jumps over the lazy fox
Destination:   brown dog jumps over the lazy fox
Result:        The quick quick quick quick quick quick quick quick
Length:        50 characters
```

memset, _fmemset

Description   Set buffers to a specified character.

#include <memory.h>	Required only for function declarations
#include <string.h>	Use either STRING.H (for ANSI compatibility) or MEMORY.H

void *memset(void **dest***, int** *c***, size_t** *count* **);**

void __far * __far _fmemset(void __far **dest***, int** *c***, size_t** *count* **);**

dest	Pointer to destination
c	Character to set
count	Number of characters

Remarks   The **memset** and **_fmemset** functions set the first *count* bytes of *dest* to the character *c*.

The **_fmemset** function is a model-independent (large-model) form of the **memset** function. It can be called from any point in any program.

There is a semantic difference between the function version of **memset** and its intrinsic version. The function version supports huge pointers in compact-, large-, and huge-model programs, but the intrinsic version does not.

Return Value   The **memset** and **_fmemset** functions return the value of *dest*.

Compatibility   **memset**

Standards:	ANSI, UNIX
16-Bit:	DOS, QWIN, WIN, WIN DLL
32-Bit:	DOS32X

_fmemset

Standards: None

16-Bit: DOS, QWIN, WIN, WIN DLL

32-Bit: None

See Also   **_memccpy, memchr, memcmp, memcpy, _strnset**

Example
```
/* MEMSET.C: This program uses memset to set the first four bytes
 * of buffer to "*".
 */

#include <memory.h>
#include <stdio.h>

void main( void )
{
    char buffer[] = "This is a test of the memset function";

    printf( "Before: %s\n", buffer );
    memset( buffer, '*', 4 );
    printf( "After:  %s\n", buffer );
}
```

Output
```
Before: This is a test of the memset function
After:  **** is a test of the memset function
```

__min

Description

Returns the smaller of two values.

#include <stdlib.h>

type __**min**(*type a, type b*);

type	Any numeric data type
a, b	Values of any numeric type to be compared

Remarks

The __**min** macro compares two values and returns the value of the smaller one. The arguments can be of any numeric data type, signed or unsigned. Both arguments and the return value must be of the same data type.

Return Value

The macro returns the smaller of the two arguments.

Compatibility

Standards: None

16-Bit: DOS, QWIN, WIN, WIN DLL

32-Bit: DOS32X

See Also

__**max**

Example

```
/* MINMAX.C */
#include <stdlib.h>
#include <stdio.h>

void main( void )
{
    int a = 10;
    int b = 21;

    printf( "The larger of %d and %d is %d\n",  a, b, __max( a, b ) );
    printf( "The smaller of %d and %d is %d\n", a, b, __min( a, b ) );
}
```

Output

```
The larger of 10 and 21 is 21
The smaller of 10 and 21 is 10
```

_mkdir

Description   Creates a new directory.

#include <direct.h>   Required only for function declarations

int _mkdir(char *_dirname_);

dirname   Path name for new directory

Remarks   The **_mkdir** function creates a new directory with the specified _dirname_. Only one directory can be created at a time, so only the last component of _dirname_ can name a new directory.

The **_mkdir** function does not do any translation of path-name delimiters. All operating systems accept either "\" or "/" internally as valid delimiters within path names.

Return Value   The **_mkdir** function returns the value 0 if the new directory was created. A return value of –1 indicates an error, and **errno** is set to one of the following values:

Value	Meaning
EACCES	Directory not created. The given name is the name of an existing file, directory, or device.
ENOENT	Path name not found.

Compatibility   Standards: None
16-Bit: DOS, QWIN, WIN, WIN DLL
32-Bit: DOS32X

See Also   **_chdir, _rmdir**

Example

```
/* MAKEDIR.C */
#include <direct.h>
#include <stdlib.h>
#include <stdio.h>

void main( void )
{
   int result;

   if( _mkdir( "\\testtmp" ) == 0 )
   {
      printf( "Directory '\\testtmp' was successfully created\n" );
      system( "dir \\testtmp" );
      if( _rmdir( "\\testtmp" ) == 0 )
         printf( "Directory '\\testtmp' was successfully removed\n"  );
      else
         printf( "Problem removing directory '\\testtmp'\n" );
   }
   else
      printf( "Problem creating directory '\\testtmp'\n" );
}
```

Output

```
Directory '\testtmp' was successfully created

The volume label in drive C is ZEPPELIN
Directory of C:\TESTTMP

.              <DIR>      12-19-99  11:20a
..             <DIR>      12-19-99  11:20a
    2 File(s)   12730368 bytes free
Directory '\testtmp' was successfully removed
```

_mktemp

Description

Creates a unique filename.

#include <io.h>   Required only for function declarations

char *_mktemp(char **template***);**

template   Filename pattern

Remarks

The **_mktemp** function creates a unique filename by modifying the given *template* argument. The *template* argument has the form:

*base***XXXXXX**

where *base* is the part of the new filename that you supply, and the **X**'s are place-holders for the part supplied by **_mktemp**; **_mktemp** preserves *base* and replaces the six trailing **X**'s with an alphanumeric character followed by a five-digit value. The five-digit value is a unique number identifying the calling process. The alphanumeric character is 0 ('**0**') the first time **_mktemp** is called with a given template.

In subsequent calls from the same process with copies of the same template, **_mktemp** checks to see if previously returned names have been used to create files. If no file exists for a given name, **_mktemp** returns that name. If files exist for all previously returned names, **_mktemp** creates a new name by replacing the alphanumeric character in the name with the next available lowercase letter. For example, if the first name returned is `t012345` and this name is used to create a file, the next name returned will be `ta12345`. When creating new names, **_mktemp** uses, in order, '0' and then the lowercase letters 'a' through 'z'.

Note that the original template is modified by the first call to **_mktemp**. If you then call the **_mktemp** function again with the same template (i.e., the original one), you will get an error.

The **_mktemp** function generates unique filenames but does not create or open files.

Return Value

The **_mktemp** function returns a pointer to the modified template. The return value is **NULL** if the *template* argument is badly formed or no more unique names can be created from the given template.

Compatibility	Standards:	UNIX
	16-Bit:	DOS, QWIN, WIN, WIN DLL
	32-Bit:	DOS32X

Use **_mktemp** for compatibility with ANSI naming conventions of non-ANSI functions. Use **mktemp** and link with OLDNAMES.LIB for UNIX compatibility.

See Also   **fopen, _getpid, _open, _tempnam, tmpfile**

Example

```
/* MKTEMP.C: The program uses _mktemp to create five unique filenames.
 * It opens each filename to ensure that the next name is unique.
 */

#include <io.h>
#include <string.h>
#include <stdio.h>

char *template = "fnXXXXXX";
char *result;
char names[5][9];

void main( void )
{
    int i;
    FILE *fp;

    for( i = 0; i < 5; i++ )
    {
        strcpy( names[i], template );

        /* Attempt to find a unique filename: */
        result = _mktemp( names[i] );
        if( result == NULL )
            printf( "Problem creating the template" );
        else
        {
            if( (fp = fopen( result, "w" )) != NULL )
                printf( "Unique filename is %s\n", result );
            else
                printf( "Cannot open %s\n", result );
            fclose( fp );
        }
    }
}
```

Output

```
Unique filename is fn000686
Unique filename is fna00686
Unique filename is fnb00686
Unique filename is fnc00686
Unique filename is fnd00686
```

mktime

Description

Converts the local time to a calendar value.

#include <time.h>

time_t mktime(struct tm *_timeptr_);

timeptr   Pointer to time structure

Remarks

The **mktime** function converts the supplied time structure (possibly incomplete) pointed to by _timeptr_ into a fully defined structure with "normalized" values and then converts it to a **time_t** calendar time value. The structure for the **tm** is described in the reference page for **asctime**.

The converted time has the same encoding as the values returned by the **time** function. The original values of the **tm_wday** and **tm_yday** components of the _timeptr_ structure are ignored, and the original values of the other components are not restricted to their normal ranges.

If successful, **mktime** sets the values of **tm_wday** and **tm_yday** appropriately, and sets the other components to represent the specified calendar time, but with their values forced to the normal ranges; the final value of **tm_mday** is not set until **tm_mon** and **tm_year** are determined.

If _timeptr_ references a date before midnight, December 31, 1899, **mktime** returns −1.

Note that the **gmtime** and **localtime** functions use a single statically allocated buffer for the conversion. If you supply this buffer to **mktime**, the previous contents will be destroyed.

Return Value

The **mktime** function returns the specified calendar time encoded as a value of type **time_t**. If the calendar time cannot be represented, the function returns the value −1 cast to type **time_t**.

Compatibility

Standards: ANSI
16-Bit: DOS, QWIN, WIN, WIN DLL
32-Bit: DOS32X

See Also

asctime, gmtime, localtime, time

Example
```
/* MKTIME.C: The example takes a number of days as input and returns
 * the time, the current date, and the specified number of days.
 */

#include <time.h>
#include <stdio.h>

void main( void )
{
    struct tm when;
    time_t now, result;
    int    days;

    time( &now );
    when = *localtime( &now );
    printf( "Current time is %s\n", asctime( &when ) );
    printf( "How many days to look ahead: " );
    scanf( "%d", &days );

    when.tm_mday = when.tm_mday + days;
    if( (result = mktime( &when )) != (time_t)-1 )
        printf( "In %d days the time will be %s\n",
                days, asctime( &when ) );
    else
        perror( "mktime failed" );
}
```

Output
```
Current time is Sat Jun 19 11:45:20 1999

How many days to look ahead: 23
In 23 days the time will be Mon Jul 12 11:45:20 1999
```

modf, _modfl

Description

Split a floating-point value into fractional and integer parts.

#include <math.h>

double modf(double *x*, **double** **intptr* **);**

long double _modfl(long double *x*, **long double** **intptr* **);**

x	Floating-point value
intptr	Pointer to stored integer portion

Remarks

The **modf** functions break down the floating-point value *x* into fractional and integer parts, each of which has the same sign as *x*. The signed fractional portion of *x* is returned. The integer portion is stored as a floating-point value at *intptr*.

The **_modfl** function uses the 80-bit, 10-byte coprocessor form of arguments and return values. See the reference page on the long double functions for more details on this data type.

Return Value

The **modf** and **_modfl** functions return the signed fractional portion of *x*. There is no error return.

Compatibility

modf

Standards:	ANSI, UNIX
16-Bit:	DOS, QWIN, WIN, WIN DLL
32-Bit:	DOS32X

_modfl

Standards:	None
16-Bit:	DOS, QWIN, WIN, WIN DLL
32-Bit:	None

See Also

frexp, ldexp

Example

```
/* MODF.C */
#include <math.h>
#include <stdio.h>

void main( void )
{
    double x, y, n;

    x = -14.87654321;        /* Divide x into its fractional */
    y = modf( x, &n );       /* and integer parts            */

    printf( "For %f, the fraction is %f and the integer is %.f\n", x, y, n );
}
```

Output   For -14.876543, the fraction is -0.876543 and the integer is -14

_movedata

Description

Moves characters to another segment.

#include <memory.h>	Required only for function declarations
#include <string.h>	Use either STRING.H or MEMORY.H

void _movedata(unsigned int *srcseg*, **unsigned int** *srcoff*, **unsigned int** *destseg*,
    unsigned int *destoff*, **unsigned int** *count* **);**

srcseg	Segment address of source
srcoff	Segment offset of source
destseg	Segment address of destination
destoff	Segment offset of destination
count	Number of bytes

Remarks

The **_movedata** function copies *count* bytes from the source address specified by *srcseg*:*srcoff* to the destination address specified by *destseg*:*destoff*.

The **_movedata** function was intended to move far data in small-model programs. The newer model-independent **_fmemcpy** and **_fmemmove** functions should be used instead of the **_movedata** function. In large-model programs, the **memcpy** and **memmove** functions can also be used.

Segment values for the *srcseg* and *destseg* arguments can be obtained by using either the **_segread** function or the **_FP_SEG** macro.

The **_movedata** function does not handle all cases of overlapping moves correctly. These occur when part of the destination is the same memory area as part of the source. The **memmove** function correctly handles overlapping moves.

Return Value

None.

Compatibility

Standards:	None
16-Bit:	DOS, QWIN, WIN, WIN DLL
32-Bit:	None

See Also

_FP_OFF, **_FP_SEG**, **memcpy**, **memmove**, **_segread**

Example

```
/* MOVEDATA.C */
#include <memory.h>
#include <stdio.h>
#include <string.h>
#include <dos.h>
#include <malloc.h>

char __far *src = "This is a test.";

void main( void )
{
   char __far *dest;

   if( (dest = _fmalloc( 80 )) != NULL )
   {
      _movedata( _FP_SEG( src ),  _FP_OFF( src ),
                 _FP_SEG( dest ), _FP_OFF( dest ), _fstrlen( src ) + 1 );
      printf( "The source data at %Fp is '%Fs'\n", src, src );
      printf( "The destination data at %Fp is '%Fs'\n", dest, dest );
      _ffree( dest );
   }
}
```

Output

```
The source data at 2D0A:02B8 is 'This is a test.'
The destination data at 3D0B:0016 is 'This is a test.'
```

_moveto Functions

Description

Move current graphics positions.

#include <graph.h>

struct _xycoord __far _moveto(short *x*, **short** *y* **);**

struct _wxycoord __far _moveto_w(double *wx*, **double** *wy* **);**

x, y	View-coordinate point
wx, wy	Window-coordinate point

Remarks

The **_moveto** functions move the current position to the specified point. The **_moveto** function uses the view-coordinate point (*x*, *y*) as the current position. The **_moveto_w** function uses the window-coordinate point (*wx*, *wy*) as the current position. No drawing takes place.

The **_moveto** function operates only in graphics video modes (e.g., **_MRES4COLOR**). Because it is a graphics function, the color of text is set by the **_setcolor** function, not by the **_settextposition** function.

Return Value

The function returns the coordinates of the previous position. The **_moveto** function returns the coordinates in an **_xycoord** structure. The **_xycoord** structure, defined in GRAPH.H, contains the following elements:

Element	Description
short xcoord	*x* coordinate
short ycoord	*y* coordinate

The **_moveto_w** function returns the coordinates in an **_wxycoord** structure, defined in GRAPH.H. The **_wxycoord** structure contains the following elements:

Element	Description
double wx	*x* window coordinate
double wy	*y* window coordinate

Compatibility   Standards: None

                        16-Bit: DOS

                        32-Bit: None

See Also   **_lineto** functions, **_outgtext**

Example

```
/* MOVETO.C: This program draws line segments of different colors. */

#include <graph.h>
#include <stdlib.h>
#include <conio.h>

void main( void )
{
    short x, y, xinc, yinc, color = 1;
    struct _videoconfig v;

    /* Find a valid graphics mode. */
    if( !_setvideomode( _MAXCOLORMODE ) )
        exit( 1 );
    _getvideoconfig( &v );
    xinc = v.numxpixels / 50;
    yinc = v.numypixels / 50;

    for( x = 0, y = v.numypixels - 1; x < v.numxpixels; x += xinc, y -= yinc )
    {
        _setcolor( color++ % 16 );
        _moveto( x, 0 );
        _lineto( 0, y );
    }
    _getch();

    _setvideomode( _DEFAULTMODE );
    exit( 0 );
}
```

_msize Functions

Description

Return the size of a memory block allocated in the heap.

#include <malloc.h>   Required only for function declarations

size_t _msize(void *memblock* **);**

size_t _bmsize(__segment *seg*, **void __based(void) *** *memblock* **);**

size_t _fmsize(void __far * *memblock* **);**

size_t _nmsize(void __near * *memblock* **);**

memblock	Pointer to memory block
seg	Based-heap segment selector

Remarks

The **_msize** family of functions returns the size, in bytes, of the memory block allocated by a call to the appropriate version of the **calloc**, **malloc**, or **realloc** functions.

In large data models (compact-, large-, and huge-model programs), **_msize** maps to **_fmsize**. In small data models (tiny-, small-, and medium-model programs), **_msize** maps to **_nmsize**.

The **_nmsize** function returns the size (in bytes) of the memory block allocated by a call to **_nmalloc**, and the **_fmsize** function returns the size (in bytes) of the memory block allocated by a call to **_fmalloc** or **_frealloc**. The **_bmsize** function returns the size of a block allocated in segment *seg* by a call to **_bmalloc**, **_bcalloc**, or **_brealloc**.

The location of the memory block is indicated below:

Function	Data Segment
_msize	Depends on data model of program
_bmsize	Based heap segment specified by *seg* value
_fmsize	Far heap segment (outside default data segment)
_nmsize	Default data segment (inside near heap)

Return Value

All four functions return the size (in bytes) as an unsigned integer.

Compatibility   **_msize**

Standards: None

16-Bit: DOS, QWIN, WIN, WIN DLL

32-Bit: DOS32X

_bmsize, _fmsize, _nmsize

Standards: None

16-Bit: DOS, QWIN, WIN, WIN DLL

32-Bit: None

See Also   **calloc** functions, **_expand** functions, **malloc** functions, **realloc** functions

Example
```
/* REALLOC.C: This program allocates a block of memory for buffer
 * and then uses _msize to display the size of that block. Next, it
 * uses realloc to expand the amount of memory used by buffer
 * and then calls _msize again to display the new amount of
 * memory allocated to buffer.
 */

#include <stdio.h>
#include <malloc.h>
#include <stdlib.h>

void main( void )
{
    long *buffer;
    size_t size;

    if( (buffer = (long *)malloc( 1000 * sizeof( long ) )) == NULL )
        exit( 1 );

    size = _msize( buffer );
    printf( "Size of block after malloc of 1000 longs: %u\n", size );

    /* Reallocate and show new size: */
    if( (buffer = realloc( buffer, size + (1000 * sizeof( long )) )) == NULL )
        exit( 1 );
    size = _msize( buffer );
    printf( "Size of block after realloc of 1000 more longs: %u\n", size );

    free( buffer );
    exit( 0 );
}
```

Output
```
Size of block after malloc of 1000 longs: 4000
Size of block after realloc of 1000 more longs: 8000
```

_onexit, _fonexit

Description

Register a routine to be called at exit time.

#include <stdlib.h>

_onexit_t _onexit(_onexit_t *func* **);**

_fonexit_t __far _fonexit(_fonexit_t *func* **);**

func   Pointer to function to be called at exit

Remarks

The **_onexit** function is passed the address of a function (*func*) to be called when the program terminates normally. Successive calls to **_onexit** create a register of functions that is executed in LIFO (last-in–first-out) order. Except for DOS32X, no more than 32 functions can be registered with **_onexit**; **_onexit** returns the value **NULL** if the number of functions exceeds 32. For DOS32X, more than 32 functions can be registered. Because the heap is used, the size of the function register is only limited by available memory in the heap. The functions passed to **_onexit** cannot take parameters.

The **_fonexit** function is a far version of **_onexit**; it can be used with any memory model.

Neither **_onexit** nor **_fonexit** is part of the ANSI definition; instead, both are Microsoft extensions. The ANSI-standard **atexit** function does the same thing as **_onexit** and should be used instead of **_onexit** when ANSI portability is desired.

Return Value

Both **_onexit** and **_fonexit** return a pointer to the function if successful and return **NULL** if there is no space left to store the function pointer.

Compatibility

_onexit

Standards: UNIX

16-Bit: DOS, QWIN, WIN, WIN DLL

32-Bit: DOS32X

Use **_onexit** for compatibility with ANSI naming conventions of non-ANSI functions. Use **onexit** and link with OLDNAMES.LIB for UNIX compatibility.

_fonexit

Standards: None
16-Bit: DOS, QWIN, WIN, WIN DLL
32-Bit: None

See Also   exit

Example

```
/* ONEXIT.C */
#include <stdlib.h>
#include <stdio.h>

/* Prototypes */
void fn1( void ), fn2( void ), fn3( void ),  fn4( void );

void main( void )
{
    _onexit( fn1 );
    _onexit( fn2 );
    _onexit( fn3 );
    _onexit( fn4 );
    printf( "This is executed first.\n" );
}

void fn1()
{
    printf( "next.\n" );
}

void fn2()
{
    printf( "executed " );
}

void fn3()
{
    printf( "is " );
}

void fn4()
{
    printf( "This " );
}
```

Output

```
This is executed first.
This is executed next.
```

_open

Description

Opens a file.

#include <fcntl.h>

#include <sys\types.h>

#include <sys\stat.h>

#include <io.h>

int _open(char *filename, int oflag [[, int pmode]]);

filename	Filename
oflag	Type of operations allowed
pmode	Permission mode

Remarks

The _open function opens the file specified by filename and prepares the file for subsequent reading or writing, as defined by oflag. The oflag argument is an integer expression formed from one or more of the manifest constants defined in FCNTL.H (listed below). When two or more manifest constants are used to form the oflag argument, the constants are combined with the bitwise-OR operator (|). See "File Handling" on page 21 for a discussion of binary and text modes.

The FCNTL.H file defines the following manifest constants:

Constant	Meaning
_O_APPEND	Repositions the file pointer to the end of the file before every write operation.
_O_BINARY	Opens file in binary (untranslated) mode.
_O_CREAT	Creates and opens a new file for writing; this has no effect if the file specified by filename exists.
_O_EXCL	Returns an error value if the file specified by filename exists. Only applies when used with _O_CREAT.
_O_RDONLY	Opens file for reading only; if this flag is given, neither _O_RDWR nor _O_WRONLY can be given.
_O_RDWR	Opens file for both reading and writing; if this flag is given, neither _O_RDONLY nor _O_WRONLY can be given.
_O_TEXT	Opens file in text (translated) mode.

Constant	Meaning
_O_TRUNC	Opens and truncates an existing file to zero length; the file must have write permission. The contents of the file are destroyed. If this flag is given, you cannot specify _O_RDONLY.
_O_WRONLY	Opens file for writing only; if this flag is given, neither _O_RDONLY nor _O_RDWR can be given.

Warning! Use the _O_TRUNC flag with care, as it destroys the complete contents of an existing file.

Either _O_RDONLY, _O_RDWR, or _O_WRONLY must be given to specify the access mode. There is no default value for the access mode.

The *pmode* argument is required only when _O_CREAT is specified. If the file exists, *pmode* is ignored. Otherwise, *pmode* specifies the file's permission settings, which are set when the new file is closed for the first time. The *pmode* is an integer expression containing one or both of the manifest constants _S_IWRITE and _S_IREAD, defined in SYS\STAT.H. When both constants are given, they are joined with the bitwise-OR operator (|). The meaning of the *pmode* argument is as follows:

Value	Meaning
_S_IWRITE	Writing permitted
_S_IREAD	Reading permitted
_S_IREAD	_S_IWRITE	Reading and writing permitted

If write permission is not given, the file is read-only. With DOS, all files are readable; it is not possible to give write-only permission. Thus the modes _S_IWRITE and _S_IREAD | _S_IWRITE are equivalent.

The _open function applies the current file-permission mask to *pmode* before setting the permissions (see _umask).

The *filename* argument used in the _open function is affected by the DOS APPEND command.

Note that with DOS versions 3.0 and later, a problem occurs when SHARE is installed and a new file is opened with *oflag* set to _O_CREAT | _O_RDONLY or _O_CREAT | _O_WRONLY and *pmode* set to _S_IREAD. Under these conditions, the operating system prematurely closes the file during system calls made within _open.

To work around the problem, open the file with the *pmode* argument set to **_S_IWRITE**. Then close the file and use **_chmod** to change the access mode back to **_S_IREAD**. Another workaround is to open the file with *pmode* set to **_S_IREAD** and *oflag* set to **_O_CREAT | _O_RDWR**.

Return Value

The **_open** function returns a file handle for the opened file. A return value of –1 indicates an error, and **errno** is set to one of the following values:

Value	Meaning
EACCES	Given path name is a directory; or an attempt was made to open a read-only file for writing; or a sharing violation occurred (the file's sharing mode does not allow the specified operations).
EEXIST	The **_O_CREAT** and **_O_EXCL** flags are specified, but the named file already exists.
EINVAL	An invalid *oflag* or *pmode* argument was given.
EMFILE	No more file handles available (too many open files).
ENOENT	File or path name not found.

Compatibility

Standards: UNIX

16-Bit: DOS, QWIN, WIN, WIN DLL

32-Bit: DOS32X

Use **_open** for compatibility with ANSI naming conventions of non-ANSI functions. Use **open** and link with OLDNAMES.LIB for UNIX compatibility.

See Also

_access, _chmod, _close, _creat, _dup, _dup2, fopen, _sopen, _umask

Example

```
/* OPEN.C: This program uses _open to open a file named OPEN.C for input
 * and a file named OPEN.OUT for output. The files are then closed.
 */

#include <fcntl.h>
#include <sys\types.h>
#include <sys\stat.h>
#include <io.h>
#include <stdio.h>
```

```
void main( void )
{
    int fh1, fh2;

    fh1 = _open( "OPEN.C", _O_RDONLY );
    if( fh1 == -1 )
        perror( "open failed on input file" );
    else
    {
        printf( "open succeeded on input file\n" );
        _close( fh1 );
    }

    fh2 = _open( "OPEN.OUT", _O_WRONLY | _O_CREAT, _S_IREAD | _S_IWRITE );
    if( fh2 == -1 )
        perror( "open failed on output file" );
    else
    {
        printf( "open succeeded on output file\n" );
        _close( fh2 );
    }
}
```

Output   open succeeded on input file
open succeeded on output file

_outgtext

Description

Prints font-based text in graphics mode.

#include <graph.h>

void __ far _outgtext(const char __far *_text_);

text   Text string to output

Remarks

The **_outgtext** function outputs on the screen the null-terminated string that _text_ points to. The text is output using the current font at the current graphics position and in the current color.

No formatting is provided, in contrast to the standard console I/O library routines such as **printf**.

After it outputs the text, **_outgtext** updates the current graphics position.

The **_outgtext** function operates only in graphics video modes (e.g., **_MRES4COLOR**). Because it is a graphics function, the color of text is set by the **_setcolor** function, not by the **_settextcolor** function. Similarly, the position is affected by the **_moveto** function, not by the **_settextposition** function.

Return Value

None.

Compatibility

Standards: None
16-Bit: DOS
32-Bit: None

See Also

_moveto functions, **_setcolor**, **_setfont**

Example

```
/* OUTGTXT.C illustrates font output using functions:
 *   _registerfonts        _setfont          _outgtext
 *   _unregisterfonts      _getfontinfo      _getgtextextent
 *   _setgtextvector
 */

#include <conio.h>
#include <stdio.h>
#include <stdlib.h>
#include <string.h>
#include <graph.h>

#define NFONTS 6

unsigned char *face[NFONTS] =
{
    "Courier", "Helvetica", "Times Roman", "Modern", "Script", "Roman"
};
unsigned char *options[NFONTS] =
{
    "courier", "helv", "tms rmn", "modern", "script", "roman"
};

void main( void )
{
    unsigned char list[20];
    char fondir[_MAX_PATH];
    struct _videoconfig vc;
    struct _fontinfo fi;
    short fontnum, x, y;

    /* Read header info from all .FON files in current or given directory. */
    if( _registerfonts( "*.FON" ) <= 0 )
    {
        _outtext( "Enter full path where .FON files are located: " );
        gets( fondir );
        strcat( fondir, "\\*.FON" );
        if( _registerfonts( fondir ) <= 0 )
        {
            _outtext( "Error: can't register fonts" );
            exit( 1 );
        }
    }

    /* Set highest available graphics mode and get configuration. */
    if( !_setvideomode( _MAXRESMODE ) )
        exit( 1 );
    _getvideoconfig( &vc );
```

```
/* Display each font name centered on screen. */
for( fontnum = 0; fontnum < NFONTS; fontnum++ )
{
    /* Build options string. */
    strcat( strcat( strcpy( list, "t'" ), options[fontnum] ), "'");
    strcat( list, "h30w24b" );

    _clearscreen( _GCLEARSCREEN );
    if( _setfont( list ) >= 0 )
    {
        /* Use length of text and height of font to center text. */
        x = (vc.numxpixels / 2) - (_getgtextextent( face[fontnum] ) / 2);
        y = (vc.numypixels / 2) + (_getgtextextent( face[fontnum] ) / 2);
        if( _getfontinfo( &fi ) )
        {
            _outtext( "Error: Can't get font information" );
            break;
        }
        _moveto( x, y );
        if( vc.numcolors > 2 )
            _setcolor( fontnum + 2 );

        /* Rotate and display text. */
        _setgtextvector( 1, 0 );
        _outgtext( face[fontnum] );
        _setgtextvector( 0, 1 );
        _outgtext( face[fontnum] );
        _setgtextvector( -1, 0 );
        _outgtext( face[fontnum] );
        _setgtextvector( 0, -1 );
        _outgtext( face[fontnum] );
    }
    else
    {
        _outtext( "Error: Can't set font: " );
        _outtext( list );
    }
    _getch();
}
_unregisterfonts();
_setvideomode( _DEFAULTMODE );
exit( 0 );
}
```

_outmem

Description

Prints text of a specified length in graphics mode.

#include <graph.h>

void __far _outmem(const char __far *_text_, short _length_);

text	Text string to output
length	Length of string to output

Remarks

The **_outmem** function outputs the string that _text_ points to. The _length_ argument specifies the number of characters to output.

Unlike **_outtext**, the **_outmem** function prints all characters literally, including ASCII 10, 13, and 0 as the equivalent graphics characters. No formatting is provided. Text is printed using the current text color, starting at the current text position.

To output text using special fonts, you must use the **_outgtext** function.

Return Value

None.

Compatibility

Standards: None
16-Bit: DOS
32-Bit: None

See Also

_outtext, **_settextcolor**, **_settextposition**, **_settextwindow**

Example

```
/* OUTMEM.C illustrates:
 *     _outmem
 */

#include <stdio.h>
#include <graph.h>

void main( void )
{
    int  i, len;
    char tmp[10];

    _clearscreen( _GCLEARSCREEN );
    for( i = 0; i < 256; i++ )
    {
        _settextposition( (i % 24) + 1, (i / 24) * 7 );
        len = sprintf( tmp, "%3d %c", i, i );
        _outmem( tmp, len );
    }
    _settextposition( 24, 1 );
}
```

_outp, _outpw

Description

Outputs a byte (**_outp**) or a word (**_outpw**) at a port.

#include <conio.h>   Required only for function declarations

int **_outp**(unsigned *port*, int *databyte*);

unsigned **_outpw**(unsigned *port*, unsigned *dataword*);

port	Port number
databyte	Output value
dataword	Output value

Remarks

The **_outp** and **_outpw** functions write a byte and a word, respectively, to the specified output port. The *port* argument can be any unsigned integer in the range 0 – 65,535; *byte* can be any integer in the range 0 – 255; and *dataword* can be any value in the range 0 – 65,535.

Return Value

The functions return the data output. There is no error return.

Compatibility

Standards: None
16-Bit: DOS
32-Bit: None

See Also

_inp, _inpw

Example

```
/* OUTP.C: This program uses _inp and _outp to make sound of variable tone
 * and duration.
 */

#include <conio.h>
#include <stdio.h>
#include <time.h>

void Beep( unsigned duration, unsigned frequency ); /* Prototypes */
void Sleep( clock_t _wait );

void main ( main )
{
    Beep( 698, 700 );
    Beep( 523, 500 );
}

/* Sounds the speaker for a time specified in microseconds by duration
 * at a pitch specified in hertz by frequency.
 */
void Beep( unsigned frequency, unsigned duration )
{
    int control;

    /* If frequency is 0, Beep doesn't try to make a sound. */
    if( frequency )
    {
        /* 75 is about the shortest reliable duration of a sound. */
        if( duration < 75 )
            duration = 75;

        /* Prepare timer by sending 10111100 to port 43. */
        _outp( 0x43, 0xb6 );

        /* Divide input frequency by timer ticks per second and
         * write (byte by byte) to timer.
         */
        frequency = (unsigned)(1193180L / frequency);
        _outp( 0x42, (char)frequency );
        _outp( 0x42, (char)(frequency >> 8) );

        /* Save speaker control byte. */
        control = _inp( 0x61 );

        /* Turn on the speaker (with bits 0 and 1). */
        _outp( 0x61, control | 0x3 );
    }
```

```
        Sleep( (clock_t)duration );

        /* Turn speaker back on if necessary. */
        if( frequency )
            _outp( 0x61, control );
    }

    /* Pauses for a specified number of microseconds. */
    void Sleep( clock_t _wait )
    {
        clock_t goal;

        goal = _wait + clock();
        while( goal > clock() )
            ;
    }
```

_outtext

Description   Prints text in graphics mode.

#include <graph.h>

void __far _outtext(const char __far *_text_);

text   Text string to output

Remarks   The **_outtext** function outputs the null-terminated string that _text_ points to. No formatting is provided, in contrast to the standard console I/O library routines such as **printf**. This function will work in any screen mode.

Text output begins at the current text position.

To output text using special fonts, you must use the **_outgtext** function.

Return Value   None.

Compatibility   Standards: None
16-Bit: DOS
32-Bit: None

See Also   **_outmem, _settextcolor, _settextposition, _settextwindow, _wrapon**

Example
```
/* OUTTXT.C: This example illustrates text output functions:
 *    _gettextcolor   _getbkcolor   _gettextposition   _outtext
 *    _settextcolor   _setbkcolor   _settextposition
 */

#include <conio.h>
#include <stdio.h>
#include <graph.h>

char buffer [80];
```

```
void main( void )
{
    /* Save original foreground, background, and text position */
    short blink, fgd, oldfgd;
    long  bgd, oldbgd;
    struct _rccoord oldpos;

    /* Save original foreground, background, and text position. */
    oldfgd = _gettextcolor();
    oldbgd = _getbkcolor();
    oldpos = _gettextposition();
    _clearscreen( _GCLEARSCREEN );

    /* First time no blink, second time blinking. */
    for( blink = 0; blink <= 16; blink += 16 )
    {
        /* Loop through 8 background colors. */
        for( bgd = 0; bgd < 8; bgd++ )
        {
            _setbkcolor( bgd );
            _settextposition( (short)bgd + ((blink / 16) * 9) + 3, 1 );
            _settextcolor( 7 );
            sprintf(buffer, "Back: %d Fore:", bgd );
            _outtext( buffer );

            /* Loop through 16 foreground colors. */
            for( fgd = 0; fgd < 16; fgd++ )
            {
                _settextcolor( fgd + blink );
                sprintf( buffer, " %2d ", fgd + blink );
                _outtext( buffer );
            }
        }
    }
    _getch();

    /* Restore original foreground, background, and text position. */
    _settextcolor( oldfgd );
    _setbkcolor( oldbgd );
    _clearscreen( _GCLEARSCREEN );
    _settextposition( oldpos.row, oldpos.col );
}
```

perror

Description

Prints an error message.

#include <stdio.h>   Required only for function declarations

void perror(const char *****string);

string   String message to print

Remarks

The **perror** function prints an error message to **stderr**. The *string* argument is printed first, followed by a colon, then by the system error message for the last library call that produced the error, and finally by a newline character. If *string* is a null pointer or a pointer to a null string, **perror** prints only the system error message.

The actual error number is stored in the variable **errno** (defined in ERRNO.H). The system error messages are accessed through the variable **sys_errlist**, which is an array of messages ordered by error number. The **perror** function prints the appropriate error message by using the **errno** value as an index to **sys_errlist**. The value of the variable **sys_nerr** is defined as the maximum number of elements in the **sys_errlist** array.

To produce accurate results, **perror** should be called immediately after a library routine returns with an error. Otherwise, the **errno** value may be overwritten by subsequent calls.

Under DOS, some of the **errno** values listed in ERRNO.H are not used. These additional **errno** values are reserved for UNIX use. See "_doserrno, errno, sys_errlist, sys_nerr" on page 63 for a list of **errno** values used in DOS and the corresponding error messages. The **perror** function prints an empty string for any **errno** value not used under the operating system.

Return Value

None.

Compatibility

Standards:	ANSI, UNIX
16-Bit:	DOS, QWIN
32-Bit:	DOS32X

See Also

clearerr, ferror, strerror

Example

```
/* PERROR.C: This program attempts to open a file named NOSUCHF.ILE.
 * Since this file probably doesn't exist, an error message is displayed.
 * The same message is created using perror, strerror, and _strerror.
 */

#include <fcntl.h>
#include <sys\types.h>
#include <sys\stat.h>
#include <io.h>
#include <stdlib.h>
#include <stdio.h>
#include <string.h>

void main( void )
{
    int  fh;

    if( (fh = _open( "NOSUCHF.ILE", _O_RDONLY )) == -1 )
    {
        /* Three ways to create error message: */
        perror( "perror says open failed" );
        printf( "strerror says open failed: %s\n", strerror( errno ) );
        printf( _strerror( "_strerror says open failed" ) );
    }
    else
    {
        printf( "open succeeded on input file\n" );
        _close( fh );
    }
}
```

Output

```
perror says open failed: No such file or directory
strerror says open failed: No such file or directory
_strerror says open failed: No such file or directory
```

_pg_ analyzechart Functions

Description

Analyze a series of data.

#include <pgchart.h>

short __far _pg_analyzechart(_chartenv __far *_env_,
   char __far * __far *_categories_, float __far *_values_, short _n_);

short __far _pg_analyzechartms(_chartenv __far *_env_,
   char __far * __far *_categories_, float __far *_values_, short _nseries_, short _n_,
   short _arraydim_, char __far * __far *_serieslabels_);

env	Chart environment variable
categories	Array of category variables
values	Array of data values
nseries	Number of series to chart
_n_	Number of data values to chart
arraydim	Row dimension of data array
serieslabels	Array of labels for series

Remarks

The **_pg_analyzechart** routines analyze a single or multiple series of data without actually displaying the presentation-graphic image.

The **_pg_analyzechart** function fills the chart environment with default values for a single-series bar, column, or line chart, depending on the type specified by the call to the **_pg_defaultchart** function. The variables calculated by **_pg_analyzechart** reflect the data given in the arguments _categories_ and _values_. All arguments are the same as those used with the **_pg_chart** function.

The **_pg_analyzechartms** function fills the chart environment with default values for a multiseries bar, column, or line chart, depending on which type is specified in the **_pg_defaultchart** function. The variables calculated by **_pg_analyzechartms** reflect the data given in the arguments _categories_ and _values_. All arguments are the same as those used with the **_pg_chartms** function.

Boolean flags in the chart environment, such as **AUTOSCALE** and **LEGEND**, should be set to **TRUE** before calling either **_pg_analyzechart** function. This will ensure that the function will calculate all defaults.

For a discussion of the chart environment and related topics, see "Presentation-Graphics Functions" on page 29.

Return Value   The **_pg_analyzechart** and **_pg_analyzechartms** functions return 0 if there were no errors. A nonzero value indicates a failure.

Compatibility   Standards: None

16-Bit: DOS

32-Bit: None

See Also   **_pg_chart** functions, **_pg_defaultchart**, **_pg_initchart**

Example
```
/* PGACHART.C: This example illustrates presentation-graphics
 * analyze functions.
 * The example uses
 *     _pg_analyzechartms
 * The same principles apply for
 *     _pg_analyzepie           _pg_analyzechart
 *     _pg_analyzescatter       _pg_analyzescatterms
 */

#include <conio.h>
#include <string.h>
#include <stdlib.h>
#include <graph.h>
#include <pgchart.h>

#define FALSE   0
#define TRUE    1

/* Note data declared as a single-dimension array. The multiseries
 * chart functions expect only one dimension. See _pg_chartms
 * example for alternate method using multidimension array.
 */
#define TEAMS   4
#define MONTHS 3
float __far values[TEAMS * MONTHS] = { .435,   .522,   .671,
                                       .533,   .431,   .590,
                                       .723,   .624,   .488,
                                       .329,   .226,   .401   };
char __far *months[MONTHS] =          { "May",  "June", "July" };
char __far *teams[TEAMS] = { "Reds", "Sox", "Cubs", "Mets" };
```

```c
void main( void )
{
    _chartenv env;

    /* Find a valid graphics mode. */
    if( !_setvideomode( _MAXRESMODE ) )
        exit( 1 );

    _pg_initchart();                        /* Initialize chart system.   */
    /* Default multiseries bar chart */
    _pg_defaultchart( &env, _PG_BARCHART, _PG_PLAINBARS );
    strcpy( env.maintitle.title, "Little League Records - Default" );
    _pg_chartms( &env, months, values, TEAMS, MONTHS, MONTHS, teams );
    _getch();
    _clearscreen( _GCLEARSCREEN );

    /* Analyze multiseries bar chart with autoscale. This sets all
     * default scale values. We want y axis values to be automatic.
     */
    _pg_defaultchart( &env, _PG_BARCHART, _PG_PLAINBARS );
    strcpy( env.maintitle.title, "Little League Records - Customized" );
    env.xaxis.autoscale = TRUE;
    _pg_analyzechartms( &env, months, values, TEAMS, MONTHS, MONTHS, teams );

    /* Now customize some of the x axis values. Then draw the chart.  */
    env.xaxis.autoscale = FALSE;
    env.xaxis.scalemax = 1.0;           /* Make scale show 0.0 to 1.0.  */
    env.xaxis.ticinterval = 0.2;        /* Don't make scale too crowded. */
    env.xaxis.ticdecimals = 3;          /* Show three decimals.         */
    strcpy( env.xaxis.scaletitle.title, "Win/Loss Percentage" );
    _pg_chartms( &env, months, values, TEAMS, MONTHS, MONTHS, teams );
    _getch();

    _setvideomode( _DEFAULTMODE );
    exit( 0 );
}
```

_pg_analyzepie

Description

Analyzes a single series of data for a pie chart.

#include <pgchart.h>

short __far _pg_analyzepie(_chartenv __far *env,
    char __far * __far *categories, float __far *values,
    short __far *explode, short n);

env	Chart environment variable
categories	Array of category variables
values	Array of data values
explode	Array of explode flags
n	Number of data values to chart

Remarks

The **_pg_analyzepie** function analyzes a single series of data without actually displaying the graphic image.

The **_pg_analyzepie** function fills the chart environment for a pie chart using the data contained in the array *values*. All arguments are the same as those used in the **_pg_chartpie** function.

For a discussion of the chart environment and related topics, see "Presentation-Graphics Functions" on page 29.

Return Value

The **_pg_analyzepie** function returns 0 if there were no errors. A nonzero value indicates a failure.

Compatibility

Standards:	None
16-Bit:	DOS
32-Bit:	None

See Also

_pg_chartpie, **_pg_defaultchart**, **_pg_initchart**

Example

See the example for **_pg_analyzechart**.

_pg_analyzescatter Functions

Description
Analyze a series of data for a scatter chart.

#include <pgchart.h>

short __far _pg_analyzescatter(_chartenv __far *_env_, float __far *_xvalues_, float __far *_yvalues_, short _n_);

short __far _pg_analyzescatterms(_chartenv __far *_env_, float __far *_xvalues_, float __far *_yvalues_, short _nseries_, short _n_, short _rowdim_, char __far * __far *_serieslabels_);

env	Chart environment structure
xvalues	Array of x-axis data values
yvalues	Array of y-axis data values
_n_	Number of data values to chart
nseries	Number of series to chart
rowdim	Row dimension of data array
serieslabels	Array of labels for series

Remarks
The **_pg_analyzescatter** set of routines analyzes a single or multiple series of data without actually displaying the graphic image.

The **_pg_analyzescatter** function fills the chart environment for a single-series scatter diagram. The variables calculated by this function reflect the data given in the arguments _xvalues_ and _yvalues_. All arguments are the same as those used in the **_pg_chartscatter** function.

The **_pg_analyzescatterms** function fills the chart environment for a multiseries scatter diagram. The variables calculated by **_pg_analyzescatterms** reflect the data given in the arguments _xvalues_ and _yvalues_. All arguments are the same as those used in the function **_pg_chartscatterms**.

Boolean flags in the chart environment, such as **AUTOSCALE** and **LEGEND**, should be set to **TRUE** before calling **_pg_analyzescatterms**; this ensures that the function will calculate all defaults.

For a discussion of the chart environment and related topics, see "Presentation-Graphics Functions" on page 29.

Return Value   The **_pg_analyzescatter** and **_pg_analyzescatterms** functions return 0 if there were no errors. A nonzero value indicates a failure.

Compatibility   Standards: None
16-Bit: DOS
32-Bit: None

See Also   **_pg_chartscatter** functions, **_pg_defaultchart**, **_pg_initchart**

Example   See the example for **_pg_analyzechart**.

_pg_ chart Functions

Description

Display single-series or multiseries charts.

#include <pgchart.h>

short __far _pg_chart(_chartenv __far *_env_,
char __far * __far *_categories_, float __far *_values_, short _n_);

short __far _pg_chartms(_chartenv __far *_env_,
char __far * __far *_categories_, float __far *_values_, short _nseries_, short _n_,
short _arraydim_, char __far * __far *_serieslabels_);

env	Chart environment variable
categories	Array of category variables
values	Array of data values
_n_	Number of data values to chart
nseries	Number of series to chart
arraydim	Row dimension of data array
serieslabels	Array of labels for series

Remarks

The **_pg_chart** function displays a single-series bar, column, or line chart, depending on the type specified in the chart environment variable (_env_).

The **_pg_chartms** function displays a multiseries bar, column, or line chart, depending on the type specified in the chart environment. All the series must contain the same number of data points, specified by the argument _n_.

The array _values_ is a two-dimensional array containing all value data for every series to be plotted on the chart. Each column of _values_ represents a single series. The parameter _rowdim_ is the integer value used to dimension rows in the array declaration for _values_.

For example, the following code fragment declares the identifier `values` to be a two-dimensional floating-point array with 20 rows and 10 columns:

```
#define ARRAYDIM 20
float values [ARRAYDIM][10];
short rowdim = ARRAYDIM;
```

Note that the number of columns in the *values* array cannot exceed 10, the maximum number of data series on a single chart. Note also that `rowdim` must be greater than or equal to the argument *n*, and the column dimension in the array declaration must be greater than or equal to the argument *nseries*. If *n* and *nseries* are set to values less than the full dimensional size of the *values* array, only part of the data contained in *values* will be plotted.

The array *serieslabels* holds the labels used in the chart legend to identify each series.

For a discussion of the chart environment and related topics, see "Presentation-Graphics Functions" on page 29.

Return Value   The **_pg_chart** and **_pg_chartms** functions return 0 if there were no errors. A nonzero value indicates a failure.

Compatibility
Standards:	None
16-Bit:	DOS
32-Bit:	None

See Also   **_pg_analyzechart** functions, **_pg_defaultchart**, **_pg_initchart**

Example

```
/* PGCHART.C: This example illustrates presentation-graphics support
 * routines and single-series chart routines, including
 *    _pg_initchart  _pg_defaultchart  _pg_chart  _pg_chartpie
 */

#include <conio.h>
#include <graph.h>
#include <string.h>
#include <stdlib.h>
#include <pgchart.h>

#define COUNTRIES 5
float __far value[COUNTRIES] =      { 42.5,    14.3,    35.2,    21.3,    32.6    };
char __far *category[COUNTRIES] = { "USSR",  "France","USA",   "UK",    "Other" };
short __far explode[COUNTRIES] =  { 0,       1,       0,       1,       0       };
```

```
void main( void )
{
   _chartenv env;
   short mode = _VRES16COLOR;

   /* Find a valid graphics mode. */
   if( !_setvideomode( _MAXRESMODE ) )
      exit( 1 );

   _pg_initchart();                        /* Initialize chart system. */

   /* Single-series bar chart */
   _pg_defaultchart( &env, _PG_BARCHART, _PG_PLAINBARS );
   strcpy( env.maintitle.title, "Widget Production" );
   _pg_chart( &env, category, value, COUNTRIES );
   _getch();
   _clearscreen( _GCLEARSCREEN );

   /* Single-series column chart */
   _pg_defaultchart( &env, _PG_COLUMNCHART, _PG_PLAINBARS );
   strcpy( env.maintitle.title, "Widget Production" );
   _pg_chart( &env, category, value, COUNTRIES );
   _getch();
   _clearscreen( _GCLEARSCREEN );

   /* Pie chart */
   _pg_defaultchart( &env, _PG_PIECHART, _PG_PERCENT );
   strcpy( env.maintitle.title, "Widget Production" );
   _pg_chartpie( &env, category, value, explode, COUNTRIES );
   _getch();

   _setvideomode( _DEFAULTMODE );
   exit( 0 );
}
```

_pg_chartpie

Description   Displays a pie chart.

#include <pgchart.h>

short __far _pg_chartpie(_chartenv __far *env,
    char __far * __far *categories, float __far *values, short __far *explode,
    short n);

env	Chart environment structure
categories	Array of category labels
values	Array of data values
explode	Array of explode flags
n	Number of data values to chart

Remarks   The _pg_chartpie function displays a pie chart for the data contained in the array *values*. Pie charts are formed from a single series of data—there is no multiseries version of pie charts as there is for other chart types.

The array *explode* must be dimensioned so that its length is greater than or equal to the argument *n*. All entries in *explode* are either 0 or 1. If an entry is 1, the corresponding pie slice is displayed slightly removed from the rest of the pie.

For example, if the *explode* array is initialized as

```
short explode[5] = {0, 1, 0, 0, 0};
```

the pie slice corresponding to the second entry of the *categories* array will be displayed "exploded" from the other four slices.

For a discussion of the chart environment and related topics, see "Presentation-Graphics Functions" on page 29.

Return Value   The _pg_chartpie function returns 0 if there were no errors. A nonzero value indicates a failure.

Compatibility   Standards: None
                      16-Bit: DOS
                      32-Bit: None

See Also   **_pg_analyzepie**, **_pg_defaultchart**, **_pg_initchart**

Example   See the example for **_pg_chart**.

_pg_ chartscatter Functions

Description   Display scatter charts.

#include <pgchart.h>

short __far _pg_chartscatter(_chartenv __far *env, float __far *xvalues,
  float __far *yvalues, short n);

short __far _pg_chartscatterms(_chartenv __far *env, float __far *xvalues,
  float __far *yvalues, short nseries, short n, short rowdim,
  char __far * __far *serieslabels);

env	Chart environment structure
xvalues	Array of x-axis data values
yvalues	Array of y-axis data values
n	Number of data values to chart
nseries	Number of series to chart
rowdim	Row dimension of data array
serieslabels	Array of labels for series

Remarks   The **_pg_ chartscatter** function displays a scatter diagram for a single series
of data.

The **_pg_ chartscatterms** function displays a scatter diagram for more than one
series of data.

The arguments *xvalues* and *yvalues* are two-dimensional arrays containing data for
the *x* axis and *y* axis, respectively. Columns for each array hold data for individual
series; thus the first columns of *xvalues* and *yvalues* contain plot data for the first
series, the second columns contain plot data for the second series, and so forth.

The *n, rowdim, nseries,* and *serieslabels* arguments fulfill the same purposes as
those used in the **_pg_ chartms** function. See **_pg_ chartms** for an explanation of
these arguments.

For a discussion of the chart environment and related topics, see "Presentation-
Graphics Functions" on page 29.

Return Value

The **_pg_chartscatter** and **_pg_chartscatterms** functions return 0 if there were no errors. A nonzero value indicates a failure.

Compatibility

Standards:	None
16-Bit:	DOS
32-Bit:	None

See Also

_pg_analyzescatter functions, **_pg_defaultchart**, **_pg_initchart**

Example

See the example for **_pg_chart**.

_pg_defaultchart

Description

Initializes the chart environment.

#include <pgchart.h>

short __far _pg_defaultchart(_chartenv __far *env, short *charttype*,
  short *chartstyle*);

env	Chart environment structure
charttype	Chart type
chartstyle	Chart style

Remarks

The **_pg_defaultchart** function initializes all necessary variables in the chart environment for the chart type by the variable *charttype*.

All title fields in the environment structure are blanked. Titles should be set in the proper fields after calling **_pg_defaultchart**.

The *charttype* variable can be set to one of the following manifest constants:

Chart Type	Description
_PG_BARCHART	Bar chart
_PG_COLUMNCHART	Column chart
_PG_LINECHART	Line chart
_PG_PIECHART	Pie chart
_PG_SCATTERCHART	Scatter chart

The *chartstyle* variable specifies the style of the chart with either the number "1" or the number "2." Each of the five types of presentation-graphics charts can appear in two different chart styles, as described below:

Chart Type	Chart Style 1	Chart Style 2
Bar	Side by side	Stacked
Column	Side by side	Stacked
Line	Points with lines	Points only
Pie	Percent	No percent
Scatter	Points with lines	Points only

In a pie chart, the pieces are "exploded" according to the *explode* array argument in the **_pg_chartpie** function. In the "percent" format, percentages are printed next to each slice. Bar and column charts have only one style when displaying a single series of data. The styles "side by side" and "stacked" are applicable only when more than one series appears on the same chart. The first style arranges the bars or columns for the different series side by side, showing relative heights or lengths. The stacked style emphasizes relative sizes between bars and columns.

Return Value

The **_pg_defaultchart** function returns 0 if there were no errors. A nonzero value indicates a failure.

Compatibility

Standards:	None
16-Bit:	DOS
32-Bit:	None

See Also

_pg_getchardef, **_pg_getpalette**, **_pg_getstyleset**, **_pg_hlabelchart**, **_pg_initchart**, **_pg_resetpalette**, **_pg_resetstyleset**, **_pg_setchardef**, **_pg_setpalette**, **_pg_setstyleset**, **_pg_vlabelchart**

Example

See the example for **_pg_chart**.

_pg_getchardef

Description

Gets the pixel bitmap for the specified character.

#include <pgchart.h>

short __far _pg_getchardef(short *charnum***, unsigned char __far ***chardef* **);**

charnum	ASCII number of character
chardef	Pointer to 8-by-8 bitmap array

Remarks

The **_pg_getchardef** function retrieves the current 8-by-8 pixel bitmap for the character having the ASCII number *charnum*. The bitmap is stored in the *chardef* array.

Return Value

The **_pg_getchardef** function returns 0 if there were no errors. A nonzero value indicates an error.

Compatibility

Standards:	None
16-Bit:	DOS
32-Bit:	None

See Also

_pg_defaultchart, _pg_initchart, _pg_setchardef

_pg_getpalette

Description

Gets palette colors, line styles, and patterns.

#include <pgchart.h>

short __ far _pg_getpalette(_paletteentry __far *_palette_);

palette   Pointer to first palette structure in array

Remarks

The **_pg_getpalette** function retrieves palette colors, line styles, fill patterns, and plot characters for all palettes. The pointer *palette* points to an array of palette structures that will contain the desired palette values.

The palette used by the presentation-graphics routines is independent of the palette used by the low-level graphics routines.

Return Value

The function **_pg_getpalette** returns 0 if there were no errors, and it returns the value **_BADSCREENMODE** if current palettes have not been initialized by a previous call to **_pg_setpalette**.

Compatibility

Standards: None
16-Bit: DOS
32-Bit: None

See Also

_pg_defaultchart, _pg_initchart, _pg_resetpalette, _pg_setpalette

Example

```
/* PGGPAL.C: This example illustrates presentation-graphics palettes
 * and the routines that modify them, including
 *    _pg_getpalette    _pg_resetpalette    _pg_setstyleset
 *    _pg_getstyleset   _pg_resetstyleset   _pg_vlabelchart
 *    _pg_hlabelchart   _pg_setpalette
 */

#include <conio.h>
#include <string.h>
#include <stdlib.h>
#include <graph.h>
#include <pgchart.h>
```

```
#define TEAMS  2
#define MONTHS 3
float __far values[TEAMS][MONTHS] =    { { .435,    .522,    .671  },
                                         { .533,    .431,    .401  } };
char __far *months[MONTHS] =            { "May", "June", "July" };
char __far *teams[TEAMS] = { "Cubs", "Reds" };

_fillmap fill1 = { 0x99, 0x33, 0x66, 0xcc, 0x99, 0x33, 0x66, 0xcc };
_fillmap fill2 = { 0x99, 0xcc, 0x66, 0x33, 0x99, 0xcc, 0x66, 0x33 };
_styleset styles;
_palettetype pal;

void main( void )
{
    _chartenv env;
    short mode = _VRES16COLOR;

    /* Find a valid graphics mode. */
    if( !_setvideomode( _MAXRESMODE ) )
        exit( 1 );

    _pg_initchart();                            /* Initialize chart system.   */

    /* Modify global set of line styles used for borders, grids, and
     * data connectors. Note that this change is used before
     * _pg_defaultchart, which will use the style set.
     */
    _pg_getstyleset( styles );                  /* Get styles and modify      */
    styles[1] = 0x5555;                         /*    style 1 (used for       */
    _pg_setstyleset( styles );                  /*    borders)—then set new.  */

    _pg_defaultchart( &env, _PG_BARCHART, _PG_PLAINBARS );

    /* Modify palette for data lines, colors, fill patterns, and
     * characters. Note that the line styles are set in the palette, not
     * in the style set, so that only data connectors will be affected.
     */
    _pg_getpalette( pal );                      /* Get default palette.       */
    pal[1].plotchar = 16;                       /* Set to ASCII 16 and 17.    */
    pal[2].plotchar = 17;
    memcpy( pal[1].fill, fill1, 8 );            /* Copy fill masks to palette. */
    memcpy( pal[2].fill, fill2, 8 );
    pal[1].color = 3;                           /* Change palette colors.     */
    pal[2].color = 4;
    pal[1].style = 0xfcfc;                      /* Change palette line styles. */
    pal[2].style = 0x0303;
    _pg_setpalette( pal );                      /* Put modified palette.      */
```

```
/* Multiseries bar chart */
strcpy( env.maintitle.title, "Little League Records - Customized" );
_pg_chartms( &env, months, (float __far *)values,
            TEAMS, MONTHS, MONTHS, teams );
_getch();
_clearscreen( _GCLEARSCREEN );

/* Multiseries line chart */
_pg_defaultchart( &env, _PG_LINECHART, _PG_POINTANDLINE );
strcpy( env.maintitle.title, "Little League Records - Customized" );
_pg_chartms( &env, months, (float __far *)values,
            TEAMS, MONTHS, MONTHS, teams );

/* Print labels. */
_pg_hlabelchart( &env, (short)(env.chartwindow.x2 * .75),
                       (short)(env.chartwindow.y2 * .10),
                       12, "Up and up!" );
_pg_vlabelchart( &env, (short)(env.chartwindow.x2 * .75),
                       (short)(env.chartwindow.y2 * .45),
                       13, "Sliding down!" );
_getch();
_clearscreen( _GCLEARSCREEN );

_pg_resetpalette();                     /* Restore default palette  */
_pg_resetstyleset();                    /*    and style set.        */

/* Multiseries bar chart */
_pg_defaultchart( &env, _PG_BARCHART, _PG_PLAINBARS );
strcpy( env.maintitle.title, "Little League Records - Default" );
_pg_chartms( &env, months, (float __far *)values,
            TEAMS, MONTHS, MONTHS, teams );
_getch();
_clearscreen( _GCLEARSCREEN );

/* Multiseries line chart */
_pg_defaultchart( &env, _PG_LINECHART, _PG_POINTANDLINE );
strcpy( env.maintitle.title, "Little League Records - Default" );
_pg_chartms( &env, months, (float __far *)values,
            TEAMS, MONTHS, MONTHS, teams );
_getch();

_setvideomode( _DEFAULTMODE );
exit( 0 );
}
```

_pg_getstyleset

Description

Gets the contents of the current styleset array.

#include <pgchart.h>

void __far _pg_getstyleset(unsigned short __far *styleset);

styleset   Pointer to current styleset array

Remarks

The **_pg_getstyleset** function retrieves the contents of the current styleset array.

Return Value

None.

Compatibility

Standards: None
16-Bit: DOS
32-Bit: None

See Also

_pg_defaultchart, _pg_initchart, _pg_resetstyleset, _pg_setstyleset

Example

See the example for **_pg_getpalette**.

_pg_hlabelchart

Description

Writes text horizontally on the screen.

#include <pgchart.h>

short __far _pg_hlabelchart(_chartenv __far *env, short x, short y,
    short color, char __far *label);

env	Chart environment structure
x	*x*-coordinate for text
y	Pixel *y*-coordinate for text
color	Color code for text
label	Label text

Remarks

The **_pg_hlabelchart** function writes text horizontally on the screen. The arguments *x* and *y* are pixel coordinates for the beginning location of text relative to the upper-left corner of the chart window.

Return Value

The **_pg_hlabelchart** functions return 0 if there were no errors. A nonzero value indicates a failure.

Compatibility

Standards: None
16-Bit: DOS
32-Bit: None

See Also

_pg_defaultchart, _pg_initchart, _pg_vlabelchart

Example

See the example for **_pg_getpalette**.

_pg_initchart

Description

Initializes presentation graphics.

#include <pgchart.h>

short __far _pg_initchart(void);

Remarks

The **_pg_initchart** function initializes the presentation-graphics package. It initializes the color and style pools, resets the chartline styleset, builds default palette modes, and reads the presentation-graphics font definition from the disk. This function is required in all programs that use presentation graphics. The **_pg_initchart** function must be called before any of the other functions in the presentation-graphics library.

The **_pg_initchart** function assumes a valid graphics mode has been established. Therefore, it must be called only after a successful call to the library function **_setvideomode**.

Note The **_pg_initchart** function can only be called after using the **_setvideomode** function to establish the video mode. Also, **_pg_initchart** must be called after each change of the video mode.

Return Value

The **_pg_initchart** functions return 0 if there were no errors. A nonzero value indicates a failure.

Compatibility

Standards: None
16-Bit: DOS
32-Bit: None

See Also

_pg_defaultchart, _pg_getchardef, _pg_getpalette, _pg_getstyleset, _pg_hlabelchart, _pg_resetpalette, _resetstyleset, _pg_setchardef, _pg_setpalette, _pg_setstyleset, _pg_vlabelchart, _setvideomode

Example

See the example for **_pg_chart**.

_pg_resetpalette

Description

Resets palette colors, line styles, and patterns to default values.

#include <pgchart.h>

short __far _pg_resetpalette(void);

Remarks

The **_pg_resetpalette** function sets the palette colors, line styles, fill patterns, and plot characters for the palette to the default for the current screen mode.

The palette used by the presentation-graphics routines is independent of the palette used by the low-level graphics routines.

Return Value

The **_pg_resetpalette** function returns 0 if there were no errors. If the screen mode is not valid, the value **_BADSCREENMODE** is returned.

Compatibility

Standards: None
16-Bit: DOS
32-Bit: None

See Also

_pg_defaultchart, **_pg_getpalette**, **_pg_initchart**, **_pg_setpalette**

Example

See the example for **_pg_getpalette**.

_pg_resetstyleset

Description

Resets styleset to default values.

#include <pgchart.h>

void __far _pg_resetstyleset(void);

Remarks

The **_pg_resetstyleset** function reinitializes the styleset to the default values for the current screen mode.

Return Value

None.

Compatibility

Standards:	None
16-Bit:	DOS
32-Bit:	None

See Also

_pg_defaultchart, **_pg_getstyleset**, **_pg_initchart**, **_pg_setstyleset**

Example

See the example for **_pg_getpalette**.

_pg_setchardef

Description

Sets the pixel bit map for the specified character.

#include <pgchart.h>

short __far _pg_setchardef(short *charnum*, **unsigned char __far ****chardef* **);**

charnum	ASCII number of character
chardef	Pointer to an 8-by-8 bitmap array for the character

Remarks

The **_pg_setchardef** function sets the 8-by-8 pixel bitmap for the character with the ASCII number *charnum*. The bitmap is stored in the *chardef* array.

Return Value

The **_pg_setchardef** function returns 0 if there was no error. A nonzero value indicates an error.

Compatibility

Standards: None
16-Bit: DOS
32-Bit: None

See Also

_pg_defaultchart, **_pg_getchardef**, **_pg_initchart**

_pg_setpalette

Description   Sets palette colors, line styles, and patterns.

#include <pgchart.h>

short __far _pg_setpalette(_paletteentry __far *_palette_);

palette   Pointer to first palette structure in array

Remarks   The **_pg_setpalette** function sets palette colors, line styles, fill patterns, and plot
                    characters for all palettes. The pointer *palette* points to an array of palette struc-
                    tures that contain the desired palette values.

                    The palette used by the presentation-graphics routines is independent of the palette
                    used by the low-level graphics routines.

Return Value   The **_pg_setpalette** function returns 0 if there were no errors. If the new palettes
                    are not valid, the value **_BADSCREENMODE** is returned.

Compatibility   Standards: None
                    16-Bit: DOS
                    32-Bit: None

See Also   **_pg_defaultchart**, **_pg_getpalette**, **_pg_initchart**, **_pg_resetpalette**

Example   See the example for **_pg_getpalette**.

_pg_setstyleset

Description

Sets the current styleset.

#include <pgchart.h>

void __far _pg_setstyleset(unsigned short __far *_styleset_);

styleset   Pointer to new styleset

Remarks

The **_pg_setstyleset** function sets the current styleset.

Return Value

None.

Compatibility

Standards: None
16-Bit: DOS
32-Bit: None

See Also

_pg_defaultchart, _pg_getstyleset, _pg_initchart, _pg_resetstyleset

Example

See the example for **_pg_getpalette**.

_pg_vlabelchart

Description

Writes text vertically on the screen.

#include <pgchart.h>

short __far _pg_vlabelchart(_chartenv __far *env, short x, short y,
   short color, char __far *label);

env	Chart environment structure
x	Pixel x coordinate for text
y	Pixel y coordinate for text
color	Color code for text
label	Label text

Remarks

The **_pg_vlabelchart** function writes text vertically on the screen. The arguments x and y are pixel coordinates for the beginning location of text relative to the upper-left corner of the chart window.

Return Value

The **_pg_vlabelchart** function returns 0 if there were no errors. A nonzero value indicates a failure.

Compatibility

Standards: None
16-Bit: DOS
32-Bit: None

See Also

_pg_defaultchart, _pg_hlabelchart, _pg_initchart

Example

See the example for **_pg_getpalette**.

_pie Functions

Description   Draw wedge-shaped figures.

#include <graph.h>

short __far _pie(short *control*, short *x1*, short *y1*, short *x2*, short *y2*, short *x3*, short *y3*, short *x4*, short *y4*);

short __far _pie_w(short *control*, double *x1*, double *y1*, double *x2*, double *y2*, double *x3*, double *y3*, double *x4*, double *y4*);

short __far _pie_wxy(short *control*, struct _wxycoord __far *pwxy1*, struct _wxycoord __far *pwxy2*, struct _wxycoord __far *pwxy3*, struct _wxycoord __far*pwxy4*);

control	Fill-control constant
x1, y1	Upper-left corner of bounding rectangle
x2, y2	Lower-right corner of bounding rectangle
x3, y3	Second point of start vector (center of bounding rectangle is first point)
x4, y4	Second point of end vector (center of bounding rectangle is first point)
pwxy1	Upper-left corner of bounding rectangle
pwxy2	Lower-right corner of bounding rectangle
pwxy3	Second point of start vector (center of bounding rectangle is first point)
pwxy4	Second point of end vector (center of bounding rectangle is first point)

Remarks   The **_pie** functions draw a pie-shaped wedge by drawing an elliptical arc whose center and two endpoints are joined by lines.

The center of the pie is the center of the bounding rectangle, which is defined by points (*x1, y1*) and (*x2, y2*) for **_pie** and **_pie_w** and by points *pwxy1* and *pwxy2* for **_pie_wxy**. The pie starts where it intersects an imaginary line extending from the center of the arc through (*x3*, *y3*) for **_pie** and **_pie_w** and through *pwxy3* for **_pie_wxy**. It is drawn counterclockwise about the center of the arc, ending where it intersects an imaginary line extending from the center of the arc through (*x4*, *y4*) for **_pie** and **_pie_w** and through *pwxy4* for **_pie_wxy**.

The **_pie** routine uses the view coordinate system. The **_pie_w** and **_pie_wxy** functions use the real-valued window coordinate system. The arc is drawn using the current color. Since an arc does not define a closed area, it is not filled.

The **_wxycoord** structure is defined in GRAPH.H and contains the following elements:

Element	Description
double wx	Window *x* coordinate
double wy	Window *y* coordinate

The wedge is drawn using the current color moving in a counterclockwise direction. The *control* parameter can be one of the following manifest constants:

Constant	Action
_GFILLINTERIOR	Fills the figure using the current color and fill mask
_GBORDER	Does not fill the figure

The control option given by **_GFILLINTERIOR** is equivalent to a subsequent call to the **_floodfill** function using the approximate center of the pie as the starting point and the current color (set by **_setcolor**) as the boundary color. Use the **_getarcinfo** function to find the exact starting point.

Return Value

These functions return a nonzero value if successful; otherwise, they return 0.

Compatibility

Standards:	None
16-Bit:	DOS
32-Bit:	None

See Also

_arc functions, **_ellipse** functions, **_floodfill**, **_getarcinfo**, **_getcolor**, **_lineto** functions, **_rectangle** functions, **_setcolor**, **_setfillmask**

Example

```
/* PIE.C: This program draws a pie-shaped figure. */

#include <stdlib.h>
#include <conio.h>
#include <graph.h>

void main( void )
{
   /* Find a valid graphics mode. */
   if( !_setvideomode( _MAXRESMODE ) )
      exit( 1 );

   _pie( _GBORDER, 80, 50, 240, 150, 240, 12, 0, 150 );
   _getch();

   _setvideomode( _DEFAULTMODE );
   exit( 0 );
}
```

_polygon Functions

Description

Draw polygon shapes.

#include <graph.h>

short __far _polygon(short *control*, const struct _xycoord __far *points*,
   short *numpoints*);

short __far _polygon_w(short *control*, const double __far *points*,
   short *numpoints*);

short __far _polygon_wxy(short *control*,
   const struct _wxycoord __far *points*, short *numpoints*);

control	Fill flag
points	Pointer to an array of structures or doubles defining the polygon
numpoints	Number of points

Remarks

The **_polygon** functions draw polygons. The border of the polygon is drawn in the current color and line style. The **_polygon** routine uses the view coordinate system (expressed in **_xycoord** structures), and the **_polygon_wxy** and **_polygon_w** routines use real-valued window coordinates (expressed in **_wxycoord** structures and in pairs of double-precision floating-point values, respectively).

The argument *points* is an array of **_xycoord** or **_wxycoord** structures or pairs of doubles, each of which specifies one of the polygon's vertices. (For **_polygon_w**, *points*[0] and *points*[1] specify the *x* and *y* coordinates, respectively, of the first point.) If the first point does not equal the last point, the **_polygon** functions use them to provide a closing edge.

The argument *numpoints* indicates the number of elements (the number of vertices) in the *points* array. The minimum number of points is 3, the maximum is 16,381.

The *control* argument can be one of the following manifest constants:

Constant	Action
_GFILLINTERIOR	Fills the polygon with the current fill mask using a scan fill
_GBORDER	Does not fill the polygon

The **_setwritemode**, **_setlinestyle**, and **_setfillmask** functions all affect the output from the **_polygon** functions.

If you try to fill the polgon with the **_floodfill** function, the polygon must be bordered by a solid line-style pattern.

Return Value

The **_polygon** functions return a nonzero value if the arc is successfully drawn; otherwise, they return 0.

Compatibility

Standards: None

16-Bit: DOS

32-Bit: None

See Also

_ellipse functions, **_floodfill**, **_lineto** functions, **_pie** functions, **_rectangle** functions, **_setcolor**, **_setfillmask**, **_setlinestyle**, **_setwritemode**

Example

```
/* POLYGON.C: This program draws a star-shaped polygon. */

#include <conio.h>
#include <stdlib.h>
#include <graph.h>
#include <math.h>
#include <stdlib.h>

#define PI 3.1415

void main( void )
{
    short  side, radius = 90, x = 0, y = 0;
    double radians;
    struct _xycoord polyside[5];
    struct _videoconfig vc;

    /* Find a valid graphics mode. */
    if( !_setvideomode( _MAXRESMODE ) )
        exit( 1 );

    _getvideoconfig( &vc );
    _setvieworg( vc.numxpixels / 2, vc. numypixels / 2 );
```

```
    /* Calculate points of star every 144 degrees, then connect them. */
    for( side = 0; side < 5; side++ )
    {
        radians = 144 * PI / 180;
        polyside[side].xcoord = x + (short)(cos( side * radians ) * radius);
        polyside[side].ycoord = y + (short)(sin( side * radians ) * radius);
    }
    _polygon( _GFILLINTERIOR, polyside, 5 );

    _getch();
    _setvideomode( _DEFAULTMODE );
    exit( 0 );
}
```

pow Functions

Description

Calculate x raised to the power of y.

#include <math.h>

double pow(double x, double y);

long double _powl(long double x, long double y);

x	Number to be raised
y	Power of x

Remarks

The **pow** and **_powl** functions compute x raised to the power of y.

The **_powl** function is the 80-bit counterpart, and it uses an 80-bit, 10-byte co-processor form of arguments and return values. See the reference page on the long double functions for more details on this data type.

Return Value

The **pow** and **_powl** functions return the value of x^y. If x is not 0.0 and y is 0.0, **pow** and **_powl** return the value 1. If x is 0.0 and y is negative, **pow** and **_powl** set **errno** to **EDOM** and return 0.0. If both x and y are 0.0, or if x is negative and y is not an integer, the function prints a **_DOMAIN** error message to **stderr**, sets **errno** to **EDOM,** and returns 0.0. If an overflow results, the function sets **errno** to **ERANGE** and returns $\pm$ **HUGE_ VAL**. No message is printed on overflow or underflow.

The **pow** function does not recognize integral floating-point values greater than 2^{64}, such as `1.0E100`.

Compatibility

pow

Standards:	ANSI, UNIX
16-Bit:	DOS, QWIN, WIN, WIN DLL
32-Bit:	DOS32X

_powl

Standards:	None
16-Bit:	DOS, QWIN, WIN, WIN DLL
32-Bit:	None

See Also   **exp**, **log** functions, **sqrt**

Example

```
/* POW.C */
#include <math.h>
#include <stdio.h>

void main( void )
{
    double x = 2.0, y = 3.0, z;

    z = pow( x, y );
    printf( "%.1f to the power of %.1f is %.1f\n", x, y, z );
}
```

Output

```
2.0 to the power of 3.0 is 8.0
```

printf

Description

Prints formatted output to the standard output stream.

#include <stdio.h>

int printf(const char **format* [[, *argument*]]... **);**

| *format* | Format control |
| *argument* | Optional arguments |

Remarks

The **printf** function formats and prints a series of characters and values to the standard output stream, **stdout**. The *format* argument consists of ordinary characters, escape sequences, and (if arguments follow *format*) format specifications. The ordinary characters and escape sequences are copied to **stdout** in order of their appearance. For example, the line

```
printf("Line one\n\t\tLine two\n");
```

produces the output

```
Line one
        Line two
```

If arguments follow the *format* string, the *format* string must contain specifications that determine the output format for the arguments.

Format specifications always begin with a percent sign (%) and are read left to right. When the first format specification (if any) is encountered, the value of the first argument after *format* is converted and output accordingly. The second format specification causes the second argument to be converted and output, and so on. If there are more arguments than there are format specifications, the extra arguments are ignored. The results are undefined if there are not enough arguments for all the format specifications.

Format Specification Fields

A format specification, which consists of optional and required fields, has the following form:

%[[*flags*]] [[*width*]] [[*.precision*]] [[{ **F** | **N** | **h** | **l** | **L** }]]*type*

Each field of the format specification is a single character or a number signifying a particular format option. The simplest format specification contains only the percent sign and a *type* character (for example, %s). The optional fields, which appear before the *type* character, control other aspects of the formatting. The fields in a **printf** format specification are described in the following list:

Field	Description
type	Required character that determines whether the associated argument is interpreted as a character, a string, or a number. (See Table R.2.)
flags	Optional character or characters that control justification of output and printing of signs, blanks, decimal points, and octal and hexadecimal prefixes. (See Table R.3.) More than one flag can appear in a format specification.
width	Optional number that specifies minimum number of characters output.
precision	Optional number that specifies maximum number of characters printed for all or part of the output field, or minimum number of digits printed for integer values. (See Table R.4.)
F, N	Optional prefixes that refer to the "distance" to the object being printed (**near** or **far**). F and N are not part of the ANSI definition for **printf**. They are Microsoft extensions that should not be used if ANSI portability is desired.
h, l, L	Optional prefixes that determine the size of the argument expected, as shown below:

Prefix	Use
h	Used with the integer types **d, i, o, x,** and **X** to specify that the argument is **short int**, or with **u** to specify **short unsigned int**. If used with %**p**, it indicates a 16-bit pointer.
l	Used with **d, i, o, x,** and **X** types to specify that the argument is **long int**, or with **u** to specify **long unsigned int**; also used with **e, E, f, g,** and **G** types to specify **double** rather than **float**. If used with %**p**, it indicates a 32-bit pointer.
L	Used with **e, E, f, g,** and **G** types to specify **long double**.

If a percent sign is followed by a character that has no meaning as a format field, the character is copied to **stdout**. For example, to print a percent-sign character, use %%.

Type Field Characters

The *type* character is the only required format field for the **printf** function; it appears after any optional format fields. The *type* character determines whether the associated argument is interpreted as a character, string, or number (see Table R.2).

Table R.2 Type Characters for printf

Character	Type	Output Format
d	int	Signed decimal integer.
i	int	Signed decimal integer.
u	int	Unsigned decimal integer.
o	int	Unsigned octal integer.
x	int	Unsigned hexadecimal integer, using "abcdef."
X	int	Unsigned hexadecimal integer, using "ABCDEF."
f	double	Signed value having the form [–]*dddd.dddd*, where *dddd* is one or more decimal digits. The number of digits before the decimal point depends on the magnitude of the number, and the number of digits after the decimal point depends on the requested precision.
e	double	Signed value having the form [–]*d.dddd* **e** [*sign*]*ddd*, where *d* is a single decimal digit, *dddd* is one or more decimal digits, *ddd* is exactly three decimal digits, and *sign* is + or –.
E	double	Identical to the **e** format, except that **E**, rather than **e**, introduces the exponent.
g	double	Signed value printed in **f** or **e** format, whichever is more compact for the given value and precision. The **e** format is used only when the exponent of the value is less than –4 or greater than or equal to the *precision* argument. Trailing zeros are truncated, and the decimal point appears only if one or more digits follow it.
G	double	Identical to the **g** format, except that **G**, rather than **g**, introduces the exponent (where appropriate).
c	int	Single character.
s	String	Characters printed up to the first null character ('\0') or until the *precision* value is reached.
n	Pointer to integer	Number of characters successfully written so far to the stream or buffer; this value is stored in the integer whose address is given as the argument.
p	Far pointer to **void**	Prints the address pointed to by the argument in the form *xxxx:yyyy*, where *xxxx* is the segment and *yyyy* is the offset, and the digits *x* and *y* are uppercase hexadecimal digits; %**hp** indicates a near pointer and prints only the offset of the address.

Flag Directives

The first optional field of the format specification is *flag*. A flag directive is a character that justifies output and prints signs, blanks, decimal points, and octal and hexadecimal prefixes. More than one flag directive may appear in a format specification. (See Table R.3.)

Table R.3 Flag Characters for printf

Flag	Meaning	Default
–	Left justify the result within the given field width.	Right justify.
+	Prefix the output value with a sign (+ or –) if the output value is of a signed type.	Sign appears only for negative signed values (–).
0	If *width* is prefixed with 0, zeros are added until the minimum width is reached. If 0 and – appear, the 0 is ignored. If 0 is specified with an integer format (**i, u, x, X, o, d**), the 0 is ignored.	No padding.
blank (' ')	Prefix the output value with a blank if the output value is signed and positive; the blank is ignored if both the blank and + flags appear.	No blank appears.
#	When used with the o, **x**, or **X** format, the # flag prefixes any nonzero output value with 0, 0x, or 0X, respectively.	No blank appears.
	When used with the **e**, **E**, or **f** format, the # flag forces the output value to contain a decimal point in all cases.	Decimal point appears only if digits follow it.
	When used with the **g** or **G** format, the # flag forces the output value to contain a decimal point in all cases and prevents the truncation of trailing zeros.	Decimal point appears only if digits follow it. Trailing zeros are truncated.
	Ignored when used with **c**, **d**, **i**, **u**, or **s**.	

Width Specification

The second optional field of the format specification is the width specification. The *width* argument is a nonnegative decimal integer controlling the minimum number of characters printed. If the number of characters in the output value is less than the specified width, blanks are added to the left or the right of the values—depending on whether the – flag (for left justification) is specified—until the minimum width is reached. If *width* is prefixed with 0, zeros are added until the minimum width is reached (not useful for left-justified numbers).

The width specification never causes a value to be truncated. If the number of characters in the output value is greater than the specified width, or *width* is not given, all characters of the value are printed (subject to the precision specification).

The width specification may be an asterisk (*), in which case an **int** argument from the argument list supplies the value. The *width* argument must precede the value being formatted in the argument list. A nonexistent or small field width does not cause a truncation of a field; if the result of a conversion is wider than the field width, the field expands to contain the conversion result.

Precision Specification

The third optional field of the format specification is the precision specification. It specifies a nonnegative decimal integer, preceded by a period (.), which specifies the number of characters to be printed, the number of decimal places, or the number of significant digits. (See Table R.4.) Unlike the width specification, the precision specification can cause truncation of the output value, or rounding in the case of a floating-point value. If *precision* is specified as zero and the value to be converted is zero, the result is no characters output, as shown below:

```
printf( "%.0d", 0 );        /* No characters output */
```

The precision specification may be an asterisk (*), in which case an **int** argument from the argument list supplies the value. The *precision* argument must precede the value being formatted in the argument list.

The interpretation of the precision value and the default when *precision* is omitted depend on the type, as shown in Table R.4.

Table R.4   How printf Precision Values Affect Type

Type	Meaning	Default
d i u o x X	The precision specifies the minimum number of digits to be printed. If the number of digits in the argument is less than *precision*, the output value is padded on the left with zeros. The value is not truncated when the number of digits exceeds *precision*.	Default precision is 1.
e E	The precision specifies the number of digits to be printed after the decimal point. The last printed digit is rounded.	Default precision is 6; if *precision* is 0 or the period (.) appears without a number following it, no decimal point is printed.

Table R.4   (*continued*)

Type	Meaning	Default
f	The precision value specifies the number of digits after the decimal point. If a decimal point appears, at least one digit appears before it. The value is rounded to the appropriate number of digits.	Default precision is 6; if *precision* is 0, or if the period (.) appears without a number following it, no decimal point is printed.
g G	The precision specifies the maximum number of significant digits printed.	Six significant digits are printed, with any trailing zeros truncated.
c	The precision has no effect.	Character is printed.
s	The precision specifies the maximum number of characters to be printed. Characters in excess of *precision* are not printed.	Characters are printed until a null character is encountered.

If the argument corresponding to a floating-point specifier is infinite, indefinite, or not a number (NAN), the **printf** function gives the following output:

Value	Output
+ infinity	**1.#INF***random-digits*
– infinity	**–1.#INF***random-digits*
Indefinite	*digit.***#IND***random-digits*
NAN	*digit.***#NAN***random-digits*

Size and Distance Specification

For **printf**, the format specification fields **F** and **N** refer to the "distance" to the object being read (**near** or **far**), and **h** and **l** refer to the "size" of the object being read (16-bit **short** or 32-bit **long**). The following list clarifies this use of **F, N, h, l,** and **L**:

Program Code	Action
printf ("%Ns");	Print **near string**
printf ("%Fs");	Print **far string**
printf ("%Nn");	Store **char** count in **near int**
printf ("%Fn");	Store **char** count in **far int**
printf ("%hp");	Print a 16-bit pointer (*xxxx*)
printf ("%lp");	Print a 32-bit pointer (*xxxx:xxxx*)
printf ("%Nhn");	Store **char** count in **near short int**
printf ("%Nln");	Store **char** count in **near long int**
printf ("%Fhn");	Store **char** count in **far short int**
printf ("%Fln");	Store **char** count in **far int**

The specifications "**%hs**" and "**%ls**" are meaningless to **printf**. The specifications "**%Np**" and "**%Fp**" are aliases for "**%hp**" and "**%lp**" for the sake of compatibility with Microsoft C version 4.0.

Return Value   The **printf** function returns the number of characters printed, or a negative value in the case of an error.

Compatibility

Standards:	ANSI, UNIX
16-Bit:	DOS, QWIN
32-Bit:	DOS32X

See Also   **fprintf, scanf, sprintf, vfprintf, vprintf, vsprintf**

Example

```c
/* PRINTF.C illustrates output formatting with printf. */

#include <stdio.h>

void main( void )
{
    char   ch = 'h', *string = "computer";
    int    count = -9234;
    double fp = 251.7366;

    /* Display integers. */
    printf( "Integer formats:\n"
            "\tDecimal: %d  Justified: %.6d  Unsigned: %u\n",
            count, count, count, count );

    printf( "Decimal %d as:\n\tHex: %Xh  C hex: 0x%x  Octal: %o\n",
            count, count, count, count );

    /* Display in different radixes. */
    printf( "Digits 10 equal:\n\tHex: %i  Octal: %i  Decimal: %i\n",
            0x10, 010, 10 );

    /* Display characters. */
    printf( "Characters in field:\n%10c   %5c\n", ch, ch );

    /* Display strings. */
    printf( "Strings in field:\n%25s\n%25.4s\n", string, string );

    /* Display real numbers. */
    printf( "Real numbers:\n\t%f   %.2f   %e   %E\n", fp, fp, fp, fp );
```

```
        /* Display pointers. */
        printf( "Address as:\n\tDefault: %p  Near: %Np  Far: %Fp\n",
                &count, (int __near *)&count, (int __far *)&count );

        /* Count characters printed. */
        printf( "Display to here:\n" );
        printf( "1234567890123456%n78901234567890\n", &count );
        printf( "\tNumber displayed: %d\n\n", count );
}
```

Output

```
Integer formats:
        Decimal: -9234  Justified: -009234  Unsigned: 56302
Decimal -9234 as:
        Hex: DBEEh  C hex: 0xdbee  Octal: 155756
Digits 10 equal:
        Hex: 16  Octal: 8  Decimal: 10
Characters in field:
            h         h
Strings in field:
                 computer
                       comp
Real numbers:
        251.736600     251.74     2.517366e+002     2.517366E+002
Address as:
        Default: 141C  Near: 141C  Far: 0087:141C
Display to here:
1234567890123456789012345678901234567890
        Number displayed: 16
```

putc, putchar

Description

Writes a character to a stream (**putc**) or to **stdout** (**putchar**).

#include <stdio.h>

int **putc**(int *c*, **FILE** **stream*);

int **putchar**(int *c*);

c	Character to be written
stream	Pointer to **FILE** structure

Remarks

The **putc** routine writes the single character *c* to the output *stream* at the current position. The **putchar** routine is identical to **putc**(*c*, **stdout**).

These routines are implemented as both macros and functions. See "Choosing Between Functions and Macros" on page 9 for a discussion of how to select between the macro and function forms.

Return Value

The **putc** and **putchar** routines return the character written, or **EOF** in the case of an error. Any integer can be passed to **putc**, but only the lower 8 bits are written.

Compatibility

putc

Standards:	ANSI, UNIX
16-Bit:	DOS, QWIN, WIN, WIN DLL
32-Bit:	DOS32X

putchar

Standards:	ANSI, UNIX
16-Bit:	DOS, QWIN
32-Bit:	DOS32X

See Also

fputc, _fputchar, getc, getchar

Example   /* PUTC.C: This program uses putc to write buffer to a stream.
                  * If an error occurs, the program will stop before writing the
                  * entire buffer.
                  */

```
#include <stdio.h>

void main( void )
{
    FILE *stream;
    char *p, buffer[] = "This is the line of output\n";
    int  ch;

    /* Make standard out the stream and write to it. */
    stream = stdout;
    for( p = buffer; (ch != EOF) && (*p != '\0'); p++ )
        ch = putc( *p, stream );
}
```

Output   This is the line of output

_putch

Description   Writes a character to the console.

#include <conio.h>   Required only for function declarations

int _putch(int *c*);

c   Character to be output

Remarks   The **_putch** function writes the character *c* directly (without buffering) to the console.

Return Value   The function returns *c* if successful, and **EOF** if not.

Compatibility   Standards: None
16-Bit: DOS
32-Bit: DOS32X

See Also   **_cprintf, _getch, _getche**

Example
```
/* GETCH.C: This program reads characters from the keyboard until it
 * receives a 'Y' or 'y'.
 */

#include <conio.h>
#include <ctype.h>

void main( void )
{
    int ch;

    _cputs( "Type 'Y' when finished typing keys: " );
    do
    {
        ch = _getch();
        ch = toupper( ch );
    } while( ch != 'Y' );

    _putch( ch );
    _putch( '\r' );     /* Carriage return */
    _putch( '\n' );     /* Line feed       */
}
```

Output   Type 'Y' when finished typing keys: Y

_putenv

Description

Creates new environment variables; modifies or removes existing ones.

#include <stdlib.h>   Required only for function declarations

int _putenv(char *envstring* **);**

envstring   Environment-string definition

Remarks

The **_putenv** function adds new environment variables or modifies the values of existing environment variables. Environment variables define the environment in which a process executes (for example, the default search path for libraries to be linked with a program).

The *envstring* argument must be a pointer to a string with the form

varname=string

where *varname* is the name of the environment variable to be added or modified and *string* is the variable's value. If *varname* is already part of the environment, its value is replaced by *string*; otherwise, the new *varname* variable and its *string* value are added to the environment. A variable can be removed from the environment by specifying an empty *string*—that is, by specifying only *varname=*.

This function affects only the environment that is local to the currently running process; it cannot be used to modify the command-level environment. When the currently running process terminates, the environment reverts to the level of the parent process (in most cases, the operating system level). However, the environment affected by **_putenv** can be passed to any child processes created by **_spawn**, **_exec**, or **system**, and these child processes get any new items added by **_putenv**.

Never free a pointer to an environment entry, because the environment variable will then point to freed space. A similar problem can occur if you pass **_putenv** a pointer to a local variable, then exit the function in which the variable is declared.

The **_putenv** function operates only on data structures accessible to the run-time library and not on the environment "segment" created for a process by the operating system.

Note that environment-table entries must not be changed directly. If an entry must be changed, use **_putenv**. To modify the returned value without affecting the environment table, use **_strdup** or **strcpy** to make a copy of the string.

The **getenv** and **_putenv** functions use the global variable **environ** to access the environment table. The **_putenv** function may change the value of **environ**, thus invalidating the *envp* argument to the **main** function. Therefore, it is safer to use the **environ** variable to access the environment information.

Return Value   The **_putenv** function returns 0 if it is successful. A return value of –1 indicates an error.

Compatibility   Standards: UNIX

16-Bit: DOS, QWIN, WIN, WIN DLL

32-Bit: DOS32X

Use **_putenv** for compatibility with ANSI naming conventions of non-ANSI functions. Use **putenv** and link with OLDNAMES.LIB for UNIX compatibility.

See Also   **getenv, _searchenv**

Example
```
/* GETENV.C: This program uses getenv to retrieve the LIB environment
 * variable and then uses _putenv to change it to a new value.
 */

#include <stdlib.h>
#include <stdio.h>

void main( void )
{
    char *libvar;

    /* Get the value of the LIB environment variable. */
    libvar = getenv( "LIB" );
    if( libvar != NULL )
        printf( "Original LIB variable is: %s\n", libvar );

    /* Attempt to change path. Note that this only affects the environment
     * variable of the current process. The command processor's environment
     * is not changed.
     */
    _putenv( "LIB=c:\\mylib;c:\\yourlib" );

    /* Get new value. */
    libvar = getenv( "LIB" );
    if( libvar != NULL )
        printf( "New LIB variable is: %s\n", libvar );
}
```

Output
```
Original LIB variable is: C:\LIB
New LIB variable is: c:\mylib;c:\yourlib
```

_putimage Functions

Description

Retrieve images from a buffer.

#include <graph.h>

void __ far _putimage(short *x*, short *y*, const char __huge *image*,
    short *action*);

void __far _putimage_w(double *wx*, double *wy*, const char __huge *image*,
    short *action*);

x, y	Position of upper-left corner of image
image	Stored image buffer
action	Interaction with existing screen image
wx, wy	Position of upper-left corner of image

Remarks

The **_putimage** function transfers to the screen the image stored in the buffer that *image* points to.

In the **_putimage** function, the upper-left corner of the image is placed at the view coordinate point (*x, y*). In the **_putimage_w** function, the upper-left corner of the image is placed at the window coordinate point (*wx, wy*).

The *action* argument defines the interaction between the stored image and the one that is already on the screen. It may be any one of the following manifest constants (defined in GRAPH.H):

Constant	Meaning
_GAND	Transfers the image over an existing image on the screen. The resulting image is the logical-AND product of the two images: points that had the same color in both the existing image and the new one will remain the same color, while points that have different colors are joined by logical-AND.
_GOR	Superimposes the image onto an existing image. The new image does not erase the previous screen contents.
_GPRESET	Transfers the data point-by-point onto the screen. Each point has the inverse of the color attribute it had when it was taken from the screen by **_getimage**, producing a negative image.

Constant	Meaning
_GPSET	Transfers the data point-by-point onto the screen. Each point has the exact color attribute it had when it was taken from the screen by _getimage.
_GXOR	Causes the points on the screen to be inverted where a point exists in the *image* buffer. This behavior is like that of the cursor: when an image is put against a complex background twice, the background is restored unchanged. This allows you to move an object around without erasing the background. The _GXOR constant is a special mode often used for animation.

Return Value   None. Use the **_grstatus** function to check the result of a call to the **_putimage** functions.

Compatibility

Standards:	None
16-Bit:	DOS
32-Bit:	None

See Also   **_getimage**, **_grstatus**, **_imagesize**

Example   See the example for **_getimage**.

puts

Description	Writes a string to **stdout**.

#include <stdio.h>

int puts(const char *string **);**

string   String to be output

Remarks   The **puts** function writes *string* to the standard output stream **stdout**, replacing the string's terminating null character ('**\0**') with a newline character (**\n**) in the output stream.

Return Value   The **puts** function returns a nonnegative value if it is successful. If the function fails, it returns **EOF**.

Compatibility   Standards: ANSI, UNIX
              16-Bit: DOS, QWIN
              32-Bit: DOS32X

See Also   **fputs, gets**

Example
```
/* PUTS.C: This program uses puts to write a string to stdout. */

#include <stdio.h>

void main( void )
{
    puts( "Hello world from puts!" );
}
```

Output   Hello world from puts!

_putw

Description

Writes an integer to a stream.

#include <stdio.h>

int _putw(int *binint*, **FILE** **stream*);

binint	Binary integer to be output
stream	Pointer to **FILE** structure

Remarks

The **_putw** function writes a binary value of type **int** to the current position of *stream*. The **_putw** function does not affect the alignment of items in the stream, nor does it assume any special alignment.

The **_putw** function is provided primarily for compatibility with previous libraries. Note that portability problems may occur with **_putw**, since the size of an **int** and ordering of bytes within an **int** differ across systems.

Return Value

The **_putw** function returns the value written. A return value of **EOF** may indicate an error. Since **EOF** is also a legitimate integer value, **ferror** should be used to verify an error.

Compatibility

Standards: UNIX
16-Bit: DOS, QWIN, WIN, WIN DLL
32-Bit: DOS32X

Use **_putw** for compatibility with ANSI naming conventions of non-ANSI functions. Use **putw** and link with OLDNAMES.LIB for UNIX compatibility.

See Also

_getw

Example

```
/* PUTW.C: This program uses _putw to write a word to a stream,
 * then performs an error check.
 */

#include <stdio.h>
#include <stdlib.h>

void main( void )
{
   FILE *stream;
   unsigned u;

   if( (stream = fopen( "data.out", "wb" )) == NULL )
      exit( 1 );
   for( u = 0; u < 10; u++ )
   {
      _putw( u + 0x2132, stdout );
      _putw( u + 0x2132, stream );    /* Write word to stream. */
      if( ferror( stream ) )          /* Make error check. */
      {
         printf( "_putw failed" );
         clearerr( stream );
         exit( 1 );
      }
   }
   printf( "\nWrote ten words\n" );
   fclose( stream );
}
```

Output

```
2!3!4!5!6!7!8!9!:!;!
Wrote ten words
```

qsort

Description

Performs a quick sort.

#include <stdlib.h>	For ANSI compatibility
#include <search.h>	Required only for function declarations

void qsort(void **base*, **size_t** *num*, **size_t** *width*,
  int(__cdecl **compare* **)) (const void** **elem1*, **const void** **elem2* **));**

base	Start of target array
num	Array size in elements
width	Element size in bytes
compare	Comparison function
elem1	Pointer to the key for the search
elem2	Pointer to the array element to be compared with the key

Remarks

The **qsort** function implements a quick-sort algorithm to sort an array of *num* elements, each of *width* bytes. The argument *base* is a pointer to the base of the array to be sorted. The **qsort** function overwrites this array with the sorted elements.

The argument *compare* is a pointer to a user-supplied routine that compares two array elements and returns a value specifying their relationship. The **qsort** function calls the *compare* routine one or more times during the sort, passing pointers to two array elements on each call:

compare(**(void *)** *elem1*, **(void *)** *elem2*);

The routine must compare the elements, then return one of the following values:

Value	Meaning
< 0	*elem1* less than *elem2*
= 0	*elem1* equivalent to *elem2*
> 0	*elem1* greater than *elem2*

The array is sorted in increasing order, as defined by the comparison function. To sort an array in decreasing order, reverse the sense of "greater than" and "less than" in the comparison function.

Return Value   None.

Compatibility   Standards: ANSI, UNIX
                       16-Bit: DOS, QWIN, WIN, WIN DLL
                       32-Bit: DOS32X

See Also   **bsearch, _lsearch**

Example
```
/* QSORT.C: This program reads the command-line parameters and
 * uses qsort to sort them. It then displays the sorted arguments.
 */

#include <stdlib.h>
#include <string.h>
#include <stdio.h>

int compare( void *arg1, void *arg2 );   /* Prototype */

void main( int argc, char **argv )
{
    int i;

    /* Eliminate argv[0] from sort: */
    argv++;
    argc-;

    /* Sort remaining args using Quicksort algorithm: */
    qsort( (void *)argv, (size_t)argc, sizeof( char * ), compare );

    /* Output sorted list: */
    for( i = 0; i < argc; ++i )
        printf( "%s ", argv[i] );
    printf( "\n" );
}

int compare( void *arg1, void *arg2 )
{
    /* Compare all of both strings: */
    return _stricmp( * ( char** ) arg1, * ( char** ) arg2 );
}
```

Output
```
[C:\LIBREF] qsort every good boy deserves favor
boy deserves every favor good
```

raise

Description

Sends a signal to the executing program.

#include <signal.h>

int raise(int *sig* **);**

sig   Signal to be raised

Remarks

The **raise** function sends *sig* to the executing program. If a signal-handling routine for *sig* has been installed by a prior call to **signal**, **raise** causes that routine to be executed. If no handler routine has been installed, the default action (as listed below) is taken.

The signal value *sig* can be one of the following manifest constants:

Signal	Meaning	Default
SIGABRT	Abnormal termination.	Terminates the calling program with exit code 3.
SIGFPE	Floating-point error.	Terminates the calling program.
SIGILL	Illegal instruction. This signal is not generated by DOS, but is supported for ANSI compatibility.	Terminates the calling program.
SIGINT	CTRL+ C interrupt.	Issues INT23H.
SIGSEGV	Illegal storage access. This signal is not generated by DOS, but is supported for ANSI compatibility.	Terminates the calling program.
SIGTERM	Termination request sent to the program. This signal is not generated by DOS, but is supported for ANSI compatibility.	Ignores the signal.

Return Value

If successful, the **raise** function returns 0. Otherwise, it returns a nonzero value.

Compatibility	Standards:	ANSI
	16-Bit:	DOS, QWIN, WIN, WIN DLL
	32-Bit:	DOS32X

See Also   **abort**, **signal**

Example   See the example for **signal**.

rand

Description

Generates a pseudorandom number.

#include <stdlib.h>   Required only for function declarations

int rand(void);

Remarks

The **rand** function returns a pseudorandom integer in the range 0 to
RAND_MAX. The **srand** routine can be used to seed the pseudorandom-number
generator before calling **rand**.

Return Value

The **rand** function returns a pseudorandom number, as described above. There is
no error return.

Compatibility

Standards: ANSI, UNIX
16-Bit: DOS, QWIN, WIN, WIN DLL
32-Bit: DOS32X

See Also

srand

Example

```
/* RAND.C: This program seeds the random-number generator with the
 * time, then displays 20 random integers.
 */

#include <stdlib.h>
#include <stdio.h>
#include <time.h>

void main( void )
{
    int i;

    /* Seed the random-number generator with current time so that
     * the numbers will be different every time we run.
     */
    srand( (unsigned)time( NULL ) );

    /* Display 10 numbers. */
    for( i = 0; i < 10; i++ )
        printf( "  %6d\n", rand() );
}
```

Output

```
19471
16395
 8268
15582
 6489
28356
27042
 5276
23070
10930
```

_read

Description

Reads data from a file.

#include <io.h>   Required only for function declarations

int _read(int *handle*, **void** **buffer*, **unsigned int** *count* **);**

handle	Handle referring to open file
buffer	Storage location for data
count	Maximum number of bytes

Remarks

The **_read** function attempts to read *count* bytes into *buffer* from the file associated with *handle*. The read operation begins at the current position of the file pointer associated with the given file. After the read operation, the file pointer points to the next unread character.

Return Value

The **_read** function returns the number of bytes actually read, which may be less than *count* if there are fewer than *count* bytes left in the file, or if the file was opened in text mode (see below). The return value 0 indicates an attempt to read at end-of-file. The return value –1 indicates an error, and **errno** is set to the following value:

Value	Meaning
EBADF	The given *handle* is invalid; or the file is not open for reading; or (DOS versions 3.0 and later) the file is locked.

For 16-bit platforms, if you are reading more than 32K (the maximum size for type **int**) from a file, the return value should be of type **unsigned int** (see the example that follows). However, the maximum number of bytes that can be read from a file in one operation is 65,534, since 65,535 (or 0xFFFF) is indistinguishable from –1, and therefore cannot be distinguished from an error return.

If the file was opened in text mode, the return value may not correspond to the number of bytes actually read. When text mode is in effect, each carriage-return–line-feed (CR-LF) pair is replaced with a single line-feed character. Only the single line-feed character is counted in the return value. The replacement does not affect the file pointer.

Note that when files are opened in text mode, a CTRL+Z character is treated as an end-of-file indicator. When the CTRL+Z is encountered, the read terminates, and the next read returns 0 bytes. The **_lseek** function will clear the end-of-file indicator.

Compatibility

Standards:	UNIX
16-Bit:	DOS, QWIN, WIN, WIN DLL
32-Bit:	DOS32X

Use **_read** for compatibility with ANSI naming conventions of non-ANSI functions. Use **read** and link with OLDNAMES.LIB for UNIX compatibility.

See Also   **_creat, fread, _open, _write**

Example

```
/* READ.C: This program opens a file named READ.C and tries to read 60,000
 * bytes from that file using read. It then displays the actual
 * number of bytes read from READ.C.
 */

#include <fcntl.h>          /* Needed only for _O_RDWR definition */
#include <io.h>
#include <stdlib.h>
#include <stdio.h>

char buffer[60000];

void main( void )
{
    int fh;
    unsigned int nbytes = 60000, bytesread;

    /* Open file for input: */
    if( (fh = _open( "read.c", _O_RDONLY )) == -1 )
    {
        perror( "open failed on input file" );
        exit( 1 );
    }

    /* Read in input: */
    if( ( bytesread = _read( fh, buffer, nbytes ) ) <= 0 )
        perror( "Problem reading file" );
    else
        printf( "Read %u bytes from file\n", bytesread );

    _close( fh );
}
```

Output   Read 747 bytes from file

realloc Functions

Description

Reallocate memory blocks.

#include <stdlib.h>   For ANSI compatibility (**realloc** only)

#include <malloc.h>   Required only for function declarations

void *realloc(void **memblock***, size_t** *size* **);**

void __based(void) *_brealloc(__segment *seg*,
   void __based(void) **memblock***, size_t** *size* **);**

void __far *_frealloc(void __far **memblock***, size_t** *size* **);**

void __near *_nrealloc(void __near **memblock***, size_t** *size* **);**

memblock	Pointer to previously allocated memory block
size	New size in bytes
seg	Segment selector

Remarks

The **realloc** family of functions changes the size of a previously allocated memory block. The *memblock* argument points to the beginning of the memory block. If *memblock* is **NULL** (**_NULLOFF** for **_brealloc**), **realloc** functions in the same way as **malloc** and allocates a new block of *size* bytes. If *memblock* is not **NULL** (**_NULLOFF** for **_brealloc**), it should be a pointer returned by a prior call to **calloc**, **malloc**, or **realloc**.

The *size* argument gives the new size of the block, in bytes. The contents of the block are unchanged up to the shorter of the new and old sizes, although the new block may be in a different location.

In large data models (that is, compact-, large-, and huge-model programs), **realloc** maps to **_frealloc**. In small data models (tiny-, small-, and medium-model programs), **realloc** maps to **_nrealloc**.

The various **realloc** functions reallocate memory in the heap as specified in the following list:

Function	Heap
realloc	Depends on data model of program
_brealloc	Based heap specified by *seg* value
_frealloc	Far heap (outside default data segment)
_nrealloc	Near heap (inside default data segment)

Return Value

The **realloc** functions return a **void** pointer to the reallocated (and possibly moved) memory block.

The return value is **NULL** (**_NULLOFF** for **_brealloc**) if the size is zero and the buffer argument is not **NULL** (**_NULLOFF** for **_brealloc**), or if there is not enough available memory to expand the block to the given size. In the first case, the original block is freed. In the second, the original block is unchanged.

The storage space pointed to by the return value is guaranteed to be suitably aligned for storage of any type of object. To get a pointer to a type other than **void**, use a type cast on the return value.

Compatibility

realloc

Standards:	ANSI, UNIX
16-Bit:	DOS, QWIN, WIN, WIN DLL
32-Bit:	DOS32X

_brealloc, _frealloc, _nrealloc

Standards:	None
16-Bit:	DOS, QWIN, WIN, WIN DLL
32-Bit:	None

See Also

calloc functions, **free** functions, **malloc** functions

Example

```
/* REALLOC.C: This program allocates a block of memory for buffer
 * and then uses _msize to display the size of that block. Next, it
 * uses realloc to expand the amount of memory used by buffer
 * and then calls _msize again to display the new amount of
 * memory allocated to buffer.
 */

#include <stdio.h>
#include <malloc.h>
#include <stdlib.h>

void main( void )
{
   long *buffer;
   size_t size;

   if( (buffer = (long *)malloc( 1000 * sizeof( long ) )) == NULL )
      exit( 1 );

   size = _msize( buffer );
   printf( "Size of block after malloc of 1000 longs: %u\n", size );

   /* Reallocate and show new size: */
   if( (buffer = realloc( buffer, size + (1000 * sizeof( long )) )) == NULL )
      exit( 1 );
   size = _msize( buffer );
   printf( "Size of block after realloc of 1000 more longs: %u\n", size );

   free( buffer );
   exit( 0 );
}
```

Output

```
Size of block after malloc of 1000 longs: 4000
Size of block after realloc of 1000 more longs: 8000
```

_rectangle Functions

Description   Draw rectangles.

#include <graph.h>

short __far _rectangle(short *control*, **short** *x1*, **short** *y1*, **short** *x2*, **short** *y2* **);**

short __far _rectangle_w(short *control*, **double** *wx1*, **double** *wy1*, **double** *wx2*, **double** *wy2* **);**

short __far _rectangle_wxy(short *control*, **struct _wxycoord __far** *pwxy1, **struct _wxycoord __far** *pwxy2 **);**

control	Fill flag
x1, *y1*	Upper-left corner
x2, *y2*	Lower-right corner
wx1, *wy1*	Upper-left corner
wx2, *wy2*	Lower-right corner
pwxy1	Upper-left corner
pwxy2	Lower-right corner

Remarks   The **_rectangle** functions draw a rectangle with the current line style. The **_rectangle** function uses the view coordinate system. The view coordinate points (*x1*, *y1*) and (*x2*, *y2*) are the diagonally opposed corners of the rectangle.

The **_rectangle_w** function uses the window coordinate system. The window coordinate points (*wx1*, *wy1*) and (*wx2*, *wy2*) are the diagonally opposed corners of the rectangle.

The **_rectangle_wxy** function uses the window coordinate system. The window coordinate points (*pwxy1*) and (*pwxy2*) are the diagonally opposed corners of the rectangle. The coordinates for the **_rectangle_wxy** routine are given in terms of an **_wxycoord** structure (defined in GRAPH.H), which contains the following elements:

Element	Description
double wx	window *x* coordinate
double wy	window *y* coordinate

The *control* parameter can be one of the following manifest constants:

Constant	Action
_GFILLINTERIOR	Fills the figure, using a scanfill algorithm, with the current color using the current fill mask
_GBORDER	Does not fill the rectangle

If the current fill mask is **NULL**, no mask is used. Instead, the rectangle is filled with the current color.

If you try to fill the rectangle with the **_floodfill** function, the rectangle must be bordered by a solid line-style pattern.

Return Value

The function returns a nonzero value if the rectangle is drawn successfully, or 0 if not.

Compatibility

Standards: None

16-Bit: DOS

32-Bit: None

See Also

_arc functions, **_ellipse** functions, **_floodfill**, **_getcolor**, **_lineto** functions, **_pie** functions, **_polygon**, **_setcolor**, **_setfillmask**

Example

```
/* RECT.C: This program draws a rectangle. */

#include <conio.h>
#include <stdlib.h>
#include <graph.h>

void main( void )
{
    /* Find a valid graphics mode. */
    if( !_setvideomode( _MAXRESMODE ) )
        exit( 1 );

    _rectangle( _GBORDER, 80, 50, 240, 150 );

    _getch();

    _setvideomode( _DEFAULTMODE );
}
```

_registerfonts

Description

Initializes the fonts graphics system.

#include <graph.h>

short __far _registerfonts(const char __far *__pathname__);

pathname   Path name specifying .FON files to be registered

Remarks

The **_registerfonts** function initializes the fonts graphics system. Font files must be registered with the **_registerfonts** function before any other font-related library function (**_getgtextextent**, **_outgtext**, **_setfont**, **_unregisterfonts**) can be used.

The **_registerfonts** function reads the specified files and loads font header information into memory. Each font header takes up about 140 bytes of memory.

The *pathname* argument is the path specification and filename of valid .FON files. The *pathname* can contain standard DOS wildcards.

The font functions affect only the output from the font output function **_outgtext**; no other run-time output functions are affected by font usage.

Return Value

The **_registerfonts** function returns a positive value which indicates the number of fonts successfully registered. A negative return value indicates failure. The following negative values may be returned:

Value	Meaning
−1	No such file or directory.
−2	One or more of the .FON files was not a valid, binary .FON file.
−3	One or more of the .FON files is damaged.

Compatibility

Standards:	None
16-Bit:	DOS
32-Bit:	None

See Also

_getfontinfo, **_getgtextextent**, **_grstatus**, **_outgtext**, **_setfont**, **_unregisterfonts**

Example

See the example for **_outgtext**.

_remapallpalette, _remappalette

Description

Remap palette colors.

#include <graph.h>

short __far _remapallpalette(long __far *colors);

long __far _remappalette(short index, long color);

colors	Color value array
index	Color index to reassign
color	Color value to assign color index to

Remarks

The **_remapallpalette** function remaps the entire color palette simultaneously to the colors given in the *colors* array. The *colors* array is an array of **long** integers where the size of the array varies from 16 to 64 to 256, depending on the video mode. The number of colors mapped depends on the number of colors supported by the current video mode. The **_remapallpalette** function works in all video modes (except **_ORESCOLOR** mode), but only with EGA, MCGA, VGA, or SVGA hardware.

The default color values for color text or a 16-color graphics mode are shown below:

Number	Color	Number	Color
0	Black	8	Dark gray
1	Blue	9	Light blue
2	Green	10	Light green
3	Cyan	11	Light cyan
4	Red	12	Light red
5	Magenta	13	Light magenta
6	Brown	14	Yellow
7	White	15	Bright white

The first array element specifies the new color value to be associated with color index 0 (the background color in graphics modes). After the call to **_remapallpalette**, calls to **_setcolor** will index into the new array of colors. The mapping done by **_remapallpalette** affects the current display immediately.

The *colors* array can be larger than the number of colors supported by the current video mode, but only the first *n* elements are used, where *n* is the number of colors supported by the current video mode, as indicated by the **numcolors** element of the **_videoconfig** structure.

The **long** color value is defined by specifying three bytes of data representing the three component colors: red, green, and blue.

Each of the three bytes represents the intensity of one of the red, green, or blue component colors, and must be in the range 0–31. In other words, the low-order six bits of each byte specify the component's intensity and the high-order two bits should be zero. The fourth (high-order) byte in the **long** is unused and should be set to zero. The diagram below shows the ordering of bytes within the **long** value.

For example, to create a lighter shade of blue, start with lots of blue, add some green, and maybe a little bit of red. The three-byte color value would be:

```
blue byte          green byte          red byte
00011111           00101111            00011111
high ─────────────────> low order
```

Manifest constants are defined in GRAPH.H for the default color values corresponding to color indices 0–15 in color text modes and 16-color graphics modes, as shown below:

Index	Constant	Index	Constant
0	**_BLACK**	8	**_GRAY**
1	**_BLUE**	9	**_LIGHTBLUE**
2	**_GREEN**	10	**_LIGHTGREEN**
3	**_CYAN**	11	**_LIGHTCYAN**
4	**_RED**	12	**_LIGHTRED**
5	**_MAGENTA**	13	**_LIGHTMAGENTA**
6	**_BROWN**	14	**_YELLOW**
7	**_WHITE**	15	**_BRIGHTWHITE**

The VGA supports a palette of 262,144 (256K) colors in color modes, and the EGA supports a palette of only 64 different colors. Color values for EGA are specified in exactly the same way as with the VGA; however, the low-order four bits of each byte are simply ignored.

The **_remappalette** function assigns a new color value *color* to the color index given by *index*. This remapping affects the current display immediately.

The **_remappalette** function works in all graphics modes, but only with EGA, MCGA, VGA, or SVGA hardware. An error results if the function is called while using any other configuration.

The color value used in _**remappalette** is defined and used exactly as noted above for _**remapallpalette**. The range of color indices used with _**remappalette** depends on the number of colors supported by the video mode.

The _**remapallpalette** and _**remappalette** functions do not affect the presentation-graphics "palettes," which are manipulated with the _**pg_getpalette**, _**pg_setpalette**, and _**pg_resetpalette** functions.

If a VGA or MCGA adapter is connected to an analog monochrome monitor, the color value is transformed into its gray-scale equivalent, based on the weighted sum of its red, green, and blue components (30% red + 50% green + 11% blue).

Return Value

If successful, _**remapallpalette** returns nonzero value (short). In case of an error, _**remapallpalette** returns 0 (short).

If successful, _**remappalette** returns the color value previously assigned to *index*, or –1 if the function is inoperative (not EGA, VGA, SVGA, or MCGA), or if the color index is out of range. Note that _**remapallpalette** returns a **short** value and _**remappalette** returns a **long** value.

Compatibility

Standards:	None
16-Bit:	DOS
32-Bit:	None

See Also

_**getvideoconfig**, _**selectpalette**, _**setbkcolor**, _**setvideomode**

Example

```
/* RMPALPAL.C: This example illustrates functions for assigning
 * color values to color indices. Functions illustrated include:
 *      _remappalette            _remapallpalette
 */

#include <graph.h>
#include <conio.h>
#include <stdio.h>
#include <stdlib.h>

/* Macro for mixing Red, Green, and Blue elements of color */
#define RGB(r,g,b) (((long) ((b) << 8 | (g)) << 8 | (r))

long tmp, pal[256];

void main( void )
{
    short  red, blue, green;
    short  inc, i, mode, cells, x, y, xinc, yinc;
    char   buf[40];
    struct _videoconfig vc;
```

```
/* Make sure all palette numbers are valid. */
for( i = 0; i < 256; i++ )
    pal[i] = _BLACK;

/* Loop through each graphics mode that supports palettes. */
for( mode = _MRES4COLOR; mode <= _MRES256COLOR; mode++ )
{
    if( mode == _ERESNOCOLOR )
        mode++;
    if( !_setvideomode( mode ) )
        continue;

    /* Set variables for each mode. */
    _getvideoconfig( &vc );
    switch( vc.numcolors )
    {
        case 256:           /* Active bits in this order:          */
            cells = 13;
            inc = 12;       /* ???????? ??bbbbbb ??gggggg ??rrrrrr */
            break;
        case 16:
            cells = 4;
            if( (vc.mode == _ERESCOLOR) || (vc.mode == _VRES16COLOR) )
                inc = 16;   /* ???????? ??bb???? ??gg???? ??rr???? */
            else
                inc = 32;   /* ???????? ??Bb???? ??Gg???? ??Rr???? */
            break;
        case 4:
            cells = 2;
            inc = 32;       /* ???????? ??Bb???? ??Gg???? ??Rr???? */
            break;
        default:
            continue;
    }
    xinc = vc.numxpixels / cells;
    yinc = vc.numypixels / cells;

    /* Fill palette arrays in BGR order. */
    for( i = 0, blue = 0; blue < 64; blue += inc )
        for( green = 0; green < 64; green += inc )
            for( red = 0; red < 64; red += inc )
            {
                pal[i] = RGB( red, green, blue );
                /* Special case of using 6 bits to represent 16 colors.
                 * If both bits are on for any color, intensity is set.
                 * If one bit is set for a color, the color is on.
                 */
                if( inc == 32 )
                    pal[i + 8] = pal[i] | (pal[i] >> 1);
                i++;
            }
```

```
    /* If palettes available, remap all palettes at once. */
    if( !_remapallpalette( pal ) )
    {
        _setvideomode( _DEFAULTMODE );
        _outtext( "Palettes not available with this adapter" );
        exit( 1 );
    }

    /* Draw colored squares. */
    for( i = 0, x = 0; x < ( xinc * cells ); x += xinc )
        for( y = 0; y < ( yinc * cells); y += yinc )
        {
            _setcolor( i++ );
            _rectangle( _GFILLINTERIOR, x, y, x + xinc, y + yinc );
        }

    /* Note that for 256-color mode, not all colors are shown. The number
     * of colors from mixing three base colors can never be the same as
     * the number that can be shown on a two-dimensional grid.
     */
    sprintf( buf, "Mode %d has %d colors", vc.mode, vc.numcolors );
    _setcolor( vc.numcolors / 2 );
    _outtext( buf );
    _getch();

    /* Change each palette entry separately in GRB order. */
    for( i = 0, green = 0; green < 64; green += inc )
        for( red = 0; red < 64; red += inc )
            for(blue = 0; blue < 64; blue += inc )
            {
                tmp = RGB( red, green, blue );
                _remappalette( i, tmp );
                if( inc == 32 )
                    _remappalette( i + 8, tmp | (tmp >> 1) );
                i++;
            }
    _getch();
    }
    _setvideomode( _DEFAULTMODE );
    exit( 0 );
}
```

remove

Description   Deletes a file.

#include <stdio.h>   Required for ANSI compatibility

#include <io.h>   Use either IO.H or STDIO.H

int remove(const char *path);

path   Path name of file to be removed

Remarks   The **remove** function deletes the file specified by *path*.

Return Value   The function returns 0 if the file is successfully deleted. Otherwise, it returns −1 and sets **errno** to one of these values:

Value	Meaning
EACCES	Path name specifies a read-only file.
ENOENT	File or path name not found, or path name specifies a directory.

Compatibility   Standards: ANSI
16-Bit: DOS, QWIN, WIN, WIN DLL
32-Bit: DOS32X

See Also   **_unlink**

Example
```
/* REMOVE.C: This program uses remove to delete REMOVE.OBJ. */

#include <stdio.h>

void main( void )
{
    if( remove( "remove.obj" ) == -1 )
        perror( "Could not delete 'REMOVE.OBJ'" );
    else
        printf( "Deleted 'REMOVE.OBJ'\n" );
}
```

Output   Deleted 'REMOVE.OBJ'

rename

Description

Renames a file or directory.

#include <stdio.h>	Required for ANSI compatibility
#include <io.h>	Use either IO.H or STDIO.H

int rename(const char *****oldname***, const char *****newname*****);**

oldname	Pointer to old name
newname	Pointer to new name

Remarks

The **rename** function renames the file or directory specified by *oldname* to the name given by *newname*. The old name must be the path name of an existing file or directory. The new name must not be the name of an existing file or directory.

The **rename** function can be used to move a file from one directory to another by giving a different path name in the *newname* argument. However, files cannot be moved from one device to another (for example, from drive A to drive B). Directories can only be renamed, not moved.

Return Value

The **rename** function returns 0 if it is successful. On an error, it returns a nonzero value and sets **errno** to one of the following values:

Value	Meaning
EACCES	File or directory specified by *newname* already exists or could not be created (invalid path); or *oldname* is a directory and *newname* specifies a different path.
ENOENT	File or path name specified by *oldname* not found.
EXDEV	Attempt to move a file to a different device.

Compatibility

Standards:	ANSI
16-Bit:	DOS, QWIN, WIN, WIN DLL
32-Bit:	DOS32X

Example
```
/* RENAMER.C: This program attempts to rename a file named RENAMER.OBJ to
 * RENAMER.JBO. For this operation to succeed, a file named RENAMER.OBJ
 * must exist and a file named RENAMER.JBO must not exist.
 */

#include <stdio.h>

void main( void )
{
    int  result;
    char old[] = "RENAMER.OBJ", new[] = "RENAMER.JBO";

    /* Attempt to rename file: */
    result = rename( old, new );
    if( result != 0 )
       printf( "Could not rename '%s'\n", old );
    else
       printf( "File '%s' renamed to '%s'\n", old, new );
}
```

Output   File 'RENAMER.OBJ' renamed to 'RENAMER.JBO'

rewind

Description

Repositions the file pointer to the beginning of a file.

#include <stdio.h>

void rewind(FILE *stream **);**

stream   Pointer to **FILE** structure

Remarks

The **rewind** function repositions the file pointer associated with *stream* to the beginning of the file. A call to **rewind** is equivalent to

(void) fseek(*stream*, **0L, SEEK_SET);**

except that **rewind** clears the error indicators for the stream, and **fseek** does not. Both **rewind** and **fseek** clear the end-of-file indicator. Also, **fseek** returns a value that indicates whether the pointer was successfully moved, but **rewind** does not return any value.

You can also use the **rewind** function to clear the keyboard buffer. Use the **rewind** function with the stream **stdin**, which is associated with the keyboard by default.

Return Value

The **rewind** function has no return value.

Compatibility

Standards: ANSI, UNIX
16-Bit: DOS, QWIN, WIN, WIN DLL
32-Bit: DOS32X

Example

```
/* REWIND.C: This program first opens a file named REWIND.OUT for input and
 * output and writes two integers to the file. Next, it uses rewind to
 * reposition the file pointer to the beginning of the file and reads
 * the data back in.
 */

#include <stdio.h>

void main( void )
{
    FILE *stream;
    int data1, data2;

    data1 = 1;
    data2 = -37;

    if( (stream = fopen( "rewind.out", "w+" )) != NULL )
    {
        fprintf( stream, "%d %d", data1, data2 );
        printf( "The values written are: %d and %d\n", data1, data2 );
        rewind( stream );
        fscanf( stream, "%d %d", &data1, &data2 );
        printf( "The values read are: %d and %d\n", data1, data2 );
        fclose( stream );
    }
}
```

Output

```
The values written are: 1 and -37
The values read are: 1 and -37
```

_rmdir

Description

Deletes a directory.

#include <direct.h>   Required only for function declarations

int _rmdir(char *dirname* **);**

dirname   Path name of directory to be removed

Remarks

The **_rmdir** function deletes the directory specified by *dirname*. The directory must be empty, and it must not be the current working directory or the root directory.

Return Value

The **_rmdir** function returns the value 0 if the directory is successfully deleted. A return value of –1 indicates an error, and **errno** is set to one of the following values:

Value	Meaning
EACCES	The given path name is not a directory; or the directory is not empty; or the directory is the current working directory or the root directory.
ENOENT	Path name not found.

Compatibility

Standards: None
16-Bit: DOS, QWIN, WIN, WIN DLL
32-Bit: DOS32X

See Also

_chdir, _mkdir

Example

```
/* MAKEDIR.C */
#include <direct.h>
#include <stdlib.h>
#include <stdio.h>

void main( void )
{
    int result;

    if( _mkdir( "\\testtmp" ) == 0 )
    {
        printf( "Directory '\\testtmp' was successfully created\n" );
        system( "dir \\testtmp" );
        if( _rmdir( "\\testtmp" ) == 0 )
            printf( "Directory '\\testtmp' was successfully removed\n"  );
        else
            printf( "Problem removing directory '\\testtmp'\n" );
    }
    else
        printf( "Problem creating directory '\\testtmp'\n" );
}
```

Output

```
Directory '\testtmp' was successfully created

The volume label in drive C is ZEPPELIN.
Directory of C:\TESTTMP

    .              <DIR>      12-19-99   11:20a
    ..             <DIR>      12-19-99   11:20a
    2 File(s)   12730368 bytes free
Directory '\testtmp' was successfully removed
```

_rmtmp

Description

Removes temporary files.

#include <stdio.h>

int _rmtmp(void);

Remarks

The **_rmtmp** function is used to clean up all the temporary files in the current directory. The function removes only those files created by **tmpfile** and should be used only in the same directory in which the temporary files were created.

Return Value

The **_rmtmp** function returns the number of temporary files closed and deleted.

Compatibility

Standards:	None
16-Bit:	DOS, QWIN, WIN, WIN DLL
32-Bit:	DOS32X

See Also

_flushall, tmpfile, tmpnam

Example

```
/* TMPFILE.C: This program uses tmpfile to create a temporary file,
 * then deletes this file with _rmtmp.
 */

#include <stdio.h>

void main( void )
{
    FILE *stream;
    char tempstring[] = "String to be written";
    int  i;

    /* Create temporary files. */
    for( i = 1; i <= 10; i++ )
    {
        if( (stream = tmpfile()) == NULL )
            perror( "Could not open new temporary file\n" );
        else
            printf( "Temporary file %d was created\n", i );
    }

    /* Remove temporary files. */
    printf( "%d temporary files deleted\n", _rmtmp() );
}
```

Output

```
Temporary file 1 was created
Temporary file 2 was created
Temporary file 3 was created
Temporary file 4 was created
Temporary file 5 was created
Temporary file 6 was created
Temporary file 7 was created
Temporary file 8 was created
Temporary file 9 was created
Temporary file 10 was created
10 temporary files deleted
```

_rotl, _rotr

Description

Rotate bits to the left (**_rotl**) or right (**_rotr**).

#include <stdlib.h>

unsigned int _rotl(unsigned int *value***, int** *shift* **);**

unsigned int _rotr(unsigned int *value***, int** *shift* **);**

value	Value to be rotated
shift	Number of bits to shift

Remarks

The **_rotl** and **_rotr** functions rotate the **unsigned** *value* by *shift* bits. The **_rotl** function rotates the value left. The **_rotr** function rotates the value right. Both functions "wrap" bits rotated off one end of *value* to the other end.

Return Value

Both functions return the rotated value. There is no error return.

Compatibility

Standards: None

16-Bit: DOS, QWIN, WIN, WIN DLL

32-Bit: DOS32X

See Also

_lrotl, **_lrotr**

Example

```
/* ROT.C: This program uses _rotr and _rotl with different shift
 * values to rotate an integer.
 */

#include <stdlib.h>
#include <stdio.h>

void main( void )
{
    unsigned val = 0x0fd93;

    printf( "0x%4.4x rotated left three times is 0x%4.4x\n",
            val, _rotl( val, 3 ) );
    printf( "0x%4.4x rotated right four times is 0x%4.4x\n",
            val, _rotr( val, 4 ) );
}
```

Output   0xfd93 rotated left three times is 0xec9f
0xfd93 rotated right four times is 0x3fd9

scanf

Description
Reads formatted data from the standard input stream.

#include <stdio.h>

int scanf(const char *format* [[,*argument*]]... **);**

format	Format control
argument	Optional argument

Remarks
The **scanf** function reads data from the standard input stream **stdin** into the locations given by *argument*. Each *argument* must be a pointer to a variable with a type that corresponds to a type specifier in *format*. The format controls the interpretation of the input fields. The format can contain one or more of the following:

- White-space characters: blank (' '); tab (**\t**); or newline (**\n**). A white-space character causes **scanf** to read, but not store, all consecutive white-space characters in the input up to the next non-white-space character. One white-space character in the format matches any number (including 0) and combination of white-space characters in the input.

- Non-white-space characters, except for the percent sign (**%**). A non-white-space character causes **scanf** to read, but not store, a matching non-white-space character. If the next character in **stdin** does not match, **scanf** terminates.

- Format specifications, introduced by the percent sign (**%**). A format specification causes **scanf** to read and convert characters in the input into values of a specified type. The value is assigned to an argument in the argument list.

The format is read from left to right. Characters outside format specifications are expected to match the sequence of characters in **stdin**; the matching characters in **stdin** are scanned but not stored. If a character in **stdin** conflicts with the format specification, **scanf** terminates. The character is left in **stdin** as if it had not been read.

When the first format specification is encountered, the value of the first input field is converted according to this specification and stored in the location that is specified by the first *argument*. The second format specification causes the second input field to be converted and stored in the second *argument*, and so on through the end of the format string.

An input field is defined as all characters up to the first white-space character (space, tab, or newline), or up to the first character that cannot be converted according to the format specification, or until the field width (if specified) is reached. If there are too many arguments for the given specifications, the extra arguments are evaluated but ignored. The results are unpredictable if there are not enough arguments for the format specification.

A format specification has the following form:

%[[*]] [[*width*]] [[{**F** | **N**}]] [[{**h** | **l**}]]*type*

Each field of the format specification is a single character or a number signifying a particular format option. The *type* character, which appears after the last optional format field, determines whether the input field is interpreted as a character, a string, or a number. The simplest format specification contains only the percent sign and a *type* character (for example, %s).

Each field of the format specification is discussed in detail below. If a percent sign (%) is followed by a character that has no meaning as a format-control character, that character and the following characters (up to the next percent sign) are treated as an ordinary sequence of characters—that is, a sequence of characters that must match the input. For example, to specify that a percent-sign character is to be input, use %%.

An asterisk (*) following the percent sign suppresses assignment of the next input field, which is interpreted as a field of the specified type. The field is scanned but not stored.

The *width* is a positive decimal integer controlling the maximum number of characters to be read from **stdin**. No more than *width* characters are converted and stored at the corresponding *argument*. Fewer than *width* characters may be read if a white-space character (space, tab, or newline) or a character that cannot be converted according to the given format occurs before *width* is reached.

The optional **F** and **N** prefixes allow the user to specify whether the argument is far or near, respectively. **F** should be prefixed to an *argument* pointing to a **far** object, while **N** should be prefixed to an *argument* pointing to a **near** object. Note also that the **F** and **N** prefixes are not part of the ANSI definition for **scanf**, but are instead Microsoft extensions, which should not be used when ANSI portability is desired.

The optional prefix **l** indicates that the **long** version of the following type is to be used, while the prefix **h** indicates that the **short** version is to be used. The corresponding *argument* should point to a **long** or **double** object (with the **l** character) or a **short** object (with the **h** character). The **l** and **h** modifiers can be used with the **d, i, n, o, x,** and **u** type characters. The **l** modifier can also be used with the **e, f,** and **g** type characters. The **l** and **h** modifiers are ignored if specified for any other type.

For **scanf**, **N** and **F** refer to the "distance" to the object being read in (near or far) and **h** and **l** refer to the "size" of the object being read in (16-bit short or 32-bit long). The list below clarifies this use of **N**, **F**, **l**, and **h**:

Program Code	Action
scanf("%Ns", &x);	Read a string into near memory
scanf("%Fs", &x);	Read a string into far memory
scanf("%Nd", &x);	Read an **int** into near memory
scanf("%Fd", &x);	Read an **int** into far memory
scanf("%Nld", &x);	Read a **long int** into near memory
scanf("%Fld", &x);	Read a **long int** into far memory
scanf("%Nhp", &x);	Read a 16-bit pointer into near memory
scanf("%Nlp", &x);	Read a 32-bit pointer into near memory
scanf("%Fhp", &x);	Read a 16-bit pointer into far memory
scanf("%Flp", &x);	Read a 32-bit pointer into far memory

The type characters and their meanings are described in Table R.5.

To read strings not delimited by space characters, a set of characters in brackets ([ ]) can be substituted for the **s** (string) type character. The corresponding input field is read up to the first character that does not appear in the bracketed character set. If the first character in the set is a caret (^), the effect is reversed: the input field is read up to the first character that does appear in the rest of the character set.

Note that %[a-z] and %[z-a] are interpreted as equivalent to %[abcde...z]. This is a common **scanf** extension, but note that it is not required by the ANSI standard.

To store a string without storing a terminating null character ('\0'), use the specification %*n*c, where *n* is a decimal integer. In this case, the **c** type character indicates that the argument is a pointer to a character array. The next *n* characters are read from the input stream into the specified location, and no null character ('\0') is appended. If *n* is not specified, the default value for it is 1.

The **scanf** function scans each input field, character by character. It may stop reading a particular input field before it reaches a space character for a variety of reasons: the specified width has been reached; the next character cannot be converted as specified; the next character conflicts with a character in the control string that it is supposed to match; or the next character fails to appear in a given character set. For whatever reason, when **scanf** stops reading an input field, the next input field is considered to begin at the first unread character. The conflicting character, if there is one, is considered unread and is the first character of the next input field or the first character in subsequent read operations on **stdin**.

Table R.5   Type Characters for scanf

Character	Type of Input Expected	Type of Argument
d	Decimal integer	Pointer to **int**
o	Octal integer	Pointer to **int**
x	Hexadecimal integer[1]	Pointer to **int**
i	Decimal, hexadecimal, or octal integer	Pointer to **int**
u	Unsigned decimal integer	Pointer to **unsigned int**
U	Unsigned decimal integer	Pointer to **unsigned long**
e, E f g, G	Floating-point value consisting of an optional sign (+ or –), a series of one or more decimal digits containing a decimal point, and an optional exponent ("e" or "E") followed by an optionally signed integer value.	Pointer to **float**
c	Character. White-space characters that are ordinarily skipped are read when **c** is specified; to read the next non-white-space character, use %1s.	Pointer to **char**
s	String	Pointer to character array large enough for input field plus a terminating null character ('\0'), which is automatically appended.
n	No input read from stream or buffer.	Pointer to **int**, into which is stored the number of characters successfully read from the stream or buffer up to that point in the current call to **scanf**.
p	Value in the form *xxxx:yyyy*, where the digits *x* and *y* are uppercase hexadecimal digits.	Pointer to far pointer to **void**

[1] Since the input for a **%x** format specifier is always interpreted as a hexadecimal number, the input should not include a leading 0x. (If 0x is included, the 0 is interpreted as a hexadecimal input value.)

Return Value

The **scanf** function returns the number of fields that were successfully converted and assigned. The return value may be less than the number requested in the call to **scanf**. The return value does not include fields that were read but not assigned.

The return value is **EOF** if the end-of-file or end-of-string is encountered in the first attempt to read a character.

Compatibility	Standards:	ANSI, UNIX
	16-Bit:	DOS, QWIN
	32-Bit:	DOS32X

See Also   **fscanf, printf, sscanf, vfprintf, vprintf, vsprintf**

Example

```
/* SCANF.C: This program receives formatted input using scanf. */
#include <stdio.h>

void main( void )
{
    int    i;
    float fp;
    char   c, s[81];
    int    result;

    printf( "Enter an integer, a floating-point number, "
            "a character and a string:\n" );
    result = scanf( "%d %f %c %s", &i, &fp, &c, s );

    printf( "\nThe number of fields input is %d\n", result );
    printf( "The contents are: %d %f %c %s\n", i, fp, c, s );
}
```

Output

```
Enter an integer, a floating-point number, a character and a string:
71
98.6
h
White space stops input

The number of fields input is 4
The contents are: 71 98.599998 h White
```

_scrolltextwindow

Description

Scrolls a text window.

#include <graph.h>

void __far _scrolltextwindow(short *lines*);

lines   Number of lines to scroll

Remarks

The **_scrolltextwindow** function scrolls a text window (previously defined by the **_settextwindow** function). The *lines* argument specifies the number of lines to scroll. A positive value of *lines* scrolls the window up (the usual direction); a negative value scrolls the window down. Specifying a number larger than the height of the current text window is equivalent to calling **_clearscreen(_GWINDOW)**. A value of 0 for *lines* has no effect on the text.

Return Value

None.

Compatibility

Standards: None
16-Bit: DOS
32-Bit: None

See Also

_gettextposition, _outmem, _outtext, _settextposition, _settextwindow

Example

```
/* SCRTXWIN.C: This program displays text in text windows and then
 * scrolls, inserts, and deletes lines.
 */

#include <stdio.h>
#include <conio.h>
#include <graph.h>

void deleteline( void );
void insertline( void );
void status( char *msg );

void main( void )
{
    short row;
    char  buf[40];

    /* Set up screen for scrolling, and put text window around scroll area. */
    _settextrows( 25 );
    _clearscreen( _GCLEARSCREEN );

    for( row = 1; row <= 25; row++ )
    {
        _settextposition( row, 1 );
        sprintf( buf, "Line %c        %2d", row + 'A' - 1, row );
        _outtext( buf );
    }
    _getch();
    _settextwindow( 1, 1, 25, 10 );

    /* Delete some lines. */
    _settextposition( 11, 1 );
    for( row = 12; row < 20; row++ )
        deleteline();
    status( "Deleted 8 lines" );

    /* Insert some lines. */
    _settextposition( 5, 1 );
    for( row = 1; row < 6; row++ )
        insertline();
    status( "Inserted 5 lines" );

    /* Scroll up and down. */
    _scrolltextwindow( -7 );
    status( "Scrolled down 7 lines" );
    _scrolltextwindow( 5 );
    status( "Scrolled up 5 lines" );
    _setvideomode( _DEFAULTMODE );
}
```

```
/* Delete lines by scrolling them off the top of the current text window.
 * Save and restore original window.
 */
void deleteline()
{
    short left, top, right, bottom;
    struct _rccoord rc;

    _gettextwindow( &top, &left, &bottom, &right );
    rc = _gettextposition();
    _settextwindow( rc.row, left, bottom, right );
    _scrolltextwindow( _GSCROLLUP );
    _settextwindow( top, left, bottom, right );
    _settextposition( rc.row, rc.col );
}

/* Insert some lines by scrolling in blank lines from the top of the
 * current text window. Save and restore original window.
 */
void insertline()
{
    short left, top, right, bottom;
    struct _rccoord rc;

    _gettextwindow( &top, &left, &bottom, &right );
    rc = _gettextposition();
    _settextwindow( rc.row, left, bottom, right );
    _scrolltextwindow( _GSCROLLDOWN );
    _settextwindow( top, left, bottom, right );
    _settextposition( rc.row, rc.col );
}

/* Display and clear status in its own window. */
void status( char *msg )
{
    short left, top, right, bottom;
    struct _rccoord rc;

    _gettextwindow( &top, &left, &bottom, &right );
    _settextwindow( 1, 50, 2, 80 );
    _outtext( msg );
    _getch();
    _clearscreen( _GWINDOW );
    _settextwindow( top, left, bottom, right );
}
```

_searchenv

Description

Searches for a file using environment paths.

#include <stdlib.h>

void _searchenv(char *filename***, char** *varname***, char** *pathname* **);**

filename	Name of file to search for
varname	Environment to search
pathname	Buffer to store complete path

Remarks

The _**searchenv** routine searches for the target file in the specified domain. The *varname* variable can be any environment variable that specifies a list of directory paths, such as PATH, LIB, INCLUDE, or other user-defined variables. The _**searchenv** function is case-sensitive, so the *varname* variable should match the case of the environment variable.

The routine first searches for the file in the current working directory. If it doesn't find the file, it next looks through the directories specified by the environment variable.

If the target file is found in one of the directories, the newly created path is copied into the buffer pointed to by *pathname*. You must ensure that there is sufficient space for the constructed path name. If the *filename* file is not found, *pathname* will contain an empty null-terminated string.

Return Value

The _**searchenv** function does not return a value.

Compatibility

Standards:	None
16-Bit:	DOS, QWIN, WIN, WIN DLL
32-Bit:	DOS32X

See Also

getenv, _putenv

Example

```
/* SEARCHEN.C: This program searches for a file in a directory
 * specified by an environment variable.
 */

#include <stdlib.h>
#include <stdio.h>

void main( void )
{
    char pathbuffer[_MAX_PATH];
    char searchfile[] = "CL.EXE";
    char envvar[] = "PATH";
    /* Search for file in PATH environment variable: */
    _searchenv( searchfile, envvar, pathbuffer );
    if( *pathbuffer != '\0' )
        printf( "Path for %s: %s\n", searchfile, pathbuffer );
    else
        printf( "%s not found\n", searchfile );
}
```

Output

```
Path for CL.EXE: C:\BIN\CL.EXE
```

_segread

Description

Gets the current values of segment registers.

#include <dos.h>

void _segread(struct _SREGS *_segregs_);

segregs   Segment-register values

Remarks

The **_segread** function fills the structure pointed to by *segregs* with the current contents of the segment registers. The **_SREGS** union is described in the reference section for **_int86x**. This function is intended to be used with the **_intdosx** and **_int86x** functions to retrieve segment-register values for later use.

Return Value

None.

Compatibility

Standards: None

16-Bit: DOS, QWIN, WIN, WIN DLL

32-Bit: None

See Also

_FP_SEG, _intdosx, _int86x

Example

```
/* SEGREAD.C: This program gets the current segment values with _segread. */

#include <dos.h>
#include <stdio.h>

void main( void )
{
    struct   _SREGS segregs;
    unsigned cs, ds, es, ss;

    /* Read the segment register values */
    _segread( &segregs );
    cs = segregs.cs;
    ds = segregs.ds;
    es = segregs.es;
    ss = segregs.ss;
    printf( "CS = 0x%.4x   DS = 0x%.4x   ES = 0x%.4x   SS = 0x%.4x\n",
            cs, ds, es, ss );
}
```

Output

```
CS = 0x0047   DS = 0x0067   ES = 0x0067   SS = 0x0067

CS = 0x2bcc   DS = 0x2ce8   ES = 0x2ba3   SS = 0x2ce8
```

_selectpalette

Description

Selects a graphics palette for CGA.

#include <graph.h>

short _ _ far _selectpalette(short *number* **);**

number   Palette number

Remarks

The _**selectpalette** function works only under the video modes
_**MRES4COLOR**, _**MRESNOCOLOR**, and _**ORESCOLOR**. A CGA palette
consists of a selectable background color (Color 0) and three set colors. Under the
_**MRES4COLOR** mode, the *number* argument selects one of the four predefined
palettes shown in Table R.6.

Table R.6   _MRES4COLOR Palette Colors

	Color Index		
Palette Number	**Color 1**	**Color 2**	**Color 3**
0	Green	Red	Brown
1	Cyan	Magenta	White
2	Light green	Light red	Yellow
3	Light cyan	Light magenta	Bright white

The _**MRESNOCOLOR** video mode is used with black-and-white displays, producing palettes consisting of various shades of gray. It will also produce color
when used with a color display. The number of palettes available depends upon
whether a CGA or EGA hardware package is employed. Under a CGA configuration, only the palettes shown in Table R.7 are available. Note that although four
palette numbers are listed, palettes 0 and 1 are identical, as are palettes 2 and 3.

Table R.7   _MRESNOCOLOR Mode CGA Palette Colors

Palette Number	Color Index		
	Color 1	Color 2	Color 3
0	Blue	Red	White
1	Blue	Red	White
2	Light blue	Light red	Bright white
3	Light blue	Light red	Bright white

Under the EGA configuration, the three palettes shown in Table R.8 are available in the _**MRESNOCOLOR** video mode. Note that although four palette numbers are listed, palettes 1 and 3 are identical.

Table R.8   _MRESNOCOLOR Mode EGA Palette Colors

Palette Number	Color Index		
	Color 1	Color 2	Color 3
0	Green	Red	Brown
1	Cyan	Magenta	White
2	Light green	Light red	Yellow
3	Cyan	Magenta	White

You can use the _**ORESCOLOR** high resolution video mode for the Olivetti graphics adapters found in most Olivetti computers and in the AT&T 6300 series computers. In _**ORESCOLOR** mode, an argument number in the range 0–15 selects one of the colors listed in Table R.9. The background color is always black in this mode.

Table R.9   _ORESCOLOR Mode Colors

Index	Color	Index	Color
0	Black	8	Dark Grey
1	Blue	9	Light Blue
2	Green	10	Light Green
3	Cyan	11	Light Cyan
4	Red	12	Light Red
5	Magenta	13	Light Magenta
6	Brown	14	Yellow
7	White	15	Bright White

Return Value   The function returns the value of the previous palette. There is no error return.

Compatibility   Standards: None
              16-Bit: DOS
              32-Bit: None

See Also   **_getvideoconfig**, **_remappalette**, **_setbkcolor**, **_setvideomode**

Example
```c
/* SELPAL.C: This program changes the current CGA palette. */

#include <stdio.h>
#include <stdlib.h>
#include <conio.h>
#include <graph.h>

long bkcolor[8] = { _BLACK,   _BLUE,      _GREEN, _CYAN,
                    _RED,     _MAGENTA,   _BROWN, _WHITE };
char *bkname [] = { "BLACK", "BLUE",     "GREEN", "CYAN",
                    "RED",    "MAGENTA", "BROWN", "WHITE" };
void main( void )
{
    int i, j, k;

    if ( !_setvideomode( _MRES4COLOR ) )
    {
        printf( "No palettes available" );
        exit( 1 );
    }
    for( i = 0; i < 4; i++ )                      /* Palette loop           */
    {
        _selectpalette( i );
        for( k = 0; k < 8; k++ )                 /* Background color loop */
        {
            _clearscreen( _GCLEARSCREEN );
            _setbkcolor( bkcolor[k] );
            _settextposition( 1, 1 );
            printf( "Background: %s\tPalette: %d", bkname[k], i );
            for( j = 1; j < 4; j++ )             /* Foreground color loop */
            {
                _setcolor( j );
                _ellipse( _GFILLINTERIOR, 100, j * 30, 220, 80 + (j * 30) );
            }
            _getch();
        }
    }
    _setvideomode( _DEFAULTMODE );
    exit( 0 );
}
```

_setactivepage

Description

Sets the active page.

#include <graph.h>

short __far _setactivepage(short *page*);

page   Memory page number

Remarks

For hardware and mode configurations with enough memory to support multiple screen pages, **_setactivepage** specifies the area in memory in which output is written. The *page* argument selects the current active page. The default page number is 0.

Screen animation can be done by alternating the graphics pages displayed. Use the **_setvisualpage** function to display a completed graphics or text page while executing graphics statements in another active page.

These functions can also be used to control text output if you use the text functions **_gettextcursor**, **_settextcursor**, **_outtext**, **_settextposition**, **_gettextposition**, **_settextcolor**, **_gettextcolor**, **_settextwindow**, and **_wrapon** instead of the standard C-language I/O functions.

The CGA hardware configuration has only 16K of RAM available to support multiple video pages, and only in the text mode. The EGA and VGA configurations may be equipped with up to 256K of RAM for multiple video pages in graphics mode.

Return Value

If successful, the function returns the page number of the previous active page. If the function fails, it returns a negative value.

Compatibility

Standards: None
16-Bit: DOS
32-Bit: None

See Also

_getactivepage, **_getvisualpage**, **_setvisualpage**

Example

```
/* PAGE.C illustrates video page functions including:
 *      _getactivepage  _getvisualpage  _setactivepage  _setvisualpage
 */

#include <conio.h>
#include <graph.h>
#include <stdlib.h>

void main( void )
{
    short  oldvpage, oldapage, page, row, col, line;
    struct _videoconfig vc;
    char   buf[80];

    _getvideoconfig( &vc );
    if( vc.numvideopages < 4 )
        exit( 1 );                      /* Fail for monochrome */
    oldapage = _getactivepage();
    oldvpage = _getvisualpage();
    _displaycursor( _GCURSOROFF );

    /* Draw arrows in different place on each page. */
    for( page = 1; page < 4; page++ )
    {
        _setactivepage( page );
        _settextposition( 12, 16 * page );
        _outtext( ">>>>>>>>" );
    }

    while( !_kbhit() )
        /* Cycle through pages 1 to 3 to show moving image. */
        for( page = 1; page < 4; page++ )
            _setvisualpage( page );
    _getch();

    /* Restore original page (normally 0) to restore screen. */
    _setactivepage( oldapage );
    _setvisualpage( oldvpage );
    _displaycursor( _GCURSORON );
    exit( 0 );
}
```

_setbkcolor

Description

Sets the current background color.

#include <graph.h>

long _ _ far _setbkcolor(long *color* **);**

color   Desired color

Remarks

The _setbkcolor function sets the current background color to the color value *color*.

In a color text mode (such as **_TEXTC80**), _setbkcolor accepts (and _getbkcolor returns) a color index. The value for the default colors is given in a table in the description of the _settextcolor function. For example, _setbkcolor(2L) sets the background color to color index 2. The actual color displayed depends on the palette mapping for color index 2. The default is green in a color text mode.

In a color graphics mode (such as **_ERESCOLOR**), **_setbkcolor** accepts (and _getbkcolor returns) a color value. The value for the background color is given by the manifest constants defined in the GRAPH.H include file. For example, _setbkcolor(_GREEN) sets the background color in a graphics mode to green. These manifest constants are provided as a convenience in defining and manipulating the most common colors. The actual range of colors is, in general, much greater.

In general, whenever a color argument is long, it refers to a color value, and whenever it is short, it refers to a color index. The two exceptions are **_setbkcolor** and **_getbkcolor**.

Since the background color is color index 0, the **_remappalette** function will act identically to the **_setbkcolor** function. Unlike **_remappalette**, however, **_setbkcolor** does not require an EGA or VGA environment.

In a text mode, the **_setbkcolor** function does not affect anything already appearing on the display; only the subsequent output is affected. In a graphics mode, it immediately changes all background pixels.

Return Value   In text modes, **_setbkcolor** returns the color index of the old background color. In graphics modes, **_setbkcolor** returns the old color value of color index 0. There is no error return. Use the **_grstatus** function to check the status after a call to **_setbkcolor**.

Compatibility   Standards: None
16-Bit: DOS
32-Bit: None

See Also   **_getbkcolor**, **_grstatus**, **_remappalette**, **_selectpalette**

Example   See the example for **_getcolor**.

setbuf

Description

Controls stream buffering.

#include <stdio.h>

void setbuf(FILE * *stream* **, char *** *buffer* **);**

stream	Pointer to **FILE** structure
buffer	User-allocated buffer

Remarks

The **setbuf** function allows the user to control buffering for *stream*. The *stream* argument must refer to an open file that has not been read or written. If the *buffer* argument is **NULL**, the stream is unbuffered. If not, the buffer must point to a character array of length **BUFSIZ**, where **BUFSIZ** is the buffer size as defined in STDIO.H. The user-specified buffer, instead of the default system-allocated buffer for the given stream, is used for I/O buffering.

The **stderr** and (in DOS only) **stdaux** streams are unbuffered by default, but can be assigned buffers with **setbuf**.

The **setbuf** function has been subsumed by the **setvbuf** function, which should be the preferred routine for new code. The **setbuf** function is retained for compatibility with existing code.

Return Value

None.

Compatibility

Standards: ANSI, UNIX
16-Bit: DOS, QWIN, WIN, WIN DLL
32-Bit: DOS32X

See Also

fclose, fflush, fopen, setvbuf

Example

```
/* SETBUF.C: This program first opens files named DATA1 and DATA2.
 * Then it uses setbuf to give DATA1 a user-assigned buffer
 * and to change DATA2 so that it has no buffer.
 */

#include <stdio.h>

void main( void )
{
    char buf[BUFSIZ];
    FILE *stream1, *stream2;

    if( ((stream1 = fopen( "data1", "a" )) != NULL) &&
        ((stream2 = fopen( "data2", "w" )) != NULL) )
    {
        /* "stream1" uses user-assigned buffer: */
        setbuf( stream1, buf );
        printf( "stream1 set to user-defined buffer at: %Fp\n", buf );

        /* "stream2" is unbuffered                 */
        setbuf( stream2, NULL );
        printf( "stream2 buffering disabled\n" );
        _fcloseall();
    }
}
```

Output

```
stream1 set to user-defined buffer at: 0298:0DF2
stream2 buffering disabled
```

_setcliprgn

Description   Sets the clipping region for graphics.

#include <graph.h>

void __far _setcliprgn(short *x1*, **short** *y1*, **short** *x2*, **short** *y2* **);**

x1, *y1*	Upper-left corner of clip region
x2, *y2*	Lower-right corner of clip region

Remarks   The **_setcliprgn** function limits the display of subsequent graphics output and font text output to an area of the screen called the "clipping region." The physical points (*x1*, *y1*) and (*x2*, *y2*) are the diagonally opposed sides of a rectangle that defines the clipping region. This function does not change the view coordinate system. Rather, it merely masks the screen.

Note that the **_setcliprgn** function affects graphics and font text output only. To mask the screen for text output, use the **_settextwindow** function.

Return Value   None.

Compatibility
Standards:	None
16-Bit:	DOS
32-Bit:	None

See Also   **_settextwindow**, **_setvieworg**, **_setviewport**, **_setwindow**

Example
```
/* SCLIPRGN.C */
#include <stdlib.h>
#include <conio.h>
#include <graph.h>
```

```
void main( void )
{
    /* Find a valid graphics mode. */
    if( !_setvideomode( _MAXRESMODE ) )
        exit( 1 );

    /* Set clip region, then draw an ellipse larger than the region. */
    _setcliprgn( 0, 0, 200, 125 );
    _ellipse( _GFILLINTERIOR, 80, 50, 240, 190 );

    _getch();
    _setvideomode( _DEFAULTMODE );
    exit( 0 );
}
```

_setcolor

Description

Sets the current color.

#include <graph.h>

short __far _setcolor(short *color*);

color   Desired color index

Remarks

The **_setcolor** function sets the current color index to *color*. The *color* parameter is masked but always within range. The following graphics functions use the current color: **_arc**, **_ellipse**, **_floodfill**, **_lineto**, **_outgtext**, **_pie**, **_polygon**, **_rectangle**, and **_setpixel**.

The **_setcolor** function accepts a **short** value as an argument. It is a color index.

The default color index is the highest numbered color index in the current palette.

Note that the **_setcolor** function does not affect the output of the presentation-graphics functions.

Return Value

This function returns the previous color. If the function fails (e.g., if used in a text mode), it returns −1.

Compatibility

Standards: None
16-Bit: DOS
32-Bit: None

See Also

_arc functions, **_ellipse** functions, **_floodfill**, **_getcolor**, **_lineto** functions, **_outgtext**, **_pie** functions, **_polygon** functions, **_rectangle** functions, **_selectpalette**, **_setpixel** functions

Example

```
/* GPIXEL.C: This program assigns different colors to randomly
 * selected pixels.
 */

#include <conio.h>
#include <stdlib.h>
#include <graph.h>

void main( void )
{
    short xvar, yvar;
    struct _videoconfig vc;

    /* Find a valid graphics mode. */
    if( !_setvideomode( _MAXCOLORMODE ) )
        exit( 1 );
    _getvideoconfig( &vc );

    /* Draw filled ellipse to turn on certain pixels. */
    _ellipse( _GFILLINTERIOR, vc.numxpixels / 6, vc.numypixels / 6,
                            vc.numxpixels / 6 * 5, vc.numypixels / 6 * 5 );

    /* Draw random pixels in random colors... */
    while( !_kbhit() )
    {
        /* ...but only if they are already on (inside the ellipse). */
        xvar = rand() % vc.numxpixels;
        yvar = rand() % vc.numypixels;
        if( _getpixel( xvar, yvar ) != 0 )
        {
            _setcolor( rand() % 16 );
            _setpixel( xvar, yvar );
        }
    }

    _getch();              /* Throw away the keystroke. */
    _setvideomode( _DEFAULTMODE );
    exit( 0 );
}
```

_setfillmask

Description

Sets the fill mask.

#include <graph.h>

void __far _setfillmask(unsigned char __far *_mask_);

mask   Mask array

Remarks

The **_setfillmask** function sets the current fill mask, which determines the fill pattern. The mask is an 8-by-8 array of bits in which each bit represents a pixel. A 1 bit sets the corresponding pixel to the current color, while a 0 bit leaves the pixel unchanged. The pattern is repeated over the entire fill area.

If no fill mask is set (*mask* is **NULL**—the default), a solid (unpatterned) fill is performed using the current color.

Return Value

None.

Compatibility

Standards: None
16-Bit: DOS
32-Bit: None

See Also

_ellipse functions, **_floodfill**, **_getfillmask**, **_pie** functions, **_polygon** functions, **_rectangle** functions

Example

```
/* GFILLMSK.C: This program illustrates _getfillmask and _setfillmask. */

#include <conio.h>
#include <stdlib.h>
#include <graph.h>

void ellipsemask( short x1, short y1, short x2, short y2, char __far *newmask );

unsigned char mask1[8] = { 0x43, 0x23, 0x7c, 0xf7, 0x8a, 0x4d, 0x78, 0x39 };
unsigned char mask2[8] = { 0x18, 0xad, 0xc0, 0x79, 0xf6, 0xc4, 0xa8, 0x23 };
char oldmask[8];
```

```
void main( void )
{
   int loop;

   /* Find a valid graphics mode. */
   if( !_setvideomode( _MAXRESMODE ) )
      exit( 1 );

   /* Set first fill mask and draw rectangle. */
   _setfillmask( mask1 );
   _rectangle( _GFILLINTERIOR, 20, 20, 100, 100 );
   _getch();

   /* Call routine that saves and restores mask. */
   ellipsemask( 60, 60, 150, 150, mask2 );
   _getch();

   /* Back to original mask. */
   _rectangle( _GFILLINTERIOR, 120, 120, 190, 190 );
   _getch();

   _setvideomode( _DEFAULTMODE );
   exit( 0 );
}

/* Draw an ellipse with a specified fill mask. */
void ellipsemask( short x1, short y1, short x2, short y2, char __far *newmask )
{
   unsigned char savemask[8];

   _getfillmask( savemask );                          /* Save mask      */
   _setfillmask( newmask );                           /* Set new mask   */
   _ellipse( _GFILLINTERIOR, x1, y1, x2, y2 );        /* Use new mask   */
   _setfillmask( savemask );                          /* Restore original */
}
```

_setfont

Description

Loads a single font.

#include <graph.h>

short __far _setfont(const char __far *_options_);

options   String describing font characteristics

Remarks

The **_setfont** function finds a single font, from the set of registered fonts, that has the characteristics specified by the _options_ string. If a font is found, it is made the current font. The current font is used in all subsequent calls to the **_outgtext** function. There can be only one active font at any time.

The _options_ string is a set of characters that specifies the desired characteristics of the font. The **_setfont** function searches the list of registered fonts for a font matching the specified characteristics.

The characteristics that may be specified in the _options_ string are shown in the list below. Characteristics specified in the _options_ string are not case-sensitive or position-sensitive.

Characteristic	Description
t'_fontname_'	Typeface.
hx	Character height, where x is the number of pixels.
wy	Character width, where y is the number of pixels.
f	Find only a fixed-space font (should not be used with the **p** characteristic).
p	Find only a proportionally spaced font (should not be used with the **f** characteristic).
v	Find only a vector font (should not be used with the **r** characteristic).
r	Find only a raster-mapped (bitmapped) font (should not be used with the **v** characteristic).
b	Select a best fit font.
nx	Select font number x, where x is less than or equal to the value returned by the **_registerfonts** function. Use this option to "step through" an entire set of fonts or to save or restore a previously set font.

You can request as many options as desired, except with **n**x, which should be used alone. If mutually exclusive options are requested (such as the pair **f/p** or **r/v**), the _setfont function ignores them. There is no error detection for incompatible parameters used with **n**x.

Options can be separated by blanks in the *options* string. Any other character is ignored by _setfont.

The **t** (the typeface specification) in *options* is specified as a "t" followed by *fontname* in single quotes. Choose *fontname* from the following list:

Fontname	Description
Courier	Fixed-width bitmapped font with serifs
Helv	Sans serif proportional bitmapped font
Tms Rmn	Proportional bitmapped font with serifs
Script	Proportional vector-mapped font of slanted characters formed from nearly continuous lines
Modern	Proportional vector-mapped font without serifs
Roman	Proportional vector-mapped font with serifs

A **b** in the *options* field causes the _setfont routine to automatically select the "best fit" font that matches the other characteristics you have specified. If the **b** parameter is specified and at least one font is registered, _setfont will always be able to set a font and will return 0 to indicate success.

You can also specify a pixel width and height for fonts. If a nonexistent value is chosen for either, and the **b** option is specified, the _setfont function will choose the closest match. A smaller font size has precedence over a larger size. For example, if _setfont requests Helv 12 with best fit, and only Helv 10 and Helv 14 are available, _setfont will select Helv 10.

In selecting a font, the _setfont routine uses the following precedence (rated from highest precedence to lowest):

1. Pixel height

2. Typeface

3. Pixel width

4. Fixed or proportional font

If a nonexistent value is chosen for pixel height and width, the _setfont function will apply a magnification factor to a vector-mapped font to obtain a suitable font size. This automatic magnification does not apply if the **r** (raster-mapped font) option is specified, or if a specific typeface is requested and no best fit (**b**) option is specified.

If you specify the **n**x parameter, **_setfont** will ignore any other specified options and supply only the font number corresponding to x.

Note that the font functions affect only the output from the font output function **_outgtext**; no other run-time output functions are affected by font usage.

Return Value

The **_setfont** function returns an index that is suitable for use with **n**x to indicate success or a negative value to indicate an error. An error occurs if a request for a specific font fails and the **b** option was not specified, or if fonts have not yet been registered.

Compatibility

Standards: None
16-Bit: DOS
32-Bit: None

See Also

_getfontinfo, _getgtextextent, _outgtext, _registerfonts, _unregisterfonts

Example

See the example for **_outgtext**.

_setgtextvector

Description

Changes the orientation of font text output.

#include <graph.h>

struct _xycoord __far _setgtextvector(short *x*, short *y*);

x, y   Integers specifying font rotation

Remarks

The **_setgtextvector** function sets the current orientation for font text output to the vector specified by *x* and *y*. The current orientation is used in calls to the **_outgtext** function.

The values of *x* and *y* define the vector which determines the direction of rotation of font text on the screen. The text-rotation options are shown below:

(x, y)	Text Orientation
(0, 0)	Unchanged
(1, 0)	Horizontal text (default)
(0, 1)	Rotated 90 degrees counterclockwise
(−1, 0)	Rotated 180 degrees
(0, −1)	Rotated 270 degrees counterclockwise

If other values are input, only the sign of the input is used. For example, (−3, 0) is interpreted as (−1, 0).

Return Value

The **_setgtextvector** function returns the previous vector in a structure of **_xycoord** type. If you pass the **_setgtextvector** function the values (0, 0), the function returns the current vector values in the **_xycoord** structure.

Compatibility

Standards: None
16-Bit: DOS
32-Bit: None

See Also

_getfontinfo, _getgtextextent, _grstatus, _outgtext, _registerfonts, _setfont, _unregisterfonts

Example

See the example for **_outgtext**.

setjmp

Description

Saves the current state of the program.

#include <setjmp.h>

int setjmp(jmp_buf *env* **);**

env   Variable in which environment is stored

Remarks

The **setjmp** function saves a stack environment that can be subsequently restored using **longjmp**. Used together this way, **setjmp** and **longjmp** provide a way to execute a "non-local **goto**." They are typically used to pass execution control to error-handling or recovery code in a previously called routine without using the normal calling or return conventions.

A call to **setjmp** causes the current stack environment to be saved in *env*. A subsequent call to **longjmp** restores the saved environment and returns control to the point just after the corresponding **setjmp** call. All variables (except register variables) accessible to the routine receiving control contain the values they had when **setjmp** was called.

Warning! Neither the **setjmp** nor the **longjmp** function is compatible with the C++ language.

Return Value

The **setjmp** function returns 0 after saving the stack environment. If **setjmp** returns as a result of a **longjmp** call, it returns the *value* argument of **longjmp**, or if the *value* argument of **longjmp** is 0, **setjmp** returns 1. There is no error return.

Compatibility

Standards: ANSI, UNIX
16-Bit: DOS, QWIN, WIN, WIN DLL
32-Bit: DOS32X

See Also

longjmp

Example

See the example for **_fpreset**.

_setlinestyle

Description

Sets the line style.

#include <graph.h>

void __far _setlinestyle(unsigned short *mask* **);**

mask   Desired line-style mask

Remarks

Some graphics routines (**_lineto**, **_polygon**, and **_rectangle**) draw straight lines on the screen. The type of line is controlled by the current line-style mask.

The **_setlinestyle** function selects the mask used for line drawing. The *mask* argument is a 16-bit array, where each bit represents a pixel in the line being drawn. If a bit is 1, the corresponding pixel is set to the color of the line (the current color). If a bit is 0, the corresponding pixel is left unchanged. The template is repeated for the entire length of the line.

The default mask is 0xFFFF (a solid line).

Return Value

None.

Compatibility

Standards: None
16-Bit: DOS
32-Bit: None

See Also

_getlinestyle, **_lineto** functions, **_polygon** functions, **_rectangle** functions

Example

See the example for **_getlinestyle**.

setlocale

Description

Defines the locale.

#include <locale.h>

char *setlocale(int *category***, const char ****locale* **);**

category	Category affected by locale
locale	Name of the locale that will control the specified category

Remarks

The **setlocale** function sets the categories specified by *category* to the locale specified by *locale*. The "locale" refers to the locality (country and language) for which certain aspects of your program can be customized. Some locale-dependent aspects include the formatting of dates and the display format for monetary values.

The **setlocale** function is used to set or get the program's current entire locale or simply portions of the locale information. The *category* argument specifies which portion of a program's locale information will be affected. The macros used for the *category* argument are listed below:

Category	Parts of Program Affected
LC_ALL	All categories listed below.
LC_COLLATE	The **strcoll** and **strxfrm** functions.
LC_CTYPE	The character-handling functions (except for **isdigit**, **isxdigit**, **mbstowcs**, and **mbtowc**, which are unaffected).
LC_MONETARY	Monetary formatting information returned by the **localeconv** function.
LC_NUMERIC	Decimal point character for the formatted output routines (such as **printf**), for the data conversion routines, and for the nonmonetary formatting information returned by the **localeconv** function.
LC_TIME	The **strftime** function.

The *locale* argument is a pointer to a string that specifies the name of the locale. If *locale* points to an empty string, the locale is the implementation-defined native environment. A value of "C" specifies the minimal ANSI conforming environment for C translation. This is the only locale supported in Microsoft C version 6.0 and Microsoft C/C++ version 7.0.

If the *locale* argument is a null pointer, **setlocale** returns a pointer to the string associated with the category of the program's locale. The program's current locale setting is not changed.

Return Value

If a valid locale and category are given, **setlocale** returns a pointer to the string associated with the specified category for the previous locale. If the locale or category is invalid, the **setlocale** function returns a null pointer and the program's current locale settings are not changed.

The pointer to a string returned by **setlocale** can be used in subsequent calls to restore that part of the program's locale information, assuming that your program does not alter the pointer or the string. Later calls to **setlocale** will overwrite the string; you can use the **_strdup** function to save a specific locale string.

Compatibility

Standards: ANSI
16-Bit: DOS, QWIN, WIN, WIN DLL
32-Bit: DOS32X

See Also

localeconv, mblen, mbstowcs, mbtowc, strcoll, strftime, strxfrm, wcstombs, wctomb

_setmode

Description

Sets the file translation mode.

#include <fcntl.h>

#include <io.h>   Required only for function declarations

int _setmode (int *handle*, **int** *mode* **);**

handle	File handle
mode	New translation mode

Remarks

The **_setmode** function sets to *mode* the translation mode of the file given by *handle*. The mode must be one of the following manifest constants:

Constant	Meaning
_O_TEXT	Sets text (translated) mode. Carriage-return–line-feed (CR-LF) combinations are translated into a single line-feed (LF) character on input. Line-feed characters are translated into CR-LF combinations on output.
_O_BINARY	Sets binary (untranslated) mode. The above translations are suppressed.

The **_setmode** function is typically used to modify the default translation mode of **stdin**, **stdout**, **stderr**, **stdaux**, and **stdprn**, but can be used on any file. If **_setmode** is applied to the file handle for a stream, the **_setmode** function should be called before any input or output operations are performed on the stream.

Return Value

If successful, **_setmode** returns the previous translation mode. A return value of –1 indicates an error, and **errno** is set to one of the following values:

Value	Meaning
EBADF	Invalid file handle
EINVAL	Invalid *mode* argument (neither **_O_TEXT** nor **_O_BINARY**)

Compatibility

Standards: None

16-Bit: DOS, QWIN, WIN, WIN DLL

32-Bit: DOS32X

See Also   _creat, fopen, _open

Example

```
/* SETMODE.C: This program uses _setmode to change stdin from text
 * mode to binary mode.
 */

#include <stdio.h>
#include <fcntl.h>
#include <io.h>

void main( void )
{
   int result;

   /* Set "stdin" to have binary mode: */
   result = _setmode( _fileno( stdin ), _O_BINARY );
   if( result == -1 )
      perror( "Cannot set mode" );
   else
      printf( "'stdin' successfully changed to binary mode\n" );
}
```

Output

```
'stdin' successfully changed to binary mode
```

_set_new_handler Functions

Description

Transfer control to your error-handling mechanism if the **new** operator fails to allocate memory.

#include <new.h>

_PNH _set_new_handler(_PNH *pNewHandler* **);**

_PNH _set_nnew_handler(_PNH *pNewHandler* **);**

_PNH _set_fnew_handler(_PNH *pNewHandler* **);**

_PNHH _set_hnew_handler(_PNHH *pNewHandler* **);**

_PNHB _set_bnew_handler(_PNHB *pNewHandler* **);**

pNewHandler   Pointer to a function that you write

Remarks

Use the C++ **_set_new_handler** function to gain control if the **new** operator fails to allocate memory. The run-time system automatically calls **_set_new_handler** when **new** fails.

To use **_set_new_handler**, you must write an exception-handling function and then pass it as an argument to **_set_new_handler**. To facilitate the easy declaration of this new handler, three pointer-to-function types—**_PNH**, **_PNHH**, and **_PNHB**—are defined in NEW.H and described in the following table:

Type	Description
_PNH	Pointer to a function that returns type **int** and takes an argument of type **size_t**. Use **size_t** to specify the amount of space to be allocated.
_PNHH	Pointer to a function that returns type **int** and takes two arguments— the type **unsigned long** and the type **size_t** arguments specified to the huge **new** operator.
_PNHB	Pointer to a function that returns type **int** and takes two arguments— the type **__segment** and the type **size_t** arguments specified to the based **new** operator. Your function must ensure the correct binding of the segment variable to its return value.

Basically, **_set_new_handler** is a garbage collection scheme. The run-time system retries allocation each time your function returns a nonzero value and fails **new** if your function returns 0.

An occurrence of one of the **_set_new_handler** functions in a program registers the exception-handling function specified in the argument list with the run-time system:

```
#include <new.h>

int handle_program_memory_depletion( size_t )
{
    // Your code
}

void main( void )
{
    _set_new_handler( handle_program_memory_depletion );
    int *pi = new int[BIG_NUMBER];
}
```

You can save the function address that was last passed to the **_set_new_handler** function and then reinstate it at a later time:

```
_PNH old_handler = _set_new_handler( my_handler );
    // Code that requires my_handler
    _set_new_handler( old_handler )
    // Code that requires old_handler
```

The **_set_new_handler** function is defined in five different forms that allow you to manage the heap for five different memory models:

Prototype	Purpose
_PNH _set_new_handler(_PNH);	Default new handler
_PNH _set_nnew_handler(_PNH);	Manages the near heap
_PNH _set_fnew_handler(_PNH);	Manages the far heap
_PNHH _set_hnew_handler(_PNHH);	Manages the huge heap
_PNHB _set_bnew_handler(_PNHB);	Manages based heaps

The **_set_new_handler** function automatically maps to either the **_set_nnew_handler** or the **_set_fnew_handler** function, depending on the default data model.

If the default memory model is either small or medium, you can call **_set_fnew_handler** to manage the far heap. If the default memory model is either compact or large, you can call **_set_nnew_handler** to manage the near heap.

You can explicitly call the **_set_hnew_handler** and the **_set_bnew_handler** functions to manage both the huge and based heaps.

In a multithreaded environment, handlers are maintained separately for each process and thread. Each new process lacks installed handlers. Each new thread gets a copy of its parent thread's new handlers. Thus, each process and thread is in charge of its own free-store error handling.

Return Value

The **_set_new_handler** function returns a pointer to the allocated program memory if successful. It returns a 0 if it's unsuccessful.

Compatibility

_set_new_handler

Standards: None

16-Bit: DOS, WIN, WIN DLL

32-Bit: DOS32X

_set_bnew_handler, _set_fnew_handler, _set_hnew_handler, _set_nnew_handler

Standards: None

16-Bit: DOS, WIN, WIN DLL

32-Bit: None

See Also

_bfreeseg, _bheapseg, calloc, delete, free, malloc, new, realloc

For more information on the **new** and **delete** operators, see Chapter 5 of the *C++ Language Reference* (in the Microsoft C/C++ version 7.0 documentation set).

Example

```
/* HANDLER.CPP: This program uses _set_new_handler to print an
 * error message if the new operator fails.
 */

#include <stdio.h>
#include <new.h>

/* Allocate memory in chunks of size MemBlock. */
const size_t MemBlock = 1024;

/* Allocate a memory block for the printf function to use in case
 * of memory allocation failure; the printf function uses malloc.
 * The failsafe memory block must be visible globally because the
 * handle_program_memory_depletion function can take one
 * argument only.
 */
char * failsafe = new char[128];
```

```
/* Declare a customized function to handle memory-allocation failure.
 * Pass this function as an argument to _set_new_handler.
 */
int handle_program_memory_depletion( size_t );

void main( void )
{
    // Register existence of a new memory handler.
    _set_new_handler( handle_program_memory_depletion );
    size_t *pmemdump = new size_t[MemBlock];
    for( ; pmemdump != 0; pmemdump = new size_t[MemBlock] );
}

int handle_program_memory_depletion( size_t size )
{
    // Release character buffer memory.
    delete failsafe;
    printf( "Allocation failed, " );
    printf( "%u bytes not available.\n", size );
    // Tell new to stop allocation attempts.
    return 0;
}
```

_setpixel Functions

Description   Set a pixel to the current color.

#include <graph.h>

short __far _setpixel(short *x*, **short** *y* **);**

short __far _setpixel_w(double *wx*, **double** *wy* **);**

x, *y*	Target pixel
wx, *wy*	Target pixel

Remarks   The **_setpixel** and the **_setpixel_w** functions set a pixel at a specified location to the current color.

The **_setpixel** function sets the pixel at the view-coordinate point (*x*, *y*) to the current color.

The **_setpixel_w** function sets the pixel at the window-coordinate point (*wx*, *wy*) to the current color.

Return Value   The function returns the previous value of the target pixel. If the function fails (for example, the point lies outside of the clipping region), it will return –1.

Compatibility   Standards: None
16-Bit: DOS
32-Bit: None

See Also   **_getpixel** functions, **_setcolor**

Example

```
/* GPIXEL.C: This program assigns different colors to randomly
 * selected pixels.
 */

#include <conio.h>
#include <stdlib.h>
#include <graph.h>

void main( void )
{
   short xvar, yvar;
   struct _videoconfig vc;

   /* Find a valid graphics mode. */
   if( !_setvideomode( _MAXCOLORMODE ) )
      exit( 1 );
   _getvideoconfig( &vc );

   /* Draw filled ellipse to turn on certain pixels. */
   _ellipse( _GFILLINTERIOR, vc.numxpixels / 6, vc.numypixels / 6,
                             vc.numxpixels / 6 * 5, vc.numypixels / 6 * 5 );

   /* Draw random pixels in random colors... */
   while( !_kbhit() )
   {
      /* ...but only if they are already on (inside the ellipse). */
      xvar = rand() % vc.numxpixels;
      yvar = rand() % vc.numypixels;
      if( _getpixel( xvar, yvar ) != 0 )
      {
         _setcolor( rand() % 16 );
         _setpixel( xvar, yvar );
      }
   }

   _getch();              /* Throw away the keystroke. */
   _setvideomode( _DEFAULTMODE );
   exit( 0 );
}
```

_settextcolor

Description

Sets the current text color.

#include <graph.h>

short __far _settextcolor(short *index*);

index   Desired color index

Remarks

The _**settextcolor** function sets the current text color to the color index specified by *index*. The default text color is the same as the maximum color index for the current video mode.

The _**settextcolor** routine sets the color for the _**outtext** and _**outmem** functions only. It does not affect the color of the **printf** function or the color of text output with the _**outgtext** font routine. Use the _**setcolor** function to change the color of font output.

In text color mode, you can specify a color index in the range 0–31. The colors in the range 0–15 are interpreted as normal (non-blinking). The normal color range is defined below:

Index	Color	Index	Color
0	Black	8	Dark gray
1	Blue	9	Light blue
2	Green	10	Light green
3	Cyan	11	Light cyan
4	Red	12	Light red
5	Magenta	13	Light magenta
6	Brown	14	Yellow
7	White	15	Bright white

Blinking is selected by adding 16 to the normal color value.

In every text mode, including monochrome, **_getvideoconfig** returns the value 32 for the number of available colors. The value 32 indicates the range of values (0–31) accepted by the **_settextcolor** function. This includes sixteen normal colors (0–15) and sixteen blinking colors (16–31). Monochrome text mode has fewer unique display attributes, so some color values are redundant. However, because blinking is selected in the same manner, monochrome text mode has the same range (0–31) as other text modes.

Return Value

The function returns the color index of the previous text color. There is no error return. Use the **_grstatus** function to check the status after a call to **_settextcolor**.

Compatibility

Standards: None
16-Bit: DOS
32-Bit: None

See Also

_gettextcolor, **_grstatus**, **_outmem**, **_outtext**

Example

```
/* OUTTXT.C: This example illustrates text output functions:
 *    _gettextcolor    _getbkcolor    _gettextposition    _outtext
 *    _settextcolor    _setbkcolor    _settextposition
 */

#include <conio.h>
#include <stdio.h>
#include <graph.h>

char buffer [80];

void main( void )
{

    /* Save original foreground, background, and text position */
    short blink, fgd, oldfgd;
    long  bgd, oldbgd;
    struct _rccoord oldpos;

    /* Save original foreground, background, and text position. */
    oldfgd = _gettextcolor();
    oldbgd = _getbkcolor();
    oldpos = _gettextposition();
    _clearscreen( _GCLEARSCREEN );
```

```
        /* First time no blink, second time blinking. */
        for( blink = 0; blink <= 16; blink += 16 )
        {
            /* Loop through 8 background colors. */
            for( bgd = 0; bgd < 8; bgd++ )
            {
                _setbkcolor( bgd );
                _settextposition( (short)bgd + ((blink / 16) * 9) + 3, 1 );
                _settextcolor( 7 );
                sprintf(buffer, "Back: %d Fore:", bgd );
                _outtext( buffer );

                /* Loop through 16 foreground colors. */
                for( fgd = 0; fgd < 16; fgd++ )
                {
                    _settextcolor( fgd + blink );
                    sprintf( buffer, " %2d ", fgd + blink );
                    _outtext( buffer );
                }
            }
        }
        _getch();

        /* Restore original foreground, background, and text position. */
        _settextcolor( oldfgd );
        _setbkcolor( oldbgd );
        _clearscreen( _GCLEARSCREEN );
        _settextposition( oldpos.row, oldpos.col );
        exit( 0 );
    }
```

_settextcursor

Description

Sets the current cursor attribute.

#include <graph.h>

short __far _settextcursor(short *attr* **);**

attr   Cursor attribute

Remarks

The **_settextcursor** function sets the cursor attribute (i.e., the shape) to the value specified by *attr*. The high-order byte of *attr* determines the top line of the cursor within the character cell. The low-order byte of *attr* determines the bottom line of the cursor.

The **_settextcursor** function uses the same format as the BIOS routines in setting the cursor. Typical values for the cursor attribute are listed below:

Attribute	Cursor Shape
0x0707	Underline
0x0007	Full block cursor
0x0607	Double underline
0x2000	No cursor

Note that this function works only in text video modes.

Return Value

The function returns the previous cursor attribute, or –1 if an error occurs (such as calling the function in a graphics screen mode).

Compatibility

Standards: None
16-Bit: DOS
32-Bit: None

See Also

_displaycursor, **_gettextcursor**

Example

```
/* DISCURS.C: This program changes the cursor shape using _gettextcursor
 * and _settextcursor, and hides the cursor using _displaycursor.
 */

#include <conio.h>
#include <graph.h>

void main( void )
{
    short oldcursor;
    short newcursor = 0x007;          /* Full block cursor */

    /* Save old cursor shape and make sure cursor is on. */
    oldcursor = _gettextcursor();
    _clearscreen( _GCLEARSCREEN );
    _displaycursor( _GCURSORON );
    _outtext( "\nOld cursor shape: " );
    _getch();

    /* Change cursor shape. */
    _outtext( "\nNew cursor shape: " );
    _settextcursor( newcursor );
    _getch();

    /* Restore original cursor shape. */
    _outtext( "\n" );
    _settextcursor( oldcursor );
}
```

_settextposition

Description

Sets the text position.

#include <graph.h>

struct _rccoord __far _settextposition(short *row*, **short** *column* **);**

row, *column*   New output start position

Remarks

The **_settextposition** function sets the current text position to the display point (*row*, *column*). The **_outtext** and **_outmem** functions (and standard console I/O routines, such as **printf**) output text at that point. Note that **_settextposition** does not affect the text position for the **_outgtext** function; use the **_moveto** function instead.

The **_rccoord** structure, defined in GRAPH.H, contains the following elements:

Element	Description
short row	Row coordinate
short col	Column coordinate

Return Value

The function returns the previous text position in an **_rccoord** structure, defined in GRAPH.H.

Compatibility

Standards: None
16-Bit: DOS
32-Bit: None

See Also

_gettextposition, _moveto, _outmem, _outtext, _settextwindow

Example

```
/* OUTTXT.C: This example illustrates text output functions:
 *    _gettextcolor   _getbkcolor   _gettextposition   _outtext
 *    _settextcolor   _setbkcolor   _settextposition
 */

#include <conio.h>
#include <stdio.h>
#include <graph.h>

char buffer [80];
```

```
void main( void )
{
    /* Save original foreground, background, and text position */
    short blink, fgd, oldfgd;
    long  bgd, oldbgd;
    struct _rccoord oldpos;

    /* Save original foreground, background, and text position. */
    oldfgd = _gettextcolor();
    oldbgd = _getbkcolor();
    oldpos = _gettextposition();
    _clearscreen( _GCLEARSCREEN );

    /* First time no blink, second time blinking. */
    for( blink = 0; blink <= 16; blink += 16 )
    {
        /* Loop through 8 background colors. */
        for( bgd = 0; bgd < 8; bgd++ )
        {
            _setbkcolor( bgd );
            _settextposition( (short)bgd + ((blink / 16) * 9) + 3, 1 );
            _settextcolor( 7 );
            sprintf(buffer, "Back: %d Fore:", bgd );
            _outtext( buffer );

            /* Loop through 16 foreground colors. */
            for( fgd = 0; fgd < 16; fgd++ )
            {
                _settextcolor( fgd + blink );
                sprintf( buffer, " %2d ", fgd + blink );
                _outtext( buffer );
            }
        }
    }
    _getch();

    /* Restore original foreground, background, and text position. */
    _settextcolor( oldfgd );
    _setbkcolor( oldbgd );
    _clearscreen( _GCLEARSCREEN );
    _settextposition( oldpos.row, oldpos.col );
}
```

_settextrows

Description

Sets the number of screen rows for text modes.

#include <graph.h>

short __far _settextrows(short *rows*);

rows   Number of text rows

Remarks

The **_settextrows** function specifies the number of screen rows to be used in text modes.

If the constant **_MAXTEXTROWS** is specified for the *rows* argument, the **_settextrows** function will choose the maximum number of rows available. In text modes, this is 50 rows on VGA, 43 on EGA, and 25 on others. In graphics modes that support 30 or 60 rows, **_MAXTEXTROWS** specifies 60 rows. In SVGA modes, **_MAXTEXTROWS** specifies the vertical resolution (as returned in a **_videoconfig struct** by the **_getvideoconfig** function) divided by 8.

Return Value

This function returns the numbers of rows set. The function returns 0 if an error occurred.

Compatibility

Standards: None
16-Bit: DOS
32-Bit: None

See Also

_getvideoconfig, _outtext, _setvideomode, _setvideomoderows

Example

```
/* STXTROWS.C: This program attempts to set the screen height. It returns
 * an errorlevel code of 1 (fail) or 0 (success) that could be tested in
 * a batch file.
 */

#include <graph.h>
#include <stdlib.h>

void main( int argc, char **argv )
{
    short rows;

    if( !(rows = atoi( argv[1] )) )
    {
        _outtext( "\nSyntax: STXTROWS [ 25 | 43 | 50 ]\n" );
        exit( 1 );
    }

    /* Make sure new rows are the same as requested rows. */
    if( _settextrows( rows ) != rows )
    {
        _outtext( "\nInvalid rows\n" );
        exit( 1 );
    }
    else
        exit( 0 );
}
```

_settextwindow

Description

Creates a text window.

#include <graph.h>

void __far _settextwindow(short *r1***, short** *c1***, short** *r2***, short** *c2* **);**

r1, *c1*	Upper-left corner of window
r2, *c2*	Lower-right corner of window

Remarks

The **_settextwindow** function specifies a window in row and column coordinates where the text output to the screen by the **_outtext** or **_outmem** function is displayed. The arguments (*r1*, *c1*) specify the upper-left corner of the text window, and the arguments (*r2*, *c2*) specify the lower-right corner of the text window.

Text is output from the top of the text window down. When the text window is full, the uppermost line scrolls up out of it.

Note that this function does not affect the output of presentation-graphics text (e.g., labels, axis marks, etc.), the output of the font display routine **_outgtext**, or the output of the standard I/O routine **printf**. Use the **_setviewport** function to control the display area for presentation graphics or fonts.

Return Value

None. Use the **_grstatus** function to check conditions of success or failure.

Compatibility

Standards: None
16-Bit: DOS
32-Bit: None

See Also

_gettextposition, _gettextwindow, _grstatus, _outmem, _outtext, _scrolltextwindow, _settextposition

Example

See the example for **_scrolltextwindow**.

setvbuf

Description

Controls stream buffering and buffer size.

#include <stdio.h>

int setvbuf(FILE **stream*, **char** **buffer*, **int** *mode*, **size_t** *size* **);**

stream	Pointer to **FILE** structure
buffer	User-allocated buffer
mode	Mode of buffering: **_IOFBF** (full buffering), **_IOLBF** (line buffering), **_IONBF** (no buffer)
size	Size of buffer

Remarks

The **setvbuf** function allows the program to control both buffering and buffer size for *stream*. The *stream* must refer to an open file that has not been read from or written to since it was opened. The array pointed to by *buffer* is used as the buffer, unless it is **NULL**, and an automatically allocated buffer *size* bytes long is used.

The mode must be **_IOFBF**, **_IOLBF**, or **_IONBF**. If *mode* is **_IOFBF** or **_IOLBF**, then *size* is used as the size of the buffer. If *mode* is **_IONBF**, the stream is unbuffered and *size* and *buffer* are ignored.

Values for *mode* and their meanings are:

Type	Meaning
_IOFBF	Full buffering; that is, *buffer* is used as the buffer and *size* is used as the size of the buffer. If *buffer* is **NULL**, an automatically allocated buffer *size* bytes long is used.
_IOLBF	With DOS, the same as **_IOFBF**.
_IONBF	No buffer is used, regardless of *buffer* or *size*.

The legal values for *size* are greater than 0 and less than 32,768.

Return Value

The return value for **setvbuf** is 0 if successful, and a nonzero value if an illegal type or buffer size is specified.

Compatibility   Standards: ANSI, UNIX

                      16-Bit: DOS, QWIN, WIN, WIN DLL

                      32-Bit: DOS32X

See Also   **fclose, fflush, fopen, setbuf**

Example
```c
/* SETVBUF.C: This program opens two streams named stream1 and stream2.
 * It then uses setvbuf to give stream1 a user-defined buffer of 1024
 * bytes and stream2 no buffer.
 */

#include <stdio.h>

void main( void )
{
   char buf[1024];
   FILE *stream1, *stream2;

   if( ((stream1 = fopen( "data1", "a" )) != NULL) &&
       ((stream2 = fopen( "data2", "w" )) != NULL) )
   {
      if( setvbuf( stream1, buf, _IOFBF, sizeof( buf ) ) != 0 )
         printf( "Incorrect type or size of buffer for stream1\n" );
      else
         printf( "'stream1' now has a buffer of 1024 bytes\n" );
      if( setvbuf( stream2, NULL, _IONBF, 0 ) != 0 )
         printf( "Incorrect type or size of buffer for stream2\n" );
      else
         printf( "'stream2' now has no buffer\n" );
      _fcloseall();
   }
}
```

Output
```
'stream1' now has a buffer of 1024 bytes
'stream2' now has no buffer
```

_setvideomode

Description

Sets the video mode.

#include <graph.h>

short __far _setvideomode(short *mode* **);**

mode   Desired mode

Remarks

The **_setvideomode** function selects a screen mode appropriate for a particular hardware/display configuration. The *mode* argument can be one of the manifest constants shown in Tables R.10 and R.11 and defined in GRAPH.H. Table R.10 describes only standard hardware; however, display hardware that is strictly compatible with IBM, Hercules, or Olivetti hardware should also work as described.

Table R.10   Manifest Constants for Screen Mode

Mode	Type[1]	Size[2]	Colors[3]	Adapter[4]
_DEFAULTMODE	Mode existing at startup			
_MAXRESMODE	Highest resolution in graphics mode			
_MAXCOLORMODE	Maximum colors in graphics mode			
_TEXTBW40	BW/T	40 columns	32	CGA
_TEXTC40	C/T	40 columns	32	CGA
_TEXTBW80	BW/T	80 columns	32	CGA
_TEXTC80	C/T	80 columns	32	CGA
_MRES4COLOR	C/G	320×200	4	CGA
_MRESNOCOLOR	BW/G	320×200	4	CGA
_HRESBW	BW/G	640×200	2	CGA
_TEXTMONO	M/T	80 columns	32	MDPA
_HERCMONO[5]	M/G/Hercules graphics	720×348	2	HGC
_MRES16COLOR	C/G	320×200	16	EGA
_HRES16COLOR	C/G	640×200	16	EGA
_ERESNOCOLOR	M/G	640×350	4	EGA
_ERESCOLOR	C/G	640×350	16/4	EGA

Table R.10 (*continued*)

Mode	Type[1]	Size[2]	Colors[3]	Adapter[4]
_VRES2COLOR	C/G	640 × 480	2	VGA
_VRES16COLOR	C/G	640 × 480	16	VGA
_MRES256COLOR	C/G	320 × 200	256	VGA
_ORESCOLOR	C/G	640 × 400	1 of 16	OGA

[1] M indicates monochrome, BW indicates monochrome, C indicates color output, T indicates text, and G indicates graphics generation.

[2] For text modes, size is given in characters (number of columns). For graphics modes, size is given in pixels (horizontal × vertical).

[3] For monochrome displays, the number of colors is the number of attributes or shades of gray.

[4] Adapters are the IBM (and compatible) Monochrome Adapter (MDPA), Color Graphics Adapter (CGA), Enhanced Graphics Adapter (EGA), Video Graphics Array (VGA), Hercules-compatible adapter (HGC), and Olivetti-compatible adapter (OGA).

[5] In **_HERCMONO** mode, the text dimensions are 80 columns by 25 rows, with a 9 by 14 character box. The bottom two scan lines of row 25 are not visible.

Table R.11 lists the manifest constants that support the Super VGA screen modes specified by the Video Electronic Standards Association (VESA). Other nonstandard Super VGA modes may also be supported. Note that some, or all, of these manifest constants may be supported by graphics cards that support the VESA Super Video standard VS891001. Other modes may also be supported; a TSR driver may be required. For more details on these constants, see Chapter 9 of *Programming Techniques* (in the Microsoft C/C++ version 7.0 documentation set).

Table R.11   VESA Manifest Constants for Screen Mode

Mode	VESA No.	Type[1]	Size	Colors	Adapter
_ORES256COLOR	0x0100	C/G	640 × 400	256	SVGA
_VRES256COLOR	0x0101	C/G	640 × 480	256	SVGA
_SRES16COLOR[2]	0x0102	C/G	800 × 600	16	SVGA
_SRES256COLOR[2]	0x0103	C/G	800 × 600	256	SVGA
_XRES16COLOR[3]	0x0104	C/G	1024 × 768	16	SVGA
_XRES256COLOR[3]	0x0105	C/G	1024 × 768	256	SVGA
_ZRES16COLOR[4]	0x0106	C/G	1280 × 1024	16	SVGA
_ZRES256COLOR[4]	0x0107	C/G	1280 × 1024	256	SVGA

[1] C indicates color output and G indicates graphics generation.

[2] Requires NEC MultiSync 3D or equivalent or better.

[3] Requires NEC MultiSync 4D or equivalent or better.

[4] Requires NEC MultiSync 5D or equivalent or better.

Warning! Do not attempt to set _SRES16COLOR, _SRES256COLOR, _XRES16COLOR, _XRES256COLOR, _ZRES16COLOR, or _ZRES256COLOR without ensuring that your monitor can safely handle that resolution. Otherwise, you may risk damaging your display monitor! Consult your owner's manual for details.

_MAXRESMODE and _MAXCOLORMODE

The two special modes _MAXRESMODE and _MAXCOLORMODE select the highest resolution or greatest number of colors available with the current hardware, respectively. These two modes fail for adapters that do not support graphics modes. They never select _SRES, _XRES, or _ZRES mode.

Table R.12 lists the video mode selected for different adapter and monitor combinations when _MAXRESMODE or _MAXCOLORMODE is specified:

Table R.12   Modes Selected by _MAXRESMODE and _MAXCOLORMODE

Adapter/Monitor	_MAXRESMODE	_MAXCOLORMODE
MDPA	fails	fails
HGC	_HERCMONO	_HERCMONO
CGA color[1]	_HRESBW	_MRES4COLOR
CGA noncolor[1]	_HRESBW	_MRESNOCOLOR
OCGA	_ORESCOLOR	_MRES4COLOR
OEGA color	_ORESCOLOR	_ERESCOLOR
EGA color 256K	_HRES16COLOR	_HRES16COLOR
EGA color 64K	_HRES16COLOR	_HRES16COLOR
EGA ecd 256K	_ERESCOLOR	_ERESCOLOR
EGA ecd 64K	_ERESCOLOR	_HRES16COLOR
EGA mono	_ERESNOCOLOR	_ERESNOCOLOR
MCGA	_VRES2COLOR	_MRES256COLOR
VGA	_VRES16COLOR	_MRES256COLOR
OVGA	_VRES16COLOR	_MRES256COLOR
SVGA	_VRES256COLOR[2]	_VRES256COLOR[2]

[1] Color monitor is assumed if the startup text mode was _TEXTC80 or _TEXTC40 or if the startup mode was graphics mode. Composite or other noncolor CGA monitor is assumed if startup mode was _TEXTBW80 or _TEXTBW40.

[2] If _VRES256COLOR is supported by the adapter/monitor combination. If not, _MAXCOLORMODE will be either _ORES256COLOR (if supported) or _MRES256COLOR and _MAXRESMODE will be _VRES16COLOR.

Hercules Support

You must install the Hercules driver MSHERC.COM before running your program. Type MSHERC to load the driver. This can be automated by adding a line to your AUTOEXEC.BAT file.

If you have both a Hercules monochrome card and a color video card, you should install MSHERC.COM with the /H (/HALF) option. The /H option causes the driver to use one instead of two graphics pages. This prevents the two video cards from attempting to use the same memory. You do not need to use the /H option if you have only a Hercules card. See your Hercules hardware manuals for more details on compatibility.

To use a mouse, you must follow special instructions for Hercules cards in *Microsoft Mouse Programmer's Reference Guide*. (This is sold separately; it is not supplied with either Microsoft C/C++ or the mouse package.)

Return Value   The function returns the number of text rows if the function is successful. If an error is encountered (that is, the mode selected is not supported by the current hardware configuration), the function returns 0.

Compatibility

Standards:	None	
16-Bit:	DOS	
32-Bit:	None	

See Also   **_getvideoconfig**, **_settextrows**, **_setvideomoderows**

Example

```
/* SVIDMODE.C: This program sets a video mode from a string given on the
 * command line.
 */

#include <graph.h>
#include <stdlib.h>
#include <string.h>

short modes[] = { _TEXTBW40,     _TEXTC40,       _TEXTBW80,
                  _TEXTC80,      _MRES4COLOR,    _MRESNOCOLOR,
                  _HRESBW,       _TEXTMONO,      _HERCMONO,
                  _MRES16COLOR,  _HRES16COLOR,   _ERESNOCOLOR,
                  _ERESCOLOR,    _VRES2COLOR,    _VRES16COLOR,
                  _MRES256COLOR, _ORESCOLOR
                };
char *names[] = { "TEXTBW40",     "TEXTC40",       "TEXTBW80",
                  "TEXTC80",      "MRES4COLOR",    "MRESNOCOLOR",
                  "HRESBW",       "TEXTMONO",      "HERCMONO",
                  "MRES16COLOR",  "HRES16COLOR",   "ERESNOCOLOR",
                  "ERESCOLOR",    "VRES2COLOR",    "VRES16COLOR",
                  "MRES256COLOR", "ORESCOLOR"
                };
```

```
void error( char *msg );

void main( int argc, char *argv[] )
{
    short i, num = sizeof( modes ) / sizeof( short );
    struct _videoconfig vc;

    if( argc < 2 )
        error( "No argument given" );

    /* If matching name found, change to corresponding mode. */
    for( i = 0; i < num; i++ )
    {
        if( !_strcmpi( argv[1], names[i] ) )
        {
            _setvideomode( modes[i] );
            _outtext( "New mode is: " );
            _outtext( names[i] );
            exit( 0 );
        }
    }
    error( "Invalid mode string" );
}

void error( char *msg )
{
    _outtext( msg );
    exit( 1 );
}
```

_setvideomoderows

Description

Sets the video mode and number of text rows for text modes.

#include <graph.h>

short __ far _setvideomoderows(short *mode*, **short** *rows* **);**

mode	Desired mode
rows	Number of text rows

Remarks

The **_setvideomoderows** function selects a screen mode for a particular hardware/display combination. The manifest constants for the screen mode are given in the reference pages for **_setvideomode**. The **_setvideomoderows** function also specifies the number of text rows to be used in a text mode. If the constant **_MAXTEXTROWS** is specified for the *rows* argument, the **_setvideomoderows** function will choose the maximum number of rows available. In text modes, this is 50 rows on VGA, 43 on EGA, and 25 on others. In graphics modes that support 30 or 60 rows, **_MAXTEXTROWS** specifies 60 rows. In SVGA modes, **_MAXTEXTROWS** specifies the vertical resolution (as returned in a **_videoconfig struct** by the **_getvideoconfig** function) divided by 8.

Return Value

The **_setvideomoderows** function returns the numbers of rows set. The function returns 0 if an error occurred (e.g., if the mode is not supported).

Compatibility

Standards:	None
16-Bit:	DOS
32-Bit:	None

See Also

_getvideoconfig, **_settextrows**, **_setvideomode**

Example   `/* SVMROWS.C */`

```
#include <stdlib.h>
#include <conio.h>
#include <graph.h>

void main( void )
{
   struct _videoconfig config;

   /* Set 43-line graphics mode if available. */
   if( !_setvideomoderows( _ERESCOLOR, 43 ) )
   {
      _outtext( "EGA or VGA required" );
      exit( 1 );
   }
   _getvideoconfig( &config );

   /* Set logical origin to center and draw a rectangle. */
   _setlogorg( config.numxpixels / 2 - 1, config.numypixels / 2 - 1 );
   _rectangle( _GBORDER, -80, -50, 80, 50 );

   _getch();
   _setvideomode( _DEFAULTMODE );
   exit( 0 );
}
```

_setvieworg

Description

Moves the view-coordinate origin to the specified physical point.

#include <graph.h>

struct _xycoord __far _setvieworg(short *x*, short *y*);

x, y   New origin point

Remarks

The **_setvieworg** function moves the view-coordinate origin (0, 0) to the physical point (*x*, *y*).

The **_xycoord** structure, defined in GRAPH.H, contains the following elements:

Element	Description
short xcoord	*x* coordinate
short ycoord	*y* coordinate

The **_setvieworg** function replaces the **_setlogorg** function of Microsoft C version 5.1.

Return Value

The function returns the physical coordinates of the previous view origin in an **_xycoord** structure, defined in GRAPH.H.

Compatibility

Standards:	None	
16-Bit:	DOS	
32-Bit:	None	

See Also

_getphyscoord, _getviewcoord, _getwindowcoord, _setcliprgn, _setviewport

Example

```
/* SVORG.C: This program sets the view origin to the center of
 * the screen, then draws a rectangle using the new origin.
 */

#include <stdlib.h>
#include <conio.h>
#include <graph.h>

void main( void )
{
    struct _videoconfig config;

    /* Find a valid graphics mode. */
    if( !_setvideomode( _MAXRESMODE ) )
      exit( 1 );
    _getvideoconfig( &config );

    /* Set view origin to the center of the screen. */
    _setvieworg( config.numxpixels / 2, config.numypixels / 2 );
    _rectangle( _GBORDER, -80, -50, 80, 50 );

    _getch();
    _setvideomode( _DEFAULTMODE );
    exit( 0 );
}
```

_setviewport

Description

Creates a viewport.

#include <graph.h>

void __far _setviewport(short *x1*, **short** *y1*, **short** *x2*, **short** *y2* **);**

x1, *y1*	Upper-left corner of viewport
x2, *y2*	Lower-right corner of viewport

Remarks

The **_setviewport** function redefines the graphics viewport. The **_setviewport** function defines a clipping region in exactly the same manner as **_setcliprgn**, and then sets the view-coordinate origin to the upper-left corner of the region. The physical points (*x1*, *y1*) and (*x2*, *y2*) are the diagonally opposed corners of the rectangular clipping region. Any window transformation done with the **_setwindow** function applies only to the viewport and not to the entire screen. The default viewport is the entire screen.

Return Value

None. Use the **_grstatus** function to check for conditions of success or failure.

Compatibility

Standards:	None
16-Bit:	DOS
32-Bit:	None

See Also

_grstatus, _setcliprgn, _setvieworg, _setwindow

Example

```
/* SVIEWPRT.C: This program sets a viewport and then draws a rectangle
 * around it and an ellipse in it.
 */

#include <conio.h>
#include <stdlib.h>
#include <graph.h>

void main( void )
{
    /* Find a valid graphics mode. */
    if( !_setvideomode( _MAXRESMODE ) )
        exit( 1 );

    _setviewport( 100, 100, 200, 200 );
    _rectangle( _GBORDER, 0, 0, 100, 100 );
    _ellipse( _GFILLINTERIOR, 10, 10, 90, 90 );

    _getch();
    _setvideomode( _DEFAULTMODE );
    exit( 0 );
}
```

_setvisualpage

Description

Sets the visual page.

#include <graph.h>

short __far _setvisualpage(short *page* **);**

page   Visual page number

Remarks

For hardware configurations that have enough memory to support multiple-screen pages, the **_setvisualpage** function selects the current visual page. The *page* argument specifies the current visual page. The default page number is 0.

Return Value

The function returns the number of the previous visual page. If the function fails, it returns a negative value.

Compatibility

Standards: None
16-Bit: DOS
32-Bit: None

See Also

_getactivepage, **_getvisualpage**, **_setactivepage**, **_setvideomode**

Example

See the example for **_setactivepage**.

_setwindow

Description

Defines a graphics window coordinate system.

#include <graph.h>

short __far _setwindow(short *finvert***, double** *wx1***, double** *wy1***, double** *wx2***,**
**   double** *wy2* **);**

finvert	Invert flag
wx1, *wy1*	Upper-left corner of window
wx2, *wy2*	Lower-right corner of window

Remarks

The **_setwindow** function defines a window viewport. The arguments (*wx1*, *wy1*)
specify the upper-left corner of the window, and the arguments (*wx2*, *wy2*) specify
the lower-right corner of the window.

The *finvert* argument specifies the direction of the coordinates. If *finvert* is **TRUE**,
the *y* axis increases from the screen bottom to the screen top (Cartesian coordinates). If *finvert* is **FALSE**, the *y* axis increases from the screen top to the screen
bottom (screen coordinates).

Any window transformation done with the **_setwindow** function applies only to
the viewport and not to the entire screen.

If *wx1* equals *wx2* or *wy1* equals *wy2*, the function will fail.

Note that this function only affects output functions suffixed with **_w** or **_wxy**.

Return Value

The function returns a nonzero value if successful. If the function fails (e.g., if it is
not in a graphics mode), it returns 0.

Compatibility

Standards:	None
16-Bit:	DOS
32-Bit:	None

See Also

_arc functions, **_ellipse** functions, **_getwindowcoord**, **_lineto** functions,
_pie functions, **_setviewport**, functions suffixed with **_w** or **_wxy**

Example

```
/* SWINDOW.C: This program illustrates translation between window,
 * view, and physical coordinates. Functions used include:
 *      _setwindow          _getwindowcoord
 *      _getphyscoord       _getviewcoord_wxy
 */

#include <conio.h>
#include <stdlib.h>
#include <graph.h>

enum boolean { FALSE, TRUE };
enum display { MOVE, DRAW, ERASE };

void main( void )
{
    struct _xycoord view, phys;
    struct _wxycoord oldwin, newwin;
    struct _videoconfig vc;
    double xunit, yunit, xinc, yinc;
    short  color, key, fintersect = FALSE, fdisplay = TRUE;

    /* Find a valid graphics mode. */
    if( !_setvideomode( _MAXRESMODE ) )
       exit( 1 );
    _getvideoconfig( &vc );

    /* Set a window using real numbers. */
    _setwindow( FALSE, -125.0, -100.0, 125.0, 100.0 );

    /* Calculate the size of one pixel in window coordinates.
     * Then get the current window coordinates and color.
     */
    oldwin = _getwindowcoord( 1, 1 );
    newwin = _getwindowcoord( 2, 2 );
    xunit = xinc = newwin.wx - oldwin.wx;
    yunit = yinc = newwin.wy - oldwin.wy;
    newwin = oldwin = _getcurrentposition_w();
    color = _getcolor();

    while( 1 )
    {
        /* Set flag according to whether current pixel is on, then
         * turn pixel on.
         */
        if( _getpixel_w( oldwin.wx, oldwin.wy ) == color )
           fintersect = TRUE;
        else
           fintersect = FALSE;
        _setcolor( color );
        _setpixel_w( oldwin.wx, oldwin.wy );
```

```
/* Get and test key. */
key = _getch();
switch( key )
{
    case 27:                            /* ESC Quit                  */
        _setvideomode( _DEFAULTMODE );
        exit( 0 );
    case 32:                            /* SPACE    Move no color    */
        fdisplay = MOVE;
        continue;
    case 0:                             /* Extended code - get next */
        key = _getch();
        switch( key )
        {
            case 72:                    /* UP          -y            */
                newwin.wy -= yinc;
                break;
            case 77:                    /* RIGHT    +x               */
                newwin.wx += xinc;
                break;
            case 80:                    /* DOWN        +y            */
                newwin.wy += yinc;
                break;
            case 75:                    /* LEFT     -x               */
                newwin.wx -= xinc;
                break;
            case 82:                    /* INS      Draw white       */
                fdisplay = DRAW;
                continue;
            case 83:                    /* DEL      Draw black       */
                fdisplay = ERASE;
                continue;
        }
        break;
}

/* Translate window coordinates to view, view to physical.
 * Then check physical to make sure we're on screen. Update screen
 * and position if we are. Ignore if not.
 */
view = _getviewcoord_wxy( &newwin );
phys = _getphyscoord( view.xcoord, view.ycoord );
if( (phys.xcoord >= 0) && (phys.xcoord < vc.numxpixels) &&
    (phys.ycoord >= 0) && (phys.ycoord < vc.numypixels) )
{
    /* If display on, draw to new position, else move to new. */
    if( fdisplay != MOVE )
    {
        if( fdisplay == ERASE )
            _setcolor( 0 );
        _lineto_w( newwin.wx, newwin.wy );
    }
```

```
                    else
                    {
                        _setcolor( 0 );
                        _moveto_w( newwin.wx, newwin.wy );

                        /* If there was no intersect, erase old pixel. */
                        if( !fintersect )
                            _setpixel_w( oldwin.wx, oldwin.wy );
                    }
                    oldwin = newwin;
                }
            else
                newwin = oldwin;
        }
    exit( 0 );
}
```

_setwritemode

Description   Sets the current logical mode for line drawing.

#include <graph.h>

short __far _setwritemode(short *action* **);**

action   Interaction with existing screen image

Remarks   The **_setwritemode** function sets the current logical write mode, which is used when drawing lines with the **_lineto**, **_polygon**, and **_rectangle** functions.

The *action* argument defines the write mode. The possible values are **_GAND**, **_GOR**, **_GPRESET**, **_GPSET**, and **_GXOR**. See the description of the **_putimage** functions for more details on these manifest constants.

Return Value   The **_setwritemode** function returns the previous write mode, or −1 if an error occurs.

Compatibility   Standards: None
16-Bit: DOS
32-Bit: None

See Also   **_getwritemode**, **_grstatus**, **_lineto** functions, **_polygon** functions, **_putimage** functions, **_rectangle** functions, **_setcolor**, **_setlinestyle**

Example   See the example for **_getwritemode**.

signal

Description

Sets interrupt signal handling.

#include <signal.h>

void (__cdecl *signal(int *sig***, void(__cdecl ***func* **)**
    (int *sig* **⟦, int** *subcode* **⟧))) (int** *sig* **);**

sig	Signal value
func	Function to be executed
subcode	Optional subcode to the signal number

Remarks

The **signal** function allows a process to choose one of several ways to handle an interrupt signal from the operating system.

The *sig* argument must be one of the manifest constants described in Table R.13 and defined in SIGNAL.H.

Table R.13   Signals and Responses

Value	Mode	Meaning	Default Action
SIGABRT	Real	Abnormal termination	Terminates the calling program with exit code 3
SIGFPE	Real	Floating-point error	Terminates the calling program with exit code 3
SIGILL	Real	Illegal instruction	Terminates the calling program with exit code 3
SIGINT	Real	CTRL+C signal	Terminates the calling program with exit code 3
SIGSEGV	Real	Illegal storage access	Terminates the calling program with exit code 3
SIGTERM	Real	Termination request	Terminates the calling program with exit code 3

Note that **SIGILL**, **SIGSEGV**, and **SIGTERM** are not generated with DOS. They are included for ANSI compatibility. Thus, you can set signal handlers for these signals via **signal**, and you can also explicitly generate these signals by calling **raise.**

Note also that signal settings are not preserved in child processes created by calls to **_exec** or **_spawn**. The signal settings are reset to the default in the child process.

The action taken when the interrupt signal is received depends on the value of *func*. The *func* argument must be either a function address or one of the manifest constants defined in SIGNAL.H and listed below:

SIG_DFL

Uses system-default response. The system-default response for all signals is to abort the calling program. The calling process is terminated with exit code 3, and control returns to DOS. If the calling program uses stream I/O, buffers created by the run-time library are not flushed, but buffers created by the operating system are flushed.

SIG_IGN

Ignores interrupt signal. This value should never be given for **SIGFPE**, since the floating-point state of the process is left undefined.

Function address

Installs the specified function as the handler for the given signal.

For all signals except **SIGFPE**, the function is passed the *sig* argument **SIGINT** and executed.

For **SIGFPE** signals, the function is passed two arguments; namely **SIGFPE** and the floating-point error code identifying the type of exception that occurred.

For **SIGFPE**, the function pointed to by *func* is passed two arguments, **SIGFPE** and an integer error subcode, **FPE_***xxx*; then the function is executed. (See the include file FLOAT.H for definitions of the **FPE_***xxx* subcodes.) The value of *func* is not reset upon receiving the signal. In C programs, **SIGFPE** is the only constant available when the **_WINDOWS** constant is defined. The **_WINDOWS** constant is defined by CL options /GA, /GD, /GE, /GW, and /Gw. To recover from floating-point exceptions, use **setjmp** in conjunction with **longjmp**. (See the example under **_fpreset**.) If the function returns, the calling process resumes execution with the floating-point state of the process left undefined.

If the function returns, the calling process resumes execution immediately following the point at which it received the interrupt signal. This is true regardless of the type of signal or operating mode.

Before the specified function is executed with DOS versions 3.x or earlier, the value of *func* is set to **SIG_DFL**. The next interrupt signal is treated as described above for **SIG_DFL**, unless an intervening call to **signal** specifies otherwise. This allows the program to reset signals in the called function.

Since signal-handler routines are normally called asynchronously when an interrupt occurs, it is possible that your signal-handler function will get control when a run-time operation is incomplete and in an unknown state. Certain restrictions therefore apply to the functions that can be used in your signal-handler routine:

1. Do not issue low-level or standard input and output routines (e.g., **printf**, **_read**, **_write**, **fread**).

2. Do not call heap routines or any routine that uses the heap routines (e.g., **malloc**, **_strdup**, **_putenv**).

3. Do not use any function that generates a system call (e.g., **_getcwd**, **time**).

4. Do not use the **longjmp** function unless the interrupt is caused by a floating-point exception (i.e., *sig* is **SIGFPE**). In this case, the program should first re-initialize the floating-point package by means of a call to **_fpreset**.

5. Do not use any overlay routines.

Note With DOS, a program must contain floating-point code if it is to trap the **SIGFPE** exception with the signal function. If your program does not have floating-point code and it requires the run-time library's signal-handling code, simply declare a volatile double and initialize it to zero:

```
volatile double d = 0.0f;
```

Return Value	The **signal** function returns the previous value of *func* associated with the given signal. For example, if the previous value of *func* was **SIG_IGN**, the return value will be **SIG_IGN**.
	A return value of **SIG_ERR** indicates an error, and **errno** is set to **EINVAL**.
Compatibility	Standards: ANSI, UNIX
	16-Bit: DOS, QWIN, WIN, WIN DLL
	32-Bit: DOS32X
See Also	**abort**, **_exec** functions, **exit**, **_exit**, **_fpreset**, **_spawn** functions

Example

```
/* SIGNAL.C illustrates setting up signal interrupt routines. Functions
 * illustrated include signal and raise.
 *
 * Since C I/O functions are not safe inside signal routines, the code
 * uses conditionals to use system-level DOS services. Another option
 * is to set global flags and do any I/O operations outside the
 * signal handler.
 */

#include <stdio.h>
#include <conio.h>
#include <signal.h>
#include <process.h>
#include <stdlib.h>
#include <dos.h>
#include <bios.h>

void ctrlchandler( int sig );              /* Prototypes */
void safeout( char *str );
int  safein( void );

void main( void )
{
    int ch;
    /* Install signal handler to modify CTRL+C behavior. */
    if( signal( SIGINT, ctrlchandler ) == SIG_ERR )
    {
        fprintf( stderr, "Couldn't set SIGINT\n" );
        abort();
    }

    /* Loop prints message to screen asking user to
     * enter Cntl+C--at which point the ctrlchandler
     * signal handler takes control.
     */
    do
    {
        printf( "Press Ctrl+C to enter handler.\n" );
    }
    while( ch = _getch());   /* Discard keystokes */
}

/* A signal handler must take a single argument. The argument can be
 * tested within the handler and thus allows a single signal handler
 * to handle several different signals. In this case, the parameter
 * is included to keep the compiler from generating a warning but is
 * ignored because this signal handler only handles one interrupt:
 * SIGINT (Ctrl+C).
 */
```

```
void ctrlchandler( int sig )
{
    int c;
    char str[] = " ";

    /* Disallow CTRL+C during handler. */
    signal( SIGINT, SIG_IGN );
    safeout( "User break - abort processing (y|n)? " );
    c = safein();
    str[0] = c;
    // safeout( str );
    safeout( "\r\n" );
    if( (c == 'y') || (c == 'Y') )
        abort();
    else
    {
        /* The CTRL+C interrupt must be reset to our handler since
         * by default it is reset to the system handler.
         */
        signal( SIGINT, ctrlchandler );
        safeout( "Press Ctrl+C to enter handler.\r\n" );
    }
}

/* Outputs a string using system level calls. */
void safeout( char *str )
{
    union _REGS inregs, outregs;

    inregs.h.ah = 0x0e;
    while( *str )
    {
        inregs.h.al = *str++;
        _int86( 0x10, &inregs, &outregs );
    }
}

/* Inputs a character using system level calls. */
int safein()
{
    return _bios_keybrd( _KEYBRD_READ ) & 0xff;
}
```

Output

```
Press Ctrl+C to enter handler.
^C
User break - abort processing (y|n)? y
abnormal program termination
```

sin Functions

Description   Calculate sines and hyperbolic sines.

#include <math.h>

double sin(double *x* **);**

double sinh(double *x* **);**

long double _sinl(long double *x* **);**

long double _sinhl(long double *x* **);**

x   Angle in radians

Remarks   The **sin** and **sinh** functions find the sine and hyperbolic sine of *x*, respectively. The **_sinl** and **_sinhl** functions are the 80-bit counterparts and use an 80-bit, 10-byte coprocessor form of arguments and return values. See the reference page on the long double functions for more details on this data type.

Return Value   The **sin** functions return the sine of *x*. If *x* is large, a partial loss of significance in the result may occur, and **sin** generates a **_PLOSS** error. If *x* is so large that significance is completely lost, the **sin** function prints a **_TLOSS** message to **stderr** and returns 0. In both cases, **errno** is set to **ERANGE**.

The **sinh** function returns the hyperbolic sine of *x*. If the result is too large, **sinh** sets **errno** to **ERANGE** and returns ± **HUGE_VAL**. Error handling can be changed with the **_matherr** function.

Compatibility   **sin, sinh**

Standards: ANSI, UNIX
16-Bit: DOS, QWIN, WIN, WIN DLL
32-Bit: DOS32X

_sinl, _sinhl

Standards: None

16-Bit: DOS, QWIN, WIN, WIN DLL

32-Bit: None

See Also   **acos** functions, **asin** functions, **atan** functions, **cos** functions, **tan** functions

Example
```
/* SINCOS.C: This program displays the sine, hyperbolic sine, cosine,
 * and hyperbolic cosine of pi / 2.
 */

#include <math.h>
#include <stdio.h>

void main( void )
{
    double pi = 3.1415926535;
    double x, y;

    x = pi / 2;
    y = sin( x );
    printf( "sin( %f ) = %f\n", x, y );
    y = sinh( x );
    printf( "sinh( %f ) = %f\n",x, y );
    y = cos( x );
    printf( "cos( %f ) = %f\n", x, y );
    y = cosh( x );
    printf( "cosh( %f ) = %f\n",x, y );
}
```

Output
```
sin( 1.570796 ) = 1.000000
sinh( 1.570796 ) = 2.301299
cos( 1.570796 ) = 0.000000
cosh( 1.570796 ) = 2.509178
```

_sopen

Description

Opens a file for file sharing.

#include <fcntl.h>
#include <sys\types.h>
#include <sys\stat.h>
#include <share.h>
#include <io.h>   Required only for function declarations

int _sopen(char *filename*, **int** *oflag*, **int** *shflag* [[, **int** *pmode*]]);

filename	Filename
oflag	Type of operations allowed
shflag	Type of sharing allowed
pmode	Permission setting

Remarks

The **_sopen** function opens the file specified by *filename* and prepares the file for subsequent shared reading or writing, as defined by *oflag* and *shflag*. The integer expression *oflag* is formed by combining one or more of the following manifest constants, defined in the file FCNTL.H. When two or more constants are used to form the argument *oflag*, the constants are combined with the bitwise-OR operator (|).

Constant	Meaning
_O_APPEND	Repositions the file pointer to the end of the file before every write operation.
_O_BINARY	Opens file in binary (untranslated) mode. (See **fopen** for a description of binary mode.)
_O_CREAT	Creates and opens a new file. This has no effect if the file specified by *filename* exists.
_O_EXCL	Returns an error value if the file specified by *filename* exists. This applies only when used with **_O_CREAT**.
_O_RDONLY	Opens file for reading only. If this flag is given, neither the **_O_RDWR** flag nor the **_O_WRONLY** flag can be given.
_O_RDWR	Opens file for both reading and writing. If this flag is given, neither **_O_RDONLY** nor **_O_WRONLY** can be given.

Constant	Meaning
_O_TEXT	Opens file in text (translated) mode. (See **fopen** for a description of text mode.)
_O_TRUNC	Opens and truncates an existing file to 0 bytes. The file must have write permission; the contents of the file are destroyed.
_O_WRONLY	Opens file for writing only. If this flag is given, neither **_O_RDONLY** nor **_O_RDWR** can be given.

The argument *shflag* is a constant expression consisting of one of the following manifest constants, defined in SHARE.H. If SHARE.COM (or SHARE.EXE for some versions of DOS) is not installed, DOS ignores the sharing mode. (See your system documentation for detailed information about sharing modes.)

Constant	Meaning
_SH_COMPAT	Sets compatibility mode. This is the sharing mode used in the **_open** function in DOS.
_SH_DENYRW	Denies read and write access to file.
_SH_DENYWR	Denies write access to file.
_SH_DENYRD	Denies read access to file.
_SH_DENYNO	Permits read and write access.

The **_sopen** function should be used only with DOS version 3.0 and later. Under earlier versions of DOS, the *shflag* argument is ignored.

The *pmode* argument is required only when **_O_CREAT** is specified. If the file does not exist, *pmode* specifies the file's permission settings, which are set when the new file is closed for the first time. Otherwise, the *pmode* argument is ignored. The *pmode* argument is an integer expression that contains one or both of the manifest constants **_S_IWRITE** and **_S_IREAD**, defined in SYS\STAT.H. When both constants are given, they are combined with the bitwise-OR operator (|). The meaning of the *pmode* argument is as follows:

Value	Meaning
_S_IWRITE	Writing permitted
_S_IREAD	Reading permitted
_S_IREAD	**_S_IWRITE**	Reading and writing permitted

If write permission is not given, the file is read-only. With DOS, all files are readable; it is not possible to give write-only permission. Thus, the modes **_S_IWRITE** and **_S_IREAD | _S_IWRITE** are equivalent.

Note that with DOS versions 3.x with SHARE installed, a problem occurs when opening a new file with **_sopen** under the following sets of conditions:

- With *oflag* set to **_O_CREAT | _O_RDONLY** or **_O_CREAT | _O_WRONLY**, *pmode* set to **_S_IREAD**, and *shflag* set to **_SH_COMPAT**.

- With *oflag* set to any combination that includes **_O_CREAT | _O_RDWR**, *pmode* set to **_S_IREAD**, and *shflag* set to anything other than **_SH_COMPAT**.

In either case, the operating system will prematurely close the file during system calls made within **_sopen**, or the system will generate a sharing violation (INT 24H). To avoid the problem, open the file with *pmode* set to **_S_IWRITE**. After closing the file, call **_chmod** and change the mode back to **_S_IREAD**. Another solution is to open the file with *pmode* set to **_S_IREAD**, *oflag* set to **_O_CREAT | _O_RDWR**, and *shflag* set to **_SH_COMPAT**.

The **_sopen** function applies the current file-permission mask to *pmode* before setting the permissions (see **_umask**).

Return Value

The **_sopen** function returns a file handle for the opened file. A return value of –1 indicates an error, and **errno** is set to one of the following values:

Value	Meaning
EACCES	Given path name is a directory; or the file is read-only but an open for writing was attempted; or a sharing violation occurred (the file's sharing mode does not allow the specified operations; DOS versions 3.0 and later only).
EEXIST	The **_O_CREAT** and **_O_EXCL** flags are specified, but the named file already exists.
EINVAL	An invalid *oflag* or *shflag* argument was given.
EMFILE	No more file handles available (too many open files).
ENOENT	File or path name not found.

Compatibility

Standards: None

16-Bit: DOS, QWIN, WIN, WIN DLL

32-Bit: DOS32X

See Also

_close, _creat, fopen, _fsopen, _open, _umask

Example

See the example for **_locking**.

_spawn Functions

Description   Create and execute a new child process for DOS.

#include <stdio.h>

#include <process.h>

int _spawnl(int *mode*, char *cmdname*, char *arg0*, char *arg1*, ... char *argn*, NULL);

int _spawnle(int *mode*, char *cmdname*, char *arg0*, char *arg1*, ... char *argn*, NULL, char **envp*);

int _spawnlp(int *mode*, char *cmdname*, char *arg0*, char *arg1*, ... char *argn*, NULL);

int _spawnlpe(int *mode*, char *cmdname*, char *arg0*, char *arg1*, ... char *argn*, NULL, char **envp*);

int _spawnv(int *mode*, char *cmdname*, char **argv*);

int _spawnve(int *mode*, char *cmdname*, char **argv*, char **envp*);

int _spawnvp(int *mode*, char *cmdname*, char **argv*);

int _spawnvpe(int *mode*, char *cmdname*, char **argv*, char **envp*);

mode	Execution mode for parent process
cmdname	Path name of file to be executed
arg0, ... argn	List of pointers to arguments
argv	Array of pointers to arguments
envp	Array of pointers to environment settings

Remarks

The **_spawn** family of functions creates and executes a new child process. Enough memory must be available for loading and executing the child process. The *mode* argument determines the action taken by the parent process before and during **_spawn**. The following values for *mode* are defined in PROCESS.H:

Value	Meaning
_P_OVERLAY	Overlays parent process with child, destroying the parent (same effect as **_exec** calls).
_P_WAIT	Suspends parent process until execution of child process is complete (synchronous _spawn).

The *cmdname* argument specifies the file which will be executed as the child process, and can specify a full path (from the root), a partial path (from the current working directory), or just a filename. If *cmdname* does not have a filename extension or does not end with a period (.), the **_spawn** function first tries the .COM extension, then the .EXE extension, and finally the .BAT extension. This ability to spawn batch files is new beginning with Microsoft C version 6.0.

If *cmdname* has an extension, only that extension is used. If *cmdname* ends with a period, the **_spawn** calls search for *cmdname* with no extension. The **_spawnlp**, **_spawnlpe**, **_spawnvp**, and **_spawnvpe** routines search for *cmdname* (using the same procedures) in the directories specified by the PATH environment variable.

If *cmdname* contains a drive specifier or any slashes (i.e., if it is a relative path name), the **_spawn** call searches only for the specified file and no path searching is done.

Arguments for the Child Process

Arguments are passed to the child process by giving one or more pointers to character strings as arguments in the **_spawn** call. These character strings form the argument list for the child process. The combined length of the strings forming the argument list for the child process must not exceed 128 bytes in real mode. The terminating null character ('\0') for each string is not included in the count, but space characters (automatically inserted to separate arguments) are included.

The argument pointers may be passed as separate arguments (**_spawnl**, **_spawnle**, **_spawnlp**, and **_spawnlpe**) or as an array of pointers (**_spawnv**, **_spawnve**, **_spawnvp**, and **_spawnvpe**). At least one argument, *arg0* or *argv*[0], must be passed to the child process. By convention, this argument is the name of the program as it might be typed on the command line by the user. (A different value will not produce an error.) In real mode, the *argv*[0] value is supplied by the operating system and is the fully qualified path name of the executing program. In protected mode, it is usually the program name as it would be typed on the command line.

The **_spawnl**, **_spawnle**, **_spawnlp**, and **_spawnlpe** calls are typically used in cases where the number of arguments is known in advance. The *arg0* argument is usually a pointer to *cmdname*. The arguments *arg1* through *argn* are pointers to the character strings forming the new argument list. Following *argn*, there must be a **NULL** pointer to mark the end of the argument list.

The **_spawnv**, **_spawnve**, **_spawnvp**, and **_spawnvpe** calls are useful when the number of arguments to the child process is variable. Pointers to the arguments are passed as an array, *argv*. The argument *argv*[0] is usually a pointer to a path name in real mode or to the program name in protected mode, and *argv*[1] through *argv*[n] are pointers to the character strings forming the new argument list. The argument *argv*[n+1] must be a **NULL** pointer to mark the end of the argument list.

Environment of the Child Process

Files that are open when a **_spawn** call is made remain open in the child process. In the **_spawnl**, **_spawnlp**, **_spawnv**, and **_spawnvp** calls, the child process inherits the environment of the parent. The **_spawnle**, **_spawnlpe**, **_spawnve**, and **_spawnvpe** calls allow the user to alter the environment for the child process by passing a list of environment settings through the *envp* argument. The argument *envp* is an array of character pointers, each element of which (except for the final element) points to a null-terminated string defining an environment variable. Such a string usually has the form

NAME=*value*

where NAME is the name of an environment variable and *value* is the string value to which that variable is set. (Note that *value* is not enclosed in double quotation marks.) The final element of the *envp* array should be **NULL**. When *envp* itself is **NULL**, the child process inherits the environment settings of the parent process.

The **_spawn** functions can pass the child process all information about open files, including the translation mode, through the **C_FILE_INFO** entry in the environment that is passed in real mode.

The startup code normally processes this entry and then deletes it from the environment. However, if a **_spawn** function spawns a non-C process, this entry remains in the environment. Printing the environment shows graphics characters in the definition string for this entry, since the environment information is passed in binary form in real mode. It should not have any other effect on normal operations. In protected mode, the environment information is passed in text form and therefore contains no graphics characters.

You must explicitly flush (using **fflush** or **_flushall**) or close any stream prior to the **_spawn** function call.

Starting with Microsoft C version 6.0, you can control whether or not the open file information of a process will be passed to its child processes. The external variable **_fileinfo** (declared in STDLIB.H) controls the passing of **C_FILE_INFO** information. If **_fileinfo** is 0, the **C_FILE_INFO** information is not passed to the child processes. If **_fileinfo** is not 0, **C_FILE_INFO** is passed to child processes.

By default, **_fileinfo** is 0 and thus the **C_FILE_INFO** information is not passed to child processes. There are two ways to modify the default value of **_fileinfo**:

- Link the supplied object file FILEINFO.OBJ into your program. Use the /NOE option to avoid multiple symbol definitions.
- Set the **_fileinfo** variable to a nonzero value directly within your C program.

Return Value

The return value from a synchronous **_spawn** (**_P_WAIT** specified for *mode*) is the exit status of the child process.

The exit status is 0 if the process terminated normally. The exit status can be set to a nonzero value if the child process specifically calls the **exit** routine with a non-zero argument. If the child process did not explicitly set a positive exit status, a positive exit status indicates an abnormal exit with an **abort** or an interrupt. A return value of –1 indicates an error (the child process is not started). In this case, **errno** is set to one of the following values:

Value	Meaning
E2BIG	In DOS, the argument list exceeds 128 bytes, or the space required for the environment information exceeds 32K.
EINVAL	The *mode* argument is invalid.
ENOENT	The file or path name is not found.
ENOEXEC	The specified file is not executable or has an invalid executable-file format.
ENOMEM	Not enough memory is available to execute the child process.

Note that signal settings are not preserved in child processes created by calls to **_spawn** routines. The signal settings are reset to the default in the child process.

Compatibility

Standards: None

16-Bit: DOS

32-Bit: DOS32X

To ensure proper overlay initialization and termination, do not use the **setjmp** or **longjmp** function to enter or leave an overlay routine.

See Also   **abort, atexit, _exec** functions, **exit, _exit, _onexit, system**

Example
```
/* SPAWN.C: This program accepts a number in the range 1 - 8 from the
 * command line. Based on the number it receives, it executes one of the
 * eight different procedures that spawn the process named child. For
 * some of these procedures, the CHILD.EXE file must be in the
 * same directory; for others, it only has to be in the same path.
 */

#include <stdio.h>
#include <process.h>

char *my_env[] =
{
   "THIS=environment will be",
   "PASSED=to child.exe by the",
   "_SPAWNLE=and",
   "_SPAWNLPE=and",
   "_SPAWNVE=and",
   "_SPAWNVPE=functions",
   NULL
};

void main( int argc, char *argv[] )
{
   char *args[4];
   int  result;

   /* Set up parameters to be sent: */
   args[0] = "child";
   args[1] = "spawn??";
   args[2] = "two";
   args[3] = NULL;
   switch (argv[1][0])    /* Based on first letter of argument */
   {
      case '1':
         _spawnl( _P_WAIT, argv[2], argv[2], "_spawnl", "two", NULL );
         break;
      case '2':
         _spawnle( _P_WAIT, argv[2], argv[2], "_spawnle", "two",
                  NULL, my_env );
         break;
      case '3':
         _spawnlp( _P_WAIT, argv[2], argv[2], "_spawnlp", "two", NULL );
         break;
      case '4':
         _spawnlpe( _P_WAIT, argv[2], argv[2], "_spawnlpe", "two",
                  NULL, my_env );
         break;
      case '5':
         _spawnv( _P_OVERLAY, argv[2], args );
         break;
```

```
        case '6':
            _spawnve( _P_OVERLAY, argv[2], args, my_env );
            break;
        case '7':
            _spawnvp( _P_OVERLAY, argv[2], args );
            break;
        case '8':
            _spawnvpe( _P_OVERLAY, argv[2], args, my_env );
            break;
        default:
            printf( "SYNTAX: SPAWN <1-8> <childprogram>\n" );
            exit( 1 );
    }
    printf( "\n\nReturned from SPAWN!\n" );
}
```

_splitpath

Description

Breaks a path name into components.

#include <stdlib.h>

void _splitpath(char *_path_, char *_drive_, char *_dir_, char *_fname_, char *_ext_);

path	Full path name
drive	Drive letter
dir	Directory path
fname	Filename
ext	File extension

Remarks

The **_splitpath** routine breaks a full path name into its four components. The _path_ argument should point to a buffer containing the complete path name. The maximum size necessary for each buffer is specified by the manifest constants **_MAX_DRIVE**, **_MAX_DIR**, **_MAX_FNAME**, and **_MAX_EXT**, defined in STDLIB.H. The other arguments point to the buffers used to store the path-name elements:

Buffer	Description
drive	Contains the drive letter followed by a colon (:) if a drive is specified in _path_.
dir	Contains the path of subdirectories, if any, including the trailing slash. Forward slashes (/), backslashes (\ ), or both may be present in _path_.
fname	Contains the base filename without any extensions.
ext	Contains the filename extension, if any, including the leading period (.).

The return parameters will contain empty strings for any path-name components not found in _path_. You can pass a **NULL** pointer to **_splitpath** for any component you don't wish to receive.

Return Value

None.

Compatibility

Standards: None

16-Bit: DOS, QWIN, WIN, WIN DLL

32-Bit: DOS32X

See Also   _fullpath, _makepath

Example
```
/* MAKEPATH.C */
#include <stdlib.h>
#include <stdio.h>

void main( void )
{
    char path_buffer[_MAX_PATH];
    char drive[_MAX_DRIVE];
    char dir[_MAX_DIR];
    char fname[_MAX_FNAME];
    char ext[_MAX_EXT];

    _makepath( path_buffer, "c", "\\c70\\clibref\\", "makepath", "c" );
    printf( "Path created with _makepath: %s\n\n", path_buffer );
    _splitpath( path_buffer, drive, dir, fname, ext );
    printf( "Path extracted with _splitpath:\n" );
    printf( "  Drive: %s\n", drive );
    printf( "  Dir: %s\n", dir );
    printf( "  Filename: %s\n", fname );
    printf( "  Ext: %s\n", ext );
}
```

Output
```
Path created with _makepath: c:\c70\clibref\makepath.c

Path extracted with _splitpath:
  Drive: c:
  Dir: \c70\clibref\
  Filename: makepath
  Ext: .c
```

sprintf, _snprintf

Description

Write formatted data to a string.

#include <stdio.h>

int sprintf(char *buffer, const char *format [[, argument]] ...);

int _snprintf(char *buffer, size_t count, const char *format [[, argument]] ...);

buffer	Storage location for output
format	Format-control string
argument	Optional arguments
count	Maximum number of bytes to store

Remarks

The **sprintf** function formats and stores a series of characters and values in *buffer*. Each *argument* (if any) is converted and output according to the corresponding format specification in the *format*. The format consists of ordinary characters and has the same form and function as the *format* argument for the **printf** function. (See **printf** for a description of the format and arguments.) A null character is appended to the end of the characters written, but is not counted in the return value.

The **_snprintf** function differs from **sprintf** in that it stores no more than *count* characters to *buffer*.

Return Value

Both the **sprintf** and **_snprintf** functions return the number of characters stored in *buffer*, not counting the terminating null character. For **_snprintf**, if the number of bytes required to store the data exceeds *count*, then *count* bytes of data are stored in *buffer* and –1 is returned.

Compatibility

sprintf

Standards:	ANSI, UNIX
16-Bit:	DOS, QWIN, WIN
32-Bit:	DOS32X

_snprintf

Standards: None

16-Bit: DOS, QWIN, WIN

32-Bit: DOS32X

See Also   **fprintf, printf, sscanf**

Example
```
/* SPRINTF.C: This program uses sprintf to format various data and
 * place them in the string named buffer.
 */

#include <stdio.h>

void main( void )
{
   char  buffer[200], s[] = "computer", c = 'l';
   int   i = 35, j;
   float fp = 1.7320534;
   /* Format and print various data: */
   j  = sprintf( buffer,     "\tString:    %s\n", s );
   j += sprintf( buffer + j, "\tCharacter: %c\n", c );
   j += sprintf( buffer + j, "\tInteger:   %d\n", i );
   j += sprintf( buffer + j, "\tReal:      %f\n", fp );

   printf( "Output:\n%s\ncharacter count = %d\n", buffer, j );
}
```

Output
```
Output:
        String:    computer
        Character: l
        Integer:   35
        Real:      1.732053

character count = 71
```

sqrt, _ sqrtl

Description

Calculate the square root.

#include <math.h>

double sqrt(double *x* **);**

long double _ sqrtl(long double *x* **);**

x   Nonnegative floating-point value

Remarks

The **sqrt** functions calculate the square root of *x*. The **_ sqrtl** function is the 80-bit counterpart and uses an 80-bit, 10-byte coprocessor form of arguments and return values.

Return Value

The **sqrt** functions return the square-root result. If *x* is negative, the function prints a **_ DOMAIN** error message to **stderr**, sets **errno** to **EDOM**, and returns 0.

Error handling can be modified by using the **_ matherr** or **_ matherrl** routine.

Compatibility

sqrt

Standards:	ANSI, UNIX
16-Bit:	DOS, QWIN, WIN, WIN DLL
32-Bit:	DOS32X

_ sqrtl

Standards:	None
16-Bit:	DOS, QWIN, WIN, WIN DLL
32-Bit:	None

See Also

exp, log, _ matherr, pow

Example   /* SQRT.C: This program calculates a square root. */

```
#include <math.h>
#include <stdio.h>
#include <stdlib.h>

void main( void )
{
    double question = 45.35, answer;

    answer = sqrt( question );
    if( errno == EDOM )
        printf( "Domain error\n" );
    else
        printf( "The square root of %.2f is %.2f\n", question, answer );
}
```

Output   The square root of 45.35 is 6.73

srand

Description

Sets a random starting point.

#include <stdlib.h>   Required only for function declarations

void srand(unsigned int *seed* **);**

seed   Seed for random-number generation

Remarks

The **srand** function sets the starting point for generating a series of pseudorandom integers. To reinitialize the generator, use 1 as the *seed* argument. Any other value for *seed* sets the generator to a random starting point.

The **rand** function is used to retrieve the pseudorandom numbers that are generated. Calling **rand** before any call to **srand** will generate the same sequence as calling **srand** with *seed* passed as 1.

Return Value

None.

Compatibility

Standards:	ANSI, UNIX
16-Bit:	DOS, QWIN, WIN, WIN DLL
32-Bit:	DOS32X

See Also

rand

Example

```
/* RAND.C: This program seeds the random number generator with the
 * time, then displays 20 random integers.
 */

#include <stdlib.h>
#include <stdio.h>
#include <time.h>

void main( void )
{
    int i;

    /* Seed the random number generator with current time so that
     * the numbers will be different every time we run.
     */
    srand( (unsigned)time( NULL ) );

    /* Display 10 numbers. */
    for( i = 0; i < 10; i++ )
        printf( "  %6d\n", rand() );
}
```

Output

```
19471
16395
 8268
15582
 6489
28356
27042
 5276
23070
10930
```

sscanf

Description

Reads formatted data from a string.

#include <stdio.h>

int sscanf(const char *_buffer_, const char *_format_ [[, _argument_]] ...);

buffer	Stored data
format	Format-control string
argument	Optional arguments

Remarks

The **sscanf** function reads data from _buffer_ into the locations given by each _argument_. Every _argument_ must be a pointer to a variable with a type that corresponds to a type specifier in _format_. The format controls the interpretation of the input fields and has the same form and function as the _format_ argument for the **scanf** function; see **scanf** for a complete description of _format_.

Return Value

The **sscanf** function returns the number of fields that were successfully converted and assigned. The return value does not include fields that were read but not assigned.

The return value is **EOF** for an attempt to read at end-of-string. A return value of 0 means that no fields were assigned.

Compatibility

Standards:	ANSI, UNIX
16-Bit:	DOS, QWIN, WIN
32-Bit:	DOS32X

See Also

fscanf, scanf, sprintf

Example

```
/* SSCANF.C: This program uses sscanf to read data items from
 * a string named tokenstring, then displays them.
 */

#include <stdio.h>

void main( void )
{
    char   tokenstring[] = "15 12 14...";
    char   s[81];
    char   c;
    int    i;
    float  fp;

    /* Input various data from tokenstring: */
    sscanf( tokenstring, "%s", s );
    sscanf( tokenstring, "%c", &c );
    sscanf( tokenstring, "%d", &i );
    sscanf( tokenstring, "%f", &fp );

    /* Output the data read */
    printf( "String    = %s\n", s );
    printf( "Character = %c\n", c );
    printf( "Integer:  = %d\n", i );
    printf( "Real:     = %f\n", fp );
}
```

Output

```
String    = 15
Character = 1
Integer:  = 15
Real:     = 15.000000
```

_stackavail

Description

Gets the size of the stack available.

#include <malloc.h>   Required only for function declarations

size_t _stackavail(void);

Remarks

The **_stackavail** function returns the approximate size (in bytes) of the stack space available for dynamic memory allocation with **_alloca**.

Return Value

The **_stackavail** function returns the size in bytes as an unsigned integer value.

Compatibility

Standards: None
16-Bit: DOS, QWIN, WIN, WIN DLL
32-Bit: None

Example

```
/* ALLOCA.C: Checks the stack space available before and after using
 * _alloca to allocate space on the stack. As _alloca is incompatible
 * with optimizing, compile with optimizations disabled (/Od).
 */
#include <malloc.h>
#include <stdio.h>

void main( void )
{
    char *buffer;

    printf( "Bytes available on stack: %u\n", _stackavail() );

    /* Allocate memory for string. */
    buffer = _alloca( 120 * sizeof( char ) );
    printf( "Enter a string: " );
    gets( buffer );
    printf( "You entered: %s\n", buffer );

    printf( "Bytes available on stack: %u\n", _stackavail() );
}
```

Output

```
Bytes available on stack: 2028
Enter a string: How much stack space will this string take?
You entered: How much stack space will this string take?
Bytes available on stack: 1902
```

_stat

Description

Gets status information on a file.

#include <sys\types.h>

#include <sys\stat.h>

int _stat(char *_pathname_, struct _stat *_buffer_);

pathname	Path name of existing file
buffer	Pointer to structure that receives results

Remarks

The **_stat** function obtains information about the file or directory specified by _pathname_ and stores it in the structure pointed to by _buffer_. The **_stat** structure, defined in the file SYS\STAT.H, includes the following fields:

Field	Value
st_atime	Time of last access of file.
st_ctime	Time of creation of file.
st_dev	Drive number of the disk containing the file (same as **st_rdev**). Real mode only.
st_mode	Bit mask for file-mode information. The **_S_IFDIR** bit is set if _pathname_ specifies a directory; the **_S_IFREG** bit is set if _pathname_ specifies an ordinary file. User read/write bits are set according to the file's permission mode; user execute bits are set according to the filename extension.
st_mtime	Time of last modification of file.
st_nlink	Always 1.
st_rdev	Drive number of the disk containing the file (same as **st_dev**). Real mode only.
st_size	Size of the file in bytes.

Note that if _pathname_ refers to a device, the size and time fields in the **_stat** structure are not meaningful. Also, as STAT.H uses the **dev_t** type, which is defined in TYPES.H, you must include TYPES.H before STAT.H in your code.

Return Value

The **_stat** function returns 0 if the file-status information is obtained. A return value of –1 indicates an error; also, **errno** is set to **ENOENT**, indicating that the filename or path name could not be found.

Compatibility

Standards: UNIX

16-Bit: DOS, QWIN, WIN, WIN DLL

32-Bit: DOS32X

Use **_stat** for compatibility with ANSI naming conventions of non-ANSI functions. Use **stat** and link with OLDNAMES.LIB for UNIX compatibility.

See Also   **_access, _fstat**

Example

```
/* STAT.C: This program uses the _stat function to report information
 * about the file named STAT.C.
 */

#include <time.h>
#include <sys\types.h>
#include <sys\stat.h>
#include <stdio.h>

void main( void )
{
    struct _stat buf;
    int  fh, result;
    char buffer[] = "A line to output";

    /* Get data associated with "stat.c": */
    result = _stat( "stat.c", &buf );

    /* Check if statistics are valid: */
    if( result != 0 )
       perror( "Problem getting information" );
    else
    {
       /* Output some of the statistics: */
       printf( "File size     : %ld\n", buf.st_size );
       printf( "Drive         : %c:\n", buf.st_dev + 'A' );
       printf( "Time modified : %s", ctime( &buf.st_atime ) );
    }
}
```

Output

```
File size     : 761
Drive         : C:
Time modified : Mon Jun 14 12:20:08 1999
```

_status87

Description   Gets the floating-point status word.

#include <float.h>

unsigned int _status87(void);

Remarks   The **_status87** function gets the floating-point status word. The status word is a combination of the 8087/80287/80387 status word and other conditions detected by the 8087/80287/80387 exception handler, such as floating-point stack overflow and underflow.

Return Value   The bits in the value returned indicate the floating-point status. See the FLOAT.H include file for a complete definition of the bits returned by **_status87**.

Note that many of the math library functions modify the 8087/80287 status word, with unpredictable results. Return values from **_clear87** and **_status87** become more reliable as fewer floating-point operations are performed between known states of the floating-point status word.

Compatibility   Standards: None
                      16-Bit: DOS, QWIN, WIN, WIN DLL
                      32-Bit: DOS32X

See Also   **_clear87, _control87**

Example
```
/* STATUS87.C: This program creates various floating-point errors and
 * then uses _status87 to display messages indicating these problems.
 * Compile this program with optimizations disabled (/Od). Otherwise,
 * the optimizer will remove the code related to the unused floating-
 * point values.
 */

#include <stdio.h>
#include <float.h>
```

```
void main( void )
{
    double a = 1e-40, b;
    float  x, y;

    printf( "Status = %.4x - clear\n",_status87() );

    /* Assignment into y is inexact & underflows: */
    y = a;
    printf( "Status = %.4x - inexact, underflow\n", _status87() );

    /* y is denormal: */
    b = y;
    printf( "Status = %.4x - inexact underflow, denormal\n", _status87() );

    /* Clear user 8087: */
    _clear87();
}
```

Output

```
Status = 0000 - clear
Status = 0030 - inexact, underflow
Status = 0032 - inexact underflow, denormal
```

strcat, _fstrcat

Description

Append a string.

#include <string.h>   Required only for function declarations

char *strcat(char *string1, const char *string2);

char __far * __far _fstrcat(char __far *string1, const char __far *string2);

string1   Destination string

string2   Source string

Remarks

The **strcat** and **_fstrcat** functions append *string2* to *string1*, terminate the resulting string with a null character, and return a pointer to the concatenated string (*string1*).

The **strcat** and **_fstrcat** functions operate on null-terminated strings. The string arguments to these functions are expected to contain a null character ('\0') marking the end of the string. No overflow checking is performed when strings are copied or appended.

The **_fstrcat** function is a model-independent (large-model) form of the **strcat** function. The behavior and return value of **_fstrcat** are identical to those of the model-dependent function **strcat**, with the exception that the arguments and return values are far pointers.

Return Value

The return values for these functions are described above.

Compatibility

strcat

Standards: ANSI, UNIX
16-Bit: DOS, QWIN, WIN, WIN DLL
32-Bit: DOS32X

_fstrcat

Standards: None

16-Bit: DOS, QWIN, WIN, WIN DLL

32-Bit: None

See Also   **strncat, strncmp, strncpy, _strnicmp, strrchr, strspn**

Example
```
/* STRCPY.C: This program uses strcpy and strcat to build a phrase. */

#include <string.h>
#include <stdio.h>

void main( void )
{
    char string[80];

    strcpy( string, "Hello world from " );
    strcat( string, "strcpy " );
    strcat( string, "and " );
    strcat( string, "strcat!" );
    printf( "String = %s\n", string );
}
```

Output
```
String = Hello world from strcpy and strcat!
```

strchr, _fstrchr

Description   Find a character in a string.

#include <string.h>   Required only for function declarations

char *strchr(const char **string***, int** *c* **);**

char __far * __far _fstrchr(const char __far **string***, int** *c* **);**

string	Source string
c	Character to be located

Remarks   The **strchr** and **_fstrchr** functions return a pointer to the first occurrence of *c* (converted to **char**) in *string*. The converted character *c* may be the null character (**'\0'**); the terminating null character of *string* is included in the search. The function returns **NULL** if the character is not found.

The **strchr** and **_fstrchr** functions operate on null-terminated strings. The string arguments to these functions are expected to contain a null character (**'\0'**) marking the end of the string.

The **_fstrchr** function is a model-independent (large-model) form of the **strchr** function. The behavior and return value of **_fstrchr** are identical to those of the model-dependent function **strchr**, with the exception that the arguments and return values are far.

Return Value   The return values for these functions are described above.

Compatibility   **strchr**

Standards:	ANSI, UNIX
16-Bit:	DOS, QWIN, WIN, WIN DLL
32-Bit:	DOS32X

_fstrchr

Standards:	None
16-Bit:	DOS, QWIN, WIN, WIN DLL
32-Bit:	None

See Also   **strcspn, strncat, strncmp, strncpy, _strnicmp, strpbrk, strrchr, strspn, strstr**

Example

```c
/* STRCHR.C: This program illustrates searching for a character with
 * strchr (search forward) or strrchr (search backward).
 */

#include <string.h>
#include <stdio.h>

int  ch = 'r';
char string[] = "The quick brown dog jumps over the lazy fox";
char fmt1[] =   "         1         2         3         4         5";
char fmt2[] =   "12345678901234567890123456789012345678901234567890";

void main( void )
{
   char *pdest;
   int result;

   printf( "String to be searched: \n\t\t%s\n", string );
   printf( "\t\t%s\n\t\t%s\n\n", fmt1, fmt2 );
   printf( "Search char:\t%c\n", ch );

   /* Search forward. */
   pdest = strchr( string, ch );
   result = pdest - string + 1;
   if( pdest != NULL )
      printf( "Result:\tfirst %c found at position %d\n\n", ch, result );
   else
      printf( "Result:\t%c not found\n" );

   /* Search backward. */
   pdest = strrchr( string, ch );
   result = pdest - string + 1;
   if( pdest != NULL )
      printf( "Result:\tlast %c found at position %d\n\n", ch, result );
   else
      printf( "Result:\t%c not found\n" );
}
```

Output

```
String to be searched:
                The quick brown dog jumps over the lazy fox
                         1         2         3         4         5
                12345678901234567890123456789012345678901234567890

Search char:    r
Result: first r found at position 12

Result: last r found at position 30
```

strcmp, _fstrcmp

Description

Compare strings.

#include <string.h>   Required only for function declarations

int strcmp(const char **string1***, const char ****string2***);**

int __far _fstrcmp(const char __far **string1***, const char __far ****string2***);**

string1	String to compare
string2	String to compare

Remarks

The **strcmp** and **_fstrcmp** functions compare *string1* and *string2* lexicographically and return a value indicating their relationship, as follows:

Value	Meaning
< 0	*string1* less than *string2*
= 0	*string1* identical to *string2*
> 0	*string1* greater than *string2*

The **strcmp** and **_fstrcmp** functions operate on null-terminated strings. The string arguments to these functions are expected to contain a null character ('**\0**') marking the end of the string.

The **_fstrcmp** function is a model-independent (large-model) form of the **strcmp** function. The behavior and return value of **_fstrcmp** are identical to those of the model-dependent function **strcmp**, with the exception that the arguments are far pointers.

Both the **_stricmp** function (described later in this book) and the **_strcmpi** function compare strings by first converting them to their lowercase forms.

Note that two strings containing characters located between 'Z' and 'a' in the ASCII table ('[', '\', ']', '^', '_', and '`') compare differently depending on their case. For example, the two strings, `"ABCDE"` and `"ABCD^"`, compare one way if the comparison is lowercase (`"abcde"` > `"abcd^"`) and compare the other way (`"ABCDE"` < `"ABCD^"`) if it is uppercase.

Return Value

The return values for these functions are described above.

Compatibility   **strcmp**

Standards: ANSI, UNIX
16-Bit: DOS, QWIN, WIN, WIN DLL
32-Bit: DOS32X

_fstrcmp

Standards: None
16-Bit: DOS, QWIN, WIN, WIN DLL
32-Bit: None

See Also   **memcmp, _memicmp, strncat, strncmp, strncpy, _strnicmp, strrchr, strspn**

Example
```
/* STRCMP.C */
#include <string.h>
#include <stdio.h>

char string1[] = "The quick brown dog jumps over the lazy fox";
char string2[] = "The QUICK brown dog jumps over the lazy fox";

void main( void )
{
    char tmp[20];
    int result;

    /* Case sensitive */
    printf( "Compare strings:\n\t%s\n\t%s\n\n", string1, string2 );
    result = strcmp string1, string2 );
    if( result > 0 )
        strcpy( tmp, "greater than" );
    else if( result < 0 )
        strcpy( tmp, "less than" );
    else
        strcpy( tmp, "equal to" );
    printf( "\tstrcmp:   String 1 is %s string 2\n", tmp );

    /* Case insensitive (could use equivalent _stricmp) */
    result = _stricmp( string1, string2 );
    if( result > 0 )
        strcpy( tmp, "greater than" );
    else if( result < 0 )
        strcpy( tmp, "less than" );
    else
        strcpy( tmp, "equal to" );
    printf( "\t_stricmp:   String 1 is %s string 2\n", tmp );
}
```

Output

```
Compare strings:
        The quick brown dog jumps over the lazy fox
        The QUICK brown dog jumps over the lazy fox

        strcmp:   String 1 is greater than string 2
        _stricmp:  String 1 is equal to string 2
```

strcoll

Description   Compares strings using locale-specific information.

#include <string.h>   Required only for function declarations

int strcoll(const char *string1**, const char ***string2**);**

string1   String to compare
string2   String to compare

Remarks   The **strcoll** function compares *string1* and *string2* in a manner determined by the **LC_COLLATE** macro and returns a value indicating their relationship, as follows:

Value	Meaning
< 0	*string1* less than *string2*
= 0	*string1* identical to *string2*
> 0	*string1* greater than *string2*

For more information on the **LC_COLLATE** macro, see the **setlocale** function.

The **strcoll** function operates on null-terminated strings. The string arguments to these functions are expected to contain a null character ('\0') marking the end of the string.

The **strcoll** function differs from **strcmp** in that it uses locale-specific information to provide locale-specific collating sequences.

Return Value   The return value for this function is described above.

Compatibility   Standards: ANSI
16-Bit: DOS, QWIN, WIN, WIN DLL
32-Bit: DOS32X

See Also   **localeconv, setlocale, strcmp, strncmp, strxfrm**

strcpy, _ fstrcpy

Description   Copy a string.

#include <string.h>   Required only for function declarations

char *strcpy(char *string1**, const char ***string2**);**

char _ _ far * _ _ far _ fstrcpy(char _ _ far *string1**, const char _ _ far ***string2**);**

string1   Destination string
string2   Source string

Remarks   The **strcpy** function copies *string2*, including the terminating null character, to the location specified by *string1*, and returns *string1*.

The **strcpy** and **_ fstrcpy** functions operate on null-terminated strings. The string arguments to these functions are expected to contain a null character ('**\0**') marking the end of the string. No overflow checking is performed when strings are copied or appended.

The **_ fstrcpy** function is a model-independent (large-model) form of the **strcpy** function. The behavior and return value of **_ fstrcpy** are identical to those of the model-dependent function **strcpy**, with the exception that the arguments and return values are far pointers.

Return Value   The return values for these functions are described above.

Compatibility   **strcpy**

Standards: ANSI, UNIX
16-Bit: DOS, QWIN, WIN, WIN DLL
32-Bit: DOS32X

_ fstrcpy

Standards: None
16-Bit: DOS, QWIN, WIN, WIN DLL
32-Bit: None

See Also   **strcat, strcmp, strncat, strncmp, strncpy, _ strnicmp, strrchr, strspn**

Example   ```
/* STRCPY.C: This program uses strcpy and strcat to build a phrase. */

#include <string.h>
#include <stdio.h>

void main(void)
{
   char string[80];

   strcpy(string, "Hello world from ");
   strcat(string, "strcpy ");
   strcat(string, "and ");
   strcat(string, "strcat!");
   printf("String = %s\n", string);
}
```

**Output**     ```
String = Hello world from strcpy and strcat!
```

strcspn, _fstrcspn

Description

Find a substring in a string.

#include <string.h>   Required only for function declarations

size_t **strcspn**(const char *string1*, const char *string2*);

size_t __far **_fstrcspn**(const char __far *string1*, const char __far *string2*);

string1	Source string
string2	Character set

Remarks

The **strcspn** functions return the index of the first character in *string1* belonging to the set of characters specified by *string2*. This value is equivalent to the length of the initial substring of *string1* consisting entirely of characters not in *string2*. Terminating null characters are not considered in the search. If *string1* begins with a character from *string2*, **strcspn** returns 0.

The **strcspn** and **_fstrcspn** functions operate on null-terminated strings. The string arguments to these functions are expected to contain a null character ('\0') marking the end of the string.

The **_fstrcspn** function is a model-independent (large-model) form of the **strcspn** function. The behavior and return value of **_fstrcspn** are identical to those of the model-dependent function **strcspn**, with the exception that the arguments and return values are far.

Return Value

The return values for these functions are described above.

Compatibility

strcspn

Standards:	ANSI, UNIX
16-Bit:	DOS, QWIN, WIN, WIN DLL
32-Bit:	DOS32X

_fstrcspn

Standards: None

16-Bit: DOS, QWIN, WIN, WIN DLL

32-Bit: None

See Also   **strncat, strncmp, strncpy, _strnicmp, strrchr, strspn**

Example
```
/* STRCSPN.C */
#include <string.h>
#include <stdio.h>

void main( void )
{
    char string[] = "xyzabc";
    int  pos;

    pos = strcspn( string, "abc" );
    printf( "First a, b or c in %s is at character %d\n", string, pos );
}
```

Output   First a, b or c in xyzabc is at character 3

_strdate

Description

Copies a date to a buffer.

#include <time.h>

char *_strdate(char *_datestr_);

datestr   Current date

Remarks

The **_strdate** function copies the date to the buffer pointed to by _datestr_, formatted

mm/dd/yy

where mm is two digits representing the month, dd is two digits representing the
day of the month, and yy is the last two digits of the year. For example, the string

12/05/99

represents December 5, 1999.

The buffer must be at least nine bytes long.

Return Value

The **_strdate** function returns a pointer to the resulting text string _datestr_.

Compatibility

Standards: None
16-Bit: DOS, QWIN, WIN, WIN DLL
32-Bit: DOS32X

See Also

asctime, ctime, gmtime, localtime, mktime, time, _tzset

Example
```
/* STRTIME.C */
#include <time.h>
#include <stdio.h>

void main( void )
{
    char dbuffer [9];
    char tbuffer [9];

    _strdate( dbuffer );
    printf( "The current date is %s \n", dbuffer );
    _strtime( tbuffer );
    printf( "The current time is %s \n", tbuffer );
}
```

Output
```
The current date is 06/20/99
The current time is 09:33:13
```

_strdup Functions

Description

Duplicate strings.

#include <string.h> Required only for function declarations

char *_strdup(const char *string);

char __far * __far _fstrdup(const char __far *string);

char __near * __far _nstrdup(const char __far *string);

string Source string

Remarks

The **_strdup** function allocates storage space (with a call to **malloc**) for a copy of *string* and returns a pointer to the storage space containing the copied string. The function returns **NULL** if storage cannot be allocated.

The **_fstrdup** and **_nstrdup** functions provide complete control over the heap used for string duplication. The **_strdup** function returns a pointer to a copy of the string argument. The space for the string is allocated from the heap specified by the memory model in use. In large data models (that is, compact-, large-, and huge-model programs), **_strdup** allocates space from the far heap. In small data models (tiny-, small-, and medium-model programs), **_strdup** allocates space from the near heap.

The **_strdup**, **_fstrdup**, and **_nstrdup** functions operate on null-terminated strings. The string arguments to these functions are expected to contain a null character ('\0') marking the end of the string.

The **_fstrdup** function returns a far pointer to a copy of the string allocated in far memory (the far heap). As with the other model-independent functions, the syntax and semantics of these functions correspond to those of **_strdup** except for the sizes of the arguments and return values. The **_nstrdup** function returns a near pointer to a copy of the string allocated in the near heap (in the default data segment).

Return Value

The return values for these functions are described above.

Compatibility   **_strdup**

Standards: None

16-Bit: DOS, QWIN, WIN, WIN DLL

32-Bit: DOS32X

_fstrdup, _nstrdup

Standards: None

16-Bit: DOS, QWIN, WIN, WIN DLL

32-Bit: None

See Also   strcat, strcmp, strncat, strncmp, strncpy, _strnicmp, strrchr, strspn

Example
```
/* STRDUP.C */
#include <string.h>
#include <stdio.h>
#include <conio.h>
#include <dos.h>

void main( void )
{
    char buffer[] = "This is the buffer text";
    char *newstring;

    printf( "Original: %s\n", buffer );
    newstring = _strdup( buffer );
    printf( "Copy:     %s\n", newstring );
}
```

Output
```
Original: This is the buffer text
Copy:     This is the buffer text
```

strerror, _strerror

Description

Gets a system error message (**strerror**) or prints a user-supplied error message (**_strerror**).

#include <string.h>   Required only for function declarations

char *strerror(int *errnum* **);**

char *_strerror(char * *string* **);**

errnum	Error number
string	User-supplied message

Remarks

The **strerror** function maps *errnum* to an error-message string, returning a pointer to the string. The function itself does not actually print the message; for that, you need to call an output function such as **fprintf**:

```
if (( _access( "datafile",2 )) == -1 )
    fprintf( stderr, strerror(NULL) );
```

If *string* is passed as **NULL**, **_strerror** returns a pointer to a string containing the system error message for the last library call that produced an error. The error-message string is terminated by the newline character (**'\n'**).

If *string* is not equal to **NULL**, then **_strerror** returns a pointer to a string containing (in order) your string message, a colon, a space, the system error message for the last library call producing an error, and a newline character. Your string message can be a maximum of 94 bytes long.

Unlike **perror**, **_strerror** alone does not print any messages. To print the message returned by **_strerror** to **stderr**, your program will need an **fprintf** statement, as shown in the following lines:

```
if (( _access( "datafile",2 )) == -1 )
    fprintf( stderr, _strerror(NULL) );
```

The actual error number for **_strerror** is stored in the variable **errno**. The system error messages are accessed through the variable **sys_errlist**, which is an array of messages ordered by error number. The **_strerror** function accesses the appropriate error message by using the **errno** value as an index to the variable **sys_errlist**. The value of the variable **sys_nerr** is defined as the maximum number of elements in the **sys_errlist** array.

To produce accurate results, **_strerror** should be called immediately after a library routine returns with an error. Otherwise, the **errno** value may be overwritten by subsequent calls.

Note that the **_strerror** function under Microsoft C version 5.0 is identical to the version 4.0 **strerror** function. The name was altered to permit the inclusion in Microsoft C version 5.0 of the ANSI-conforming **strerror** function. The **_strerror** function is not part of the ANSI definition but is instead a Microsoft extension to it; it should not be used where portability is desired. For ANSI compatibility, use **strerror** instead.

Return Value   The **strerror** and **_strerror** functions return a pointer to the error-message string. The string can be overwritten by subsequent calls to **strerror** or **_strerror**, respectively.

Compatibility   **strerror**

Standards:	ANSI
16-Bit:	DOS, QWIN, WIN, WIN DLL
32-Bit:	DOS32X

_strerror

Standards:	None
16-Bit:	DOS, QWIN, WIN, WIN DLL
32-Bit:	DOS32X

See Also   **clearerr, ferror, perror**

Example   See the example for **perror**.

strftime

Description

Formats a time string.

#include <time.h>   Required only for function declarations

size_t strftime(char *string*, **size_t** *maxsize*, **const char** *format*,
     const struct tm *timeptr* **);**

string	Output string
maxsize	Maximum length of string
format	Format control string
timeptr	**tm** data structure

Remarks

The **strftime** function formats the **tm** time value in *timeptr* according to the supplied *format* argument and stores the result in the buffer *string*. At most, *maxsize* characters are placed in the string.

The *format* argument consists of one or more codes; as in **printf**, the formatting codes are preceded by a **%** sign. Characters that do not begin with a **%** sign are copied unchanged to *string*. The **LC_TIME** category of the current locale affects the output formatting of **strftime**.

The formatting codes for **strftime** are listed below:

Format	Description
%a	Abbreviated weekday name
%A	Full weekday name
%b	Abbreviated month name
%B	Full month name
%c	Date and time representation appropriate for the locale
%d	Day of the month as a decimal number (01 – 31)
%H	Hour in 24-hour format (00 – 23)
%I	Hour in 12-hour format (01 – 12)
%j	Day of the year as a decimal number (001 – 366)
%m	Month as a decimal number (01 – 12)
%M	Minute as a decimal number (00 – 59)
%p	Current locale's AM/PM indicator for a 12-hour clock

Format	Description
%S	Second as a decimal number (00 – 59)
%U	Week of the year as a decimal number; with Sunday as the first day of the week (00 – 51)
%w	Weekday as a decimal number (0 – 6; Sunday is 0)
%W	Week of the year as a decimal number; with Monday as the first day of the week (00 – 51)
%x	Date representation for current locale
%X	Time representation for current locale
%y	Year without the century as a decimal number (00 – 99)
%Y	Year with the century as a decimal number
%z	Time zone name or abbreviation; no characters if time zone is unknown
%%	Percent sign

Return Value

The **strftime** function returns the number of characters placed in *string* if the total number of resulting characters, including the terminating null, is not more than *maxsize*.

Otherwise, **strftime** returns 0, and the contents of the string are indeterminate.

Compatibility

Standards: ANSI

16-Bit: DOS, QWIN, WIN

32-Bit: DOS32X

See Also

localeconv, setlocale, strcoll, strxfrm

Example

See the example for **time**.

_stricmp, _fstricmp

Description

Perform a lowercase comparison of strings.

#include <string.h>   Required only for function declarations

int _stricmp(const char * *string1* **, const char *** *string2* **);**

int __far _fstricmp(const char __far * *string1* **, const char __far *** *string2* **);**

string1	String to compare
string2	String to compare

Remarks

The **_stricmp** and **_fstricmp** functions perform a lexicographical comparison of lowercase versions of *string1* and *string2* and return a value indicating their relationship, as follows:

Value	Meaning
< 0	*string1* less than *string2*
= 0	*string1* identical to *string2*
> 0	*string1* greater than *string2*

Note that two strings containing characters located between 'Z' and 'a' in the ASCII table ('[', '\', ']', '^', '_', and '`') compare differently depending on their case. For example, the two strings, `"ABCDE"` and `"ABCD^"`, compare one way if the comparison is lowercase (`"abcde"` > `"abcd^"`) and compare the other way (`"ABCDE"` < `"ABCD^"`) if it is uppercase.

The **_stricmp** and **_fstricmp** functions operate on null-terminated strings. The string arguments to these functions are expected to contain a null character (**'\0'**) marking the end of the string.

The **_fstricmp** function is a model-independent (large-model) form of the **_stricmp** function. The behavior and return value of **_fstricmp** are identical to those of the model-dependent function **_stricmp**, with the exception that the arguments are far pointers.

The **_strcmpi** function is functionally equivalent to **_stricmp**. It is included in STRING.H for compatibility with previous versions of Microsoft C. The preferred form is **_stricmp**.

The **strcmp** function is a case-sensitive version of **_stricmp**.

Return Value   The return values for these functions are described above.

Compatibility   **_stricmp**

Standards: None
16-Bit: DOS, QWIN, WIN, WIN DLL
32-Bit: DOS32X

_fstricmp

Standards: None
16-Bit: DOS, QWIN, WIN, WIN DLL
32-Bit: None

See Also   **memcmp, _memicmp, strcat, strcpy, strncat, strncmp, strncpy, _strnicmp, strrchr, _strset, strspn**

Example   See the example for **strcmp**.

strlen, _fstrlen

Description

Get the length of a string.

#include <string.h>   Required only for function declarations

size_t strlen(const char **string**);

size_t _fstrlen(const char __far **string**);

string   Null-terminated string

Remarks

The **strlen** and **_fstrlen** functions return the length in bytes of *string*, not including the terminating null character (**'\0'**).

The **_fstrlen** function is a model-independent (large-model) form of the **strlen** function. The behavior and return value of **_fstrlen** are identical to those of the model-dependent function **strlen**, with the exception that the argument is a far pointer.

Return Value

These functions return the string length. There is no error return.

Compatibility

strlen

Standards:	ANSI, UNIX
16-Bit:	DOS, QWIN, WIN, WIN DLL
32-Bit:	DOS32X

_fstrlen

Standards:	None
16-Bit:	DOS, QWIN, WIN, WIN DLL
32-Bit:	None

Example

```
/* STRLEN.C */
#include <string.h>
#include <stdio.h>
#include <conio.h>
#include <dos.h>

void main( void )
{
    char buffer[61] = "How long am I?";
    int  len;

    len = strlen( buffer );
    printf( "'%s' is %d characters long\n", buffer, len );
}
```

Output

```
'How long am I?' is 14 characters long
```

_ strlwr, _ fstrlwr

Description

Convert a string to lowercase.

#include <string.h>   Required only for function declarations

char *_strlwr(char *_string_);

char __far * __far _fstrlwr(char __far *_string_);

string   String to be converted

Remarks

The **_ strlwr** and **_ fstrlwr** functions convert any uppercase letters in the given null-terminated _string_ to lowercase. Other characters are not affected.

The **_ fstrlwr** function is a model-independent (large-model) form of the **_ strlwr** function. The behavior and return value of **_ fstrlwr** are identical to those of the model-dependent function **_ strlwr**, with the exception that the argument and return values are far pointers.

Return Value

These functions return a pointer to the converted string. There is no error return.

Compatibility

_ strlwr

Standards: None
16-Bit: DOS, QWIN, WIN, WIN DLL
32-Bit: DOS32X

_ fstrlwr

Standards: None
16-Bit: DOS, QWIN, WIN, WIN DLL
32-Bit: None

See Also

_ strupr

Example

```
/* STRLWR.C: This program uses _strlwr and _strupr to create
 * uppercase and lowercase copies of a mixed-case string.
 */

#include <string.h>
#include <stdio.h>

void main( void )
{
    char string[100] = "The String to End All Strings!";
    char *copy1, *copy2;

    copy1 = _strlwr( _strdup( string ) );
    copy2 = _strupr( _strdup( string ) );
    printf( "Mixed: %s\n", string );
    printf( "Lower: %s\n", copy1 );
    printf( "Upper: %s\n", copy2 );
}
```

Output

```
Mixed: The String to End All Strings!
Lower: the string to end all strings!
Upper: THE STRING TO END ALL STRINGS!
```

strncat, _fstrncat

Description   Append characters of a string.

#include <string.h>   Required only for function declarations

char *strncat(char * *string1* **, const char *** *string2* **, size_t** *count* **);**

char __far * __far _fstrncat(char __far * *string1* **, const char __far *** *string2* **, size_t** *count* **);**

string1	Destination string
string2	Source string
count	Number of characters appended

Remarks   The **strncat** and **_fstrncat** functions append, at most, the first *count* characters of *string2* to *string1*, terminate the resulting string with a null character ('**\0**'), and return a pointer to the concatenated string (*string1*). If *count* is greater than the length of *string2*, the length of *string2* is used in place of *count*.

The **_fstrncat** function is a model-independent (large-model) form of the **strncat** function. The behavior and return value of **_fstrncat** are identical to those of the model-dependent function **strncat**, with the exception that all the pointer arguments and return values are far pointers.

Return Value   The return values for these functions are described above.

Compatibility   **strncat**

Standards: ANSI, UNIX
16-Bit: DOS, QWIN, WIN, WIN DLL
32-Bit: DOS32X

_fstrncat

Standards: None
16-Bit: DOS, QWIN, WIN, WIN DLL
32-Bit: None

See Also   **strcat, strcmp, strcpy, strncmp, strncpy, _strnicmp, strrchr, _strset, strspn**

Example

```
/* STRNCAT.C */
#include <string.h>
#include <stdio.h>

void main( void )
{
    char string[80] = "This is the initial string!";
    char suffix[] = " extra text to add to the string...";

    /* Combine strings with no more than 19 characters of suffix: */
    printf( "Before: %s\n", string );
    strncat( string, suffix, 19 );
    printf( "After:  %s\n", string );
}
```

Output

```
Before: This is the initial string!
After:  This is the initial string! extra text to add
```

strncmp, _fstrncmp

Description

Compare characters of two strings.

#include <string.h>   Required only for function declarations

int strncmp(const char *string1*, **const char** *string2*, **size_t** *count* **);**

int _ _far _fstrncmp(const char _ _far *string1*, **const char _ _far** *string2*, **size_t** *count* **);**

string1	String to compare
string2	String to compare
count	Number of characters compared

Remarks

The **strncmp** and **_fstrncmp** functions lexicographically compare, at most, the first *count* characters of *string1* and *string2* and return a value indicating the relationship between the substrings, as listed below:

Value	Meaning
< 0	*string1* less than *string2*
= 0	*string1* equivalent to *string2*
> 0	*string1* greater than *string2*

The **_strnicmp** function is a case-insensitive version of **strncmp**.

The **_fstrncmp** function is a model-independent (large-model) form of the **strncmp** function. The behavior and return value of **_fstrncmp** are identical to those of the model-dependent function **strncmp**, with the exception that all the arguments and return values are far.

Return Value

The return values for these functions are described above.

Compatibility

strncmp

Standards: ANSI, UNIX

16-Bit: DOS, QWIN, WIN, WIN DLL

32-Bit: DOS32X

_fstrncmp

Standards: None

16-Bit: DOS, QWIN, WIN, WIN DLL

32-Bit: None

See Also   **strcat, strcmp, strcpy, strncat, strncpy, strrchr, _strset, strspn**

Example
```c
/* STRNCMP.C */
#include <string.h>
#include <stdio.h>

char string1[] = "The quick brown dog jumps over the lazy fox";
char string2[] = "The QUICK brown fox jumps over the lazy dog";

void main( void )
{
   char tmp[20];
   int result;

   printf( "Compare strings:\n\t\t%s\n\t\t%s\n\n", string1, string2 );

   printf( "Function:\tstrncmp (first 10 characters only)\n" );
   result = strncmp( string1, string2 , 10 );
   if( result > 0 )
      strcpy( tmp, "greater than" );
   else if( result < 0 )
      strcpy( tmp, "less than" );
   else
      strcpy( tmp, "equal to" );
   printf( "Result:\t\tString 1 is %s string 2\n\n", tmp );

   printf( "Function:\t_strnicmp (first 10 characters only)\n" );
   result = _strnicmp( string1, string2, 10 );
   if( result > 0 )
      strcpy( tmp, "greater than" );
   else if( result < 0 )
      strcpy( tmp, "less than" );
   else
      strcpy( tmp, "equal to" );
   printf( "Result:\t\tString 1 is %s string 2\n\n", tmp );
}
```

Output
```
Compare strings:
                The quick brown dog jumps over the lazy fox
                The QUICK brown fox jumps over the lazy dog

Function:       strncmp (first 10 characters only)
Result:         String 1 is greater than string 2

Function:       _strnicmp (first 10 characters only)
Result:         String 1 is equal to string 2
```

strncpy, _fstrncpy

Description   Copy characters of one string to another.

#include <string.h>   Required only for function declarations

char *strncpy(char *string1, const char *string2, size_t count);

char __far * __far _fstrncpy(char __far *string1, const char __far *string2,
    size_t count);

string1   Destination string
string2   Source string
count   Number of characters copied

Remarks   The **strncpy** and **_fstrncpy** functions copy count characters of string2 to string1
and return string1. If count is less than the length of string2, a null character ('\0')
is not appended automatically to the copied string. If count is greater than the
length of string2, the string1 result is padded with null characters ('\0') up to
length count.

Note that the behavior of **strncpy** and **_fstrncpy** is undefined if the address
ranges of the source and destination strings overlap.

The **_fstrncpy** function is a model-independent (large-model) form of the **strncpy**
function. The behavior and return value of **_fstrncpy** are identical to those of the
model-dependent function **strncpy**, with the exception that all the arguments and
return values are far.

Return Value   The return values for these functions are described above.

Compatibility   **strncpy**

Standards: ANSI, UNIX
16-Bit: DOS, QWIN, WIN, WIN DLL
32-Bit: DOS32X

_fstrncpy

Standards: None

16-Bit: DOS, QWIN, WIN, WIN DLL

32-Bit: None

See Also   **strcat, strcmp, strcpy, strncat, strncmp, _strnicmp, strrchr, _strset, strspn**

Example

```c
/* STRNCPY.C */
#include <string.h>
#include <stdio.h>

void main( void )
{
    char string[100] = "Cats are nice usually";

    printf("Before: %s\n", string );
    strncpy( string, "Dogs", 4 );
    strncpy( string + 9, "mean", 4 );
    printf("After:  %s\n", string );
}
```

Output

```
Before: Cats are nice usually
After:  Dogs are mean usually
```

_strnicmp, _fstrnicmp

Description   Compare characters of two strings without regard to case.

#include <string.h>   Required only for function declarations

int _strnicmp(const char *_string1_, const char *_string2_, size_t _count_);

int __far _fstrnicmp(const char __far *_string1_, const char __far *_string2_, size_t _count_);

string1	String to compare
string2	String to compare
count	Number of characters compared

Remarks   The **_strnicmp** and **_fstrnicmp** functions lexicographically compare (without regard to case), at most, the first _count_ characters of _string1_ and _string2_ and return a value indicating the relationship between the substrings, as listed below:

Value	Meaning
< 0	_string1_ less than _string2_
= 0	_string1_ equivalent to _string2_
> 0	_string1_ greater than _string2_

The **strncmp** function is a case-sensitive version of **_strnicmp**.

Note that two strings containing characters located between 'Z' and 'a' in the ASCII table ('[', '\', ']', '^', '_', and '`') compare differently depending on their case. For example, the two strings, `"ABCDE"` and `"ABCD^"`, compare one way if the comparison is lowercase (`"abcde"` > `"abcd^"`) and compare the other way (`"ABCDE"` < `"ABCD^"`) if it is uppercase.

The **_fstrnicmp** function is a model-independent (large-model) form of the **_strnicmp** function. The behavior and return value of **_fstrnicmp** are identical to those of the model-dependent function **_strnicmp**, with the exception that all the arguments and return values are far.

Return Value   The return values for these functions are described above.

Compatibility

_ strnicmp

Standards:	None
16-Bit:	DOS, QWIN, WIN, WIN DLL
32-Bit:	DOS32X

_ fstrnicmp

Standards:	None
16-Bit:	DOS, QWIN, WIN, WIN DLL
32-Bit:	None

See Also   **strcat, strcmp, strcpy, strncat, strncpy, strrchr, _ strset, strspn**

Example   See the example for **strncmp**.

_strnset, _fstrnset

Description   Initialize characters of a string to a given character.

#include <string.h>   Required only for function declarations

char *_strnset(char *_string_**, int** _c_**, size_t** _count_ **);**

char _ _ far * _ _ far _fstrnset(char _ _ far *_string_**, int** _c_**, size_t** _count_ **);**

string	String to be initialized
_c_	Character setting
count	Number of characters set

Remarks   The **_strnset** and **_fstrnset** functions set, at most, the first _count_ characters of _string_ to _c_ (converted to **char**) and return a pointer to the altered string. If _count_ is greater than the length of _string_, the length of _string_ is used in place of _count_.

The **_fstrnset** function is a model-independent (large-model) form of the **_strnset** function. The behavior and return value of **_fstrnset** are identical to those of the model-dependent function **_strnset**, with the exception that all the arguments and return values are far.

Return Value   The return values for these functions are described above.

Compatibility   **_strnset**

Standards: None
16-Bit: DOS, QWIN, WIN, WIN DLL
32-Bit: DOS32X

_fstrnset

Standards: None
16-Bit: DOS, QWIN, WIN, WIN DLL
32-Bit: None

See Also   **strcat, strcmp, strcpy, _strset**

Example

```
/* STRNSET.C */
#include <string.h>
#include <stdio.h>

void main( void )
{
    char string[15] = "This is a test";

    /* Set not more than 4 characters of string to be *'s */
    printf( "Before: %s\n", string );
    _strnset( string, '*', 4 );
    printf( "After:  %s\n", string );
}
```

Output

```
Before: This is a test
After:  **** is a test
```

strpbrk, _fstrpbrk

Description

Scan strings for characters in specified character sets.

#include <string.h>   Required only for function declarations

char *strpbrk(const char **string1***, const char ****string2* **);**

char __far * __far _fstrpbrk(const char __far **string1***,**
  const char __far *string2 **);**

string1	Source string
string2	Character set

Remarks

The **strpbrk** function finds the first occurrence in *string1* of any character from *string2*. The terminating null character ('**\0**') is not included in the search.

The **_fstrpbrk** function is a model-independent (large-model) form of the **strpbrk** function. The behavior and return value of **_fstrpbrk** are identical to those of the model-dependent function **strpbrk**, with the exception that all the arguments and return values are far.

Return Value

These functions return a pointer to the first occurrence of any character from *string2* in *string1*. A **NULL** return value indicates that the two string arguments have no characters in common.

Compatibility

strpbrk

Standards:	ANSI, UNIX
16-Bit:	DOS, QWIN, WIN, WIN DLL
32-Bit:	DOS32X

_fstrpbrk

Standards:	None
16-Bit:	DOS, QWIN, WIN, WIN DLL
32-Bit:	None

See Also

strchr, strrchr

Example

```
/* STRPBRK.C */
#include <string.h>
#include <stdio.h>

void main( void )
{
    char string[100] = "The 3 men and 2 boys ate 5 pigs\n";
    char *result;

    /* Return pointer to first 'a' or 'b' in "string"  */
    printf( "1: %s\n", string );
    result = strpbrk( string, "0123456789" );
    printf( "2: %s\n", result++ );
    result = strpbrk( result, "0123456789" );
    printf( "3: %s\n", result++ );
    result = strpbrk( result, "0123456789" );
    printf( "4: %s\n", result );
}
```

Output

```
1: The 3 men and 2 boys ate 5 pigs

2: 3 men and 2 boys ate 5 pigs

3: 2 boys ate 5 pigs

4: 5 pigs
```

strrchr, _fstrrchr

Description

Scan a string for the last occurrence of a character.

#include <string.h>   Required only for function declarations

char *strrchr(const char **string***, int** *c* **);**

char __far * __far _fstrrchr(const char __far **string***, int** *c* **);**

string	Searched string
c	Character to be located

Remarks

The **strrchr** function finds the last occurrence of *c* (converted to **char**) in *string*. The string's terminating null character ('\0') is included in the search. (Use **strchr** to find the first occurrence of *c* in *string*.)

The **_fstrrchr** function is a model-independent (large-model) form of the **strrchr** function. The behavior and return value of **_fstrrchr** are identical to those of the model-dependent function **strrchr**, with the exception that all the pointer arguments and return values are far pointers.

Return Value

These functions return a pointer to the last occurrence of the character in the string. A **NULL** pointer is returned if the given character is not found.

Compatibility

strrchr

Standards:	ANSI, UNIX
16-Bit:	DOS, QWIN, WIN, WIN DLL
32-Bit:	DOS32X

_fstrrchr

Standards:	None
16-Bit:	DOS, QWIN, WIN, WIN DLL
32-Bit:	None

See Also

strchr, strcspn, strncat, strncmp, strncpy, _strnicmp, strpbrk, strspn

Example

```
/* STRCHR.C: This program illustrates searching for a character with
 * strchr (search forward) or strrchr (search backward).
 */

#include <string.h>
#include <stdio.h>

int  ch = 'r';
char string[] = "The quick brown dog jumps over the lazy fox";
char fmt1[] =   "         1         2         3         4         5";
char fmt2[] =   "12345678901234567890123456789012345678901234567890";

void main( void )
{
   char *pdest;
   int result;

   printf( "String to be searched: \n\t\t%s\n", string );
   printf( "\t\t%s\n\t\t%s\n\n", fmt1, fmt2 );
   printf( "Search char:\t%c\n", ch );

   /* Search forward. */
   pdest = strchr( string, ch );
   result = pdest - string + 1;
   if( pdest != NULL )
      printf( "Result:\tfirst %c found at position %d\n\n", ch, result );
   else
      printf( "Result:\t%c not found\n" );

   /* Search backward. */
   pdest = strrchr( string, ch );
   result = pdest - string + 1;
   if( pdest != NULL )
      printf( "Result:\tlast %c found at position %d\n\n", ch, result );
   else
      printf( "Result:\t%c not found\n" );
}
```

Output

```
String to be searched:
                The quick brown dog jumps over the lazy fox
                         1         2         3         4         5
                12345678901234567890123456789012345678901234567890

Search char:    r
Result: first r found at position 12

Result: last r found at position 30
```

_ strrev, _ fstrrev

Description

Reverse characters of a string.

#include <string.h>   Required only for function declarations

char *_ strrev(char *_string_);

char _ _far * _ _far _fstrrev(char _ _far *_string_);

string   String to be reversed

Remarks

The **_ strrev** function reverses the order of the characters in _string_. The terminating null character ('**\0**') remains in place.

The **_ fstrrev** function is a model-independent (large-model) form of the **_ strrev** function. The behavior and return value of **_ fstrrev** are identical to those of the model-dependent function **_ strrev**, with the exception that the argument and return value are far pointers.

Return Value

These functions return a pointer to the altered string. There is no error return.

Compatibility

_ strrev

Standards:	None
16-Bit:	DOS, QWIN, WIN, WIN DLL
32-Bit:	DOS32X

_ fstrrev

Standards:	None
16-Bit:	DOS, QWIN, WIN, WIN DLL
32-Bit:	None

See Also

strcpy, _ strset

Example

```
/* STRREV.C: This program checks an input string to see whether it is a
 * palindrome: that is, whether it reads the same forward and backward.
 */

#include <string.h>
#include <stdio.h>

void main( void )
{
    char string[100];
    int result;

    printf( "Input a string and I will tell you if it is a palindrome:\n" );
    gets( string );

    /* Reverse string and compare (ignore case): */
    result = _strcmpi( string, _strrev( _strdup( string ) ) );
    if( result == 0 )
        printf( "The string \"%s\" is a palindrome\n\n", string );
    else
        printf( "The string \"%s\" is not a palindrome\n\n", string );
}
```

Output

```
Input a string and I will tell you if it is a palindrome:
Able was I ere I saw Elba
The string "Able was I ere I saw Elba" is a palindrome
```

_strset, _fstrset

Description

Set characters of a string to a character.

#include <string.h>   Required only for function declarations

char *_strset(char **string***, int** *c* **);**

char __far * __far _fstrset(char __far **string***, int** *c* **);**

string   String to be set

c   Character setting

Remarks

The **_strset** function sets all of the characters of *string* to *c* (converted to **char**), except the terminating null character ('**\0**').

The **_fstrset** function is a model-independent (large-model) form of the **_strset** function. The behavior and return value of **_fstrset** are identical to those of the model-dependent function **_strset**, with the exception that the pointer arguments and return value are far pointers.

Return Value

These functions return a pointer to the altered string. There is no error return.

Compatibility

_strset

Standards: None
16-Bit: DOS, QWIN, WIN, WIN DLL
32-Bit: DOS32X

_fstrset

Standards: None
16-Bit: DOS, QWIN, WIN, WIN DLL
32-Bit: None

See Also

memset, strcat, strcmp, strcpy, _strnset

Example

```
/* STRSET.C */
#include <string.h>
#include <stdio.h>

void main( void )
{
   char string[] = "Fill the string with something";

   printf( "Before: %s\n", string );
   _strset( string, '*' );
   printf( "After:  %s\n", string );
}
```

Output

```
Before: Fill the string with something
After:  *****************************
```

strspn, _fstrspn

Description   Find the first substring.

#include <string.h>   Required only for function declarations

size_t strspn(const char *string1, const char *string2);

size_t __far _fstrspn(const char __far *string1, const char __far *string2);

string1   Searched string

string2   Character set

Remarks   The **strspn** function returns the index of the first character in *string1* that does not belong to the set of characters specified by *string2*. This value is equivalent to the length of the initial substring of *string1* that consists entirely of characters from *string2*. The null character ('**\0**') terminating *string2* is not considered in the matching process. If *string1* begins with a character not in *string2*, **strspn** returns 0.

The **_fstrspn** function is a model-independent (large-model) form of the **strspn** function. The behavior and return value of **_fstrspn** are identical to those of the model-dependent function **strspn**, with the exception that the arguments are far pointers.

Return Value   These functions return an integer value specifying the length of the segment in *string1* consisting entirely of characters in *string2*.

Compatibility   **strspn**

Standards: ANSI, UNIX
16-Bit: DOS, QWIN, WIN, WIN DLL
32-Bit: DOS32X

_fstrspn

Standards: None

16-Bit: DOS, QWIN, WIN, WIN DLL

32-Bit: None

See Also   **strcspn, strncat, strncmp, strncpy, _strnicmp, strrchr**

Example
```c
/* STRSPN.C: This program uses strspn to determine the length of
 * the segment in the string "cabbage" consisting of a's, b's, and c's.
 * In other words, it finds the first non-abc letter.
 */

#include <string.h>
#include <stdio.h>

void main( void )
{
    char string[] = "cabbage";
    int  result;

    result = strspn( string, "abc" );
    printf( "The portion of '%s' containing only a, b, or c "
            "is %d bytes long\n", string, result );
}
```

Output   The portion of 'cabbage' containing only a, b, or c is 5 bytes long

strstr, _fstrstr

Description   Find a substring.

#include <string.h>   Required only for function declarations

char *strstr(const char **string1***, const char ****string2***);**

char __far * __far _fstrstr(const char __far **string1***,**
    const char __far **string2***);**

string1	Searched string
string2	String to search for

Remarks   The **strstr** function returns a pointer to the first occurrence of *string2* in *string1*.

The **_fstrstr** function is a model-independent (large-model) form of the **strstr** function. The behavior and return value of **_fstrstr** are identical to those of the model-dependent function **strstr**, with the exception that the arguments and return value are far pointers.

Return Value   These functions return either a pointer to the first occurrence of *string2* in *string1*, or **NULL** if they do not find the string.

Compatibility   **strstr**

Standards: ANSI
16-Bit: DOS, QWIN, WIN, WIN DLL
32-Bit: DOS32X

_fstrstr

Standards: None
16-Bit: DOS, QWIN, WIN, WIN DLL
32-Bit: None

See Also   **strcspn, strncat, strncmp, strncpy, _strnicmp, strpbrk, strrchr, strspn**

Example

```
/* STRSTR.C */
#include <string.h>
#include <stdio.h>

char str[] =     "lazy";
char string[] = "The quick brown dog jumps over the lazy fox";
char fmt1[] =     "         1         2         3         4         5";
char fmt2[] =     "12345678901234567890123456789012345678901234567890";

void main( void )
{
   char *pdest;
   int  result;

   printf( "String to be searched:\n\t%s\n", string );
   printf( "\t%s\n\t%s\n\n", fmt1, fmt2 );

   pdest = strstr( string, str );
   result = pdest - string + 1;
   if( pdest != NULL )
      printf( "%s found at position %d\n\n", str, result );
   else
      printf( "%s not found\n", str );
}
```

Output

```
String to be searched:
        The quick brown dog jumps over the lazy fox
                 1         2         3         4         5
        12345678901234567890123456789012345678901234567890

lazy found at position 36
```

_strtime

Description   Copies the time to a buffer.

#include <time.h>

char *_strtime(char *timestr **);**

timestr   Time string

Remarks   The **_strtime** function copies the current time into the buffer pointed to by
timestr. The time is formatted as

hh:mm:ss

where hh is two digits representing the hour in 24-hour notation, mm is two digits
representing the minutes past the hour, and ss is two digits representing seconds.
For example, the string

18:23:44

represents 23 minutes and 44 seconds past 6:00 PM.

The buffer must be at least nine bytes long.

Return Value   The **_strtime** function returns a pointer to the resulting text string *timestr*.

Compatibility   Standards: None
16-Bit: DOS, QWIN, WIN, WIN DLL
32-Bit: DOS32X

See Also   **asctime, ctime, gmtime, localtime, mktime, time, _tzset**

Example

```
/* STRTIME.C */
#include <time.h>
#include <stdio.h>

void main( void )
{
    char dbuffer [9];
    char tbuffer [9];

    _strdate( dbuffer );
    printf( "The current date is %s \n", dbuffer );
    _strtime( tbuffer );
    printf( "The current time is %s \n", tbuffer );
}
```

Output

```
The current date is 06/20/99
The current time is 09:33:13
```

strtod, strtol, _strtold, strtoul

Description

Convert strings to a double-precision (**strtod**), long-double-precision (**_strtold**), long-integer (**strtol**), or unsigned long-integer (**strtoul**) value.

#include <stdlib.h>

double strtod(const char **nptr,* **char** ***endptr* **);**

long strtol(const char **nptr,* **char** ***endptr,* **int** *base* **);**

long double _strtold(const char **nptr,* **char** ***endptr* **);**

unsigned long strtoul(const char **nptr,* **char** ***endptr,* **int** *base* **);**

nptr	String to convert
endptr	Pointer to character that stops scan
base	Number base to use

Remarks

The **strtod**, **_strtold**, **strtol**, and **strtoul** functions convert a character string to a double-precision value, a long-double value, a long-integer value, or an unsigned long-integer value, respectively. The input string is a sequence of characters that can be interpreted as a numerical value of the specified type.

These functions stop reading the string at the first character they cannot recognize as part of a number. This may be the null character ('\0') at the end of the string. With **strtol** or **strtoul**, this terminating character can also be the first numeric character greater than or equal to *base*. If *endptr* is not **NULL**, a pointer to the character that stopped the scan is stored at the location pointed to by *endptr*. If no conversion could be performed (no valid digits were found or an invalid base was specified), the value of *nptr* is stored at the location pointed to by *endptr*.

The **strtod** and **_strtold** functions expect *nptr* to point to a string with the following form:

[[*whitespace*]] [[*sign*]] [[*digits*]] [[*.digits*]] [[{**d** | **D** | **e** | **E**}[[*sign*]]*digits*]]

A *whitespace* consists of space and tab characters, which are ignored; *sign* is either plus (**+**) or minus (**–**); and *digits* are one or more decimal digits. If no digits appear before the decimal point, at least one must appear after the decimal point. The decimal digits can be followed by an exponent, which consists of an introductory letter (**b**, **D**, **e**, or **E**) and an optionally signed decimal integer.

The first character that does not fit this form stops the scan.

The **strtol** function expects *nptr* to point to a string with the following form:

[[*whitespace*]] [[*sign*]] [[**0**]] [[{ **x** | **X** }]] [[*digits*]]

The **strtoul** function expects *nptr* to point to a string having this form:

[[*whitespace*]] [[{ **+** | **-** }]] [[**0**]] [[{ **x** | **X** }]] [[*digits*]]

If *base* is between 2 and 36, then it is used as the base of the number. If *base* is 0, the initial characters of the string pointed to by *nptr* are used to determine the base. If the first character is 0 and the second character is not 'x' or 'X', then the string is interpreted as an octal integer; otherwise, it is interpreted as a decimal number. If the first character is '0' and the second character is 'x' or 'X', then the string is interpreted as a hexadecimal integer. If the first character is '1' through '9', then the string is interpreted as a decimal integer. The letters 'a' through 'z' (or 'A' through 'Z') are assigned the values 10 through 35; only letters whose assigned values are less than *base* are permitted.

The **strtoul** function allows a plus (+) or minus (–) sign prefix; a leading minus sign indicates that the return value is negated.

Return Value

The **strtod** and **_strtold** functions return the value of the floating-point number, except when the representation would cause an overflow, in which case they return ± **HUGE_VAL**. The functions return 0 if no conversion could be performed or an underflow occurred.

The **strtol** function returns the value represented in the string, except when the representation would cause an overflow, in which case it returns **LONG_MAX** or **LONG_MIN**. The function returns 0 if no conversion could be performed.

The **strtoul** function returns the converted value, if any. If no conversion can be performed, the function returns 0. The function returns **ULONG_MAX** on overflow.

In all four functions, **errno** is set to **ERANGE** if overflow or underflow occurs.

Compatibility

strtod, strtol

Standards:	ANSI, UNIX
16-Bit:	DOS, QWIN, WIN, WIN DLL
32-Bit:	DOS32X

_strtold

Standards: None

16-Bit: DOS, QWIN, WIN, WIN DLL

32-Bit: None

strtoul

Standards: ANSI

16-Bit: DOS, QWIN, WIN, WIN DLL

32-Bit: DOS32X

See Also   **atof, atol**

Example
```
/* STRTOD.C: This program uses strtod to convert a string to a
 * double-precision value; strtol to convert a string to long
 * integer values; and strtoul to convert a string to unsigned
 * long-integer values.
 */

#include <stdlib.h>
#include <stdio.h>

void main( void )
{
    char    *string, *stopstring;
    double  x;
    long    l;
    int     base;
    unsigned long ul;

    string = "3.1415926This stopped it";
    x = strtod( string, &stopstring );
    printf( "string = %s\n", string );
    printf("   strtod = %f\n", x );
    printf("   Stopped scan at: %s\n\n", stopstring );

    string = "-10110134932This stopped it";
    l = strtol( string, &stopstring, 10 );
    printf( "string = %s\n", string );
    printf("   strtol = %ld\n", l );
    printf("   Stopped scan at: %s\n\n", stopstring );
```

```
        string = "10110134932";
        printf( "string = %s\n", string );
        /* Convert string using base 2, 4, and 8: */
        for( base = 2; base <= 8; base *= 2 )
        {
            /* Convert the string: */
            ul = strtoul( string, &stopstring, base );
            printf( "   strtol = %ld (base %d)\n", ul, base );
            printf( "   Stopped scan at: %s\n", stopstring );
        }
    }
}
```

Output
```
string = 3.1415926This stopped it
    strtod = 3.141593
    Stopped scan at: This stopped it

string = -10110134932This stopped it
    strtol = -2147483647
    Stopped scan at: This stopped it

string = 10110134932
    strtol = 45 (base 2)
    Stopped scan at: 34932
    strtol = 4423 (base 4)
    Stopped scan at: 4932
    strtol = 2134108 (base 8)
    Stopped scan at: 932
```

strtok, _fstrtok

Description

Find the next token in a string.

#include <string.h>   Required only for function declarations

char *strtok(char *string1, const char *string2);

char __far * __far _fstrtok(char __far *string1, const char __far *string2);

string1   String containing token(s)

string2   Set of delimiter characters

Remarks

The **strtok** function reads string1 as a series of zero or more tokens and string2 as the set of characters serving as delimiters of the tokens in string1. The tokens in string1 may be separated by one or more of the delimiters from string2.

The tokens can be broken out of string1 by a series of calls to **strtok**. In the first call to **strtok** for string1, **strtok** searches for the first token in string1, skipping leading delimiters. A pointer to the first token is returned. To read the next token from string1, call **strtok** with a **NULL** value for the string1 argument. The **NULL** string1 argument causes **strtok** to search for the next token in the previous token string. The set of delimiters may vary from call to call, so string2 can take any value.

The **_fstrtok** function is a model-independent (large-model) form of the **strtok** function. The behavior and return value of **_fstrtok** are identical to those of the model-dependent function **strtok**, with the exception that the arguments and return value are far pointers.

Note that calls to these functions will modify string1, since each time **strtok** is called it inserts a null character ('\0') after the token in string1.

Return Value

The first time **strtok** is called, it returns a pointer to the first token in string1. In later calls with the same token string, **strtok** returns a pointer to the next token in the string. A **NULL** pointer is returned when there are no more tokens. All tokens are null-terminated.

Compatibility	**strtok**	
	Standards:	ANSI, UNIX
	16-Bit:	DOS, QWIN, WIN, WIN DLL
	32-Bit:	DOS32X

_fstrtok

	Standards:	None
	16-Bit:	DOS, QWIN, WIN, WIN DLL
	32-Bit:	None

See Also   strcspn, strspn

Example

```
/* STRTOK.C: In this program, a loop uses strtok to print all the tokens
 * (separated by commas or blanks) in the string named "string".
 */

#include <string.h>
#include <stdio.h>

char string[] = "A string\tof ,,tokens\nand some  more tokens";
char seps[]   = " ,\t\n";
char *token;

void main( void )
{
    printf( "%s\n\nTokens:\n", string );

    /* Establish string and get the first token: */
    token = strtok( string, seps );
    while( token != NULL )
    {
        /* While there are tokens in "string" */
        printf( " %s\n", token );
        /* Get next token: */
        token = strtok( NULL, seps );
    }
}
```

Output   A string   of ,,tokens
and some   more tokens

Tokens:
A
string
of
tokens
and
some
more
tokens

_strupr, _fstrupr

Description

Convert a string to uppercase.

#include <string.h>   Required only for function declarations

char *_strupr(char **string**);

char __far * __far _fstrupr(char __far **string**);

string   String to be capitalized

Remarks

These functions convert any lowercase letters in the string to uppercase. Other characters are not affected.

The **_fstrupr** function is a model-independent (large-model) form of the **_strupr** function. The behavior and return value of **_fstrupr** are identical to those of the model-dependent function **_strupr**, with the exception that the argument and return value are far pointers.

Return Value

These functions return a pointer to the converted string. There is no error return.

Compatibility

_strupr

Standards:	None
16-Bit:	DOS, QWIN, WIN, WIN DLL
32-Bit:	DOS32X

_fstrupr

Standards:	None
16-Bit:	DOS, QWIN, WIN, WIN DLL
32-Bit:	None

See Also

_strlwr

Example

```
/* STRLWR.C: This program uses _strlwr and _strupr to create
 * uppercase and lowercase copies of a mixed-case string.
 */

#include <string.h>
#include <stdio.h>

void main( void )
{
    char string[100] = "The String to End All Strings!";
    char *copy1, *copy2;

    copy1 = _strlwr( _strdup( string ) );
    copy2 = _strupr( _strdup( string ) );
    printf( "Mixed: %s\n", string );
    printf( "Lower: %s\n", copy1 );
    printf( "Upper: %s\n", copy2 );
}
```

Output

```
Mixed: The String to End All Strings!
Lower: the string to end all strings!
Upper: THE STRING TO END ALL STRINGS!
```

strxfrm

Description

Transforms a string based on locale-specific information.

#include <string.h>   Required only for function declarations

size_t strxfrm(char * *string1***, const char *** *string2***, size_t *** *count* **);**

string1	String to which transformed version of *string2* is returned
string2	String to transform
count	Maximum number of characters to be placed in *string1*

Remarks

The **strxfrm** function transforms the string pointed to by *string2* into a new collated form that is stored in *string1*. No more than *count* characters (including the null character) are transformed and placed into the resulting string.

The transformation is made using the locale-specific information set by the **setlocale** function.

After the transformation, a call to **strcmp** with the two transformed strings will yield identical results to a call to **strcoll** applied to the original two strings.

The value of the following expression is the size of the array needed to hold the transformation of the source string:

```
1 + strxfrm( NULL, string, 0 )
```

Currently, the run-time library supports the "C" locale only; thus **strxfrm** is equivalent to the following:

```
strncpy( _string1, _string2, _count );
return( strlen( _string2 ) );
```

Return Value

The **strxfrm** function returns the length of the transformed string, not counting the terminating null character. If the return value is greater than or equal to *count*, the contents of *string1* are unpredictable.

Compatibility	Standards:	ANSI
	16-Bit:	DOS, QWIN, WIN, WIN DLL
	32-Bit:	DOS32X

See Also   **localeconv, setlocale, strcmp, strncmp, strcoll**

_swab

Description

Swaps bytes.

#include <stdlib.h>   Required only for function declarations

void _swab(char **src***, char ****dest***, int** *n* **);**

src	Data to be copied and swapped
dest	Storage location for swapped data
n	Number of bytes to be copied and swapped

Remarks

The **_swab** function copies *n* bytes from *src*, swaps each pair of adjacent bytes, and stores the result at *dest*. The integer *n* should be an even number to allow for swapping. The **_swab** function is typically used to prepare binary data for transfer to a machine that uses a different byte order.

Return Value

None.

Compatibility

Standards: UNIX
16-Bit: DOS, QWIN, WIN, WIN DLL
32-Bit: DOS32X

Use **_swab** for compatibility with ANSI naming conventions of non-ANSI functions. Use **swab** and link with OLDNAMES.LIB for UNIX compatibility.

Example

```
/* SWAB.C */
#include <stdlib.h>
#include <stdio.h>

char from[] = "BADCFEHGJILKNMPORQTSVUXWZY";
char to[] =   ".........................";

void main( void )
{
   printf( "Before:\t%s\n\t%s\n\n", from, to );
   _swab( from, to, sizeof( from ) );
   printf( "After:\t%s\n\t%s\n\n", from, to );
}
```

Output

```
Before: BADCFEHGJILKNMPORQTSVUXWZY
        .........................

After:  BADCFEHGJILKNMPORQTSVUXWZY
        ABCDEFGHIJKLMNOPQRSTUVWXYZ
```

system

Description

Executes a command.

#include <process.h>	Required only for function declarations
#include <stdlib.h>	Use STDLIB.H for ANSI compatibility

int system(const char **command***);**

command	Command to be executed

Remarks

The **system** function passes *command* to the command interpreter, which executes the string as an operating-system command. The **system** function refers to the COMSPEC and PATH environment variables that locate the command-interpreter file (the file named COMMAND.COM in DOS). If *command* is a pointer to an empty string, the function simply checks to see whether or not the command interpreter exists.

Return Value

If *command* is **NULL** and the command interpreter is found, the function returns a nonzero value. If the command interpreter is not found, it returns the value 0 and sets **errno** to **ENOENT**. If *command* is not **NULL**, the **system** function returns the value 0 if the command interpreter is successfully started.

A return value of –1 indicates an error, and **errno** is set to one of the following values:

Value	Meaning
E2BIG	In DOS, the argument list exceeds 128 bytes, or the space required for the environment information exceeds 32K.
ENOENT	The command interpreter cannot be found.
ENOEXEC	The command-interpreter file has an invalid format and is not executable.
ENOMEM	Not enough memory is available to execute the command; or the available memory has been corrupted; or an invalid block exists, indicating that the process making the call was not allocated properly.

Compatibility	Standards:	ANSI, UNIX
	16-Bit:	DOS
	32-Bit:	DOS32X

See Also   _exec functions, **exit**, _exit, _spawn functions

Example   ```
/* SYSTEM.C: This program uses system to TYPE its source file. */

#include <process.h>

void main(void)
{
    system("type system.c");
}
```

**Output**      ```
/* SYSTEM.C: This program uses system to TYPE its source file. */

#include <process.h>

void main( void )
{
    system( "type system.c" );
}
```

tan Functions

Description

Calculate the tangent (**tan** and **_tanl**) and hyperbolic tangent (**tanh** and **_tanhl**).

#include <math.h>

double tan(double *x* **);**

double tanh(double *x* **);**

long double _tanl(long double *x* **);**

long double _tanhl(long double *x* **);**

x   Angle in radians

Remarks

The **tan** functions return the tangent or hyperbolic tangent of their arguments. The list below describes the differences between the various tangent functions:

Function	Description
tan	Calculates tangent of *x*
tanh	Calculates hyperbolic tangent of *x*
_tanl	Calculates tangent of *x* (80-bit version)
_tanhl	Calculates hyperbolic tangent of *x* (80-bit version)

The **_tanl** and **_tanhl** functions are the 80-bit counterparts and use an 80-bit, 10-byte coprocessor form of arguments and return values. See the reference page on the long double functions for more details on this data type.

Return Value

The **tan** function returns the tangent of *x*. If *x* is large, a partial loss of significance in the result may occur; in this case, **tan** sets **errno** to **ERANGE** and generates a **_PLOSS** error. If *x* is so large that significance is totally lost, **tan** prints a **_TLOSS** error message to **stderr**, sets **errno** to **ERANGE**, and returns 0. Error handling can be modified by using the **_matherr** function.

There is no error return for **tanh**.

Compatibility   **tan, tanh**

Standards: ANSI, UNIX

16-Bit: DOS, QWIN, WIN, WIN DLL

32-Bit: DOS32X

_tanl, _tanhl

Standards: None

16-Bit: DOS, QWIN, WIN, WIN DLL

32-Bit: None

See Also   **acos** functions, **asin** functions, **atan** functions, **cos** functions, **sin** functions

Example
```
/* TAN.C:  This program displays the tangent of pi / 4 and the hyperbolic
 * tangent of the result.
 */

#include <math.h>
#include <stdio.h>

void main( void )
{
   double pi = 3.1415926535;
   double x, y;

   x = tan( pi / 4 );
   y = tanh( x );
   printf( "tan( %f ) = %f\n", x, y );
   printf( "tanh( %f ) = %f\n", y, x );
}
```

Output
```
tan( 1.000000 ) = 0.761594
tanh( 0.761594 ) = 1.000000
```

_tell

Description   Gets the position of the file pointer.

#include <io.h>   Required only for function declarations

long _tell(int *handle* **);**

handle   Handle referring to open file

Remarks   The **_tell** function gets the current position of the file pointer (if any) associated with the *handle* argument. The position is expressed as the number of bytes from the beginning of the file.

Return Value   A return value of –1L indicates an error, and **errno** is set to **EBADF** to indicate an invalid file-handle argument. On devices incapable of seeking, the return value is undefined.

Compatibility   Standards: None
16-Bit: DOS, QWIN, WIN, WIN DLL
32-Bit: DOS32X

See Also   **ftell, _lseek**

Example
```
/* TELL.C:  This program uses _tell to tell the file pointer position
 * after a file read.
 */

#include <io.h>
#include <stdio.h>
#include <fcntl.h>
```

```
void main( void )
{
    int  fh;
    long position;
    char buffer[500];

    if( (fh = _open( "tell.c", _O_RDONLY )) != -1 )
    {
      if( _read( fh, buffer, 500 ) > 0 )
          printf( "Current file position is: %d\n", _tell( fh ) );

      _close( fh );
    }
}
```

Output   Current file position is: 425

_tempnam, tmpnam

Description

Create temporary filenames.

#include <stdio.h>

char *_tempnam(char *_dir_, char *_prefix_);

char *tmpnam(char *_string_);

string	Pointer to temporary name
dir	Target directory to be used if TMP not defined
prefix	Filename prefix

Remarks

The **tmpnam** function generates a temporary filename that can be used to open a temporary file without overwriting an existing file. This name is stored in _string_. If _string_ is **NULL**, then **tmpnam** leaves the result in an internal static buffer. Thus, any subsequent calls destroy this value. If _string_ is not **NULL**, it is assumed to point to an array of at least **L_tmpnam** bytes (the value of **L_tmpnam** is defined in STDIO.H). The function will generate unique filenames for up to **TMP_MAX** calls.

The character string that **tmpnam** creates consists of the path prefix, defined by the entry **P_tmpdir** in the file STDIO.H, followed by a sequence consisting of the digit characters '0' through '9'; the numerical value of this string can range from 1 to 65,535. Changing the definitions of **L_tmpnam** or **P_tmpdir** in STDIO.H does not change the operation of **tmpnam**.

The **_tempnam** function allows the program to create a temporary filename for use in another directory. This filename will be different from that of any existing file. The _prefix_ argument is the prefix to the filename. The **_tempnam** function uses **malloc** to allocate space for the filename; the program is responsible for freeing this space when it is no longer needed. The **_tempnam** function looks for the file with the given name in the following directories, listed in order of precedence:

Directory Used	Conditions
Directory specified by TMP	TMP environment variable is set, and directory specified by TMP exists.
dir argument to **_tempnam**	TMP environment variable is not set, or directory specified by TMP does not exist.

Directory Used	Conditions
P_tmpdir in STDIO.H	The *dir* argument is **NULL**, or *dir* is name of nonexistent directory.
Current working directory	**P_tmpdir** does not exist.

If the search through the locations listed above fails, **_tempnam** returns the value **NULL**.

Return Value

The **tmpnam** and **_tempnam** functions both return a pointer to the name generated, unless it is impossible to create this name or the name is not unique. If the name cannot be created or if a file with that name already exists, **tmpnam** and **_tempnam** return the value **NULL**.

Compatibility

_tempnam

Standards: UNIX

16-Bit: DOS, QWIN, WIN, WIN DLL

32-Bit: DOS32X

Use **_tempnam** for compatibility with ANSI naming conventions of non-ANSI functions. Use **tempnam** and link with OLDNAMES.LIB for UNIX compatibility.

tmpnam

Standards: ANSI, UNIX

16-Bit: DOS, QWIN, WIN, WIN DLL

32-Bit: DOS32X

See Also   **tmpfile**

Example

```
/* TEMPNAM.C: This program uses tmpnam to create a unique filename in
 * the current working directory, then uses _tempnam to create a unique
 * filename with a prefix of stq.
 */

#include <stdio.h>
```

```
void main( void )
{
    char *name1, *name2;

    /* Create a temporary filename for the current working directory: */
    if( ( name1 = tmpnam( NULL ) ) != NULL )
        printf( "%s is safe to use as a temporary file.\n", name1 );
    else
        printf( "Cannot create a unique filename\n" );

    /* Create a temporary file name in temporary directory with the
     * prefix "stq". The actual destination directory may vary depending
     * on the state of the TMP environment variable and the global variable
     * P_tmpdir.
     */
    if( ( name2 = _tempnam( "c:\\tmp", "stq" ) ) != NULL )
        printf( "%s is safe to use as a temporary file.\n", name2 );
    else
        printf( "Cannot create a unique filename\n" );
}
```

Output

```
\2 is safe to use as a temporary file.
C:\TMP\stq2 is safe to use as a temporary file.
```

time

Description

Gets the system time.

#include <time.h>   Required only for function declarations

time_t time(time_t *_timer_);

timer   Storage location for time

Remarks

The **time** function returns the number of seconds elapsed since midnight (00:00:00), December 31, 1899, Universal Coordinated Time, according to the system clock. The system time is adjusted according to the **_timezone** system variable, which is explained under **_tzset**.

The return value is stored in the location given by _timer_. This parameter may be **NULL**, in which case the return value is not stored.

Return Value

The **time** function returns the time in elapsed seconds. There is no error return.

Compatibility

Standards: ANSI, UNIX
16-Bit: DOS, QWIN, WIN, WIN DLL
32-Bit: DOS32X

See Also

asctime, _ftime, gmtime, localtime, _tzset, _utime

Example

```
/* TIMES.C illustrates various time and date functions including:
 *      time            _ftime          ctime           asctime
 *      localtime       gmtime          mktime          _tzset
 *      _strtime        _strdate        strftime
 *
 * Also the global variable:
 *      _tzname
 */

#include <time.h>
#include <stdio.h>
#include <sys\types.h>
#include <sys\timeb.h>
#include <string.h>

void main( void )
{
    char tmpbuf[128], ampm[] = "AM";
    time_t ltime;
    struct _timeb tstruct;
    struct tm *today, *gmt, xmas = { 0, 0, 12, 25, 11, 91 };

    /* Set time zone from TZ environment variable. If TZ is not set,
     * PST8PDT is used (Pacific standard time, daylight savings).
     */
    _tzset();

    /* Display DOS-style date and time. */
    _strtime( tmpbuf );
    printf( "DOS time:\t\t\t\t%s\n", tmpbuf );
    _strdate( tmpbuf );
    printf( "DOS date:\t\t\t\t%s\n", tmpbuf );

    /* Get UNIX-style time and display as number and string. */
    time( &ltime );
    printf( "Time in seconds since GMT 1/1/70:\t%ld\n", ltime );
    printf( "UNIX time and date:\t\t\t%s", ctime( &ltime ) );

    /* Display GMT. */
    gmt = gmtime( &ltime );
    printf( "Greenwich Mean Time:\t\t\t%s", asctime( gmt ) );

    /* Convert to time structure and adjust for PM if necessary. */
    today = localtime( &ltime );
    if( today-tm_hour  12 )
    {
        strcpy( ampm, "PM" );
        today-tm_hour -= 12;
    }
```

```
/* Note how pointer addition is used to skip the first 11 characters
 * and printf is used to trim off terminating characters.
 */
printf( "12-hour time:\t\t\t\t%.8s %s\n",
        asctime( today ) + 11, ampm );

/* Print additional time information. */
ftime( &tstruct );
printf( "Plus milliseconds:\t\t\t%u\n", tstruct.millitm );
printf( "Zone difference in seconds from GMT:\t%u\n", tstruct.timezone );
printf( "Time zone name:\t\t\t%s\n", tzname[0] );
printf( "Daylight savings:\t\t\t%s\n", tstruct.dstflag ? "YES" : "NO" );

/* Make time for noon on Christmas, 1991. */
if( mktime( &xmas ) != (time_t)-1 )
    printf( "Christmas\t\t\t\t%s\n", asctime( &xmas ) );

/* Use time structure to build a customized time string. */
today = localtime( &ltime );

/* Use strftime to build a customized time string. */
strftime( tmpbuf, 128,
          "Today is %A, day %d of %B in the year %Y.\n", today );
printf( tmpbuf );
}
```

Output

```
DOS time:                               17:36:10
DOS date:                               12/15/99
Time in seconds since GMT 1/1/70:       -1398750726
UNIX time and date:                     Wed Dec 15 17:36:10 1999
Greenwich Mean Time:                    Thu Dec 16 00:36:10 1999
12-hour time:                           05:36:10 PM
Plus milliseconds:                      90
Zone difference in seconds from GMT:    480
Time zone name:                         PST
Daylight savings:                       NO
Christmas                               Wed Dec 25 12:00:00 1999

Today is Wednesday, day 15 of December in the year 1999.
```

tmpfile

Description   Creates a temporary file.

#include <stdio.h>

FILE *tmpfile(void);

Remarks   The **tmpfile** function creates a temporary file and returns a pointer to that stream. If the file cannot be opened, **tmpfile** returns a **NULL** pointer.

This temporary file is automatically deleted when the file is closed, when the program terminates normally, or when **_rmtmp** is called, assuming that the current working directory does not change. The temporary file is opened in **w+b** (binary read/write) mode.

Return Value   If successful, the **tmpfile** function returns a stream pointer. Otherwise, it returns a **NULL** pointer.

Compatibility   Standards: ANSI, UNIX
    16-Bit: DOS, QWIN, WIN, WIN DLL
    32-Bit: DOS32X

See Also   **_rmtmp, _tempnam, tmpnam**

Example
```
/* TMPFILE.C: This program uses tmpfile to create a temporary file,
 * then deletes this file with _rmtmp.
 */

#include <stdio.h>
```

```
void main( void )
{
    FILE *stream;
    char tempstring[] = "String to be written";
    int  i;

    /* Create temporary files. */
    for( i = 1; i <= 10; i++ )
    {
        if( (stream = tmpfile()) == NULL )
            perror( "Could not open new temporary file\n" );
        else
            printf( "Temporary file %d was created\n", i );
    }

    /* Remove temporary files. */
    printf( "%d temporary files deleted\n", _rmtmp() );
}
```

Output

```
Temporary file 1 was created
Temporary file 2 was created
Temporary file 3 was created
Temporary file 4 was created
Temporary file 5 was created
Temporary file 6 was created
Temporary file 7 was created
Temporary file 8 was created
Temporary file 9 was created
Temporary file 10 was created
10 temporary files deleted
```

__toascii, tolower, toupper Functions

Description   Convert characters.

#include <ctype.h>

int __toascii(int *c*);

int tolower(int *c*);

int _tolower(int *c*);

int toupper(int *c*);

int _toupper(int *c*);

c   Character to be converted

Remarks   The **__toascii**, **tolower**, **_tolower**, **toupper**, and **_toupper** routines and their
associated macros convert a single character, as described below:

Function	Macro	Description
__toascii	**__toascii**	Converts *c* to ASCII character
tolower	**tolower**	Converts *c* to lowercase if appropriate
_tolower	**_tolower**	Converts *c* to lowercase
toupper	**toupper**	Converts *c* to uppercase if appropriate
_toupper	**_toupper**	Converts *c* to uppercase

The **__toascii** routine sets all but the low-order 7 bits of *c* to 0, so that the converted value represents a character in the ASCII character set. If *c* already represents an ASCII character, *c* is unchanged.

The **tolower** routine converts *c* to lowercase if *c* represents an uppercase letter.
Otherwise, *c* is unchanged.

The **_tolower** routine is a version of **tolower** to be used only when *c* is known to
be uppercase. The result of **_tolower** is undefined if *c* is not an uppercase letter.

The **toupper** routine convers *c* to uppercase if *c* represents an lowercase letter.
Otherwise, *c* is unchanged.

The **_toupper** routine is a version of **toupper** to be used only when c is known to be lowercase. The result of **_toupper** is undefined if c is not a lowercase letter.

These routines are implemented both as functions and as macros. To conform to the ANSI specification, the **tolower** and **toupper** routines are also implemented as functions. The function versions can be used by removing the macro definitions through **#undef** directives or by not including CTYPE.H. Function declarations of **tolower** and **toupper** are given in STDLIB.H.

If the /Za compile option is used, the macro form of **toupper** or **tolower** is not used because it evaluates its argument more than once. Since the arguments are evaluated more than once, arguments with side effects would produce potentially bad results.

Return Value   The **__toascii, tolower, _tolower, toupper**, and **_toupper** routines return the converted character c. There is no error return.

Compatibility   **__toascii, _tolower, _toupper**

Standards: UNIX

16-Bit: DOS, QWIN, WIN, WIN DLL

32-Bit: DOS32X

Use **__toascii** for compatibility with ANSI naming conventions of non-ANSI functions. Use **toascii** and link with OLDNAMES.LIB for UNIX compatibility.

tolower, toupper

Standards: ANSI, UNIX

16-Bit: DOS, QWIN, WIN, WIN DLL

32-Bit: DOS32X

See Also   **is** functions

Example

```
/* TOUPPER.C: This program uses toupper and tolower to analyze all
 * characters between 0x0 and 0x7F. It also applies _toupper and _tolower
 * to any code in this range for which these functions make sense.
 */

#include <conio.h>
#include <ctype.h>
#include <string.h>

char msg[] = "Some of THESE letters are Capitals\r\n";
char *p;
```

```
void main( void )
{
   _cputs( msg );

   /* Reverse case of message. */
   for( p = msg; p < msg + strlen( msg ); p++ )
   {
      if( islower( *p ) )
         _putch( _toupper( *p ) );
      else if( isupper( *p ) )
         _putch( _tolower( *p ) );
      else
         _putch( *p );
   }
}
```

Output

```
Some of THESE letters are Capitals
sOME OF these LETTERS ARE cAPITALS
```

_tzset

Description

Sets time environment variables.

#include <time.h>   Required only for function declarations

void _tzset(void);

int _daylight   Global variables set by function
long _timezone
char *_tzname[2]

Remarks

The **_tzset** function uses the current setting of the environment variable TZ to assign values to three global variables: **_daylight**, **_timezone**, and **_tzname**. These variables are used by the **_ftime** and **localtime** functions to make corrections from Universal Coordinated Time (UCT) to local time, and by **time** to compute UCT from system time.

Use the following syntax to set the TZ environment variable:

set TZ=_tzn_[[+ | –]]_hh_[[:_mm_[[:_ss_]]]][[_dzn_]]

The _tzn_ must be a three-letter time-zone name, such as PST, followed by an optionally signed number, + –_hh_, giving the difference in hours between UCT and local time. To specify the exact local time, the hours can be followed by minutes, :_mm_; seconds, :_ss_; and a three-letter daylight-saving-time zone, _dzn_, such as PDT. Separate hours, minutes, and seconds with colons (:). If daylight saving time is never in effect, as is the case in certain states and localities, set TZ without a value for _dzn_.

If the TZ value is not currently set, the default is PST8PDT, which corresponds to the Pacific time zone.

Based on the TZ environment variable value, the following values are assigned to the variables **_daylight**, **_timezone**, and **_tzname** when **_tzset** is called:

Variable	Value
_daylight	Nonzero value if a daylight-saving-time zone is specified in the TZ setting; otherwise, 0
_timezone	Difference in seconds between GMT and local time
_tzname[0]	String value of the three-letter time-zone name from the TZ environmental variable
_tzname[1]	String value of the daylight-saving-time zone, or an empty string if the daylight-saving-time zone is omitted from the TZ environmental variable

The default for **_daylight** is 1; for **_timezone**, 28,800; for **_tzname**[0], PST; and for **_tzname**[1], PDT. This corresponds to "PST8PDT."

If the DST zone is omitted from the TZ environmental variable, the **_daylight** variable will be 0 and the **_ftime**, **gmtime**, and **localtime** functions will return 0 for their DST flags.

Return Value   None.

Compatibility   Standards: UNIX

16-Bit: DOS, QWIN, WIN, WIN DLL

32-Bit: DOS32X

Use **_tzset** for compatibility with ANSI naming conventions of non-ANSI functions. Use **tzset** and link with OLDNAMES.LIB for UNIX compatibility.

See Also   asctime, **_ftime**, **gmtime**, **localtime**, **time**

Example
```
/* TZSET.C: This program first sets up the time zone by placing the variable
 * named TZ=EST5 in the environment table. It then uses _tzset to set the
 * global variables named _daylight, _timezone, and _tzname.
 */

#include <time.h>
#include <stdlib.h>
#include <stdio.h>
```

```
void main( void )
{
   if( _putenv( "TZ=EST5EDT" ) == -1 )
   {
      printf( "Unable to set TZ\n" );
      exit( 1 );
   }
   else
   {
      _tzset();
      printf( "_daylight = %d\n", _daylight );
      printf( "_timezone = %ld\n", _timezone );
      printf( "_tzname[0] = %s\n", _tzname[0] );
   }
   exit( 0 );
}
```

Output

```
_daylight = 1
_timezone = 18000
_tzname[0] = EST
```

_ultoa

Description

Converts an unsigned long integer to a string.

#include <stdlib.h>   Required only for function declarations

char *_ultoa(unsigned long *value*, **char ****string*, **int** *radix* **);**

value	Number to be converted
string	String result
radix	Base of *value*

Remarks

The **_ultoa** function converts *value* to a null-terminated character string and stores the result (up to 33 bytes) in *string*. No overflow checking is performed. The *radix* argument specifies the base of *value*; it must be in the range 2–36.

Return Value

The **_ultoa** function returns a pointer to *string*. There is no error return.

Compatibility

Standards: None
16-Bit: DOS, QWIN, WIN, WIN DLL
32-Bit: DOS32X

See Also

_itoa, _ltoa

Example

```
/* ITOA.C: This program converts integers of various sizes to strings
 * in various radixes.
 */

#include <stdlib.h>
#include <stdio.h>
```

```
void main( void )
{
    char buffer[20];
    int  i = 3445;
    long l = -344115L;
    unsigned long ul = 1234567890UL;

    _itoa( i, buffer, 10 );
    printf( "String of integer %d (radix 10): %s\n", i, buffer );
    _itoa( i, buffer, 16 );
    printf( "String of integer %d (radix 16): 0x%s\n", i, buffer );
    _itoa( i, buffer, 2  );
    printf( "String of integer %d (radix 2): %s\n", i, buffer );

    _ltoa( l, buffer, 16 );
    printf( "String of long int %ld (radix 16): 0x%s\n", l, buffer );

    _ultoa( ul, buffer, 16 );
    printf( "String of unsigned long %lu (radix 16): 0x%s\n", ul, buffer );
}
```

Output

```
String of integer 3445 (radix 10): 3445
String of integer 3445 (radix 16): 0xd75
String of integer 3445 (radix 2): 110101110101
String of long int -344115 (radix 16): 0xfffabfcd
String of unsigned long 1234567890 (radix 16): 0x499602d2
```

_umask

Description

Sets the default file-permission mask.

#include <sys\types.h>
#include <sys\stat.h>
#include <io.h>   Required only for function declarations

int _umask(int *pmode* **);**

pmode   Default permission setting

Remarks

The **_umask** function sets the file-permission mask of the current process to the mode specified by *pmode*. The file-permission mask is used to modify the permission setting of new files created by **_creat**, **_open**, or **_sopen**. If a bit in the mask is 1, the corresponding bit in the file's requested permission value is set to 0 (disallowed). If a bit in the mask is 0, the corresponding bit is left unchanged. The permission setting for a new file is not set until the file is closed for the first time.

The argument *pmode* is a constant expression containing one or both of the manifest constants **_S_IREAD** and **_S_IWRITE**, defined in SYS\STAT.H. When both constants are given, they are joined with the bitwise-OR operator (|). The meaning of the *pmode* argument is as follows:

Value	Meaning
_S_IREAD	Reading not allowed (file is write-only)
_S_IWRITE	Writing not allowed (file is read-only)

For example, if the write bit is set in the mask, any new files will be read-only.

Note that with DOS, all files are readable—it is not possible to give write-only permission. Therefore, setting the read bit with **_umask** has no effect on the file's modes.

Return Value

The **_umask** function returns the previous value of *pmode*. There is no error return.

Compatibility	Standards:	UNIX
	16-Bit:	DOS, QWIN, WIN, WIN DLL
	32-Bit:	DOS32X

Use **_umask** for compatibility with ANSI naming conventions of non-ANSI functions. Use **umask** and link with OLDNAMES.LIB for UNIX compatibility.

See Also   **_chmod, _creat, _mkdir, _open**

Example
```
/* UMASK.C: This program uses _umask to set the file-permission mask so
 * that all future files will be created as read-only files. It also
 * displays the old mask.
 */

#include <sys\types.h>
#include <sys\stat.h>
#include <io.h>
#include <stdio.h>

void main( void )
{
    int oldmask;

    /* Create read-only files: */
    oldmask = _umask( _S_IWRITE );
    printf( "Oldmask = 0x%.4x\n", oldmask );
}
```

Output
```
Oldmask = 0x0000
```

ungetc

Description

Pushes a character back onto the stream.

#include <stdio.h>

int ungetc(int *c*, **FILE** **stream* **);**

c	Character to be pushed
stream	Pointer to **FILE** structure

Remarks

The **ungetc** function pushes the character *c* back onto *stream* and clears the end-of-file indicator. The stream must be open for reading. A subsequent read operation on the stream starts with *c*. An attempt to push **EOF** onto the stream using **ungetc** is ignored. The **ungetc** function returns an error value if nothing has yet been read from *stream* or if *c* cannot be pushed back.

Characters placed on the stream by **ungetc** may be erased if **fflush**, **fseek**, **fsetpos**, or **rewind** is called before the character is read from the stream. The file-position indicator will have the same value it had before the characters were pushed back. On a successful **ungetc** call against a text stream, the file-position indicator is un-specified until all the pushed-back characters are read or discarded. On each successful **ungetc** call against a binary stream, the file-position indicator is stepped down; if its value was 0 before a call, the value is undefined after the call.

Results are unpredictable if the **ungetc** function is called twice without a read operation between the two calls. After a call to the **fscanf** function, a call to **ungetc** may fail unless another read operation (such as the **getc** function) has been performed. This is because the **fscanf** function itself calls the **ungetc** function.

Return Value

The **ungetc** function returns the character argument *c*. The return value **EOF** indicates a failure to push back the specified character.

Compatibility

Standards:	ANSI, UNIX
16-Bit:	DOS, QWIN, WIN, WIN DLL
32-Bit:	DOS32X

See Also

getc, getchar, putc, putchar

Example

```
/* UNGETC.C: This program first converts a character representation of an
 * unsigned integer to an integer. If the program encounters a character
 * that is not a digit, the program uses ungetc to replace it in the stream.
 */

#include <stdio.h>
#include <ctype.h>

void main( void )
{
    int ch;
    int result = 0;

    printf( "Enter an integer: " );

    /* Read in and convert number: */
    while( ((ch = getchar()) != EOF) && isdigit( ch ) )
        result = result * 10 + ch - '0';        /* Use digit. */
    if( ch != EOF )
        ungetc( ch, stdin );                     /* Put non-digit back. */
    printf( "Number = %d\nNext character in stream = '%c'\n",
            result, getchar() );
}
```

Output

```
Enter an integer: 521a
Number = 521
Next character in stream = 'a'
```

_ungetch

Description   Pushes back the last character read from the console.

#include <conio.h>   Required only for function declarations

int _ungetch(int *c* **);**

c   Character to be pushed

Remarks   The **_ungetch** function pushes the character *c* back to the console, causing *c* to be
the next character read by **_getch** or **_getche**. The **_ungetch** function fails if it is
called more than once before the next read. The *c* argument may not be **EOF**.

Return Value   The **_ungetch** function returns the character *c* if it is successful. A return value of
EOF indicates an error.

Compatibility   Standards: None
16-Bit: DOS
32-Bit: DOS32X

See Also   **_cscanf, _getch, _getche**

Example
```
/* UNGETCH.C: In this program, a white-space delimited token is read
 * from the keyboard. When the program encounters a delimiter,
 * it uses _ungetch to replace the character in the keyboard buffer.
 */

#include <conio.h>
#include <ctype.h>
#include <stdio.h>
```

```
void main( void )
{
    char buffer[100];
    int count = 0;
    int ch;

    ch = _getche();
    while( isspace( ch ) )           /* Skip preceding white space. */
        ch = _getche();
    while( count < 99 )              /* Gather token. */
    {
        if( isspace( ch ) )         /* End of token. */
            break;
        buffer[count++] = ch;
        ch = _getche();
    }
    _ungetch( ch );                 /* Put back delimiter. */
    buffer[count] = '\0';           /* Null terminate the token. */
    printf( "\ntoken = %s\n", buffer );
}
```

Output   White
token = White

_unlink

Description

Deletes a file.

#include <io.h>	Required only for function declarations
#include <stdio.h>	Use either IO.H or STDIO.H

int _unlink(const char *filename);

filename	Name of file to remove

Remarks

The **_unlink** function deletes the file specified by *filename*.

Return Value

If successful, **_unlink** returns 0; otherwise, it returns −1 and sets **errno** to one of the following constants:

Value	Meaning
EACCES	Path name specifies a read-only file
ENOENT	File or path name not found, or path name specified a directory

Compatibility

Standards: UNIX

16-Bit: DOS, QWIN, WIN, WIN DLL

32-Bit: DOS32X

Use **_unlink** for compatibility with ANSI naming conventions of non-ANSI functions. Use **unlink** and link with OLDNAMES.LIB for UNIX compatibility.

See Also

_close, remove

Example   /* UNLINK.C: This program uses _unlink to delete UNLINK.OBJ. */

```
#include <stdio.h>

void main( void )
{
    if( _unlink( "_unlink.obj" ) == -1 )
        perror( "Could not delete 'UNLINK.OBJ'" );
    else
        printf( "Deleted 'UNLINK.OBJ'\n" );
}
```

Output   Deleted 'UNLINK.OBJ'

_unregisterfonts

Description   Frees memory used by fonts.

#include <graph.h>

void __far _unregisterfonts(void);

Remarks   The **_unregisterfonts** function frees memory previously allocated and used by the **_registerfonts** function. The **_unregisterfonts** function removes the header information for all fonts and unloads the currently selected font data from memory.

Any attempt to use the **_setfont** function or the **_outgtext** function after calling **_unregisterfonts** results in an error.

Return Value   None.

Compatibility   Standards: None
16-Bit: DOS
32-Bit: None

See Also   _getfontinfo, _getgtextextent, _outgtext, _registerfonts, _setfont

Example   See the example for **_outgtext**.

_utime

Description

Sets the file modification time.

#include <sys\types.h>

#include <sys\utime.h>

int _utime(char *filename, struct _utimbuf *times);

filename	Filename
times	Pointer to stored time values

Remarks

The **_utime** function sets the modification time for the file specified by filename. The process must have write access to the file; otherwise, the time cannot be changed.

Although the **_utimbuf** structure contains a field for access time, only the modification time is set with DOS. If times is a **NULL** pointer, the modification time is set to the current time. Otherwise, times must point to a structure of type **_utimbuf**, defined in SYS\UTIME.H. The modification time is set from the **modtime** field in this structure.

Return Value

The **_utime** function returns the value 0 if the file-modification time was changed. A return value of –1 indicates an error, and **errno** is set to one of the following values:

Value	Meaning
EACCES	Path name specifies directory or read-only file
EINVAL	Invalid argument; the times argument is invalid
EMFILE	Too many open files (the file must be opened to change its modification time)
ENOENT	File or path name not found

Compatibility

Standards:	UNIX
16-Bit:	DOS, QWIN, WIN, WIN DLL
32-Bit:	DOS32X

Use **_utime** for compatibility with ANSI naming conventions of non-ANSI functions. Use **utime** and link with OLDNAMES.LIB for UNIX compatibility.

See Also   asctime, ctime, _fstat, _ftime, gmtime, localtime, _stat, time

Example
```
/* UTIME.C: This program uses _utime to set the file-modification time to
 * the current time.
 */

#include <stdio.h>
#include <stdlib.h>
#include <sys\types.h>
#include <sys\utime.h>

void main( void )
{
   /* Show file time before and after. */
   system( "dir _utime.c" );
   if( _utime( "_utime.c", NULL ) == -1 )
     perror( "_utime failed\n" );
   else
     printf( "File time modified\n" );
   system( "dir _utime.c" );
}
```

Output
```
The volume label in drive C is ZEPPELIN.
Directory of C:\LIBREF

UTIME    C       397   6-20-99   2:11p
    1 File(s)   12974080 bytes free
File time modified

The volume label in drive C is ZEPPELIN.
Directory of C:\LIBREF

UTIME    C       397   6-20-99   2:12p
    1 File(s)   12974080 bytes free
```

va_arg, va_end, va_start

Description   Access variable-argument lists.

#include <stdarg.h>   Required for ANSI compatibility

#include <varargs.h>   Required for UNIX V compatibility

#include <stdio.h>

type **va_arg(** **va_list** *arg_ptr*, *type* **);**

void va_end(**va_list** *arg_ptr* **);**

void va_start(**va_list** *arg_ptr* **);**   UNIX version

void va_start(**va_list** *arg_ptr*, *prev_param* **);**   ANSI

arg_ptr	Pointer to list of arguments
prev_param	Parameter preceding first optional argument (ANSI only)
type	Type of argument to be retrieved

Remarks   The **va_arg**, **va_end**, and **va_start** macros provide a portable way to access the arguments to a function when the function takes a variable number of arguments. Two versions of the macros are available: the macros defined in STDARG.H conform to the ANSI C standard, and the macros defined in VARARGS.H are compatible with the UNIX System V definition. The macros are listed below:

Macro	Description
va_alist	Name of parameter to called function (UNIX version only)
va_arg	Macro to retrieve current argument
va_dcl	Declaration of **va_alist** (UNIX version only)
va_end	Macro to reset *arg_ptr*
va_list	The **typedef** for the pointer to list of arguments
va_start	Macro to set *arg_ptr* to beginning of list of optional arguments (UNIX version only)

Both versions of the macros assume that the function takes a fixed number of required arguments, followed by a variable number of optional arguments. The required arguments are declared as ordinary parameters to the function and can be accessed through the parameter names. The optional arguments are accessed through the macros in STDARG.H or VARARGS.H, which set a pointer to the first optional argument in the argument list, retrieve arguments from the list, and reset the pointer when argument processing is completed.

The ANSI C standard macros, defined in STDARG.H, are used as follows:

1. All required arguments to the function are declared as parameters in the usual way. The **va_dcl** macro is not used with the STDARG.H macros.

2. The **va_start** macro sets *arg_ptr* to the first optional argument in the list of arguments passed to the function. The argument *arg_ptr* must have **va_list** type. The argument *prev_param* is the name of the required parameter immediately preceding the first optional argument in the argument list. If *prev_param* is declared with the **register** storage class, the macro's behavior is undefined. The **va_start** macro must be used before **va_arg** is used for the first time.

3. The **va_arg** macro does the following:

   ■ Retrieves a value of *type* from the location given by *arg_ptr*

   ■ Increments *arg_ptr* to point to the next argument in the list, using the size of *type* to determine where the next argument starts

   The **va_arg** macro can be used any number of times within the function to retrieve arguments from the list.

4. After all arguments have been retrieved, **va_end** resets the pointer to **NULL**.

The UNIX System V macros, defined in VARARGS.H, operate in a slightly different manner, as follows:

1. Any required arguments to the function can be declared as parameters in the usual way.

2. The last (or only) parameter to the function represents the list of optional arguments. This parameter must be named **va_alist** (not to be confused with **va_list**, which is defined as the type of **va_alist**).

3. The **va_dcl** macro appears after the function definition and before the opening left brace of the function. This macro is defined as a complete declaration of the **va_alist** parameter, including the terminating semicolon; therefore, no semicolon should follow **va_dcl**.

4. Within the function, the **va_start** macro sets *arg_ptr* to the beginning of the list of optional arguments passed to the function. The **va_start** macro must be used before **va_arg** is used for the first time. The argument *arg_ptr* must have **va_list** type.

5. The **va_arg** macro does the following:

- Retrieves a value of *type* from the location given by *arg_ptr*
- Increments *arg_ptr* to point to the next argument in the list, using the size of *type* to determine where the next argument starts

The **va_arg** macro can be used any number of times within the function to retrieve the arguments from the list.

6. After all arguments have been retrieved, **va_end** resets the pointer to **NULL**.

Return Value   The **va_arg** macro returns the current argument; **va_start** and **va_end** do not return values.

Compatibility

Standards:	ANSI, UNIX
16-Bit:	DOS, QWIN, WIN, WIN DLL
32-Bit:	DOS32X

See Also   **vfprintf**

Example

```
/* VA.C: The program below illustrates passing a variable number of arguments
 * using the following macros:
 *       va_start              va_arg              va_end
 *       va_list               va_decl (UNIX only)
 */

#include <stdio.h>
#define ANSI                 /* Comment out for UNIX version        */
#ifdef ANSI                  /* ANSI compatible version             */
#include <stdarg.h>
int average( int first, ... );
#else                        /* UNIX compatible version             */
#include <varargs.h>
int average( va_list );
#endif

void main( void )
{
    /* Call with 3 integers (-1 is used as terminator). */
    printf( "Average is: %d\n", average( 2, 3, 4, -1 ) );

    /* Call with 4 integers. */
    printf( "Average is: %d\n", average( 5, 7, 9, 11, -1 ) );

    /* Call with just -1 terminator. */
    printf( "Average is: %d\n", average( -1 ) );
}
```

```
                /* Returns the average of a variable list of integers. */
                #ifdef ANSI              /* ANSI compatible version    */
                int average( int first, ... )
                {
                    int count = 0, sum = 0, i = first;
                    va_list marker;

                    va_start( marker, first );        /* Initialize variable arguments. */
                    while( i != -1 )
                    {
                        sum += i;
                        count++;
                        i = va_arg( marker, int);
                    }
                    va_end( marker );                     /* Reset variable arguments.     */
                    return( sum ? (sum / count) : 0 );
                }
                #else       /* UNIX compatible version must use old-style definition. */
                int average( va_alist )
                va_dcl
                {
                    int i, count, sum;
                    va_list marker;

                    va_start( marker );               /* Initialize variable arguments. */
                    for( sum = count = 0; (i = va_arg( marker, int)) != -1;  count++ )
                        sum += i;
                    va_end( marker );                      /* Reset variable arguments.     */
                    return( sum ? (sum / count) : 0 );
                }
                #endif
```

Output

```
Average is: 3
Average is: 8
Average is: 0
```

vfprintf, vprintf, vsprintf, _vsnprintf

Description   Write formatted output using a pointer to a list of arguments.

#include <stdio.h>

#include <varargs.h>   Required for UNIX System V compatibility

#include <stdarg.h>   Required for ANSI compatibility

int vfprintf(FILE **stream***, const char ****format***, va_list** *argptr* **);**

int vprintf(const char **format***, va_list** *argptr* **);**

int vsprintf(char **buffer***, const char ****format***, va_list** *argptr* **);**

int _vsnprintf(char **buffer***, size_t** *count***, const char ****format***, va_list** *argptr* **);**

stream	Pointer to **FILE** structure
format	Format control
argptr	Pointer to list of arguments
buffer	Storage location for output
count	Maximum number of bytes

Remarks   The **vfprintf**, **vprintf**, and **vsprintf** functions format data and output data to the file specified by *stream*, to standard output, and to the memory pointed to by *buffer*, respectively. The **_vsnprintf** function differs from **vsprintf** in that it writes not more than *count* bytes to *buffer*. These functions are similar to their counterparts **fprintf**, **printf**, and **sprintf**, but each accepts a pointer to a list of arguments instead of an argument list.

The *format* argument has the same form and function as the *format* argument for the **printf** function; see **printf** for a description of *format*.

The *argptr* parameter has type **va_list**, which is defined in the include files VARARGS.H and STDARG.H. The *argptr* parameter points to a list of arguments that are converted and output according to the corresponding format specifications in the format.

Return Value   The return value for **vprintf**, **vsprintf**, and **_vsnprintf** is the number of characters written, not counting the terminating null character. For **_vsnprintf**, if the number of bytes to write exceeds *buffer*, then *count* bytes are written and −1 is returned. If successful, the **vfprintf** return value is the number of characters written. If an output error occurs, it is a negative value.

Compatibility   **vfprintf, vsprintf**

Standards: ANSI, UNIX
16-Bit: DOS, QWIN, WIN
32-Bit: DOS32X

vprintf

Standards: ANSI, UNIX
16-Bit: DOS, QWIN
32-Bit: DOS32X

_vsnprintf

Standards: None
16-Bit: DOS, QWIN
32-Bit: DOS32X

See Also   **fprintf, printf, sprintf, va_arg, va_end, va_start**

Example

```
/* VPRINTF.C shows how to use vprintf functions to write new versions
 * of printf. The vsprintf function is used in the example.
 */

#include <stdio.h>
#include <graph.h>
#include <string.h>
#include <stdarg.h>
#include <malloc.h>

int wprintf( short row, short col, short clr, long bclr, char *fmt, ... );

void main( void )
{
    short fgd = 0;
    long  bgd = 0L;

    _clearscreen( _GCLEARSCREEN );
    _outtext( "Color text example:\n\n" );

    /* Loop through 8 background colors. */
    for( bgd = 0L; bgd < 8; bgd++ )
    {
        wprintf( (int)bgd + 3, 1, 7, bgd, "Back: %d Fore:", bgd );

        /* Loop through 16 foreground colors. */
        for( fgd = 0; fgd < 16; fgd++ )
            wprintf( -1, -1, fgd, -1L, " %2d ", fgd );
    }
}

/* Full-screen window version of printf that takes row, column, textcolor,
 * and background color as its first arguments, followed by normal printf
 * format strings (except that \t is not handled). You can specify -1 for
 * any of the first arguments to use the current value. The function returns
 * the number of characters printed, or a negative number for errors.
 */
int wprintf( short row, short col, short clr, long bclr, char *fmt, ... )
{
    struct  _rccoord tmppos;
    short   ret, size;
    va_list marker;
    char    *buffer;

    /* It's probably safe to use a buffer length of 512 bytes or five times
     * the length of the format string.
     */
    size = strlen( fmt );
    size = (size > 512) ? 512 : size * 5;
    if( (buffer = (char *)malloc( size )) == NULL )
        return -1;
```

```
        /* Set text position. */
        tmppos = _gettextposition();
        if( row < 1 )
            row = tmppos.row;
        if( col < 1 )
            col = tmppos.col;
        _settextposition( row, col );

        /* Set foreground and background colors. */
        if( clr >= 0 )
            _settextcolor( clr );
        if( bclr >= 0 )
            _setbkcolor( bclr );

        /* Write text to a string and output the string. */
        va_start( marker, fmt );
        ret = vsprintf( buffer, fmt, marker );
        va_end( marker );
        _outtext( buffer );
        free( buffer );
        return ret;
}
```

_vfree

Description

Deallocates a virtual memory block.

#include <vmemory.h>

void __far _vfree(_vmhnd_t *handle* **);**

handle	Handle to previously allocated virtual memory block

Remarks

The **_vfree** function deallocates a virtual memory block. The argument *handle* points to a virtual memory block previously allocated through a call to **_vmalloc** or **_vrealloc**. The number of bytes freed is the number of bytes specified when the block was allocated (or reallocated, in the case of **_vrealloc**). The block must be unlocked before it is freed; use **_vlockcnt** to ensure that the block is unlocked. After the call, the freed block is available for reuse by the virtual heap.

Return Value

None.

Compatibility

Standards:	None
16-Bit:	DOS
32-Bit:	None

See Also

_vlock, _vlockcnt, _vmalloc, _vrealloc, _vunlock

Example

See the example for **_vmalloc**.

_vheapinit

Description

Initializes the virtual memory manager.

#include <vmemory.h>

int _ _far _vheapinit(unsigned int *dosmin*, **unsigned int** *dosmax*,
  unsigned int *swaparea* **);**

dosmin	Minimum amount of DOS memory that must be available for the virtual memory manager to install itself, in paragraphs
dosmax	Maximum amount of DOS memory that the virtual memory manager can use, in paragraphs
swaparea	Type of auxiliary memory to use

Remarks

The **_vheapinit** routine initializes the virtual memory manager in preparation for future allocations. It must be called before any virtual memory blocks are requested.

The **_vheapinit** function may round up the minimum value specified. After rounding, if the minimum amount of DOS memory is not available, **_vheapinit** does not initialize the virtual memory manager and returns 0. The virtual memory manager requires several kilobytes to function effectively.

If **_VM_ALLDOS** is specified for the *dosmax* argument, the virtual memory manager uses all available DOS memory.

The *swaparea* argument specifies which types of auxiliary memory the virtual memory manager can use to hold blocks of memory that are swapped out. The argument can be one or more of the following manifest constants, combined with the bitwise-OR operator (|):

Value	Meaning
_VM_EMS	Use expanded memory
_VM_XMS	Use extended memory
_VM_DISK	Use disk space
_VM_ALLSWAP	(_VM_EMS | _VM_XMS | _VM_DISK)

If not all of the specified forms of storage are available, the virtual memory manager uses what is available.

After the program is done using virtual memory, it must call **_vheapterm** to terminate the virtual memory manager. A program can contain multiple pairs of **_vheapinit** / **_vheapterm** calls.

Warning! If the program terminates without a call to **_vheapterm**, various system memory resources may not be available to subsequent programs.

To specify that no minimum amount of memory is required for installation of the virtual memory manager and to use all available DOS memory in the virtual heap and all auxiliary storage, use the following command:

```
if( _vheapinit( 0, _VM_ALLDOS, _VM_ALLSWAP) == 0 )
    /* Error */
```

Return Value

The **_vheapinit** function returns a nonzero value if the virtual memory manager was successfully initialized. Otherwise, it returns 0.

Compatibility

Standards: None

16-Bit: DOS

32-Bit: None

See Also

_vheapterm

Example

See the example for **_vmalloc**.

_vheapterm

Description

Terminates the virtual memory manager.

#include <vmemory.h>

void __far _vheapterm(void);

Remarks

The **_vheapterm** function terminates the virtual memory manager and releases all resources that it used.

Warning! If the program terminates without a call to **_vheapterm**, various system memory resources may not be available to subsequent programs.

If the virtual memory manager has not been initialized or has already been terminated when **_vheapterm** is called, the function returns immediately.

Return Value

None.

Compatibility

Standards: None
16-Bit: DOS
32-Bit: None

See Also

_vheapinit

Example

See the example for **_vmalloc**.

_vload

Description

Loads a virtual memory block into DOS memory.

#include <vmemory.h>

void __far *__far _vload(_vmhnd_t *handle*, **int** *dirty*);

handle	Handle to previously allocated virtual memory block
dirty	Flag indicating whether the block should be written out or discarded when swapping occurs

Remarks

The **_vload** function loads a virtual memory block into DOS memory and returns a far pointer to it. The argument *handle* points to a virtual memory block previously allocated through a call to **_vmalloc** or **_vrealloc**.

The block of memory is not locked and may be swapped out if the virtual memory manager needs the memory. Consequently, the pointer returned by **_vload** is valid only until the next call to the virtual memory manager.

The *dirty* flag indicates whether the block of memory should be written out or discarded when swapping occurs. It can have one of the following values:

Value	Meaning
_VM_CLEAN	Discard contents of block when swapping occurs
_VM_DIRTY	Write contents of block to auxiliary memory when swapping occurs

Return Value

The **_vload** function returns a far pointer to DOS memory if the virtual memory block is successfully loaded. If insufficient DOS memory is available, **_vload** returns **NULL**.

Compatibility

Standards:	None
16-Bit:	DOS
32-Bit:	None

See Also

_vlock, _vmalloc, _vunlock

Example

```
/* VLOAD.C: This program loads a block of virtual memory with _vload,
 * writes to it, and loads in a new block. It then reloads the first block
 * and verifies that its contents haven't changed.
 */

#include <stdio.h>
#include <stdlib.h>
#include <vmemory.h>

void main( void )
{
    int i, flag;
    _vmhnd_t handle1,
             handle2;
    int __far *buffer1;
    int __far *buffer2;

    if ( !_vheapinit( 0, _VM_ALLDOS, _VM_XMS | _VM_EMS ) )
    {
        printf( "Could not initialize virtual memory manager. \n" );
        exit( -1 );
    }

    if ( ( (handle1 = _vmalloc( 100 * sizeof(int) )) == _VM_NULL ) ||
         ( (handle2 = _vmalloc( 100 * sizeof(int) )) == _VM_NULL )   )
    {
        _vheapterm();
        exit( -1 );
    }

    printf( "Two blocks of virtual memory allocated.\n" );

    if ( (buffer1 = (int __far *)_vload( handle1, _VM_DIRTY )) == NULL )
    {
        _vheapterm();
        exit( -1 );
    }

    printf( "buffer1 loaded: valid until next call to VM manager.\n" );
    for ( i = 0; i  100; i++ )          /* write to buffer1 */
        buffer1[i] d= i;

    if ( (buffer2 = (int __far *)_vload( handle2, _VM_DIRTY )) == NULL )
    {
        _vheapterm();
        exit( -1 );
    }

    printf( "buffer2 loaded. buffer 1 no longer valid.\n" );
```

```
            if ( (buffer1 = (int __far *)_vload( handle1, _VM_CLEAN )) == NULL )
            {
                _vheapterm();
                exit( -1 );
            }

            printf( "buffer1 reloaded.\n" );

            flag = 0;
            for ( i = 0; i  100; i++ )
                if ( buffer1[i] != i )
                    flag = 1;

            if ( !flag )
                printf( "Contents of buffer1 verified.\n" );

            _vfree( handle1 );
            _vfree( handle2 );
            _vheapterm();
            exit( 0 );
        }
```

Output   Two blocks of virtual memory allocated.
              buffer1 loaded: valid until next call to VM manager.
              buffer2 loaded. buffer 1 no longer valid.
              buffer1 reloaded.
              Contents of buffer1 verified.

_vlock

Description

Loads a virtual memory block into DOS memory and locks it.

#include <vmemory.h>

void __far *__far _vlock(_vmhnd_t *handle* **);**

handle   Handle to previously allocated virtual memory block

Remarks

The **_vlock** function loads a virtual memory block into DOS memory, locks it, and returns a far pointer to it. The argument *handle* points to a virtual memory block previously allocated through a call to **_vmalloc** or **_vrealloc**.

A locked virtual memory block will not be swapped out until it is unlocked. A virtual memory block can be locked up to 255 times. The pointer returned by **_vlock** remains valid until an equal number of unlock operations is performed.

Since DOS memory may be scarce, try to keep the number of blocks locked at one time to a minimum and use **_vunlock** to unlock them as soon as possible.

Return Value

The **_vlock** function returns a far pointer to DOS memory if the virtual memory block is successfully loaded and locked. If insufficient DOS memory is available, **_vload** returns **NULL**.

Compatibility

Standards: None
16-Bit: DOS
32-Bit: None

See Also

_vlockcnt, _vmalloc, _vunlock

Example

```
/* VLOCK.C: This program locks a block of virtual memory using _vlock,
 * writes to it, loads in a new block with _vload, and then verifies
 * that the contents of the locked block are still accessible. It then
 * unlocks the block with _vunlock.
 */

#include <stdio.h>
#include <stdlib.h>
#include <vmemory.h>

void main( void )
{
    int i, flag;
    _vmhnd_t handle1,
             handle2;
    int __far *buffer1;
    int __far *buffer2;

    if ( !_vheapinit( 0, _VM_ALLDOS, _VM_XMS | _VM_EMS ) )
    {
        printf( "Could not initialize virtual memory manager. \n" );
        exit( -1 );
    }

    if ( ( (handle1 = _vmalloc( 100 * sizeof(int) )) == _VM_NULL ) ||
         ( (handle2 = _vmalloc( 100 * sizeof(int) )) == _VM_NULL )   )
    {
        _vheapterm();
        exit( -1 );
    }

    printf( "Two blocks of virtual memory allocated.\n" );

    if ( (buffer1 = (int __far *)_vlock( handle1 )) == NULL )
    {
        _vheapterm();
        exit( -1 );
    }

    printf( "buffer1 locked: valid until unlocked.\n" );
    for ( i = 0; i  100; i++ )        // write to buffer1
        buffer1[i] = i;

    if ( (buffer2 = (int __far *)_vload( handle2, _VM_DIRTY )) == NULL )
    {
        _vheapterm();
        exit( -1 );
    }
```

```
            printf( "buffer2 loaded. buffer 1 still valid.\n" );

            flag = 0;
            for ( i = 0; i  100; i++ )
                if ( buffer1[i] != i )
                    flag = 1;

            if ( !flag )
                printf( "Contents of buffer1 verified.\n" );

            _vunlock( handle1, _VM_DIRTY );
            _vfree( handle1 );
            _vfree( handle2 );
            _vheapterm();
            exit( 0 );
        }
```

Output
```
Two blocks of virtual memory allocated.
buffer1 locked: valid until unlocked.
buffer2 loaded. buffer 1 still valid.
Contents of buffer1 verified.
```

_vlockcnt

Description

Returns the number of times a virtual memory block was locked.

#include <vmemory.h>

unsigned int __far _vlockcnt(_vmhnd_t *handle* **);**

handle   Handle to previously allocated virtual memory
                                   block

Remarks

The **_vlockcnt** function returns the number of times a virtual memory block has
been locked. The argument *handle* points to a virtual memory block previously
allocated through a call to **_vmalloc** or **_vrealloc**. Use the **_vlockcnt** function to
ensure that a block is unlocked before it is freed (using **_vfree**).

Return Value

The **_vlockcnt** function returns the number of locks held on the specified virtual
memory block.

Compatibility

Standards: None
16-Bit: DOS
32-Bit: None

See Also

_vlock, _vmalloc, _vunlock

Example

```
/* VCNT.C: This program locks a block of virtual memory five times with
 * _vlock, and then unlocks it five times with _vunlock, calling
 * _vlockcnt after each operation to report the number of locks held.
 */

#include <stdio.h>
#include <stdlib.h>
#include <vmemory.h>
```

```
void main( void )
{
    int i, count;
    _vmhnd_t handle;
    int __far *buffer;

    if ( !_vheapinit( 0, _VM_ALLDOS, _VM_XMS | _VM_EMS ) )
    {
        printf( "Could not initialize virtual memory manager. \n" );
        exit( -1 );
    }

    if ( (handle = _vmalloc( 100 * sizeof(int) )) == _VM_NULL )
    {
        _vheapterm();
        exit( -1 );
    }

    printf( "Block of virtual memory allocated.\n" );

    printf( "Locking...\n" );
    for ( i = 0; i  5; i++ )
    {
        if ( (buffer = (int __far *)_vlock( handle )) == NULL )
        {
            _vheapterm();
            exit( -1 );
        }

        count = _vlockcnt( handle );
        printf( "%d locks held.\n", count );
    }

    printf("Unlocking...\n" );
    for ( i = 0; i  5; i++ )
    {
        _vunlock( handle, _VM_CLEAN );

        count = _vlockcnt( handle );
        printf( "%d locks held.\n", count );
    }

    _vfree( handle );
    _vheapterm();
    exit( 0 );
}
```

Output   Block of virtual memory allocated.
Locking...
1 locks held.
2 locks held.
3 locks held.
4 locks held.
5 locks held.
Unlocking...
4 locks held.
3 locks held.
2 locks held.
1 locks held.
0 locks held.

_vmalloc

Description

Allocates a virtual memory block.

#include <vmemory.h>

_vmhnd_t __far _vmalloc(unsigned long *size*);

size   Bytes to allocate

Remarks

The **_vmalloc** function allocates a virtual memory block of at least *size* bytes. The actual size of the allocated block may be larger than *size* bytes to allow the virtual memory manager to operate more efficiently; use **_vmsize** to find the actual size of the block.

The value returned by **_vmalloc** is a handle that uniquely identifies the virtual memory block. This value is not an address and cannot be used to access memory directly. The value must be passed to either the **_vload** or **_vlock** function to obtain a valid address.

Return Value

The **_vmalloc** function returns a handle to the allocated virtual memory block, or **_VM_NULL** if insufficient memory is available or if the requested block size is too large to load into DOS memory.

Compatibility

Standards: None
16-Bit: DOS
32-Bit: None

See Also

_vfree, _vmsize, _vrealloc

Example

```
/* VMALLOC.C: This program initializes the virtual memory manager with
 * _vheapinit and allocates a block of virtual memory with _vmalloc.
 * It then frees the memory with _vfree, and terminates the virtual
 * memory manager with _vheapterm.
 */

#include <stdio.h>
#include <stdlib.h>
#include <vmemory.h>

void main( void )
{
    _vmhnd_t handle;

    if ( !_vheapinit( 0, _VM_ALLDOS, _VM_XMS | _VM_EMS ) )
    {
        printf( "Could not initialize virtual memory manager.\n" );
        exit( -1 );
    }

    printf( "Requesting 100 bytes of virtual memory.\n" );
    if ( (handle = _vmalloc( 100 )) == _VM_NULL )
    {
        _vheapterm();
        exit( -1 );
    }

    printf( "Received block of virtual memory.\n" );
    _vfree( handle );
    _vheapterm();
    exit( 0 );
}
```

Output

```
Requesting 100 bytes of virtual memory.
Received block of virtual memory.
```

_vmsize

Description

Returns the size of a virtual memory block.

#include <vmemory.h>

unsigned long __far _vmsize(_vmhnd_t *handle* **):**

handle   Handle to previously allocated virtual memory
                                      block

Remarks

The **_vmsize** function returns the size, in bytes, of a virtual memory block. The argument *handle* points to a virtual memory block previously allocated through a call to **_vmalloc** or **_vrealloc**. The size returned may be larger than the size requested in the call to **_vmalloc** or **_vrealloc**.

Return Value

The **_vmsize** function returns the size (in bytes) of the specified virtual memory block as an unsigned long.

Compatibility

Standards: None
16-Bit: DOS
32-Bit: None

See Also

_vmalloc

Example

See the example for **_vrealloc**.

_vrealloc

Description

Reallocates a virtual memory block.

#include <vmemory.h>

_vmhnd_t __far _vrealloc(_vmhnd_t *handle*, **unsigned long** *size* **);**

handle	Handle to previously allocated virtual memory block
size	New size in bytes

Remarks

The **_vrealloc** function changes the size of a virtual memory block. If *handle* is **_VM_NULL**, **_vrealloc** behaves in the same way as **_vmalloc** and allocates a new block of *size* bytes. If *handle* is not **_VM_NULL**, it must point to a virtual memory block previously allocated through a call to **_vmalloc** or **_vrealloc**.

The *size* argument gives the new size of the block, in bytes. The size of the block may be larger than *size* bytes to allow the virtual memory manager to operate more efficiently; use **_vmsize** to find the actual size of the block. The contents of the block are unchanged up to the shorter of the new and old sizes, although the new block may be in a different location.

Return Value

The **_vrealloc** functions returns a handle to the reallocated (and possibly moved) virtual memory block.

The return value is **_VM_NULL** if the size specified is zero and the handle argument is not **_VM_NULL**. In this case, the original block is freed.

The return value is also **_VM_NULL** if there is not enough available memory to expand the block to the requested size, if the requested block size is too large to load into DOS memory, or if the given handle is still locked. In these cases, the original block is still valid.

Compatibility

Standards:	None
16-Bit:	DOS
32-Bit:	None

See Also

_vfree, _vmalloc, _vmsize

Example

```
/* VRSIZE.C: This program allocates a block of virtual memory with
 * _vmalloc and uses _vmsize to display the size of that block. Next,
 * it uses _vrealloc to expand the amount of virtual memory and calls
 * _vmsize again to display the new amount of memory allocated.
 */

#include <stdio.h>
#include <stdlib.h>
#include <vmemory.h>

void main( void )
{
    _vmhnd_t handle;
    unsigned long block_size;

    if ( !_vheapinit( 0, _VM_ALLDOS, _VM_XMS | _VM_EMS ) )
    {
        printf( "Could not initialize virtual memory manager.\n" );
        exit( -1 );
    }

    printf( "Requesting 100 bytes of virtual memory.\n" );
    if ( (handle = _vmalloc( 100 )) == _VM_NULL )
    {
        _vheapterm();
        exit( -1 );
    }

    block_size = _vmsize( handle );
    printf( "Received %d bytes of virtual memory.\n", block_size );

    printf( "Resizing block to 200 bytes.\n" );
    if ( (handle = _vrealloc( handle, 200 )) == _VM_NULL )
    {
        _vheapterm();
        exit( -1 );
    }

    block_size = _vmsize( handle );
    printf( "Block resized to %d bytes.\n", block_size );

    _vfree( handle );
    _vheapterm();
    exit( 0 );
}
```

Output

```
Requesting 100 bytes of virtual memory.
Received 100 bytes of virtual memory.
Resizing block to 200 bytes.
Block resized to 200 bytes.
```

_vunlock

Description

Unlocks a virtual memory block.

#include <vmemory.h>

void __far _vunlock(_vmhnd_t *handle*, int *dirty*);

handle	Handle to previously allocated virtual memory block
dirty	Flag indicating whether block should be written out or discarded when swapping occurs

Remarks

The **_vunlock** function unlocks a virtual memory block. The argument *handle* points to a virtual memory block previously allocated through a call to **_vmalloc** or **_vrealloc** and locked through a call to **_vlock**.

If multiple locks are held on the virtual memory block, the block's lock count is decremented by one. If the block's lock count goes to zero, the block can be swapped out by the virtual memory manager. The pointer returned by **_vlock** when the block was first locked then becomes invalid.

The *dirty* flag indicates whether the block should be written out or discarded when swapping occurs. It can have one of the following values:

Value	Meaning
_VM_CLEAN	Discard contents of block when swapping occurs
_VM_DIRTY	Write contents of block to auxiliary memory when swapping occurs

Return Value

None.

Compatibility

Standards:	None
16-Bit:	DOS
32-Bit:	None

See Also

_vlock, _vlockcnt, _vmalloc

Example

See the example for **_vlock**.

_wabout

Description

Sets the string that appears in the About dialog box of a QuickWin program.

#include <io.h>

int _wabout(char *_string_);

string   Pointer to a null-terminated string

Remarks

The **_wabout** function sets the string that appears in the About dialog box of a QuickWin program. This routine is used only in QuickWin programs; it is not part of the Windows API. For full details about QuickWin, see Chapter 8 of _Programming Techniques_ (in the Microsoft C/C++ version 7.0 documentation set).

When the user chooses the About command from the Help menu, a dialog box appears containing the string set with **_wabout**. If a QuickWin program does not include a call to **_wabout**, information about QuickWin itself is displayed by default.

The maximum string length is 256 bytes.

Return Value

If successful, **_wabout** returns 0. A nonzero return value indicates an error.

Compatibility

Standards:	None
16-Bit:	QWIN
32-Bit:	None

See Also

_fwopen, _wclose, _wgetexit, _wgetfocus, _wgetscreenbuf, _wgetsize, _wmenuclick, _wopen, _wsetexit, _wsetfocus, _wsetscreenbuf, _wsetsize, _wyield

Example

```
/* WABOUT.C - Demonstrate setting the About dialog box
 * string with _wabout
 */

#include <stdio.h>
#include <io.h>

char string[512];

void main( void )
{
    int nRes;

    for ( ; ; )
    {
        printf( "\nEnter the About string: " );
        scanf("%s", string);
        printf( "\nAbout string = %s\n", string );

        printf( "Setting about string..." );
        nRes = _wabout( string );
        printf( "\n_wabout result = %i\n", nRes );

        printf( "\nTry 'About' in the Help menu\n" );
    }
}
```

_wclose

Description   Closes a QuickWin window's file handle.

#include <io.h>

int _wclose(int *wfh*, int *persist*);

| *wfh* | File handle to a QuickWin window |
| *persist* | Flag indicating whether the window stays on the screen after closing |

Remarks   The **_wclose** function closes a QuickWin window. The window must have been previously opened with the QuickWin function **_wopen**. This routine is used only in QuickWin programs; it is not part of the Windows API. For full details about QuickWin, see Chapter 8 of *Programming Techniques* (in the Microsoft C/C++ version 7.0 documentation set).

To close a window opened with **_wopen**, pass its file handle to **_wclose**. To close a window opened with **_fwopen**, call the STDIO.H function **fclose**.

The *persist* flag can have one of the following values:

Value	Meaning
_WINNOPERSIST	Erase the closed window
_WINPERSIST	Leave the window on the screen

If the window remains on the screen, another **_wclose** call to the same file handle with **_WINNOPERSIST** removes it. While the window remains visible, the user can copy and paste text in it, choose QuickWin menus, and operate the window's scroll bars.

Regardless of which *persist* option is used, the window's file handle is closed to all further I/O. If a window is opened with the same title as a window closed with persistence, it will be a different window. Windows closed with persistence count against the total number of open windows (20 by default).

Return Value   If successful, **_wclose** returns 0. A return value of –1 indicates an error; **errno** is set to **EBADF**, indicating an invalid file-handle argument.

Compatibility	Standards:	None
	16-Bit:	QWIN
	32-Bit:	None

See Also   _fwopen, _wabout, _wgetexit, _wgetfocus, _wgetscreenbuf, _wgetsize, _wmenuclick, _wopen, _wsetexit, _wsetfocus, _wsetscreenbuf, _wsetsize, _wyield

Example

```
/* WCLOSE.C - Demonstrate closing QuickWin windows */

#include <fcntl.h>
#include <stdio.h>
#include <io.h>

#define PERSISTFLAG _WINNOPERSIST
#define OPENFLAGS   _O_RDWR

void main( void )
{
    int wfh;     /* File handle for window */
    int nRes;    /* Window write results */
    int wc;      /* Window closure results */
    struct _wopeninfo wininfo; /* Open information */

    /* Set up window open information */
    wininfo._version = _WINVER;
    wininfo._title = "Window Closing";
    wininfo._bufsize = _WINBUFDEF;

    /* Open a window with _wopen */
    wfh = _wopen( &wininfo, NULL, OPENFLAGS );
    if( wfh == -1 )
    {
        printf( "***ERROR: On _wopen\n" );
        exit( -1 );
    }

    /* Write in the window */
    nRes = write( wfh, "Windows Everywhere!\n", 20 );

    /* Close the window with _wclose */
    wc = _wclose( wfh, PERSISTFLAG );

    exit( 0 );
}
```

wcstombs, _fwcstombs

Description

Convert a sequence of wide characters to a corresponding sequence of multibyte characters.

#include <stdlib.h>

size_t wcstombs(char *_mbstr_, const wchar_t *_wcstr_, size_t _count_);

size_t __far _fwcstombs(char __far *_mbstr_, const wchar_t __far *_wcstr_, size_t _count_);

mbstr	The address of a sequence of multibyte characters
wcstr	The address of a sequence of wide characters
count	The number of bytes to convert

Remarks

The **wcstombs** function converts _count_ or fewer wide characters pointed to by _wcstr_ to the corresponding multibyte characters and stores the results in the _mbstr_ array.

If **wcstombs** encounters the wide-character null character (**L'\0'**) either before or when _count_ occurs, it converts it to the multibyte null character (a 16-bit 0) and stops. Thus, the multibyte character string at _mbstr_ is null-terminated only if **wcstombs** encounters a wide-character null character during conversion. If the sequences pointed to by _wcstr_ and _mbstr_ overlap, the behavior of **wcstombs** is undefined.

The **_fwcstombs** function is a model-independent (large-model) form of the **wcstombs** function.

Return Value

If either **wcstombs** or **_fwcstombs** successfully converts the multibyte string, it returns the number of converted multibyte characters, excluding the wide-character null character. If either function encounters a wide character that cannot be converted to a multibyte character, it returns –1 cast to type **size_t**.

Compatibility   **wcstombs**

Standards: ANSI

16-Bit: DOS, QWIN, WIN, WIN DLL

32-Bit: DOS32X

_fwcstombs

Standards: None

16-Bit: DOS, QWIN, WIN, WIN DLL

32-Bit: None

See Also   **mblen, mbstowcs, mbtowc, wctomb, MB_CUR_MAX, MB_LEN_MAX**

Example
```
/* WCSTOMBS.CPP illustrates the behavior of the wcstombs function */

#include <stdio.h>
#include <stdlib.h>

void main( void )
{
    int     i;
    char    *pmbbuf   = (char *)malloc( MB_CUR_MAX );
    wchar_t *pwcEOL   = L'\0';
    wchar_t *pwchello = L"Hello, world.";

    printf( "Convert entire wide-character string:\n" );
    i = wcstombs( pmbbuf, pwchello, MB_CUR_MAX );
    printf( "\tCharacters converted: %u\n", i );
    printf( "\tMultibyte character: %s\n\n", pmbbuf );

    printf( "Attempt to convert null character:\n" );
    i = wcstombs( pmbbuf, pwcEOL, MB_CUR_MAX );
    printf( "\tCharacters converted: %u\n", i );
    printf( "\tMultibyte character: %s\n\n", pmbbuf );
}
```

Output
```
Convert entire wide-character string:
    Characters converted: 1
    Multibyte character: H

Attempt to convert null character:
    Characters converted: 0
    Multibyte character:
```

wctomb, _fwctomb

Description

Convert a wide character to the corresponding multibyte character.

#include <stdlib.h>

int wctomb(char **mbchar***, wchar_t** *wchar* **);**

int __far _fwctomb(char __far **mbchar***, wchar_t** *wchar* **);**

mbchar	The address of a multibyte character
wchar	A wide character

Remarks

The **wctomb** function converts its *wchar* argument to the corresponding multibyte character and stores the result at *mbchar*.

The **_fwctomb** function is a model-independent (large-model) form of the **wctomb** function. It can be called from any point in any program.

Return Value

If either **wctomb** or **_fwctomb** converts the wide character to a multibyte character, it returns the number of bytes—which is never greater than **MB_CUR_MAX**—in the wide character. If *wchar* is the wide-character null character (**L'\0'**), **wctomb** returns 0. If the conversion is not possible in the current locale, **wctomb** returns –1.

Compatibility

wctomb

Standards:	ANSI
16-Bit:	DOS, QWIN, WIN, WIN DLL
32-Bit:	DOS32X

_fwctomb

Standards:	None
16-Bit:	DOS, QWIN, WIN, WIN DLL
32-Bit:	None

See Also

mblen, mbstowcs, mbtowc, wcstombs, MB_CUR_MAX, MB_LEN_MAX

Example   /* WCTOMB.CPP illustrates the behavior of the wctomb function */

```
#include <stdio.h>
#include <stdlib.h>

void main( void )
{
    int i;
    wchar_t wc = L'a';
    char *pmbnull = NULL;
    char *pmb = (char *)malloc( sizeof( char ) );

    printf( "Convert a wide character:\n" );
    i = wctomb( pmb, wc );
    printf( "\tCharacters converted: %u\n", i );
    printf( "\tMultibyte character: %.1s\n\n", pmb );

    printf( "Attempt to convert when target is NULL:\n" );
    i = wctomb( pmbnull, wc );
    printf( "\tCharacters converted: %u\n", i );
    printf( "\tMultibyte character: %.1s\n", pmbnull );
}
```

Output
```
Convert a wide character:
    Characters converted: 1
    Multibyte character: a

Attempt to convert when target is NULL:
    Characters converted: 0
    Multibyte character: (null)
```

_wgetexit

Description

Returns a value that indicates how a QuickWin program will behave when the **exit** function is called.

#include <io.h>

int _wgetexit(void);

Remarks

QuickWin programs can optionally keep their windows on the screen after termination. How a program will behave at exit time depends on its current exit behavior setting. The **_wgetexit** function lets you examine the current exit behavior setting. This routine is used only in QuickWin programs; it is not part of the Windows API. For full details about QuickWin, see Chapter 8 of *Programming Techniques* (in the Microsoft C/C++ version 7.0 documentation set).

If the companion function **_wsetexit** has been called previously, **_wgetexit** returns the value that it set. This can be one of the following values:

Value	Meaning
_WINEXITPROMPT	Prompt the user at exit time to determine whether the windows stay on the screen
_WINEXITNOPERSIST	The windows do not stay on the screen and there is no prompt to the user
_WINEXITPERSIST	The windows stay on the screen at exit

If **_wsetexit** has not been called previously, the **_wgetexit** function returns **_WINEXITPERSIST**, the default exit behavior. For a description of how to use this exit behavior, see **_wsetexit**.

Return Value

If successful, **_wgetexit** returns the current exit behavior setting value: **_WINEXITPROMPT**, **_WINEXITNOPERSIST**, or **_WINEXITPERSIST**. A return value of −1 indicates an error.

Compatibility

Standards: None
16-Bit: QWIN
32-Bit: None

See Also

_fwopen, _wabout, _wclose, _wgetfocus, _wgetscreenbuf, _wgetsize, _wmenuclick, _wopen, _wsetexit, _wsetfocus, _wsetscreenbuf, _wsetsize, _wyield

Example

```
/* FWOPEN.C - Demonstrate opening QuickWin windows with _fwopen
 * Also demonstrate setting and getting exit behavior for QuickWin
 */

#include <io.h>
#include <stdio.h>

#define OPENFLAGS "w"                 /* Access permission */

void main( void )
{
    struct _wopeninfo wininfo;        /* Open information */
    char wintitle[32]="QuickWin ";    /* Title for window */
    FILE *wp;                         /* FILE ptr to window */
    int nRes;                         /* I/O result */

    /* Set up window info structure for _fwopen */
    wininfo._version = _WINVER;
    wininfo._title = wintitle;
    wininfo._wbufsize = _WINBUFDEF;

    /* Check current 'exit behavior' setting */
    /* Test should be true, since default is _WINEXITPERSIST */
    /* So set new behavior to prompt user */
    if( _wgetexit == _WINEXITPERSIST )
        _wsetexit( _WINEXITPROMPT );

    /* Create a new window */
    /* NULL second argument accepts default size/position */
    wp = _fwopen( &wininfo, NULL, OPENFLAGS );
    if( wp == NULL )
    {
        printf( "***ERROR: _fwopen\n" );
        exit( -1 );
    }

    /* Write in the window */
    nRes = fprintf( wp, "Hello, QuickWin!\n" );

    /* Close the window */
    nRes = fclose( wp );

    /* On exiting anywhere, user is prompted
     *  to keep window on screen or not
     */
    exit( 0 );
}
```

_wgetfocus

Description

Gets a file handle to the currently active QuickWin window.

#include <io.h>

int _wgetfocus(void);

Remarks

The **_wgetfocus** function determines which of a QuickWin program's child (document) windows is active (has the program's "focus"). The routine returns the file handle of the active child window. If the entire application is not active, the routine returns the handle of the child window that would be active if the application were active. This routine is used only in QuickWin programs; it is not part of the Windows API. For full details about QuickWin, see Chapter 8 of *Programming Techniques* (in the Microsoft C/C++ version 7.0 documentation set).

If the active window is a closed child window kept on the screen with the **_WINPERSIST** flag (see **_wclose**), **_wgetfocus** fails.

Return Value

If successful, **_wgetfocus** returns the file handle of the active child window. A return value of –1 indicates an error.

Compatibility

Standards: None
16-Bit: QWIN
32-Bit: None

See Also

_fwopen, _wabout, _wclose, _wgetexit, _wgetscreenbuf, _wgetsize, _wmenuclick, _wopen, _wsetexit, _wsetfocus, _wsetscreenbuf, _wsetsize, _wyield

Example

```
/* WGETFOC.C - Demonstrate testing which QuickWin window is the
 * active window with _wgetfocus
 */

#include <io.h>
#include <stdio.h>

#define NUMWINS     4      /* Number of windows */
#define OPENFLAGS   "w"    /* Access permission */
```

```
void main( void )
{
    int i, nRes;
    int sf, gf;          /* Set/Get focus results */
    FILE *wins[NUMWINS];  /* Array of file pointers */

    /* Open NUMWINS windows */
    /* NULL arguments accept default characteristics */
    for( i = 0; i < NUMWINS; i++ )
    {
        wins[i] = _fwopen( NULL, NULL, OPENFLAGS );
        if( wins[i] == NULL )
        {
            printf( "***ERROR: On _fwopen #%i\n", i );
            exit( -1 );
        }
        /* Write in each window */
        nRes = fprintf( wins[i], "Windows!\n" );
    }

    /* Tile child windows with _wmenuclick */
    nRes = _wmenuclick( _WINTILE );
    if( nRes == -1 )
    {
        printf( "***ERROR: _wmenuclick\n" );
        exit( -1 );
    }

    /* Pass the focus from window to window */
    for( i = 0; i < NUMWINS; i++ )
    {
        sf = _wsetfocus( _fileno( wins[i] ) );
        gf = _wgetfocus();
        if(( sf == -1 ) || ( gf == -1 )
           || ( gf != _fileno( wins[i] ) ) )
        {
            printf( "***ERROR: _wsetfocus/_wgetfocus\n" );
            exit( -1 );
        }
    }

    nRes = _fcloseall();

    exit( 0 );
}
```

_wgetscreenbuf

Description

Gets a QuickWin window's current screen-buffer size.

#include <io.h>

long _wgetscreenbuf(int *wfh* **);**

wfh   File handle to a QuickWin window

Remarks

The **_wgetscreenbuf** function returns the size of a QuickWin window screen buffer. This routine is used only in QuickWin programs; it is not part of the Windows API. For full details about QuickWin, see Chapter 8 of *Programming Techniques* (in the Microsoft C/C++ version 7.0 documentation set).

Each QuickWin child window has a buffer in which the screen-display text for the window is stored. The buffer size determines how much text is retained and thus how much output can be viewed by scrolling back through the window.

By default, the screen-buffer size is 2,048 bytes, but this value can be changed. See **_wsetscreenbuf**.

Return Value

If successful, the **_wgetscreenbuf** function returns the current screen-buffer size (in bytes) or the value **_WINBUFINF**. (A value of **_WINBUFINF** signifies that the size of the screen buffer is unlimited.) A return value of −1 indicates an error.

Compatibility

Standards: None
16-Bit: QWIN
32-Bit: None

See Also

_fwopen, _wabout, _wclose, _wgetexit, _wgetfocus, _wgetsize, _wmenuclick, _wopen, _wsetexit, _wsetfocus, _wsetscreenbuf, _wsetsize, _wyield

Example

```
/* WGSCRBUF.C - Demonstrate examining the current size of a
 * QuickWin window's screen buffer
 */

#include <io.h>
#include <stdio.h>

#define NUMWINS      4     /* Number of windows */
#define OPENFLAGS   "w"    /* Access permission */

void main( void )
{
    int nSize;                /* Size of screen buffer */
    int nRes;                 /* Write result */
    FILE *wp;                 /* File pointer */

    /* Open a window */
    /* NULL arguments accept default characteristics */
    wp = _fwopen( NULL, NULL, OPENFLAGS );
    if( wp == NULL )
    {
        printf( "***ERROR:_fwopen\n" );
        exit( -1 );
    }

    /* Get the size of its screen buffer */
    nSize = _wgetscreenbuf( _fileno( wp ) );
    nRes = fprintf( wp, "Screen buffer holds %i chars\n", nSize );

    nRes = _wclose( _fileno( wp ), _WINPERSIST );

    exit( 0 );
}
```

_wgetsize

Description

Gets a QuickWin window's current size and position on the screen.

#include <io.h>

int _wgetsize(int *wfh*, **int** *reqtype*, **struct _wsizeinfo ***wsize **);**

wfh	File handle to a QuickWin window
reqtype	Type of request
wsize	Pointer to a **_wsizeinfo** structure

Remarks

The **_wgetsize** function returns the size and position of the specified child window. This routine is used only in QuickWin programs; it is not part of the Windows API. For full details about QuickWin, see Chapter 8 of *Programming Techniques* (in the Microsoft C/C++ version 7.0 documentation set).

The *wfh* argument is a handle to the window file. Use the manifest constant **_WINFRAMEHAND** as the value of *wfh* to query the size and position of the parent frame (client or application window). The maximum size of the parent frame may vary according to the hardware specifications of your terminal.

The *reqtype* argument is the type of request, which can have one of two values:

Value	Meaning
_WINCURRREQ	Return the current size of the window
_WINMAXREQ	Return the maximum size that the window can grow to (which cannot exceed the current size of the parent frame)

The *wsize* argument is a pointer to a **_wsizeinfo** structure (declared in IO.H) that returns the size and position information. The structure contains a **_type** field that has one of the following values on return:

Value	Meaning
_WINSIZEMIN	Window is minimized
_WINSIZEMAX	Window is maximized
_WINSIZECHAR	Window is of the size specified in the structure's remaining members

If the type returned is **_WINSIZECHAR**, the **_x**, **_y**, **_h**, and **_w** values in the remainder of the structure specify the coordinates of the upper-left corner and the height and width of the window (in characters). Size returned always indicates the "client space" available in the parent frame, which means that it does not include space occupied by title bars and other parts of the window.

Return Value   If successful, **_wgetsize** returns 0 and fills in the **_wsizeinfo** structure. A return value of −1 indicates an error.

Compatibility   Standards: None
16-Bit: QWIN
32-Bit: None

See Also   **_fwopen**, **_wabout**, **_wclose**, **_wgetexit**, **_wgetfocus**, **_wgetscreenbuf**, **_wmenuclick**, **_wopen**, **_wsetexit**, **_wsetfocus**, **_wsetscreenbuf**, **_wsetsize**, **_wyield**

Example
```
/* WGETSIZE.C - Demonstrate getting the
 * size of a QuickWin window on the screen
 */

#include <io.h>
#include <stdio.h>

#define OPENFLAGS    "w"           /* Access permission */
#define PERSISTFLAG _WINPERSIST   /* Keep on screen */

void main( void )
{
    int nRes;                  /* Result */
    FILE *wp;                  /* File pointer */
    struct _wsizeinfo ws;      /* Size information */

    /* Open a window */
    /* NULL arguments accept default characteristics */
    wp = _fwopen( NULL, NULL, OPENFLAGS );
    if( wp == NULL )
    {
        printf( "***ERROR:_fwopen\n" );
        exit( -1 );
    }
```

```
    /* Get the window's size and screen position */
    ws._version = _WINVER;
    nRes = _wgetsize( _fileno( wp ), _WINCURRREQ, &ws );
    if( nRes == -1 )
    {
        printf( "***ERROR: _wgetsize\n" );
        exit( -1 );
    }
    nRes = fprintf( wp, "Size:\n" );
    nRes = fprintf( wp, "  Upper Left: x = %d\n", ws._x );
    nRes = fprintf( wp, "              y = %d\n", ws._y );
    nRes = fprintf( wp, "  Width:      w = %d\n", ws._w );
    nRes = fprintf( wp, "  Height:     h = %d\n", ws._h );

    nRes = _wclose( _fileno( wp ), PERSISTFLAG );

    exit( 0 );
}
```

_wmenuclick

Description

Chooses a QuickWin menu item.

#include <io.h>

int _wmenuclick(int *menuitem* **);**

menuitem   Constant specifying which menu command to
                                  execute

Remarks

The **_wmenuclick** function emulates the user choosing a command from the
QuickWin Window menu. This routine is used only in QuickWin programs; it is
not part of the Windows API. For full details about QuickWin, see Chapter 8 of
Programming Techniques (in the Microsoft C/C++ version 7.0 documentation set).

The *menuitem* argument is a manifest constant specifying one of four available
menu commands:

Value	Meaning
_WINTILE	Tile the program's child windows
_WINCASCADE	Cascade the program's child windows
_WINARRANGE	Arrange icons at the bottom of the client window area
_WINSTATBAR	Toggle the status bar

These are the only menu commands you can choose. Calling the function with one
of these values performs the menu action.

Return Value

If successful, **_wmenuclick** returns 0. A return value of −1 indicates an error.

Compatibility

Standards: None
16-Bit: QWIN
32-Bit: None

See Also

**_fwopen, _wabout, _wclose, _wgetexit, _wgetfocus, _wgetscreenbuf,
_wgetsize, _wopen, _wsetexit, _wsetfocus, _wsetscreenbuf, _wsetsize**

Example

```
/* WMENUCLK.C - Demonstrate choosing a menu
 * command with the QuickWin _wmenuclick function
 */
```

```c
#include <io.h>
#include <stdio.h>

#define NUMWINS      4      /* Number of windows */
#define OPENFLAGS    "w"    /* Access permission */

void main( void )
{
    int i, nRes;
    int wm;                 /* Menu click result */
    int sf, gf;             /* Set/Get focus results */
    FILE *wins[NUMWINS];    /* Array of file pointers */

    /* Open NUMWINS windows */
    /* NULL arguments accept default characteristics */
    for( i = 0; i < NUMWINS; i++ )
    {
        wins[i] = _fwopen( NULL, NULL, OPENFLAGS );
        if( wins[i] == NULL )
        {
            printf( "***ERROR: On _fwopen #%i\n", i );
            exit( -1 );
        }
        /* Write in each window */
        nRes = fprintf( wins[i], "Windows!\n" );
    }

    /* Tile child windows with _wmenuclick */
    wm = _wmenuclick( _WINTILE );
    if( wm == -1 )
    {
        printf( "***ERROR: _wmenuclick\n" );
        exit( -1 );
    }

    /* Pass the focus from window to window */
    for( i = 0; i < NUMWINS; i++ )
    {
        sf = _wsetfocus( _fileno( wins[i] ) );
        gf = _wgetfocus();
        if(( sf == -1 ) || ( gf == -1 )
            || ( gf != _fileno( wins[i] ) ) )
        {
            printf( "***ERROR: _wsetfocus/_wgetfocus\n" );
            exit( -1 );
        }
    }

    nRes = _fcloseall();

    exit( 0 );
}
```

_wopen

Description

Opens a QuickWin window.

#include <io.h>

int _wopen(struct _wopeninfo *wopeninfo*,
   struct _wsizeinfo *wsizeinfo*, **int** *oflag* **);**

wopeninfo	Pointer to a **_wopeninfo** structure
wsizeinfo	Pointer to a **_wsizeinfo** structure
oflag	Type of operations allowed

Remarks

The **_wopen** function opens a QuickWin window, returning a file handle to the window. This routine is used only in QuickWin programs; it is not part of the Windows API. For full details about QuickWin, see Chapter 8 of *Programming Techniques* (in the Microsoft C/C++ version 7.0 documentation set).

The **_wopeninfo** and **_wsizeinfo** structures, declared in IO.H, are used to pass window initialization information, including the window's initial size and position on the screen. You can pass **NULL** for the **_wsizeinfo** argument to accept QuickWin size and positioning defaults, or you can declare a variable of type **_wsizeinfo** and fill in its fields with initial values. You must declare a variable of type **_wopeninfo** and fill in its fields.

For both the **_wopeninfo** and **_wsizeinfo** variables, set the **_version** field to **_WINVER**, which is defined in IO.H.

For the **_wopeninfo** variable, assign a null-terminated string to the **_title** field containing the desired window title. You can also optionally set the size of the window's screen buffer in the **_wbufsize** field. The default is 2,048 bytes, but you can pass some other number or the value **_WINBUFINF**. The value **_WINBUFINF** imposes no limit on the buffer size.

For the **_wsizeinfo** variable, if you choose to pass size information, assign one of the following values to the **_type** field:

Value	Meaning
_WINSIZEMIN	Minimize the window
_WINSIZEMAX	Maximize the window
_WINSIZECHAR	Use character coordinates for the window size

If the type is **_WINSIZECHAR**, you must supply the **_x**, **_y**, **_h**, and **_w** values in the remainder of the structure. They specify the upper-left corner and the height and width of the window (in characters).

The **_wopen** function is a low-level I/O call. It accepts the following access flags: **_O_BINARY**, **_O_RDONLY**, **_O_RDWR**, **_O_TEXT**, **_O_WRONLY**.

These flags can be combined with the bitwise-OR operator (|). See **_open** for additional information about the flags.

Unlike the **_open** function, **_wopen** does not accept the **_O_CREAT**, **_O_TRUNC**, or **_O_EXCL** flag. Using one of these flags results in an error.

Return Value

If successful, **_wopen** returns a QuickWin file handle. A return value of –1 indicates an error; **errno** is set to one of the following values:

Value	Meaning
EINVAL	An invalid *oflag* argument was given
EMFILE	No more file handles available (too many open files)

Compatibility

Standards: None

16-Bit: QWIN

32-Bit: None

See Also

_fwopen, **_wabout**, **_wclose**, **_wgetexit**, **_wgetfocus**, **_wgetscreenbuf**, **_wgetsize**, **_wmenuclick**, **_wsetexit**, **_wsetfocus**, **_wsetscreenbuf**, **_wsetsize**, **_wyield**

Example

```
/* WOPEN.C - Demonstrate opening a QuickWin
 * window with _wopen
 */

#include <fcntl.h>
#include <io.h>
#include <stdio.h>

#define PERSISTFLAG   _WINNOPERSIST
#define OPENFLAGS     _O_RDWR
```

```c
void main( void )
{
    int wfh;                    /* File handle for window */
    int nRes;                   /* Window write results */
    struct _wopeninfo wininfo;  /* Open information */

    /* Set up window open information */
    wininfo._version = _WINVER;
    wininfo._title = "Window Closing";
    wininfo._wbufsize = _WINBUFDEF;

    /* Open a window with _wopen */
    /* NULL second argument accepts default size */
    wfh = _wopen( &wininfo, NULL, OPENFLAGS );
    if( wfh == -1 )
    {
        printf( "***ERROR: On _wopen\n" );
        exit( -1 );
    }

    /* Write in the window */
    nRes = write ( wfh, "Windows Everywhere!\n", 20 );

    /* Close the window with _wclose */
    nRes = _wclose( wfh, PERSISTFLAG );

    exit( 0 );
}
```

_wrapon

Description

Controls word wrap.

#include <graph.h>

short __ far _wrapon(short *option* **);**

option	Wrap condition

Remarks

The **_wrapon** function controls whether text output with both the **_outmem** and the **_outtext** functions wraps to a new line or is simply clipped when the text output reaches the edge of the defined text window. The *option* argument can be one of the following manifest constants:

Constant	Meaning
_GWRAPOFF	Truncates lines at window border
_GWRAPON	Wraps lines at window border

Note that this function does not affect the output of presentation-graphics routines or font routines.

Return Value

The function returns the previous value of *option*. There is no error return.

Compatibility

Standards:	None
16-Bit:	DOS, QWIN, WIN, WIN DLL
32-Bit:	None

See Also

_outtext, _outmem, _scrolltextwindow, _settextwindow

Example

```
/* WRAPON.C */

#include <conio.h>
#include <graph.h>

void main( void )
{
   _wrapon( _GWRAPON );
   while( !_kbhit() )
      _outtext( "Wrap on!   " );
   _getch();
   _outtext( "\n\n" );

   _wrapon( _GWRAPOFF );
   while( !_kbhit() )
      _outtext( "Wrap off!   " );
   _getch();
   _outtext( "\n\n" );
}
```

Output

```
Wrap on!  Wrap on!  Wrap on!  Wrap on!  Wrap on!  Wrap on!  Wrap on!  Wrap
on!  Wrap on!  Wrap on!  Wrap on!  Wrap on!  Wrap on!  Wrap on!  Wrap on!
Wrap on!  Wrap on!  Wrap on!  Wrap on!  Wrap on!  Wrap on!  Wrap on!  Wr
ap on!  Wrap on!  Wrap on!  Wrap on!  Wrap on!  Wrap on!  Wrap on!  Wrap o
n!  Wrap on!  Wrap on!

Wrap off! Wrap off! Wrap off! Wrap off! Wrap off! Wrap off! Wrap off! Wrap
```

_write

Description

Writes data to a file.

#include <io.h>   Required only for function declarations

int _write(int *handle*, **void** **buffer*, **unsigned int** *count* **);**

buffer	Data to be written
count	Number of bytes

Remarks

The **_write** function writes *count* bytes from *buffer* into the file associated with *handle*. The write operation begins at the current position of the file pointer (if any) associated with the given file. If the file is open for appending, the operation begins at the current end of the file. After the write operation, the file pointer is increased by the number of bytes actually written.

Return Value

The **_write** function returns the number of bytes actually written. The return value may be positive but less than *count* (for example, when **_write** runs out of disk space before *count* bytes are written).

A return value of –1 indicates an error. In this case, **errno** is set to one of the following values:

Value	Meaning
EBADF	Invalid file handle or file not opened for writing
ENOSPC	No space left on device

For 16-bit platforms, if you are writing more than 32K (the maximum size for type **int**) to a file, the return value should be of type **unsigned int**. (See the example that follows.) However, the maximum number of bytes that can be written to a file at one time is 65,534, since 65,535 (or 0xFFFF) is indistinguishable from –1 and would return an error.

If the file is opened in text mode, each line-feed character is replaced with a carriage-return–line-feed pair in the output. The replacement does not affect the return value.

When writing to files opened in text mode, the **_write** function treats a CTRL+Z character as the logical end-of-file. When writing to a device, **_write** treats a CTRL+Z character in the buffer as an output terminator.

Compatibility	Standards:	UNIX
	16-Bit:	DOS, QWIN, WIN, WIN DLL
	32-Bit:	DOS32X

Use **_write** for compatibility with ANSI naming conventions of non-ANSI functions. Use **write** and link with OLDNAMES.LIB for UNIX compatibility.

See Also   **fwrite, _open, _read**

Example

```
/* WRITE.C: This program opens a file for output and uses _write to
 * write some bytes to the file.
 */

#include <io.h>
#include <stdio.h>
#include <stdlib.h>
#include <fcntl.h>
#include <sys\types.h>
#include <sys\stat.h>

char buffer[] = "This is a test of 'write' function";

void main( void )
{
    int fh;
    unsigned byteswritten;

    if( (fh = _open( "write.o", _O_RDWR | _O_CREAT,
                            _S_IREAD | _S_IWRITE )) != -1 )
    {
        if(( byteswritten = _write( fh, buffer, sizeof( buffer ))) == -1 )
            perror( "Write failed" );
        else
            printf( "Wrote %u bytes to file\n", byteswritten );

        _close( fh );
    }
}
```

Output   Wrote 35 bytes to file

_wsetexit

Description

Specifies what a QuickWin application does when it exits (with a call to the **exit** function).

#include <io.h>

int _wsetexit(int *exb* **);**

exb   Desired exit behavior type

Remarks

QuickWin programs can optionally keep their windows on the screen after termination. How a program behaves at exit time depends on its current exit behavior setting. The **_wsetexit** function sets the exit behavior setting. This routine is used only in QuickWin programs; it is not part of the Windows API. For full details about QuickWin, see Chapter 8 of *Programming Techniques* (in the Microsoft C/C++ version 7.0 documentation set).

The **_wsetexit** function takes one of three arguments:

Value	Meaning
_WINEXITPROMPT	Prompt the user at exit time to determine whether the windows stay on the screen
_WINEXITNOPERSIST	The windows do not stay on the screen and there is no prompt to the user
_WINEXITPERSIST	The windows stay on the screen at exit

If **_WINEXITPERSIST** is passed, or if **_WINEXITPROMPT** is passed and the user chooses to keep the windows on the screen, the windows stay visible, their contents can be copied and pasted, and their scroll bars can be used, but the windows are closed to further I/O. See **_wclose**. The default exit behavior is **_WINEXITPERSIST** if you do not call **_wsetexit**.

Return Value

If successful, **_wsetexit** returns 0. A return value of –1 indicates an error.

Compatibility   Standards: None

16-Bit: QWIN

32-Bit: None

See Also   **_fwopen, _wabout, _wclose, _wgetexit, _wgetfocus, _wgetscreenbuf, _wgetsize, _wmenuclick, _wopen, _wsetfocus, _wsetscreenbuf, _wsetsize, _wyield**

Example
```c
/* FWOPEN.C - Demonstrate opening QuickWin windows with _fwopen
 * Also demonstrate setting and getting exit behavior for QuickWin
 */

#include <io.h>
#include <stdio.h>

#define OPENFLAGS "w"                /* Access permission */

void main( void )
{
    struct _wopeninfo wininfo;      /* Open information */
    char wintitle[32]="QuickWin ";  /* Title for window */
    FILE *wp;                       /* FILE ptr to window */
    int nRes;                       /* I/O result */

    /* Set up window info structure for _fwopen */
    wininfo._version = _WINVER;
    wininfo._title = wintitle;
    wininfo._wbufsize = _WINBUFDEF;

    /* Check current 'exit behavior' setting */
    /* Test should be true, since default is _WINEXITPERSIST */
    /* So set new behavior to prompt user */
    if( _wgetexit == _WINEXITPERSIST )
        _wsetexit( _WINEXITPROMPT );

    /* Create a new window */
    /* NULL second argument accepts default size/position */
    wp = _fwopen( &wininfo, NULL, OPENFLAGS );
    if( wp == NULL )
    {
        printf( "***ERROR: _fwopen\n" );
        exit( -1 );
    }
```

```
        /* Write in the window */
        nRes = fprintf( wp, "Hello, QuickWin!\n" );

        /* Close the window */
        nRes = fclose( wp );

        /* On exiting anywhere, user is prompted
         *  to keep window on screen or not
         */

        exit( 0 );
}
```

_wsetfocus

Description

Makes a QuickWin window the active (focused) window.

#include <io.h>

int _wsetfocus(int *wfh* **);**

wfh   File handle to a QuickWin window

Remarks

The **_wsetfocus** function makes a QuickWin window the active window (sets the program's focus to the window). This routine is used only in QuickWin programs; it is not part of the Windows API. For full details about QuickWin, see Chapter 8 of *Programming Techniques* (in the Microsoft C/C++ version 7.0 documentation set).

If the application has focus, the window gets focus. If not, the window will get the focus when the application gets focus.

If the program has other child windows, the focused window moves in front of them and is highlighted. This does not automatically direct I/O to the window. All I/O calls specify which window they are directed to by passing a stream pointer or file handle as an argument.

Return Value

If successful, **_wsetfocus** returns 0. A return value of –1 indicates that the focus failed to change.

Compatibility

Standards: None
16-Bit: QWIN
32-Bit: None

See Also

_fwopen, _wabout, _wclose, _wgetexit, _wgetfocus, _wgetscreenbuf, _wgetsize, _wmenuclick, _wopen, _wsetexit, _wsetscreenbuf, _wsetsize, _wyield

Example

```
/* WSETFOC.C - Demonstrate making a new QuickWin window the active
 * window with _wsetfocus
 */
```

```
#include <io.h>
#include <stdio.h>

#define NUMWINS     4       /* Number of windows */
#define OPENFLAGS   "w"     /* Access permission */

void main( void )
{
   int i, nRes;
   int sf, gf;             /* Set/Get focus results */
   FILE *wins[NUMWINS];    /* Array of file pointers */

   /* Open NUMWINS windows */
   /* NULL arguments accept default characteristics */
   for( i = 0; i < NUMWINS; i++ )
   {
      wins[i] = _fwopen( NULL, NULL, OPENFLAGS );
      if( wins[i] == NULL )
      {
         printf( "***ERROR: On _fwopen #%i\n", i );
         exit( -1 );
      }
      /* Write in each window */
      nRes = fprintf( wins[i], "Windows!\n" );
   }

   /* Tile child windows with _wmenuclick */
   wm = _wmenuclick( _WINTILE );
   if( wm == -1 )
   {
      printf( "***ERROR: _wmenuclick\n" );
      exit( -1 );
   }

   /* Pass the focus from window to window */
   for( i = 0; i < NUMWINS; i++ )
   {
      sf = _wsetfocus( _fileno( wins[i] ) );
      gf = _wgetfocus();
      if(( sf == -1 ) || ( gf == -1 )
         || ( gf != _fileno( wins[i] ) ) )
      {
         printf( "***ERROR: _wsetfocus/_wgetfocus\n" );
         exit( -1 );
      }
   }

   nRes = _fcloseall();

   exit( 0 );
}
```

_wsetscreenbuf

Description   Sets a QuickWin window's screen-buffer size.

#include <io.h>

int _wsetscreenbuf(int *wfh*, **long** *bufsiz* **);**

wfh	File handle to a QuickWin window
bufsiz	Desired size of the window's screen buffer (in bytes)

Remarks   The **_wsetscreenbuf** function sets the size of a QuickWin window's screen buffer to *bufsiz* bytes. This size determines how much text is retained in the buffer and thus how much text you can scroll back through. This routine is used only in QuickWin programs; it is not part of the Windows API. For full details about QuickWin, see Chapter 8 of *Programming Techniques* (in the Microsoft C/C++ version 7.0 documentation set).

The *bufsiz* argument can be specified as a number or as one of the following values:

Value	Meaning
_WINBUFDEF	Use the default window screen-buffer size (2,048 bytes)
_WINBUFINF	Use a window screen buffer of unlimited size

The buffer size simply limits how big the buffer can become. The buffer is always allocated dynamically, so that it fits its contents. Specifying **_WINBUFINF** puts no upper limit on buffer size. The buffer may grow within the limits of available memory.

Return Value   If successful, **_wsetscreenbuf** returns 0. A return value of −1 indicates an error.

Compatibility

Standards:	None
16-Bit:	QWIN
32-Bit:	None

See Also   _fwopen, _wabout, _wclose, _wgetexit, _wgetfocus, _wgetscreenbuf, _wgetsize, _wmenuclick, _wopen, _wsetexit, _wsetfocus, _wsetsize

Example

```
/* WSSCRBUF.C - Demonstrate setting the size of a QuickWin window's
 * screen buffer
 * Note: The size is set here to an amount smaller than the default
 * size, but you can set it larger as well
 */

#include <io.h>
#include <stdio.h>

#define NUMWINS     4       /* Number of windows */
#define OPENFLAGS   "w"     /* Access permission */
#define NUMLINES    100     /* Lines of text to write */

void main( void )
{
    int i;                  /* Loop variable */
    int nSize;              /* Old size of screen buffer */
    int nWinBufSize = 1500L; /* New size */
    int nRes;               /* Result */
    FILE *wp;               /* File pointer */

    /* Open a window */
    /* NULL arguments accept default characteristics */
    wp = _fwopen( NULL, NULL, OPENFLAGS );
    if( wp == NULL )
    {
        printf( "***ERROR:_fwopen\n" );
        exit( -1 );
    }

    /* Get the size of its screen buffer */
    nSize = _wgetscreenbuf( _fileno( wp ) );
    nRes = fprintf( wp, "Screen buffer holds %i chars\n", nSize );

    /* Reset the screen buffer size */
    nRes = _wsetscreenbuf( _fileno( wp ), nWinBufSize );

    /* Write many lines in the window */
    for( i = 0; i < NUMLINES; i++ )
    {
        nRes = fprintf( wp, "%i Windows!\n", i );
    }
    nRes = fprintf( wp, "\nWhen the program ends, click 'No'\n" );
    nRes = fprintf( wp, "and try using the scroll bars\n" );

    nRes = _wclose( _fileno( wp ), _WINPERSIST );

    exit( 0 );
}
```

_wsetsize

Description

Sets the size and screen position of a QuickWin window.

#include <io.h>

int _wsetsize(int wfh, struct _wsizeinfo *_wsize_);

wfh	File handle to a QuickWin window
wsize	Pointer to a **_wsizeinfo** structure

Remarks

The **_wsetsize** function sets the size and position of a QuickWin window. This routine is used only in QuickWin programs; it is not part of the Windows API. For full details about QuickWin, see Chapter 8 of *Programming Techniques* (in the Microsoft C/C++ version 7.0 documentation set).

The *wsize* argument points to a **_wsizeinfo** structure (declared in IO.H) containing the new size and position information. The structure contains a **_type** field that can have one of the following values:

Value	Meaning
_WINSIZEMIN	Minimize the window
_WINSIZEMAX	Maximize the window
_WINSIZRESTORE	Restore a previously minimized window
_WINSIZECHAR	Use character coordinates for the window size

If the type is **_WINSIZECHAR**, you must supply the **_x**, **_y**, **_h**, and **_w** values in the remainder of the structure. They specify the upper-left corner and the height and width of the window (in characters).

Return Value

If successful, **_wsetsize** returns 0. A return value of –1 indicates an error.

Compatibility

Standards:	None
16-Bit:	QWIN
32-Bit:	None

See Also   _fwopen, _wabout, _wclose, _wgetexit, _wgetfocus, _wgetscreenbuf,
_wgetsize, _wmenuclick, _wopen, _wsetexit, _wsetfocus, _wsetscreenbuf,
_wyield

Example

```c
/* WSETSIZE.C - Demonstrate setting the
 * size of a QuickWin window on the screen
 */

#include <io.h>
#include <stdio.h>

#define OPENFLAGS    "w"           /* Access permission */
#define PERSISTFLAG _WINPERSIST  /* Keep on screen */

void main( void )
{
    int nRes;               /* Result */
    FILE *wp;               /* File pointer */
    struct _wsizeinfo ws;   /* Size information */

    /* Open a window */
    /* NULL arguments accept default characteristics */
    wp = _fwopen( NULL, NULL, OPENFLAGS );
    if( wp == NULL )
    {
        printf( "***ERROR:_fwopen\n" );
        exit( -1 );
    }

    /* Minimize the window to an icon */
    ws._version = _WINVER;
    ws._type = _WINSIZEMIN;

    nRes = _wsetsize( _fileno( wp ), &ws );
    if( nRes == -1 )
    {
        printf( "***ERROR: _wsetsize\n" );
        exit( -1 );
    }

    nRes = _wclose( _fileno( wp ), PERSISTFLAG );

    exit( 0 );
}
```

_wyield

Description

Yields processor control from a QuickWin program for Windows queue servicing.

#include <io.h>

void _wyield(void);

Remarks

The **_wyield** function yields control to Windows in order to give processor time to other Windows applications. This routine is used only in QuickWin programs; it is not part of the Windows API. For full details about QuickWin, see Chapter 8 of *Programming Techniques* (in the Microsoft C/C++ version 7.0 documentation set).

A Windows application must service its message queue periodically to ensure smooth appearance and performance. Well-behaved QuickWin applications yield time to other applications and allow the user to switch tasks without having to wait for the QuickWin program to complete lengthy processing.

The compiler attempts to issue "yield for queue servicing" calls at appropriate times. But in some cases a program requires additional yield calls, particularly during lengthy processing loops. If Windows appears sluggish when running a QuickWin program, insert **_wyield** calls into the program to improve Windows' responsiveness. Note that when an application is servicing the message queue (yielding) it can be told to stop so the user can work with another running Windows application.

Return Value

None.

Compatibility

Standards:　None
16-Bit:　　QWIN
32-Bit:　　None

See Also

_fwopen, _wabout, _wclose, _wgetexit, _wgetfocus, _wgetscreenbuf, _wgetsize, _wmenuclick, _wopen, _wsetexit, _wsetfocus, _wsetscreenbuf, _wsetsize

Example

```
/* WYIELD.C - Demonstrate yielding processor time from a
 *  QuickWin program so that other Windows programs can
 *  process their message queues; uses _wyield
 */

#include <io.h>

void compute( int a );          /* Function prototype */

void main( void )
{
    int l;

    for( l = 0; l <= 10000; l++ )
    {
        compute( l );            /* Time-consuming function you supply */
        if( l % 1000 )
            _wyield();           /* Yield once every 1000 loops */
    }
}

void compute( int a )
{
    /* Intensive computations */
}
```

Index

Essential References for the
Windows™ Programmer

PROGRAMMING WINDOWS,™ 2nd ed.
Charles Petzold

This edition of *Programming Windows*—completely updated and revised to highlight version 3 capabilities—is packed with keen insight, tried-and-true programming techniques, scores of complete sample programs written in C, and straightforward explanations of the Microsoft Windows programing environment. Topics cover Dynamic Data Exchange (DDE), the Multiple Document Interface (MDI) features, reading input, using resources, the Graphics Device Interface (GDI), and data exchange and links. *Programming Windows* is the most author-itative, example-packed, and thorough resource for programmers new to the Microsoft Windows version 3 graphical environment, those familiar with earlier versions, and anyone looking for information on the dynamics and structure of the Microsoft Windows environment.

960 pages $29.95 ($39.95 Canada)
Note: New edition covering Windows 3.1 available in April 1992.

THE MICROSOFT® VISUAL BASIC™ WORKSHOP
John Clark Craig

Create Windows applications quickly with Microsoft Visual Basic and *The Microsoft Visual Basic Workshop*. Whether you're a new or experienced Windows programmer, you'll find this book-and-disk package invaluable. It includes dozens of ready-to-use Visual Basic routines and applications that can be easily incorporated into your Windows programming projects. The author provides helpful overviews of both Visual Basic and event-driven programming. Also covered are advanced programming concepts—using Dynamic Data Exchange with the Windows Applications Programming Interface, creating Dynamic Link Libraries, and using Windows graphics.
NOTE: Both executable and source-code files are included so you can preview Visual Basic if you don't already own it!

320 pages; includes one 5¹/₄ 1.2 MB disk $34.95 ($44.95 Canada)

MICROSOFT® WINDOWS™ 3 DEVELOPER'S WORKSHOP
Richard Wilton

This example-packed programming resource provides rich and detailed discussions of some of the central—and most complex—areas of programming for Windows. Wilton addresses topics that concern every serious Windows programmer: debugging, building custom controls, interprocess communication through Dynamic Data Exchange, using Dynamic Link Libraries, and tapping into the added functionality of Windows' DDE programming interface, the DDE Management Library. Wilton takes a practical, problem-solving approach, explaining how to combine effective programming practices with good design.

352 pages $24.95 ($32.95 Canada)

*Microsoft Press books are available wherever quality computer books are sold. Prices are subject to change.
Or call **1-800-MSPRESS** for ordering information or placing credit card orders.*
*Please refer to **BBK** when placing your order.*

* In Canada, contact Macmillan Canada, Attn: Microsoft Press Dept., 164 Commander Blvd., Agincourt, Ontario, Canada M1S 3C7.
In the U.K., contact Microsoft Press, 27 Wrights Lane, London W8 5TZ.

Great Programming Resources from Microsoft Press

ANSI AND ISO STANDARD C PROGRAMMER'S REFERENCE

P. J. Plauger and Jim Brodie

A conveniently organized, indispensable reference with all the information you need
to read and write programs that conform to the approved ANSI and ISO standard for the
C programming language. Written by two members of the ANSI-authorized C Programming
Language Standards Committee, this book provides precise explanations of all the Standard C
elements and important guidelines for proper implementation of the language. Scores
of railroad-track diagrams illustrate the syntax rules.

288 pages $19.95 ($24.95 Canada)

MICROSOFT® MS-DOS® PROGRAMMER'S REFERENCE

This is Microsoft's official reference to the MS-DOS operating system—an absolute
necessity for every MS-DOS programmer. This comprehensive resource is updated to
version 5 and provides easy access to essential information about the structure of MS-DOS
and its programming interface. The heart of this book is a comprehensive reference to hundreds
of MS-DOS system interrupts and functions. There are details on syntax and usage along with
information on special notes, warnings, and version compatibility. The coverage of Interrupt 21h
functions is indispensable to assembly language programmers. The *Microsoft MS-DOS
Programmer's Reference* contains a wealth of information covering: the file system ■ register
contents ■ device drivers ■ software interrupts ■ function definitions ■ data structures ■ task-
switching protocol ■ control blocks and work areas ■ EXE file structure and loading ■ error
codes ■ character input and output ■ font-file formats ■ national language support

472 pages $24.95 ($32.95 Canada)

MICROSOFT® MOUSE PROGRAMMER'S REFERENCE, 2nd ed.

This is the official documentation for programming the Microsoft Mouse. It provides
all the software and how-to information you need to incorporate a sophisticated mouse
interface for MS-DOS operating system-based programs. Fully updated to cover Microsoft
BallPoint mouse and the mouse driver version 8, this new edition includes: sample programs
that demonstrate mouse programming in six PC programming languages; a complete reference
to all mouse function calls; an overview of mouse programming; detailed information about
writing and using mouse menu programs; comprehensive index; and much more. The two
5 1/4-inch companion disks include sample mouse menus, MOUSE.LIB and EGA.LIB, and a
collection of valuable programming examples in interpreted Basic, Microsoft QuickBasic,
Microsoft C, Microsoft QuickC, Microsoft Macro Assembler, FORTRAN, and Pascal.

352 pages with two 5 1/4-inch disks $34.95 ($44.95 Canada)

Microsoft Press books are available wherever quality computer books are sold. Prices are subject to change.
*Or call **1-800-MSPRESS** for ordering information or placing credit card orders.*
*Please refer to **BBK** when placing your order.*

* In Canada, contact Macmillan Canada, Attn: Microsoft Press Dept., 164 Commander Blvd., Agincourt, Ontario, Canada M1S 3C7.
In the U.K., contact Microsoft Press, 27 Wrights Lane, London W8 5TZ.

SPECIAL OFFER
Companion Disk for
MICROSOFT C/C++
RUN-TIME LIBRARY REFERENCE

Microsoft Press has created a companion disk for *Microsoft C/C++ Run-Time Library Reference, 2nd ed.* This disk, available in 5 ¼-inch and 3½-inch format, contains nearly 300 example programs from the book. You can use code fragments from the companion disk for commercial or personal purposes without infringing on the copyright of the book.

Domestic Ordering Information:
To order, use the special reply card opposite. If the card has already been used, please send $19.95, plus sales tax in the following states if applicable: AZ, CA, CO, CT, DC, FL, GA, HI, ID, IL, IN, IA, KS, KY, ME, MD, MA, MI, MN, MO, NE, NV, NJ, NM, NY, NC, OH, OK, PA, RI, SC, TN, TX, VA, WA, WV, WI. Microsoft reserves the right to correct tax rates and/or collect the sales tax assessed by additional states as required by law, without notice. Please add $2.50 per disk set for domestic postage and handling charges. Mail your order to: **Microsoft Press, Attn: Companion Disk Offer, 21919 20th Ave SE, Box 3011, Bothell, WA 98041-3011**. Specify 5 ¼-inch or 3 ½-inch format. Payment must be in U.S. funds. You may pay by check or money order (payable to Microsoft Press) or by American Express, VISA, or MasterCard; please include credit card number, expiration date, and cardholder signature. Allow 2–3 weeks for delivery.

Foreign Ordering Information (except within the U.K. and Canada., see below):
Follow procedures for domestic ordering. Add $15.00 per disk set for foreign postage and handling.

U.K. Ordering Information:
Send your order in writing along with £18.95 (includes VAT) to: Microsoft Press, 27 Wrights Lane, London W8 5TZ. You may pay by check or money order (payable to Microsoft Press) or by American Express, VISA, MasterCard, or Diners Club; please include credit card number, expiration date, and cardholder signature. Specify 5 ¼-inch or 3 ½-inch format.

Canadian Ordering Information:
Send your order in writing along with $27.95 (includes GST) to: Macmillan Canada, Attn: Microsoft Press Department, 164 Commander Blvd., Agincourt, Ontario, Canada M1S 3C7. You may pay by check or money order (payable to Microsoft Press) or by VISA or MasterCard; please include credit card number, expiration date, and cardholder signature. Specify 5 ¼-inch or 3 ½-inch format.

Microsoft Press Companion Disk Guarantee:
If a disk is defective, a replacement disk will be sent. Please send the defective disk along with your packing slip (or copy) to: Microsoft Press, Consumer Sales, One Microsoft Way, Redmond, WA 98052-6399. If you have questions or comments about the files on the disk, send them to: Languages User Education, Microsoft Corporation, One Microsoft Way, Redmond, WA 98052-6399.